THE BIBLE
AND
THE ANCIENT NEAR EAST

The Bible and the Ancient Near East

Collected Essays

by

J. J. M. Roberts

EISENBRAUNS
WINONA LAKE, INDIANA
2002

Printed in the United States of America.

Library of Congress Cataloging-in-Publication Data

Roberts, J. J. M. (Jimmy Jack McBee), 1939–
The Bible and the ancient Near East : collected essays / by J. J. M. Roberts.
p. cm.
Includes bibliographical references and indexes.
ISBN 1-57506-066-3 (hardcover : alk. paper)
1. Bible. O.T.—Criticism, interpretation, etc. 2. Middle East—Religion. I. Title.
BS1171.3.R63 2002
221.6′7—dc21
2002012640

The paper used in this publication meets the minimum requirements of the American National Standard for Information Sciences—Permanence of Paper for Printed Library Materials, ANSI Z39.48-1984. ♾™

Contents

Part 3
Solving Difficult Problems: New Readings of Old Texts

Part 4
Kingship and Messiah

Part 5
Interpreting Prophecy

Indexes

Preface

Patrick D. Miller

No development in biblical studies over the last century has been more important than the study of the many texts and artifacts from the ancient world that have been unearthed to shed light on the past and provoke new thinking about the Bible. Uppermost among these discoveries are the Qumran scrolls, but they are only among the best known. The sheer quantity of material from the time and locale in which the Bible took shape is far beyond the capacity of any single scholar to control and use. Among those scholars who have spent their lifetime in the study of the ancient texts to see what light they shed on Scripture, few have been as productive and successful as J. J. M. Roberts. Mastering Greek and Hebrew in college and seminary courses, he turned to the study of the languages and texts of ancient Mesopotamia and Palestine in his doctoral study. His dissertation was a study of the Old Akkadian pantheon that has remained the definitive treatment of the topic in the thirty years since its publication. He has continued to teach courses and seminars in the languages of the ancient Near East and in the interpretation of the texts as they illumine the world, thought, and religious practice of the Old Testament.

There are at least three possible avenues of research for biblical scholars as they approach the extra-biblical languages and texts. One is so to engage these texts that one becomes a student and interpreter of the texts in themselves, thus becoming essentially an assyriologist or an egyptologist, even a ugaritologist. The demands placed upon anyone who would interpret the ancient texts in knowledgeable and sophisticated fashion are such that it is not surprising that a number of people who begin as biblical scholars end up as assyriologists. Another approach is to gather together the many examples of words, concepts, and practices that parallel material from the Bible. Both of these approaches to the literature of the ancient Near East are valuable and necessary. Careful interpretation of texts and artifacts on the basis of years of study of the language, iconography, or archaeology of the ancient Near East is a sine qua non for being able to draw upon that material for illuminating the Bible. So also the scrutiny of the thousands of pieces of data to uncover materials that reflect something of what is found in the Bible, or may be associated with it in some way or another, serves to create a store of resources of potential usefulness for understanding biblical texts.

What finally matters, however, is the capacity to see what is important in the connections, to discern from the sea of data what is really relevant to understanding the biblical text and provides either a corrective to current interpretation or fresh insight into the biblical text. Few persons have done this last task better than Roberts—both correction of existing views and new understanding. This volume brings together a large number of his essays in this vein, most of them previously published in scattered collections and journals, so that they may be more accessible to biblical interpreters. Several of them deal with large methodological questions or with substantive matters of theology and practice shared by Mesopotamian and Israelite literature and religion.

In all of these, Roberts is careful about generalizing out of the literature or religion as a whole. His focus tends to be on particular texts. In most instances, he will seek to draw together a complex of texts from different genres or periods around a particular issue, such as the significance of the downfall of a cultic center, a matter much attested in Mesopotamian literature and, of course, central to Israel's history and its theological interpretation ("Nebuchadnezzar I's Elamite Crisis in Theological Perspective"). Throughout these foundational essays, Roberts queries the common tendency to claim uniqueness for Israel's theological expressions or to set myth (Near Eastern) and history (Israelite) over against each other, a tendency still evident in the scholarly literature and in its appropriation by those outside the field of Old Testament studies ("Myth Versus History: Relaying the Comparative Foundations"). What Roberts seeks and demonstrates in many instances is a kind of "thick description" through a complex of texts in order to avoid oversimplification and to show the breadth of perspective in the Near Eastern literature. One may also compare his work to a slice through the mound of literary remains at a particular point, that is, around a particular topic, theme, or motif, whether of a very broad sort—for example, myth and history or divine freedom versus cultic manipulation—or of a more pointed nature, as in his studies of the motifs of the hand of the god, the weeping god, and divine deceit.

Not infrequently, Roberts addresses major issues of debate or matters on which the issue of uniqueness has been ardently argued. A good example is his critique of the presumed difference between the manipulation of the deity by cultic apparatus and magic in Mesopotamian religion and the careful preservation of the freedom of God in Israelite worship ("Divine Freedom and Cultic Manipulation in Israel and Mesopotamia"). In the process of demonstrating the oversimplification in this reading of the two religious cultures, Roberts shows his capacity to read the texts of "pagan" religion empathetically while not using such reading as a polemical or ideological tool against Israelite religion.

The interpretation of the notion of the king as son of the deity has regularly been understood as an adoptive notion in contrast to more mythopoeic and presumably cruder ideas of the god as giving birth to the king, as, for example, in

Egyptian thought. In his essay on Isa 9:5, Roberts challenges the assumption of adoption as the relationship but also provides a reinterpretation of the birth imagery in Egyptian theology. Along the way, he uncovers the arbitrariness evidenced when interpreters decree some language to be metaphorical and acceptable—for example, adoption—while other language is to be regarded as literal and thus more crude and not as acceptable—birth, for instance.

The effort to counter denigrations and misreadings of Near Eastern literature and its differences from Israelite literature does not mean Roberts simply regards them as identical. He regularly uncovers both continuity and discontinuity in the relationships, as one would expect for the literature of a nation with a long history but one that was always in interaction with many other national communities. In his masterful and sweeping perusal of the various genres of biblical literature in relation to Near Eastern literature ("The Bible and the Literature of the Ancient Near East"), for example, Roberts provides a concise survey of psalmic and prayer literature that brings a large amount of material into manageable scope. This survey, complemented by the essay on "The Ancient Near Eastern Environment" with its extensive bibliography, identifies many similarities in form, some of which have been further developed in his own work (see, for example, the treatment of the weeping god motif in Jeremiah in relation to the lament tradition of the ancient Near East in this volume) as well as in that of his students.[1] Along the way, however, Roberts identifies significant differences that arise primarily from the more polytheistic theological context of the Mesopotamian literature. Implicit in such an analysis, though never explicitly articulated, is the conclusion that one cannot easily read Israelite literature—and Roberts would probably say this is true of extrabiblical or epigraphic Hebrew also—as ever being polytheistic in orientation. The growing tendency to revert to earlier models of an early and widespread polytheistic character to Israelite religion in its formative period does not appear to be substantiated in these essays if one reads between the lines of Roberts's work—an important outcome for a body of scholarly contributions that so thoroughly identifies the continuities between Near Eastern and Israelite literature.

Of particular significance among these probes into major issues and themes is Roberts's essay on divine deceit, a subject he anticipates taking up in more detail. A comparative work again, this essay asks the provocative theological questions: Can one trust the gods? Can one trust God? To the first question he answers "probably not." His answer to the second question may be surprising

1. F. W. Dobbs-Allsopp, *Weep, O Daughter of Zion: A Study of the City-Lament Genre in the Hebrew Bible* (Biblica et Orientalia 44; Rome: Pontifical Biblical Institute, 1993); and Walter C. Bouzard, *We Have Heard with Our Ears, O God: Sources of the Communal Laments in the Psalms* (SBLDS 159; Atlanta: Scholars Press, 1997).

but arises out of a careful look at some of the more difficult prophetic texts where the issue of false prophecy is to the fore.

Here, as in other essays, Roberts has delved deeply into prophetic literature. Already having written a commentary on Nahum, Habakkuk, and Zephaniah and presently preparing the commentary on Isaiah for the Hermeneia series, Roberts's interest in prophecy as reflected in these essays has several features that draw one to them. Most evident is the careful use of the comparative data already indicated. But the focus of attention is often on the nature of prophecy and the question of what is true and authentic prophecy and how one discerns that. Roberts is not afraid to tackle the difficult problems in understanding prophecy. Alongside the discussion of whether the divine word can be trusted one finds a helpful attempt to deal with one of the issues that has always perplexed devout readers of the Bible. In the essay "A Christian Perspective on Prophetic Prediction," Roberts takes up the questions: Did the prophets predict the future? If they did, were their predictions accurate? Such questions are often ignored in the scholarly study of the prophets. Roberts addresses them directly and provides a complex answer that draws on the range of prophetic writings to show that the questions can be answered, but not with a simple yes or no.

In some ways, the pièce de résistance of this volume is the only previously unpublished work, "The Mari Prophetic Texts in Transliteration and English Translation." The study of Israelite prophecy has been greatly enhanced by the publication of a large number of texts from Mesopotamia dealing with prophetic phenomena, especially Neo-Assyrian texts and texts uncovered and published over the last fifty years from the excavations at the ancient city of Mari. The latter group of texts has not been available in English translation except for William Moran's publication of only a portion of them in the journal *Biblica*—the portion of texts that had appeared in French at that time. A number of new texts have been published and improvements have been made in the readings of earlier texts together with significant joins of texts. A new English edition of the whole corpus is thus a need that has now been fulfilled in this volume. Roberts's aim in this the largest essay in the book is different from most of the other essays. He seeks to provide a basic resource for carrying on the comparative work exemplified in this collection. Thus he provides a transliteration and translation of all the texts together with the necessary bibliographical data for consulting the original or critical edition of the different texts. The reader will find helpful the brief annotations at the beginning, summarizing each text and in a number of instances suggesting "possible points of comparative relevance" between these texts and selected Old Testament texts. One expects there will be more from Roberts in the future on some of these points. Meanwhile, those who want a complete corpus of these prophetic texts, in which the English translation can be compared with the Akkadian text, now have such a resource available for understanding Mari prophecy on its own terms but especially for drawing upon it to understand Israelite prophecy, divination, and related phenomena more clearly.

Along with his continuing interest in and contributions to the study of prophecy in Israel and the ancient Near East, Roberts has devoted much attention to the origins and character of the royal theology of ancient Israel, as indicated by the essays in part 4 of this collection. Focusing upon both the place of the king and the election of Zion as God's dwelling place, Roberts has provided a kind of mini-handbook on the royal theology in the series of articles on that subject included here. He argues and proposes intelligible and rationalized views about the origin of the royal theology, criticizing the arguments in favor of an origin in Jebusite or Canaanite pre-Israelite Jerusalem or in a much later time, specifically the exile and after ("The Davidic Origin of the Zion Tradition"). Mythic and comparative motifs were drawn upon in the development of the royal theology, as Roberts demonstrates especially with regard to the election of Zion ("Zion in the Theology of the Davidic-Solomonic Empire"). But the significant play of such mythological motifs does not necessarily mean that the royal theology as a whole came from outside Israelite experience. On the contrary, Roberts seeks to show how it is best understood as arising out of the Davidic-Solomonic era (see also "The Religio-Political Setting of Psalm 47").

In all of the essays on royal theology, Roberts joins *historical* and *theological* issues, attending to matters of origin and development while laying out the theology and significance of the motifs investigated. Even his investigation of an apparently small issue, the interpretation of Isa 28:16, opens up a much wider discussion of the Zion tradition and its place in Isaiah's theological message ("Yahweh's Foundation in Zion [Isa 28:16]"). Not surprisingly, here as well as elsewhere in these essays (for example, "The Divine King and the Human Community in Isaiah's Vision of the Future"), one finds valuable insight into the theology of Isaiah, in whom the royal theology found its strongest prophetic voice. This combination of historical and theological interests is characteristic of Roberts's work as a whole but is especially evident in his treatment of the royal theology. Against the efforts of several scholars to identify kingship as a "pagan" phenomenon and a negative development in Israelite history and religion, Roberts argues passionately for the importance of the monarchy—despite its obvious distortions and abuses—for the whole of biblical theology ("In Defense of the Monarchy: The Contribution of Israelite Kingship to Biblical Theology"). At a time when various ideological readings of the Scriptures denigrate the development of kingship in ancient Israel as a distortion of normative Yahwism, one hears in these essays a strong voice in behalf of the centrality of the royal ideology for the faith of Israel and the theological developments that arose out of that faith ("The Old Testament Contribution to Messianic Expectations").

Finally, while Roberts's treatment of the larger issues may catch the reader's attention more quickly, his smaller essays addressing particular words and debated texts exemplify careful philological work and provide new interpretations that are well grounded or, in some cases, new grounds for older interpretations. The latter is well illustrated in his use of Akkadian texts to interpret the lament of Ps 22:17c [Eng. 16c], making good sense out of an enigmatic and probably corrupt text ("A New Root for an Old Crux, Ps 32:17c") and the puzzling reference to "young lions" in Ps 34:11 [Eng. 10] ("The Young Lions of Psalm 34:11"). Exemplary of his new interpretations is his demonstration, on the basis of Near Eastern literature, that every colon of the enigmatic verse in Ps 74:9 may be understood in relation to Israelite oracular practice ("Of Signs, Prophets, and Time Limits: A Note on Ps 74:9). The apparently narrow focus opens up larger issues having to do with prophecy and the communication of divine oracles (see also "Blindfolding the Prophet: Political Resistance to First Isaiah's Oracles in the Light of Ancient Near Eastern Attitudes toward Oracles"). The reader should be alerted to the fact that Roberts's treatment of seemingly small points often leads into matters of greater substance than one might have expected from the starting point.

There are many things to whet the interests of readers who plunge into these essays. What may be most important is the way they provide both method and substance. Here one learns by example what sound philological and historical critical research is all about and why it matters (for a more reflective treatment of what Roberts exemplifies in these essays, see the final piece on "Historical-Critical Method, Theology, and Contemporary Exegesis"). The result, however, is anything but a proposal about method. More important in the long run are the substantive historical and theological results from such careful critical study. The reader will understand the Bible better when these essays have been read and absorbed.

Acknowledgments

Grateful acknowledgment for permission to republish articles that first appeared elsewhere is hereby noted:

Chapter 1: "The Ancient Near Eastern Environment," was previously published in *The Hebrew Bible and Its Modern Interpreters* (ed. Dougas A. Knight and Gene M. Tucker; Philadelphia: Fortress / Chico, Calif.: Scholars Press, 1985) 75–121.

Chapter 2: "The Bible and the Literature of the Ancient Near East," was previously published in *Harper's Bible Commentary* (ed. Paul J. Achtemeier; San Francisco: Harper, 1988) 33–41; rev. ed.: *The HarperCollins Bible Commentary* (San Francisco: HarperSanFrancisco, 2000) 50–57.

Chapter 3: "Myth versus History: Relaying the Comparative Foundations," was previously published in *The Catholic Biblical Quarterly* 38 (1976) 1–13.

Chapter 4: "Divine Freedom and Cultic Manipulation in Israel and Mesopotamia," was previously published in *Unity and Diversity: Essays in the History, Literature, and Religion of the Ancient Near East* (ed. H. Goedicke and J. J. M. Roberts; Baltimore: Johns Hopkins University Press, 1975) 181–90.

Chapter 5: "Nebuchadnezzar I's Elamite Crisis in Theological Perspective," was previously published in *Essays on the Ancient Near East in Memory of Jacob Joel Finkelstein* (ed. Maria de J. Ellis; Memoirs of the Connecticut Academy of Arts and Sciences 19; Hamden, Conn.: Archon, 1977) 183–87.

Chapter 6: "The Hand of Yahweh," was previously published in *Vetus Testamentum* 21 (1971) 244–51.

Chapter 7: "A New Parallel to 1 Kings 18:28–29," was previously published in *Journal of Biblical Literature* 89 (1970) 76–77.

Chapter 8: "The King of Glory," was previously published in *The Princeton Seminary Bulletin* n.s. 3/1 (1980) 5–10.

Chapter 9: "Job and the Israelite Religious Tradition," was previously published in *Zeitschrift für die Alttestamentliche Wissenschaft* 89 (1977) 107–14.

Chapter 10: "Job's Summons to Yahweh: The Exploitation of a Legal Metaphor," was previously published in *Restoration Quarterly* 16 (1974) 159–65.

Chapter 11: "Does God Lie? Divine Deceit as a Theological Problem in Israelite Prophetic Literature," was previously published in *Congress Volume: Jerusalem* (VTSup 40; Leiden: Brill, 1988) 211–20.

Chapter 12: "The Motif of the Weeping God in Jeremiah and Its Background in the Lament Tradition of the Ancient Near East," was previously published in *Old Testament Essays* 5 (1992) 361–74.

Chapter 13: "Whose Child Is This? Reflections on the Speaking Voice in Isaiah 9:5," was previously published in *Harvard Theological Review* 90 (1997) 115–29.

Chapter 14: "The Mari Prophetic Texts in Transliteration and English Translation" is published here for the first time.

Chapter 15: "A New Root for an Old Crux, Psalm 32:17c," was previously published in *Vetus Testamentum* 23 (1973) 247–52.

Chapter 16: "The Young Lions of Psalm 34:11," was previously published in *Biblica* 54 (1973) 265–67.

Chapter 17: "The Religio-political Setting of Psalm 47," was previously published in *Bulletin of the American Schools of Oriental Research* 221 (1976) 129–32.

Chapter 18: "Of Signs, Prophets, and Time Limits: A Note on Psalm 74:9," was previously published in *Catholic Biblical Quarterly* 39 (1977) 474–81.

Chapter 19: "Blindfolding the Prophet: Political Resistance to First Isaiah's Oracles in the Light of Ancient Near Eastern Attitudes toward Oracles," was previously published in *Oracles et Prophéties dans l'Antiquité: Actes du Colloque de Strasbourg 15-17 juin 1995* (ed. Jean-Georges Heintz; Université des Sciences Humaines de Strasbourg, Travaux du Centre de Recherche sur le Proche-Orient et la Grèce Antiques 15; Srasbourg: De Boccard, 1997) 135–46.

Chapter 20: "Yahweh's Foundation in Zion (Isaiah 28:16)," was previously published in *Journal of Biblical Literature* 106 (1987) 27–45.

Chapter 21: "The Davidic Origin of the Zion Tradition," was previously published in *Journal of Biblical Literature* 92 (1973) 329–44.

Chapter 22: "Zion in the Theology of the Davidic-Solomonic Empire," was previously published in *Studies in the Period of David and Solomon and Other Essays* (ed. T. Ishida; Winona Lake, Ind.: Eisenbrauns, 1982) 93–108.

Chapter 23: "The Divine King and the Human Community in Isaiah's Vision of the Future," was previously published in *The Quest for the Kingdom of God: Studies in Honor of George E. Mendenhall* (ed. H. B. Huffmon, F. A. Spina, and A. R. W. Green; Winona Lake, Ind.: Eisenbrauns, 1983) 127–36.

Chapter 24: "In Defense of the Monarchy: The Contribution of Israelite Kingship to Biblical Theology," was previously published in *Ancient Israelite Religion: Essays in Honor of Frank Moore Cross* (ed. P. D. Miller, P. D. Hanson, and S. D. McBride; Philadelphia: Fortress, 1987) 377–96.

Chapter 25: "The Old Testament's Contribution to Messianic Expectations," was previously published in *The Messiah: Developments in Earliest Judaism and Christianity* (ed. J. H. Charlesworth; Minneapolis: Fortress, 1992) 39–51.

Chapter 26: "Historical-Critical Method, Theology, and Contemporary Exegesis," was previously published in *Biblical Theology: Problems and Perspectives in Honor of J. Christian Beker* (ed. S. J. Kraftchick, C. D. Myers Jr., and B. C. Ollenburger; Nashville: Abingdon, 1995) 131–41.

Chapter 27: "A Christian Perspective on Prophetic Prediction," was previously published in *Interpretation* 33 (1979) 240–53.

Part 1

Fundamental Issues

Chapter 1

The Ancient Near Eastern Environment

In 1951, W. F. Albright contributed two chapters to H. H. Rowley's *The Old Testament and Modern Study*, the second of which was entitled, "The Old Testament and the Archaeology of the Ancient East." Albright used the term "archaeology" to include the reading and interpretation of orthographic remains, and it was this textual evidence that was central in his survey of scholarly advances in the understanding of the ancient Near East that shed light on biblical studies. Thus his article provides a convenient starting point for the present survey of the field, which will emphasize the main corpora of Near Eastern texts and the main currents of their interpretation that have influenced Old Testament studies in the three decades since Albright's essay. Many of the new insights that the ancient Near Eastern environment has offered to biblical studies stem from further work in areas that Albright had already seen as important, and some of these insights confirm his earlier and often brilliant intuitions. In other cases, new discoveries that seemed to promise much have turned out to be largely sterile, at least regarding biblical studies, while some areas that had appeared to be mined out have begun to yield new treasures to more recent investigators. Moreover, there have been new textual discoveries, some of such an age and wealth as would have astounded even Albright.

I. Collections of Texts

Byblos, Alalakh, Nuzi

Albright called the finds at Byblos disappointing (1951: 29), and nothing during this intervening period has changed that judgment The Phoenician inscriptions discovered there have contributed to our understanding of the Phoenician language and orthography, but the religious or historical content of these texts is quite inconsequential (see below). The earlier Byblian syllabic remains undeciphered despite the persistent efforts of Mendenhall and others.

The excavations at Alalakh appeared more promising. Albright had the statue of Idri-mi (Smith), which shed light on life in Northern Syria and Palestine around 1450 B.C.E., but the subsequent publication of the Alalakh tablets (Wiseman 1953, 1954, 1959a, 1959b) provided relatively little of direct bearing on biblical studies. Their main contribution was to provide a better understanding of the historical and sociological developments in Syria against which some of the later biblical statements could be seen in a clearer light (Wiseman 1967; Mendelsohn 1955, 1959; and Dietrich 1966, 1969). The distribution of these texts between the seventeenth and fifteenth centuries, for example, revealed an increasing Hurrian element in the population as well as changes in the structure of the society such as the rise of the *maryannu* chariot-warrior class. Apart from Idri-mi's autobiography, the treaty texts (Wiseman 1953: 25–32), and one text in which a camel was mistakenly alleged to appear (Wiseman 1959a: 29; Lambert 1960a), the Alalakh tablets have not figured largely in specifically biblical discussions.

The Nuzi texts are a different matter. The publication of these texts has continued apace until now about four thousand of the approximately five thousand tablets recovered from Yoghlan Tepe (ancient Nuzi) and Kirkuk (ancient Arrapkha) have appeared (Eichler 1976: 635; for a comprehensive bibliography see Dietrich 1972b). Additional Nuzi-type texts have also been discovered at Tell-al-Fahhar and Tell er-Rimah (Eichler 1976: 635). E. A. Speiser thought that these texts provided the legal background for understanding many of the customs reflected in the patriarchal narratives. He, along with Cyrus Gordon (1954), A. E. Draffkorn-Kilmer (1957), and others (Eichler 1976: 636), espoused this view in a number of detailed articles (Speiser 1955, 1963) and popularized it in his influential commentary on Genesis (1964). The conclusions of Speiser and company were generally accepted among the students of Albright, and this view was disseminated further in the writings of G. E. Wright and in both editions of John Bright's *A History of Israel* (1959: 71, 1972: 68). It was also adopted by de Vaux in his early study on the Hebrew patriarchs (1946, 1948, 1949). Only recently have scholars begun reevaluating the worth of these Nuzi parallels for understanding the Bible (de Vaux 1971: 224–43).

Critics have contested the importance of the Nuzi parallels from the Mesopotamian side on two grounds: they have argued either (1) that the interpretation assigned to Nuzi texts is itself untenable, in which case the parallel can no longer be drawn, or (2) that the given Nuzi custom is not unique but simply a reflection of general Mesopotamian legal practice, in which case the parallel, although it still exists, loses much of its value for historical reconstruction (Eichler 1976: 635, Thompson: 294). As examples of the first type of argument, one may cite the role of the Nuzi house gods and the sistership contracts. It now appears that the household gods did not function as tokens of inheritance rights; hence the explanation of Rachel's theft of the teraphim based on that understanding of Nuzi law falls to the ground (Greenberg 1962). New evidence has also weakened the view that a husband at Nuzi could enhance his wife's standing in Hurrian society by adopting her as his sister prior to marrying her (Skaist: 17; Eichler 1977), thus casting doubt on Speiser's explanation of the origin of the stories in which a patriarch claims his wife as his sister. As examples of the second type of argument, one may point to the discussion of the customs of inheritance and concubinage. Scholars have questioned whether the right of the firstborn or the practice of a childless wife providing her husband with a slave to bear children for her are limited to Nuzi (Eichler 1976). Alleged parallels have been sought elsewhere, in the Old Babylonian and Old Assyrian periods, or even in much later periods (Van Seters 1968, 1969, 1975: 70, 91). Moreover, the value of such parallels has also been questioned from the biblical side, particularly in the new exegetical program espoused by Childs. Do these parallels aid in the exegetical task, or is their value limited to historical reconstruction? Do they really enlighten the reader to what the present biblical text is trying to say, or are they important only for the historical and necessarily hypothetical reconstruction of earlier forms of the tradition? If the latter, can one show how this earlier form of the tradition was transformed into the present text? If there is an unbridgeable gap between the reconstructed "historical" kernel or earlier form of the tradition and the text to be exegeted, one may well question whether such reconstruction is anything more than a futile exercise of the creative imagination. It is too early to say whether this reaction to the earlier excessive stress on the Nuzi parallels is itself excessive, but future biblical scholarship will have to be more critical in the treatment of all alleged parallels.

Ugarit

Albright's estimate of the importance of Ugaritic for the future development of biblical studies has proved correct. Since he wrote, Ugaritology has developed into a quasi-independent specialization, and new texts as well as many new tools have contributed to the better elucidation of these difficult texts. The most important texts earlier known, as well as some previously unedited alphabetic texts, were published in a fine edition by A. Herdner (1963). Other new alphabetic texts were published under the editorship of C. Schaeffer in *PRU* II, V, and VI, in *Ugaritica* V, and in works by Virolleaud, Fisher (1971), Herdner (1972), Caquot and Masson (1977), and Bordreuil. The most important editions of syllabic texts appeared in *PRU* III, IV, VI, and in *Ugaritica* V. Whitaker produced a very useful concordance of the alphabetic Ugaritic literature; M. Dietrich and others contributed a basic bibliography (1973) as well as a concordance to the differing and often confusing systems for numbering the texts (1972a). A specialized new annual, *Ugarit-Forschungen*, edited by Bergerhof and others, was introduced in 1969, and it now runs to ten volumes. Craigie began editing "Newsletter for Ugaritic Studies" in 1972, and it has proved very helpful in keeping up with what is going on in the field. Cyrus Gordon's periodically updated *Ugaritic Textbook* still provides the best grammatical introduction to Ugaritic as well as the best glossary. The glossary, however, should be supplemented with Aistleitner's dictionary, and G. R. Driver's *Canaanite Myths and Legends* also contains a glossary as well as a helpful discussion and translation of the more important mythological and epic texts known at the time. The last work has just recently been revised and reedited by J. C. L. Gibson. H. L. Ginsberg's translation of the Ugaritic myths, epics, and legends in *ANET* remains one of the most useful, but the more recent translation by Caquot, Sznycer, and Herdner as well as Coogan's popular treatment should also be mentioned.

The study of Ugaritic language and literature has had an impact on several areas of biblical studies. The light that the Ugaritic texts have thrown on Canaanite religion and culture has provided a helpful foil against which to discuss Israelite religion, and numerous studies have been devoted to Ugaritic religion (Pope 1955; Kapelrud 1969; Oldenburg; Gese 1970; de Moor 1970, 1971, 1972; Cassuto; van Zijl) and to a comparison of Ugaritic and Israelite beliefs (Kaiser; Habel; Gray 1965; Kapelrud 1963; Schmidt; Clifford; Miller 1973b; Albright 1968; Cross 1973). Sometimes an excessive emphasis has been placed on the undeniable contrast between Israelite and Canaanite beliefs, but in the better treatments of the subject attention has been given to the elements of continuity between Israel and her pagan environment as well as to those features of discontinuity (Miller 1973a).

The Ugaritic language has also contributed to a better understanding of Hebrew lexicography, syntax, and prosody. A glance through the third edition of Köhler-Baumgartner's *Hebräisches und aramäisches Lexikon zum Alten Testament* is enough to form some conception of the influence of Ugaritic studies on recent Hebrew lexicography. To cite one example (although it is taken from that part of the alphabet not yet reached by Köhler-Baumgartner's third edition), the forms תשתע and ונשתעה, found in Isa 40:10, 23, were erroneously listed under the root שעה in BDB (1043) despite the fact that both forms occurred in parallel with the root ירא. When the Ugaritic cognate *t̠tʿ* also appeared in parallel with *yrʾ*, it was finally realized that שתע was, in fact, a separate verb, synonymous with ירא, meaning "to fear." Many other lexicographical suggestions derived from Ugaritic may be found in the writings of M. Dahood and his students (see Martinez), although by no means all are persuasive. James Barr (39–61) has strongly criticized Dahood's lack of sound method in his lexicographical suggestions, and the criticism was certainly telling at points. Barr demonstrated, for instance, that Dahood's attractive interpretation of מגן as "suzerain"—in this case based on Phoenician material rather than Ugaritic—was unfortunately devoid of any textual foundation, being based merely on a misunderstood passage in a French article (Barr: 45–48).

In the area of syntax Ugaritic's enclitic *-m* (C. H. Gordon 1965: 103–4), emphatic *l-* and *k-* (1965: 76), *l-* meaning "from" (1965: 92), and its use of both imperfect and perfect forms for past tense in poetry (1965: 114), to mention only a few items, have led to the discovery of these same features in Hebrew and in many cases have thereby explained long-standing cruxes in the biblical texts (Hummel; Hoetscher; Gordis; Fitzmyer; Held 1962; Moran 1961). Unfortunately, enthusiasm for the Ugaritic explanation has led Dahood and his students to introduce these and other far less certain features of the biblical text even at those points where the traditional text presents no difficulties. An atomistic approach to both the Ugaritic texts and the biblical text compounds the problem. One can never be sure that a proposed rendering of a Ugaritic passage cited by Dahood as support for a new rendering of the biblical text really makes any sense in the original Ugaritic context unless one goes to the trouble of working through the extended context of the Ugaritic passage for oneself. For this reason Dahood's very suggestive and stimulating commentary on Psalms (1966–70) is also extremely frustrating. It is almost as though the writer abdicated responsibility to be self-critical of new insights and foisted off the whole burden of that onerous task on the unfortunate reader.

Much of the recent discussion of the relative date of early Israelite poetry hinges on the comparative data provided by Ugaritic. Albright had already laid the theoretical basis for this attempt at typological-sequence dating of Hebrew poetry at the beginning of our period (1944, 1950), but his work has been followed up in that of his students Cross and Freedman (1948, 1950; Cross 1955 1968; Freedman 1971, 1972, 1976) and has received independent confirmation in the recent work of D. A. Robertson. The underlying assumption is that poetry, like any other human activity, will show a typological development over a period of time. By comparing undated Hebrew poetry with Ugaritic poetry of the middle of the second millennium and with dated Hebrew poetry of the eighth century and later, one can establish a relative chronology of the undated material based on its closer resemblances to one end or the other of the scale. Robertson worked exclusively with linguistic features in his analysis, while Albright, Cross, and Freedman also noted prosodic patterns—types of parallelism, meter, etc.—and historical allusions. Freedman's latest work in this area (1976) adds the criterion of divine epithets. Despite the different criteria, all agree in dating Exod 15:1–18 to the premonarchical period. There is less agreement on some of the other texts, but Judges 5, the Balaam oracles in Numbers 23–24, Genesis 49, Deuteronomy 32 (significant variation) and 33, Psalm 18 (= 1 Samuel 22), 29, and 68 are generally considered relatively ancient. D. W. Goodwin's unfortunate attack on the method of Albright and his students was demolished in a devastating response by Cross and Freedman (1972). Goodwin simply restated older views without refuting the arguments against them and without considering the new inscriptional evidence that had accumulated in the interval since the last article he considered had appeared. While many European critics still do not accept the datings proposed by Cross and Freedman, discounting Goodwin's feeble attempt, no reasoned critique of the approach has appeared. Norin, who does take the method seriously in his recent study of Exodus 15, ends up by accepting a very early date for the original form of that poem.

Dating is only one area in which the stylistic analysis of Ugaritic poetry has contributed to a better understanding of Hebrew material. The discovery in Ugaritic of so-called parallel pairs of A and B words, i.e., the regular recurrence in the same sequence of parallel words in parallel stichs (Held 1957), led to the study of the same phenomenon in Hebrew poetry (Boling; Melamed) and eventually to the major research tool edited by Fisher (1972–75). Some of the recent stylistic study of Hebrew poetry, in fact, with its attention to chiastic arrangement, inclusio, and other features, received its stimulus from earlier work on Ugaritic.

Although some critics have made unsound use of the Ugaritic material or overplayed its importance to the virtual exclusion of other comparative material and others have warned of the dangers of pan-Ugaritism (Donner 1967; van der Lugt), it is unlikely that biblical studies can or should return to a pre-Ugaritic approach. The advances have been many and substantial. If one may hazard a personal opinion, however, despite the new texts and the mass of secondary literature the work of translating Ugaritic has not progressed substantially beyond the point represented by Ginsberg's *ANET* translation. Much remains obscure, and the proliferation of secondary studies has convincingly removed relatively few of these lexical obscurities. One wonders how much farther one can press without substantial new additions to our corpus of Ugaritic texts. Such is certainly possible. In the meantime biblical studies could profit from a far more self-critical application of those insights that Ugaritic studies have already provided.

Mari

Albright was also on target in his estimate of the importance of the Mari texts for biblical studies. The texts continue to appear with no immediate end in sight. So far thirteen volumes of autographed copies have appeared in the series *ARM*, and the companion translation series *ARMT* now numbers eighteen volumes, although two of these do not contain texts. In addition numerous other texts have been published in various journals, and these are now listed in *ARMT* 17/1. Well over a thousand letters and two thousand economic, juridical, and administrative texts have been published. Most of the texts date to a relatively short span (1800–1760 B.C.E.) during the Old Babylonian period, which makes Old Babylonian Mari one of the best-documented societies in antiquity. This material is important for OT studies not only for general historical background but also because Israel's ancestors probably originated among just such tribal groups as are described in the Mari texts. Biblical tradition places Abraham's family in Harran prior to his migration to Canaan, and part of his family, with which the patriarchs maintained contact, remained in the region. This same Harran region figures prominently in the Mari texts as an area in which nomadic groups moved. Moreover, there are linguistic, sociological, and religious connections between Israel and the Amorites of the Mari texts that have been taken to suggest a genetic link. Even if this link cannot be established, the well-documented character of the tribal society at Mari provides important comparative material for understanding the early tribal society in premonarchic Israel.

The question of the linguistic classification of the Semitic but non-Akkadian language attested at Mari in many of the proper names as well as in certain lexicographical items has been hotly debated (Moran 1961: 56–57). Theo Bauer had classified similar names from previously known Old Babylonian sources as East Canaanite, and M. Noth invoked the term proto-Aramaic. But H. B. Huffmon's fundamental study of the Mari names (1965), I. J. Gelb's analysis of Amorite grammar (1958), and G. Buccellati's work on the Amorites of the Ur III period have demonstrated the value of retaining the traditional designation Amorite. This language was, as Moran so aptly puts it, "an ancient and venerable uncle of both Canaanite and Aramaic, who was, it should be stressed, a colorful personality with an individuality bordering on eccentricity" (1961: 57). These linguistic studies are important for OT scholarship, even if one cannot make this Northwest Semitic language the immediate ancestor of either Canaanite or Aramaic. Many of the names in the early patriarchal tradition seem to come from the same linguistic strata as the Amorite names, and that has encouraged scholars to connect the migrations of the patriarchs to the Amorite movements of the beginning of the second millennium (de Vaux 1971: 193–94). Such a view also finds support in Malamat's comparative study of early Israelite and Mari tribal society based largely on the series of West Semitic terms used at Mari to denote tribal units, forms of settlements, and positions of authority (1967). In the religious realm, one may point to the appearance of prophetic phenomena at Mari closely paralleling the later phenomena in Israel. The majority of these prophetic texts have been superbly translated and discussed from the Assyriological side by Moran (1969b, with references to the earlier literature), and their relationship to the Hebrew Bible has been investigated in detail by J.-G. Heintz, F. Ellermeier (with reference to the many earlier studies), and most recently by E. Noort. In the meantime an additional dream text has appeared (Dossin), although it does not change the overall picture presented by the texts. One should also note the resemblances between the ban in Mari and in early Israel (Malamat 1966).

Despite the many points of contact between later Israel and the Amorite society reflected in the Mari texts, however, there remains a significant chronological gap. The oldest biblical narratives are hardly earlier than the tenth century, some eight hundred years after the Mari period, and it is likely that the biblical narrators of the patriarchal stories have telescoped into three generations a process of centuries. The "Patriarchal Age" as a concrete and well-defined period of time, therefore, is problematic, and that in turn renders the quest for a genetic relationship problematic, although not impossible (Malamat 1967: 131).

In any case the discovery of the Mari texts has provided scholars with a far better analogy for understanding the tribal society of the patriarchs and of later premonarchic Israel than the earlier model provided by the bedouin of the classical Arabic sources. J.-R. Kupper's fundamental study showed that the seminomads of the Mari region were primarily sheep and goat herders and therefore were tied to the margins of the cultivated lands. Moreover, as later studies particularly emphasized (Luke; Rowton 1967, 1973a, 1973b, 1974, 1976; Liverani 1970, 1973; Dever; Matthews), the nomads of the Mari region were in a constant symbiotic relationship with the settled agricultural towns and villages, and there was movement back and forth between the two sides of this dimorphic society. The impact of these studies on the Hebrew Bible has up to now focused largely on the period of the conquest and settlement. These studies served to lessen the contrast between the seminomadic Israelite shepherds infiltrating into Canaan and the Canaanite farmers already settled in the land (Gottwald 1974, 1975). This is particularly true of Luke's study, since he denied that the Mari material reflected the influx of any significant new element of population.

Taken with the anarchic portrayal of Canaanite society pictured in the Amarna letters, this new conception provided support for the thesis of Luke's teacher, Mendenhall, that the Israelite conquest of Palestine was by revolution rather than by settlement (1962; see also de Geus). There was neither invasion nor piecemeal infiltration, but a peasant revolt against the oppressive structures of Canaanite feudal society. Gottwald has corrected and further elaborated Mendenhall's views in his massive new book (1979), but while very suggestive the work fails to live up to its advance billing. The sociological jargon and Marxist ideology double the size of the book without making it any more convincing, and the sometimes arbitrary treatment of the biblical material—e.g., his discussion of the meaning of ישב (1979: 519–34)—objectionable in itself, becomes even more objectionable in a work as polemical as this.

Other scholars who have maintained a more traditional picture of Amorite movement into Mesopotamia have seen the long-term infiltration of Amorites into the Fertile Crescent as support for an analogous, largely peaceful infiltration of Israel into Canaan (Weippert). One may question, however, whether either of these treatments has dealt adequately with the Mesopotamian evidence. There may have been Amorite elements in Mesopotamia for a very long time, but prosopography gives evidence for a heavy new influx in the Ur III and Isin-Larsa period, and some of the evidence suggests invasion rather than simple infiltration. One cannot simply ignore references to the "Amorite wall which keeps the nomads far away" or to the "Amorites who break in like a south-storm" or to "Amorites, people from the steppe, have pressed into the settled land" (Edzard 1957: 33–34). One should also be a bit more cautious about totally dismissing the evidence from the literary texts; even if they do reflect urban prejudices against the outsider, those prejudices, however warped, are rooted in experience. Moreover, one should note the number of military titles in the Old Babylonian period that are composed with MARTU as one element (Edzard 1957: 37; Sasson [12 n. 4] discusses only three of these titles: GAL.MAR.TU, UGULA.MAR.TU, and DUB.SAR.MAR.TU). One should also note the reference to the "council of the Amorites" in one of the letters inadequately edited by K. A. Al-A'dami (19: IM 49341, Pl. 1), which suggests an Amorite tribal organization that extended beyond the individual city-state, at least in the period before the Amorites were totally assimilated into the Mesopotamian city-state system. That in turn calls to mind possible analogies to the Israelite tribal assemblies and their conflict with particular Canaanite city-states.

However much or little the new sociological model of Luke, Gottwald, and Rowton has to be revised back toward more traditional models, one can only agree with Dever, against Van Seters (1975: 17) and Thompson (85–88), that "the Mari material provides the best available data . . . for promising research on patriarchal backgrounds" (116–17). As a final point one should note the similarity between the Amorite genealogical traditions and the early genealogical traditions of the Bible (Kraus 1965b; Finkelstein 1966; Malamat 1968). Wilson's recent study of these has shed new light on the function of the genealogical material (1977), and if, as seems likely, the Tudija of the Assyrian genealogical tradition has now turned up as a historical personage in the Ebla texts (Pettinato 1976e: 48), it means that these genealogical traditions in the Bible must be treated with new respect as historiographical sources whether that was their original function or not.

Ebla

The mention of Ebla invokes the most sensational discovery of epigraphic remains in the Near East since Albright's essay. Tell Mardikh, ancient Ebla, is situated in Syria about thirty-five miles (sixty kilometers) southwest of Aleppo and sixty miles (one hundred kilometers) northeast of Ugarit. There in 1974, after ten seasons of relatively modest finds, the Italian excavators, under the direction of P. Matthiae, discovered an archive of some forty-two cuneiform tablets and fragments dating to the last half of the third millennium B.C.E. The following year they uncovered some sixteen thousand additional tablets and fragments of the same period. The story of this remarkable discovery has been widely reported in the popular press, in semipopular journals (Matthiae 1976b; Pettinato 1976e; LaFay), and in a notably well-informed, well-documented semipopular book (Bermant and Weitzman), so it need not be repeated here.

The implications of this discovery for biblical scholarship, however, do merit discussion.

There is no question that this discovery will force fundamental revisions in scholarly reconstructions of the early history of the ancient Near East. Syria no longer remains a silent bridge between the two great literate, riverine cultures of Egypt and Mesopotamia. It is clear from the Ebla discoveries that Syria had an advanced and vigorous culture of its own. Ebla itself was a powerful kingdom, treated on an equal footing with the most powerful states of the time (Gelb 1977: 15), and the many references to other Syrian and Palestinian cities reported in the texts (Pettinato 1976e: 46) probably indicate an economic network with other flourishing urban centers. Thus these texts will enable the future historian to correct and fill in the rather sketchy picture of early Syro-Palestinian history provided up to now by archaeology and the relatively few relevant texts from Egypt and Mesopotamia.

Since the general history of the ancient Near East provides the setting in which biblical scholars do their work, these advances in our understanding offered by the Ebla texts will certainly affect the direction of biblical studies. Much that has been written recently on the direct connections between Ebla and the Bible, however, seems curiously premature. While various scholars have seen photographs of some of the tablets, only a few have been adequately published (Pettinato 1976c and 1977); for the rest one is dependent on Pettinato's reports, based on his preliminary readings. Preliminary readings normally require significant corrections after more extensive study, however, so they offer a very insecure foundation for elaborate hypothetical reconstructions. D. N. Freedman's recent (1978) defense of the historical accuracy of Genesis 14 on the basis of an unpublished Ebla tablet is a case in point. This tablet, TM.75.G.1860, which was reported to list the cities of the plain in the same order as Genesis 14 (i.e., Sodom, Gomorrah, Admah, Zeboiim, and Bela), provides the key for his whole reconstruction, including his attempt to redate Abraham to the mid-third millennium B.C.E. Yet, prior to the publication of his article, in time to include it in a box insert, Freedman received a letter from M. Dahood informing him that Pettinato had changed his reading of the third and fourth city names and that, in any case, the third and fourth city names were not in the same tablet (143). In short, Freedman's premature reconstruction was left hanging in the air.

Equally premature is Dahood's attempt (1978) to explain anomalous Ugaritic forms from the newly discovered Eblaite language. Pettinato has established that the Ebla scribes used the Sumerian writing system in an Old Akkadian syllabary to write their own Eblaite language and that this language was a Semitic language (1975). It remains debatable, however, whether this language should be classified as proto-Canaanite. Gelb has argued on the data presented by Pettinato that Eblaite's closest affinities are with Old Akkadian and Amorite (1977: 28). His view has also been criticized; indeed Ullendorf (154) argues that from Gelb's own assessment there is insufficient ground for choosing either Akkadian or Ugaritic as having the closer affinities with Eblaite; the question should be considered unanswerable until more texts are published and available for grammatical analysis. Up to now the analyses of Eblaite have been based primarily on information derived from proper names, but proper names are notoriously difficult to interpret even when their reading is not in doubt. When too few texts have been published to provide any control on which syllabic values one should assign to multiple-value signs, such analysis becomes even more problematic. This is why many cuneiformists remain unconvinced by Pettinato's claim that the divine name Ya(w), a shortened form of Yahweh, has appeared in the Ebla tablets (1976e: 49). Even if the reading *-yà* were correct, one need not explain the element as a divine name, but one should note that the sign in the Old Akkadian syllabary has the more common values *ni*, *lí*, and *ì* (Gelb 1961: 81–82). While it is doubtful in most cases whether Pettinato's reading *-yà* will survive closer scrutiny, his case would be much stronger if this element ever appeared as an independent name, not just as an element of a composite personal name.

Unfortunately, the premature rhapsodies over the connections between Ebla and the Bible have not only contaminated popular literature on the Bible with possible misinformation that may persist indefinitely; they have also created political problems that can only hinder the scholarly evaluation of the new evidence from Ebla. The Syrians, who are perhaps too sensitive to the possible political implications of these ancient texts (all of which seem very remote, if not absurd, to the average Western scholar), were very disturbed by Freedman and Pettinato's emphasis on the importance of these texts for biblical studies (Shanks: 48–50). This, together with the quarrel between Pettinato and Matthiae over the dating of the texts, has led to Pettinato's fall from favor. The publication of the texts has been taken out of his hands and assigned to an international committee composed of G. Buccellati, D. O. Edzard, P. Fronzaroli, P. Garelli, H. Klengel, J.-R. Kupper, G. Pettinato, F. Rashid, and E. Sollberger under the presidency of Matthiae (Matthiae 1978: 334). Although Pettinato was assigned several volumes of texts, continuing difficulties have led him to resign from the committee, and Shanks, in reporting this development, hints at an intentional suppression of certain crucial Ebla texts by the Syrians (43–50). Such a fear seems a trifle premature. There has almost always been a big gap between new discoveries and adequate publications; many of the most important Dead Sea scrolls still have not appeared. One ought to give the committee a chance to do their work without further poisoning the air by conspiracy theories. On the other hand, scholars have a legitimate interest in the prompt publication of important new discoveries. One can only hope that the committee, with the support of the Syrian authorities, will provide a new model of scholarly responsibility by the rapid publication of these important new texts. In the meantime scholars would do well to learn from the debates over past discoveries. Sensational interpretations have seldom stood the test of time. The cautious interpretation is more useful because it is most often more nearly correct.[1]

Amarna

Work has continued on the Amarna tablets. These cuneiform texts discovered in Egypt in 1887 consist primarily of diplomatic correspondence between the Egyptian courts of Amenophis III and Amenophis IV (Akhenaten) and their allies or vassals in Western Asia. Since many of them come from vassal kings in Palestine and are often written in a barbaric Akkadian that betrays the native West Semitic language of the writer, these texts are important for the history, culture, and languages of Palestine in the period prior to the Israelite conquest. Following up on suggestions of Albright, Moran has contributed a number of important studies (1950b, 1960, 1961, 1969a, 1973, 1975a, 1975b), of which one should especially note his still unpublished dissertation on the Byblos dialect (1950a). He has also promised a new translation of all the Amarna texts, but this has not yet appeared. Rainey published a supplement (1970) to Knudtzon's still basic edition, and one should also note the historical studies of Campbell (1964, 1965), Kitchen, Klengel (1964, 1965–70), and Helck (1971). Space forbids listing all the other studies that have appeared, scattered through the journals, but one should mention the discovery of some new Amarna-type tablets at ancient Kumidi (Edzard 1973; Wilhelm).

The Amarna material has figured largely in such historical questions as the nature of the Israelite occupation or conquest of Palestine and the disputed relationship between the widely attested *ʿapiru* and the Hebrew. Both questions continue to occupy biblical scholars. Bottéro (1954) and Greenberg (1955) both argued for a sociological understanding of the term *ʿapiru*, but de Vaux in his last treatment of the topic still argued for an ethnic interpretation of the designation (1971: 106–12). Nonetheless, the ethnic interpretation is clearly a

1. Since this manuscript was completed, the discussion on Ebla has continued. Robert Biggs published a thoughtful review of the present state of the discussion. There occurred an interchange of views between Alfonso Archi, Pettinato's replacement as epigrapher for the excavation, and Pettinato (1980); this debate was represented, partly in summary and partly in detail, along with photographs of several texts in *BA* 43 (1980) 200–216. Even more significant is Pettinato's decision to proceed with the publication of the texts despite the creation of the international committee. So far two volumes have appeared in the series, Materiali epigrafici di Ebla, published by the University of Naples Press. The first is a catalogue of the texts, *Catalogo dei testi cuneiformi di Tell Mardikh-Ebla* (1979), and the second is a transliteration and translation of fifty economic texts with extensive commentary. *Testi amministrativi della biblioteca L. 2769* (1980). Additional volumes are in preparation. Although one could wish that the volumes would include photographs, it is very encouraging that the texts are beginning to appear.

minority point of view. Gottwald (1979) hardly even acknowledges its existence in his extensive discussion of *ʿapiru* and *ʿibrî*.

II. Areas of Research

For the later periods there has not been any comparable publication of new collections of texts. This is one reason why comparative work on the Hebrew Bible has tended to concentrate on the extrabiblical material from the second millennium rather than on the first millennium, even though the Hebrew Bible itself is basically a literary product of the first millennium. Another reason for this paradoxical state of affairs is the scholarly fascination with origins, and Israel's origins were indubitably in the second millennium. Important work has been done in the later periods, however, and it will be mentioned in the following survey of the major areas of Near Eastern research bearing on the Hebrew Bible.

Historiography

Although they do not compare in sheer quantity to the mass of new texts from the second and third millenniums B.C.E., there have appeared some new texts from the later periods that affect the study of ancient Israel. One thinks especially of the discovery of the continuation of the Neo-Babylonian chronicle (Wiseman 1961), which has enabled biblical scholars to reconstruct the late history of Judah with far more accuracy (Bright 1972: 323 nn. 40–41; Malamat 1974). One should also note the inscription of Adad-nirari III (Page), which mentions the tribute of Joash of Samaria, thus adding a complicating factor to the already troublesome chronology of the divided kingdom (Donner 1970; Tadmor 1973). The major advances in the understanding of the historiographical material, however, have come from new studies of earlier known material. One thinks of the historical studies of Tadmor (1961, 1970, 1975) and Brinkman (1964, 1968), Borger's edition of the Esarhaddon inscriptions (1956), Borger's (1961) and Schramm's introductions to the Assyrian royal inscriptions, Grayson's new translations of the Assyrian inscriptions (1972, 1976), his new edition of the Assyrian and Babylonian chronicles (1975a), and his smaller study of related historiographical literature (1975b).

Grayson's work on the broader historiographical literature has a bearing on two related questions. He rejected the view, recently resurrected by Lambert (1972), that the Babylonian chronicles simply arose out of Mesopotamian divination (1966). Grayson's more pronounced appreciation of the Mesopotamian historiographic achievement together with his new edition of the chronicles, following the important discussion of Albrektson, raises the possibility of a more adequate comparison of Israelite and Mesopotamian historiography. A significant attempt has been made along this line by Cancik, although he primarily concentrates on the comparison of Hittite and Israelite material.

One should also mention Gese's earlier study (1958a), but the task more likely requires a new approach with a much broader base (Roberts 1976).

The other question raised by Grayson's work is closely connected; it is the question of the genre and function of a particular historiographical work. Here Egyptian, Hittite, and Mesopotamian parallels may all be helpful in gaining a better understanding of the Israelite historiographical literature. A. Hermann, followed by S. Herrmann (1953/54; 1973: 212), argued for the Israelite adaptation of the Egyptian *Königsnovelle* in explaining 2 Samuel 7 and 1 Kings 8. Although the analysis as they present it can be criticized both from the standpoint of its applicability to the alleged biblical parallels (Kutsch 1961), a more careful analysis on both sides of the comparative equation, such as in the recent work of M. Görg, may yet yield positive results. On the Hittite side one may point to the history of David's rise to power. Tsevat justly criticized Wolf 's failure to apply sound form-critical method in his study, but that weakness should not be allowed to obscure Wolf 's valid insights. Hoffner has returned to the question with positive results in his "Propaganda and Political Justification in Hittite Historiography" (1975b), and P. Machinist has similarly stressed the political aspect of an important piece of Mesopotamian historiographical literature in his treatment of the epic of Tukulti-Ninurta. Finally, one may note the comparative use of Mesopotamian texts of various genres dealing with the return of captured images in the recent discussion of the ark narrative in 1 Samuel (Miller and Roberts, with the earlier literature cited there) and T. W. Mann's similarly extensive use of comparative material in his study of the typology of exaltation.

At this point one may also refer to the interpretative work done on the Phoenician, Aramaic, Moabite, Ammonite, Edomite, and Hebrew inscriptions. Their interpretation has affected the reconstruction of Israel's history and religion, and it has improved the linguistic understanding of the Hebrew and Aramaic languages in which the OT text is written. (See the chapter by Dever in this volume [[not reproduced here]].)

Religion

Hymns and Prayers. The study of Israelite hymns and prayers went through a period in the 1920s and the 1930s when a great deal of attention was paid to Egyptian and Mesopotamian parallels. In the 1940s attention was shifted to the newly discovered Ugaritic parallels (Patton; Coppens). Although only a few Ugaritic texts have been published that could by any stretch of the imagination be called hymns or prayers, it is this concern for Ugaritic parallels that still dominates the important Psalms commentary of Dahood.

In the meantime, however, a revival of interest in the more strictly comparative material of the broader Near Eastern region has taken place. Falkenstein and von Soden's translation of Sumerian and Akkadian hymns and prayers provided a handy tool for comparing a wide range of hymns and prayers, while Ebeling's edition of the Akkadian *šu-illa* prayers gave biblical scholars access to a large corpus of one general class—whether one can speak of one genre is questionable (Lambert 1974–77)—of prayers comparable to the individual lament of the biblical psalms. The publication of the Sultantepe tablets (Gurney and Finkelstein; Gurney and Hulin) supplemented this collection with a number of nicely preserved duplicates as well as some new texts and generated new interest in Akkadian hymns and prayers. Lambert published three long literary prayers of the Babylonians in 1960, and similar individual articles continue to appear in the Assyriological literature to the present. One may note particularly Lambert's article on the DINGIR.ŠÀ.DIB.BA prayers (1974) and von Soden's recent treatment of two royal Assyrian prayers to Ištar (1974–77).

In 1962 E. R. Dalglish wrote a valuable comparative study on Palms 51 in which he tried to apply form-critical principles to the Mesopotamian as well as the biblical material. Following this, Hallo pointed to the importance of the Sumerian material as providing a point of comparison or the interpretation of the biblical text (1968). He was primarily concerned with the individual prayer, but he discussed other genres as well, and one should especially note the congregational lament. Several of these have been recently published (Kramer 1969a: 611–19; Kutscher), but they have yet to be fully utilized in the exegetical treatment of this genre of psalms to which the book of Lamentations also belongs. One should also note the renewed work on the Egyptian comparative material by Barucq and the possibility for comparison with the Hittite material, which has never been fully exploited (Gurney 1948; Güterbock; Houwink ten Cate).

Gerstenberger's recent work on Psalms (1971) is a major advance in the right direction. In the meantime, however, a whole spate of new tools that should ease the task of the biblical scholar attempting to understand the psalms in the light of the general Near Eastern background has appeared. Werner Mayer's excellent new study of the *šu-illa* prayers, heavily influenced as it is by biblical form criticism, particularly that of Gerstenberger, should make it easier for the biblical scholar to make methodologically legitimate comparisons. The additional texts available to Mayer, some of which are now published in copies by Loretz and Mayer, make Mayer's study the most complete and accurate treatment of the *šu-illa* prayers and a necessary supplement and corrective to both Ebeling's edition and the earlier form-critical study of Kunstmann. Nonetheless, Mayer's volume is not the final word; there are still unpublished texts, and the form-critical work has not yet been carried through with the thoroughness it deserves (Lambert 1974–77). Returning to the positive, one should note the new French translation of Babylonian hymns and prayers by M.-J. Seux. Taken together with the older works, it and Mayer's volume provide the biblical scholar with a rich corpus for comparative purposes. Moreover, Jan Assmann's new translation of Egyptian hymns and prayers opens up new possibilities for serious comparative work on the Egyptian side as well. The number of texts represented and the clear types into which they fall should make form-critical analysis relatively easy and thereby provide some of the methodological control necessary for worthwhile comparative work.

Myth, Ritual, Magic

The period since Albright wrote has seen the recovery of significant portions of the Babylonian creation epic (Lambert and Parker; Grayson 1969), publication of the Atrahasis (Lambert and Millard) and Erra epics (Cagni 1969, 1970), and smaller additions to other Babylonian epics and myths (Grayson 1969; Hecker). One should also note the appearance of a number of Sumerian (Kramer 1969b; Alster 1972; Ferrara; Cooper 1978; Farber-Flügge) and Hittite (Hoffner 1975a) myths and epics.

The Atrahasis epic, in particular, has had an important influence on biblical studies since this epic connects the creation of humanity and the flood in a historical sequence just as the Genesis account does. Comparative studies between the two texts have concentrated on the reason for the flood in the two narratives. One school of thought sees a similarity in that the flood in both stories is caused by human evil. This is not so clear in the Babylonian account, but such an interpretation is assigned to the text based on a moral understanding of the "noise" made by humanity. Such an interpretation tries to connect the motif of "noise" to the "outcry" of the Sodom and Gomorrah story and, in fact, often sees this later story as a simple variant of the basically similar flood story (Pettinato 1971b). The other, far more persuasive, school of thought sees rather a contrast between the biblical and Mesopotamian reasons for the flood. The biblical account blames the flood on moral evil (Frymer-Kensky), but the Atrahasis epic sees the problem in what one might call natural evil, in the problem of overpopulation (Draffkorn-Kilmer 1972; Moran 1971). Needless to say, the nature of the deity involved in the two accounts varies considerably. For the view of creation and the position of the gods in Atrahasis, note especially the articles of Moran (1970) and Jacobsen (1977) where earlier literature is discussed.

The creation epic has also figured prominently in biblical discussions, particularly in the ongoing debate over the alleged enthronement festival in Israel. There is no room to enter into that debate, which is well treated in the fine comparative study by Lipiński, except to note the new material relevant to the discussion that has emerged from the extrabiblical material. The myth and ritual school's view of a pattern of divine kingship common to the whole Near East was severely criticized by Frankfort, who pointed to striking differences between the Egyptian and Mesopotamian views of the king. Even the divinity of the Egyptian king, however, has been questioned. Goedicke stressed the divinity of the office of the king rather than his person, and Posener has been even more critical of the alleged divinity of the Pharaoh. Such criticism has reduced the contrast between Egyptian and Mesopotamian conceptions of kingship, but at the same time it has also reduced the "divine" element in both conceptions, a central tenet of the myth and ritual school. Moving to the Mesopotamian side, reconstructions of the Babylonian new year festival have tended to ignore regional and temporal differences in the quest for a common pattern, and the resulting reconstructions are therefore subject to question. To mention only one point, most reconstructions include the death and resurrection of Marduk, but the one text that was thought to tell of Marduk's resurrection has been shown by von Soden to be something quite different (1952–55, 1957). The text actually uses mythological material to justify Sennacherib's sack of Babylon. A similar use of mythological material to interpret or justify historical events for political reasons can be seen in the much earlier Sumerian composition *The Exaltation of Inanna* (Hallo and van Dijk; cf. Roberts 1973: 341), and Jacobsen has argued that it is a significant feature in most of the combat myths of later Mesopotamian history (1975: 72–77). Even the great creation epic was written, according to Jacobsen, to celebrate a historical event: Babylon's victory over the Sealand (1975: 76). Such a development obviously has significant implications for biblical studies where one can find a similar political use of myth (Roberts 1973).

The numerous ritual texts from the ancient Near East also have a potential value for biblical scholarship that has not yet been fully exploited. *Maqlu* (Meier) and *Shurpu* (Reiner) have been mined for their rich contribution to curse formulas (Hillers 1964), and Jacob Milgrom, in particular, has drawn upon Hittite material in explaining Israelite ritual (1970, 1976a, 1976b), but much remains unused. In addition to the Mari prophecies and the Neo-Assyrian prophetic texts, for instance, the enormous amount of new material on Babylonian divinatory practice (RAI 14, 1966; Bottéro 1974 and bibliography) would appear to be ready-made for the new interest in the "social location" of the Israelite prophets. It has not been totally overlooked (Long 1973), but this discussion has seemed to prefer more remote, relatively modern analogies (Long 1977). These analogies have their place, but there is much that one can still learn from the more ancient parallels (Roberts 1977a; Barré). A fine summary and a good use of this material can be found in Robert Wilson's new monograph (1980). One should also note the potential value of such ritual series as the "opening of the mouth" ceremony (Borger 1975: 85) for gaining a better understanding of ancient Near Eastern idolatry and hence of the prophetic polemic against idolatry.

Law

The major collections of Near Eastern law were already known at the time Albright wrote, but our understanding of them has increased in the intervening period. New translations or editions of some of the collections have appeared (Yaron; Cardascia; Finet), but even more important, detailed interpretative work such as that of Finkelstein (1973) has opened our eyes to the significance of these corpora as collections, or perhaps even revisions, of traditional case law, and has made clear the basic continuity of the biblical collections with these antecedents. F. R. Kraus's (1958, 1965a) and Finkelstein's (1965) treatments of the Babylonian mišarum edicts, moreover, have provided possible legal parallels for such Israelite institutions as the Sabbath Year and the Jubilee Year, which were once regarded as purely utopian constructs.

Albrecht Alt's classic study of the origins of Israelite law remains a formative influence although it has required significant modification. On form-critical grounds he made a sharp distinction between casuistic or case law, common to the ancient Near Eastern legal tradition and adapted from it by Israel, and the so-called apodictic or categorical law, typified by the Ten Commandments, which he regarded as uniquely Israelite and derived from religious instruction in the cult. Several criticisms have been leveled against his category of apodictic law (Nielsen: 56–93). The category as he defines it is not a unit, since some radically different formulations have been subsumed under one category. Moreover, the apodictic command is neither peculiarly Israelite nor necessarily cultic—examples have been found in Near Eastern laws, ritual instructions, and Hittite treaties. These observations could be accommodated by slight modifications of Alt's theory, but E. Gerstenberger (1965) raised a more fundamental objection when he denied that the apodictic command originated in a cultic setting and argued instead that it arose in the ethos of early Israelite tribal society as instruction given by clan heads and elders to the youth (*Sippenweisheit*). His treatment was suggestive and has been favorably received by many scholars, but there are serious grammatical difficulties with Gerstenberger's attempt to remove the distinction between the Hebrew negatives לא and אל (Bright 1973). If that distinction cannot be erased, most of Gerstenberger's examples of apodictic law in the wisdom collections vanish, and Bright's alternate explanation of an original Israelite setting in the covenant stipulations, later transmitted in various channels—cultic recitation, priestly instruction, prophetic word, legal debates among the village elders, and family instruction—appears a more adequate model for understanding the origins and development of this kind of legal material.

Covenant

No area of the Near Eastern background of the Hebrew Bible has been more discussed in recent years than the international treaty. Since Mendenhall initiated the biblical discussion with his little booklet in 1955, the comparative treaty material has multiplied dramatically. McCarthy was able to take account of most of the new material in his standard treatment of the question (1963), but new material since then, such as the Hittite version of the Aziru treaty (Freydank), forced McCarthy to revise some of his earlier conclusions in his more recent work (1972). McCarthy's very thorough work tended to dampen discussion of these parallels despite the fact that many of the scholars who had worked on this material earlier were far from agreeing with McCarthy's assessment of the material (Huffmon 1966; Huffmon and Parker; Hillers 1969; Mendenhall 1973). This, in turn, has resulted in a perceptible shift in much OT discussion of covenant back to a narrowly biblical base, which can be seen in Kutsch's widely quoted definition of ברית as "obligation" (1967) and in Perlitt's return to Wellhausen's view of covenant as a late theological novelty in Israel. This is a false step, an attempt to gain a bogus security in the constricted womb of pure OT studies. Whatever the excesses of the comparative work done on biblical covenant and Near Eastern treaty, it should have made clear that the reality involved could not be apprehended by a simple syntactical study of a single Hebrew word (see McCarthy 1974: 103). If genuine progress is to be made in this area, it will come from a continued firsthand acquaintance with the extrabiblical material conjoined with careful analysis of the biblical texts. Examples of this type of approach may be seen in M. Weinfeld's interesting comparison of the Davidic covenant to the royal grant and in P. Riemann's thoughtful reappraisal of the Mosaic covenant.

Wisdom

The wisdom literature is another area in which our understanding of the Near Eastern background has advanced significantly in the last three decades. Edmund Gordon's *Sumerian Proverbs*, recently supplemented by Alster (1978), and W. G. Lambert's *Babylonian Wisdom Literature* (1960b) were significant milestones in a better understanding of the Mesopotamian material, but one must also note Kramer's treatment of the Sumerian "Man and his God" (1955, 1969c) and Nougayrol's publication of "Une version ancienne du 'Juste souffrant' " (1952). These together with the new texts discovered at Ugarit (Nougayrol 1968: 265–300)—providing, among other things, evidence of a possible cultural link between Canaan and the Babylonian tradition—testified to a long intellectual tradition in which the problem of individual suffering was treated, and they thus have an important bearing on the interpretation of Job (Roberts 1977b; see more recently Müller). Sjöberg's studies on the Sumerian schools (1972, 1973, 1975a, 1975b) helped to clarify the part these may have played in the continuity of that tradition. A number of summarizing studies appeared (Kuhl 1953, 1954; Gray 1970), including the oft-cited work by Gese (1958b). At the same time significant work was also being done on the Egyptian wisdom material. Williams (1961) and Couroyer (1963, 1968) refuted Drioton's (1957, 1959) attempt to trace the Wisdom of Amenemope back to a Semitic original. Gardiner's work on the onomastica was used by von Rad to explain Job 38. Other currents in Egyptian wisdom literature were mediated to biblical scholars in the works of McKane, Schmid, and Gemser.

Some of the attempts to explain biblical material from the background of international wisdom, however, seem a bit excessive. One may question whether Israelite wisdom had any conception equivalent to the Egyptian *maat*, and certainly the influence of the Egyptian encyclopaedic lists on biblical literature has been highly overrated. Hillers has shown that the background for Psalm 148, far from being sought in the Egyptian lists, may be found in a hymnic tradition reaching back to pre-Israelite Mesopotamia and Egypt, in which other gods, as deified elements of creation, join in praising the deity being worshiped (1978).

Love Poetry

One should also look at the recent attempts to find a background for understanding the Song of Songs. Gerleman has stressed the Egyptian parallels, and the recent work of White has added some relevant material (Williams 1977: 499). Schmökel (1952, 1956) and Cooper (1971) have pointed to cuneiform parallels, and if one takes at all seriously the possibility that these songs originated in a fertility cult, one cannot overlook the rather peculiar "love" lyrics published by Lambert (1975). All of this material, together with a mass of nontextual comparative evidence, has been assembled in the massive new commentary by Pope (1977), but it is still too early to say how much this will clarify the text of this most peculiar of biblical books.

Collections of Pictures and Texts in Translation

Finally, one should note the major collections of ancient Near Eastern texts and pictures relating to the Bible. The two standard collections have been those of Gressmann (1926, 1927) and Pritchard (1969). A bit less expensive is Beyerlin's collection of texts made for the ATD series, which has now been translated into English for the OT Library series. D. Winton Thomas edited a collection of texts prepared by the Society for Old Testament Study, and Kurt Galling's collection of historical texts should also be mentioned. Although the iconographic evidence has never been entirely ignored in OT scholarship, it has never received quite the same serious treatment that has been accorded the ancient Near Eastern texts. This exclusively textual orientation has been a serious flaw in the approach of many biblical scholars. Spalinger's study (1978) of a Canaanite human sacrifice depicted on an Egyptian relief points up the value of the pictorial evidence for understanding the OT backgrounds. Even more impressive, however, has been Othmar Keel's series of exciting exegetical studies (1974, 1977a, 1977b) which have systematically incorporated the pictorial evidence, including that of the seals, into the exegetical process. This is perhaps the most promising direction taken in recent biblical scholarship's use of the comparative material. One can only hope that scholars will begin to give serious attention to nonepigraphic evidence in a more self-critical fashion.

III. Summary

It is difficult in a summary statement to do justice to the complexity of the ebb and flow of the study of OT backgrounds over the last thirty years. The tendency has been to overstress the importance of the background material in the first flush of discovery, and then, when the flaws in the early interpretations have become obvious, to swing to the other extreme of largely ignoring the comparative material. Very often in this latter phase of the discussion many of the biblical scholars involved no longer controlled the primary sources for the extrabiblical evidence. This lack of firsthand acquaintance with the nonbiblical material is a growing problem in the field. It is partly a reflex of the growing complexity of the broader field of ancient Near Eastern studies: no one can master the whole field any longer. Partly it reflects a conscious theological decision about the appropriate task of the OT scholar (Childs), and partly it may reflect a loss of nerve, a decision to settle for a more controllable albeit more restricted vision.

In any case, the perceptible shift away from the larger picture bodes ill for the exegetical task. The concern for biblical backgrounds has had its abuses and exaggerations. There is a need for a far more rigorous attempt to understand both the OT material and the nonbiblical material in their own settings, and before making comparative judgments one should also be clear that the material being compared or contrasted is really comparable (Saggs: 1–29). But, despite the abuses and the need for a more self-critical methodology, the attention to extrabiblical sources has brought new understanding to the biblical text. If it has never proven a particular interpretation, it has certainly ruled out some and suggested others. However, if this light from the East is to continue shining and grow brighter, biblical scholars must continue to be conversant with fields outside their own discipline. To some extent one can and must depend on experts in these related fields, but unless one has some firsthand acquaintance with the texts and physical remains with which these related fields deal, one will hardly be able to choose which expert's judgment to follow. There is no substitute for knowledge of the primary sources.

Bibliography

Aistleitner, Joseph
1963 *Wörterbuch der Ugaritischen Sprache.* Berichte über die Verhandlungen der Sächsischen Akademie der Wissenschaften zu Leipzig. Phil.-hist. Klasse 106/3. Berlin: Akademie Verlag.

Al-A'dami, Khalid Ahmad
1967 "Old Babylonian Letters from ed-Der." *Sumer* 23: 151–66.
Albrektson, Bertil
1967 *History and the Gods: An Essay on the Idea of Historical Events as Divine Manifestations in the Ancient Near East and in Israel.* Lund: CWK Gleerup.
Albright, William F.
1944 "The Oracles of Balaam." *JBL* 63: 207–33.
1950 "The Psalm of Habakkuk." Pp. 1–18 in *Studies in Old Testament Prophecy.* Edinburgh: T. & T. Clark.
1951 "The Old Testament and the Archaeology of the Ancient East." Pp. 27–47 in *The Old Testament and Modern Study.* Ed. H. H. Rowley. Oxford: Clarendon.
1968 *Yahweh and the Gods of Canaan.* Garden City, NY: Doubleday.
Alster, Bendt
1972 *Dumuzi's Dream: Aspects of Oral Poetry in a Sumerian Myth.* Mesopotamia, 1. Copenhagen: Akademisk Forlag.
1978 "Sumerian Proverb Collection Seven." *RA* 72: 97–112.
Alt, Albrecht
1934 *Die Ursprünge des israelitischen Rechts.* Berichte über die Verhandlungen der Sächsischen Akademie der Wissenschaften zu Leipzig. Phil.-hist. Klasse 86/1. Leipzig: S. Hirzel. Reprinted pp. 278–332 in *Kleine Schriften zur Geschichte des Volkes Israel*, 1. Munich: C. H. Beck, 1968.
Archi, Alfonso
1979 "The Epigraphic Evidence from Ebla and the Old Testament." *Bib* 60: 556–66.
Archives royales de Mari I–
1946 Textes cunéiformes, Musée du Louvre, XXII–. Paris: Paul Geuthner.
Archives royales de Mari, transcrite et traduite, I–XIX
1950–1977 Ed. André Parrot and Georges Dossin. Paris: Imprimerie Nationale.
Assman, Jan
1975 *Ägyptische Hymnen und Gebete.* Zurich and Munich: Artemis-Verlag.
Barr, James
1974 "Philology and Exegesis: Some General Remarks, with Illustrations from Job 3." Pp. 39–61 in *Questions disputées d'Ancien Testament.* Ed. C. Brekelmans. Leuven: University Press.
Barré, M. L.
1978 "New Light on the Interpretation of Hosea vi 2." *VT* 28: 129–41.
Barucq, André
1962 *L'expression de la louange divine et de la prière dans la Bible et en Égypte.* Bibliothèque d'étude, 33. Cairo: Institut français d'archéologie orientale.
Bauer, Theodor
1926 *Die Ostkanaanäer.* Leipzig: Asia Major.
Bergerhof, K., M. Dietrich, O. Loretz, and J. C. de Moor
1969 *Ugarit-Forschungen.* Neukirchen-Vluyn: Neukirchener Verlag.
Bermant, Chaim, and Michael Weitzman
1979 *Ebla: An Archaeological Enigma.* London: Weidenfeld and Nicolson.

Beyerlin, Walter, ed.

1978 *Near Eastern Texts Relating to the Old Testament.* Philadelphia: Westminster.

Biggs, Robert

1980 "The Ebla Tablets: An Interim Perspective." *BA* 43: 76–86.

Boling, Robert G.

1960 " 'Synonymous' Parallelism in the Psalms." *JSS* 5: 221–55.

Bordreuil, Pierre

1975 "Nouveaux textes économiques en cunéiformes alphabétiques de Ras Shamra-Ougarit (34e campagne 1973)." *Sem* 25: 19–29.

Borger, Riekele

1956 *Die Inschriften Asarhaddons, Königs von Assyrien.* AfO Beih, 9. Graz: E. Weidner.

1961 *Einleitung in die assyrischen Königsinschriften*, I. Leiden: E. J. Brill.

1967–1975 *Handbuch der Keilschriftliteratur*, I–III. Berlin and New York: Walter de Gruyter.

Bottéro, Jean

1954 *Le problème des Habiru à la 4e Rencontre assyriologique internationale.* Cahiers de la Société asiatique, 12. Paris: Imprimerie Nationale.

1974 "Symptômes, signes, écritures en Mésopotamie ancienne." Pp. 70–197 in *Divination et Rationalité.* Paris: Éditions du Seuil.

Bright, John

1959 *A History of Israel.* Philadelphia: Westminster. 2d ed., 1972.

1973 "The Apodictic Prohibition: Some Observations." *JBL* 92: 185–204.

Brinkman, J. A.

1964 "Merodach-Baladan II." Pp. 6–53 in *Studies Presented to A. L. Oppenheim.* Chicago: Oriental Institute.

1968 *A Political History of Post-Kassite Babylonia 1158–722 B.C.* AnOr 43. Rome: Pontifical Biblical Institute.

Buccellati, Giorgio

1966 *The Amorites of the Ur III Period.* Naples: Istituto Orientale di Napoli.

Cagni, Luigi

1969 *L'epopea di Erra.* Studi Semitici 34. Rome: Istituto di Studi del Vicino Oriente.

1970 *Das Erra-Epos Keilschrifttext.* Rome: Pontifical Biblical Institute.

Campbell, Edward F., Jr.

1964 *The Chronology of the Amarna Letters.* Baltimore: Johns Hopkins University Press.

1965 "Shechem in the Amarna Archive." Pp. 191–207 in *Shechem: The Biography of a Biblical City.* Ed. G. E. Wright. New York and Toronto: McGraw-Hill.

Cancik, Hubert

1976 *Grundzüge der hethitischen und alttestamentlichen Geschichtsschreibung.* Wiesbaden: Otto Harrassowitz.

Caquot, André, Maurice Sznycer, and Andrée Herdner

1974 *Textes Ougaritiques: I. Mythes et Légendes.* Paris: Éditions du Cerf.

Caquot, André, and Emilia Masson

1977 "Tablettes Ougaritiques du Louvre." *Sem* 27: 5–19.

Cardascia, Guillaume
1969 *Les lois assyriennes.* Littératures anciennes du proche-orient. Paris: Éditions du Cerf.
Cassuto, Umberto
1971 *The Goddess Anath.* Jerusalem: Magnes. Hebrew original in 1951.
Childs, Brevard S.
1979 *Introduction to the Old Testament as Scripture.* Philadelphia: Fortress.
Clifford, Richard J.
1972 *The Cosmic Mountain in Canaan and the Old Testament.* Cambridge, MA: Harvard University Press.
Cohen, Mark E.
1974 *Balag-Compositions: Sumerian Lamentation Liturgies of the Second and First Millennium B.C.* Sources from the Ancient Near East, 1/2. Malibu, CA: Undena.
Coogan, Michael David
1978 *Stories from Ancient Canaan.* Philadelphia: Westminster.
Cooper, Jerrold S.
1971 "New Cuneiform Parallels to the Song of Songs." *JBL* 90: 157–62.
1978 *The Return of Ninurta to Nippur.* AnOr 52. Rome: Pontifical Biblical Institute.
Coppens, Joseph
1946 "Les parallèles du Psautier avec les textes de Ras Shamra-Ougarit." *Bulletin d'histoire et d'exégèse de AT* 18: 113–42.
Couroyer, B.
1963 'L'origine égyptienne de la Sagesse d'Amenemopé." *RB* 70: 208–24.
1968 "Amenemopé XXIV, 13–18." *RB* 75: 549–61.
Craigie, P. E., ed.
1972– *Newsletter for Ugaritic Studies.* Calgary, Alberta, Canada: Religious Studies Program, University of Calgary.
Cross, Frank M.
1954 "The Evolution of the Proto-Canaanite Alphabet." *BASOR* 132: 15–24.
1955 "The Song of Miriam." *JNES* 14: 237–50.
1961 "The Development of the Jewish Scripts." Pp. 133–302 in *The Bible and the Ancient Near East: Essays in Honor of William Foxwell Albright.* Ed. G. E. Wright. Garden City, NY: Doubleday.
1967 "The Origin and Early Evolution of the Alphabet." Pp. 8–24 in *E. L. Sukenik Memorial Volume (1899–1953).* Eretz-Israel 8. Jerusalem: Israel Exploration Society.
1968 "Song of the Sea and Canaanite-Myth." *JTC* 5: 1–25.
1973 *Canaanite Myth and Hebrew Epic.* Cambridge, MA: Harvard University Press.
1974 "Leaves from an Epigraphist's Notebook." *CBQ* 36: 486–94.
Cross, Frank M., and David N. Freedman
1948 "The Blessing of Moses." *JBL* 67: 191–210.
1950 *Studies in Ancient Yahwistic Poetry.* Baltimore: Authors. Published as SBLDS 21. Missoula, MT: Scholars Press.

1952 *Early Hebrew Orthography: A Study of the Epigraphic Evidence.* New Haven: American Oriental Society.
1972 "Some Observations on Early Hebrew." *Bib* 53: 413–20.

Dahood, Mitchell
1966–1970 *Psalms.* 3 vols. AB 16, 17, 17a. Garden City, NY: Doubleday.
1978 "Ebla, Ugarit and the Old Testament." Pp. 81–112 in *Congress Volume: Göttingen, 1977.* VTSup 29. Leiden: E. J. Brill.

Dalglish, Edward R.
1962 *Psalm Fifty-One in the Light of Ancient Near Eastern Patternism.* Leiden: E. J. Brill.

Dever, William G.
1977 "Palestine in the Second Millennium BCE: The Archaeological Picture." Pp. 70–120 in *Israelite and Judaean History.* Ed. J. H. Hayes and J. M. Miller. Philadelphia: Westminster.

Dietrich, Manfred, and O. Loretz
1966, 1969 "Die soziale Struktur von Alalah und Ugarit." *WO* 3: 188–205; 5: 57–93.
1972a *Konkordanz der ugaritischen Textzählungen.* AOAT 19. Kevelaer: Verlag Butzon und Bercker.
1972b *Nuzi-Bibliographie.* AOAT Sonderreihe 11. Kevelaer: Verlag Butzon und Bercker.
1973 *Ugarit-Bibliographie 1928–66.* AOAT 20. Kevelaer: Verlag Butzon und Bercker.

Donner, Herbert
1967 "Ugaritismen in der Psalmenforschung." *ZAW* 79: 322–50.
1970 "Adadnirari III und die Vasallen des Westens." Pp. 49–59 in *Archäologie und Altes Testament* (Festschrift Kurt Galling). Ed. A. Kuschke and E. Kutsch. Tübingen: J. C. B. Mohr.

Dossin, G.
1975 "Tablettes de Mari." *RA* 69: 23–30.

Draffkorn-Kilmer, Anne E.
1957 "*Ilāni/Elohim.*" *JBL* 76: 216–24.
1972 "The Mesopotamian Concept of Overpopulation and its Solution as Represented in the Mythology." *Or* 41: 160–77.

Drioton, Etienne
1957 "Sur la Sagesse d'Aménémopé." Pp. 254–80 in *Mélanges bibliques redigés en l'honneur de André Robert.* Ed. H. Cazelles. Paris: Bloud & Gay.
1959 "Le livre des Proverbes et la Sagesse d'Aménémopé." Pp. 229–41 in *Sacra Pagina: Miscellanea biblica congressus internationalis Catholici de re biblica,* vol. 1. Ed. J. Coppens. BETL 12. Gembloux: Duculot; Paris: Gabalda.

Driver, G. R.
1956 *Canaanite Myth and Legends.* Old Testament Studies, 3. Edinburgh: T. & T. Clark.

Ebeling, Erich
1953 *Die akkadische Gebetsserie 'Handerhebung' von neuem gesammelt und herausgegeben.* Berlin: Akademie Verlag.
Edzard, Dietz Otto
1957 *Die 'zweite Zwischenzeit' Babyloniens.* Wiesbaden: Otto Harrassowitz.
1973 "Die Tontafeln von Kämid el-Löz." Pp. 50–62 in *Kamid el-Loz-Kumidi.* Ed. D. O. Edzard et al. Saarbrücker Beiträge zur Altextumskunde, 7. Bonn: Rudolf Habelt.
Eichler, Barry L.
1973 *Indenture at Nuzi: The Personal Tidennūtu Contract and its Mesopotamian Analogues.* New Haven and London: Yale University Press.
1976 "Nuzi." Pp. 635–36 in *IDBSup.*
1977 "Another Look at Nuzi Sisterhood Contracts." Pp. 45–59 in *Essays on the Ancient Near East in Memory of Jacob Joel Finkelstein.* Ed. Maria de Jong Ellis. Memoirs of the Connecticut Academy of Arts and Sciences, 19. Hamden, CT: Archon Books.
Ellermeier, Friedrich
1968 *Prophetie in Mari und Israel.* Herzberg am Harz: E. Jungfer.
Falkenstein, Adam, and Wolfram von Soden
1953 *Sumerische und akkadische Hymnen und Gebete.* Zurich and Stuttgart: Artemis-Verlag.
Farber-Flügge, Gertrud
1973 *Der Mythos "Inanna und Enki" unter besonderer Berücksichtigung der Liste der me.* Studia Pohl 10. Rome: Pontifical Biblical Institute.
Ferrara, A. J.
1973 *Nanna-Suen's Journey to Nippur.* Studia Pohl: Series Maior, 2. Rome: Pontifical Biblical Institute.
Finet, André
1973 *Le code de Hammurapi.* Littératures anciennes du proche-orient. Paris: Éditions du Cerf.
Finkelstein, J. J.
1965 "Some New *Misharum* Material and its Implications." Pp. 233–46 in *Studies in Honor of Benno Landsberger on His Seventy-Fifth Birthday, April 21, 1965.* AS 16. Chicago: University of Chicago Press.
1966 "The Genealogy of the Hammurapi Dynasty." *JCS* 20: 95–118.
1973 "The Goring Ox: Some Historical Perspectives on Deodards, Forfeitures, Wrongful Death and the Western Notion of Sovereignty." *Temple Law Quarterly* 46: 169–290.
Fisher, Loren R., ed.
1971 *The Claremont Ras Shamra Tablets.* AnOr 48. Rome: Pontifical Biblical Institute.
1972, 1975 *Ras Shamra Parallels: The Texts from Ugarit and the Hebrew Bible.* 2 vols. Rome: Pontifical Biblical Institute.
Fitzmyer, Joseph A.
1956 "*le* as a Proposition and a Particle in Micah 5,1(5,2)." *CBQ* 18: 10–13.

Frankfort, Henri

1948 *Kingship and the Gods.* Chicago: University of Chicago Press.

Freedman, David N.

1971 Prolegomenon to G. B. Gray's *The Forms of Hebrew Poetry.* New York: Ktav.

1972 "Psalm XXIX in the Hebrew Poetic Tradition." *VT* 22: 144–45.

1976 "Divine Names and Titles in Early Hebrew Poetry." Pp. 55–102 in *Magnalia Dei: The Mighty Acts of God: Essays on the Bible and Archaeology in Memory of G. Ernest Wright.* Ed. F. M. Cross, W. E. Lemke, P. D. Miller. Garden City, NY: Doubleday.

1977 "A Letter to the Readers." *BA* 40: 2–4.

1978 "The Real Story of the Ebla Tablets: Ebla and the Cities of the Plain." *BA* 41: 143–64.

Freedman, Nadezhda

1977 "The Nuzi Ebla." *BA* 40: 32–33.

Freydank, Helmut

1960 "Eine hethitische Fassung des Vertrags zwischen dem Hethiterkönig Šuppiluliuma und Aziru von Amurru." *MIO* 7: 35–81.

Frymer-Kensky, T.

1977 "The Atrahasis Epic and Its Significance for our Understanding of Genesis 1–9." *BA* 40: 147–55.

Galling, Kurt

1950 *Textbuch zur Geschichte Israels.* Tübingen: J. C. B. Mohr. 2d ed., 1968.

Gardiner, Alan H.

1947 *Ancient Egyptian Onomastica* 1–3. London: Oxford University Press.

Gelb, Ignace J.

1958 *La lingua degli Amoriti.* Rendiconti delle sedute Del' accademia Nazionale dei Lincei. Class di Science morali, storiche e filologiche, XIII: 143–64. Atti della Accademia Nazionale dei Lincei.

1961 *Old Akkadian Writing and Grammar.* 2d ed. Chicago: University of Chicago Press.

1977 "Thoughts About Ibla: A Preliminary Evaluation, March, 1977." *Syro-Mesopotamian Studies* 1: 113–30.

Gemser B.

1960 "The Instructions of Onchsheshonqy and Biblical Wisdom Literature." Pp. 102–28 in *Congress Volume: Oxford, 1959.* VTSup 7. Leiden: E. J. Brill.

Gerleman, Gillis

1965 *Ruth: Das Hohelied.* BKAT 18. Neukirchen-Vluyn: Neukirchener Verlag.

Gerstenberger, Erhard

1965 *Wesen und Herkunft des "apodiktischen Rechts."* WMANT 20. Neukirchen-Vluyn: Neukirchener Verlag. *Der bittende Mensch: Bittritual und Klagelied des Einzelnen im Alten Testament.* Habil.-Schrift, Heidelberg. Now published: WMANT 51. Neukirchen-Vluyn: Neukirchener Verlag.

Gese, Hartmut

1958a "Geschichtliches Denken im Alten Orient und im Alten Testament." *ZTK* 55: 127–45.

1958b *Lehre und Wirklichkeit in der alten Weisheit.* Tübingen: J. C. B. Mohr.
1970 "Die Religionen Altsyriens." *Die Religionen der Menschheit* X, 2: 1–232.

Geus, C. H. J. de
1976 *The Tribes of Israel.* Assen and Amsterdam: Van Gorcum.

Gibson, J. C. L.
1978 *Canaanite Myths and Legends.* Edinburgh: T. & T. Clark.

Ginsberg, H. L.
1955 "Ugaritic Myths, Epics and Legends." Pp. 129–55 in *ANET.* 2d ed. Ed. J. Pritchard. Princeton: Princeton University Press.

Goedicke, Hans
1960 *Die Stellung der Königs im alten Reich.* Ägyptologische Abhandlungen, 2. Wiesbaden: Otto Harrassowitz.

Goodwin, Donald Watson
1969 *Text-Restoration Methods in Contemporary U.S.A. Biblical Scholarship.* Pubblicazioni del Seminario di Semitistica, Ricerche 5. Naples: Istituto Orientale di Napoli.

Gordis, Robert
1943 "The Asseverative Kaph in Ugaritic and Hebrew." *JAOS* 63: 176–78.

Gordon, Cyrus H.
1940 "Biblical Customs and the Nuzi Tablets." *BA* 3: 1–12.
1954 "The Patriarchal Narratives." *JNES* 13: 56–59.
1965 *Ugaritic Textbook.* AnOr 38. Rome: Pontifical Biblical Institute.

Gordon, Edmund I.
1959 *Sumerian Proverbs: Glimpses of Everyday Life in Ancient Mesopotamia.* Philadelphia: University Museum.

Görg, Manfred
1975 *Gott-König-Reden in Israel und Ägypten.* BWANT 105. Stuttgart: W. Kohlhammer.

Gottwald, Norman K.
1974 "Were the Early Israelites Pastoral Nomads?" Pp. 223–55 in *Rhetorical Criticism: Essays in Honor of James Muilenburg.* Ed. J. J. Jackson and M. Kessler. PTMS 1. Pittsburgh: Pickwick.
1975 "Domain Assumptions and Societal Models in the Study of Pre-Monarchic Israel." Pp. 89–100 in *Congress Volume: Edinburgh, 1974.* VTSup 28. Leiden: E. J. Brill.
1979 *The Tribes of Yahweh: A Sociology of the Religion of Liberated Israel 1250–1050 B.C.E.* Maryknoll, NY: Orbis Books.

Gray, John
1957 *The Legacy of Canaan.* VTSup 5. Leiden: E. J. Brill. 2d ed., 1965.
1970 "The Book of Job in the Context of Near Eastern Literature." *ZAW* 82: 251–69.

Grayson, Albert K.
1966 "Divination and the Babylonian Chronicles." Pp. 69–76 in *La divination en Mesopotamie ancienne*, XIV[e]. Rencontre Assyriologique Internationale. Paris: Presses Universitaires de France.

1969 "Akkadian Myths and Epics." Pp. 501–18 in *ANET.* Ed. J. Pritchard. Princeton: Princeton University Press.

1972, 1976 *Assyrian Royal Inscriptions*, 1–2. Records of the Ancient Near East. Wiesbaden: Otto Harrassowitz.

1975a *Assyrian and Babylonian Chronicles.* Texts from Cuneiform Sources, 5. Locust Valley, NY: J. J. Augustin.

1975b *Babylonian Historical-Literary Texts.* Toronto and Buffalo: University of Toronto Press.

Green, Margaret Whitney

1975 "Eridu in Sumerian Literature." Ph.D. dissertation, Department of Near Eastern Languages and Civilizations, University of Chicago.

Greenberg, Moshe

1955 *The Hab/piru.* New Haven: American Oriental Society.

1962 "Another Look at Rachel's Theft of the Teraphim." *JBL* 81: 239–48.

Gressmann, Hugo

1926 *Altorientalische Texte zum Alten Testament*, 2d ed. Berlin and Leipzig: Walter de Gruyter.

1927 *Altorientalische Bilder zum Alten Testament.* Berlin and Leipzig: Walter de Gruyter.

Gröndahl, Franke

1967 *Die Personennamen der Texte aus Ugarit.* Studia Pohl 1. Rome: Pontifical Biblical Institute.

Gurney, Oliver R.

1948 "Hittite Prayers of Mursili II." *Annals of Archaeology and Anthropology* 27: 1–163.

Gurney, Oliver R., and J. J. Finkelstein

1957 *The Sultantepe Tablets*, I. London: British Institute of Archaeology at Ankara.

Gurney, Oliver R., and P. Hulin

1964 *The Sultantepe Tablets*, II. London: British Institute of Archaeology at Ankara.

Güterbock, H. G.

1958 "The Composition of Hittite Prayers to the Sun." *JAOS* 78: 237–45.

Habel, Norman

1964 *Yahweh Versus Baal.* New York: Bookman Associates.

Hallo, William W.

1968 "Individual Prayer in Sumerian: The Continuity of a Tradition." Pp. 71–89 in *Essays in Memory of E. A. Speiser.* Ed. W. W. Hallo. *JAOS* 88/1 and AOS 53.

1976 "The Royal Correspondence of Larsa: A Sumerian Prototype for the Prayer of Hezekiah?" Pp. 209–24 in *Kramer Anniversary Volume.* AOAT 25. Neukirchen-Vluyn: Neukirchener Verlag.

Hallo, William W., and J. J. A. van Dijk

1968 *The Exaltation of Inanna.* New Haven and London: Yale University.

Hecker, Karl

1974 *Untersuchungen zur akkadischen Epik.* AOAT Sonderreihe. Neukirchen-Vluyn: Neukirchener Verlag.

Heintz, Jean-Georges
1969 "Oracles prophétiques et 'guerre sainte' selon les archives royales de Mari et l'Ancien Testament." Pp. 112–38 in *Congress Volume: Rome, 1968*. VTSup 17. Leiden: E. J. Brill.
Helck, Wolfgang
1971 *Die Beziehungen Ägyptens zu Vorderasien im 3. und 2. Jahrtausend v. Chr.* 2d. ed. Ägyptologische Abhandlungen, 5. Wiesbaden: Otto Harrassowitz.
Held, Moshe
1957 "Studies in Ugaritic Lexicography and Poetic Style." Ph.D. dissertation, Johns Hopkins University.
1962 "The YQTL-QTL (QTL-YQTL) Sequence of Identical Verbs in Biblical Hebrew and in Ugaritic." Pp. 281–90 in *Studies and Essays in Honor of Abraham A. Neuman*. Ed. M. Ben-Horin, B. D. Weinryb, and S. Zeitlin. Leiden: E. J. Brill.
Herdner, Andrée
1963 *Corpus des tablettes en cunéiformes alphabétiques découvertes à Ras Shamra–Ugarit de 1929 à 1939*. MRS 10. Paris: Imprimerie Nationale.
1972 "Une prière à Baal des Ugaritiens en danger." *CRAIBL*, 693–97, 698–703.
Hermann, Alfred
1938 "Die ägyptische Königsnovelle." Leipziger Ägyptologische Studien, 10. Glückstadt: Augustin.
Hermann, Siegfried
1953/1954 "Die Königsnovelle in Ägypten und in Israel." *Wissenschaftliche Zeitschrift der Karl-Marx-Universität.* 3: 33–44, 87–91.
1973 *Geschichte Israels in alttestamentlicher Zeit.* Munich: Chr. Kaiser.
Hillers, Delbert R.
1964 *Treaty-Curses and the Old Testament Prophets.* BibOr 16. Rome: Pontifical Biblical Institute.
1969 *Covenant: The History of a Biblical Idea.* Baltimore: Johns Hopkins University Press.
1978 "A Study of Psalm 148." *CBQ* 40: 322–34.
Hoffner, H. A., Jr.
1975a "Hittite Mythological Texts: A Survey." Pp. 136–45 in *Unity and Diversity.* Ed. H. Goedicke and J. J. M. Roberts. Baltimore and London: Johns Hopkins University Press.
1975b "Propaganda and Political Justification in Hittite Historiography." Pp. 49–62 in *Unity and Diversity.*
Hoftijzer, J., and G. van der Kooij
1976 *Aramaic Texts from Deir ʿAlla.* Leiden: E. J. Brill.
Houwink ten Cate, Ph. H. J.
1969 "Hittite Royal Prayer." *Numen* 16: 81–98.
Huffmon, Herbert B.
1965 *Amorite Personal Names in the Mari Texts.* Baltimore: Johns Hopkins University Press.
1966 "The Treaty Background of Hebrew Yădaʿ." *BASOR* 181: 31–37.

Huffmon, Herbert B., and Simon B. Parker

1966 "A Further Note on the Treaty Background of Hebrew Yădaʿ." *BASOR* 184: 36–38.

Hummel, H. D.

1957 "Enclitic *mem* in Early Northwest Semitic, especially Hebrew." *JBL* 76: 85–107.

Jacobsen, Thorkild

1975 "Religious Drama in Ancient Mesopotamia." Pp. 65–97 in *Unity and Diversity.* Ed. H. Goedicke and J. J. M. Roberts. Baltimore and London: Johns Hopkins University Press.

1977 "Inuma ilu awilum." Pp. 113–17 in *Essays on the Ancient Near East in Memory of Jacob Joel Finkelstein.* Memoirs of the Connecticut Academy of Arts and Sciences, 19. Hamden, CT: Archon Books.

Kaiser, Otto

1962 *Die mythische Bedeutung des Meeres in Ägypten, Ugarit, und Israel.* 2d ed. BZAW 78. Berlin: A. Töpelmann.

Kapelrud, Arvid S.

1963 *The Ras Shamra Discoveries and the Old Testament.* Norman: University of Oklahoma Press.

1969 *The Violent Goddess.* Oslo: Universitetsforlaget.

Keel, Othmar

1969 *Feinde und Gottesleugner.* Stuttgart: Katholisches Bibelwerk.

1974 *Wirkmächtige Siegeszeichen im Alten Testament.* OBO 5. Göttingen: Vandenhoeck & Ruprecht.

1977a *Vögel als Boten.* OBO 14. Göttingen: Vandenhoeck & Ruprecht.

1977b *Jahwe-Visionen und Siegelkunst.* SBS 84/85. Stuttgart: Katholisches Bibelwerk.

1978 *The Symbolism of the Biblical World.* New York: Seabury. German original in 1972.

Kitchen, Kenneth A.

1962 *Suppiluliuma and the Amarna Pharaohs.* Liverpool: Liverpool University.

Klengel, Evelyn, and Horst Klengel

1970 *Die Hettiter: Geschichte und Umwelt.* Vienna and Munich: Verlag Anton Scholl.

Klengel, Horst

1964 "Aziru von Amurru und seine Rolle in der Geschichte der Amarnazeit." *MIO* 10: 57–83.

1965, 1969, 1970 *Geschichte Syriens im 2. Jahrtausend v.u.Z,* 1–3. Berlin: Akademie Verlag.

1972 *Zwischen Zelt und Palast—die Begegnung von Nomaden und Sesshaften im alten Vorderasien.* Leipzig: Koehler & Ameorng.

Knudtzon, Jorgen Alexander

1915 *Die El-Amarna-Tafeln,* 1–2. Vorderasiatische Bibliothek, 2. Leipzig: J. C. Hinrichs. Photostatic reprint. Aaden: Otto Zeller, 1964.

Koehler, Ludwig, and Walter Baumgartner
1967– *Hebräisches und aramäisches Lexikon zum Alten Testament.* Leiden: E. J. Brill.
Kramer, Samuel Noah
1955 " 'Man and His God': A Sumerian Variation on the 'Job' Motif." Pp. 170–82 in *Wisdom in Israel and in the Ancient Near East.* Ed. M. Noth and D. W. Thomas. VTSup 3. Leiden: E. J. Brill.
1969a "Lamentation over the Destruction of Sumer and Ur." Pp. 611–19 in *ANET.* Ed. J. B. Pritchard. Princeton: Princeton University Press.
1969b "The Curse of Agade: The Ekur Avenged." Pp. 646–51 in *ANET.* Ed. J. B. Pritchard. Princeton: Princeton University Press.
1969c " 'Man and His God': A Sumerian Variation of the 'Job' Motif." Pp. 589–91 in *ANET.* Ed. J. B. Pritchard. Princeton: Princeton University Press.
Kraus, Fritz R.
1958 *Ein Edikt des Königs Ammi-saduqa von Babylon.* Studia et documenta ad iuru orientis antiqui pertinentia, 5. Leiden: E. J. Brill.
1965a "Ein Edikt des Königs Samsu-iluna von Babylon." Pp. 225–31 in *Studies in Honor of Benno Landsberger on His Seventy-Fifth Birthday, April 21, 1965.* AS 16. Chicago: University of Chicago Press.
1965b *Könige, die in Zelten wohnten.* Mededelingen der Koninklijke Nederlandse Akademie van Wetenschappen (Afd. Letterkunde, N. R. 28/2). Amsterdam: Noord-Hollandsche Uitgevers Maatschappij.
Kuhl, C.
1953 "Neuere Literarkritik des Buches Hiob." *TRu* 21: 163–205, 257–317.
1954 "Von Hiobbuche und seinen Problemen." *TRu* 22: 261–316.
Kümmel, Hans Martin
1965 *Ersatzrituale für den hethitischen König.* Studien zu den Bogazköy-Texten. Wiesbaden: Otto Harrassowitz.
Kunstmann, Walter G.
1932 *Die babylonische Gebetsbeschwörung.* Leipzig: J. C. Hinrichs.
Kupper, Jean-Robert
1957 *Les nomades en Mésopotamie au temps des rois de Mari.* Bibliothèque de la Faculté de Philosophie et Lettres de l'Université de Liège, Fascicule 142. Paris: Société d'Édition "Les Belles Lettres."
Kutsch, E.
1961 "Die Dynastie von Gottes Gnaden." *ZTK* 58: 137–53.
1967 "Gesetz und Gnade. Probleme des alttestamentlichen Bundesgriffs." *ZAW* 79: 18–35.
Kutscher, R.
1975 *Oh Angry Sea (a-ab-ba/hu-luh-ha): The History of a Sumerian Congregational Lament.* New Haven and London: Yale University Press.
LaFay, Howard
1978 "Ebla, Splendor of an Unknown Empire." *National Geographic* 154: 730–59.
Lambert, W. G.
1959/1960 "Three Literary Prayers of the Babylonians." *AfO* 19: 47–66.

1960a "The Domesticated Camel in the Second Millennium—Evidence from Alalakh and Ugarit." *BASOR* 160: 42–43. *Babylonian Wisdom Literature.* Oxford: Clarendon.

1972 "Destiny and Divine Intervention in Babylon and Israel." *OTS* 17: 65–72.

1974 "DINGIR.ŠÀ.DIB.BA Incantations." *JNES* 33: 267–322.

1974–1977 Review of Werner Mayer, *Untersuchungen zur Formensprüche der babylonische "Gebetsbeschwörungen."* *AfO* 25: 197–99.

1975 "The Problem of the Love Lyrics." Pp. 98–135 in *Unity and Diversity.* Ed. H. Goedicke and J. J. M. Roberts. Baltimore and London: Johns Hopkins University Press.

Lambert, W. G., and Alan R. Millard

1969 *Atra-hasis: The Babylonian Story of the Flood.* Oxford: Clarendon.

Lambert, W. G., and Simon B. Parker

1966 *Enuma Eliš: The Babylonian Epic of Creation, the Cuneiform Text.* Oxford: Clarendon.

Lehmann, Johannes

1975 *Die Hethiter. Volk der tausend Götter.* Munich and Vienna: C. Bertelsmann Verlag.

Lipiński, Edouard

1965 *La royauté de Yahwe dans la poésie et le culte de l'ancien Israël.* Brussels: Paleis der Academiën.

Liverani, M.

1970 "Per una considerazione storica del problema amorreo." *OrAnt* 9: 5–27.

1973 "The Amorites." Pp. 100–133 in *Peoples of Old Testament Times.* Ed. D. J. Wiseman. Oxford: Clarendon.

Long, Burke O.

1973 "The Effect of Divination upon Israelite Literature." *JBL* 92: 489–97.

1977 "Prophetic Authority as Social Reality." Pp. 3–20 in *Canon and Authority: Essays in Old Testament Religion and Theology.* Ed. G. W. Coats and B. O. Long. Philadelphia: Fortress.

Loretz, Oswald, and W. B. Mayer

1978 *Šu-ila-Gebete.* Supplement zu L. W. King. *Babylonian Magic and Sorcery.* AOAT 34. Neukirchen-Vluyn: Neukirchener Verlag.

Lugt, P. van der

1974 "The Spectre of Pan-Ugaritism." *BO* 31: 3–26.

Luke, John T.

1965 "Pastoralism and Politics in the Mari Period: A Re-Examination of the Character and Political Significance of the Major West Semitic Tribal Groups on the Middle Euphrates, c. 1828–1753 B.C." Ph.D. dissertation, University of Michigan.

McCarthy, Dennis J.

1963 *Treaty and Covenant: A Study in Form in the Ancient Oriental Documents and the Old Testament.* AnBib 21. Rome: Pontifical Biblical Institute.

1972 *Old Testament Covenant: A Survey of Current Opinions.* Atlanta: John Knox.

1974 "Covenant-relationships." Pp. 91–103 in *Questions disputées d'Ancien Testament, Méthode et Théologie.* Ed. C. Brekelmans. BETL 33. Leuven: University Press.

Machinist, P.

1976 "Literature as Politics: The Tukulti-Ninurta Epic and the Bible." *CBQ* 38: 455–82.

McKane, William

1970 *Proverbs: A New Approach.* OTL. Philadelphia: Westminster.

Malamat, Abraham

1966 "The Ban in Mari and in the Bible." Pp. 40–49 in *Biblical Essays.* University of Stellenbosch.

1967 "Aspects of Tribal Societies in Mari and Israel." Pp. 129–38 in *XVe Rencontre Assyriologique Internationale: La civilisation de Mari.* Ed. J. R. Kupper. Paris: Société d'Édition "Les Belles Lettres."

1968 "King Lists of the Old Babylonian Period and Biblical Genealogies." *JAOS* 88: 163–73.

1974 "The Twilight of Judah: In the Egyptian-Babylonian Maelstrom." Pp. 123–45 in *Congress Volume: Edinburgh, 1974.* VTSup 28. Leiden: E. J. Brill.

Mann, Thomas W.

1977 *Divine Presence and Guidance in Israelite Traditions: The Typology of Exaltation.* Baltimore and London: Johns Hopkins University Press.

Martinez, Ernest R.

1967 *Hebrew-Ugaritic Index to the Writings of Mitchell J. Dahood.* Rome: Pontifical Biblical Institute.

Marzal, Angel

1976 *Gleanings from the Wisdom of Mari.* Studia Pohl 11. Rome: Pontifical Biblical Institute.

Matthews, Victor Harold

1978 *Pastoral Nomadism in the Mari Kingdom (ca. 1830–1760 B.C.).* ASOR Dissertation Series, 3. Cambridge, MA: ASOR.

Matthiae, Paola

1973 "Ebla nel periodo delle dinastie amoree e della dinastia di Akkadi-Scoperte archaeologiche recenti a tell Mardikh." *Or* 44: 337–60.

1976a "Aspetti amministrativi e topografici di Ebla nel II millennio Av. Cr.: B. Considerazioni archeologiche." *RSO* 50: 16–30.

1976b "Ebla in the Late Early Syrian Period: The Royal Palace and the State Archives." *BA* 39: 94–113.

1978 "Tell Mardikh-Ebla." *Or* 47: 334–35.

Mayer, Werner

1976 *Untersuchungen zur Formenspräche der babylonischen "Gebetsbeschwörungen."* Studia Pohl, Series Maior 5. Rome: Pontifical Biblical Institute.

Meier, Gerhard

1937 *Die assyrische Beschwörungssammlung Maqlû. AfO* Beih. 2. Berlin: Selbstverlag des Herausgebers.

Melamed, E. Z.
1961 "Break-up of Stereotype Phrases as an Artistic Device in Biblical Poetry." Pp. 115–53 in *Studies in the Bible.* Ed. C. Rabin. Scripta Hierosolymitana, 8. Jerusalem: Magnes.
Mendelsohn, I.
1955 "On Slavery in Alalakh." *IEJ* 5: 65–72.
1959 "On Marriage at Alalakh." Pp. 351–57 in *Essays on Jewish Life and Thought.* New York: Columbia University Press.
Mendenhall, George E.
1955 *Law and Covenant in Israel and the Ancient Near East.* Pittsburgh: Biblical Colloquium.
1962 "The Hebrew Conquest of Palestine." *BA* 25: 66–87.
1973 *The Tenth Generation: The Origins of the Biblical Tradition.* Baltimore and London: Johns Hopkins University Press.
Milgrom, Jacob
1970 *Studies in Levitical Terminology,* 1. Berkeley: University of California Press.
1976a *Cult and Conscience: The Asham and the Priestly Doctrine of Repentance.* SJLA 18. Leiden: E. J. Brill.
1976b "The Concept of *MAʿAL* in the Bible and the Ancient Near East." *JAOS* 96: 236–47.
Miller, Patrick D., Jr.
1973a "God and the Gods." *Affirmation* 1/5: 37–62.
1973b *The Divine Warrior in Early Israel.* Cambridge: Harvard University Press.
Miller, Patrick D., Jr., and J. J. M. Roberts
1977 *The Hand of the Lord.* Baltimore and London: Hopkins University Press.
Moor, Johannes C. de
1970 "The Semitic Pantheon of Ugarit." *UF* 2: 187–228.
1971 *The Seasonal Pattern in the Ugaritic Myth of Baʿlu.* AOAT 16. Kevelaer: Verlag Butzon & Bercker.
1972 *New Year with Canaanites and Israelites.* Kampen: J. H. Kok.
Moran, William L.
1950a "A Syntactical Study of the Dialect of Byblos as Reflected in the Amarna Tablets." Ph.D. dissertation, Johns Hopkins University.
1950b "The Use of Canaanite Infinitive Absolute as a Finite Verb in the Amarna Letters from Byblos." *JCS* 4: 169–72.
1960 "Early Canaanite *yaqtula.*" *Or* 29: 1–19.
1961 "The Hebrew Language in its Northwest Semitic Background." Pp. 54–72 in *The Bible and the Ancient Near East.* Ed. G. E. Wright. Garden City, NY: Doubleday.
1969a "The Death of Abdi-Asirta." Pp. 94–99 in *W. F. Albright Volume.* Ed. A. Malamat. Eretz-Israel 9. Jerusalem: Israel Exploration Society.
1969b "New Evidence from Mari on the History of Prophecy." *Bib* 50: 15–56.
1970 "The Creation of Man in Atrahasis I 192–248." *BASOR* 200: 48–56.
1971 "Atrahasis: The Babylonian Story of the Flood." *Bib* 52: 51–61.
1973 "The Dual Personal Pronouns in Western Peripheral Akkadian." *BASOR* 211: 50–53.

1975a "The Syrian Scribe of the Jerusalem Amarna Letters." Pp. 146–66 in *Unity and Diversity*. Ed. H. Goedicke and J. J. M. Roberts. Baltimore and London: Johns Hopkins University Press.

1975b "Amarna Glosses." *RA* 69: 147–58.

Müller, Hans-Peter

1978 *Das Hiobproblem.* Darmstadt: Wissenschaftliche Buchgesellschaft.

Nielsen, Eduard

1965 *The Ten Commandments in New Perspective: A Traditio-Historical Approach* SBT 2/7. London: SCM.

Noetscher, F.

1953 "Zum emphatischen Lamed." *VT* 3: 372–80.

Noort, Edward

1977 *Untersuchungen zum Gottesbescheid in Mari: Die "Mariprophetie" in der alttestamentlichen Forschung.* AOAT 202. Neukirchen-Vluyn: Neukirchener Verlag.

Norin, Stig I. L.

1977 *Er spaltete das Meer: Die Auszugsüberlieferung in Psalmen und Kult des alten Israel.* ConBOT 9. Lund: CWK Gleerup.

Noth, Martin

1961 *Die Ursprünge des alten Israel im Lichte neuer Quellen.* Arbeitsgemeinschaft für Forschung des Landes Nordrhein-Westfalen Geisteswissenschaften 94. Cologne and Opladen: Westdeutscher Verlag.

Nougayrol, J.

1952 "Une version ancienne du 'juste souffrant.'" *RB* 59: 239–50.

1968 "Choix de textes littéraires." Pp. 265–319 in *Ugaritica* V. MRS 16. Paris: Imprimerie Nationale.

Oldenburg, U.

1969 *The Conflict between El and Baʿal in Canaanite Religion.* Leiden: E. J. Brill.

Page, S.

1968 "A Stela of Adad-nirari III and Nergal-ereš from Tell al Rimah." *Iraq* 30: 139–53.

Patton, John H.

1944 *Canaanite Parallels in the Book of Psalms.* Baltimore: Johns Hopkins University Press.

Perlitt, Lothar

1969 *Bundestheologie im Alten Testament.* WMANT 36. Neukirchen-Vluyn: Neukirchener Verlag.

Petschow, H.

1965 "Zur Systematik und Gesetztechnik im Codex Hammurabi." *ZA* 57: 146–72.

Pettinato, Giovanni

1971a *Das altorientalische Menschenbild und die sumerischen und akkadischen Schöpfungsmythen.* Abhandlungen der Heidelberger Akademie der Wissenschaften, Philosophisch-historische Klasse. Heidelberg: Carl Winter—Universitätsverlag.

1971b "Die Bestrafung des Menschengeschlechts durch die Sintflut." *Or* 37: 165–200.

1975 "Testi cuneiformi del 3. millennio in paleo-cananeo rinvenuti nella campagna 1974 a Tell Mardikh-Ebla." *Or* 44: 361–74.
1976a "Aspetti amministrativi e topografici di Ebla nel III millennio Av. Cr.: A. Documentazione epigraffici." *RSO* 50: 1–14.
1976b "Carchimiš-KĀR-kamiš: Le prime attestagioni den III Millennio." *OrAnt* 15: 11–15.
1976c "Ed lu e ad Ebla: La recostruzione delle prime 63 righe sulla base di TM.75.G.1488." *OrAnt* 15: 169–78.
1976d "Ibla (Ebla) A. Philologisch." *RLA* 5: 9–13.
1976e "The Royal Archives of Tell Mardikh-Ebla." *BA* 39: 44–52.
1977 "Al Calendario di Ebla al Tempo del Re Ibbi-Sipis sulla base di Tm. 75.G.427." *AfO* 25: 1–36.
1980 "Ebla e la Bibbia." *OrAnt* 19: 49–72.

Pope, Marvin H.
1955 *El in the Ugaritic Texts.* VTSup 2. Leiden: E. J. Brill.
1977 *Song of Songs.* AB 7C. Garden City, NY: Doubleday.

Posener, Georges
1960 *De la divinité du Pharaon.* Cahiers de la Société Asiatique, 15. Paris: Imprimerie Nationale.

Pritchard, James B.
1969 *Ancient Near Eastern Texts.* 3d ed. Princeton: Princeton University Press.

Rad, Gerhard von
1955 "Hiob xxxviii und die altägyptische Weisheit." Pp. 293–391 in *Wisdom in Israel and in the Ancient Near East.* Ed. M. Noth and D. W. Thomas. VTSup 3. Leiden: E. J. Brill.

Rainey, Anson F.
1970 *El Amarna Tablets 359–379.* AOAT 8. Neukirchen-Vluyn: Neukirchener Verlag.
1976 "Tell el Amarna." P. 869 in *IDBSup.*

Reiner, Erica
1958 *Šurpu: A Collection of Sumerian and Akkadian Incantations. AfO* Beiheft, 11. Graz. Reprinted, Osnabrück: Biblio-Verlag, 1970.

Rencontre Assyriologique Internationale 14
1966 *La divination en Mésopotamie ancienne et dans les régions voisines.* Paris: Presses Universitaires de France.

Riemann, P. A.
1976 "Covenant, Mosaic." Pp. 192–97 in *IDBSup.*

Roberts, J. J. M.
1973 "The Davidic Origin of the Zion Tradition." *JBL* 92: 329–44.
1976 "Myth *Versus* History: Relaying the Comparative Foundations." *CBQ* 38: 1–13.
1977a "Of Signs, Prophets, and Time Limits: A Note on Ps 74: 9." *CBQ* 39: 474–81.
1977b "Job and the Israelite Religious Tradition." *ZAW* 89: 107–14.

Robertson, David A.
1972 *Linguistic Evidence in Dating Early Hebrew Poetry.* SBLDS 3. Missoula, MT: Scholars Press.

Römer, Willem H. Ph.
1971 *Frauenbriefe über Religion, Politik und Privatleben in Mari.* AOAT 12. Neukirchen-Vluyn: Neukirchener Verlag.
Rowton, M. B.
1967 "The Physical Environment and the Problem of the Nomads." Pp. 109–21 in *XVe Rencontre Assyriologique Internationale: La civilisation de Mari.* Ed. J. R. Kupper. Paris: Société d'Édition "Les Belles Lettres."
1973a "Autonomy and Nomadism in Western Asia." *Or* 42: 247–58.
1973b "Urban Autonomy in a Nomadic Environment." *JNES* 32: 201–15.
1974 "Enclosed Nomadism." *Journal of Economic and Social History of the Orient* 17: 1–30.
1976 "Dimorphic Structure and the Problem of the ʿApirû-ʾIbrîm." *JNES* 35: 13–20.
Saggs, H. W. F.
1978 *The Encounter with the Divine in Mesopotamia and Israel.* London: Athlone.
Sasson, Jack
1969 *The Military Establishments at Mari.* Studia Pohl 3. Rome: Pontifical Biblical Institute.
Schaeffer, Claude F. A., ed.
1955– *Ugaritica* V. MRS 16. Paris: Imprimerie Nationale.
1968 *Le palais royal d'Ugarit* I–VI. MRS. Pais: Imprimerie Nationale.
Schmid, Hans H.
1966 *Wesen und Geschichte der Weisheit: Eine Untersuchung zur altorientalischen und israelitischen Weisheitsliteratur.* BZAW 101. Berlin: A. Töpelmann.
Schmidt, Werner H.
1966 *Königtum Gottes in Ugarit und Israel.* 2d ed. BZAW 80. Berlin: A. Töpelmann.
Schmökel, Hartmut
1952 "Zur kultischen Deutung des Hoheliedes." *ZAW* 64: 148–55.
1956 *Heilige Hochzeit und Hoheslied.* Abhandlungen für die Kunde des Morgenlandes, 23/1. Wiesbaden: Deutsche Morgenländische Gesellschaft.
Schramm, Wolfgang
1973 *Einleitung in die assyrischen Königsinschriften*, 2. Leiden: E. J. Brill.
Seux, Marie-Joseph
1976 *Hymnes et prières aux dieux de Babylonie et d'Assyrie.* Paris: Éditions du Cerf.
Shanks, Hershel
1979 "Syria Tries to Influence Ebla Scholarship." *BARev* 5/2: 37–50.
Sjöberg, A. W.
1972 "In Praise of the Scribal Art." *JCS* 24: 126–31.
1973 "Der Vater und sein missratener Sohn." *JCS* 25: 105–69.
1975a "Der Examenstext A." *ZA* 64: 137–76.
1975b "The Old Babylonian Ebuda." Pp. 159–70 in *Sumerological Studies in Honor of Thorkild Jacobsen on his Seventieth Birthday, June 7, 1974.* AS 20. Chicago and London: University of Chicago Press.

Skaist, A.
1969 "The Authority of the Brother at Arrapha and Nuzi." *JAOS* 89: 10–17.
Smith, Sidney
1949 *The Statue of Idri-mi.* London: British Institute of Archaeology in Ankara.
Soden, Wolfram von
1952–1955 "Gibt es ein Zeugnis, dass die Babylonier an Marduks Wiederauferstehung glaubten?" *ZA* 16–17: 130–66.
1957 "Ein neues Bruchstück des assyrischen Kömmentars zum Marduk-Ordal." *ZA* 52: 224–34.
1965 "Das Fragen nach der Gerechtigkeit Gottes im Alten Orient." *MIO* 96: 41–59.
1971 "Der grosse Hymnus an Nabu." *ZA* 61: 44–71.
1974–1977 "Zwei Königsgebete an Ištar aus Assyrien." *AfO* 25: 37–49.
Spalinger, A. J.
1973 "Aspects of the Military Documents of the Ancient Egyptians." Ph.D. dissertation, Yale University.
1978 "A Canaanite Ritual Found in Egyptian Reliefs." *The Society for the Study of Egyptian Antiquities Journal* 8/2: 47–60.
Speiser, E. A.
1940 "Of Shoes and Shekels." *BASOR* 77: 15–18.
1955 "I Know not the Day of my Death." *JBL* 74: 252–56.
1963 "The Wife-Sister Motif in the Patriarchal Narratives." Pp. 15–28 in *The Lown Institute Studies and Texts*: Volume 1. *Biblical and Other Studies.* Ed. A. Altmann. Cambridge, MA: Harvard University Press.
1964 *Genesis.* AB 1. Garden City, NY: Doubleday.
Szlechter, Emile
1951 *Les lois d'Ešnunna.* Paris: Centre National de la Recherche Scientifique.
Tadmor, Hayim
1958 "The Campaigns of Sargon II of Assur: A Chronological Historical Study." *JCS* 12: 22–40, 77–100.
1961 "Azriyau of Yaudi." Pp. 232–71 in *Studies in the Bible.* Ed. C. Rabin. Scripta Hierosolymitana, 8. Jerusalem: Magnes.
1970 "*Hʾrwt lšwrwt hptyḥh šl hḥwzh hʾrmw myspyrh.*" Pp. 397–401 in *Samuel Yeivin Jubilee Volume.* Jerusalem: Israel Society for Biblical Research (Hebrew).
1973 "The Historical Inscriptions of Adad-nirari III." *Iraq* 35: 141–50.
1975 "Assyria and the West: The Ninth Century and its Aftermath." Pp. 36–48 in *Unity and Diversity.* Ed. H. Goedicke and J. J. M. Roberts. Baltimore and London: Johns Hopkins University Press.
Thomas, D. Winton
1958 *Documents from Old Testament Times.* London: Thomas Nelson & Sons.
Thompson, Thomas L.
1974 *The Historicity of the Patriarchal Narratives: The Quest for the Historical Abraham.* BZAW 133. Berlin: Walter de Gruyter.

Tocci, Franco Michelini
1960 *La siria nell'eta di Mari.* Studi Semitici 3. Rome: Centro di Studi Semitici, University of Rome.
Tsevat, Matitiahu
1968 Review of H. M. Wolf's *The Apology of Hattusilis. . . . JBL* 87: 458–61.
Ullendorff, Edward
1978 Review of I. J. Gelb, "Thoughts about Ibla. . . ." *JSS* 23: 151–54.
Van Seters, John
1968 "The Problem of Childlessness in Near Eastern Law and the Patriarchs of Israel." *JBL* 87: 401–8.
1969 "Jacob's Marriages and the Ancient Near East." *HTR* 62: 377–95.
1975 *Abraham in History and Tradition.* New Haven and London: Yale University Press.
Vaux, Roland de
1946, 1948, 1949 "Les patriarches hébreux et les découvertes modernes." *RB* 53: 321–48; 55: 321–47; 56: 5–36.
1971 *Histoire ancienne d'Israel.* Paris: Gabalda. English trans., 1978.
Virolleaud, Charles
1960 "Un nouvel épisode du mythe ugaritique de Baal." *CRAIBL*: 180–86.
Weinfeld, M.
1976 "Covenant, Davidic." Pp. 188–92 in *IDBSup.*
Weippert, Manfred
1967 *Die Landnahme der israelitischen Stämme in der neueren wissenschaftlichen Diskussion.* FRLANT 92. Göttingen: Vandenhoeck & Ruprecht. English trans., 1971.
Whitaker, Richard E.
1972 *A Concordance of the Ugaritic Literature.* Cambridge, MA: Harvard University Press.
White, John B.
1978 *A Study of the Language of Love in the Song of Songs and Ancient Egyptian Poetry.* SBLDS 38. Missoula, MT: Scholars Press.
Wilhelm, G.
1973 "Ein Brief der Amarna Zeit aus Kāmid el-Lōz (KL 72: 600)." *ZA* 63: 69–75.
Williams, Ronald J.
1961 "The Alleged Semitic Original of the *Wisdom of Amenemope.*" *JEA* 47: 100–106.
1977 "II. Ägypten und Israel." Pp. 492–505 in *TRE* 1/4. Berlin and New York: Walter de Gruyter.
Wilson, Robert R.
1977 *Genealogy and History in the Biblical World.* New Haven and London: Yale University Press.
1980 *Prophecy and Society in Ancient Israel.* Philadelphia: Fortress.
Wiseman, Donald J.
1953 *The Alalakh Tablets.* London: British Institute of Archaeology in Ankara.
1954 "Supplementary Copies of Alalakh Tablets." *JCS* 8: 1–30.

1959a "Ration Lists from Alalakh VII." *JCS* 13: 19–33.
1959b "Ration Lists from Alalakh IV." *JCS* 13: 50–62.
1961 *Chronicles of Chaldaean Kings (626–556 B.C.) in the British Museum.* London: Trustees of the British Museum.
1967 "Alalakh." Pp. 119–35 in *Archaeology and Old Testament Study.* Ed. D. Winton Thomas. Oxford: Clarendon.
1976 "Alalakh Texts." Pp. 16–17 in *IDBSup.*

Wolf, Herbert Marlin
1967 *The Apology of Hattusilis Compared with Other Political Self-Justifications of the Ancient Near East.* Ann Arbor: University Microfilms.

Yaron, Reuven
1969 *The Laws of Eshnunna.* Jerusalem: Magnes.

Zijl, Peter J. van
1972 *Baal.* AOAT 10. Kevelaer: Verlag Butzon und Bercker.

Chapter 2

The Bible and the Literature of the Ancient Near East

Introduction

Scholars have always been aware that the biblical literature resembled in some respects other ancient literature, and even precritical commentators made comparisons between the biblical and extrabiblical literature. Until Napoleon's campaign in Egypt, however, the earliest extensive sources available for comparison were the classical sources in Greek and Latin. Champollion's decipherment of Egyptian hieroglyphics in 1823, the decipherment of Akkadian in the 1850s, and the subsequent discovery and decipherment of Sumerian, Hittite, Ugaritic, and an increasing number of early West Semitic inscriptions have radically changed this situation. This recovery of the ancient Near Eastern literature contemporary with and even a millennium older than the earliest OT writings has provided an important new framework within which to study OT literature.

A perusal of the collection of ancient Near Eastern texts translated into English in the third edition of *Ancient Near Eastern Texts* (J. B. Pritchard, ed.), though it is by no means complete, can give one some idea of the scope and significance of this body of ancient literature. The value of ancient Near Eastern literature for the interpretation of the OT is profound, and that value is immediately apparent when one studies OT law, psalmody, or wisdom literature.

Law and Covenant

In addition to numerous legal formulations scattered throughout the Pentateuch, the OT contains three major bodies of law: the so-called Book of the Covenant (Exod 21:1–23:33), the Holiness Code (Leviticus 17–26), and the Deuteronomic Law Code (Deuteronomy 12–26). Prior to V. Scheil's publication of the stele of Hammurabi's law code in 1902, the study of these biblical collections was carried out in what one could well call a cultural vacuum. As late as 1861 an important German commentator in his treatment of the goring ox law (Exod 21:28–36) could claim that of all ancient peoples only Israel had a law that held owners responsible if their animals killed or injured another person. The reason for this difference, he claimed, was because no other people had recognized that humans were made in the image of God.

Such a claim would be impossible for a responsible contemporary critic, because the cultural vacuum has been filled. The modern student of OT law has several major collections of cuneiform law with which to compare the biblical material. There are the Sumerian laws of Ur Nammu and Lipit Ishtar, the Old Babylonian laws of Eshnunna and Hammurabi, the Middle Assyrian laws from Asshur, the Hittite law code, and a small collection of Late Babylonian laws. Apart from the Late Babylonian collection, all these collections are prior in date to the period of composition of the biblical collections of law. Not only are these collections of cuneiform law older than the legal collections in the OT, comparative study shows that they constitute particular embodiments of a common law tradition that, for all its local and temporal variations, was basically shared throughout the region of Mesopotamia, Syria, and Palestine. The formal similarity between these written collections suggests that the act of making such written collections had itself become, probably under strong Mesopotamian influence, part of this widespread legal tradition.

To return to the goring ox law, far from the value placed on human life in this law being unique to the biblical material, a comparison with Eshnunna laws 53–55 and Hammurabi laws 250–52 shows that the biblical law is just a slightly different formulation of a much older law embodying the same legal principle. The slight differences in formulation do not suggest any superior evaluation of human life. Moreover, a comparative study of these laws demonstrates that the respect for human life reflected in the biblical law is not dependent on the theological doctrine of creation in the image of God. Respect for human life was part of the legal tradition in the Near East and in Israel well before the formulation of the doctrine of the image of God in Genesis 1. Its author has simply undergirded received ethical and legal mores with theological reflection.

Such theological elaboration of the received ethical and legal mores is paradigmatic for the whole development of biblical law. Very little in biblical law is unique to Israel. Even the Ten Commandments, delivered to the Israelites at Mount Sinai/Horeb by the voice of Yahweh, contain little that would not have been acknowledged everywhere else in the Near East. Apart from the limitation of worship to the one God, the prohibitions of images, and perhaps the observance of the Sabbath, these commands simply embody in a very pithy formulation the ethical standards common in the region. As we know from Mesopotamian sources, other religious communities had their own sacred days of abstention from work, so the only significant elements of uniqueness in the Ten Commandments are closely tied to the monotheistic thrust of Israelite religion. Even the biblical laws concerning the Sabbatical and Jubilee years (Exod 23:11; Leviticus 25; Deut 15:1–4), long considered utopian and unenforceable, may have their roots in much earlier Mesopotamian legal tradition. Throughout the Old Babylonian period the Babylonian government issued periodic *mesharum*-edicts (Akkadian) at fairly regular intervals canceling debts and otherwise easing the economic plight of the impoverished elements of Babylonian society. The Israelite Sabbatical Year, which seems to have the same purpose and recurs at about the same interval, appears to be an Israelite adaptation of this *mesharum*-edict tradition. The Jubilee Year probably represents a later easing of the Sabbatical Year requirements by lengthening the period between such attempts at economic redress.

In the light of this older legal tradition, the role of Moses as lawgiver must be reevaluated. His work must be seen as in some sense analogous to that of Hammurabi. Neither was primarily engaged in the formulation of brand-new laws. Both were responsible for a new collection, revision, and necessary updating of laws already current in the legal tradition of the people or the region.

On the other hand, Moses appears to have placed Israelite law in a new religious context. While the gods, and particularly Shamash, the god of justice, appear as the ultimate source and guarantors of Mesopotamian law, the revision and promulgation of particular collections is primarily the work of the king. Divine revelation of the individual commandments is not stressed, and the concept of the commandments as the stipulations of a covenant between the gods and the people is simply unknown in Mesopotamia. In Israel, on the contrary, not only the major collections of law, but almost all laws are considered stipulations in the covenant that Yahweh graciously entered into with Israel under the mediatorship of Moses. As a part of God's covenant they were given to Moses by direct revelation from God. The tensions, contradictions, and redundancies in the biblical legal material give ample evidence of later revisions and additions just as one finds such revisions in earlier Mesopotamian law. But while a new Mesopotamian ruler could issue a new collection of law in his own name, there was tremendous pressure in Israel to attribute all law, no matter how late, to Moses. Divine sanction for the law was more secure if the laws were seen as a part of the covenant stipulations God revealed to Moses on the sacred mountain.

Covenant, then, is an important ingredient in Israel's concept of law. The Bible speaks of God's covenant with Noah, with Abraham, with David and his house, with particular priestly families, and of the covenant with Israel given at Sinai or Horeb, but the search for ancient Near Eastern analogues has not produced any clear examples of a covenant between a god and his people or even a very convincing example of a covenant between a god and his chosen king. On the contrary, the evidence suggests that Israel adapted political language dealing with contractual relations between human parties to describe the religio-political relationship between God and his people or between God and his chosen representatives. The study of ancient Near Eastern political treaties of various types, however, has been very fruitful for a clearer understanding of Israelite covenant theology. Despite the ongoing debate and many unresolved questions, few would deny that the careful study of the many political treaties from the ancient Near East has aided in the understanding of Israelite covenant theology, especially as it is formulated in Deuteronomy. The study of royal grants given by Babylonian and Assyrian kings to chosen officials to reward meritorious service to the crown has also proven fruitful in providing a possible political model for the Davidic type covenant.

Because Israelite law was set within the context of covenant and obedience to it was seen as the appropriate religious response to Yahweh's gracious deeds on behalf of Israel, the content of that law came to include specifically religious and ritual obligations, and in the course of time some of the legal collections were elaborated in a hortatory style. The ancient Near Eastern law codes have nothing that would correspond to the ritual demands found in the Book of the Covenant (Exod 23:14–19), much less to the detailed laws for the various kinds of sacrifice legislated in the book of Leviticus. For parallels to this type of ritual instruction, one must turn from the ancient law codes to the Hittite instruction texts or to the Akkadian, Egyptian, Hittite, and Ugaritic ritual texts. There one will find much helpful material for understanding this genre of biblical law.

Psalmody

The biblical psalms have very important parallels in the hymns and prayers preserved in the surrounding Near Eastern cultures. Egypt and Mesopotamia provide both the greatest number of these texts and the most important ones as well. Given the striking number of parallels between Israelite religious poetry and Ugaritic poetry, one would expect that Canaanite hymns and prayers would be even closer to the biblical texts. Israel's hymnic tradition probably developed largely under the influence of Canaanite poetic canons. It has been seriously argued that Psalm 29, for instance, is just a superficially edited Canaanite hymn originally addressed to Baal. Unfortunately, the many texts uncovered at Ugarit included only one Ugaritic text that could legitimately be considered a hymn, and there were no examples of prayers. Canaan proper has yielded even less, not much more than a few phrases gleaned from the Amarna letters. Some of the West Semitic inscriptions have properly been compared to the individual prayers of thanksgiving, but the corpus of the relevant inscriptions is quite small and therefore less helpful than could be wished. There are a significant number of Hittite prayers that should be considered and apparently some Hurrian prayers, though the present stage of our knowledge of Hurrian provides no adequate base for the use of these texts in comparative study.

Mesopotamian

There is still much work to be done in the study of Mesopotamian hymns and prayers, but the large corpus of Mesopotamian texts contains clear counterparts to Israelite hymns and individual laments. Both the resemblances and the differences should be noted.

Apart from stylistic differences in the poetic canons that govern Sumerian, Akkadian, and Hebrew poetry, the major discontinuities between Mesopotamian and Israelite psalmody can be attributed to the fundamental distinction between monotheistic and polytheistic religion. Mesopotamian texts make far greater use of divine epithets in the praise of their deities, and the invocation of the deity in Mesopotamian individual laments is normally extended with a long introductory section of praise built up of such epithets. This is in sharp contrast to the Israelite laments, which typically begin the lament proper with a very simple and short invocation of Yahweh. The difference probably arises from the need of the polytheist to clearly specify which god is being invoked, but this difference does not justify denigrating the introductory praise in the Mesopotamian texts as mere calculated flattery. The motif in Mesopotamian prayers of calling upon one god to intercede with another god is obviously rooted in polytheism, and the pervasiveness of the set formulas that occur in many Mesopotamian prayers expressing fear over bad omens or blaming one's suffering on the work of sorcerers owes a great deal to the multiplicity of independent powers in a polytheistic universe.

Despite these obvious differences, Mesopotamian hymns and prayers share much in common with their Israelite counterparts. Many of the same motifs and metaphors are found in the prayers of both cultures. The psychological approach to the deity is hardly distinguishable. Mesopotamian hymns tend to focus on what Claus Westermann, in studying the biblical hymns, has called "descriptive praise," the praise of the deity for what the deity customarily does or is, rather than focusing on what Westermann calls "narrative praise," praising the deity by narrating a particular action of the deity. There are exceptions, however, such as the hymn to Marduk celebrating his victory over Elam at the time of Nebuchadnezzar I.

Some differences are actually more apparent than real. Akkadian *shu-illa* prayers are typically accompanied by ritual directions following a ruled line at the end of the prayer. These normally indicate that the prayer was to be recited several times as accompaniment to a sacrificial offering. Biblical psalms lack such ritual directions, but it is clear from references in the Psalms and the historical books that the biblical laments and thanksgiving songs were also accompanied by sacrifice. In fact, the same Hebrew term, *todah*, designates both the thanksgiving song and the thanksgiving sacrifice. It is important to remember that, both when studying the Psalms and when studying the rules for sacrifice in Leviticus. The relative separation of word and ritual act in the biblical sources is a literary phenomenon that does not reflect what actually went on in worship. In addition to the brief ritual directions that accompany Mesopotamian prayers, Mesopotamia also provides us with more extended rituals for particular cultic celebrations, and these enable us to get a glimpse of how hymns and prayers of different genres could actually form a part of the same cultic celebration—a key point in Sigmund Mowinckel's cult-centered approach to the Psalms. Finally, one should note the occurrence in Mesopotamian prayers of the formula identifying the speaker in the form "I so-and-so, the son of so-and-so. . . ." These prayers were obviously intended for repeated use by different individuals; the supplicant needed only to insert his or her own name at the appropriate place. Such a formula is not found in the biblical psalms, but their stereotypical nature points to the same intention for their repeated use by different individuals in roughly analogous situations. In neither case, however, does such public use imply any lack of sincerity in the spirituality expressed in the text of the Mesopotamian or Israelite prayer. The works of professional composers of psalms were presumably preserved in both cultures precisely because they articulated for the masses their inchoate religious sensibilities. One must take the words of these prayers seriously.

Egyptian

Egyptian hymns and prayers also provide important parallels for the study of the biblical material. Psalm 104 is widely regarded as modeled on Amenophis IV's famous hymn to the sun god, and Egyptian enthronement hymns are helpful in the comparative study of the Israelite enthronement ritual and in the exegesis of such texts as Psalms 2, 110, and Isa 9:1–6. Given the large number of Egyptian hymns and prayers belonging to carefully differentiated genres now available for study, the next few years should see significant progress in the comparative study of these texts.

Hittite

There are also a number of Hittite prayers that may be profitably studied for comparative purposes—one thinks especially of the plague prayers of the Hittite king Mursilis. Mursilis' religious interpretation of the plague as a judgment on his Hittite people because of their breach of a treaty with Egypt under an earlier Hittite king provides an interesting commentary on David's religious interpretation of the drought in his days as a judgment on Israel because of Saul's breach of the ancient treaty with the Gibeonites (2 Sam 21:1–14). Moreover, Mursilis' pathetic appeal to the gods at least to tell him, through one or another of the various means of revelation, why they were angry, provides a striking parallel to the biblical statement that when Saul inquired of

Yahweh, "Yahweh did not answer him, either by dreams, or by Urim, or by prophets" (1 Sam 28:6).

Sumerian

Finally, one should mention the Sumerian laments over the destruction of important cult centers. These laments, such as the famous lament over the destruction of Ur, provide interesting parallels to the biblical book of Lamentations and to the Israelite public laments found scattered in the Psalms and elsewhere in the Bible. Motifs from pre-Israelite traditions of public lament very similar to those found in the Sumerian laments are adapted by such prophets as Jeremiah to give profound pathos to his description of Yahweh's anguish over the sin of his people.

Wisdom Literature

Wisdom literature tends to be international in character, so it is not surprising to find striking Egyptian and Mesopotamian parallels to the biblical books of Proverbs, Job, and, to a lesser extent, Ecclesiastes. Mesopotamia provides several collections of moral admonitions similar to parts of Proverbs and Ecclesiastes, and there is a large collection of Sumerian and bilingual proverbs, though proverbs do not seem to have represented an important genre of Akkadian Babylonian literature. The numerous Egyptian works giving the "instructions" of a famous vizier, king, or wise man of the past are even more impressive as parallels to Proverbs. One of them, "The Instruction of Amen-em-Opet," appears to have been the literary model for structuring Prov 22:17–24:22, though the passage in Proverbs can hardly be considered a direct paraphrase of the Egyptian text, much less a straight translation. Recent comparative study has shown the influence of Mesopotamian texts as well as a number of other Egyptian texts on Prov 22:17–24:22. Its author was apparently well versed in a variety of international wisdom traditions and simply used Amen-em-Opet to provide a model structure in which to incorporate insights drawn from various sources. One should also mention the Aramaic proverbs preserved in the story of the Assyrian Sage Ahiqar.

The Mesopotamian texts dealing with the problem of the righteous sufferer give one a glimpse of the intellectual tradition within which the book of Job fits. It is a long tradition that includes an early Sumerian composition and an Old Babylonian Akkadian text. Its most elaborate literary expressions, however, are found in the long poem "I Will Praise the Lord of Wisdom" (*Ludlul bel nemeqi*) and "The Babylonian Theodicy," a text constructed in the form of a cycle of dialogues between the righteous sufferer and a friend. Other texts resembling *Ludlul*, though considerably shorter, have been found among the

Akkadian documents from Ugarit. *Ludlul* and the texts similar to it have many points of contact with individual prayers of lament. In fact, *Ludlul* could be analyzed as the literary expansion of an individual thanksgiving song that incorporates major elements of the lament in its description of the evil from which the deity has delivered the worshiper. Such an analysis is very suggestive in explaining the development of the wisdom psalm from the individual thanksgiving song. In contrast to *Ludlul*, "The Babylonian Theodicy" owes more to the tradition of scribal-school debates with their convention of insulting or ironic address to one's opponent in the debate. The book of Job seems to have been influenced by both strands in the tradition. It has incorporated the psalmic lament motifs found in the *Ludlul* strand, but it has structured them in an expanded symposium inspired by the "Theodicy" strand.

Other Genres in Genesis–Numbers

Outside of law, psalmody, and wisdom literature, one would be hard pressed to find Near Eastern parallels to the larger Israelite compositions. There is really nothing comparable in the preserved writings of the surrounding cultures to Genesis–Numbers or the Deuteronomistic History (Deuteronomy–2 Kings). For that matter, even individual books within these compilations have no real ancient Near Eastern counterparts. Nor do the books of the writing prophets or the book of Chronicles. What one can speak of are parallels to smaller genres used in the composition of these larger works.

Mythological Texts

The primeval history in the early chapters of Genesis contains a number of shorter stories with clear parallels in the surrounding cultures. The two creation stories (Gen 1:1–2:4; 2:4–3:24) share certain features with some of the large number of creation stories known from Mesopotamia and Egypt. Given the structural similarities, the differences in detail between these accounts and the biblical stories are helpful in specifying the issue addressed in the Genesis accounts. The comparison of Gen 1:1–2:4a with the Babylonian creation poem the *Enuma elish*, for instance, suggests a conscious polemic on the part of the biblical writer against the polytheistic theology reflected in this Babylonian myth. This account has been stripped of almost all the traces of the cosmogonic battle found in the Babylonian story, despite the fact that a similar form of this cosmogonic myth of the origin of world order was well known in Israel (Ps 74:12–17; Isa 27:1–2; 51:9–10; Job 9:13; 26:12–13). The closest parallels to the Israelite cosmogonic myth come from the Baal Epic at Ugarit—though the preserved Ugaritic texts do not explicitly tie Baal's defeat of the sea dragon to creation—but there are also Egyptian and Hittite texts of a similar character.

The Fall story in Genesis 2–3 has no clear analogues, and the story of the first murder (Genesis 4) is only loosely paralleled by a Mesopotamian account of a debate between the shepherd and the farmer as to which of the two professions was superior. This debate between professions is a genre known in both Mesopotamia and Egypt, but the typical texts end on a far friendlier note than the Cain and Abel story. It is not until one reaches the Flood story that the external parallels are again compelling. The Genesis Flood story (chaps. 6–9) appears to be derived from Mesopotamian tradition, where the Flood story is known in a Sumerian version, in the Akkadian version found in the Atrahasis Epic, and in the well-known version of the Gilgamesh Epic. The Atrahasis Epic is particularly important because it shows that Genesis' linking of the creation of humankind and the Flood story in a history that leads to the present structures of society was not a unique achievement of Israelite theology. This move finds a remarkable, if partial, parallel in the Babylonian Epic. The Atrahasis Epic fills out the history between the creation of humankind and the Flood differently than the Genesis account does, and the Atrahasis Epic does not continue with an account of the origin of the various languages. But its linking of creation and the Flood account, with strong etiological elements similar to those found in the biblical Fall story, provides a theological interpretation of humankind's place in this world analogous to one level of the biblical text. The motif of the confusion of the languages does seem to be mentioned in a Sumerian myth, and the somewhat mysterious figure of Nimrod, mentioned without elaboration in Genesis, may have its background in very popular Akkadian heroic legends about Sargon the Great or Naram-sin. Moreover, the Akkadian genealogies of the Hammurabi dynasty and of the ancestors of the Assyrian kings have proven very helpful in the study of the background and function of the biblical genealogies in Genesis.

Patriarchal Stories

One can find parallels to motifs in the patriarchal stories in Genesis 12–50, but the parallels do not extend much beyond that level. The concern for a male heir integral to the patriarchal narratives is also reflected in the Keret and Daniel epics from Ugarit. The Egyptian story of Sinuhe has certain points of similarity to the story of Jacob's flight from Canaan to escape Esau's anger. Both Sinuhe and Jacob flee to another country where they stay for an extended period, marry into the family of the wealthy patron who receives them, and prosper in their new surroundings before returning to the land from which they had fled. The story of Moses' flight to Midian in the book of Exodus also follows this line with some variation. The Moses story does not emphasize the refugee's financial success in his new country, but it is closer to the Sinuhe narrative in the political motivation for the flight. In this connection one should also mention Idrimi's autobiographical account of his flight from and eventual return to his ancestral Aleppo.

The revelatory importance of dreams in these stories and elsewhere in the OT has many parallels in the ancient Near Eastern literature, and such texts as the Assyrian Dream Book show a very similar pattern of interpretation to that reflected in the Bible. One should also mention the Egyptian tale of the two brothers that provides an oft-cited but rather remote parallel to the incident with Potiphar's wife in the Joseph story. On the whole, however, the narrative art reflected in the patriarchal stories has no real counterpart in the preserved literature of the surrounding cultures.

Moses' Birth

There are more points of contact with elements in the other pentateuchal books. The parallel between the Akkadian birth story of Sargon the Great and the Exodus account of Moses' birth is particularly striking. In both stories a baby boy who cannot be kept by the real parents is placed in a reed basket and left in the water at the edge of a river. Eventually the child is discovered by someone else who adopts thc child and raises it as his or her own.

Construction of a Sanctuary

The Near Eastern parallels to the legal and ritual material have already been noted, but there are also Near Eastern texts that provide parallels to the Exodus account of the building of the tabernacle, to the accounts in Kings and Chronicles of the building of Solomon's Temple, and to Ezekiel's description of the future Temple. One thinks especially of the Sumerian text of Gudea in which King Gudea of Lagash relates how he was given the command in a dream to (re)build the temple of the city god Ningirsu. Gudea asks for further instruction, which the god provides, and after very careful preparation the temple is constructed, Ningirsu and his fellow deities are brought into the temple, and the gods bless the king. The text and the statues of Gudea showing him holding the divine blueprint given him by the gods reveal the very ancient background to the biblical references that speak of God's blueprint for the tabernacle (Exod 25:9, 40) or for the Temple (1 Chr 28:11–19).

The concern for building or rebuilding the temple precisely according to the pattern originally given by the deity is reflected in "The Curse of Agade," an early Sumerian text that attributes the fall of the Akkad dynasty to Naram-sin's offense against Enlil's temple in Nippur. Naram-sin did major repair work on Enlil's temple, but according to this text he did it without sufficient regard to Enlil's wishes. The temple was a microcosm of the world, and Naram-sin's abuse of various parts of the temple resulted in dislocations in their macrocosmic counterparts in the external world. Thus when grain was cut in the gate where grain is not to be cut, grain was cut off from the land, etc. The same concern is still reflected in the late Neo-Babylonian building inscriptions that stress how the king rebuilt the temple precisely upon the original foundation trenches. If one missed the original line by so much as a finger's breadth, the results could be disastrous, resulting in the early collapse of the restored building. This understanding of the importance of following the divine pattern in temple construction is part of the background to the famous passage about God's foundation stone in Zion (Isa 28:16–17). With regard to the detailed descriptions of the tabernacle and Temple and their contents, one should note that the building inscriptions of the Assyrian and Babylonian kings sometimes contain rather detailed descriptions of the architectural features of the temples they built.

The biblical story about the Mesopotamian prophet Balaam whom the Moabite king Balak hired to curse Israel (Numbers 22–24) has been placed in a new light by the Aramaic wall inscriptions from Deir Alla that also mention this prophet. These texts are in a poor state of preservation and their precise date (ca. seventh century B.C.) is still disputed, but they indicate that a non-Israelite tradition about the seer Balaam was known in the Transjordan area among a presumably non-Israelite population group well before the period of the exile.

Other Genres in the Deuteronomistic History

The Mesopotamians, Hittites, and Egyptians all composed annals and chronicles, but none of these texts that have been preserved compare in scope or in complexity with the account of Israel's history that scholars have designated the Deuteronomistic History and that includes the books of Deuteronomy, Joshua, Judges, 1 and 2 Samuel, and 1 and 2 Kings. That difference remains even though some of these Near Eastern historiographical texts resemble the Deuteronomistic History in important features. The Assyrian Synchronistic History, for example, narrates the history of Assyro-Babylonian relations from ca. 1500 to 783 B.C., discussing each Assyrian king treated—only those who had relations with Babylon are included—along with his Babylonian contemporary or contemporaries. This synchronistic treatment is similar, though not identical, to the Deuteronomistic historian's synchronistic handling of the Israelite and Judean kings from ca. 922 to 722 B.C. Moreover, the Deuteronomistic historian's penchant for judging a king's reign and explaining his successes or failures on the very narrow ground of his religious performance is paralleled by a similar pattern in the Babylonian Weidner Chronicle. This text judges individual kings and explains their fate on the basis of their treatment of Marduk's temple Esagila in Babylon.

Despite such similarities, the biblical text appears far more complex. The Deuteronomistic historian's preservation and incorporation of major preformed blocks of earlier narratives with quite different agendas have given the biblical text an ambiguity that suggests a far more profound appreciation of the complexities of historical phenomena. One need only consider the account of the rise of kingship in 1 Samuel, with its disconcerting juxtaposition of pro- and antimonarchical sources, or the account of Solomon's reign in 1 Kings 1–11, with its peculiar mixture of lavish praise and harsh condemnation, in some cases with regard to the same actions, to illustrate the point. Just as in the case of Genesis–Numbers, the Near Eastern parallels tend to be parallels to some of these earlier narratives preserved in the Deuteronomistic History or to much smaller units or motifs.

The story of the Philistine capture and return of the Ark of the covenant has been compared to Babylonian accounts of the return of the cult statue of Marduk to Babylon after a period of foreign exile. The account of David's rise to power in 1 Samuel and the account of Solomon's succession to David's throne in 2 Samuel 9–20 and 1 Kings 1–2 have been explained as originally apologetic writings commissioned by these kings to justify their irregular accession to the throne on the analogy of such Near Eastern texts as the Hittite "Apology of Hattusilis III." One could also compare the Telepinus edict and Esarhaddon's account of his accession to the throne of Assyria after the assassination of his father, Sennacherib. Still at the level of genre, some scholars would see the Egyptian *Königsnovelle*, a narrative recounting a Pharaoh's accession to the throne, as a major influence on the narrative about Solomon's dream at Gibeon, but this is denied by other scholars.

At the level of the much smaller units of narrative, and especially at the level of the individual motif, the amount of comparative material is overwhelming. To take only one example, the narratives about military campaigns, which abound in the Bible and in Near Eastern literature, share many of the same ideas and motifs. It is clear from the Moabite stele of King Mesha and from numerous Mesopotamian texts, for instance, that the practices generally associated with "holy war" in Israel were not unique to Israel. The understanding of the outcome of battle as reflecting a judicial decision of the gods was also widespread, and stories about a city being taken by a stratagem are common.

Finally, one should note how the Deuteronomistic historian and many other biblical writers cite written correspondence of various sorts. The large collections of official and private letters from Mesopotamia, Egypt, Ugarit, and Palestine—including the Hebrew inscriptions from Arad and Lachish—have given a clear picture of the conventions governing actual letter writing, thus enabling scholars to better evaluate such literary citations.

Prophecy

The phenomenon of prophecy was widespread in the ancient Near East. Prophets or prophet-like figures are attested among the Canaanites, the Arameans, the Hittites, in Mesopotamia, and in Egypt, but nowhere else did they leave a literary deposit comparable in any way to the books of the classical Israelite prophets. The Egyptian "Admonitions of Ipu-wer" and "The Prophecy of Neferti" are probably the two longest non-Israelite documents claimed by scholars as prophetic works, but their identification as prophetic is disputed. The latter is often regarded as political propaganda disguised as prophecy but actually composed after the events prophesied and the former could be treated as political advice from a royal counselor. Caution is also in order in comparing the so-called "Prophecy of Marduk" from Mesopotamia to the biblical material. This text, in which Marduk explains away the ancient capture of his statue by the Hittites and the Assyrians as a business trip and a vacation that he decided to take but then treats the more recent capture of his statue by the Elamites as his judgment on sinful Babylon with which he has become angry, has points of contact with Israelite prophetic theology, especially in its theological interpretation of past history and in its insistence that the deity is in full control of that history. Marduk's promise for the restoration of Babylon even appears to be predictive, if scholars are correct in dating the text prior to Nebuchadnezzar I's conquest of Elam. On the other hand, the text does not mention any human intermediary through whom this revelation of Marduk was given, and its treatment of history might suggest a closer parallel to apocalyptic works such as Daniel in which the major part of "prophecy" is actually prophecy after the event. The Assyrian prophecy texts translated by Pfeiffer and Biggs in Pritchard's *Ancient Near Eastern Texts* may also be regarded as apocalyptic texts, if they are not simply omen apodoses.

In contrast, the collection of oracles concerning Esarhaddon attributed to various prophetic figures, but apparently all speaking in the name of the goddess Ishtar of Arbela, do appear to be genuine prophetic oracles, and the manner of their collection is suggestive for the study of the preservation and collection of the prophetic material in Israel. The Assyrian collection reflects no clear organizing principle, though it appears to be a collection made for some official purpose, and the concern to identify the speaker of the individual oracles may signal a legal responsibility that the prophet bore for his words. This would correspond to the earlier practice at Mari of taking legal symbols from the prophet, thus holding the prophet responsible for the reliability of his or her prophetic message. The Assyrian collection is rather short, however, and, unlike the majority of the prophetic books in the Bible, it does not even purport to be the collection of the oracles of a single prophet.

If the literary parallels to the prophetic books of the Bible are less than impressive, the same cannot be said for prophetic phenomena in general, nor for the content of particular oracles. Many of the motifs found in Israelite oracles are also attested in the oracles from the surrounding cultures. One thinks, for instance, of the common admonition "Fear not!" followed by a promise of divine assistance. It is found in the response of the Aramaic prophets to King Zakir of Hamath and Luʿath, and it is very common in the Assyrian oracles.

The some twenty-eight prophetic texts in the Mari correspondence from the first half of the second millennium B.C. are particularly significant, both in the range of their parallels to the later biblical material and in their occurrence in an area and among a population group that might suggest some cultural link between the Mari phenomenon and the later Israelite development. In contrast to the traditional Mesopotamian preference for the technical, institutionalized practice of divination as the chosen means of obtaining communications from the divine world, Mari prophecy depends on inspiration and the initiative of a deity. The Mari prophets see themselves as the messengers or mouthpieces of the deity, speaking for the deity in the first person. Moreover, the reception of the prophetic message takes place in what may be defined broadly as an ecstatic state—a state characterized by somewhat abnormal behavior, if one may judge by the use of the same root to refer to the behavior both of the prophet and of the insane. In all these respects, prophecy at Mari resembles prophecy as it is known in the biblical texts.

Even at Mari, however, technical divination remains the favorite means of obtaining communications from the divine world. The authenticity of prophetic messages was tested by having the divination priests take the omens in the normal way and then comparing their results with the prophetic message. This preference for technical divination of various sorts as the primary means of revelation may account for the relative sparsity of literary collections of prophetic oracles. Mesopotamia's cultural equivalent to the biblical prophet as the central mediator between the divine and human worlds was the divination priest, and the cultural equivalent to the biblical prophetic book is perhaps the Mesopotamian omen collection, of which there are many very extensive examples. Such collections, if they ever existed in Israel, were not preserved in the canonical Israelite literature. The omen collections and the collections of incantations represent the two genres of literature that are very important in Mesopotamia, but are conspicuous by their absence from the Bible.

Other Writings

Of the biblical writings not yet discussed, the one with the closest Near Eastern parallels is the Song of Songs. Both secular Egyptian love poetry and more religious love poetry from Mesopotamia have been compared to it. The memoirs of Nehemiah have been compared to votive inscriptions of Mesopotamian kings and officials who wanted their deeds on behalf of the god to be remembered and rewarded. Books like Ruth and Esther, on the other hand, present literary genres with no clear counterparts in the early ancient Near Eastern literature. Finally, the anti-Babylonian stories in the book of Daniel may reflect a late development of the Persian-sponsored anti-Nabonidus propaganda of the Marduk priests of Babylon. The particular development of these stories in Daniel, however, reflects a changed literary world. A literature of the powerless or stateless has taken the place of the older literature rooted in the national state. There is an analogy for this in the Aramaic story of Ahiqar, but this major shift in the kind of Israelite literature produced in the late postexilic period (second century B.C.) marks the end of the biblical period.

Bibliography

Hoftijzer, J., and G. Van der Kooij. *Aramaic Texts from Deir ʿAlla.* Leiden: Brill, 1976.

Lambert, W. G., and A. R. Millard. *Atra-Hasis: The Babylonian Story of the Flood.* Oxford: Clarendon, 1969.

Mowinckel, S. *The Psalms in Israel's Worship.* Nashville, TN: Abingdon, 1967.

Pritchard, J. B. *Ancient Near Eastern Texts Relating to the Old Testament.* 3d ed. Princeton, NJ: Princeton University Press, 1969.

Roberts, J. J. M. "The Ancient Near Eastern Environment." In *The Hebrew Bible and Its Modern Interpreters.* Edited by D. A. Knight and G. M. Tucker. Chico, CA: Scholars Press, 1985. Pp. 75–121.

Westermann, C. *Praise and Lament in the Psalms.* Atlanta, GA: John Knox, 1981.

Chapter 3

Myth versus History: Relaying the Comparative Foundations

While one may speak of the decline, if not the demise, of biblical theology, certain of its main emphases live on in contemporary OT scholarship. One of these is the almost exclusive concentration of theological significance on those features of biblical faith which are, or are purported to be, unique to Israel. Another is the fascination with history as the almost essential element in any authentic theological formulation. Both of these emphases mesh in the popular contrast between Israelite history and Pagan myth. In spite of the recent strictures of James Barr[1] and Bertil Albrektson,[2] the view that history was the constitutive genre of Israel's religious expression while myth exercised that function in contemporary paganism, still dominates the field. Moreover, it has survived this recent criticism with only the slightest adjustments and without the more detailed analysis of the comparative material that the criticism should have provoked.[3] Whether dealing with the cult or with comparative historiography, OT scholars still tend to simply presuppose the old dichotomy or, at best, to sketch it with broad and rather dubious generalizations.

---

1. James Barr, *Old and New in Interpretation: A Study of the Two Testaments* (London: SCM Press, 1966) 65–102.

2. Bertil Albrektson, *History and the Gods: An Essay on the Idea of Historical Events as Divine Manifestations in the Ancient Near East and in Israel* (Lund: CWK Gleerup, 1967).

3. The most detailed criticism of Albrektson's book that this writer is aware of was given by W. G. Lambert in a review in *Or* 39 (1970) 170–77 and a subsequent article, "Destiny and Divine Intervention in Babylon and Israel," *OTS* 17 (1972) 65–72, but even this treatment is inadequate in its review of the evidence. Despite some good observations, Lambert finds the differences between Israel and Babylon too easily, at the expense of the Babylonians and often by applying a double standard (see below, n. 19). Moreover, some of Lambert's remarks on Babylonian historiography are of doubtful validity. The derivation of the Babylonian chronicles from omen observations, for instance, has been rejected by A. K. Grayson, who is currently reediting all the chronicles ("Divination and the Babylonian Chronicles," *La divination en Mésopotamie ancienne* [XIVe Rencontre Assyriologique Internationale; Paris: Presses Universitaires de France, 1966] 76).

Historiography

An instructive example of this procedure in dealing with comparative historiography is provided by Paul Hanson's otherwise stimulating article on the origins of apocalyptic.[4] A careful examination of his presentation, therefore, will demonstrate some of the inadequacies of the oversimplified myth-versus-history model still characteristic of much current comparative theology.[5]

Hanson, following a widely held position,[6] asserts that a "true historiography developed first in Israel";[7] neither Egypt nor Mesopotamia developed a "historiography in the true sense of the word."[8] The validity of such a judgment depends, of course, on how one defines a "true historiography." Hanson does not stop to define his usage, much less to defend it, but several statements scattered through the first part of his article give a reasonably clear picture of what he means by a genuine historiography:

> Thus an idea of history did not develop in Egyptian religion, for without an historical realm of men, distinct from the cosmic realm of the gods, without a dividing line between gods and men, no concept of a development through history was possible.[9]

> An historical sequence spanning centuries in an unbroken development . . . [10]

> No common line connects these separate phases in an unbroken development.[11]

> This idea of history represents a true historiography for it traces the events of Israel's experience from a distinct beginning point, follows them down through a progression in time, and looks to a future unfolding of that history. This historiography first became possible in Israel because human history was consigned to a sphere which, though not unrelated to, was yet distinct from the cosmic realm of myth; for Old Testament faith attributes to man freedom of will either to fol-

4. "Jewish Apocalyptic Against Its Near Eastern Environment," *RB* 78 (1971) 31–58.

5. It should be noted that Hanson's present views would require some revision of his earlier presentation. His paper was sharply criticized when it was presented at the Colloquium for Old Testament Research after already being accepted for publication, and he had obviously rethought many of his views by the time I found the opportunity to discuss an earlier draft of this paper with him two years later. Needless to say, the present paper profited greatly from that delightfully stimulating discussion.

6. Noth's judgment is probably an accurate reflection of Old Testament scholarship in general: "Die *altorientalische Welt* mit ihrem grossen Reichtum an schriftlichem Aufzeichnungen hat eigentliche Werke der G(eschichtsschreibung) nicht hervorgebracht," *RGG* II (1958^3) 1498. Similar views may also be found outside the field, among Assyriologists and Egyptologists.

7. *RB* 78 (1971) 40.

8. Ibid., 37–40.

9. Ibid., 37.

10. Ibid., 38.

11. Ibid., 39.

> low directives from the deity, or to follow a course of his own. History is thus the account of the relationship between two distinct entities: Yahweh the god who inhabits the cosmic realm and Israel a people dwelling on the earth. The basis of this relationship is a Covenant established between Yahweh and Israel, a Covenant guaranteeing blessing for obedience, curse for disobedience. History thus traces the working out of this relationship, which already at an early date is seen as moving toward a fulfillment of the covenant.[12]

If one may construct a composite definition from these various statements, it would appear that a true historiography requires the tracing of the experiences of a human society that is free to follow its own course from a distinct beginning point through a significant progression in time, perhaps spanning centuries, in an unbroken development that looks forward to yet a future unfolding.

This writer cannot accept such a definition of a "true historiography." Hanson's definition confuses a *literary* category (historiography), which could include more than one genre, with a particular, though not self-evident, *philosophical* concept of history.[13] It reflects the same parochial outlook which has led some western historians to dismiss as basically unhistorical not only the ancient Near East, but the classical civilization of Greece and Rome as well.[14] Moreover, if one took the definition seriously, it would disqualify much of modern historiography as well as ancient. Does the determinism in Marxist historiography, for instance, leave sufficient room for "a human society that is free to follow its own course"? Or is modern positivistic historiography sufficiently teleological? Does all modern historiography show an unbroken development spanning centuries or even generations? There are "histories" of World War II which trace its origins far beyond the immediate outbreak of hostilities and unfold its implications for the post-war period, but there are also "histories" of particular campaigns which involve a very limited time span, sometimes only a few weeks. Is this common use of the term history illegitimate? History and historiography are notoriously difficult terms to define to anyone else's satisfaction,[15] but any definition which fails to correspond with common usage and automatically excludes some modern and many ancient attempts to record and understand the past must be viewed with

12. Ibid., 40–41.

13. Cf. J. J. Finkelstein, "Mesopotamian Historiography," *Proceedings of the American Philosophical Society* 107 (1963) 461–62.

14. Ibid., especially 461, n. 3.

15. Historiography I would define as a literary phenomenon involving the recording and analysis, explicit or *implicit*, of past events. As such it would include a number of literary genres—king lists, chronicles, annals, epics, royal apologies, etc. This would correspond, to some extent at least, with the broader definition of history favored by Finkelstein (ibid., 462). Perhaps one should also include history as a particular historiographical genre, but I am unable to offer any defensible definition of such a genre at this point.

suspicion. Adequate comparative analysis of the theological significance of history is rendered impossible from the outset if one cancels half the evidence by an *a priori* and partisan definition.

Nonetheless, if Hanson's definition of historiography accurately reflected the contrast between Israel's views and those of her neighbors, one might speak more modestly, but still impressively of Israel's *distinctive* historiography. There are weaknesses in his comparative analysis, however, which makes it doubtful whether either the Israelite or the Mesopotamian material has been correctly characterized.[16]

To begin with, there are Mesopotamian historiographical works which do treat long periods of time.[17] One can rightly fault them for their jumpy, episodic character, but before one is too harsh, he should take another look at J, the Deuteronomistic History, and Chronicles. These are not exactly models of smooth, unbroken historical development either.[18] One may admit a relative superiority to the Israelite works, but one does not thereby neutralize this cuneiform evidence that the Mesopotamian saw a continuity in history. The Sumerian King List's attempt to force the various contemporary dynasties into a single temporal sequence,[19] a tendency also found in the deuteronomistic his-

16. One could also raise questions about his characterization of the Egyptian material, but that would take the discussion too far afield.

17. One could cite the various Assyrian and Babylonian chronicles which will soon appear in a new edition by A. K. Grayson (in the series *Texts from Cuneiform Sources* [Locus Valley, J. J. Augustin] as well as the Sumerian (Thorkild Jacobsen, *The Sumerian King List* (Assyriological Studies 11; Chicago: University of Chicago Press, 1939]) and Assyrian (I. J. Gelb, "Two Assyrian King Lists," *JNES* 13 [1954] 209–30) king lists. One may object to such a comparison on the grounds that chronicles and king lists simply record events or historical relationships without analyzing or interpreting them. This objection, however, does not hold for every chronicle, and even when a chronicle or king list lacks an explicit analysis or interpretation, its very arrangement of the material often bears eloquent, if implicit, testimony to its author's analysis of the meaning of the events or relationships he records. See, for example, Jacobsen's study of the methodology of the author of the Sumerian King List (ibid., 138–64). Cf. also R. R. Wilson, "The Old Testament Genealogies in Recent Research," *JBL* 94 (1975) 169–89, particular 184.

18. One may well question whether the Deuteronomistic History, which simply incorporates whole blocks of disparate, preexisting literary material within a rather loose and easily distinguishable editorial framework, really passes Hanson's own test for true historiography.

19. F. R. Kraus, "Zur Liste der älteren Könige von Babylonien," *ZA* NF 16 (1952) 48–49. When Lambert cites this as an example of the unhistorical motivations behind Mesopotamian texts containing historical materials (*OTS* 17 [1972] 70–71) while ignoring the similar phenomenon in the biblical writer, he is surely applying a double standard. His whole attempt to discredit Mesopotamian historical works on the basis of the motivation behind them seems strained (ibid.). Not only would much, if not all, of the biblical material fail such a test—the Throne Succession narrative was hardly written as an impartial account of events from purely historical motives—but such a criterion ignores the variety of motivations even within modern historiography. See the collection of essays edited by Fritz Stern,

torian's treatment of the judges, may be an effort to sharpen up just such a continuity.

One must also object to Hanson's claim that the OT faith was unique in attributing to man the "freedom of will either to follow directives from the deity, or to follow a course of his own."[20] Even in early Mesopotamia the events of human history were not merely a reflection of the decisions and actions of the gods.[21] Man was not totally passive.[22] In the Curse of Agade, Inanna turns against her city Akkad for no apparent reason just as Harmut Gese has pointed out,[23] but Gese neglected to mention that the final denouement in the story is provoked by two human actions: (1) Naram-Sin's defiance of Enlil in ignoring the oracles and destroying the Ekur, and (2) the continuing supplications of the inhabitants of Nippur.[24] This is even clearer in the later form of this tradition where Naram-Sin's disasters are traced to his impiety in refusing to await a clear oracle from the deity.[25] One could multiply the examples where the disaster having overtaken a king or country, while it may have been decreed in the council of the gods, was, nonetheless, the result of that king or country's rebellion against the gods. The Assyrian victory over the Babylonian king in the Tukulti-Ninurta epic is a case in point.[26] The battle is interpreted as a judicial decision rendered by the gods in Tukulti-Ninurta's favor, but precisely because Kashtiliash had sinned in breaking the covenant made in the name of the gods.[27] Moreover, the refusal of the Mesopotamians to attribute every alteration in the prosperity of a community to human freedom may be seen as

The Varieties of History from Voltaire to the Present (Cleveland and New York: Meridian Books, World Publishing Co., 1956) and Maurice Mandelbaum's masterful study of nineteenth-century historicism, *History, Man and Reason* (Baltimore and London: The Johns Hopkins Press, 1971).

20. *RB* 78, 40.

21. Contra Hanson, ibid., 38.

22. Contra Harmut Gese, "Geschichtliches Denken im Alten Orient und im Alten Testament," *ZTK* 44 (1958) 133.

23. Ibid.

24. S. N. Kramer, *ANET* (1969) 648–50, lines 91–150, 200–20.

25. O. R. Gurney and J. J. Finkelstein, *The Sultantepe Tablets* I (Occasional Publications of the British Institute of Archaeology at Ankara 3; London, 1957) Nr. 30:72–92; O. R. Gurney, "The Sultantepe Tablets (Continued): IV. The Cuthaean Legend of Naram-Sin," *Anatolian Studies* 5 (1955) 102–3:72–92.

26. A new edition of the Tukulti-Ninurta Epic is being prepared by Peter Machinist, a student at Yale. For the time being see R. Campbell Thompson, "The British Museum Excavations at Nineveh, 1931–32," *Annals of Archaeology and Anthropology* 20 (1933) 116–26, Pls. CI–CIV; "The Excavations on the Temple of Nabu at Nineveh," *Archeologia* 79 (1929) 126–33; E. Ebeling, *Bruchstücke eines politischen Propagandagedichtes aus einer assyrischen Kanzlei* (*MVAG* 12/2; Leipzig, 1938); and especially W. G. Lambert, "Three Unpublished Fragments of the Tukulti-Ninurta Epic," *AfO* 18 (1957) 38–51.

27. Lambert's Col. I 32–47 (BM 98730); III 20–55; V 23–45.

evidence of a profoundly empirical view. Human folly is not the only cause for the decline of a community, and sometimes a community *is* powerless to control its own fate. The willingness to admit as much should not be taken as a less historical viewpoint than a dogmatism which attempts to explain the unexplainable in terms of sin and punishment.

Neither can one agree with Hanson's view that man and god were distinct entities in Israel, but not in Mesopotamia.[28] One need only recall the alewife's admonition to Gilgamesh to see the falsity of this distinction:

> Gilgamesh, whither rovest thou?
> The life thou pursuest thou shalt not find.
> When the gods created mankind,
> Death for mankind they set aside,
> Life in their own hands they retained.[29]

A clearer demarcation between god and man would be hard to find. Nor can I see how Hanson's comparison of Babylonian and Israelite creation accounts alters this.[30] Babylonian man may be made of divine substance, albeit mixed with clay, but how does this differ fundamentally from the Yahwist's man, who is made of clay but given life by the influx of divine breath and who lacks only immortality to rival the gods (Gen 3:22). The difference is too subtle to follow.

There is a similar difficulty with his related claim that in Israelite historiography, "For the first time in the Near East, the cosmic realm and the realm of the real world are recognized as two truly distinct realms."[31] What he means by this is perhaps best expressed by his later statement:

> The Israelite's world was the human sphere, and it was within this realm, distinct from the cosmic realm of deity, and through historical events, that he believed Yahweh related himself to his people for the sake of his covenant. Further indicative of Israel's unique historiography, in these events Yahweh related himself through human instruments like Moses, thereby recognizing the integrity of the human order.[32]

As a characterization of Israelite historiography in general, this will simply not stand up. To begin with his reference to Moses, the epic's portrayal of Yahweh's role in the Exodus and Wanderings material with its plagues, its fiery pillar, its theophany on the mountain, and its man-devouring earth is anything but a paradigm that "recognizes the integrity of the human order." Moreover, the Deuteronomistic History, which Hanson sees as in one respect the logical conclusion of the prophetic historiography,[33] preserves many passages where

28. *RB* 78, 41–42.
29. B. Meissner, *MVAG* 7 (1902) 15, III 1–5; E. A. Speiser, *ANET* (1955) 90.
30. *RB* 78, 41, n. 22.
31. Ibid., 41.
32. Ibid., 42–43.
33. Ibid., 46.

the cosmic background to "historical" events is made quite explicit. One thinks especially of Yahweh's role in the conquest,[34] the defeat of Dagon in the history of the ark, Samuel's victory over the Philistines, Micaiah ben-Imlah's vision of the heavenly court, the fiery chariots and horsemen of Elisha, and the miraculous deliverance of Jerusalem in Hezekiah's day. Of course, not every event in the Deuteronomistic History is given a cosmic background, but neither is every event in Mesopotamian historical accounts, and the human instrumentality in the activity of the Mesopotamian gods is often quite explicit.[35] Actually, it is only in the "Throne Succession Narrative" that Yahweh recedes behind the scenes and while still directing history, permits a relatively genuine integrity to the human order. Interestingly enough, this most "secularized," most "humanistic" of all the Israelite historical documents precedes the prophets, which forces one to question whether, in fact, the prophets were the ones responsible for historicizing Israel's religion.[36]

One must also reject Hanson's repeated assertions that Mesopotamian historiography, just because it saw historical events within a cosmic framework, was reflecting timeless episodes.[37] The rise and fall of empires may reflect decisions in a divine council, but that does not rule out historical sequence, and one cannot, without more ado, designate these activities of the gods as timeless. To cite the Curse of Agade again, the account of the rise and fall of the Akkadian capitol is introduced by placing it in a temporal sequence with earlier empires:

> After the frowning forehead of Enlil
> Had killed (the people of) Kish like the "Bull of Heaven,"
> After he had ground the house of Erech into dust, like a giant bull,
> From below to above, Enlil
> Had given him lordship and kingship,
> Then did holy Inanna, the shrine of Agade
> Erect as her noble chamber,
> In Ulmash did she set up a throne.[38]

34. Hanson mentions one of these passages (Josh 10:8–14) as an example of an archaic league tradition where the vision of divine activity on a cosmic level is largely untranslated into the terms of real history (ibid., 43).

35. This can be seen, for example, by comparing two parallel accounts of Asshurbanipal's campaign against the rebellious Arabs under Uaiteʾ. In one account Ishtar "rains down fire upon Arabia" (Maximilian Streck, *Assurbanipal und die letzten assyrischen Könige bis zum Untergange Nineveh's* [Vorderasiatische Bibliothek: Leipzig: J. C. Hinrichs, 1916] 78: 79–82); in the other Asshurbanipal's troops set the Arabs's tents on fire (ibid., 132–34, vii 97–viii 19). See my discussion in *The Earliest Semitic Pantheon* (Baltimore and London: The Johns Hopkins University Press, 1972), 25–26.

36. As Hanson asserts, *RB* 78, 46.

37. Ibid., 40.

38. Kramer, *ANET* (1969) 647.

There are texts in which the activities of the gods do appear timeless, where one is dealing with "primordial events," but that is not always the case. Activity on the cosmic plane need not be timeless. The intervention of the deity in avenging a breach of covenant, for example, while it gives a cosmic dimension to historical events necessarily ties these cosmic actions to a definite temporal sequence. The transgression must precede the punishment.

Furthermore, one should note that the Israelite tendency to historicize myth by making mythical episodes like creation and the flood links in the historical chain has been anticipated by the Mesopotamians. The Sumerian King List, for instance, incorporates the flood as just another event in the historical sequence,[39] and the same attitude is expressed in other texts as well.[40] Whatever one may say about creation, the flood was not simply an episode in the timeless adventures of the gods, but a real event in the history of man which followed the primacy of Shuruppak and preceded that of Kish. The Atrahasis epic, however, links the creation of man with the flood in one continuous narrative, and that raises the question whether one can even speak of the Mesopotamian view of the creation of man in totally non-historical categories.

Finally, one must question the ease with which Hanson dismisses the theological significance of creation for the Yahwist.[41] It is not Yahweh's covenant with Abraham which first brought deity and man into a relationship according to the Yahwist. The first man Adam already had a relationship to Yahweh, and while the expulsion from the garden may have strained it, Yahweh did not withdraw from the relationship. Cain and Abel bring him sacrifices (Gen 4:3–4), men call upon his name after the birth of Seth's son (Gen 4:26), and Noah apparently already observed the cultic distinctions between clean and unclean animals (Gen 7:2). Abraham does receive a special call (Gen 12:1–3), but there is not the slightest reason for seeing this call as the beginning of Abraham's relation to Yahweh. From all appearances Abraham responds not to a hitherto unknown deity—there is no disclosure of the divine name—but to the same deity that he had always known, and who had been worshipped in the same way since time immemorial. The historical reality was quite different, and other OT traditions seem closer to the historical truth, but the Yahwist's theology has to be interpreted in the context of his own historical reconstruction, not that of E or P, much less Noth or Bright.

This criticism of Hanson's comparative analysis should not be construed as an attempt to level through real differences between Israelite and Pagan historiography. There may be significant ones, and they may point to a distinctive

39. Jacobsen, *Sumerian King List*, 77:39–42.

40. Asshurbanipal boasts of being able to read difficult cuneiform texts written before the flood (Streck, *Asshurbanipal*, 256:17–18, and discussion in n. 6).

41. *RB* 78, 41.

centrality of history in Israel's religion, but as yet no one has worked out such comparative differences on an adequate exegetical base. Von Rad has correctly pointed to the repeated attempts of Israelite writers to theologically understand their past,[42] but any thorough comparative study must balance this against the parallel endeavors to grasp the theological significance of the past among Israel's neighbors. One thinks particularly of the Weidner Chronicle with its deuteronomistic-like evaluation of past kings on the basis of their cultic performance,[43] but one could also point to less ambitious attempts to understand the theological implications of shorter periods and individual episodes.[44]

One such episode is worth examining in detail—Sennacherib's savage destruction and attempted obliteration of Babylon, a destruction which according to Sennacherib's own inscription involved the smashing of the Babylonian gods[45] and was intended to blot out the memory of the site of Babylon and its temples forever.[46] Such an action could hardly be justified without divine sanction. Sennacherib's inscriptions make it clear the move was undertaken in response to Assur's command.[47] This theological understanding of the event is made even more explicit in the mythological text earlier, but erroneously thought to contain an account of Marduk's resurrection.[48] This text, no doubt commissioned by Sennacherib, recounts how a divine court headed by Assur condemned Marduk for wrongdoing.[49]

---

42. Gerhard von Rad, *Weisheit in Israel* (Neukirchen-Vluyn: Neukirchener Verlag, 1970) 368, n. 3.

43. Eva Osswald, "Altorientalische Parallelen zur deuteronomistischen Geschichtsbetrachtung," *Mitteilungen des Instituts für Orientforschung* 15 (1969) 286–96; Hans-Gustav Güterbock, "Die historische Tradition und ihre literarische Gestaltung bei Babyloniern und Hethitern bis 1200," *ZA* NF 8 (1934) 47–57.

44. To cite only a few, note Yasmah-Adad's historical sketch of the relations between the ruling houses of Mari and Assyria (*ARM* I, 3), the various attempts to explain the fall of the Sargonic empire (cf. above, nn. 24–25), and the several texts dealing with the return of Marduk from Elam (W. G. Lambert, "Enmeduranki and Related Matters," *JCS* 21 [1967] 126–31; Johannes Hehn, "Hymnen und Gebete an Marduk," *Beiträge zur Assyriologische* 5 [1906] 326–29, 339–44; L. W. King, *Cuneiform Texts from Babylonian Tablets in the British Museum* [London, 1901], Pl. 48).

45. D. D. Luckenbill, *The Annals of Sennacherib* (*OIP* II; Chicago: University of Chicago Press, 1924) 83:48.

46. Ibid., 84:53–54.

47. Ibid., 84:54–55; 138:44–45.

48. W. von Soden, "Gibt es ein Zeugnis dass die Babylonier an Marduks Wiederauferstehung glaubten?" *ZA* NF 16–17 (1952–55) 130–66; "Ein neues Bruchstück des assyrischen Kommentars zum Marduk-Ordal," *ZA* NF 18–19 (1957–59) 224–34.

49. Cf. the latest discussion by Thorkild Jacobsen, "Religious Drama in Ancient Mesopotamia," in *Unity and Diversity: Essays in the History, Literature, and Religion of the Ancient Near East*, ed. by H. Goedicke and J. J. M. Roberts (Baltimore: The Johns Hopkins University Press, 1975) 73–74.

The same event, however, is completely reinterpreted in the reign of Esarhaddon, Sennacherib's successor. Under the rule of a former king, so the new explanation stated, the Babylonians became wicked and provoked Marduk to punish them.[50] Without mentioning Sennacherib, his devastation of Babylon was attributed directly to Marduk.[51] A similar understanding of the event is found in Assurbanipal's inscriptions,[52] but alongside this view is a more ambiguous interpretation according to which Marduk, during the reign of a former king, went to live with his father in Assur[53]—a motif which, while compatible with Marduk's voluntary destruction of his own city, nevertheless moves toward the earlier view of Sennacherib in underscoring Marduk's subordination to Assur.

Much later, long after Assyria has disappeared from the scene, Nabonidus is still reflecting on the theological significance of Sennacherib's action and, one must add, in a way which reveals the openness of that past event to a future unfolding.[54] According to Nabonidus, Marduk was angry with his land and used the Assyrian king to punish it. Sennacherib treated the land according to the anger of Marduk. Here, in contrast to Esarhaddon and Assurbanipal's treatments, the human agent in the destruction of Babylon is not passed over in silence. The Assyrian was Marduk's tool for punishing Babylon, but that in no way justified Sennacherib's behavior. Nabonidus makes it clear that Sennacherib was guilty of great sacrilege even in the carrying out of Marduk's angry decree, and when the god's anger with Babylon subsided, the agent of his anger was punished in turn. One can hardly ignore the striking parallel in theology to Isaiah's theological treatment of historical events in Israel involving the same Assyrian king.[55]

Marduk's revenge, however, also took the form of sacrilege, this time against the gods of Assyria, and Nabonidus, who was a polytheist worried about the feelings of the other gods and who had no illusions as to the fate of the human agents of divine outrages, disassociates himself completely from these actions. It was not the Babylonians but the Uman-manda who were the human agents of Marduk's avenging wrath.

---

50. R. Borger, *Die Inscriften Asarhaddons, Königs von Assyrien* (*AfO* Beiheft 9; Graz: E. Weidner, 1956) 12–14, Episodes, 2–5.

51. This explanation probably originated among the Babylonians themselves as Morton Cogan suggests (*Imperialism and Religion* [Missoula: Scholars Press, 1974] 13).

52. M. Streck, *Assurbanipal und die letzten assyrischen Könige bis zum Untergange Niniveh's*, II (*VAB* 7; Leipzig: J. C. Hinrich, 1916) 262:29.

53. Ibid., 244:37–41.

54. Stephen Langdon, *Die neubabylonischen Königsinschriften* (*VAB* 4; Leipzig: J. C. Hinrich, 1912) 270ff., Nabonid Nr. 8; translated in *ANET* (1955^2) 308–11.

55. See especially Isa 10:12–19.

Cult

If historiography does not privilege easy access to a theologically marketable contrast, however, neither does the cult. Frank Cross's treatment of the central events celebrated in the Israelite cult, combining as it does the valid insights of both the Myth-and-Ritual and the History-of-Salvation schools, is brilliant.[56] What is lacking, however, is an adequate pole for comparison. The problem is not in Cross's treatment of the Ugaritic material, which is admirable, but in the nature of the evidence itself. The absence of hymns and prayers from the Ugaritic corpus leaves our knowledge of the Canaanite cult too incomplete to confidently dismiss the category of history as theologically irrelevant to Canaanite religion.

Certainly the Mesopotamian cult, where the evidence is far more abundant, cannot be so easily dismissed as completely ahistorical, entirely dominated by myth. Such a view of the Mesopotamian cult, though it is still widely held and while it has a certain validity when applied to the earliest reconstructable forms of Mesopotamian piety, ignores the later developments which altered the earlier meanings of Mesopotamian rites as surely as the latter Israelite historical reinterpretations changed the meanings of the Israelite festivals.[57] Thorkild Jacobsen's earlier treatment of the Mesopotamian festival had already intimated such a development, but his recently published contribution to the Albright symposium volume presents a more detailed exposition of the subject.[58] In it he argues that the battle drama of the first millennium was the vehicle for a political-historical viewpoint.[59] The *Enuma Elish*, for example, celebrated the historical achievement of the unification of the Babylonian world after the conquest of the Sealand.[60] This historical interpretation was superimposed upon the originally agricultural Akitu festival, making it a national festival.[61] The battle for unification, however, was given cosmic scope and made primeval through the mythical language.[62]

Assuming Jacobsen's analysis is correct, there are two observations one should make. In the first place, one should note that the Mesopotamians, like the Israelites, celebrated historical events in their cult. On the other hand, one must admit that the common practice of giving these historical events religious significance by translating them into the cosmic language of myth is far more

56. F. M. Cross, *Canaanite Myth and Hebrew Epic* (Cambridge: Harvard University Press, 1973) 77–111.

57. See my comments in "Divine Freedom and Cultic Manipulation in Israel and Mesopotamia," *Unity and Diversity*, 182–83.

58. Thorkild Jacobsen, *Unity and Diversity*, 65–97.

59. Ibid., 72–77.

60. Ibid., 76.

61. Ibid.

62. Ibid.

pervasive an influence in Mesopotamia than in Israel. The Assyrian justification for the sack of Babylon in the text recounting Marduk's trial for treason[63] can be closely paralleled by the justification for the Davidic empire in Yahweh's trial of the pagan gods in Psalm 82,[64] but it is more difficult to find Mesopotamian religious texts that speak of historical events in non-mythological language. They are not entirely lacking—one could cite the bilingual prayer of Tukulti-Ninurta that complains of revolting vassals[65] or the hymn to Marduk that celebrates his defeat of the Elamites[66]—but they are comparatively rare. Nonetheless, without overstressing this historical element in the Mesopotamian cult, one should recognize its presence and adjust one's comparative analysis accordingly. Whether the Canaanite cult had any historical concerns comparable to the Mesopotamian is uncertain, but since epic is "a well-known literary genre in ancient Canaanite (Ugaritic) religious literature,"[67] the possibility cannot be excluded until there is much more evidence.

Conclusion

That some contrast involving the myth-history tension existed between Israel's theology and that of her neighbors seems to me self-evident, and the preceding discussion is not intended to obscure that contrast. If my argument has been sound, however, the earlier comparative treatments have been grossly oversimplified, and thus provide no solid basis for elaborating what precisely that contrast was. Thus, the task of clarifying that contrast remains.

In my opinion, this task requires a new approach.[68] Broad generalizations, whether based on historiographical literature or cultic practices, are of little help. What is at issue is the relative theological significance of history to Israel and her neighbors, and about the only avenue we have for grasping this comparative significance is through its expression in the respective literatures. That means, however, that we must begin with individual texts and only move to broader generalizations with caution. The comparative study of the historiographical literature must consider the theological treatment of individual episodes and motifs before moving to the larger complexes and the overall

63. See above, nn. 48–49.

64. J. J. M. Roberts, "The Davidic Origin of the Zion Tradition," *JBL* 92 (1973) 340–41.

65. Erich Ebeling, *Keilschrifttexte aus Assur religiösen Inhalts* (Ausgrabungen der deutschen Orient-Gesellschaft in Assur, E; Inschriften; ed. F. Delitzsch; Leipzig: Hinrichs, 1919) 128, 129 fragments 1–2; H. Gressmann (ed.), *Altorientalische Texte zum Alten Testament* (Berlin and Leipzig: Walter de Gruyter and Co., 1926²) 263–65.

66. J. Hehn, *Beiträge zur Assyriologie* 5 (1906) 326–29.

67. Cross, *Canaanite Myth and Hebrew Epic*, ix.

68. Since this paper was first drafted, several comparative studies have appeared which do move in the direction I think necessary, though none that I know of are concerned with precisely this problem.

meanings of these works. One must be aware of the possible mythological use of history as well as the historical use of myth. Moreover, the investigation cannot be limited to the historiographical material. An adequate comparative study must examine the theological interpretations of historical events across the whole spectrum of literary genres native to the cultures being compared. One way of doing this is to take a typical event such as the fall of a royal cult center and then to trace the theological reflections on that event through the literature of both cultures. Other techniques for getting at the problem will undoubtedly emerge in the ensuing discussion, and eventually one must construct a new synthesis—hopefully one that will recognize the theological value of both what is unique to the biblical faith and what it shares in common with the Ancient Near Eastern religions. The present task, however, is to relay the foundations.

Chapter 4

Divine Freedom and Cultic Manipulation in Israel and Mesopotamia

The reemergence of biblical theology in the years following World War I brought with it a renewed interest in the uniqueness of the biblical faith.[1] In terms of Old Testament studies, that meant an attempt to isolate the distinctively Israelite elements in Israel's religion from those elements which Israel held in common with her polytheistic neighbors.[2] G. E. Wright's *The Old Testament against Its Environment* exemplifies well the mood and method of this theological approach to the Old Testament, and the title of his study would make an appropriate designation for this important aspect of the biblical theology movement.[3]

In spite of significant differences between Wright and other Old Testament theologians belonging to the movement, there seems to be a general consensus among them with regard to two fundamental contrasts between Israel and her neighbors: (1) Israel's religion was *historically oriented* and primarily concerned with bringing man's will into line with Yahweh's will, while the polytheistic religions were ahistorical, focusing on man's attempt to integrate himself into the rhythm of nature.[4] (2) The pagan ritual was an attempt to gain control over or manipulate the gods by *sympathetic magic*, while in Israel the cult by its emphasis on historical recitation, imaginative memory, and thanksgiving served to clarify God's will to man and to renew man's commitment to that will.[5] Thus, according to these scholars, the superficial similarities between Israel's religion and that of the surrounding nations obscures a far more profound discontinuity between the faith of Israel and that of the nations.

---

1. Brevard S. Childs gives a very good historical sketch of this movement, with a necessary distinction between the European development in the 1920s and the American Biblical Theology Movement of the 1940s and later (*Biblical Theology in Crisis* [Philadelphia: The Westminster Press, 1970] 1–31).

2. Ibid., 47–50.

3. G. E. Wright, *The Old Testament against Its Environment*, Studies in Biblical Theology No. 2 (London: SCM Press LTD, 1950).

4. Ibid., 22–23.

5. Ibid., 101.

There is no doubt a significant element of truth in this comparative analysis—Israelite religion is undeniably different—and the analysis lent itself, as Childs notes, to a "hard-hitting, impressive new form of apologetic for Biblical religion."[6] The consequent popularizing, however, revealed certain weaknesses in the analysis that are not totally absent from the more sophisticated treatments, and it was inevitable that a reaction would set in. It came, along with a general decline in biblical theology,[7] in a two-pronged attack on the first thesis. Bertil Albrektson demonstrated that the pagan gods also act quite decisively in history,[8] and James Barr seriously questioned whether history was really as important a theological category to the ancient Israelites as the modern biblical theologians had made it.[9] Even if these critics have overstated their case, it seems relatively clear that the radical contrast between the polytheistic gods of nature and the Israelite god of history must be softened considerably.

As far as I am aware, the second thesis, which predicates a similarly radical distinction between the Israelite cult that preserves divine freedom and the pagan cult that seeks to manipulate the deity, has not received the same critical attention. Were the pagan gods, in fact, more susceptible to manipulation than Yahweh, and was the pagan cult a more blatant attempt to gain control over the deity than the Israelite cult? I think not.

To begin with, one must insist on a far more basic similarity in religious motivation between Israel and her neighbors than Wright's analysis would seem to allow. Despite whatever difference in historical emphasis there may have been between the Israelite and pagan cults, the rationale for serving the deity, especially on the individual level, was essentially the same in Israel as elsewhere. If one may generalize it, Satan's question about Job is very much to the point: "Does man fear God for nought?" The answer to this question in both Israel and Mesopotamia, to pick a specific area for comparison, was of course, "No!" Obedience to the deity, whether in ethical matters or in purely ritual concerns, paid. This is evident from the *Counsels of Wisdom* on the Mesopotamian side,[10] and one need only look at the covenant blessings to see how fundamental a role the incentive of profit or reward played in Israelite theology.[11]

6. Childs, *Biblical Theology in Crisis*, 49.

7. Childs has vividly described this breakdown in the biblical theology movement (ibid., 51–87).

8. Bertil Albrektson, *History and the Gods: An Essay on the Idea of Historical Events as Divine Manifestations in the Ancient Near East and in Israel* (Lund: CWK Gleerup, 1967).

9. James Barr, *Old and New in Interpretation: A Study of the Two Testaments* (London: SCM Press LTD, 1966) 65–102.

10. W. G. Lambert, *Babylonian Wisdom Literature* (Oxford: Clarendon Press, 1960) 101–3:57–65; 105:135–47.

11. Deut 28:1–14.

Moreover, the rewards sought by the Mesopotamian and the Israelite differed very little, if at all. Both wanted long life, good health, numerous children (especially male children), material prosperity, deliverance from foreign enemies, peace and stability at home, and general well-being which would include what a modern would call mental health. Forgiveness of sins, for which both the Israelite and the Mesopotamian prayed, was related to these more concrete blessings, since it was only through the right relationship with the deity that these blessings flowed to man. If that relationship were broken through sin, the blessings would be lost.

In view of this basic identity in the ultimate goal of Mesopotamian and Israelite religiosity, the contrast Wright draws between the polytheist who saw the problem of life as an integration with the forces of nature and the Israelite who saw it as an adjustment to the will of God,[12] if it has any validity at all, is simply a contrast in the means used to attain the same end. When Wright speaks of an integration with nature in polytheism, he is, of course, referring to the origin of the polytheistic gods in the numinous awareness of the powers in nature, and the human need to bring oneself and these sometimes conflicting powers into a life-giving harmony. But, more than that, the polytheist accomplished this "integration with nature"—as the term "integration" itself suggests—by entering into the world of these powers, identifying himself with them, and through imitative action, forcing them to do what he wanted. As evidence for this fundamental role of sympathetic magic in polytheistic religion, Wright points especially to the underlying meaning of the major festivals of the pagan world.[13] Unfortunately, his argument is flawed here by a methodological inconsistency. When discussing the Israelite festivals, he emphasizes, not the original meanings of these celebrations, but the later Israelite historical reinterpretations, and in so doing he stresses the important point that even when rites and festivals are preserved in outwardly the same form, they do not always retain their earlier meanings.[14] Yet he completely overlooks this important insight when he discusses the pagan festivals. Of course, he did not have the benefit of Professor Jacobsen's paper on Mesopotamian religious drama,[15] but even in the *Intellectual Adventure of Ancient Man*, which Wright used extensively, there was already a clear intimation that Mesopotamian religion could not be understood as a static entity:[16]

> Though these functions of the human state have been integrated to some degree with the view of the universe as a state . . . the deeper significance, the inner

12. Wright, *The Old Testament Against Its Environment*, 23.
13. Ibid., 93–95.
14. Ibid., 98–101.
15. See pp. 65–97 of this volume.
16. Thorkild Jacobsen, "Mesopotamia," in *The Intellectual Adventure of Ancient Man*, ed. Henri and H. A. Frankfort (Chicago: University of Chicago Press, 1946) 200.

> sense of these festivals, lies outside of and is not truly founded in the view of the universe as a state. It should therefore not cause wonder that they cannot stand out in true perspective in a presentation of that view; that they represent an older layer of "speculative" thought.
>
> According to the view of the world as a state, man is the slave of the great cosmic forces; he serves them and obeys them; and his only means of influencing them is by prayer and sacrifice, that is, by persuasion and gifts. According to the older view which created the festivals, man could himself become god, could enter into the identity of the great cosmic forces in the universe which surrounded him, and could thus sway it by action, not merely by supplication.

The point is, had Wright chosen as his object of comparison the later Mesopotamian view of the world rather than the more primitive, he would not have been able to paint such a sharp contrast between the pagan who could control the deity by sympathetic magic and the Israelite who could only adjust himself to Yahweh's will.

In the later Mesopotamian development, while the element of sympathetic magic never totally disappeared, the means by which one attempted to gain the desired blessings were modeled far more on the psychological devices one used with human superiors in line with the strong anthropomorphic and sociomorphic conception of the gods that had largely displaced their primary identification with natural powers. Note, for instance, the famous Old Babylonian letter which a certain suppliant addressed to his personal god:[17]

> To the god my father speak: thus says Apiladad, your servant: Why have you neglected me so? Who is going to give you one who can take my place? Write to the god Marduk, who is fond of you, that he may break my bondage; then I shall see your face and kiss your feet! Consider also my family, grown-ups and little ones; have mercy on me for their sake, and let your help reach me!

With great sensitivity Jacobsen has captured the psychological pressures this sulking worshiper is applying to his personal god:[18]

> His feelings are hurt because he thinks his god neglects him. He hints that such neglect is very unwise on the part of the god, for faithful worshipers are hard to get and difficult to replace. But if the god will only comply with his wishes, then he will be there right away and adore him. Finally, he works on the god's pity: the god must consider that there is not only himself but that he has a family and poor little children who also suffer with him.

One should also note, as Jacobsen does, that the man asks his god to write to Marduk for him.[19] Just as men call upon other men to intercede for them in the

17. *YOS*, 2, 141; *The Intellectual Adventure of Ancient Man*, ed. Frankfort and Frankfort, 205–6.

18. Ibid., 205.

19. Ibid.

affairs of men, so the polytheist asks individual gods to use their influence on other gods in his behalf. In this case the personal god is called upon to use his connections with Marduk; in other cases a god like Marduk is asked to placate the personal deity who has deserted his ward in anger.

The ancient Mesopotamian also used various gifts, offerings, and promises of such to obtain the desired response from his divine overlords. One can hardly dismiss such practices as simply calculated bribery, but human nature being what it is, this approach to the deity always runs the risk of sinking to that level, and Mesopotamian literature offers some graphic examples of just such a corruption. In the Atra-ḫasîs epic, for instance, when Enlil decides to solve the noise problem by eliminating mankind through the plague, the people at Enki's counsel ignore their own gods and goddesses and shower all their gifts on Namtara, the god of plague. The maneuver has the intended effect of both pleasing and embarrassing Namtara, and he lifts the plague.[20] Subsequently the same ploy is used with success on Adad.[21]

But what normally strikes the Old Testament theologian as the most significant contrast between Israelite religion, which also had its sacrifices, free-will offerings, and vows, is the sometimes explicit statement that the Mesopotamian gods actually needed these gifts.[22] In the Atra-ḫasîs epic, for instance, after the flood has done away with the human slaves of the gods, there is no one left to provide them cult, and they sit weeping, their lips feverishly athirst, their stomachs cramped with hunger.[23] And everyone is familiar with the scene where the hero of the flood offers his sacrifice upon disembarking, whereupon the gods sniff the smell and gather like flies over the offering.[24] Or no less famous, the response of the slave when his master decides not to offer sacrifice:[25]

> Do not sacrifice, sir, do not sacrifice.
> You can teach your god to run after you like a dog.

Nevertheless, I think one should be more cautious than scholars sometimes are in citing such examples as evidence that the pagans could coerce or manipulate their gods while such would be unheard of in Israel. Do these passages in fact reflect normative Mesopotamian theology? Or could one with equal right quote Job 9:22–24 as the normative Israelite view on Yahweh's justice?

> It is all one; therefore I say, he destroys both the blameless and the wicked. When disaster brings sudden death, he mocks at the calamity of the innocent. The earth

20. W. G. Lambert and A. R. Millard, *Atra-ḫasīs: The Babylonian Story of the Flood* (Oxford: Clarendon Press, 1969) 68:378–71:413.

21. Ibid., 74:9–77:35.

22. Wright, *The Old Testament Against Its Environment*, 103.

23. Lambert and Millard, *Atra-ḫasīs*, 96–97:12–22.

24. *Gilgamesh*, XI, 155–61.

25. *BWL*, 148–49:60–61.

> is given into the hand of the wicked; he covers the faces of its judges—if it is not he, who then is it?

But perhaps that is straining the argument.

It is true that the Israelites explicitly denied that Yahweh ate the sacrificial offerings,[26] and since there was no image of Yahweh, it was not easy to think of him as actually wearing the votive offerings of clothing, jewelry, and the like—in Mesopotamia these were directly connected with the care for the image.[27] But, apart from these rather crude anthropomorphisms which are to a certain degree tied to the presence of a physical image, all the Mesopotamian devices for influencing the god mentioned above are also present in the Old Testament in one form or another.

The highly stereotyped descriptions of physical and mental anguish characteristic of the individual psalms of lament clearly function to provoke Yahweh's compassion, and the use of vows and votive offerings in the Old Testament is too well known to need comment.

Because of Israel's monotheistic faith one would not expect a worshiper to call upon other gods to intercede with Yahweh, though intercessory spirits may be known in Late Israelite sources,[28] but to a large extent the same function is performed in Israel by men who stand in a particularly close relationship to Yahweh, such as Moses, Samuel, or one of the prophets.[29] Thus the use of influential mediators in approaching the deity with a request is a motif common to both Israel and Mesopotamia; the details are just altered to fit the differing theological systems.

Moreover, one should remember that physical needs are not the only needs an anthropomorphic god may have. If Yahweh could not be touched by the hunger and thirst that tormented the pagan deities deprived of their cult, his "spiritual" needs for praise and glory provided the Israelite with essentially the same bargaining point. Over and over again Yahweh is asked to do something for his "name's sake."[30] He must protect his name's honor:

> Remember your servants, Abraham, Isaac, and Jacob; do not regard the stubbornness of this people, or their wickedness, or their sin, lest the land from which you brought us say, "Because Yahweh was not able to bring them into the land which he promised them, or because he hated them, he has brought them out to kill them in the wilderness." (Deut 9:27–28; see Exod 32:11–12)

26. Ps 50:9–13.

27. W. F. Leemans, *Ishtar of Lagaba and her Dress*, SLB I (Leiden: E. J. Brill, 1952); A. L. Oppenheim, "The Golden Garments of the Gods," *JNES* 8 (1949) 172–93.

28. See Zech 3:1; Dan 12:1; and Job 9:33; 16:19; 19:25; 33:23 (Job may not be such a late source).

29. Exod 32:30–32; 1 Sam 12:23; Gen 27:7; Jer 15:1.

30. Pss 31:3; 69:6–7; 109:21.

Yahweh's need for praise and glory also finds expression in the Psalms where the psalmist, just as the Babylonian letter writer, sometimes reminds the deity that he is in danger of losing a valuable worshiper:

> Turn, O Yahweh, save my life; deliver me for the sake of your steadfast love. For in death no one remembers you; in sheol who praises you? (Ps 6:5–6)

Or again:

> What profit is there in my blood, if I go down to the pit? Will the dust praise you? Will it declare your faithfulness? (Ps 30:10; see 88:11–13)[31]

No doubt it is in this context that one should judge those passages in the Psalms where a request is concluded by such words as, "Then my tongue shall proclaim your righteousness, your praise all the day long."[32] As in the Babylonian *shu-ila* prayers, which characteristically end with a very similar vow,[33] the implication is that if the deity will give the man what he wants, the man will give the deity the praise he desires.

Moreover, strange as it may seem, the presence of such vows and other psychological pressure techniques in both Israelite and Mesopotamian prayers gives the lie, I think, to the widespread attempt on the part of Old Testament scholars to draw a sharp distinction between the manipulative quality of Mesopotamian and Israelite prayers. Arnold Gamper,[34] for instance, basing himself on G. R. Castellino's work,[35] refers to the prevailing Mesopotamian conception of the magical effect of prayer. "The thing prayed for," he says, "followed mechanically, as it were, out of the performance of the prescribed ritual."[36] If that were true, why bother making vows or indulging in the other psychological means of persuasion of which Akkadian prayers are full? At some point in the history of Mesopotamian religion the content of those prayers must have been taken seriously. After all, the appended ritual in many cases involves no more than a simple sacrificial offering, which in itself hardly implies a magical manipulation of the deity. Comparable ritual directions are lacking in the Old Testament Psalms, of course, but one should not

31. This motif is given a new twist in Ben Sira 17:25–28, where it has become a motivation for man to repent. If he does not, he will miss the joys of taking part in worship. This new use of the motif is obviously secondary to the usage in the Psalms, however, so it is illegitimate to reinterpret these earlier passages in the light of this later use of the motif.

32. Pss 35:17–18, 28; 22:22; 61:9.

33. Walter G. Kunstmann, *Die babylonische Gebetsbeschwörung*, LSS NF 2 (Leipzig: J. C. Hinrichsische Buchhandlung, 1932) 39–42.

34. *Gott als Richter in Mesopotamien und im Alten Testament, zum Verständnis einer Gebetsbitte* (Innsbruck: Universitätsverlag Wagner, 1966) 7.

35. *Le Lamentazioni individuali e gli Inni in Babilonia e in Israele* (Torino: Società Editrice Internazionale, 1940) XX, n. 4.

36. Gamper, *Gott als Richter*, 7.

make too much of this fact. One cannot safely argue on this basis—particularly for the preexilic period—that the Old Testament Psalms were recited independently of any ritual. In fact it seems clear that at least some of the Psalms were originally composed to accompany the sacrificial ritual—one thinks particularly of the correspondence between the *tôdāh*-prayer and the *tôdāh*-offering.[37]

Even Wright's argument from the Old Testament's prohibition against magic and divination is strangely inconclusive for his thesis. In the first place, only one page after saying, ". . . the pagan world of magic and divination is simply incompatible with the worship of Yahweh,"[38] he must temper this judgment by admitting that official Yahwism did contain some elements which "we would consider magical practices or things verging closely thereon."[39] Among the more important elements he puts in this category are the Israelite purification laws, the power of the spoken word in blessings and curses, the use of sacred lots for divining Yahweh's will, and the goat for Azazel in the Day of Atonement ritual.[40] He does not really explain why these exceptions do not invalidate his thesis, but his discussion of Azazel, his comments on the use of Urim and Thummin, and his treatment of Samuel the seer, who revealed secrets for a fee, suggest that these elements were simply feeble survivals from a pagan background which, for the most part, either died out early in Israelite history, or whose inner meaning was reinterpreted.[41]

Once again, however, the logic of historical development is just as applicable to Mesopotamia as it is to Israel. Even when one turns to those Mesopotamian incantations which strike us as the least prayer-like, and whose accompanying ritual seems most clearly to have originated in the realm of sympathetic magic, one must still reckon with the possibility that the original significance of the rite has been overlaid with a new interpretation. In some cases where such rituals are given a mythological interpretation, it is clear that the two do not really correspond, that the later interpretation has altered the purely magical significance of the original rite.[42] In other words one cannot simply assume from the character of the ritual that the Mesopotamian understood his incantation as a device for bypassing the divine will and achieving his desired ends by his own actions.

To illustrate this last point one need only compare 2 Kgs 13:15–19:

---

37. Lev 7:11; 22:29; Amos 4:5; 2 Chr 29:31; 33:16; Pss 50:14, 23; 56:13; 107:22; 116:17.

38. Wright, *The Old Testament Against Its Environment*, 86–87.

39. Ibid., 88.

40. Ibid., 88–92.

41. Ibid.

42. W. G. Lambert, "Myth and Ritual as Conceived by the Babylonians," *JSS* 13 (1968) 110–11.

> And Elisha said to him, "Take a bow and arrows"; so he took a bow and arrows. Then he said to the king, "Draw the bow"; so he drew the bow, and Elisha placed his hands upon the king's hands. Then he said, "Open the window eastward"; and he opened it. Elisha said, "Shoot!"; and he shot. He said, "Yahweh's arrow of victory, the arrow of victory over Aram! You will smite the Arameans in Aphek until you have annihilated them." Then he said, "Take the arrows"; and he took them. He said to the king of Israel, "Strike the ground"; and he struck the ground three times and stopped. Then the man of God became angry with him and said, "You should have struck five or six times, then you would have smitten Aram until you had annihilated them, but now you will only smite Aram three times."

This text with its precise ritual directions, its account of their execution, and its incantation-like recitation—"Yahweh's arrow of victory, the arrow of victory over Aram! You will smite the Arameans in Aphek until you have annihilated them"—shows striking similarities to Mesopotamian incantations. Nor is it unique. It does not differ radically from other accounts of prophetic symbolic acts.[43] On the surface it seems to portray a purely magical rite, yet few Old Testament scholars would be satisfied with an explanation of this passage which saw in it an attempt to bypass Yahweh's will. Whether explicit or not, the magic is subservient to Yahweh's purposes. The prophet speaks and acts in the name of and as the agent of Yahweh, not according to his own will; hence, as Fohrer argues, this and other symbolic acts of the prophets have only a "broken" or "dialectical" relationship to magic.[44] I would agree, but precisely the same argument may be made for the Mesopotamian material. The Mesopotamian incantation expert, the *āšipu*, also derived his authority from the gods and spoke their words in their name.[45] The priest acted not on his own, but as the agent of the gods, as the legitimation theme found in many incantation texts makes clear.[46]

The empirical experience of the Mesopotamians, as we shall see, must have made it clear that even the most meticulous performance of incantations and rituals could not guarantee with mechanical certainty the desired end. Those rituals which end with a positive statement that the desired blessing will be achieved do not really alter this fact.[47] They simply state the expectations of the specialist, presumably based on prior experience, and no doubt, like the

43. G. Fohrer, "Prophetie und Magie," *ZAW* 78 (1966) 32.

44. Ibid., 28, 34.

45. Edith K. Ritter, "Magical-Expert (= *Āšipu*) and Physician (= *Asû*): Notes on Two Complementary Professions in Babylonian Medicine," *AS* 16 (Chicago: University of Chicago Press, 1965) 299–321, esp. 321.

46. Adam Falkenstein, *Die Haupttypen der sumerischen Beschwörung*, LSS NF 11 (Leipzig: August Pries, 1931) 23–27, 70–74; see *BWL* 49:15, 25–28; 51:41–44.

47. E. Ebeling, *Keilschrifttexte aus Assur religiösen Inhalts* I, Wissenschaftliche Veröffentlichung der Deutschen Orient-Gesellschaft 28 (Leipzig: J. C. Hinrichs, 1919) Nr. 43; E. Ebeling, "Assyrische Beschwörungen," *ZDMG* 69 (1915) 92–95.

optimistic prognostications of modern physicians, these expectations were often disappointed.[48]

Moreover, Wright and other Old Testament theologians have basically misunderstood divination, at least as far as the normal Mesopotamian practice is concerned, when they describe it as a way of tricking or coercing the deity into revelation.[49] It may be that the origins of divination go back to a view of the world in which its very structure is thought to contain a clue to the future—a clue which one may discover by examining some microcosmic reflection of that world such as the entrails of a sacrificial lamb, but in the later period, as one text says, it is the god who writes the message of the future in the entrails.[50] The Old Babylonian prayer of the divination priest recently published by Goetze is enlightening in this regard.[51] Running like a thread through the whole text, or at least the part Goetze published, is the constantly recurring and only slightly varied refrain in which the priest appeals to the various gods: "In the ritual act I prepare, in the extispicy I perform put you truth!"[52] This repeated plea, not only for an answer, but for a true answer, should make it clear that the success of divination depended on the good will of the deity. Even the pagan deities could refuse to respond to man's appeal. The omens did not always turn out favorably, and often enough, they were totally unclear—the gods simply refused to answer.[53] To quote a Hittite example, Mursilis, as his plague prayers eloquently testify, had no easier time evoking a revelatory response from his gods than the tragic Saul did from Yahweh.[54]

In the final analysis, whatever the differences between Israelite religion and that of their pagan neighbors, and I do not mean to unduly minimize them, neither the pagan nor the Israelite could really control the divine world. In spite of all the means of persuasion available to humans, the inscrutable gods sometimes turned a deaf ear to their human subjects. Not even the most submissive and conscientious obedience to the divine will could guarantee the desired blessings—covenant or no covenant.[55] The good man sometimes suffered while the wicked man prospered, and as a result of this observation, drawn

48. Note the preferences to unsuccessful treatment in Ritter, *AS* 16, 315–17, and see *BWL* 45:108:11.

49. Wright, *The Old Testament Against Its Environment*, 87.

50. O. R. Gurney and J. J. Finkelstein, *The Sultantepe Tablets* I, Occasional Publications of the British Institute of Archaeology at Ankara 3 (London, 1957) 60:15 and duplicates.

51. A. Goetze, "An Old Babylonian Prayer of the Divination Priest," *JCS* 22 (1968) 25–29.

52. Ibid., lines 11ff., 17–18, 31–33, 40–41, 48–49, 52–53, 56–57, 64–66.

53. Note especially the use of this motif in the Kuthean legend about Narām-Sîn (*STT* 1, 30:72–92; O. R. Gurney, *Anatolian Studies* 5 [1955] 102–3:72–92).

54. *ANET* 394–96.

55. Whatever advantages covenant provided the Israelite over his pagan contemporary, it did not provide the individual with certainty of success. Josiah's fate makes that too painfully clear.

from the actual experience of life, some thinkers in Mesopotamia as well as Israel, moved toward a more profound view of the relationship between obedience and the divine blessings.[56] Man in the finiteness of his knowledge and power was simply unable to strip the deity of his freedom. This insight is most clearly stated in the wisdom literature of both cultures, but at least a rudimentary awareness of its truth can be detected even in the more strictly cultic texts of both Israel and Mesopotamia.

56. See especially *Ludlul Bēl Nēmeqi* and the Babylonian *Theodicy* (*BWL* 21–91) for Mesopotamia, and Job for the Old Testament.

Nebuchadnezzar I's Elamite Crisis in Theological Perspective

In an earlier paper I have argued that an adequate comparative study of biblical and Mesopotamian views of history "must examine the theological interpretations of historical events across the whole spectrum of literary genres native to the cultures being compared."[1] I suggested that one way of doing this "is to take a typical event such as the fall of a royal cult center and then to trace the theological reflections on that event through the literature of both culture."[2] This paper will make a beginning toward that larger project by examining the Babylonian reflections on one particular sequence of events. Since J. J. Finkelstein, though his main research was concentrated elsewhere, always maintained an interest in the nature of Mesopotamian historical thought[3] and the light Mesopotamian studies could shed on biblical material,[4] it is with genuine pleasure that I dedicate this preliminary study to his memory.

The crisis brought on by the Elamite sack of Babylon, the plunder of its gods—particularly the removal of the statue of Marduk—and the ultimate resolution of this crisis by Nebuchadnezzar I's conquest of Elam and subsequent return of Marduk was widely celebrated in Babylonian literature.[5] It is referred to in two contemporary inscriptions of Nebuchadnezzar I;[6] it is the occasion of a "prophecy" of Marduk;[7] it is the subject of at least one and probably two epics of uncertain date;[8] and it may be celebrated in an unusual historical

1. J. J. M. Roberts, "Myth Versus History: Relaying the Comparative Foundations," *CBQ* 38 (1976) 1–13.

2. *CBQ* 38 (1976) 1–13.

3. See, for instance, his important article, "Mesopotamian Historiography," *PAPS* 107 (1963).

4. See, for an example, his article "An Old Babylonian Herding Contract and Genesis 31:38f.," *JAOS* 88 (1968) 30–36.

5. For the history, see J. A. Brinkman, *A Political History of Post-Kassite Babylonia*, *AnOr* 43 (Rome: Pontifical Biblical Institute, 1968) 104–10.

6. L. W. King, *Babylonian Boundary-Stones* (London: British Museum, 1912) nos. 6 and 24.

7. Rykle Borger, "Gott Marduk und Gott-König Šulgi als Propheten: Zwei prophetische Texte," *BiOr* 28 (1971) 3–24.

8. K.3426 and K.2660. For bibliography on these texts see Brinkman, *Political History*, p. 328, nos. 4.3.8 and 4.3.9. K.3426 (= CT 13 48) mentions Nebuchadnezzar by name, but

hymn to Marduk.[9] Despite Brinkman's doubts, two bilingual poems—or two fragments of the same larger work—probably refer to the same events.[10] The so-called Kedorlaomer texts also seem to deal with this historical era,[11] and, finally, there are additional references to it in omen texts.[12] In short, thanks to the abundance and diverse genres of our sources, we are able to see this sequence of events from several different viewpoints. Thus it provides us with a model example of the ways in which the Babylonians interpreted the fall and subsequent restoration of a royal cult center involving the removal and return of its divine images. Even if some of the sources used actually refer to a later conflict with the Elamites, it will not significantly affect the results, since this concrete historical sequence is chosen merely as an example of the typical interpretation.

The two contemporary inscriptions are perhaps the least theological in their treatments of the events. One simply states that Nebuchadnezzar went to Elam, smote it, took the hand of Marduk, and returned this god together with the goddess Eriya to Babylon.[13] The second, however, is not without theological interest. According to it, Marduk, the king of the gods, gave Nebuchadnezzar the command, and he took up arms to *avenge* Akkad.[14] The historical background for such vengeance is not given—the contemporaries of Nebuchadnezzar hardly needed an explanation—but it clearly implies that the Elamites had sinned against Marduk and his land in the past. After its report of Marduk's command, the text then describes the ensuing campaign. Its primary concern is to glorify Nebuchadnezzar and his servant LAK-ti-Marduk, for whose benefit the *kudurru* containing the inscription was set up, by relating

K.2660 (=3 R 38 no. 2) may be about a somewhat later king, though Nebuchadnezzar still appears the most likely candidate.

9. DT 71; copy in BA 5 386–87. Manfred Weippert wants to connect it to Assurbanipal's defeat of the Elamites, and he points out that the name of the deity praised does not occur on the preserved part of the text (*ZAW* 84 [1972] 482 nn. 108–9), but the hymn's resemblance to the other texts celebrating the success of Nebuchadnezzar I argues for the earlier date.

10. K.344+BM 99067 (= 4R^2 20 no. 1+AJSL 35 [1918] 139) is accepted by Brinkman and listed with bibliography in *Political History*, p. 329, no. 4.3.10. His reservations about the second text (ibid., p. 19, n. 81) may well have been dispelled by W. G. Lambert's masterful edition of the text which utilized additional pieces not known to Brinkman at the time ("Enmeduranki and Related Matters," *JCS* 21 [1967] 126–31). If both these texts deal with Nebuchadnezzar I's Elamite war, as they probably do, it is hard to dissociate DT 71, discussed above, from the same event.

11. A. Jeremias, "Die sogenannten Kedorlaomer-Texte," *MVAG* 21 (1916) 69–97. Pinches' copies in *JTVI* 29 (1897) 43–90 were not available to me.

12. See Brinkman, *Political History*, p. 328, no. 4.3.6 and p. 329, no. 4.3.11.

13. BBSt. 24 obv. 7–12.

14. BBSt. 6 i 12–13: *ūtaʾʾiršuma šar ilāni Marduk ana turri gimilli māt Akkadī ušatbâ kakkēšu.*

their endurance and courage in the face of great adversity. Two further theological statements are made, however. The difficult march is achieved because "the gods carry" Nebuchadnezzar.[15] Moreover, the outcome of the battle was decided by the command of Ishtar and Adad; thus Nebuchadnezzar routed Ḫulteludish, king of Elam, who then disappeared permanently.[16]

Far more interesting theologically is the prophecy text recently re-edited by Borger.[17] This text has Marduk narrate past history in autobiographical form down to the time just prior to Nebuchadnezzar's Elamite campaign. As far as the often fragmentary text allows one to judge, the emphasis is on the earlier "trips" of Marduk's statue. Muršilis' capture and removal of Marduk's statue becomes a business trip ordered by Marduk himself to establish trade connections between Babylon and Ḫatti:[18]

> I gave the command. I went to the land of Ḫatti. I questioned Ḫatti. The throne of my Anu-ship I set up within it. I dwelt within it for 24 years, and I established within it the caravan trade of the Babylonians.

A sojourn in Assyria, no doubt reflecting Tukulti-Ninurta's removal of the Marduk statue following his victory over Kashtiliash, is also mentioned, but the reason for this trip is obscured by a break.[19] Marduk's favorable treatment of Assyria, however, suggests it was presented as a peaceful visit.[20]

Nevertheless, Marduk makes it clear that he was in charge of the situation; he may have gone away on trips, but he always returned:[21]

> I am Marduk the great lord. I alone am lord of destinies and decisions. Who has taken this road? Wherever I went, from there I returned.

This strong affirmation of Marduk's control of history following the recitation of past events involving the removal of Marduk's statue from Babylon prepares the stage for the god's interpretation of a more recent disaster, one apparently still too disquieting to be easily dismissed as a business trip—the Elamite conquest of Babylon and plunder of Marduk's statue. Marduk does not refer to the event as a defeat. Indeed Marduk asserts he himself gave the command for his departure from Babylon as well as for Babylon's subsequent misfortunes:[22]

15. BBSt. 6 i 22: *illak šarru nasqu ilāni našûšu.*

16. BBSt. 6 i 40–41: *ina pi Ištar u Adad ilāni bēlī tāḫāzi ulteshir Ḫulteludiš šar māt Elamti ītemid šadāšu.* Adad's help in this victory is also alluded to in another inscription of Nebuchadnezzar. See *BiOr* 7 (1950) 42–46 and plates I–III, and the additional references listed in Brinkman, *Political History*, pp. 325–26, no. 4.2.1.

17. *BiOr* 28 (1971) 3–24.

18. *BiOr* 28 (1971) 5:13–19.

19. *BiOr* 28 (1971) 6, the beginning lines of K.7065.

20. *BiOr* 28 (1971) 7:12′.

21. *BiOr* 28 (1971) 7:18′–21′a.

22. *BiOr* 28 (1971) 7:21′b–24′.

> I myself gave the command. I went to the land of Elam, and all the gods went with me—I alone gave the command. The food offerings of the temples I alone cut off.

Marduk's very insistence on this point, however, suggests there were those who questioned this interpretation of history. Perhaps this doubt took concrete form as less than enthusiastic support by the nobility, army, or populace for Nebuchadnezzar's proposed Elamite campaign.[23] The campaign appears to have suffered initial setbacks which one of the later texts attributed to the baleful opposition of the rebellious god Erra.[24] Whether Nebuchadnezzar's contemporaries, like the later writer, interpreted this setback as a thwarting of Marduk's will by a rival god is uncertain, but it certainly could have raised questions about Marduk's control of history.[25]

---

23. CT 13 48:1–3 speaks of Nebuchadnezzar terrifying his nobles by his rage over Babylon's predicament, and though the text does not have that in mind, they were probably frightened by what Nebuchadnezzar intended to do about the situation. At any rate, 3R 38 no. 2 rev. 6′–8′ pictures the panic and despair which gripped even the Babylonian king prior to the first engagement.

24. 3R 38 no. 2 rev. 9′–11′:

> [*itt*]*i sitāt nišî ina rēš Uknê ūqūsuma*
> [*ul itū*]*ramma kî la libbi ilī Erra gašri ilī*
> [*qur*]*ādīya unappiṣ*
>
> [wit]h the rest of the people I waited for him alongside the Kerkha river.
> [. . . did not] turn back, but Erra, strongest of the gods, against the will of the gods
> shattered my [war]riors.

The text goes on to describe the effects of the plague and the fear which caused Nebuchadnezzar to withdraw, first to Kar-Dur-Apil-Sin, and subsequently from there as well (lines 12′–16′).

25. A unique biblical passage which contains a remark bearing some resemblance to this interference by a rival deity is the peculiar notice at the end of 2 Kings 3. Following Yahweh's oracle promising victory (3:18–19), the Israelites and their allies relentlessly annihilate the Moabites (vv. 20–26) until, in a final act of desperation, the Moabite king sacrifices his eldest son and successor to his throne on the city wall (v. 27a). The result of that offering, presumably made to his own god, is then stated in a peculiarly succinct manner (v. 27b):

> *wyhy qṣp gdwl ʿl yśrʾl wyśw mʿlyw wyšbw lʾrṣ*
>
> And great wrath fell upon Israel, so they withdrew from him and returned home.

Yahweh is not mentioned as the agent of this wrath, and this raises some suspicion that the deuteronomic historian's source blamed Israel's discomfiture, not on Yahweh, but on the intervention of a Moabite deity well known in Israel.

If the Bible provides only the vaguest parallel to Erra's interference with the divine assembly's will, it provides very clear parallels to Marduk's insistent claim that he was the author of Babylon's defeat by Elam. A very instructive text in this regard is Ezek 8:1–11:23.

According to Marduk, however, the time of his sojourn outside Babylon was over, he longed for his city, and he summoned the gods to once more bring their tribute to Babylon.[26] At this point, then, the actual prophecy begins:[27] a king will arise in Babylon who will renew the sanctuaries, and bring Marduk back. Happy conditions will once again exist in Babylon. In the process, this king, with whom Marduk and all the gods are in covenant, will thoroughly destroy Elam.[28] One could question whether this prophecy is not in fact a *vaticinium ex eventu*, particularly since it exists only in late copies, but the tone of the document argues for dating the original prior to Nebuchadnezzar I's Elamite victories.[29] Otherwise it is difficult to explain the great concern to underscore

Yahweh was irritated because the Israelites left in Jerusalem were saying "Yahweh does not see; Yahweh has left the country" (8:12, 9:9). This view may have been based partly on the Babylonians' plundering of the temple treasures, presumably including the ark, in 597 B.C. (2 Kgs 24:13). There is certainly evidence for a belief that equated the loss of the ark with the loss of Yahweh's presence (1 Sam 4:21–22), and it may have been to counter this popular view that the importance of the ark was discounted in the oracle preserved in Jer 3:16. At any rate, the saying that offended Yahweh, whatever its origin, denied Yahweh's control of history. He was no longer in charge of Jerusalem's fate. In response to his challenge Ezekiel asserts that Yahweh himself was planning the city's destruction (8:18ff.). This point is underscored with graphic symbolism when the fire that is to fall on the city is taken from between the cherubim, that is, from the fiery glory of the divine presence itself (10:2, 6).

Whether Ezekiel's prophecy convinced many of his contemporaries that the final destruction of Jerusalem was Yahweh's own work, perfectly compatible with his control of history, may be doubted, particularly in view of the unbelief confronted by the later Second Isaiah. (It must have been easier for the Babylonians to believe Marduk's happier prophecy with its similar claims, at least following Elam's defeat.) Ezekiel's oracle did, however, catch the imagination of later writers struggling to explain subsequent disasters in a way consonant with God's sovereignty. The author of the Syriac Apocalypse of Baruch, for instance, has Yahweh reassure Baruch that "the enemy will not overthrow Zion, nor shall they burn Jerusalem" (5:3). In fulfillment of that promise God first sends an angel who removes the most holy objects—the veil, the ark, its cover, the two tablets, the holy raiment of the priests, the altar of incense, the forty-eight precious stones of the high priest's adornment, and all the holy vessels—from the temple and commits them to the earth's keeping (6:5–10). Then four angels with burning lamps who have been standing at the four corners of Jerusalem overthrew its wall and burned the temple (6:4; 7:1–8). Only then are the human enemies of Jerusalem permitted to enter the city; its destruction is really the work of God alone (8:2–5).

26. *BiOr* 28 (1971) 8:12–17.

27. *BiOr* 28 (1971) 8:19ff.

28. *BiOr* 28 (1971) 11:21′–23′.

29. Borger leaves open both possibilities, *BiOr* 28 (1971) 21. There is certainly no valid *a priori* reason for rejecting this text as a genuine prophecy. Genuine prophecies promising victory to the king are well known from Mari and the later Assyrian oracles, and they often contain elements which function to allay doubts or fear in the king's mind. Marduk's insistence on his control of history may have had the same function in our text, particularly if it were composed in an attempt to get Nebuchadnezzar to move against Elam. Moreover, the promises made do not read like a description after the fact. Where they rise above vague traditional *topoi*, they read more like a priestly program than historical reality.

Marduk's control of history; after Nebuchadnezzar's successful execution of Marduk's orders such concern would have had little point. Thus the text would appear to be a genuine "prophecy of salvation" seeking credence by an appeal to past history.[30] As such, it would, of course, antedate Nebuchadnezzar's own inscriptions and perhaps provide part of the background for his statement that Marduk ordered him to avenge Akkad.

The other treatments of these historical events are neither identical to one another, nor do they all represent the same literary genres, but for the sake of convenience, they may all be discussed together without serious distortion of the evidence. Taken together, they provide us with a kind of schema for the interpretation of the various moments in the sequence from cause to disaster to resolution.

Several of the texts, at least as far as they are preserved, ignore the origin of the problem,[31] but one which traces its development through the reigns of several kings appears to place the blame on the "wicked Elamites,"[32] a motif that finds numerous echoes in the other texts.[33] Another text, however, while it holds no higher opinion of the Elamites, finds the cause in the Babylonians' own sins which provoked Marduk to anger and led him to command the gods to desert the land.[34] As a result, the people were incited to sin, became godless, and evil multiplied.[35] At this stage the Elamites entered to devastate the land, destroy the cult centers, and carry off the gods.[36] According to another text this evil took place according to the plan of Marduk.[37]

The removal of Marduk's statue, however, created some problems for this view. The text that places the blame on the Elamites uses language so similar to the Erra epic in describing Marduk's departure from the seat of his dominion that one must doubt that its author attributed the event to Marduk's own plan-

30. Yahweh argues in much the same way in Second Isaiah (41:2–4; 42:24–25; 46:9–13; 51:12–16; 52:4–12; 54:7–17).

31. CT 13 48; 4R^2 20 no. 1 and duplicates; and DT 71.

32. 3R 38 no. 2, especially obv. 4′–5′:

> [*ša*] *eli abbēšu arna⟨šu⟩ šūturu šurbû ḫīṭušu kabtu*
> [*lemn*]*ēti ukappida ana māt Akkadī ibtani teqītu*
>
> [(Kudur-naḫḫunti) . . . who]se sin was far greater than that of his forefathers, whose heavy crime exceeded theirs,
> [. . .] planned wicked things against the land of Akkad, plotted insolence.

33. 4R^2 20 no. 1:12–13; DT 71:14–17, 10–12; *JCS* 21 (1967) 129:23; *MVAG* 21 (1916) 86:33; 90:33.

34. *JCS* 21 (1967) 128:15–18a.

35. *JCS* 21 (1967) 128:18b–22.

36. *JCS* 21 (1967) 129:23–24.

37. *MVAG* 21 (1916) 88:4–5: *nakru Elamû urriḫ lemnētu u Bēl ana Bābili ušakpidu lemuttu*, "The Elamite enemy hastened his evil work, and Bel instigated evil against Babylon."

ning.[38] At worst he was taken into exile by force; at best, like the hapless victim of Erra's duplicity in the Erra epic, he was tricked. Even the text which traces the cause of the disaster to the Babylonians' sin leaves the impression that the Elamites carried the destruction further than Marduk intended, though Marduk remained in control of the situation.[39] After describing the behavior of the wicked Elamites, it significantly adds the comment, "Marduk . . . observed everything."[40] Such a motif could be merged with the interpretation that attributed the disaster to the god's planning,[41] but the text that actually talks about Marduk's planning underscores Marduk's control in a different, but highly effective manner. According to it, the wicked Elamite, when he entered the sanctuary to work his design on Marduk, was so terrified by the divine statue's splendor that he withdrew and tried to force a third party, the native priest, to do his dirty work.[42] Though this stands in marked contradiction to another text's statement that the Elamite did not fear Marduk's great divinity,[43] it effectively conveys the impression that the Elamites' removal of the statue was possible only by Marduk's acquiescence, and even then was not accomplished without considerable trepidation.

As a result of these disasters there was great lamentation in Babylon.[44] In his lament, king Nebuchadnezzar describes the pitiful situation in Babylon.[45] "How long," he asks Marduk, "will you live in an enemy land?"[46] He implores Marduk, "Remember Babylon the well-favored, turn your face to Esagil which

38. 3R 38 no. 2 obv. 10′: [*Marduk bē*]*la rabâ iddeki ina šubat* [*šarrūtīšu*], "The great lord [Marduk] he made rise from the throne of [his majesty]." This points more to a forcible removal than the passage in the Erra epic, where Erra tricks Marduk into leaving by promising him that he would mind the world while Marduk was away, see L. Cagni, *L'Epopea di Erra*, Studi Semitici 34 (Rome: Istituto di Studi del Vicino Oriente, 1969) 76–69, I 168–92. Both texts, however, speak of Erra acting against the will of the gods. See note 24 above, and compare Erra I 102: *bēlum Erra minsu and ilāni* [*lemut*]*tim tak*[*pud*]. "Lord Erra, why have you planned evil against the gods?"

39. *JCS* 21 (1967) 129:25.

40. Ibid. One may compare this with Isaiah's oracle against Assyria in Isa 10:5–19.

41. As is true of the Isaiah passage mentioned above and in Nabonidus' very similar treatment of Sennacherib's desecration of Babylon (*MVAG* 1/1 [1896] 73ff. i 18–41; translated in *ANET*[2] [1955] 309). See my discussion in *CBQ* 38 (1976) 1–13.

42. *MVAG* 21 (1916) 86:20–29. The statue in question is actually referred to as that of En-nun-dagal-la, one of the lesser members of Marduk's divine entourage (CT 24 28:64; 15: 9), but A. Jeremias suggested that this name may be used here as simply another name for Marduk (*MVAG* 21 [1916] 87 n. 3).

43. DT 71:15–16.

44. 4R[2] 20 no. 1:5–10; CT 13 48:5–7.

45. CT 13 48:6–7: *aḫulap ina mātiya šaknū bakê u sapādu / aḫulap ina nišiya šaknū numbê u bakê*, "Be merciful! In my land there is weeping and mourning. Be merciful! Among my people there is wailing and weeping."

46. CT 13 48:8: *adi mati bēl Bābili ina māti nakiri ašbāti*? Cf. the similar "how long" formulations found in Israelite public laments (Pss 74:10; 79:5; 80:5).

you love."[47] The royal epic that mentions the initial disaster speaks of the people looking for Marduk's sign,[48] and after that setback, lamentation is renewed.[49] The end of this particular text is not preserved, so we can only guess at the outcome, but in the other texts, Nebuchadnezzar's prayer was heard.[50] The other epic relates that Marduk gave a favorable response, commanded Nebuchadnezzar to bring him back to Babylon, and promised him Elam as his reward.[51]

The description of Marduk's revenge on Elam is most detailed in the hymn to Marduk, perhaps because the other texts are broken in precisely the places where this material would have been recorded.[52] It is striking that the hymn, in contrast to Nebuchadnezzar's inscriptions, ignores the king's role in the defeat of Elam, and attributes the whole victory to the deity.[53] The Elamite did not reverence Marduk's great divinity, but blasphemed.[54] He became haughty, trusted in himself, forgot Marduk's divinity, and broke his oath.[55] Thus the devastation wrought on Elam was a just punishment for the Elamite's sin. As

47. CT 13 48:9–10: [*li*]*b*?-*bal*-[*k*]*it ina libbīka Bābili banûmma* / [*an*]*a Esagil ša tarammu šusḫira panīka*. Compare this to the following biblical passages: *zkr ʿdtk qnyt qdm / gʾlt šbṭ nḥltk / hr ṣywn zh šknt bw*, "Remember your congregation which you acquired long ago, the tribe of your possession which you redeemed, Mount Zion in which you dwelt" (Ps 74:2); *ʾlhym ṣbʾwt šwb nʾ / hbṭ mšmym wrʾh / wpqd gpn zʾt*, "God of hosts, turn back. Look from heaven and visit this vine" (Ps 80:15).

48. 3R 38 no. 2 rev. 5′: *išteniʾū dīn Mar*[*duk*]. For the reading of the divine name as Marduk, see Brinkman, *Political History*, p. 106, n. 575. What the Babylonians sought was an omen that the period of Marduk's wrath was over, but apparently they were disappointed. Compare Ps 74:9: *ʾtwtynw lʾ rʾynw / ʾyn ʿwd nbyʾ / wlʾ ʾtnw ywdʿ ʿd mh*, "We have not seen our signs, there is no longer a prophet, and there is no one with us who knows, 'How long'."

49. 3R 38 no. 2 rev. 17′–24′.

50. 4R² 20 no. 1:9–11; DT 71:10–12; and CT 13 48:11.

51. CT 13 48:12–18. The oracle is also mentioned in BBSt. 6 i 12–13 (see n. 14 above), and in *BiOr* 7 (1950) pl. III 16 (see Brinkman, *Political History*, p. 106, n. 575).

52. 4R² 20 no. 1, while it contains the king's lament and Marduk's positive response, has no picture of the devastation of Elam. It moves immediately from positive response to a description of Marduk's return. This is surprising, and it may suggest that the description of devastation (lines 1–4) found before the lament (lines 5ff.) actually pictures Marduk's treatment of Elam. If so, the lament would be for a positive oracle to return the divine statue rather than for victory over the Elamites. Note that after Agum-kakrime received divine orders to return Marduk on an earlier occasion, he still went to the trouble of consulting Šamaš (5R 33 i 44–ii 8), and we actually have several inquiry texts in which Assurbanipal seeks divine approval for his plans to return Marduk to Babylon (J. A. Knudtzon, *Assyrische Gebete an den Sonnengott* [Leipzig, 1893] nos. 104, 105, and 149).

53. It might be well to rethink Israel's hymnic celebration of the deliverance at the Reed Sea in that light.

54. DT 71 obv. 14–15: [*Elam*]*ū ša la pitluḫu rabītu ilūssu* [*eli*] *ilūtišu ṣīrtu iqbû mēriḫtu*.

55. DT 71 rev. 10–12: [. . .] *ušarriḫa ramānšu* [. . .] *ittaklu emūqu* [. . . *l*]*a iḫsusa ilūtka*; rev. 19–20: [. . .] *zikirka kabtu* [. . .] *ḫu la*? *aṣ-ṣu-ru ma-mit-su*.

a result of the victory, of course, Marduk returned in triumph and splendor to his own city and temple.[56]

Though the omen texts add little to the preceding sketch, one should perhaps note the temporal element mentioned in the apodosis of one:[57]

> . . . , the Umman-manda will arise and rule the land. The gods will depart from their daisies, and Bel will go to Elam. It is said that after 30 years vengeance will be exercised, and the gods will return to their place.

This calls to mind the statement in the prophetic text, "I fulfilled my years";[58] it speaks to the lamenting question, "How long?"[59]; and it has an analogue in the later tradition of Marduk's decision to leave Babylon for 70 years,[60] which in turn may be compared to Jeremiah's famous prophecy of the 70 year captivity.[61]

---

56. 4R² 20 no. 1:12f.

57. 3R 61 no. 2:21′–22′: *Umman-manda itebbīma māta ibēl parakkī ilū itebbûma Bēl ana Elamti illak iqqabbi ina* 30 *šanāti tuqtû uttarru ilū rabūtu* ⟨*ana*⟩ *ašrīsunu iturrū*. See Brinkman, *Political History*, p. 108, n. 585.

58. *BiOr* 28 (1971) 8:12: *ūmīya umallīma šanātiya umallīma*. The idea that there were predetermined limits to the periods of divine wrath which could be discovered through omens or oracles (see n. 48 above) was widespread. Cf. Nabonidus' statement: 21 *šanāti qirib Aššur irtame šubassu imlū ūmū ikšuda adannu inūḫma uzzašu libbi šar ilī bēl bēli Esagil u Bābil iḫsus šubat bēlūtīšu*, "For 21 years he (Marduk) established his seat in Assur, but when the days were fulfilled and the set time arrived, his anger abated, and the heart of the king of the gods, the lord of lords, remembered Esagil and Babylon, the seat of his lordship" (*MVAG* 1/1 [1896] 73ff. i 23–24).

59. This was a crucial question during times of tribulation, whether those tribulations affected a group (see notes 46 and 48, above), or only a single individual. As an example of the latter, see the lament of the sufferer in Ludlul, *u adanna siliʾtīya bārû ul iddin*, "Nor has the diviner put a time limit on my illness," *BWL* 44–45:111. When a time limit was given, and it passed without the hoped-for change, that was the source of even greater discouragement: *akšudma ana balāṭ adanna īteq*, "I survived to the next year; the appointed time passed" *BWL* 38–39:1.

This may be another part of the background to the Israelites' discouraging assessment: "Yahweh has left the country," discussed in note 25 above. Ezekiel's oracle in which this sentiment is expressed is dated to the sixth month of the sixth year (Ezek 8:1), or exactly two years and one month after Hananiah gave his famous oracle in which Yahweh promised, "Within two years I will bring back to this place all the vessels of Yahweh's house, which Nebuchadnezzar king of Babylon took away from this place and carried to Babylon . . ." (Jer 28:1–4; LXX preserves the original date formula in v. 1). With the failure of so much of the favorable prophecies of that period (Jer 27:16ff.), it is no wonder that the psalmist could say, "We have not seen our signs, there is no longer a prophet, and there is no one with us who knows 'How long' " (Ps 74:9). It was not so much that there were no prophets, it is simply that their words had failed, and they had lost credibility.

60. R. Borger, *Die Inschriften Asarhaddons, Königs von Assyrien*, AfO Beiheft 9 (Graz, 1956) 14–15, Episodes 6–10.

61. Jer 29:10.

The preceding discussion is by no means a sufficient foundation upon which to base wide ranging comparative judgments on the theological significance of history in Mesopotamia and Israel. I have dealt with only one example of one typical event in Mesopotamia, and I have limited my discussion of the comparative biblical material, giving only the briefest hints as to where I think one should turn for the most relevant parallels. In my judgment, however, it is this kind of detailed examination of individual episodes which must be extended further, both on the Mesopotamian and biblical sides, before comparative judgments can be either significant or meaningful, much less serve as fundamental elements of interpretive constructs.[62] If the discussion has persuaded anyone to take a fresh look at the way history was theologically interpreted in Mesopotamia or Israel, it has accomplished its modest goal.

62. See my critical remarks on one such construct in *CBQ* 38 (1976) 1–13. For the application of this approach to biblical material see the forthcoming monograph jointly authored by P. D. Miller, Jr. and this writer, *The Hand of the Lord: A Study of 1 Sam. 2:12–17,* 22–25, 27–36, 4:1b–7:1.

Part 2

Themes and Motifs

Chapter 6
The Hand of Yahweh

The expression, "the hand of Yahweh was upon him," and related phrases occur a number of times in the Old Testament literature to designate one aspect of prophetic experience.[1] Scholars differ, however, in their definitions of the precise experience involved. I. P. Seierstad argues that the expression does not refer to any specific empirical fact but merely serves to attribute the particular extraordinary event, whether the marvelous running feat of Elijah or Ezekiel's reception of the divine word, to the intervention of Yahweh.[2] Other scholars, probably the majority, take the expression as a rather specific reference to an ecstatic or trance state, though these terms harbor their own ambiguities.[3] Duhm further specifies the ecstatic state designated by the expression as "a halfway cataleptic condition which the human spirit because of a psychological reaction resists as a violence inflicted upon it."[4] Lindblom also connects the expression to a very specific phenomenon—"the feeling of a psychophysical convulsion or cramps so common in ecstatic experience."[5]

When one moves from the question of the phenomenon designated by the expression to the question of the origin of the expression itself, there is even less unanimity, and a large part of the blame for this state of affairs is due to the reluctance of scholars to pursue the investigation on a broad enough basis. Lindblom, for instance, argues that "the origin of the idea of Yahweh's hand is a physical sensation of being seized and pressed by an external power connected with the ecstatic experience,"[6] though this explanation completely ignores the large number of non-prophetic contexts in which the same expression

---

1. Ezek 1:3; 3:14, 22; 8:1; 33:22; 37:1; 40:1; 1 Kgs 18:46; 2 Kgs 3:15; Isa 8:11; Jer 15:17.

2. *Die Offenbarungserlebnisse der Propheten Amos, Jesaja und Jeremia* (Oslo, 1965) 172.

3. P. Volz, *Der Geist Gottes* (Tübingen, 1910) 68, n. 1; G. Hölscher, *Die Profeten* (Leipzig, 1914) 24; A. Bertholet, *Hesekiel*, *HAT* 13 (Tübingen, 1936) 13; G. A. Cooke, *The Book of Ezekiel*, *ICC* (New York, 1937) 6; W. Eichrodt, *Der Prophet Hesekiel*, *ATD* (Göttingen, 1959) 5; W. Zimmerli, *Ezekiel*, *BK* XIII-1 (Neukirchen, 1959) 49–50.

4. *Das Buch Jesaja*, *HK* (Göttingen, 1914f.) 59.

5. *Prophecy in Ancient Israel* (Philadelphia, 1962) 58.

6. Op. cit., 175.

occurs. Even Zimmerli, who presents the most thorough discussion of the expression known to this writer and who at least considers all the biblical occurrences of the expression, not just those directly related to prophecy, fails to take account of the non-biblical parallels.[7] He notes that the outstretched hand and arm of Yahweh play a significant role in the exodus accounts and suggests that this is the source for the strong emphasis on the language of the hand and arm of Yahweh in the Old Testament.[8] Moreover, since the peculiarly prophetic use of the expression only occurs with the name Yahweh, never with the generic word God, he concludes that the expression is a "genuine Israelite formulation," and, according to Zimmerli, "That could support the conjecture of a derivation of this whole surprising manner of speech from the imagery of the Exodus tradition."[9]

This whole line of argument would have been more difficult had Zimmerli considered the non-biblical parallels. For the expression, "hand of *x*," where *x* represents a divine name or the generic word god, occurs in Akkadian with a large number of different divine names. In the Akkadian "diagnostic" texts edited by Labat, for instance, about forty different deities, as well as several demons, the underworld, the sanctuary, and men (sorcerers) appear as the *x* in the expression.[10] While Labat doubts that the "hand" of a god is specifically tied to the notion of sickness, it is clear that it designates the "disastrous manifestation of the supernatural power."[11] And, in spite of Labat's doubts, sickness or plague is the normal form this "manifestation" assumes in the Akkadian texts where the implications of the "hand" of the god are spelled out.

Without attempting to be exhaustive a few of the better examples may be cited. In a context where he is describing his affliction, the sufferer in *Ludlul bēl nēmeqi* says of the god: *kabtat qāssu ul aleʾi našâša*, "His hand was heavy (upon me), I could not bear it."[12] The commentary text from this passage gives *dannu* as a synonym of *kabtu*,[13] and another text from Mari uses this other root in precisely the same fashion. In *ARM* X, 87, the woman, Šattukiyazi, is complaining because Zimri-Lim sent her to Sagaratum even though the omens were bad and the king knew the omens were bad:

[i-na]-an-na a-na Sa-ga-ra-tim^{ki}	Now to Sagaratum
[at-ta-a]l-kam-ma	I have come, but
[i]š-[t]u u_4*mi-im*	from the day

7. Op. cit., 47–50.
8. Ibid., 47.
9. Ibid., 48.
10. R. Labat, *Traité akkadien de diagnostics et pronostics médicaux* (Paris and Leiden, 1951) xxi–xxiii.
11. Ibid., xxiii.
12. W. G. Lambert, *Babylonian Wisdom Literature* (Oxford, 1960) 48–49:1.
13. Ibid.

[*ša*? *a*]*t-ta-al-kam*	I came here,
[*ma-a*]*r-ṣa-ku*	I have been sick.
[ ] *1-ŠU 2-ŠU dan-nu-ma*	. . . .
[u^4?] *qa-at Ištar-ra-da-na-ma*	and it is the hand of Ištara-danna,
u_4 *be-li i-di*	and my lord knows
ki-ma qa-at Ištar-ra-da-na	that the hand of Ištara-danna
e-li-ya da-an-na-at	is strong upon me.

It is clear that *qāt Ištara-danna* refers to Šattukiyazi's illness, because the letter continues, *inanna šumma libbi bēlīya warkāt murṣim annîm liprus* . . . , "Now if it pleases my lord, let him look into the background of this illness. . . ." Though the text does not use the precise expression, the reference to the plague in *ARM* III, 61:9–13, is undoubtedly drawn from the same circle of ideas: *šanītam ina Kulḫitim ilum ana akāl alpi u awīlūtim qātam iškun ina ūmim* 2 3 *awīlū imutū*, "Another thing, in Kulḫitum the god has placed (his) hand to devour cattle and men. Every day two or three men die." One should also note Lambert's discussion of the expression *lišaqqil qāssu*, "let him lift/ remove his hand," in the Atra-ḫasīs epic, where it is clear that Atra-ḫasīs and his fellow men are trying to get Namtara to lift the plague.[14]

Moreover, the expression is found in the West with the same meaning. It occurs in an Amarna letter from Cyprus: *šumma ina mātīya qāti Rašap*[15] *bēlīya gabba awīlī ša mātīya idūk* . . . *aššum qāti Rašap ibašši ina mātīya u ina bītīya aššatīya māru ibašši ša mīt inanna aḫīya*, "Behold, in my land the hand of *Rašap*, my lord, has killed all the men of my land . . . because the hand of Rašap was in my land, and in my house my wife had a son who is now dead, my brother."[16] It is also found in a Ugaritic letter: *šmʿt . ḫtʾi . nḫtʾu . ht hm. ʾin mm nḫtʾu.w.lʾak ʿmy.w.yd ʾilm . p . kmtm ʿz . mʾid*, "You have heard of the blows by which we have been shattered (ruined) indeed, behold, there is

14. W. G. Lambert, *Atra-ḫasīs* (Oxford, 1969) 66–71, lines 360–412, and pp. 155f., n. 384. The verb *šuqqulu* with the meaning "lift" or "remove" is now also attested in *ARM* X, 92:8, where Shewirum-ubrat exclaims in the midst of her complaint to Zimri-Lim: *di-ma-ti-ya šu-uq-*qi_2*-il*, "Remove my tears!" Cf. *CAD* D, p. 147: *ina panīka abtiki šumma ilānika ina panīka ana rēme* [*is*]*-sak-nu-u-ni di-a-ti-ya šaqqil* . . . , "I wept before you, remove my tears if your gods have caused me to find mercy before you. . . . "

15. The reading Rašap for ^{d}*MAŠ.MAŠ* is based on the equation Rašap = Nergal in the god list from Ugarit (*Ugaritica* V, pp. 45:26, 57), where Rašap clearly represents Mesopotamian Nergal's West Semitic counterpart, who is well attested in the Ugaritic personal names (ibid., 57; F. Gröndahl, *Die Personennamen der Texte aus Ugarit* (Rome, 1967) 181–82). Since Cyprus is more closely connected to Ugarit than to Mesopotamia both geographically and linguistically (note the West Semitic use of *šumma* like asseverative *kî*), it seems probable to me that the West Semitic name was intended by the ideogram. Cf. already Nougayrol's reading of the name ^{d}*MAŠ.MAŠ-a-bu* as *Rašap-abu* (*Ugaritica* V, 57).

16. *EA* 35:13–14, 37–39.

nothing (left)—we are ruined! So send (help) to me. And the hand of the god(s)[17] is very strong here like death."[18]

The basis for this usage lies in the very concrete use of the word "hand" to designate the physical member with which men or gods (anthropomorphically conceived) perform an action, as the numerous Akkadian idioms with *qātum* clearly indicate.[19] Precisely the same situation exists in the biblical material, however, where one not only finds analogues to most of the Akkadian idioms,[20] but where one can see the same idea of the "disastrous manifestation of the supernatural power" as the dominant connotation of the "hand of Yahweh."[21] Just as the god at Mari "placed his hand to devour cattle and men," so Yahweh "sent forth" or "stretched out" his hand and smote peoples, nations, animals, etc.[22] Moreover, plague or sickness remains the normal form in

---

17. The use of this expression with a plural, gods, is not expected, so I prefer to take *ʾilm* either as *ʾil* + enclitic *mem*, or better as a morphological plural with singular meaning like Hebrew *ʾĕlōhîm.*

18. A. Herdner, *Corpus des tablettes en cunéiformes alphabetiques* (Paris, 1963), no. 53:7–13. The translation follows Albright (*BASOR* 82, pp. 47–48), except for the expression *kmtm*, for which see the parallel in Song of Songs 8:6, which was pointed out to the writer by D. Hillers.

19. E. Dhorme, *L'emploi métaphorique des noms de parties du corps en Hébreu et en Akkadien* (Paris, 1963) 144–50. In addition to those noted by Dhorme one should also mention the idioms *qātam ummudu*, "to lay on hands," either for magic purposes or as a legal gesture of ownership or protection (*CAD* E, p. 144), *ana + infinitive qātam šakānum*, "to place the hand to do x," to indicate the initiation of an action (*ARMT* XV, p. 247), and the various expressions for handiwork: *binût qāti*, *epšēt qāti*, *lipit qāti*, and *šikin qāti.*

20. Dhorme, loc. cit.; Zimmerli, op. cit., 47–48. Note especially Zimmerli's comment: "The hand is the organ with which Yahweh demonstrates the historical power of his word of promise" (ibid.).

21. Occasionally the expression "hand of the god" has a good sense: *awīlum ša Ištar qāti Ištar* [*el*]*īšu ummuda*[*t*], "This man belongs to Ištar, Ištar's protection is upon him" (*CAD* E, p. 144), to which compare כי־תנוח יד־יהוה בהד הזה, "For the hand of Yahweh rests upon this mountain. . . . " (Isa 25:10); but normally this has to be indicated in both Hebrew and Akkadian by the addition of an adjective meaning good, favorable, or the like: כיד אלהיו הטובה עליו (Ezra 7:9; 8:18, 22; Neh 2:8, 18), to which compare *ana qātī damqāti ša ilīšu lippaqid* (*CT* 17, 22 iii 145f., and passim; *CAD* D, p. 73). The very necessity of adding this additional modifier points up the basically negative understanding of the divine manifestation implied in the simple expression.

22. With שלח note Exod 9:15: כיעתה שלחת את־ידי ואך אותך ואת־עמך בדבר, "For now I should have put forth my hand and smitten you and your people with the plague . . ." (cf. Exod 3:20; 24:11; Job 1:11; 2:5; Ps 138:7); and with נטה see Isa 5:25ff.: על־כן הרה אף יהוה בעמו ויט ידו עליו ויכהו, "Therefore the anger of Yahweh burned against his people, and he stretched out his hand upon them and smote them. . . ." (cf. Exod 7:5; Isa 31:3; Jer 6:12; 15:6; 51:26; Ezek 6:14; 14:9, 13; 16:27; 25:7, 13, 16, passim). The other Akkadian examples of the expression cited above can also be paralleled from the Bible: *qāti Rašap ibašši ina mātīya* / ותהי יד־יהוה בעיר (1 Sam 5:9); *qāti Rašap . . . idūk* / ידו נגעה בנו (1 Sam 6:9), יד־אלוה נגעה בי (Job 19:21); *kabtat qāssu* / תכבד יד־יהוה (1 Sam 5:6); *qāt Ištara-danna elīya dannat* /

which this "manifestation" finds expression. This is clear not only from statistical considerations but also from the way in which דֶּבֶר is sometimes used almost as a gloss on יד־יהוה: הנה יד־יהוה הויה במקנך אשר בשדה בסוסים בחמרים בגמלים בבקר ובצאן דֶּבֶר כבד מאד, "Now the hand of Yahweh is about to be upon your livestock which is in your fields, upon the horses, the asses, the camels, the cattle, and the sheep—a very grievous plague.[23]

When the peculiarly prophetic use of the expression, "hand of Yahweh," is seen in this broader perspective, the question of its origin must be reexamined. It is true that a similar prophetic use of the expression is not attested (at least up to now) outside of Israel, but it is just as clear that this specialized use is a secondary development of an expression that is still most commonly used to designate the "disastrous manifestation of the supernatural power" especially as seen in sickness or plague. Such a secondary development, however, would presumably imply some relationship between the more general and the newer, more specific usage. Zimmerli seems to find that connection in a consciously theological exploitation of the imagery of the Exodus tradition where the more general meaning of the expression is well attested, but this primary meaning is also attested elsewhere in the biblical material, in Canaanite, and Akkadian as well. It was part of the lexical stock of the language spoken by the Israelites, and, though there are many literary allusions to the Exodus tradition in which the expression occurs, the expression was neither created by the Exodus tradition, nor is it legitimate to assume that there is an allusion to the Exodus tradition every time the expression occurs in the Bible. Moreover, there is nothing in the prophetic use of the expression that requires or even suggests that one thinks of the Exodus—unless one assigns that weight to the mere occurrence of the name Yahweh in the expression. One must look elsewhere, therefore, for the semantic link between "hand of Yahweh" as "illness" and "hand of Yahweh" in the specifically prophetic meaning.

Another explanation for this semantic development is suggested by H. Grapow's discussion of the similar Egyptian expression, "man in the hand of the God."[24] The phrase designates an insane person, but Grapow sees a clear

קשתה ידו עלינו (1 Sam 5:7); *lišaqqil qāssu* / יקל את־ידו מעליכם (1 Sam 6:5), לא־תסור ידו מכם (1 Sam 6:3).

23. Exod 9:3; cf. the reversal of salvation history in Jer 21:5–6: ונלחמתי אני אתכם ביד נטויה ובזרוע חזקה ובאף ובחמה ובקצף גדול: והכיתי את־יושבי העיר הזאת ואת האדם ואת־הבהמה בדבר גדול ימתו:, "And I will fight against you with an outstretched hand and a strong arm, with anger and rage and great wrath; and I will smite the inhabitants of this city, both men and beasts. They will die in a great plague." Note also the occurrence of the expression in certain Psalms where sickness seems to be the cause of the individual's lament (32:4; 38:3–4; 39:11; H. Gunkel, *Einleitung in die Psalmen* (Göttingen, 1966[2]) 190–91).

24. H. Grapow, *Kranker, Krankheiten, und Arzt, Grundriss der Medizin der Alten Ägypter* III (Berlin, 1956) 38. The writer is indebted to H. Goedicke for this reference.

connection between this phrase and the description of the ecstatic in the Journey of Wen-Amon, since the raving of the ecstatic and the madness of the insane person were both brought about by seizure of the deity.[25] A similar situation, of course, exists in the Semitic world where in both Hebrew and Akkadian the same verb is used for the behavior of a madman and the ecstatic behavior of the prophet.[26] Moreover, it is well known that the prophets' contemporaries called them madmen.[27] In the Semitic languages the expression "hand of the god" is not attested with the specific meaning "insane," but the expression is not tied to any one specific illness, and there is no apparent reason why symptoms of mental illness, many of which can occur in other illnesses, e.g., the delirious raving of a person with a high fever, should not be subsumed under this expression. It is possible, then, that the expression, "hand of Yahweh," was applied to the prophetic phenomenon precisely because that phenomenon bore a remarkable similarity to the symptoms of human illness normally designated by the expression. In support of this view one should note that Jeremiah speaks of his prophetic experience of the "hand of Yahweh" in language strikingly similar to that used by the sufferer in certain Psalms:

> I did not sit in the company of the merry-makers,
> nor did I rejoice.
> Because of your hand (מפני ידך) I sat alone,
> for you filled me with indignation (זעם).
> Why is my pain unceasing
> and my wound incurable, refusing to be healed?
> Will you be to me like a deceitful brook,
> like waters that fail?[28]

If the preceding argument is sound, the development of the peculiarly prophetic use of the expression "hand of Yahweh" is dependent on a similarity between the prophetic phenomenon designated by the expression and certain symptoms of a pathological nature. Thus the expression can hardly be interpreted with Seierstad as simply assigning a particular extraordinary event to the intervention of Yahweh. The semantic development suggested rather supports those who see the expression as referring to some kind of ecstatic experience of the prophet. While this writer cannot accept Lindblom's immediate derivation of the expression from the prophet's own experience and is there-

25. Ibid.
26. Hebrew התנבא; Akkadian *namḫû*.
27. Hos 9:7; Jer 29:26; 2 Kgs 9:11.
28. Jer 15:17–18. Cf. Ps 38:3–4: "For your arrows have descended into me; your hand has come down upon me (ותנחת עלי ידך). There is no soundness in my flesh from before your wrath (מפני זעמך); there is no well-being in my bones from before my sin." Note also Ps 32:3–4, and the comments of Zimmerli, op. cit., p. 49.

fore dubious about the specificity with which he and Duhm describe the psycho-physical sensations involved, it does seem clear that they are right in connecting the expression to concrete manifestations of a physical or psycho-physical nature.

Chapter 7
A New Parallel to 1 Kings 18:28–29

1 Kgs 18:28–29 describes how the prophets of Baal, according to their custom (כְּמִשְׁפָּטָם), lacerated themselves with swords and lances, either as a result of or as an attempt to induce a "prophetic" frenzy.[1] Zech 13:6 probably contains an allusion to a similar practice among certain Israelite prophets,[2] but apart from these two passages the rite is never connected to prophecy in the OT.[3] Elsewhere self-laceration (הִתְגֹּדֵד) appears merely as a sign of mourning, particularly in the context of funerary rites, though even here its pagan background led to the proscription of the practice.[4] Thus the limited attestation of "prophetic" self-laceration in the OT and its total absence in contemporary inscriptions forced the commentators to turn to late hellenistic sources for convincing parallels to explain the behavior of the prophets of Baal.[5]

These late parallels are still significant, but now the excavations at Ugarit have provided us with a much earlier parallel. It occurs in an Akkadian wisdom text copied ca. 1300 B.C. but composed originally, according to Nougayrol, in the Old Babylonian or early Cassite period.[6] The text, which is very similar to *Ludlul* in many respects, begins after an initial break by recounting the failure of the cultic experts to diagnose the sick man's problem. Then it proceeds to describe the preparations for burying the man. It is in this context that our line occurs:

aḫḫūʾa (ŠEŠ-u$_2$-a) ki-ma maḫ-ḫe-e [d]a-mi-šu-nu ra-am-ku
My brothers bathed in their own blood like (an) ecstatic(s).[7]

---

1. According to the wording of the text the self-laceration precedes the ecstatic behavior designated by the verb וַיִּתְנַבְּאוּ, but one wonders if the prophets were not already a bit overwrought when they began cutting.

2. See the commentaries.

3. 1 Kgs 20:35–37 is sometimes quoted as an example, but it does not involve self-laceration, and the wounding of the prophet functions quite differently in that story.

4. Hos 7:14 (emended); Jer 16:6; 41:5; 47:5; Deut 14:1; and Lev 19:28 (וְשֶׂרֶט לֹא תִתְּנוּ בִּבְשַׂרְכֶם).

5. The references cited most often are Apuleius, *Metamorphoses* 8:27–28, and Lucian, *De Dea Syra* 36, 50, but cf. R. de Vaux, "Les prophètes de Baal sur le Mont Carmel," *Bulletin du Musée de Beyrouth*, 5 (1944) 7–20.

6. *Ugaritica V, Mission de Ras Shamra XVI* (1968) 265–73, no. 162 (R.S. 25.460).

7. Line 11′.

In his comments on this line Nougayrol refers to an Esarhaddon passage, though he notes it is not really parallel,[8] but he does not cite either the Mari texts where the verb *maḫû* is used of the ecstatic trance of a prophet[9] or our biblical passage. The parallel to 1 Kgs 18:28 is very close, however, since Nougayrol's new text, just as the biblical material, portrays self-laceration as a feature common to both ecstatic prophecy and burial rites.

Unfortunately the evidence does not allow us to pinpoint the specific geographical area in which this extreme form of ecstatic behavior occurred. While the text was preserved at Ugarit, the date of its original composition and the language in which it is written point toward a more easterly location for its place of composition and thus for the customs it describes. Moreover, the rather surprising absence of terms for prophet or prophecy in the fairy large Ugaritic corpus seems to exclude Ugarit as a place where ecstatic phenomena could provide material for such a comparison. The region from Aleppo to Mari, where ecstatic prophecy is attested in the Old Babylonian period, is more likely, but one should note that the term for ecstatic at Mari was vocalized differently, viz., *muḫḫûm*, and so far there is little evidence at Mari of the extreme frenzy that self-laceration implies.[10]

8. Op. cit., 270.

9. For these texts see now W. L. Moran, "New Evidence from Mari on the History of Prophecy," *Biblica* 50 (1969) 15–56.

10. Moran, op. cit., pp. 27–28.

Chapter 8
The King of Glory

Psalm 24 reads as follows:

> To Yahweh belongs the earth and its fulness,
> the world and those who dwell therein;
> for he has founded it upon the seas,
> and established it upon the rivers.
> Who shall ascend the Mountain of Yahweh?
> And who shall stand in his holy place?
> He who has clean hands and a pure heart,
> who does not lift up his soul to what is false,
> and does not swear deceitfully.
> He will receive blessing from Yahweh
> and vindication from the God of his salvation.
> Such is the generation of those who seek him,
> who seek the face of the God of Jacob.[1]
> Lift up your heads, O gates!
> and be lifted up, O ancient doors!
> that the King of glory may come in.
> Who is the king of glory?
> Yahweh, strong and mighty,
> Yahweh, mighty in battle!
> Lift up your heads, O gates!
> and be lifted up, O ancient doors!
> that the king of glory may come in.
> Who is this king of glory?
> Yahweh of hosts.
> He is the king of glory!

Twice in this relatively short Psalm, Psalm 24, the question is asked, "Who is the king of glory?" The Psalmist responds with an answer that may have been totally adequate in the ancient Near Eastern world of polytheism. The king of glory is Yahweh. That is, he is not Baal or El as the Canaanites might claim.

1. Reading *pny ʾlhy yʿqb* by emendation. The MT is clearly corrupt.

He is not Dagan as the Philistines say. Or Chemosh of the Moabites or Milcom of the Ammonites. The real king of glory is Yahweh. But note that the answer of the Psalmist is not simply Yahweh. The divine name is amplified by a series of epithets: Yahweh, strong and mighty, Yahweh, might in battle, Yahweh of hosts. This suggests that a modern, living in a world where the straightforward gods of ancient polytheism have been replaced by far more nebulous forces of history, society, or psyche, might rephrase the question to obtain a more relevant answer. Put bluntly, "Who is Yahweh?" Or perhaps more adequately, what is the nature of the God whose triumph our Psalmist is celebrating?

In the first place, one should note the continuity between Yahweh and the older gods whom he displaced. This is clear from the strange metaphor in verses 7 and 9: "Lift up your heads, O gates! Ancient Palestinian gates had no parts that moved up and down. The command to lift up their heads, therefore, is a secondary metaphor, borrowed from another setting. F. M. Cross has identified that setting with a passage in the Canaanite Baal epic.[2] When the assembly of the gods was cowed by the messengers of Prince Sea and hung their heads in subjection, Baal encouraged them to resist under his leadership with these very words: "Lift up your heads, O gods. . . ."[3] The Israelite poet has put Yahweh in place of Baal and the temple gates in place of the divine council, but the basic pattern of the Baal myth is retained. Just as Baal returned in triumph from his victory over Prince Sea, Judge River, to be proclaimed king of the Gods, so Yahweh returns from triumph in battle to be proclaimed king of glory. Moreover, verse 2 grounds Yahweh's sovereignty on his *founding* the world upon the seas and rivers. The motif here suggests a mythological background in which creation followed Yahweh's victory over seas and rivers, conceived as cosmogonic enemies like the Prince Sea, Judge River, of the Canaanite myth. Such a view is clearly expressed in Ps 74:12–17:

> But you, O God, are my king from of old;
> you bring salvation upon the earth.
> It was you who split open the sea by your power;
> you broke the heads of the sea monsters on the waters.
> It was you who crushed the heads of Leviathan
> and gave him as food to the creatures of the desert.
> It was you who opened up springs and streams;
> you dried up the ever flowing rivers.
> The day is yours, and yours also the night;
> you established the sun and moon.

2. *Canaanite Myth and Hebrew Epic* (Cambridge: Harvard University Press, 1973) 97–98.

3. Andrée Herdner, *Corpus des tablettes en cunéiformes alphabétiques* (MRS X; Paris: Paul Geuthner, 1963) 2, i 27.

> It was you who set all the boundaries of the earth;
> you made both summer and winter.

Note here how the theme of the God's victory over the sea dragons is followed by the theme of creation. This is clear in the reference to day and night, sun and moon, but it also is what is intended in the reference to opening of springs and streams. The closest parallel is in the Babylonian creation epic where Marduk splits open his slain foe, Tiamat, the Sea, and then proceeds to create the world out of her carcass, including the rivers which flow from her eyes and the springs which were opened up from other parts of her anatomy. The extant Canaanite texts so far published are lacking any creation account, but Thorkild Jacobsen has shown that the Babylonian myth was borrowed from the West,[4] so it is likely that the Canaanites had a tradition of Baal creating the world out of the carcass of Prince Sea, Judge River, and it is this tradition that Israel appropriated in speaking of Yahweh's founding the world on the seas and establishing it on the rivers.

If we may drop the ancient mythological language for the moment in favor of a more current jargon, the Canaanites worshipped Baal as the god who established and preserves order in the world. The powers of chaos, dissolution, and evil personified by the unruly Sea had been defeated and were kept under restraint by this god. This aspect of ancient polytheism was simply taken up and only slightly modified by the new Yahwistic faith. It was Yahweh, not Baal, who established the orders of creation and made possible a fruitful life in a relatively harmonious universe. But the element of continuity remains
strong. In both Israel and Canaan people were aware that the possibility f
meaningful existence—both of the human and non-human creation—was d
pendent on the ordering grace of divine power.

The epithets attached to the name Yahweh in our Psalm point in anothe
rection, however. They are military metaphors and theoretically could re
Yahweh's display of power in his cosmogonic war against Prince Sea,
the Israelite literature preserved for us their actual referent is quite di
So, for instance, in Exodus 15, the oldest Israelite poem we possess,
is celebrated as "a man of war" (v. 3), but in reference to his historic
over the Egyptians, not in reference to the cosmogonic wars of
myth. There was also an ancient poetic collection known as the S
Wars of Yahweh (Num 21:14), and to judge by the quotation from
these poems dealt with the Israelite struggle to conquer Palestine
Judg 3:1 calls the "wars of Canaan." The later wars of Saul an
also called the wars of Yahweh (1 Sam 18:17; 25:28), howev
these may also have been celebrated in this ancient poetic c

4. "The Battle Between Marduk and Tiamat," *JAOS* 88 (196) 104

over, the metaphor of Yahweh as king owes a great deal of its popularity to David's imperial expansion that, for a brief period, elevated Jerusalem to an imperial capital and brought widespread recognition to Yahweh, the imperial deity.[5] Psalm 47, for instance, celebrates God as the great king over all the earth who had subdued the nations to Israel and calls upon these subject nations and their gods to join in the worship of Yahweh.[6]

In other words, the epithets attached to Yahweh in Psalm 24, when read in the light of Israelite literature, give a historical dimension to this God.[7] Yahweh is the god who delivered Israel from Egyptian bondage, carved them out a homeland in Palestine, and raised them to an imperial power of the first rank. In more abstract terms, this king of glory is a God who involves himself in political processes. His role is not limited to establishing an ordered universe or controlling the rhythms of nature like some ancient caricature of the Deist's god. Yahweh, the warrior, is no pacifist, nor has he, like some of his worshippers, conceded the world of politics and diplomacy to less scrupulous rivals.[8]

Here, too, there is an element of continuity. Yahweh had his rivals in the ancient world. He was not the only god of the Ancient Near East who "acted in history."[9] Part of Israel's struggle with her environment was centered around precisely this question. Which god really did control history? Was it Yahweh, or Asshur, or Marduk? From the modern point of view, it really would not matter very much if one could simply change the names and be left with essentially the same deity. But the element of continuity does not extend that far.

Psalm 24 adds another qualification to its delineation of the king of glory when it raises the question of this god's demands on his worshippers, "Who shall ascend the mountain of Yahweh? And who shall stand in his holy place?" The Psalmist's answer makes it clear that Yahweh's demands are not limited

---

5. J. J. M. Roberts, "The Davidic Origin of the Zion Tradition," *JBL* 92 (1973) 329–44.

6. Roberts, "The Religio-Political Setting of Psalm 47," *BASOR* 221 (1976) 129–32.

7. The term *ʿzwz* is used only here as an epithet of Yahweh. *Gbwr* is more common. It is used of Yahweh in the context of his defeat of the Philistines (Ps 78:65–66); it appears as an epithet for him in the Zion tradition (Isa 10:21; Zeph 3:17); and it is often used of him in reference to the exodus or new exodus (Deut 10:17; Isa 42:13; Jer 32:18; Neh 9:32). The closest parallel to *gbwr mlḥmh* is *ʾyš mlḥmh*, which occurs in passages dealing with the exodus (Exod 15:3) and the new exodus (Isa 42:13). *ʾlhy yʿqb*, though based on an emendation in our passage, presents an interesting anomaly. Ostensibly a northern term, while it does occur in passages from the exodus tradition (Exod 3:6, 15; 4:5; Ps 81:2, 5), it is also an epithet very much at home in the Zion tradition, cultivated in the south (2 Sam 23:1; Isa 2:3; Pss 20:2; 46:8, 12; 76:7; 84:9; 94:7).

8. One can only agree with Patrick D. Miller, Jr., when he argues that any serious theology of the OT must give significant attention to the conception of God as warrior, *The Divine Warrior in Early Israel* (Cambridge: Harvard University Press, 1973) 171.

9. J. J. M. Roberts, "Myth *Versus* History," *CBQ* 38 (1976) 1–13; H. W. F. Saggs, *The Encounter with the Divine in Mesopotamia and Israel* (London: Athlone Press, 1978) 64–92; and the earlier literature cited in these sources.

to the sphere of irrational taboos; they are primarily ethical or moral, and they address the individual, not just the group. Both these points are worth stressing. Yahweh is the great God who created and sustains the natural order, and he is the God of history who directs the destiny of nations and peoples, but he is also the personal God of the individual man or woman. Job, Psalms, and Proverbs are as much a part of the canon as Exodus, Samuel, or Kings. The same God who saved and guided the nation of Israel in her struggles also comes as savior and guide to the individual Israelite in all the particularity of that individual's personal struggles.

Yet Yahweh, the personal God, comes with demands, and the nature of those demands are worth noting. The Psalmist speaks of innocent hands and a pure heart. That is, correct outward actions that are a true reflection of the inward intent of the heart. And there is a particular stress on honesty, especially in the matter of swearing oaths. All of which underscores an overriding concern for justice and integrity in the affairs of men and women. Again Yahweh is not totally unique in this regard. Through the ancient Near East the gods were the guarantors of justice and the sanctioning powers behind the moral laws that regulated human society.

Nonetheless, there are a number of subtle differences that do distinguish Yahweh from his rivals. In the Near East the divine functions were diffuse. Typically one god was creator, another was the imperial god, another was the god of Justice, and another was the personal god. In the Babylonian creation epic, for example, Marduk creates the world, but it is Ea who creates mankind. The lines were fluid and there was some movement toward monotheism, but the essence of polytheism is a division of labor, and that essence was never overcome in any lasting way in the Near East outside of Israel. In contrast, Yahweh, the king of glory, took over all the divine functions so completely that there was no room left for anything like the traditional pantheon. As creator he transcended the created order in a way that few of his rivals ever could. Many of them were, after all, personified parts of the universe itself—Shamash the sun, Sin the moon, Anu the heavens, to mention only the most obvious.

The very character of the events that led to the formation of the people of Israel marked Yahweh as a God of justice who saves the oppressed, and this insight into his character was crystallized in a formal covenant that kept his demands before the people.[10] Thus Yahweh, the national god of Israel, could never be reduced to simply a personification of the national will. His ethical demands remained a constant corrective to the very human tendency to identify national policy with the divine will. Moreover, Yahweh's concern, as a personal god, for the individual, stood in judgment on any tendency to deify

10. Delbert R. Hillers, *Covenant: The History of a Biblical Idea* (Baltimore: The Johns Hopkins Press, 1969).

the state at the expense of the individual or to reduce piety to ceremonies of state. At the same time, since Yahweh was the national God and the upholder of social norms as well as the personal God, there was protection against the perversion of religion into a purely inward, personal piety.

In short, Yahweh incorporated in one deity the valid but scattered insights of ancient Near Eastern religion, and so transcended the inherent limitations of contemporary polytheism. The various aspects of his dominion were often in tension, but a community faithful to this God could never resolve this tension by simply dismissing any of these aspects of the divine rule. Of course, even when one has stressed God's sovereignty in nature and history, in the life of the community and of the individual, one has not fully answered our initial question. The Christian will ultimately feel that our Psalmist's identification of the king of glory is painfully inadequate. The nature of the deity we worship cannot be fully grasped without the revelation through the son: "no one knows the father except the son and anyone to whom the son chooses to reveal him" (Matt 11:27). Nevertheless, the partial insights of the ancient Psalmist remain valid. While the Christian can say more about the king of glory, he can say no less and still be faithful to the Christian God.

Chapter 9
Job and the Israelite Religious Tradition

Despite J. Barr,[1] history's stranglehold on biblical theology and Old Testament scholarship in general remains unbroken. Even the recent vogue for Wisdom literature has not succeeded in loosing history's grip. On the contrary, some of the leading devotees of Wisdom seem determined to legitimate their now fashionable specialty by removing its damning stigma of *Geschichtslosigkeit*. Whether one does it by writing a history of the Wisdom literature itself[2] or by seeking to demonstrate Wisdom's influence on the historiographical literature[3]—no one to my knowledge has tried to demonstrate the converse, historiographical influence on Wisdom—history remains the touchstone of a genuine, normative, biblical theology.[4]

This persisting theological tyranny of history is certainly a factor in Job studies. Apart from M. Pope's commentary,[5] most recent interpretations of Job seem unduly influenced by an assumed historical background extraneous to

1. *Old and New in Interpretation*, 1966, 65–102.

2. H. H. Schmid, *Wesen und Geschichte der Weisheit*, 1966.

3. Works attempting to do this have proliferated so fast in recent years it is difficult to keep up with them all. As examples, however, one should note J. L. McKenzie, "Reflections on Wisdom," *JBL* 86 (1967), 1–9; R. N. Whybray, *The Succession Narrative*, 1968; and H.-J. Hermisson, "Weisheit und Geschichte," in *Probleme biblischer Theologie* (ed. H. W. Wolff), 1971, 136–54. Other examples are cited and discussed in J. L. Crenshaw's excellent critique of this trend ("Method in Determining Wisdom Influence upon 'Historical' Literature," *JBL* 88, 1969, 129–42) and in W. Brueggemann's more favorable summary (*In Man We Trust*, 1972, 134–38). Note also G. von Rad's critical comment (*Weisheit in Israel*, 1970, 373–74 n. 9) on H.-J. Hermisson's earlier work (*Studien zur israelitischen Spruchweisheit*, 1968, 126–27, 133) and H.-J. Hermisson's response in *Weisheit und Geschichte*, 148 n. 17 and 153 n. 21. R. N. Whybray has now returned to the problem in *The Intellectual Tradition in the Old Testament*, 1974.

4. This is particularly evident in W. Brueggemann's "radical" promotion of wisdom in his: *In Man We Trust*. Despite his intention to draw attention to this neglected side of biblical faith, he constantly treats wisdom as though it were meaningful only in a *particular* historical context. Thus he must fix all the wisdom material in specific historical contexts even where the evidence is far from convincing. Note, moreover, how he rejects the either-or choice between the God of history and mother earth with the comment that "*in history* there is another option" (p. 46 [emphasis mine]).

5. *Job*, The Anchor Bible, 1973^3.

the text of the book.[6] In its most extreme form this predilection for history reduces Job to a mere cipher for Israel, and his theological problem becomes the problem of understanding Israel's national experience.[7] The number of scholars who would defend this extreme view is small, but basically the same theological bias for history finds expression in other, more subtle ways. It is evident, for instance, in F. M. Cross's attempt to read Job as repudiating the God of history for an El or Baal-type god of myth,[8] a view that necessitates placing the book against an interpretative background provided by Israel's *corporate* history. In fact, even among those scholars who take more seriously the individualistic nature of the problem as presented in Job, few have avoided the temptation to historicize. Nearly everyone tries to fit Job into the unilinear typological sequence of theological development provided by datable Hebrew prophecy and historiography. This is evident from, among other things, the constantly repeated claim that Job presupposes an individual doctrine of retribution first introduced in Israel during the period of Ezekiel.[9] What justification is there, however, for the assumption that one may string Job on the same typological continuum with such disparate material as the historiographic and prophetic works? Or what legitimacy can an interpretative background of history claim in the absence of any clear textual references to that history?

---

6. This will be illustrated in the following discussion, but as a preliminary example one may note J. Lévêque's repeated references to "l'Alliance" (*Job et son dieu*, I–II 1970, 178. 276. passim). One would be hard pressed to find a single *textual* reference to the covenant in the whole book of Job.

7. D. Napier comes very close to this view in his *Song of the Vineyard*, 1962, 335. 338: . . . but the work as a whole unmistakably reflects Israel's own corporate catastrophic experience of the bitter sixth century. The "biography" of Job is like the "biography" of the Servant of Second Isaiah: both are created and conditioned out of Israel's anguished existence through destruction and exile. . . . Here again it is Job/Israel—as it was Jacob/Israel, Servant/Israel. Biblical Theology is a product of history. It is the historical experience of a people that predominantly shapes the faith of the Old Testament.

Compare also C. L. Feinberg, "Job and the Nation Israel," *Bibliotheca Sacra* 96 (1939), 405–11; 97 (1940, 27–33. 211–16; and Margarete Susman, *Das Buch Hiob und das Schicksal des jüdischen Volkes*, 1948.

8. *Canaanite Myth and Hebrew Epic*, 1973, 344.

9. E. Dhorme, *A Commentary on the Book of Job*, 1967, cxxix–cxxx; A. Weiser, *The Old Testament: Its Formation and Development*, 1966, 292; H. H. Rowley, *Job*, The Century Bible, 1970, 22; O. Eißfeldt, *The Old Testament: An Introduction*, 1965, 467; and C. Kuhl, *Neuere Literarkritik des Buches Hiob*, ThR NF 21 (1953), 316–17. R. Gordis, while acknowledging the individual was never wholly submerged in the destiny of the nation, also places Job in the early days of the second temple "when the concern with the individual became paramount in religious thought" (*The Book of God and Man: A Study of Job*, 1965, 147–52.216), and even G. Fohrer, who notes the influence of ancient Near Eastern wisdom on Job's doctrine of retribution, still makes the Joban formulation dependent on deuteronomic theology (*Das Buch Hiob*, KAT 16, 1963, 140).

The subjective nature of all these attempts to interpret Job by reference to a particular historical background is underscored by the total lack of consensus in the dating of the book. Recent scholars have suggested dates as early as the eleventh or tenth centuries[10] and as late as the fourth century.[11] In view of this seven-hundred-year discrepancy it should be obvious that most of the criteria advanced for dating carry little conviction.[12] The chronological significance of the so-called Aramaisms is a moot point,[13] and the numerous attempts to demonstrate literary dependency have either failed to show more than the common use of traditional motifs,[14] or have left the direction of dependency—a notoriously double-edged blade—ambiguous,[15] or the dependency has been useless for dating because the other text in the comparison is itself undatable.[16] More promising have been D. N. Freedman's observations on Job's orthographic peculiarities[17] and D. A. Robertson's study of linguistic criteria,[18] but even these remain inconclusive. Both are made problematic by the long history of textual transmission, and D. A. Robertson's inability to resolve the problem of con-

10. D. A. Robertson, *Linguistic Evidence in Dating Early Hebrew Poetry*, 1972, 155.

11. O. Eißfeldt, *The Old Testament*, 470.

12. Cf. C. Kuhl, *ThR* NF 21, 314–16.

13. Given the long period of relations between Israel and the Arameans, the probability of dialectical variations within pre-exilic Hebrew, and the relatively small, basically religious corpus of classical Hebrew preserved in our sources, the identification of a syntactical construction or a lexical item as a *post-exilic* borrowing from Aramaic is a very uncertain business. See N. H. Snaith, *The Book of Job: Its Origin and Purpose*, 1968, 104–12, and contrast M. Wagner, *Die lexikalischen und grammatikalischen Aramaismen im alttestamentlichen Hebräisch*, 1966.

14. In some cases it can be demonstrated that these traditional motifs antedate any Israelite sources. Job 5:18, for instance, shares the motif of the deity as the "smiter who heals" with Deut 32:39, Hos 6:1 and Isa 30:26, but precisely the same motif occurs in the text from Ugarit RS 25.460 (*Ugaritica* V, no. 162: 34–39):

> He smote me, but he took pity on me.
> He . . . me, but he bound me up.
> He broke me, but he . . . me.
> He loosed me, but he joined me back together.
> He poured me out, but he gathered me up.
> He threw me down, but he raised me up. (Cf. W. von Soden, *UF* 1, 1969, 191ff)

It also occurs in Ludlul IV 9–10: "[He who] smote me, Marduk, he restored me" (*BWL* 58–59). One should also note my comments on the traditional background of the use of lion imagery to picture the wicked (*Biblica* 54, 1973, 265–67, especially 266 n. 2).

15. As an example, see the discussions on the relationship between Job 3:3ff. and Jer 20: 14–15. Of course, some scholars would classify the relationship between these passages as simply the common use of a traditional motif.

16. Here one can point to the parody of Ps 8:5–6 in Job 7:17–18.

17. D. N. Freedman, "Orthographic Peculiarities in the Book of Job," *Eretz Israel* 9 (1969), 35–44.

18. D. A. Robertson, *Linguistic Evidence*.

scious archaisms places the use of his criteria under an added liability. Moreover, neither presents a broad enough base to be finally convincing.

One cannot use the date of the book, therefore, to provide a ready-made background for its interpretation, and lacking this, an historical framework is hard to establish, since Job simply ignores Israel's epic and prophetic traditions. That he ignores Israel's epic traditions is hardly debatable. Possible allusions to these traditions are very rare and never certain. The land which was given to the fathers (15:19) is not necessarily Palestine,[19] and *ʾereṣ* in 9:24 is undetermined and should probably be translated "earth."[20] Job 5:9–27 and 12: 14–25 discuss God's great deeds in nature and among men, but there is no direct reference to events of Israelite history, or in fact to any specific history. The writer is simply describing the customary actions of God, and the content of these passages can be closely paralleled in Mesopotamian texts.[21] The denial of the sexual abuse of strangers (31:31–34) might be interpreted as indicating a knowledge of the Lot or Levite stories, and Job 42:2 has been taken as a play on Gen 11:6, but in neither case is such a conclusion required.

There is more room for discussion when it comes to the question of possible prophetic influence, but one must be quite clear what is at issue here. I have no doubt Job is an Israelite work. Job's oath that he was innocent of astral worship (31:26–28) makes that clear. The listing of moral norms in 22:6–9 and 24:2–17 are less distinctively Israelite, but together with Job's unquestioned dependence on Israel's psalmic tradition they support the Israelite identity of the author. Nevertheless, by itself, this general "Yahwistic" background of the work does not imply any real dependency on the prophetic tradition. Such telltale signs of national identity are no more than one might expect to find in the writing of any religious Israelite from the very beginning of Israel as a cultic community, and certainly from the time of Solomon onward. The prophets did not create Israel's religion.

If one could show Job's literary dependency on specific prophetic texts, or better, on several texts from a single prophetic book, the situation would be different. Then one would be fully justified in speaking of prophetic influence on Job. But, at best, such attempts have proven indecisive.[22] R. H. Pfeiffer's convincing demonstration of Job's priority over Deutero-Isaiah removed the only compelling example.[23] One should not rule out the *possibility* of some literary use of the earlier prophets, and as I have argued elsewhere,[24] it may be

19. M. Pope, *Job*, 1973³, 116.

20. Ibid., 73.

21. Cf. for example, W. G. Lambert, "Three Literary Prayers of the Babylonians," *AfO* 19 (1959/60), 63:45–49; 65:3–16; and 66:8–9.

22. C. Kuhl, *ThR* NF 21, 315–16.

23. R. H. Pfeiffer, "The Dual Origin of Hebrew Monotheism," *JBL* 46 (1927), 202–6.

24. "Job's Summons to Yahweh: The Exploitation of a Legal Metaphor," *Restoration Quarterly* 16 (1973), 159–65.

that Job's use of legal metaphor owes something to the covenant lawsuit—note Job's objection to God's dual role as litigant and judge (9:12–35, 13:20–22) as well as Zophar's reference to heaven and earth as witnesses (20:27)[25]—but such evidence is both too ambiguous and too slim to establish any significant prophetic influence on the book.

These observations do not mean the author of Job was ignorant of Israel's epic and prophetic traditions, but they do prohibit using those traditions as a background, even as a negative background, for interpreting the book. Given Job's literary form as a dialogue, one can hardly speak of the author's repudiation of views simply passed over in silence. One may agree with F. M. Cross that "the God who called Israel out of Egypt, who spoke by prophet, the covenant god of Deuteronomy, did not reveal himself to Job,"[26] but what F. M. Cross fails to stress is that such a God did not reveal himself to Job's friends either. His friends do not appeal to the sacred history, and they seem as much at home with the god of myth as Job is.[27]

Neither party in the debate sounds anything like the classical prophets, and Job, even at his blasphemous worst, bears only the faintest resemblance to those prophetic opponents we sometimes encounter in dialogues embedded in prophetic books. Moreover, the repeated characterization of the friends' theology as deuteronomic ignores the lack of any covenantal context and fails to do justice to the highly individualistic nature of the friends' doctrine of retribution. One cannot identify a theology as deuteronomic simply because it holds that God rewards the good man and punishes the bad. Such a view was widespread, if not universal, in the ancient Near East, even among people who had no covenant with their gods. It is the common property of both Israelite and Mesopotamian hymnology and wisdom, and one need not look outside these traditions to find the views Job is reacting against.

If one simply sticks to the text, the poetic dialogue presents the problem as that of a religious individual who was experiencing what appeared to him as undeserved suffering. There is no hint that the suffering extended beyond his immediate family; indeed 19:13–17 implies that even within his own household Job's agony was his alone. A similar theme appears numerous times in Israelite and Mesopotamian individual laments, and C. Westermann has drawn attention to our author's extensive use of this genre in the composition of his

25. H. Richter's attempt (*Studien zu Hiob*, 1959) to derive all the legal imagery in Job from the everyday litigation in the village gate is hardly satisfactory. It is very doubtful that the village courts ever permitted one of the litigants to serve as the judge in his own case, and heaven and earth, to judge by Near Eastern analogies, were not frequent witnesses in ordinary lawsuits. Zophar's statement suggests a borrowing of imagery originally at home in the covenant lawsuit, but it cannot be pressed to make his theology covenantal.

26. *Canaanite Myth and Hebrew Epic*, 344.

27. Note 26:5–14, which M. Pope assigns to Bildad's last speech.

work.[28] The same motifs also appear in the narrative portions of the individual thanksgiving song, however, and several of the Mesopotamian "wisdom" texts often compared to Job actually belong to this genre.[29] Their resemblance to Job stems not from wisdom per se, but from their roots in the existential experience of rejection, lament, and restoration.

With this cultic tradition the poet has combined several wisdom elements. The proverbial literature of moral exhortation certainly lies behind the friends' clearcut, moralistic, and highly individualistic doctrine of divine retribution, and one can recognize the background of the school debate in his choice of the literary form of the dialogue. At this point the author of Job was clearly working within a long literary tradition. Not only do both these elements have Mesopotamian antecedents, they had already been combined prior to Job in the *Babylonian Theodicy.* This work, remarkably similar to Job in the problem it discusses, in its literary structure, and even in some of its imagery, must have exercised at least an indirect influence on the biblical work.

The biblical author was far more than a mere imitator, however. He radically extended the literary model provided by the tradition, stretching the dialogue to its limits by the addition of two extra speakers, and he sharpened the focus on the problem by setting this expanded dialogue within the framework of the old Job legend. Far more significant, however, was his profoundly successful joining of the cultic and wisdom traditions.[30] It is as though he combined the best qualities of *Ludlul* and the *Babylonian Theodicy* in a single work. In so doing he preserved the full pathos of the lament while keeping the

---

28. C. Westermann, *Der Aufbau des Buches Hiob*, 1956, 25–55. In his excellent article: "The Book of Job in the Context of Near Eastern Literature," *ZAW* 82 (1970), 251–69, J. Gray has noted some points of connection between the "sapiential Book of Job" and the "Plaint of the Sufferer in Hebrew tradition" (261–62), but he fails to note the similar material in Mesopotamian laments. Consider, for example, the plaint in a prayer to Nabu:

> In my youth I called upon. . . .
> (Now) I am old (and) my hands are open to all the gods.
> I have exhausted myself with gestures of humility.
> (Yet) before men I am like straw.
> My days have fled, my years have come to an end,
> I have not seen good, I have not received pity.
> (E. Ebeling, *Die akkadische Gebetsserie "Handerhebung,"* 1953, 10–11)

This passage which dwells on the contrast between the pious behavior of the sufferer and his lot in life offers only one of the many motifs common to the Mesopotamian laments and the more specifically wisdom treatment of the worthy sufferer, but further elaboration will have to be reserved for another paper.

29. Ludlul and RS 25.460 (*Ugaritica* V, No. 162) may be analyzed this way, though Ludlul could be seen as incorporating more than one genre.

30. This is anticipated in the Mesopotamian tradition, but the author of Job carries it through much more successfully. Cf. J. Gray, *ZAW* 82, 268.

movement and clash of ideas integral to the dialogue. It enabled him to show that the traditional wisdom theology, pushed uncritically to its logical limits, would end by transforming would-be comforters into the slandering enemies so well-known from the individual laments. Finally, his use of hymnic material, particularly the mythic motifs of theophany and cosmogony, lends a grandeur to the poet's work which surpasses anything in the Babylonian parallels. It almost compensates for the inevitable intellectual disappointment at his resolution of the problem.

Assuming these observations are correct, the actual date of the composition of Job is largely irrelevant for its exegesis. If its author stood in a long literary tradition in which basically the same problem had been dealt with before, and if the human experience necessary for this problem to arise in Israel was independent of any necessary connection to the national history,[31] it is illegitimate to read that history into the book simply because the book could have come into its present form during an acute national crisis. Not every work written in a period of great upheaval deals with or is strongly influenced by that upheaval, not even when the work could plausibly be interpreted in that fashion. To cite a modern analogy, J. R. R. Tolkien's "The Lord of the Rings" was written between 1936–1949, most of it during World War II, yet the author insists that little or nothing in the work was modified or significantly influenced by that experience.[32] One can object, of course, in the fashion typical of critics, that the author is the last person to consult about the meaning of his work. Yet one can hardly dispute J. R. R. Tolkien's claim that in the case of a critic and a writer whose lifespans only partially overlap, the movements of thought or the events of the time common to both are not necessarily the most powerful influences on that writer. As J. R. R. Tolkien shrewdly observes, having already lived through World War I, he did not need World War II to experience the hideous oppression of war. If the critic of a contemporary writer can be misled by a superficial application of the historical method, the biblical scholar, who is in a far less enviable position with regard to evidence, must certainly beware. The historical method has its own peculiar temptations toward eisegesis.

31. Cf. the excellent characterization of the intellectual tradition behind Job given in R. N. Whybray's latest book (*The Intellectual Tradition in the Old Testament*, 1974, 69–70).

32. *The Lord of the Rings*, 1965, xi–xii.

Chapter 10

Job's Summons to Yahweh: The Exploitation of a Legal Metaphor

Legal metaphors are extremely popular in the theological language of the Old Testament.[1] In part this popularity of legal language merely reflects Israel's Near Eastern background, where the idea of the deity as judge was both ancient and widespread.[2] Partly it is a more uniquely Israelite phenomenon, stemming from early Israel's creative adaptation of the international treaty form to give institutional expression to her new relation with Yahweh.[3] Much of the legal imagery of the Psalms comes out of the first background,[4] while the legal terminology of the prophets, particularly in the prophetic *rîb*, must often be traced back to covenantal theology.[5] Nevertheless, the imagery from both backgrounds is often mixed, so one must be wary of pushing for pure forms.

This warning is especially appropriate in connection with the book of Job, where the legal imagery flourishes, but often in unconventional ways. It is to such an unconventional usage of legal metaphor that this study, presented in memory of my friend and respected teacher the late Dr. J. W. Roberts, is directed.

> If I say, "I will forget my complaint,
> I will relax my face and smile,
> I become afraid of all my sufferings.
> I know you will not acquit me.
> I am already found guilty;
> Why should I struggle in vain.

---

1. B. Gemser, "The *rib*—or Controversy-Pattern in Hebrew Mentality," *SVT* 3 (1955) 120–37.

2. Arnold Gamper, *Gott als Richter in Mesopotamien und im Alten Testament: zum Verständnis eines Gebetsbitte* (Innsbruck: Universitätsverlag Wagner, 1966).

3. The vast literature on covenant is still expanding and cannot be listed here. For the sake of the novice, however, one should mention Delbert R. Hillers' *Covenant: The History of a Biblical Idea* (Baltimore: The Johns Hopkins Press, 1969), which is undoubtedly the best introduction to the subject.

4. Gamper, op. cit.

5. Julien Harvey, *Le plaidoyer prophétique contre Israël après la rupture de l'alliance* (Studia travaux de recherche, 22; Bruges-Paris: Desclée de Brouwer//Montréal: Les Éditions Bellarmin, 1967).

Were I to wash myself with soapwort,
Cleanse my hands with lye;
You would dunk me in filth,
And my clothes would abhor me.
For he is not a man, like me, whom I could challenge:
"Let us go to court together (*nbwʾ yḥdw bmšpṭ*)."
Would there were an umpire between us
That he might place his hand on us both.
Let him put aside his club,
And let his terror not dismay me.
Then I would speak and not fear him,
Though I am not just before him.[6] (Job 9:27–35)

This passage is loaded with unconventional thoughts, but let us focus first on the expression Job uses in his hypothetical summons to God, "Let us go to court together (*nbwʾ yḥdw bmšpṭ*)." This expression, while unexceptional when used of two humans, runs counter to normal usage when applied to God. *Bwʾ bmšpṭ ʿm/ʾt*, "to enter into litigation with," or *hbyʾ bmšpṭ*, "to bring into litigation," when used with God as the subject, normally designates an experience to be avoided if possible. The Psalmist prays to be delivered from it: "Do not enter into judgment with your servant (*w ʾl tbwʾ bmšpṭ ʾt ʿbdk*), for no living being can be in the right before you" (Ps 143:2). Isaiah threatens the leaders of Israel with its imminence, "Yahweh is about to take the stand to prosecute, He is about to stand to judge his people, Yahweh is entering into litigation with the elders of his people and their princes (*yhwh bmšpṭ ybwʾ ʿm . . .*)" (Isa 3:13, 14).

And Qohelet uses it as a warning to temper any libertine misunderstanding of his philosophy of life:

Rejoice, young man, in your youth,
And let your heart cheer you in the days of your youth.
Walk in the ways of your heart and in the sight of your eyes,
But know that for all these things God will bring you into
  judgment (*ybyʾ k hʾ lhym bmšpṭ*). (Qoh 11:9)[7]

The reason for this rather negative evaluation of such an experience is clearly expressed in Eliphaz's sharp rebuke to Job: "Is it because of your piety

6. For the rendering of this last line, see Anton C. M. Blommerde, *Northwest Semitic Grammar and Job* (Biblica et Orientalia 22; Rome: Pontifical Biblical Institute, 1969), 57, 58. There are other difficulties in the text as well, but for the sake of economy I have limited my textual notes to those places where my rendering departs radically from any of the commonly accepted translations. For the rest the reader should consult the commentaries, especially Marvin Pope's in the *Anchor Bible* series.

7. The other occurrence of this expression in Qoh 12:14 probably has a somewhat different implications.

he reproves you (*ykyḥk*)? That he enters into litigation with you (*ybwʾ ʿmk bmšpṭ*)" (Job 22:4)? Up to this point in the dialogue God has not deigned to speak with Job, so the reference cannot be to an oral rebuke. The only tangible expression of Yahweh's reproof or litigation lay in the sufferings Job was enduring. Such suffering was interpreted in traditional Israelite thought, as in Near Eastern thought in general, as God's judgment on a sinner. Thus the metaphor "to bring/enter into judgment," when used with God as the subject, meant, translated into literal prose, "to suffer some kind of pain or disaster." Naturally that is an experience to be avoided and one which invites its use as a warning.

Job follows this normal usage of the metaphor when he complains what man is too ephemeral a creature, his life too brief, for God to waste time bringing him to court (14:1–3), but in the passage quoted earlier (9:32), the poet has Job express a quite different sentiment. Under certain circumstances he would actually initiate litigation with God! Obviously Job is using the expression with a different meaning here—he certainly does not want more suffering. And if one considers the circumstances in which this summons would be offered, one can see what Job has done to the metaphor. He has simply transferred it, untranslated, out of the realm of metaphor into that of literal prose. While traditional language spoke metaphorically of God entering into judgment with man, Job pleads that he literally do so in a tangible, equitable fashion.

This implies, among other things, that God make himself visible to his opponent at law. Part of Job's complaint is his inability to find God. He touches on this problem of God's invisibility earlier in the same chapter, "Lo, he passes by me, but I cannot see him; He moves on by, but I cannot perceive him" (9:11), but his clearest exposition of it is in Job 23:3–9:

Would that I knew where to find him
That I might come to his tribunal.
I would lay my case before him,
Would fill my mouth with arguments.
I want to know what words he would answer me.
I want to consider what he would say to me.
Would he contend with me in his great strength?
No, he would pay attention to me.
There the upright could reason with him
And I could carry my case through successfully.
Lo, I go forward, but he is not there,
Backwards, but I cannot see him.
I turn right, but I do not spy him.[8]

8. It would also be possible to translate the terms "forward," "backwards," "left," and "right," in accordance with their use in Hebrew to designate the cardinal points of the compass, as "east," "west," "north," and "south," respectively.

It is not enough, however, for God to show himself to his opponent. He must restrain himself, forego the use of his awesome, intimidating power, in order that Job may reason with him unafraid, as an equal:

Only two things do not do to me,
Then I will not hide from your face:
Remove your hand from upon me,
And let your terror not dismay me.
Then call, and I will answer,
Or let me speak, and you reply. (13:20–22)

Otherwise justice cannot be achieved, for God would simply terrorize his opponent into accepting his verdict:

If he carries off, who can challenge him,
Who can say to him, "What are you doing?"
A god could not turn back his anger,
The helpers of Rahab groveled beneath him.
How then could I challenge him?
Choose my words with him?
Though in the right I could not answer;
I would have to entreat my judge.[9]
If I summoned, and he answered,
I do not believe he would heed my voice.
He would bruise me with a tempest
And multiply my wounds without cause.
He would not permit me to catch my breath.
Yea, he would sate me with bitterness.
Be it power, he is strongest;
Or litigation, who could arraign him?
Though I were innocent, his mouth would declare me guilty.
Though I were blameless, he would pronounce me perverse. (9:12–20)

In stressing this need for Yahweh to exercise self-control, the poet appears to have picked upon a logical weakness in legal imagery dear to the prophets. The whole presentation in Job 9 may, in fact, be read as a critical reflection on the famous passage in Isa 1:18–20:[10]

---

9. This translation follows the MT vocalization *limšōpĕṭî*, but takes the *mem* as the enclitic expansion of the preposition, i.e., *lm špṭy.* Cf. the use of *lmw* in 27:14, 29:21; 38:40; and 40:4.

10. Both have a summons to litigation (Isa 1:18//Job 9:32), both stress the impossibility of man's cleansing himself before God (Isa 1:18 [see next note]//Job 9:30–31), and both make it evident, though in radically different ways, that Yahweh's will cannot be thwarted (Isa 1:19–20// for Job, see below).

> Come and let us reason together, says Yahweh.
> If your sins be as scarlet, shall they become white as snow?[11]
> If they are red like crimson, shall they become as wool?
> If you are willing and obedient, you will eat the good of the land,
> But if you refuse and rebel, you will be devoured by the sword,
> For the mouth of Yahweh has spoken.

The late President Johnson once quoted the first line of this text in an appeal for national unity only to have a querulous critic point to its conclusion. The appeal to sweet reasonableness ends in a threat! Agree with me or be damned!

Actually the word translated "reason together" (*nwkḥh*) properly means "to dispute together in court," but that only gives more point to the critic's cynicism. Yahweh is both an interested party in the lawsuit and the judge! This is hardly a fair arrangement for Yahweh's opponents at law, yet this rather bizarre pattern constantly appears in the prophetic *rîb*s. It can only be explained, I think, by the covenantal background to these prophetic lawsuits. In the international treaties the gods who served as witnesses also acted as judges, in the event the treaty was broken, either by deciding the outcome of the battle which was almost sure to follow, or by afflicting the guilty side with natural disaster.[12] But Israel, when it adapted this political form to express its religious commitment to Yahweh, obviously could not assimilate these pagan gods—one finds only attenuated accommodations to the pressure of the form.[13] Thus Yahweh, one party to the treaty, also had to assume the responsibility of the gods to see that it was observed. As a result, the lawsuits based on this covenant model place Yahweh in this same invidious dual role. This is sometimes obscured by the appeal to various parties as witnesses, but ultimately it is always Yahweh, the litigant, who pronounces judgment on the guilty.

---

11. For this rendering of this and the following line see Hans Wildberger, *Jesaja* (BK X/I; Neukirchen-Vluyn: Neukirchener Verlag, 1972), 52–53, especially the following:

> Since Yahweh summons to a clarification before the judgment, he must say why that is necessary. Against the prophet's preaching one will have raised the objection that the possibility of reparation for the guilt of sin exists, and indeed through cultic rites, be they sacrifice or ritual washings. It is not the forgiveness of sins, but the possibility of expiation that stands under discussion. Now it is fully in line with [vss.] 10–17 if here also Isaiah opposes the sharpest "No!" to a confidence rooted in the performance of cultic rites and thus destroys the certainty of salvation, so understood, as an illusion. One cannot be finished with the guilt of sin so easily, and man should not attempt to play so sacrilegious a game with God's patience (p. 53).

12. For the first note the appeal to Shamash in the Tukulti-Ninurta Epic and in Yarim-Lim's letter to Yashub-Yahad (both conveniently included in the appendix to Harvey's work, *op. cit.*, 170–73), and for the latter see Mursilis's plague prayers (*ANET*, p. 395, para. 4–10).

13. The prophetic appeal to heaven and earth as witnesses must be regarded as such.

One can see that the flaw lies at the metaphor's roots, in the imperfect analogy between the original political form and the religious use to which it was put. Other metaphors for God's relation to man such as the language of father and son do not harbor this particular weakness. Job, however, who appears to have read the Isaiah passage with the same cynical eye as Johnson's critic, is interested in exploiting the metaphor, not in explaining its flaw. How can he hope for a fair trial, if God is to be both his opponent and his judge? Thus Job presses for a third party to adjudicate his dispute with God.

This third party, variously referred to as an "umpire" (*mwkyḥ*),[14] "witness" (*ʿd* and *śhd*),[15] "interpreter" (*mlyṣ*),[16] and "redeemer" (*gʾl*),[17] has been the source of endless discussion, and the passages where this figure occurs are some of the most difficult in the book of Job. One cannot deal with them here except to say that all these terms take on more than ordinary significance when applied to this third party.

That is entirely in keeping with our poet's method. He has produced Job's summons to Yahweh with its concomitant features by exploiting ambiguities and logical weaknesses in the traditional legal metaphors. It is not surprising that these terms suffer the same creative fate.

14. Job 9:33.
15. Job 16:19.
16. Job 16:19; 33:23.
17. Job 19:25.

Chapter 11

Does God Lie?
Divine Deceit as a Theological Problem in Israelite Prophetic Literature

Can one trust the gods? This question has a strange sound to the ears of those who have been raised or trained in the Jewish or Christian traditions. First of all, there is only one God, and of course you can trust him. God does not lie; it is against his very nature. The Old Testament characterizes Yahweh as a god of truth (Ps 31:6) or faithfulness (Deut 32:4), who is just and right (Deut 32:4; Pss 92:16, 119:137, 145:17), and without iniquity (Deut 32:4; Ps 92:16). His word and judgments are straight (Ps 33:4) and true (Pss 19:10, 119:137, 151–60) and altogether righteous (Ps 19:10). He does not lie, because he is not a man that he should lie or change his mind (Num 23:19; 1 Sam 15:29); what he says he will do, and what he promises he will bring to pass (Num 23:19). The New Testament also characterizes God's word as truth (John 17:17), denies that there is any unrighteousness in him (Rom 9:14), and speaks of him as ὁ ἀψευδὴς θεὸς, "God who does not" or "cannot lie" (Titus 1:2). Finally, the author of Hebrews claims that when the divine promise is confirmed by the divine oath, these two things make it impossible for God to prove false (Heb 6:18).

Despite the initial strangeness of the question, however, it may be profitable to pursue it. The very fact that God felt constrained to swear an oath suggests that, for whatever reason, humans were inclined to distrust the divine word, even the word of promise.[1] Moreover, when one moves from the monotheistic world of Judaism and Christianity to the polytheistic world of the ancient Near Eastern matrix out of which Judaism and Christianity arose, one can see even more justification for distrusting divine promises. If the god of my city is only one god in a whole pantheon, how can I be sure that he will be able to fulfill his promises? How can I be sure that the divine assembly will not overrule his desire and even his promises to bless his city and its inhabitants?

The ancient Mesopotamian polytheist was aware of this problem, but it did not prevent him from making claims about the reliability of the word of his

1. Note God's repeated oaths in Ps 89:34–36 that he would not lie to David or change his promise, yet the point of the psalm is that God has not kept his word.

gods and goddesses similar to those found in Scripture. Thus we read of Enlil "whose word cannot be changed, whose reliable consent cannot be transgressed."[2] We read of Shamash, "whose yes remains yes, whose no, no,"[3] and "whose positive answer no god can change."[4] Similar comments are made about Ninurta, Marduk, and numerous other gods and goddesses. Yet, as the cuneiform literature shows, such claims must be taken with a grain of salt.

In the Atrahasis epic,[5] for instance, the mighty Enlil finds his exalted command thwarted at every turn by the wily Enki. Even when he forces the whole divine assembly to swear an oath not to inform mankind of the annihilating flood the gods have planned, Enki finds a way of getting around the oath and succeeds both in warning Atrahasis and in preventing Enlil from accomplishing his purpose of wiping out mankind.[6] Moreover, neither the deviousness nor the impotence of the gods always works to the benefit of mankind as they do in the Atrahasis story. In the Lamentation over the Destruction of Ur, Ningal, the city goddess of Ur, piteously implores Enlil and Anu to spare her city, but all her supplications are in vain before the implacable decision of the divine assembly.[7] In the Adapa story, the deviousness of Enki/Ea saves Adapa's life, but it prevents Adapa from gaining immortality (*ANET*, pp. 101–3). When Adapa is brought before the judgment seat of Anu, Ea teaches him how to get the gods Tammuz and Gizzida to plead his case, but Ea also tells Adapa not to accept food or drink from Anu, because it will be the food and drink of death. This, however, is a lie. Anu offers Adapa the food and drink of immortality, but Adapa, obedient to the divine lie, turns down this boon, and so Adapa, and perhaps all mankind,[8] is doomed to die. The story calls to mind the doubt the serpent created in Eve's mind in the biblical story of temptation (Gen 3:1–4).

Obviously the questions of divine power and trustworthiness were critical questions in the ancient Near Eastern world when the outcome of a person's plans depended on the decision of the gods. In Mesopotamia, the pious person did not undertake any major task without inquiring of the gods whether that task would be successful. If the answer was no or indefinite, the pious person either changed his plans or delayed them until he could obtain a positive divine response. If the omens threatened the person with death or disaster, the pious person tried to ward off the impending evil by performing the appropriate rituals to appease the angry gods. The whole system of anticipating the fu-

2. *ša qibīt pīšu la innennû u annašu kīnu la innettiqu*, *CAD* A/2, p. 134.
3. *ša annašu annu ullašu ulla*, *CAD* A/2, p. 135.
4. *ša . . . annašu ilu mamman la enû*, *CAD* A/2, p. 135.
5. W. G. Lambert and A. R. Millard, *Atra-hasīs: The Babylonian Story of the Flood* (Oxford, 1969).
6. Ibid., pp. 100–101, vi 5–19.
7. *ANET*, pp. 455–63, especially the third song, p. 458a.
8. The broken ending of the text precludes certainty on this point.

ture by divine revelation, whether that revelation came unbidden through prophets and dreams, or whether it came as a divine response to a prior question, the answer to which was derived deductively by an omen specialist like the *bārû*, depended on the trustworthiness of the divine oracle and the ability of the gods to fulfill their words, but neither was entirely self-evident.

ARM X 9, one of the Mari prophetic texts, appears to speak to the question whether the gods were able to fulfill their promises. The tablet is unfortunately broken and fragmentary, but a prophet, perhaps Qīšti-Dirītim, who is named earlier in the letter as the *āpilum* of the goddess Dirītum, has a dream or sees a vision of the divine assembly. The gods are talking about taking an oath when one of the gods, a certain Asumum, says something to the god Ea. The prophet did not hear what was said, but then the god, presumably Ea, though the antecedent is ambiguous and Asumum could be intended, rises and says, "[Before] we pronounce [the oath] let us take the dirt and jamb of the gate of Mari, dissolve them in water, and drink the water." Then Ea commands the gods, "Swear that you will not sin against the brickwork and the protective deity of Mari," and the gods and goddesses swear as Ea had commanded them.

The ritual associated with the oath bears certain interesting resemblances to the ritual associated with the oath that the woman suspected of adultery must swear in Num 5:16–28, but the function of the vision as a whole is quite different. The Mari vision clearly serves as a promise of salvation, and the certainty of that promise is underscored by the oath that all the gods and goddesses take not to sin against Mari. In the earlier oracle reported in the same letter the goddess Dirītum promised Zimri-Lim a secure throne in Mari, and this oracle underscores the certainty of that message of salvation by indicating that no god was going to annul the promised salvation by acting on his or her own to destroy Mari. The divine assembly had bound itself by oath not to sin against the city. In effect, Dirītum could fulfill her promise, because none of the other gods or goddesses could cross her without violating their solemnly sworn oath.

The ability of a god or goddess to fulfill his or her promise was not the only concern of the ancient Mesopotamian worshiper; there was also a concern whether the god or goddess was actually speaking in good faith. That concern finds eloquent expression in the Old Babylonian prayer of the *bārû* priest published by Goetze.[9] Eight times in the course of this relatively short ritual the divination priest calls upon Shamash and Adad to put truth (*kittam šuknam*) in the extispicy that the priest was performing. The same request also occurs eight times in the 142-line ritual of the diviner published by Ivan Starr,[10] and similar formulae are found in many other divination ritual texts: "place a true

9. *Journal of Cuneiform Studies* 22 (1968) 25–29.
10. *The Rituals of the Diviner* (Malibu, 1983) 30–44.

answer in the lamb I am dedicating";[11] "let there be a true answer in the inquiry I am dedicating";[12] "let them render a decision with truth and justice";[13] "let them render a decision of truth."[14] The occurrence, and particularly the repeated occurrence, of such formulae suggests a fear on the part of the priest that the gods might put a false message in the extispicy. In fact, more than one omen apodosis claims that the god will lie to the man.[15] A similar concern for the reliability of the omen finds expression in a characteristic series of clauses that form part of the oracular questions posed to Shamash in the Shamash prayers published by J. A. Knudtzon.[16] After carefully posing the question, the priest asks the god to overlook any of a long list of things that might confuse the answer. If the action was going to happen after the time limit set by the question, or if the enemy was planning the action, but was not going to carry it out, the god should ignore these complications. If the priest garbled the question, the god should overlook his mistake and answer according to the way in which the priest intended to ask the question. If the weather turned bad, or the priest wore soiled clothes, or an unclean person blundered into the ritual area, or any number of other bad things happened, the god was asked to overlook these potentially disturbing events and answer with a reliable and positive oracle (*annam kīnam apulanni*).

It is clear that the king or other individual who depended on a prophet or divination priest for a divine revelation was faced with a double problem. He had to decide whether the prophet or priest was telling the truth, and beyond that, he had to decide whether the divine message itself was trustworthy. Sargon divided his diviners into four groups when having the extispicy performed, so that he could check their answers against one another (*CAD* B, 122). At Mari one used extispicy to check whether a person who reported a revelatory dream had in fact had that dream. In *ARM* X 94:9′–12′, after reporting such a dream, the lady Shibatum urges the king, "Now let my lord have the divination priest investigate this matter. If that dream was seen, my lord, trust

11. *ina puḫād akarrabu kittam šuknam*, *RA* (= *Revue d'Assyriologie et d'archéologie Orientale*) 38 (1941) 86:23, 87:9; *RA* 32 (1935) 180:24.

12. *ina tāmīt akarrabu kitti libši*, *Journal of the Royal Asiatic Society*, Cent. Suppl. (1924) pl. 3, r. 13.

13. *ina kitti u mīšari lidīnū dīna*, Heinrich Zimmern, *Beiträge zur Kenntnis der babylonischen Religion* 2 (Leipzig, 1901) n. 97:5.

14. *lidīnū dīnam ša kittim*, *RA* 38 (1941) 87:v 6–7.

15. Note, for example, the following passages: "The god will speak with a false mouth to the man," *ilum itti awēlim piam la kīnam idabbub* (*Cuneiform Texts from Babylonian Tablets, &c., in the British Museum* 5 [London, 1898] 5:45); "The god will open a false mouth to the man," *ilum awīlam piam la kīnam ippaššu*: A. Goetze, *Old Babylonian Omen Texts, Yale Oriental Series*, Babylonian Texts 10 (New Haven, Conn., 1947) 14:4.

16. *Assyrische Gebete an den Sonnengott für Staat und königliches Haus aus der Zeit Asarhaddons und Asurbanipals* 1–2 (Leipzig, 1893).

that servant girl. . . ." Note that what is at issue is whether one could trust the person who claimed to have a revelation. Bad intelligence could lead to disaster, and even the queen could be suspected of manufacturing divine revelations. In *ARM* X 4:35–39, after reporting a very favorable revelation, Shibtu, Zimri-Lim's main wife, defends herself against the possibility of such suspicion: "Heaven forbid that my lord should say, 'With evil intentions she is making them speak.' I am not making them say anything. They are speaking on their own. They are agreeing on their own." The standard practice of taking a tuft of hair and a piece from the fringe of a prophet's garment was also apparently done in order to check whether the prophet had actually received a revelation, or whether the prophet was speaking without divine authorization.

Even if the revelatory message was demonstrated to be genuine by the convergence of more than one method of obtaining revelation or by repeated but independent inquiries of the same type, the question whether to trust the divine word still remained. In *ARM* X 4, the oracular message is that Zimri-Lim will overpower his opponent, the king of Assyria, Ishme-Dagan. As soon as the two armies approach one another, the auxiliary troops of Ishme-Dagan will desert. But Shibtu is afraid Zimri-Lim will not be convinced by this promise. After all, Zimri-Lim may say, "So what? Even if the auxiliary troops of Ishme-Dagan desert, his army is still very large, and I have no auxiliary troops to speak of." Against such doubt Shibtu tries to reassure her husband: "It is Dagan, Adad, Itur-Mer, and Belet-ekallim who go at the side of my lord, and Adad is indeed the lord of decisions." In effect, your auxiliary troops are the great gods, including the god who renders decisions about the outcome of battles.

Before turning back to the Bible, one might add as a footnote that the divine promises to Zimri-Lim were not realized. Despite a number of oracles guaranteeing his throne and his victory over Babylon, Mari fell to Hammurabi of Babylon, Mari was destroyed, and Zimri-Lim perished. So much for the oath of the divine assembly.

Moreover, despite the biblical texts that we looked at earlier, a similar problem is present in the biblical material. The issue of false prophecy was a major concern in the Old Testament, and even in the New Testament one finds the admonition to "test the spirits to see if they are from God, because many false prophets have gone out into the world" (1 John 4:1). In the Old Testament, in 1 Kings 13, we have the curious story about the hospitable old prophet from Bethel who lied to the young prophet from Judah, thus causing the young prophet's death. In 2 Kgs 19:10 and its parallel in Isa 37:10, the Assyrian Rabshakeh warns Hezekiah, "Do not let your God on whom you rely deceive you by promising that Jerusalem will not be given into the hand of the king of Assyria." Such a promise, given through prophetic oracles, was the typical response of a national god when his king was threatened by enemy forces, but no national god had yet been able to resist the Assyrian power, and Yahweh would not be able to either. The implication is that Yahweh might promise more than he could deliver, but there is no hint in the passage that Yahweh was deceiving Hezekiah with the malicious intent of getting him killed.

More interesting for our discussion, therefore, are a series of Old Testament passages in which Yahweh is characterized as the willful source of false prophecy. The most famous of these is the narrative about Micaiah ben Imlah in 1 Kings 22. King Ahab of Israel wants to take the city Ramoth-gilead away from the Arameans of Damascus, and he persuades Jehoshaphat of Judah to join him in this endeavor. Jehoshaphat, however, wants to inquire of Yahweh as to the success of the proposed endeavor before going into battle, so Ahab summons about four hundred prophets and asks them, "Shall I go to battle against Ramoth-gilead, or shall I forbear?" The prophets give a unanimously positive response: "Go up; for Yahweh will give it into the hand of the king." Jehoshaphat is not satisfied, however. Like Zimri-Lim, he may have suspected that Ahab was putting too much pressure on the prophets to give the response the king wanted to hear. Or it may have been that he simply wanted an independent confirmation of their message from another source to allay his fears. In principle this would not be unlike the Mari practice of confirming a prophetic message by an independent extispicy, or Sargon's practice of dividing his divination priests into four independent groups. At any rate, Jehoshaphat asks if there is not another prophet of Yahweh there through whom they may inquire. Ahab reluctantly agrees to summon Micaiah ben Imlah, whom Ahab dislikes intensely, because Micaiah has a history of giving unfavorable oracles. A messenger is sent to fetch Micaiah, and that messenger takes it upon himself to urge Micaiah to give a favorable oracle like all the other prophets. Micaiah rather indignantly swears that he will say only what Yahweh tells him to say, but when he comes before Ahab, he responds to the king's inquiry with a positive oracle: "Go up and triumph; Yahweh will give it into the hand of the king." Something about Micaiah's answer or the way he gives it—his tone of voice, his expression, his gesture, or something, the text does not explain just what—warns Ahab that Micaiah is lying. He rebukes Micaiah," How many times shall I adjure you that you speak to me nothing but the truth in the name of Yahweh?" The rebuke itself suggests that Micaiah had a history of lying to the king. At any rate, following the rebuke, Micaiah gives a very unfavorable oracle, and Ahab tells Jehoshaphat, "I told you so." Then Micaiah tells the two monarchs of the vision he had of the deliberations of Yahweh's divine council:

> Therefore hear the word of Yahweh: I saw Yahweh sitting on his throne, and all the host of heaven standing beside him on his right hand and on his left; and Yahweh said, "Who will deceive Ahab, that he may go up and fall at Ramoth-gilead?" And one said one thing, and another said another. Then a spirit came

> forward and stood before Yahweh, saying, "I will deceive him." And Yahweh said to him, "By what means?" And he said, "I will go forth, and will be a lying spirit in the mouth of all his prophets." And he said, "You are to deceive him, and you shall succeed; go forth and do so." Now therefore see, Yahweh has put a lying spirit in the mouth of all these your prophets; Yahweh has spoken evil concerning you.

In this story the true prophet attributes false prophecy to Yahweh's own initiative, to Yahweh's desire to deceive (*pittâ*) and overpower (*yākōl*) Ahab, so that he will go up against Ramoth-gilead and be killed.[17]

Such an explanation of false prophecy sounds strange to Western ears, but before we dismiss it as just an example of unsophisticated, popular theology, we should note that no less a figure than Jeremiah considered such an explanation quite seriously. In response to the bitter message of judgment he was given to announce to Jerusalem, Jeremiah in 4:10 cries out in surprised dismay: "Ah, my Lord Yahweh! Surely you have utterly deceived this people and Jerusalem, saying, 'It shall be well with you'; when actually the sword was at their throat." Later, when his own message of judgment was slow in finding fulfillment, Jeremiah toyed with the frightening possibility that he himself had been deceived by Yahweh. In his lament in Jer 20:7, the prophet uses the same vocabulary that we encountered in the Micaiah ben Imlah story: "O Yahweh, you have deceived me (*pittîtanî*) and I was deceived (*wā᾽eppāt*). You were stronger than I, and you have prevailed (*wattûkāl*)." From a comparison of this text with the other laments of Jeremiah, it seems clear that it was Yahweh's slowness in executing the threatened judgment that exposed the prophet to peril and made him feel that God had deliberately deceived him.[18] In Jer 15:15, he prays, "O Yahweh, you know; remember me and visit me, and take vengeance for me on my persecutors. In your forbearance take me not away; know that for your sake I bear reproach." Three verses later in 15:18, he accuses Yahweh of being "like a deceitful brook, like waters that fail." In 17:15, he quotes the words of his persecutors: "Look, they say to me, 'Where is the word of Yahweh? Let it come!' " The opposition put Jeremiah in a difficult position. He did not want to see destruction come upon his people: "I have not pressed you to send evil, nor have I desired the day of disaster, you know; that which came out of my lips was before your face" (17:16). On the other hand, if the judgment he announced did not come to pass, he was, by the standards of the Deuteronomic law code, a false prophet, and a false prophet, particularly an unpatriotic prophet who undermined the morale of the population, could be legitimately executed (Deut 18:20–22). Thus Jeremiah prays in

17. Cf. Simon J. De Vries, *Prophet Against Prophet* (Grand Rapids, 1978) 44.

18. Cf. William Holladay, *Jeremiah: Spokesman Out of Time* (New York, 1974) 101; J. A. Thompson, *The Book of Jeremiah* (Grand Rapids, 1980) 459.

17:17–18: "Be not a terror to me; you are my refuge in the day of evil. Let those be put to shame who persecute me, but let me not be put to shame; let them be dismayed, but let me not be dismayed; bring upon them the day of evil; destroy them with double destruction." And in Jer 20:10, Jeremiah's opponents, using the same vocabulary of deception found earlier in v. 7 and in 1 Kings 22, say, "Perhaps he will be deceived (*yĕputteh*), then we can overcome (*wĕnûkĕlâ*) him, and take our revenge on him."[19] Jeremiah's opponents are hardly thinking of sexual seduction, and the use of the passive, "perhaps he will be deceived," make it dubious that the opponents, who speak of their own actions with active, first-person plural verb forms, are referring to human attempts to trick Jeremiah. They are more likely expressing the hope that Jeremiah will be unmasked as a false prophet, as one deceived by God, and thus as one on whom they can take vengeance with impunity. Such an interpretation is strongly suggested by a striking parallel in Ezekiel.

In Ezek 14:1–11,[20] a group of Israelite elders comes to the prophet seeking an oracle from Yahweh. God is irritated, however, because these men come to him while still harboring their idols and sins in their heart. In indignation he asks Ezekiel, "Should I allow myself to be consulted by such men?" Then implicitly prohibiting the prophet from responding to their specific inquiry, Yahweh gives a warning instead. If anyone fails to heed this warning to repent, yet goes to the prophet to inquire of Yahweh, Yahweh further threatens:

> I Yahweh will answer him myself; and I will set my face against that man, I will make him a sign and a byword and cut him off from the midst of my people; and you shall know that I am Yahweh. And if the prophet be deceived (*yĕputteh*) and speak a word, I Yahweh have deceived (*pittêtî*) that prophet, and I will stretch out my hand against him, and will destroy him from the midst of my people Israel, and they shall bear their punishment—the punishment of the prophet and the punishment of the inquirer shall be alike. (vv. 7b–10)

This oracle is directed not only against those individuals who, while still holding onto their sins and idols, turn to Yahweh for a word about their future; it is also against those prophets who respond to the inquiries of such individuals without calling them to account for their sins and idols. The prophet who responds to such an individual has been deceived by Yahweh; that prophet will

19. William McKane's attempt to separate vv. 7–9 from 10–12 is based on the unnecessary assumption that the dominant image in vv. 7–9 is sexual seduction (see below) and does not give sufficient weight to the repetition of these key words—the assumption of multiple catchwords is strained (*Jeremiah* 1 [Edinburgh, 1986] 468–69). Far more convincing is the stylistic argument for the unity of the passage presented by D. J. A. Clines and D. M. Gunn, "Form, Occasion and Redaction in Jeremiah 20," *ZAW* 88 (1976) 390–409, especially p. 391.

20. On this passage see especially Moshe Greenberg, *Ezekiel, 1–20* (Garden City, 1983) 254.

share the inquirer's fate. In effect, the deception of the worshiper, who inquires of Yahweh while faithlessly holding onto his sins and idols, and the faithlessness of the prophet, who discharges his office without, as Micah puts it, "declaring to Jacob his transgression and to Israel his sin" (3:8), will be rewarded by Yawheh's own deception. This frightening explanation for the origin of false prophecy fits the circumstances of the Micaiah ben Imlah story and Jeremiah's complaints about the prophets of peace in his day. In both cases an unrepentant king or an unrepentant people inquired of Yahweh seeking confirmation and support for their own crooked ways. They received what they sought, a message of reassurance. But that message was as treacherous as the human hearts who sought it. The message of peace was a lie; it brought death to people and prophet alike. One could well capture the theology of such passages about divine deception in the words of the ancient hymn found in 2 Sam 22:26–27, and Ps 18:26–27:

> With the loyal you show yourself loyal; with the blameless you show yourself blameless; and with the pure you show yourself pure, but with the crooked you show yourself perverse.

In the theology of the Old Testament there comes a point at which Yahweh's patience is overtaxed. When God's people refuse to see and hear, when "they say to the seers, 'Do not see!' and to the prophets, 'Do not prophesy to us what is right; speak to us smooth things, prophesy illusions . . .' " (Isa 30:10), in God's poetic justice they eventually get what they ask for: "For Yahwch has poured out upon you a spirit of deep sleep, and has closed your eyes, the prophets, and covered your heads, the seers" (Isa 29:10). But this theology is not limited to the Old Testament; it is also found in the New Testament. It is expressed clearly in 2 Thess 2:9–12:

> The coming of the lawless one by the activity of Satan will be with all power and with pretended signs and wonders, and with all wicked deception for those who are to perish, because they refused to love the truth and so be saved. Therefore God sends upon them a strong delusion, to make them believe what is false, so that all may be condemned who did not believe the truth but had pleasure in unrighteousness.

Can one trust the gods? Probably not. They are too many, too fickle, too limited, and too devious. Can one trust God? Maybe, but only at the price of obedience and a genuine love for the truth, no matter how unpleasant that truth may be. Without those ingredients in one's response to God, the divine lie remains a distinct and terrifying possibility.

Chapter 12

The Motif of the Weeping God in Jeremiah and Its Background in the Lament Tradition of the Ancient Near East

Jeremiah makes significant use of the traditions of public lament in his prophetic message. He cites a public lament of the people in 14:7–9:[1]

> Though our sins testify against us, O Yahweh, act for the sake of your name. Indeed our apostasies are many, against you we have sinned. O hope of Israel, its saviour in time of trouble, why should you be like an alien in the land, like a traveller turning aside for the night? Why should you be like someone confused, like a warrior who is unable to save? Yet you are in our midst O Yahweh, and we are called by your name; do not forsake us!

In 9:16–19 he calls for the skilled mourning women to come lead a dirge, and he urges them to teach the traditional laments to their daughters and their neighbors:

> Thus says Yahweh of Hosts:
> Consider and summon the mourning women to come,
> and send for the skilled women to come,
> let them hurry and raise a dirge over us,
> that our eyes may run down with tears,
> and our eyelids flow with water,
> For a sound of wailing is heard from Zion:
> How we are ruined! We are utterly shamed!
> For we have left the land,
> for they have cast down our dwellings.
> Hear, O women, the word of Yahweh,
> and let your ears receive the word of his mouth;
> teach your daughters a dirge,
> and each of you teach your neighbour a lament.

In the Jeremianic texts that actually cite the words of a lament at least three different voices may be identified.

Author's note: This paper was prepared while I was in the service of the University of Stellenbosch as guest lecturer.

1. All the translations from the Hebrew are my own.

(1) There is the voice of the people which may be recognized by the use of the third person plural. The public lament in 14:7–9 cited above is a clear example of this voice.

(2) There is also a feminine voice of the city or state personified as a woman and seen as the mother of her people. A clear example of this voice may be seen in 10:17–21. The text begins with a feminine singular imperative: "Gather up your bundle from the ground, O you who live under siege!" Then, after God announces what he is going to do to the inhabitants of the land, the city or land addressed in verse 17 takes up a lament:

> Woe is me because of my hurt!
> My wound is severe.
> But I said, "Truly this is my punishment,
> and I must bear it."
> My tent is plundered and all my cords arc broken;
> my children have gone out from me, and they are no more;
> there is no one to spread my tent again,
> and to set up my curtains.
> For the shepherds were stupid,
> and did not inquire of Yahweh;
> therefore they did not prosper,
> and all their flock is scattered.

(3) Finally, there is a third voice, usually identified as the voice of the prophet. This is the voice that has led to the characterization of Jeremiah as the weeping prophet. Three passages are of primary significance in this portrait of the prophet: 8:18–9:3; 14:17–18; 4:19–21. It is Jer 8:23, in particular, which has led to the characterization of Jeremiah as "the weeping prophet" (Holladay 1986:295). There, in the context of a larger lament, the speaker, normally assumed to be Jeremiah, cries out:

> Would that my head were water, and my eye a fountain of tears, that I might weep day and night for the slain of my dear people.

Jer 14:17–18 is also commonly regarded as supporting this portrait of the prophet, particularly the command addressed to the prophet in verse 17:

> And you shall say to them this word:
> Let my eyes run down with tears night and day,
> and let them not cease.
> For the virgin daughter—my people—has been broken with a mighty blow,
> with a very grievous wound.

The lament in Jer 4:19–21 may also be cited in more general support of this portrayal, though it does not use the precise vocabulary of weeping.

The assumption that the speaker of these passages should be identified with Jeremiah has hardly been challenged in the scholarly literature, even though that identification of the speaker is less than certain. Each of these passages contains certain features that suggest the speaker is Yahweh himself, not his prophetic spokesman:

(1) the lament in 4:19–21 is concluded in verse 22 by a comment by Yahweh without any indication of a change in speaker;

(2) the lament in 8:23 is followed by a lament in 9:1–2, whose speaker must be Yahweh unless one resorts to textual emendation; and

(3) since 14:17 is introduced as a word Yahweh commands Jeremiah to speak, it is more natural to take the first person pronouns as referring to Yahweh rather than to Jeremiah. Nonetheless, few commentators have seriously suggested that these passages portray Yahweh as a weeping God. This is surprising, given the recent popularity of the theological concept of God as a God who suffers with his people. In his 1962 book on the prophets, Abraham Heschel, who was in many ways a precursor of this recent trend, emphasized God's passionate involvement with his people.[2] Heschel (1962:111 note 4) even observed that the early rabbinic commentators of the Lamentations Rabbah saw God, not the prophet, as the one weeping in Jer 8:23.[3] Yet Heschel (1962:111) was unwilling to go that far. According to Heschel, "A sense of delicacy prevented the prophet from spelling out the meaning of the word: 'Mourn My people for Me as well. . . .' These words are aglow with a divine pathos that can be reflected but not pronounced: God is mourning Himself." Thus while God's sorrow is communicated through the prophet's tears, the prophet does not dare to speak of God himself weeping. Most recent treatments of the suffering of God in the Old Testament have not gone beyond

2. Note especially the following comments: "Israel's distress was more than a human tragedy. With Israel's distress came the affliction of God, His displacement, His homelessness in the land, in the world" (p. 112). "What convulsed the prophet's whole being was God. His condition was a state of suffering in sympathy with divine pathos" (p. 118). "The modes of prophetic sympathy are determined by the modes of the divine pathos. The pathos of love and the pathos of anger awake corresponding tones in the heart of the prophet. . . . Through insight into the nexus between prophetic emotion and divine pathos, it is possible to gain a clue to the meaning behind the conflicting and confusing emotions of Jeremiah's mind" (p. 119).

3. For a translation of the relevant passages from Lamentations Rabbah, see Jacob Neusner 1989: 16, 73, 111, 182–83. Note especially the following passage (p. 182):

> "Oh that my head were waters, and my eyes a fountain of tears that I may weep day and night for the slain of the daughter of my people" (Jer 8:23). Who said this verse? If you wish to suggest that Jeremiah said it, it is not possible for someone not to eat, drink, or sleep (and only mourn and weep all day long). But it is only the Holy One, blessed be He, who said it, for he never sleeps: "Behold, he who keeps Israel neither slumbers nor sleeps" (Ps 121:4).

Heschel in this regard, though Terence Fretheim's book (1984) on the suffering of God is a welcome exception.[4]

Though most commentators give no reasoned argument for rejecting God as the weeping figure, the comments that are made suggest that the anthropomorphisms involved in such a portrait of God are simply too striking for most commentators to entertain seriously. If one could demonstrate that such imagery stood in a long tradition of public lamentation, however, it might force critics to look at this possibility with a new openness. That is the purpose of this paper.

One may begin with God's lament in Jer 12:7–13, noting especially verses 7–8:

> I have abandoned my house, I have deserted my heritage;
> I have given the beloved of my soul into the hand of her enemies.
> My heritage became to me like a lion in the forest;
> she roared against me, therefore I hated her.

There is no question that God is the speaker of this lament. Nor is there any question that it combines the motif of divine abandonment and harsh judgment on God's people with the motif of his love for them. The expression *yedidû napšî*, 'the beloved of my soul', shows clearly enough that God's judgment on his people is not that of an uninvolved schoolmaster. God is passionately devoted to his people, but their hostility toward him has driven him to punish them.

This combination of a deity's abandonment of his or her people despite the deity's passionate love for them has a very old history in the lament literature of the ancient Near East. It is particularly well illustrated in the abundant lament literature from ancient Mesopotamia. It is a standard feature in the five classic Sumerian city laments:[5] (1) the Lamentation over Ur (LU), (2) the Lamentation over Sumer and Ur (LSU), (3) the Lamentation over Nippur (LN); (4) the Lamentation over Eridu (LEr), and (5) the Lamentation over Uruk (LW).[6] Each of these lamentations, all of which seem to date to the same

4. Note especially his comments on pp. 160–61:

> The suffering of prophet and God are so interconnected that it is difficult to sort out who is speaking in many texts. Nor should one try to make too sharp a distinction. As if with one voice, prophet and God express their anguish over the suffering of the people. . . . These texts should be interpreted in terms of the prophet's embodiment of God's mourning. . . . At the least, Jeremiah's mourning is an embodiment of the anguish of God, showing the people the genuine pain God feels over the hurt that his people are experiencing.

5. For this analysis of the classic city laments see Green 1984:253–79, especially p. 253.
6. For this listing see Vanstiphout 1980:83–89.

general period, some years after the fall of Ur III (2006 B.C.) and prior to the end of the reign of Ishme-Dagan of Isin (1953–1935 B.C.),[7] follows the same general thematic pattern with individual differences in focus and elaboration (cf. Green 1984:253–79, especially 253). Together they present the collapse and the revival of Sumer in five major themes: destruction, assignment of responsibility, abandonment, restoration, and return (Green 1984:253–79). The decision to destroy the city is normally made by Enlil and the other high gods in the divine council. The god and goddess of the affected city often try to change the council's mind, but to no avail, and though they weep bitterly over the fate of their city, they must nonetheless leave the city, abandoning it to its fate. A few citations will suffice to show how these laments combine the weeping of these deities with their abandonment of their cities.

The Lamentation over Ur begins with a long list of deities that have abandoned their houses (Pritchard 1969:455–63). The city is then called upon to set up a bitter lament, and in response to that lament the god weeps: "Thy lament which is bitter—how long will it grieve thy weeping lord? Thy lament which is bitter—how long will grieve the weeping Nanna?" (Pritchard 1969:456). In the third section of the lament the city goddess speaks: "To Anu the water of my eye verily I poured out; to Enlil I in person verily made supplication" (Pritchard 1969:458). When this was to no avail, she had to leave her city. "Its lady like a flying bird departed from her city; Ningal like a flying bird departed from her city" (Pritchard 1969:459). Or again, "Mother Ningal in her city like an enemy stood aside. The woman loudly utters the wail for her attacked house; the princess in Ur, her attacked shrine, bitterly cries . . ." (Pritchard 1969:460). "Her eyes are flooded with tears; bitterly she weeps" (Pritchard 1969:461). Her people complain, "O my queen, verily thou art one who has departed from the house; thou art one who has departed from the city. How long, pray, wilt thou stand aside in the city like an enemy? O Mother Ningal, how long wilt thou hurl challenges in the city like an enemy? Although thou art a queen beloved of her city, thy city . . . thou hast abandoned; Although thou art a queen beloved of her people, thy people . . . thou hast abandoned" (Pritchard 1969:462).

There are similar descriptions of Enki and Damgalnunna, the god and goddess of Eridu, in the Eridu Lament:[8]

> Its lord stayed outside his city as if it were an alien city. He wept bitter tears. Father Enki stayed outside his city as if it were an alien city. He wept bitter tears. For the sake of his harmed city, he wept bitter tears. Its lady, like a flying bird, left her city. The mother of the Lofty Temple, the pure one, Damgalnunna, left her city. (Green 1978:133, lines 10–15)

7. Compare Piotr Michalowski (1989:6).
8. For the translation of this lament, see Green 1978:127–67.

The anguish of both god and goddess is expressed in exceedingly graphic terms:

> Its lady, the faithful cow, the compassionate one, the pure one, Damgalnunna, claws at her breast, claws at her eyes. She utters a frenzied cry. She held dagger and sword in her two hands—they clash together. She tears out her hair like rushes, uttering a bitter lament. . . . Enki, king of the Abzu, felt distressed, felt anxious. At the words of his beloved, he wailed to himself. He lay down and fasted. (Green 1978:139–41)

The Lamentation over Sumer and Ur gives a long list of gods and goddesses who leave their dwellings, all the while mourning for their city. With some small variations the formula runs as follows:

> Zababa took an unfamiliar path away from his beloved dwelling, Mother Bau was lamenting bitterly in her Urukug: "Alas, the destroyed city, my destroyed temple!" bitterly she cries. (Michalowski 1989:42–43, lines 116–18)

When Enlil rejects the moon god's plea for pity on his city, the moon god's reaction is described as follows:

> Then, (upon hearing this), His Majesty, the Noble Son, became distraught, Lord Ashimbabbar, the Noble Son, grieved, Nanna, who loves his city, left his city, Suen took an unfamiliar path away from his beloved Ur, Ningal . . . in order to go to an alien place, quickly clothed herself (and) left the city. (All) the Anunna stepped outside of Ur. (Michalowski 1989:58–61, lines 371–77)

One could go on, but these citations should be sufficient to make the point that the motif of the weeping deity who must abandon its city is a common feature of these classic Sumerian city laments. Moreover this feature is preserved in the later, more general Balag laments that began to be composed in the Old Babylonian period around 1900 B.C. and which continued to be copied and used in the cult into the Seleucid era (Cohen 1988:39). One example of this motif from one of these later Balags must suffice:

> Nammu, the mother of Enki, went out from the city. Her hands become heavy through wailing. She cries bitter tears. She beats her chest like a holy drum. She cries bitter tears. "Enki keeps away from Eridu!" "Damgalnunna keeps away from Eridu! Oh my city!" she says. "The ruined city! My destroyed house!" shall I call out faithfully. (Cohen 1988:85)

Mesopotamian laments of the motif of the weeping god who nonetheless abandons his beloved people do not necessarily prove that the motif was known in the west, in Canaan and Israel. Given our limited extrabiblical West Semitic sources and the nature of our biblical sources, it is difficult to be certain of the degree of Mesopotamian influence on the West Semitic lament tradition. Nonetheless, there are indications that such influence, whenever it originated, did exist.[9] The Mesopotamian Balag laments were used in ceremonies during the razing of sacred buildings in need of repair, lest the deity become angry at the tearing down of his sacred house (Cohen 1988:39; Gwaltney 1983:197–98). Many of these Balag laments were also paired with Ershemma laments in the liturgy of the gala-priests (Cohen 1988:44; Gwaltney 1983:99). The Ershemmas often combined mythological narratives with wails over catastrophes, and the capture and death of Dumuzi is one of seven mythological themes that recur in these texts (Cohen 1981:20–21). Such lamentation over the death of Dumuzi was also practiced in Jerusalem in Jeremiah's time, as Ezek 8:14 indicates:

> Then he brought me to the entrance of the north gate of the house of Yahweh; women were sitting there weeping for Tammuz.

Moreover, this reference to the women lamenting for Tammuz comes just two verses after Ezeḳiel quotes a saying of his people to the effect that God has abandoned his people: "For they say, 'Yahweh does not see us, Yahweh has forsaken the land' " (8:12; 9:9).

This at least suggests the possibility that aspects of the Mesopotamian lament tradition were known in the west and used by the skilled mourning women (Jer 9:17) in Israelite laments when disasters of various sorts suggested God's absence from the land. One should note that the motif of God abandoning his people plays a central role in the Israelite public lament cited in Jer 14:7–9: "Why have you become like an alien in the land, like a traveler who turned aside to spend the night?"

The presence of similar motifs and the indication that Israel was familiar with the Tammuz mythology suggest that the Mesopotamian lament tradition exercised some influence on the practice of public laments in Israel. One would hardly expect the Mesopotamian tradition to be taken over unchanged, however. In Israel, Yahweh was not only the city God of Jerusalem, he was the supreme deity. There could be no thought of a higher God imposing a judgment on Yahweh's people. The judgment must be rendered by Yahweh himself. Rather than finding the conflict between divine anger and divine compassion in the conflict between gods, Israel must root that conflict in the heart of a single deity. Moreover, since Yahweh, at least in prophetic thought, had no consort,[10] one could not take over the motif of the weeping goddess without adapting it. Israel did that by turning the weeping city goddess into the personified city as

9. The notion of any Sumerian influence on Israelite lament literature was rejected by McDaniel 1968:198–209, but his arguments are not persuasive. For the contrary opinion, see especially the judicious discussion of Gwaltney, Jr. 1983:191–211.

10. The inscriptions from Kuntillet Ajrud as well as the prophetic critiques against idolatry make it clear that in some circles of Israelite religious thought Yahweh did have a consort, his Asherah.

the mother of her people. In this light one may take a new look at the identity of the speaker in Jer 4:19–22; 8:18–9:3; and 14:17–18. All of Jer 4:19–22 may be understood as spoken by the deity. The graphic description of God's anguish in verse 19a has close parallels in the Mesopotamian lament tradition, and much of the vocabulary used is used of God elsewhere in the prophet literature:

My bowels, my bowels! I must writhe in pain!
The walls of my heart!
My heart is in tumult within me!
I cannot keep silent. (Jer 4:19)

The term *meʿim*, 'bowels', is used in Isa 63:15 and Jer 31:20 to refer to God's mercy. The latter passage is particularly striking, since it construes *meʿim* with the verb *hamah*, 'to be in tumult', and expresses a very similar thought of God's passionate love for his people:

Is Ephraim my dear son?
Is he my darling child?
As often as I speak against him,
I still remember him.
Therefore my bowels are in tumult for him;
I will surely have mercy upon him, says Yahweh. (Jer 31:20)

Moreover, the expression "to keep silence" is often used of God when confronted with serious provocation (Isa 42:14; Hab 1:13; Ps 50:21). In Isa 42:13–15, just as in our passage, God can no longer keep silent, but like a woman in travail will now cry out and avenge himself:

Yahweh goes forth like a soldier,
like a warrior he stirs up his fury;
he cries out, he shouts aloud,
he shows himself mighty against his foes.
For a long time I have held my peace,
I have kept still and restrained myself;
now I will cry out like a woman in labor,
I will gasp and pant.
I will lay waste mountains and hills,
and will dry up all their herbage;
I will turn the rivers into islands,
and dry up the pools.

The cause of God's anguish in Jeremiah 4 is the destruction that has come upon his people:

For I have heard the sound of the trumpet,
my soul the shout of war.
Disaster upon disaster is encountered,

for the whole land is plundered.
Suddenly my tents are plundered;
in a moment my curtains.
How long must I see the standard?
How long must I hear the sound of the trumpet? (4:19b–21)

While the reference to "my tents" and "my curtains" could be taken as the words of the personified city as in 10:20, the context in chapter 4 suggests that God is the speaker here. Where the city is the speaker in 10:20, God is referred to in the third person: "For the shepherds were stupid and did not inquire of Yahweh" (10:21). Jer 4:21, however, is followed by a first person reference to God without any hint of a change of speaker:

For my people are fools,
they do not know me.
They are foolish children,
they are not wise.
They are wise only to do evil,
but they do not know how to do good. (4:22)

Holladay tries to avoid this point by drawing a sharp distinction between the tone of Jer 4:19–21 and verse 22. According to Holladay (1986:147–48 and 151), the prophet's emotional outburst in 4:19–21 is followed in 4:22 by a divine response which he characterizes as a purely objective, totally unemotional response of a schoolmaster marking his students: do well—pass; do poorly—fail. Such a distinction is far from obvious. Holladay (1986:304) recognizes that God begins a lament in 9:9 and again in 12:7, when he makes the insightful comment, ". . . here is a passage in which divine pathos and judgment are blended." In my opinion the same should be said for 4:19–22.

If God is the only speaker in Jer 4:19–22, there are several changes of speaker in Jer 8:18–9:11. It begins with God expressing his grief over his people: "My joy is gone, grief is upon me, my heart is sick" (8:18). God gives the reason for this grief by quoting the cry of his people: "Hark, the cry of my poor people from far and wide in the land: 'Is Yahweh not in Zion? Is her King not in her?' " (8:19a). God is no more pleased by this comment of the people in Jeremiah than he was by the similar comment of the people in Ezek 8:12 and 9:10, and God interrupts his quotation of the people's cry with the angry question, "Why have they provoked me to anger with their images, with their foreign idols?" God then finishes quoting the people, "The harvest is past, the summer is ended, and we are not saved" (8:19b), before reverting to the theme of his own sorrow at this state of affairs:

For the hurt of my poor people I am hurt,
I mourn, and dismay has taken hold of me.
Is there no balm in Gilead?

Is there no physician there?
Why then has the health of my poor people not been restored?
O that my head were a spring of water,
and my eyes a fountain of tears,
so that I might weep day and night
for the slain of my poor people. (8:21–23)

God's sorrow is so great he expresses the desire to desert his people, for their wickedness allows God no alternative but to continue punishing them:

O that I had in the desert a traveller's lodging place,
that I might leave my people and go away from them!
For they are all adulterers, a band of traitors,
they bend their tongues like bows;
they have grown strong in the land for falsehood, and not for truth;
for they proceed from evil to evil, and they do not know me,
says Yahweh. (9:1–3)

Unless one emends the text in 9:2, it is clear that God must be the speaker in 9:1ff. But since 9:1 opens with the same idiom as the preceding verse, there is no reason to separate these two verses and assign them different speakers. In 9:3–11 God continues speaking, describing his people's sins and threatening to bring them into judgment. The MT of 9:9 has God explicitly announcing that he will take up a lamentation over his land:

I will take up weeping and wailing for the mountains,
and a lamentation for the pastures of the wilderness,
because they are laid waste so that no one passes through,
and the lowing of cattle is not heard;
both the birds of the air and the animals have fled and are gone.

Jeremiah 14:17–18 begins with God's command to his prophet to quote his word to the people. That suggests that the first person pronoun in the quotation that follows refers to God, not the prophet. It is God who is weeping. Verse 18, then, uses very anthropomorphic imagery when it speaks of God going out into the field or entering the city to see the desolation, but such imagery is not without its parallels in the older lament tradition. Note, moreover, that this description of the desolation of the land is followed by a note about the people's lack of knowledge, a motif found in the same position in this oracle that it occupies in 4:22 and 9:3. God's statement of his sorrow is then followed in 4:19 by the people's response, in which they accuse God of totally rejecting them.

If the argument of this paper is sound, the ancient Near Eastern lament tradition offered the prophet Jeremiah very striking anthropomorphic imagery for expressing God's passionate involvement with his people, and Jeremiah exploited that possibility to the full. The ancient rabbis were correct; rather than speaking of the weeping prophet, one should speak of Jeremiah's weeping

God. This portrait of a God who weeps over the people he must punish is also encountered in the figure of Jesus who laments over Jerusalem:

> Jerusalem Jerusalem, the city that kills the prophets and stones those who are sent to it! How often have I desired to gather your children together as a hen gathers her brood under her wings, and you were not willing. See your house is left to you desolate. (Matt 23:37–38)

Bibliography

Alster, B. (ed.) 1980. *Death in Mesopotamia: Papers Read at the XXVIe Recontre assyriologique internationale.* Copenhagen: Akademisk Forlag (Mesopotamia: Copenhagen Studies in Assyriology 8).

Cohen, M. E. 1981. *Sumerian Hymnology: The Ershemma.* Cincinnati: HUC (HUCAS 2).

_____. 1988. *The Canonical Lamentations of Ancient Mesopotamia I–II.* Potomac: Capital Decisions.

Fretheim, T. R. 1984. *The Suffering God: An Old Testament Perspective.* Philadelphia: Fortress (Overtures to Biblical Theology).

Green, M. W. 1978. The Eridu Lament. *JCS* 30, 127–67.

_____. 1984. The Uruk Lament. *JAOS* 104, 253–79.

Gwaltney, W. C., Jr. 1983. "The Biblical Book of Lamentations in the Context of Near Eastern Lament Literature," in Hallo, W. W., Moyer, J. C., and Perdue, L. G. (ed.) 1983:191–211.

Hallo, W. W.; Moyer, J. C.; and Perdue, L. G. (ed.) 1983. *Scripture in Context II: More Essays on the Comparative Method.* Winona Lake, Ind.: Eisenbrauns.

Heschel, A. J. 1962. *The Prophets.* New York/Evanston: Harper & Row.

Holladay, W. L. 1986. *Jeremiah I: A Commentary on the Book of Jeremiah, Chapters 1–25.* Philadelphia: Fortress.

McDaniel, T. F. 1968. The Alleged Sumerian Influence upon Lamentations. *VT* 18, 198–209.

Michalowski, P. 1989. *The Lamentation over the Destruction of Sumer and Ur.* Winona Lake, Ind.: Eisenbrauns.

Neusner, J. 1989. *Lamentations Rabbah: An Analytical Translation.* Atlanta: Scholars (Brown Judaic Studies 193).

Pritchard, J. B. (ed.) 1969. *Ancient Near Eastern Texts Relating to the Old Testament (ANET).* 3d ed. Princeton: Princeton University Press.

Vanstiphout, H. L. J. 1980. The Death of an Era: The Great Morality in Sumerian City Laments, in Alster, B. (ed). 1980:83–89.

Chapter 13

Whose Child Is This? Reflections on the Speaking Voice in Isaiah 9:5

In his 1947 article, "Das judäische Königsritual," Gerhard von Rad argued that the Judean enthronement ritual was heavily dependent on the corresponding Egyptian ritual.[1] He argued persuasively that the חק of Ps 2:7, he עדות of 2 Kgs 11:12, and the ברית of Ps 89:40 were all simply different designations of the same reality, the Judean counterpart of the Egyptian *nḫb.t*, the royal protocol that the deity writes and presents to the new king along with the crown at the time of the latter's coronation.[2] The Egyptian protocol contained the five names of the new pharaoh's titulary and the legitimation of his rule by the deity's acknowledgment of the king as the deity's child. Von Rad argued that both of these elements also appeared in the Judean ritual. Ps 2:7 quotes from the protocol marking Yahweh's legitimation of the new Davidic king as God's son, while Isa 9:5 reflects the king's divine sonship as well as his five-fold royal titulary. In making this argument, von Rad suggested that the speaker in Isa 9:5 was not the people, but the deity.[3] In 1950, von Rad's teacher, Albrecht Alt, published his justly famous study, "Befreiungsnacht und Krönungstag," in which he applied von Rad's insights to Isa 8:23–9:6 in great detail.[4] He argued that the Isaiah passage was composed for Hezekiah's enthronement, that it reflected the strong influence of Egyptian enthronement rituals, that verse 5 referred not to the birth of an actual child but to the legitimation of the new king at his coronation, and that the names are enthronement names parallel to the fivefold titulary of the Egyptian kings. Alt differed from von Rad, however, in identifying the "we" in verse 5, not as the deity but as heralds whom the Judean royal court sent to the former Israelite territories in the north in an attempt to lure them into joining Judah in accepting Hezekiah as their king.[5]

Author's note: An abbreviated version of this paper was presented in the Egyptology and the History and Culture of Ancient Israel Group at the annual meeting of the Society of Biblical Literature, New Orleans, November 23, 1996.

1. Gerhard von Rad, "Das judäische Königsritual," *ThLZ* 72/4 (1947) 211–16.
2. Ibid., 213–15.
3. Ibid., 216.
4. Albrecht Alt, "Jesaja 8, 23–9, 6. Befreiungsmacht und Krönungstag," in Walter Baumgartner, ed., *Festschrift Alfred Bertholet zum 80. Geburtstag gewidmet* (Tübingen: Mohr/Siebeck, 1950) 29–49; reprinted in Albrecht Alt, *Kleine Schriften zur Geschichte des Volkes Israel* (3 vols.; Munich: C. H. Beck'sche Verlagsbuchhandlung, 1953) 2.206–25.
5. Alt, "Befreiungsmacht und Krönungstag," 44–45 (= idem, *Kleine Schriften*, 2.221–22).

Contemporary Critique of the Alt–von Rad Consensus

Despite this slight difference in understanding, these two studies created an impressive consensus that dominated the interpretation of the Isaiah passage for a significant period. Certain weaknesses in presentation, however, left their general understanding of the passage open to criticism. In recent years critics have begun to erode the older consensus by attacking these vulnerable spots. It is, nonetheless, my contention that von Rad was fundamentally correct in his assessment of the Isaiah passage and that the apparent points of vulnerability are simply the result of von Rad failing to push his insights far enough.

While both Alt and von Rad emphasized the Egyptian influence on the Judean enthronement ritual, both also drew a sharp distinction between the Egyptian and Judean conceptions of the human king's divine sonship.[6] According to them, Egyptians understood the coronation announcement that the deity had begotten the new king mythologically: the king was the actual physical offspring of the deity and therefore shared the divine nature. In Judah, by contrast, that announcement was a legal formula of adoption. The Davidic king was not the physical offspring of Yahweh but merely the god's "adopted" son. This approach to understanding the language of Ps 2:7 seemed to work well there,[7] but it did provide an opening for critics to attack von Rad and Alt's understanding of the sonship language of Isa 9:5.

Isa 9:5 differs from Ps 2:7 in employing the passive construction and in the use of the noun ילד ("child") for the offspring of the deity. Many scholars who were willing to understand the statement in Ps 2:7 as an adoption formula could not see the Isaiah formulation in the same light.[8] According to these critics, in the accession oracle God speaks directly to the king, and the term ילד never applies to an adult king.[9] Adoption language, moreover, is always active, whereas the passive form commonly refers to actual physical birth. Pushing this argument even further, Simon Parker has pointed out that Isa 9:5 evidences features of the traditional birth announcement, a fact that he thinks

6. Von Rad, "Das judäische Königsritual," 214; Alt, "Befreiungsmacht und Krönungstag," 42–43 (= idem, *Kleine Schriften*, 2.218–19).

7. This understanding of Ps 2:7 appears already in Hermann Gunkel, *Ausgewählte Psalmen übersetzt und erklärt* (3d ed.; Göttingen: Vandenhoeck & Ruprecht, 1911) 13–14.

8. Hans-Joachim Kraus, "Jesaja 9,5–6 (6–7)," in Georg Eichholz, ed., *Herr, tue Meine Lippen auf: Eine Predigthilfe*, 5 (Wuppertal: Muller, 1961) 43–53; Theodor Lescow, "Das Geburtsmotiv in den messianischen Weissagungen bei Jesaja und Micha," *ZAW* 79 (1967) 172–207; Dieter Vieweger, "'Das Volk, das durch das Dunkel zieht . . .': Neue Überlegungen zu Jes (8, 23aβb) 9, 1–6," *BZ* n.s. 36/1 (1992) 77–86; and Paul D. Wegner, "A Re-Examination of Isaiah IX 1–6," *VT* 42 (1992) 103–12.

9. Kraus, "Jesaja 9,5–6 (6–7)," 47; Lescow, "Das Geburtsmotiv," 182–84; Vieweger, "Das Volk, das durch das Dunkel zieht . . .'," 82; Wegner, "A Re-examination," 104.

lends further support to the arguments against the adoptionist-coronation interpretation of the Isaiah passage.[10]

Still another significant objection to von Rad's interpretation is that he had to assume a change of speaker at v. 5. Verses 2–3 address Yahweh in the second person, but according to von Rad the deity is the speaker in v. 5.[11] Yet there is no orthographic marker in the text to indicate this shift in speaker.

R. A. Carlson[12] and, after him, Paul Wegner[13] also object that von Rad and Alt vastly overstated the Egyptian background to the royal names, suggesting that they more closely resemble Assyrian material, This assertion does not create serious problems for von Rad's thesis because it is patently false. Carlson's treatment of the Akkadian royal epithets as the background for the names in Isa 9:5 is hardly compelling. He quickly dismisses the explanation of the peculiar orthography in Isa 9:6 as evidence for a missing fifth name, though he offers no adequate explanation for the peculiar orthography.[14] Then he makes the presence of only four names significant for Isaiah's purpose. According to him, the prophet uses four names in response to the Assyrian king's claim to be "king of the four quarters.[15] There is absolutely nothing in the names themselves to suggest such a connection. Carlson then argues that the name *peleʾ yôʿēṣ* ("wonderful counselor") is a pun on the Assyrian king's name *Tiglat pilʾeser,*[16] but the two names have only the faintest resemblance to one another, and even then only if one ignores the first part of the Assyrian king's name. Carlson also argues with regard to the name אביעד ("father of eternity") that the epithet *abu* ("father") is proper to the Akkadian royal titulary, citing a text from Hammurabi. According to Carlson, "Tiglath-pileser may be termed *abu*, the heir of David is *ʾăbi-ʿad*, 'father forever'."[17] Isaiah, however, lived a thousand years after Hammurabi, and a search of Tiglath-pileser's inscriptions suggests the absence of *abu* among his royal epithets. Carlson asserts that his "interpretations of the Messianic titelage [sic] . . . presupposes a thorough acquaintance, on the prophet's part, with these epithets attached to the Assyrian king, namely Tiglath-pileser,"[18] but Carlson's article gives no evidence that he investigated what epithets Tiglath-pileser actually used. The most one can say

10. Simon B. Parker, "The Birth Announcement," in Lyle Eslinger and Glen Taylor, eds., *Ascribe to the Lord: Biblical & Other Studies in Memory of Peter C. Craigie* (JSOTSup 67; Sheffield: JSOT Press, 1988) 137.

11. Von Rad, "Das judäische Königsritual," 216.

12. R. A. Carlson, "The Anti-Assyrian Character of the Oracle in Is. IX 1–6," *VT* 24 (1974) 130–35.

13. Wegner, "A Re-examination," 105.

14. Carlson, "The Anti-Assyrian Character," 131–32.

15. Ibid., 133.

16. Ibid., 133.

17. Ibid., 134.

18. Ibid., 134.

for Carlson's effort is that a certain very general resemblance exists between the ideas about kingship in Judah and Assyria, but one could say the same thing for Babylon, the Hittite kingdom, Ugarit, and Egypt. The actual names in Isa 9:5, however, are far more similar (both in their syntactical structure and in their meaning) to those occurring in the Egyptian royal titularies than to the royal epithets in Akkadian, Hittite, or Ugaritic texts.

Adoption and Adoption Formulae

To return to the more difficult problem, then, how is one to account for the linguistic differences between Isa 9:5 and Ps 2:7? The problem arises from the generally held assumption that the statement in Ps 2:7, "You are my son, today I have begotten you," is a legal formula of adoption. Nonetheless, despite the ubiquity of this claim in the secondary literature, the evidence for the claim is not impressive. The meager evidence has been conveniently assembled in two recent studies by Shalom M. Paul[19] and Jeffrey H. Tigay.[20] Before looking at this evidence in detail, however, one should note how foreign the metaphor of adoption was to Israel's own culture. As Paul notes, "no laws pertaining to adoption are found in the biblical legal corpora,"[21] and as Tigay observes, "the very institution of adoption was rare—if at all existent—in Israel."[22] One may well ask, then, where an Israelite or Judean theologian of the royal court would find the necessary model for the adoption metaphor.

In any case, when turning to the formulae actually attested in adoption contracts, one finds ample attestation of solemn declarations of the *dissolution* of adoptive ties. The adoption contracts often spell out the penalty if the adoptive parent renounces the adopted child or if the adopted child renounces the adoptive parent or parents. Thus the renunciation formulae *ul marī atta* ("you are not my son"), *ul abī atta* ("you are not my father"), and *ul ummī attī* ("you are not my mother") are extremely common in the documents. Despite the impression that the secondary literature leaves, however, *positive* declarations associated with the *creation* of adoptive ties are very rare, if attested at all. Scholars originally assumed the existence of such positive declarations simply on the basis of the negative declarations actually attested. Martin David in his fundamental work on Old Babylonian adoption thus argued from these negative declarations

> that in connection with the dissolution (of an adoptive relationship) originally specific formal expressions will have been used. If this is correct, however, it

---

19. Shalom M. Paul, "Adoption Formulae: A Study of Cuneiform and Biblical Legal Clauses," *Maarav* 2/2 (1979–80) 173–85.

20. Jeffrey H. Tigay, "Adoption," *EncJud* (1971) 2.300–301.

21. Paul, "Adoption Formulae," 173.

22. Tigay, "Adoption," 300–301.

> allows one to suppose that also in connection with the entrance into the adoptive relationships corresponding phrases have found employment; in other words, that the adoption contract possibly has been connected originally with the saying of solemn declarations. In connection with a giving into adoption this may have been something like: "You are his father, you are my child"; when an Arrogation (adoption of an adult) was involved: "You are my father," or "you are my child."[23]

David went on to admit, however, that these suppositions were purely hypothetical until one could find textual sources to support them.[24] David could only find two examples of such positive formulations in the Akkadian texts, and Paul in his recent summary article has only been able to add one more. I shall look at these examples in some detail but will state at the outset that none of these examples contains the positive formula *atta marī* ("you are my son"), allegedly the background to Ps 2:7.

The closest approximation to this formulation is found in the Code of Hammurabi §170:37–59:

> If a man's wife bore him children and his female slave also bore him children, if the father during his lifetime has ever said, *maru*(DUMU^{meš})-*ú-a* (§170:45), "My children!" to the children whom the slave bore him, thus having counted them with the children of the first wife, after the father has gone to (his) fate, the children of the first wife and the children of the slave shall share equally in the goods of the paternal estate, with the firstborn, the son of the first wife, receiving a preferential share.[25]

On a formal level, the formulation in the Code of Hammurabi lacks the second person independent pronoun, but more substantively, the children in this text are the physical offspring of the speaker. Taking this passage as the background to Ps 2:7 could well allow one to read the formula in the Psalm not as an attempt to deny the physical engenderment of the king by Yahweh but as an acknowledgment and legitimation of the physical kinship between Yahweh and the king that had existed even prior to this legitimation.

David's second example appears in an Old Babylonian contract in which a certain Zuḫuntum had handed over her child to the priestess Iltani for wet-nursing.[26] When Zuḫuntum was unable to pay the fee for three years of wet-nursing, she said to Iltani, "Take the child. Let him be your son" (*tablī ṣuḫaram*

23. Martin David, *Die Adoption im altbabylonischen Recht* (Leipziger Rechtswissenschaftliche Studien, 23; Leipzig: Weicher, 1927) 79.

24. Interestingly, he refused to attach much weight to Kohler's attempt to find such support in the formulaic language of Ps 2:7 ("you are my son, today I have begotten you") and Hos 2:1 ("you are not my people") since the dependency of these expressions on the Old Babylonian outlook was by no means obvious. Ibid., 79, n. 42.

25. Author's adaptation of Theophile J. Meeks' translation in *ANET* (3d ed.; 1969) 173.

26. Arthur B. Ungnad, *Vorderasiatische Schriftdenkmäler der Königlichen Museen zu Berlin* (Leipzig: Hinrichs'sche Buchhandlung, 1909) 6, nos. 10–11.

lū maruki).[27] Iltani apparently agreed, paid Zuḫuntum three shekels over and above the unpaid fee for three years of wet-nursing, and thus sealed the contract. One should note that the expression *lū maruki* ("let him be your son") is in the third person and is spoken not by the adoptive parent but by the biological parent. It may be a solemn formula—though it could just as easily be an ordinary expression—but it is not a striking parallel to Ps 2:7. Iltani apparently never said to the child during the adoption proceedings, "You are my son!" (*atta marī*).

The third example, which Paul (following Weinfeld)[28] adds, occurs in the Hittite-Akkadian bilingual of Hattušiliš I.[29] This text describes the king's adoption of an appropriate successor. Because of conflict within his family, Hattušiliš had disowned his sons and his original heir, the son of his sister, and chosen instead Muršiliš I, perhaps a grandson, to be the heir to his throne. With regard to his ultimately disinherited nephew, Hattušiliš said to his council of nobles, "Now I had named to you the young Labarna. Let him sit on the throne. I, the king, have called him son."[30] Later to the same council of nobles he said of Muršiliš, "[Now Muršiliš is my son. You must acknowledge] him [and put] him [on the throne]."[31] While this text does contain two notices of adoption, neither corresponds to Psalm 2. Both of Hattušiliš's statements address the council of nobles, and the references to the adopted sons are third-person references, not second-person address as in Ps 2:7. To repeat, there is as yet no real parallel in the Mesopotamian adoption texts to the positive, second-person formulation of Ps 2:7.

Ps 2:7, moreover, continues with the statement, "today I have begotten you," and one can probably reconstruct the same verbal expression in Ps 110:3, a related coronation psalm. If the expression, "you are my son," is an adoption formula, then how is one to explain, "today I have begotten you"? Tigay understands all of this as part of the adoption formula. "Today" he explains as a typical date formula, and says, "the next phrase may reflect the conception of adoption as a new birth. . . ."[32] His explanation, however, is very dubious. Whatever one may make of the simple use of "today" as a date for-

27. Ibid., no. 10.10–11, no. 11.8–9.

28. Moshe Weinfeld, "The Covenant of Grant in the Old Testament and in the Ancient Near East," *JAOS* 90 (1970) 191; Paul, "Adoption Formulae," 179.

29. Ferdinand Sommer and Adam Falkenstein, *Die Hethitisch-Akkadische Bilingue des Hattusili I. (Labarna II.)* (Abhandlungen der bayerischen Akademie der Wissenschaften, Philosophisch-Historische Abteilung, n.s. 16; Munich: Verlag der bayerischen Akademie der Wissenschaften, 1938).

30. *a-nu-um-ma* TUR-*am la-ba-ar-na [aq-b]i-a-ak-ku-nu-ši-im šu-ú li-it-ta-ša-ab-mi* LUGAL-*ru [al-]si-šu-ma* DUMU(?)-*am.* Ibid., Text A I, 2–4.

31. [*a-nu-um-ma* [1]*mu-ur-ši-li* DUMU-*ri ù šu-wa-a-tu lu-ú ti-da-a ù*] *šu-wa-a-tu* [*šu-ši-ba*]. The restoration is based on the parallel Hittite lines. Ibid., Text A, I 37–38.

32. Tigay, "Adoption," 300.

mula, the Akkadian verb *walādu* ("to give birth"), the equivalent of Hebrew *yālad*, never appears in any Akkadian adoption contract. Since Tigay admits that adoption was not a widespread practice in Israel, if it existed at all, whence does this peculiar use of birth language as a metaphor for adoption come? It does not come from Akkadian adoption texts.

Both Paul and Tigay follow Weinfeld in arguing that the source of this adoption language imagery is the covenants of royal grant.[33] This move, however, does not solve the problem with the birth language ("I have begotten you"), for one still finds no example of *walādu* as a metaphorical way of expressing this new adoptive relationship to the vassal even in such covenants of grant. In fact, one should be hesitant to describe the metaphorical familial language of the political sphere as adoption language at all. To refer to a suzerain as "father," a vassal as "son," or an ally as "brother" characterizes in familial terms the nature of the power relationship between the two treaty partners, but it does not imply a self-conscious adaptation of technical adoption language. The focus is on the relationship, not its genesis. The suzerain is to behave like a father to the vassal, but that does not imply actual adoption. The frequent attempts to bind the vassal to oneself in an actual family relationship most often took the form of political marriage rather than adoption.

In this connection it is worth looking at several of the key examples that Weinfeld cites of such politically motivated adoption. In discussing the language of Ps 89:21–35, he makes the following claim: " 'House' (= dynasty), land and people are then given to David as a fief and as it was the rule in the second millennium this could be legitimized only by adoption."[34] To support his claim that a king could only make a land grant in the second millennium through the fiction of adoption, Weinfeld first cites in a footnote the example of Yarim-Lim of Alalah.[35] In the texts from Alalah, one finds reference to a Yarim-Lim, son of Abba-El, and a Yarim-Lim, son of Hammurabi. Following Albrecht Alt,[36] Weinfeld assumes that these Yarim-Lims are one and the same person. Yarim-Lim's real father was Hammurabi; Abba-El was Yarim-Lim's suzerain, but, according to this thesis, "Abba-El later adopted Yarim-Lim in order to create the legal basis for installing him as king of Haleb."[37] This whole reconstruction, however, rests on thin air. In the first place, one should note that Abba-El installed Yarim-Lim as ruler of Alalaḫ long before the assumed adoption took place. This land grant to Yarim-Lim obviously did not

33. Weinfeld, "Covenant of Grant," 184–203; idem, *Deuteronomy and the Deuteronomic School* (Oxford: Clarendon, 1972) 77–81.

34. Weinfeld, "Covenant of Grant," 191.

35. Ibid., 191, n. 59.

36. Albrecht Alt, "Bemerkungen zu den Verwaltungs- und Rechtsurkunden von Ugarit und Alalach," *WO* 3 (1964) 14–17.

37. Weinfeld, "Covenant of Grant," 191, n. 59.

need the legitimation of adoption. In the second place, there is no textual reference to any adoption at all: it is just a hypothesis based on the different fathers assigned to Yarim-Lim. There is, however, no compelling reason to assume that one is dealing with a single Yarim-Lim, since that was a very popular name in the region. As both William F. Albright and Horst Klengel have persuasively argued, Abba-El of Aleppo (Ḫaleb) and Yarim-Lim of Alalaḫ were probably brothers, both sons of Hammurabi I of Aleppo, while Yarim-Lim, the son of Abba-El, is probably Yarim-Lim II of Aleppo, the real son of Abba-El and the nephew of Yarim-Lim of Alalaḫ.[38] In short, this text cited in Weinfeld's footnote provides no proof of the adoption of a political vassal or of the need for such adoption in order to legitimate a dynastic land grant.

In the text of his article, Weinfeld cites another example to make his point:

> That this is really the case here may be learned from the treaty between Šuppiluliumaš and Mattiwaza.[39] Mattiwaza, in describing how he established relations with Šuppiluliumaš, says: "(The great king) grasped me with [his ha]nd . . . and said: when I will conquer the land of Mitanni I shall not reject you, I shall make you my son, I will stand by (to help in war) and will make you sit on the throne of your father . . . the word which comes out of his mouth will not turn back."[40]

The use Weinfeld makes of this citation is misleading in the extreme. If one did not know better, one might think that the sequence, "I shall make you my son . . . and will make you sit on the throne of your father," meant that Mattiwaza would succeed to the throne of Šuppiluliumaš, his putative adoptive father. Nothing would be further from the truth. Mattiwaza was the son of Tušratta, the king of Mitanni. When Mitanni fell apart after Tušratta's disastrous war against Šuppiluliumaš, Tušratta was assassinated, and Šuttarna seized his throne. Escaping an attempt on his life, Mattiwaza was able to flee to Hittite territory where he received asylum from Šuppiluliumaš. The accounts of these events survive in the texts of the treaty between Šuppiluliumaš and Mattiwaza. There are two recensions of the treaty, one from Mattiwaza's

38. William F. Albright, "Further Observations on the Chronology of Alalakh," *BASOR* 146 (1957) 27; Horst Klengel, *Geschichte Syriens im 2. Jahrtausend v. u. Z.: Teil I-Nordsyrien* (Deutsche Akademie der Wissenschaften zu Berlin, Institut für Orientforschung, 40; Berlin: Akademie Verlag, 1965) 154–55, 208–9.

39. There is a debate among contemporary Hittite scholars whether the name Mattiwaza should be read as Kurtiwaza or Šattiwaza, but that debate is irrelevant for my argument, and to avoid introducing unnecessary confusion I have kept without prejudice the older reading that Weinfeld followed. See Emmanuel Laroche, *Les noms des Hittites* (Études Linguistiques IV; Paris: Librairie C. Klincksieck, 1966) 117; Annelies Kammenhuber, *Die Arier im Vorder-orient* (Heidelberg: Carl Winter/Universitätsverlag, 1968) 81–84; Guy Kestemont, *Diplomatique et droit international en Asie occidentale (1600–1200 av. J.C.)* (Publications de l'Institut Orientaliste de Louvain 9; Louvain-La-Neuve: Université Catholique de Louvain, Institut Orientaliste, 1974) 92 n. 15.

40. Weinfeld, "Covenant of Grant," 191.

standpoint and one from Šuppiluliumaš's.[41] Weinfeld quotes from Mattiwaza's version, but does not bother to inform the reader that Šuppiluliumaš had given his daughter in marriage to Mattiwaza, his new vassal. That is clear from the end of the latter's version of the treaty,[42] but it is even clearer from the Šuppiluliumaš version, which is worth quoting:

> After I grasped Mattiwaza, the son of Tušratta, the king, with my hand, I caused him to sit on the throne of his father. In order that the land of Mitanni, the great land, not perish, I the great king, the king of the land of Hatti, revived the land of Mitanni for the sake of my daughter. Mattiwaza, the son of Tušratta, I grasped in my hand, and I gave to him (my) daughter as his wife. And Mattiwaza, the son of the king, shall surely be king in the land of Mitanni, and the daughter of the king of the land of Hatti shall surely be queen in the land of Mitanni.[43]

The text goes on to forbid Mattiwaza from taking other wives in such a fashion as to diminish the queenly authority of Šuppiluliumaš's daughter. One should note that the term "the king" in this text, when otherwise unspecified, refers to the king of Mitanni. In other words, when the text calls Mattiwaza "the son of the king," it is referring to king Tušratta of Mitanni, not Šuppiluliumaš of Hatti. Contrary to Weinfeld, Mattiwaza's claim on the throne of Mitanni, even if Šuppiluliumaš helped him to make that claim a reality, derived from the fact that he was a real son and rightful heir of Tušratta. Mattiwaza's family tie to Šuppiluliumaš, which was based on marriage to the latter's daughter, not Weinfeld's alleged adoption, did not bolster his legal claim to the throne of Mitanni. In real adoption texts the adopted child inherits the property of his adoptive father, not his biological father; yet Mattiwaza was certainly not a candidate for the Hittite throne.

This shows the danger of putting too much weight on formulaic expressions without attention to the larger context. The Akkadian expression Šuppiluliumaš used in accepting Mattiwaza as a vassal, *ana marūtiya eppuškami* ("I will make you my son"), is an idiom attested in adoption contracts. As the preceding comparison of the two version of the treaty between Šuppiluliumaš and Mattiwaza has nevertheless shown, Šuppiluliumaš actually brought Mattiwaza into his family legally, not by adopting him, but by marrying him to a royal daughter. Dynastic marriage, not adoption, is the basis for familial language in these treaties.

This stricture is even more relevant with regard to language describing divine-human relationships. Weinfeld says, "Hattušiliš I is similarly described as

41. Ernst F. Weidner, *Politische Dokumente aus Kleinasien: Die Staatsverträge in akkadischer Sprache aus dem Archiv von Boghazköi* (Boghazköi-Studien, 8; Leipzig: Hinrichs'sche Buchhandlung, 1923) 1–37 (= no. 1), 37–57 (= no. 2).

42. Weidner, *Politische Dokumente*, 53 (11.35–39).

43. Ibid., 19 (11.56–60).

adopted and legitimized by the sun goddess of Arinna: "She put him into her bosom, grasped his hand and ran (in battle) before him'."[44] Divine nurture language often depicts the gods' concern for their favorites, but such language is not a part of the legal terminology of adoption; there is then absolutely no justification for asserting that the terminology of divine nurture and protection implies anything about adoption. One must also be very cautious in making claims about divine adoption when dealing with Mesopotamian texts that refer to the king as the "son of such and such deity." In Mesopotamia any person could claim to be the son of his or her personal deity, and Mesopotamians conceived of the personal deity as playing an important role in the physical birth of the child. This terminology has therefore little bearing on the question at issue.[45]

One must emphasize this warning against discovering the adoption metaphor everywhere that familial language occurs, because biblical scholars have become far too quick to read adoption into any biblical text that speaks of God as a parent, even in texts where the child concerned is not the king but the people of Israel in general. Paul, for example, says, "The nation 'adopted' by God is called 'Israel, my first born son' in Exod 4:22."[46] Exod 4:22 says nothing about adoption, however. The text reports God's command to Moses to speak to Pharaoh as follows:

> You will say to Pharaoh, thus says Yahweh: "Israel is my first born son, and I said to you, 'Send my son that he may serve me.' But you refused to send him. Now therefore I am about to kill your first born son."[47]

The text focuses on the relationship between Yahweh and Israel, not on how that relationship came to be. Tigay is far more careful on this point than Paul. He refers to several passages (Exod 4:22; Deut 8:5; 14:1) in speaking of the comparison of the relationship between God and Israel to that of father and son, but he immediately adds, "Usually there is no indication that this is meant in an adoptive sense. . . . "[48] Some passages may possibly use adoption language to describe the creation of the parent-child relationship between Yahweh and his people,[49] but other texts use the language of physical birth. Thus Deut 32:18 says, "You were unmindful of the Rock who bore you (*yĕlādĕkā*), and you forgot the God who gave birth to you (*mĕḥōlĕlekā*)." By no stretch of the imagination is this adoption language. It uses birth imagery to indicate the

44. Weinfeld, "Covenant of Grant," 192.

45. M. J. Seux, *Épithètes royales Akkadiennes et Sumériennes* (Paris: Letouzey et Ané, 1967) 159, n. 28.

46. Paul, "Adoption formulae," 178.

47. Exod 4:22–23.

48. Tigay, "Adoption," 300.

49. Ibid., 300. Tigay suggests this as a possibility for Jer 3:19; 31:8; and Hosea 11:1.

labor pains God suffered in creating Israel in order to revive in his apostate people a sense of responsibility toward this deity who had been so gracious to Israel in the past. In the same way, I would argue that one should take seriously the birth imagery used of the king in Ps 2:7, not strip it of its mythic power by transforming it into adoption language.

Scholars have been reluctant even to consider this possibility because of an apologetic desire to distance Israelite conceptions of the king's divine sonship as far as possible from the allegedly crudely literal Egyptian conceptions of the physical engenderment of the Egyptian king by the deity. In the grip of this apologetic fear, biblical scholars often speak as though birth imagery is inherently literal while the putative adoption imagery is clearly metaphorical. Simply to articulate this view is to recognize its falsity. Both images can be used in a literal way, but when used to speak of the deity as a parent, on any sophisticated level, both birth imagery and adoption imagery are unavoidably metaphorical. That was just as true in Egypt as it was in Judah.

The Divine Birth of the King in the Egyptian Coronation Ritual

The view that the Egyptians held a crudely literal conception of the king's physical engenderment by the deity is based primarily on the parallel accounts of the coronation of Hatshepsut and Amenhotep III,[50] and secondarily on the account of the coronation of Haremhab.[51] The first two texts contain a narrative about the god Amun taking the form of the reigning king, having intercourse with the queen, filling her with "his dew," and thus engendering the new ruler. In the case of Haremhab, the text is less sexually explicit, but it does speak of his reflecting divine qualities even as a child. It is noteworthy, however, that these texts are all unusual. In all three cases the succession was contested and irregular. Thus the accounts sought to bolster shaky claims to the throne. Even in these cases, moreover, one should not overstress the literal physicality of the deity's role in the birth process.

In the first two texts, the narrative goes on to describe how the craftsman god Khnum fashions the child. The texts fluctuate in referring to the mother as the divine Hathor or the human queen and in referring to the father as the divine Amun or the human king. Moreover, the Haremhab text refers to Haremhab at one moment as the son of Horus, the god of Hnes, but at another moment as the son of Amun. On any literal level, such fluctuation would be confusing. Claims as to the literal physicality of the conception of these royal

50. *ARE* 2.75–100, 334.

51. Ibid., 3.12–19; Alan H. Gardiner, "The Coronation of King Haremhab," *JEA* 39 (1953) 13–31.

figures by the gods are less important to their propaganda than the assertion that their special relationship to the divine world justifies their claim to the throne. That the language is actually more metaphorical than it appears at first also finds confirmation in the language of one of Akhenton's hymns to the Aton:

> Thy rays are upon thy beloved son. Thy hand has a myriad of jubilees for the King of Upper and Lower Egypt, Neferkheprure-Wanre, thy child who came forth from thy rays. Thou assignest to him thy lifetime and thy years. Thou hearest for him that which is in his heart. He is thy beloved, thou makest him like Aton. When thou risest, eternity is given him; when thou settest, thou givest him everlastingness. Thou begettest him in the morning like thine own forms; thou formest him as thy emanation, like Aton, ruler of truth, who came forth from eternity, son of Re, wearing his beauty. . . .[52]

Here the imagery centers upon the rays of the sun rather than the human intercourse and birth. Yet one should remember that the artistic representations of Akhenaton portray him in painfully human form. One should also remember that among contemporary Egyptologists the dominant view is that the Egyptians did not regard their kings in their own person as genuinely divine; at best the office was divine. To quote Ronald J. Leprohon:

> However, the evidence shows that the living pharaoh was not, as was once thought, divine in nature or a god incarnate on earth. Rather, we should think of him as a human recipient of a divine office. Any individual king was a transitory figure, while the kingship was eternal.[53]

Conclusion

If, in the light of these observations, one may take the birth imagery in the biblical text seriously and give full weight to the impressive evidence for Egyptian influence on the Judean coronation ritual, all the objections against von Rad's basic understanding of Isa 9:5 find an answer. Amun's statement to Haremhab at his coronation, "You are my son, the heir who came forth from my flesh . . . ," is strikingly parallel to Yahweh's statement to the Davidic king in Ps 2:7, "You are my son, today I have begotten you." The Egyptian coronation ritual, however, does not only have Amun making the proclamation of the king's divine sonship directly to the new pharaoh. Amun, or Thoth speaking for him, also addresses the divine council, using third-person pronouns to present the human king to them as his son. The assembly of the gods responds

52. *ARE*, 2.409.

53. Ronald J. Leprohon, "Royal Ideology and State Administration in Pharaonic Egypt," in Jack Sasson, ed., *Civilizations of the Ancient Near East* (4 vols.; New York: Scribner's, 1995) 1.275.

to the presentation, in turn, by referring to the king in the third person. In a Judean royal ritual dependent on this Egyptian model, it would thus not be surprising to find references to the king's divine birth in both direct address to the king and in third-person announcements. There is no reason to expect such announcements to be formulated only in the active voice. Furthermore, while the Egyptian texts may identify the onset of the king's divine sonship with the physical birth of the king, the actual public announcement of that divine birth comes only at his accession and coronation, that is, at the time of the promulgation of the royal titulary. That a Judean adaptation of this ceremony should take the form of a traditional birth announcement and accordingly should use vocabulary referring to a young child is not at all surprising. It does not suggest a recent birth of a new royal baby any more than the parallel birth narratives in the Egyptian enthronement texts do.

Von Rad's basic understanding of Isa 8:23–9:6 does not, moreover, require a change of speaker at v. 5. He correctly saw that in the Egyptian parallels a deity was the speaker throughout, and he also noted that it would be odd for the people, speaking of the divine birth of the king, to say, "a child has been born to us." He could not, however, explain the second person references to Yahweh in vv. 2–3, if the deity was the speaker throughout. In the Egyptian texts, however, it is not just Amun who speaks; the divine council also responds to him in the second person or describes his action in the third person, praising him for his salvation. Two examples will illustrate the point. In the text of her purification ceremony, the gods announce their satisfaction with Amun's daughter Hatshepsut:

> This thy daughter . . . who liveth, we are satisfied with her in life and peace. She is now thy daughter of thy form, whom thou hast begotten, prepared. Thou hast given her thy soul. . . . While she was in the body of her that bore her, the lands were hers, the countries were hers; all that the heavens cover, all that the sea encircles. Thou hast now done this with her, for thou knowest the two aeons. Thou hast given to her the share of Horus in life, the years of Set in satisfaction.[54]

Similarly, in Haremhab's coronation ritual the gods respond to the presentation of the new king as follows:

> Behold, Amūn is come, his son in front of him, to the Palace in order to establish his crown upon his head and in order to prolong his period like to himself. We have gathered together that we may establish for him [and as]sign to him the insignia of Rēᶜ and the years of Horus as king. . . .[55]

Given these Egyptian models, one should at least consider the possibility that the fictive speakers of the entire oracle of Isa 8:23b–9:6, represented by

54. *ARE*, 2.89.
55. Gardiner, "Coronation of King Haremhab," 14.

the first-person plural pronouns in 9:5, are the members of Yahweh's divine court. Isaiah had no qualms about attributing such speech to the divine council, since he explicitly quotes the words of the seraphim in Isa 6:3, and the later Isaianic tradition continued to put important words in the mouth of members of the divine council (see Isa 40:3). In short, one may read Isa 9:5 as reflecting the joyous assent of the divine council to the new king, Yahweh's son.

Chapter 14

The Mari Prophetic Texts in Transliteration and English Translation

Since William L. Moran published his translation of the Mari prophetic texts in 1969,[1] there has been no major English translation known to me of the corpus of prophetic texts from Mari. But since Moran's work, a significant number of new prophetic texts from Mari have been published,[2] and earlier known texts have been augmented by significant joins.[3] These newer texts have received some discussion in English articles, but the whole corpus of texts is no longer readily available in an English translation. The texts are of significant interest to both students and colleagues who are unlikely to consult them in their French editions, so this transliteration and English translation of the texts is intended to make these texts accessible to a wider scholarly public.

I have presented the transliterated text and the translated text side by side for the convenience of those who wish to check the English translation against the Akkadian text. The difference in word order and syntactical structure between English and Akkadian, however, means that one cannot always match a line of transliteration to a line of translation without producing a very awkward or confusing English translation. I have opted for what I hope will be clear English syntax, even if this means that the lines do not always correspond. I have also tried to keep the footnotes to a bare minimum. They are usually introduced when my reading or translation varies significantly from that of Durand[4] or, sometimes, from that of Moran.[5] Most of the time, my readings and restorations follow Durand. Due to constraints of space and time, it did not

---

1. W. L. Moran, "New Evidence from Mari on the History of Prophecy," *Biblica* 50 (1969): 15–56; W. L. Moran, "Akkadian Letters," in *ANET* (1969), 623–26, 629–32.

2. Jean-Mari Durand, "Le combat entre le Dieu de l'orage et la Mer," *Mari, Annales de Recherche Interdisciplinaires* 7 (1993): 39–61; Jean-Marie Durand, *Archives épistolaires de Mari I/1*, Archives royales de Mari XXVI (Paris: Éditions Recherche sur les Civilisations, 1988).

3. Bertrand Lafont, "Le roi de Mari et les prophètes du dieu Adad," *RA* 78 (1984): 7–18.

4. Jean-Marie Durand, *Archives épistolaires de Mari I/1*, Archives royales de Mari XXVI (Paris: Éditions Recherche sur les Civilisations, 1988).

5. W. L. Moran, "New Evidence from Mari on the History of Prophecy," *Biblica* 50 (1969): 15–56; W. L. Moran, "Akkadian Letters," in *ANET* (1969), 623–26, 629–32.

seem profitable to cite all the variant suggestions of other scholars, though my own work is certainly indebted to that of Ellermeier,[6] Berger,[7] Römer,[8] von Soden,[9] Heintz,[10] Dossin,[11] Sasson,[12] Malamat,[13] and others.[14] I have tried to translate the technical designations for the prophetic or priestly figures mentioned in the texts consistently with an appropriate English term rather than simply transliterating the terms. Thus *muḫḫum* and *muḫḫutum* are rendered as "ecstatic" and "female ecstatic", and *āpilum* and *āpiltum* are rendered as "respondent" and "female respondent." The first term in its masculine and feminine forms is based on an adjectival formation for designating individuals with

6. F. Ellermeier, *Prophetie in Mari und Israel*, Theol. und orientalische Arbeiten, vol. 1 (Herzberg: Erwin Jungfer, 1968).

7. P.-R. Berger, "Einige Bemerkungen zu Friedrich Ellermeier: Prophetie in Mari und Israel," *UF* 1 (1969): 207–9, 221.

8. W. H. Ph. Römer, *Frauenbriefe über Religion politik und Privatleben in Mari*, AOAT (Kevelaer / Neukirchen-Vluyn: Butzon & Bercker / Neukirchener Verlag, 1971).

9. W. von Soden, "Einige Bemerkungen zu den von Fr. Ellermeier in 'Prophetie in Mari und Israel' (Herzberg 1968) erstmalig bearbeiteten Briefen aus ARM 10," *UF* 1 (1969): 198–99.

10. J.-G. Heintz, "Oracles prophétiques et 'guerre sainte' selon les archives royales de Mari et l'Ancien Testament," *VTSup* 17 (1968): 112–38; J.-G. Heintz, "Aux origines d'une expression biblique: *ūmūšū qerbu* A.R.M., X 6, 8′?," *VT* 21 (1971): 528–40; J.-G. Heintz, "Prophetie in Mari und Israel," *Bib* 52 (1971): 543–55.

11. G. Dossin, "Sur le prophétisme à Mari," in *La divination en Mésopotomie ancienne et dans les régions voisines* (Paris: 1966), 77–86; Georges Dossin, *Correspondance Féminine Transcrite et Traduite*, Archives Royales de Mari, vol. X (Paris: Librairie Orientaliste Paul Geuthner, 1978).

12. Jack M. Sasson, "An Apocalyptic Vision from Mari?: Speculations on ARM X:9," *Mari: Annales de Recherches Interdisciplinaires* 1 (1982): 151–167; Jack M. Sasson, "Review of Willem H. Ph. Römer, Frauenbriefe über Religion, Politik und Privatleben in Mari," *BO* 28 (1971): 354–56.

13. Abraham Malamat, "Notes Brèves. 88) Parallels between the New Prophecies from Mari and Biblical Prophecy: I) Predicting the Death of a Royal Infant," *NABU* 4 (1989): 61–63; Abraham Malamat, "Notes Brèves. 89) Parallels between the New Prophecies from Mari and Biblical Prophecy: II) Material Remuneration for Prophetic Services," *NABU* 4 (1989): 63–64; Abraham Malamat, "A Mari Prophecy and Nathan's Dynastic Oracle," in *Prophecy: Essays Presented to Georg Fohrer on his Sixty-fifth Birthday*, ed. J. A. Emerton (Berlin: Walter de Gruyter, 1980), 68–82; Abraham Malamat, "Prophetic Revelations in New Documents from Mari and the Bible" (VT Sup. 15; 1965); A. Malamat, "Prophetic Revelations in New Documents from Mari and the Bible," *Eretz Israel* (1966): 207–27.

14. H. B. Huffmon, "Prophecy in the Mari Letters," *BA* 31 (1968): 101–24; E. Noort, *Üntersuchungen zum Gottesbescheid in Mari*, AOAT, vol. 202 (Neukirchen: 1977); J. F. Craghan, "The ARM 'Prophetic' Texts: Their Media', Style and Structure," *JANES* 5 (1974): 39–57; J. F. Craghan, "Mari and its Prophets. The Contribution of Mari to the Understanding of Biblical Prophecy," *BibTB* 5 (1975): 32–55. The secondary literature on the Mari prophets is quite extensive, but perhaps the best source for keeping up with it is Jean-Georges Heintz's *Bibliographie de Mari* (Wiesbaden: Otto Harrossowitz, 1990), which is periodically updated in supplements published in Akkadica, of which several have appeared.

physical or mental abnormalities; the second is simply the G active participle, "the one (male or female) who answers or responds," presumably on behalf of the deity.[15] The term *qammatum* I have not translated, since the meaning of that term remains unclear to me. Though *CAD* claims that "there is no specific evidence that he was a eunuch or a homosexual (A II, 341)," I have translated *assinnu* as "cult homosexual." Given the rather clear passages cited in *CAD*, it is unclear to me what its editors would count as "specific evidence."

The order in which I present the texts is somewhat arbitrary, though the correspondence between my numbers and the primary French publications are clearly marked. The French translation of these texts in *Prophéties et oracles*, Fasc. 1 . . . *dans le Proche Orient Ancien* (Supplément au Cahier Evangile 88; Paris, 1994), 8–74, in which these texts are supposed to be arranged in chronological order,[16] was not available to me in time to make use of it in my arrangement. For the convenience of my students and colleagues I have included two texts that are not, strictly speaking, prophetic texts from Mari. One is the Old Babylonian prophecy text from Ischali, ancient Ešnunna, published by Maria deJong Ellis,[17] and the other is the diviner's loyalty oath from Mari.

I have provided no extensive commentary to the individual texts in the transliteration and translation, but I have given brief annotations to the individual texts in the introductory list. These annotations are intended to provide a general introduction to the individual text and to indicate possible points of comparative relevance between these texts and selected Old Testament texts.

Annotated List of Texts Included

1. A.1968 = Jean-Mari Durand, "Le combat entre le Dieu de l'orage et la Mer," *Mari: Annales de Recherches Interdisciplinaires* 7 (Paris: Éditions Recherche sur les Civilisations, 1993) 39–61. [p. 166]

   This letter from Nur-Suen to Zimri-Lim contains an oracle of Abiya, the respondent of Adad of Aleppo, in which Adad recites his history of support for Zimri-Lim. He mentions anointing Zimri-Lim, and he claims to have given to Zimri-Lim his divine weapons with which Adad defeated the sea. Compare

15. See the discussion in Jean-Marie Durand, "Les prophéties des textes de Mari," in *Oracles et prophéties dans l'Antiquité: Actes de Colloque de Strasbourg 15–17 juin 1995*, ed. Jean-Georges Heintz, Université des Sciences Humaines de Strasbourg, Travaux du Centre de Recherche sur le Proche-Orient et la Grèce Antiques (Paris: de Boccard, 1997): 125.

16. Jean-Marie Durand, "Les prophéties des textes de Mari," in *Oracles et prophéties dans l'Antiquité: Actes de Colloque de Strasbourg 15–17 juin 1995*, ed. Jean-Georges Heintz, Université des Sciences Humaines de Strasbourg, Travaux du Centre de Recherche sur le Proche-Orient et la Grèce Antiques (Paris: de Boccard, 1997).

17. Maria de Jong Ellis, "The Goddess Kititum speaks to King Ibalpiel: Oracle Texts from Ishchali," *Mari: Annales de Recherches Interdisciplinaires* 5 (1987): 235–66.

Ps 89:21–26 for similar motifs of Yahweh's anointment of David and David's participation in Yahweh's continuing victory over Sea and River.

2. A.l5 = Dossin, "Une révélation du dieu Dagan à Terga," *RA* 42 (1948) 125–34. Durand, *AEM* 1/1, 233, pp. 473–67. [p. 168]

   This letter from Itur-Asdu to Zimri-Lim reports the vision of a certain Malik-Dagan which he had in the temple of Dagan at Terqa. In it Dagan commissions Malik-Dagan as his messenger to deliver his word to Zimri-Lim.

3. A.222 Dossin, *RA* 69 (1975) 28–30. Durand, *AEM* 1/1, 229. [p. 170]

   This text reports the dream of a certain woman named Ayala involving a conflict between a woman of Ṭišritum and a woman of Mari.

4. A.1121 + A.2731 = Bertrand Lafont, "Le roi de Mari et les prophètes du dieu Adad," *RA* 78 (1984) 7–18. Earlier treatments: A.112l = A. Lods and G. Dossin, "Une tablette inédite de Mari, interéssante pour l'histoire ancienne du prophétisme sémitique," *Studies in Old Testament Prophecy*, ed. by H. H. Rowley (Edinburgh: T.& T. Clark, 1957) 103–10. A.2731 sections translated by Dossin, *La divination*, 78, under the erroneous number A.2925. [p. 172]

   This letter from Nur-Suen to Zimri-Lim contains two similar oracles from Adad of Kallassu and Adad of Aleppo. Adad of Kallassu is irritated with Zimri-Lim, because despite his past support of Zimri-Lim, Zimri-Lim has not given the god what the god requested. Cf. 2 Sam 12:7–8. Adad of Aleppo also refers to his past support of Zimri-Lim, but his request is only that Zimri-Lim give justice to the oppressed.

5. A.4260 = Durand, *AEM* 1/1, 194, 417–19. Sections translated by Dossin, op. cit., p. 85. [p. 176]

   This letter from the respondent of Šamaš in Sippar to Zimri-Lim contains an oracle of Šamaš that deals primarily with the appropriate distribution of booty and offerings to various gods following a recent victory of Zimri-Lim.

6. A.455 = Durand, *AEM* 1/1, 215, pp. 443–44. Sections translated by Dossin, *La divination en Mésopotamie ancienne*, 79–80. [p. 178]

   This letter from Lanasum to Zimri-Lim reports the oracle of an ecstatic during a sacrifice to Dagan in which Dagan asks to be provided with pure water.

7. A.4865 = *ARM* II 90 = *AEM* 1/1, 220. [p. 180]

   This letter from Kibri-Dagan, governor of Terqa, to Zimri-Lim reports an oracle from the ecstatic of Dagan in which the ecstatic claims to have been sent by Dagan to demand the performance of a sacrifice for the dead.

8. A.2030 = *ARM* III 40 = *AEM* 1/1, 221. [p. 182]

   This letter from Kibri-Dagan to Zimri-Lim reports an oracle from the ecstatic of Dagan in which Dagan sends the ecstatic to demand the performance of funerary offerings for Zimri-Lim's dead father, Yaḫdun-Lim.

9. A.4934 = *ARM* III 78 = *AEM* 1/1, 221. [p. 182]

This letter from Kibri-Dagan to Zimri-Lim reports an oracle of the ecstatic in which the god threatens a calamity if a new gate is not constructed immediately.

10. A.368 = *ARM* VI 45 = *AEM* 1/1, 201. [p. 184]

This letter from Baḫdi-Lim of Mari to Zimri-Lim, who is obviously absent from Mari, mentions a report sent to him by Aḫum the priest concerning the oracle of a female ecstatic.

11. A.996 = *ARM* X 4 = *AEM* 1/1, 207. [p. 186]

This letter from Šibtu, the main wife of Zimri-Lim, to the king reports the results of oracles she obtained by questioning a man and woman after plying them with drink. The oracles are favorable for Zimri-Lim, but unfavorable to Išme-Dagan against whom Zimri-Lim was campaigning. Colorful metaphorical language is used, and Šibtu protects herself against any suspicion that she unduly influenced the outcome of the oracles. Šibtu allays Zimri-Lim's possible hesitancy to act on the message by reminding her husband that the gods are his allies in battle, a point reminiscent of holy war ideology in Israel (Deut 21:1).

12. A.3217 = *ARM* X 6 = *AEM* 1/1, 212. [p. 188]

This letter from Šibtu to Zimri-Lim reports on an oracle delivered by the cult homosexual of Annunitum concerning Ḫammurabi of Babylon. His oracle agrees with other oracles that Šibtu took by plying individuals with drink. The goddess promises that Ḫammurabi's day of death is near.

13. A.100 = *ARM* X 7 = *AEM* 1/1, 213. [p. 190]

This letter from Šibtu to Zimri-Lim reports an oracle of Annunitum that Šelibum, the cult homosexual of Annunitum, received in an ecstatic trance. It warns Zimri-Lim of a rebellion, but promises him deliverance.

14. A.671 = *ARM* X 8 = *AEM* 1/1, 214. [p. 192]

This letter from Šibtu to Zimri-Lim reports an oracle that Aḫatum, the servant girl of Dagan-Malik, had in an ecstatic trance in the temple of Annunitum. In it Annunitum addresses Zimri-Lim, complains about his neglect, yet nevertheless promises her continued love and support of Zimri-Lim against his enemies.

15. A.2233 = *ARM* X 9 = *AEM* 1/1, 208. [p. 194]

This letter from Šibtu to Zimri-Lim reports an oracle of Qišti-Diritum, the respondent of Diritum. In it Diritum promises that the lance of the Elamite enemy will be broken. The reverse of the table contains another oracle in which the gods in council, after dissolving dirt from the gateway of Mari in water and drinking it, swear an oath to do no wrong against the brickwork and protective deity of Mari. The use of dirt dissolved in water in connection with an oath reminds one of the ritual for a jealous husband in Num 5:17.

16. A.2437 = *ARM* X 10 = *AEM* 1/1, 236. [p. 196]

This letter from Šibtu to Zimri-Lim reports a dream of Kakkalidi seen in the temple of Itur-Mer. In the dream Zimri-Lim and his soldiers are on two barges blocking the river, and the soldiers proclaim the kingship as given to Zimri-Lim.

17. A.994 = *ARM* X 50 = *AEM* 1/1, 237. [p. 198]

This letter from Adad-duri to Zimri-Lim relates a very disturbing dream, the like of which Adad-duri had not seen since the fall of Yaḫdun-Lim, Zimri-Lim's father. In the dream Belet-ekallim and the other gods and goddesses were no longer present in the temple of Belet-ekallim. This alludes to the motif of the deities abandoning their city and temples prior to its fall to the enemy. Cf. Jer 9:1; 12:7; Ezek 10:1–11:23. The letter also reports another oracle of a female ecstatic of Annunitum warning Zimri-Lim to remain in Mari and to protect himself.

18. A.122 = *ARM* X 51 = *AEM* 1/1, 238. [p. 198]

This letter from Adad-duri to Zimri-Lim reports a dream of Iddin-Ili, the priest of Itur-Mer, in which the goddess Belet-biri urges Zimri-Lim to be more careful.

19. A. 3420 = *ARM* X 53 = *AEM* 1/1, 195.

This letter from Adad-duri to Zimri-Lim reports an oracle that a respondent named Iṣi-Aḫu gave in the temple of Ḫišametum. The goddess appears to refer to eating and drinking as a covenant ritual and promises to trample those who keep speaking evil against Zimri-Lim. [p. 200]

20. A.1047 = ARM X 80 = *AEM* 1/1, 197.

This letter from Inibšina to Zimri-Lim, whom she refers to as My Star, refers to an earlier oracle of Šelebum, the cult homosexual, and reports a new one brought by a *qammatum* of Dagan of Terqa. The oracle, employing a proverb about water running under an apparently solid surface covered by straw, warns Zimri-Lim against the peace overtures of the ruler of Ešnunna.

21. A.2264 = *ARM* X 81 = *AEM* 1/1, 204. [p. 202]

This letter from Inibšin to Zimri-Lim reports an oracle of Inni-bana, a female respondent, concerning the enemies of Zimri-Lim who circle around his borders.

22. A.2858 = *ARM* X 94 = *AEM* 1/1, 239. [p. 204]

This letter from Šimatum to Zimri-Lim reports a dream Šimatum had about the appropriate name to give the new daughter of Zimri-Lim and lady Tepaḫum.

23. A.907 = *ARM* X 100 = *AEM* 1/1, 232. [p. 206]

This letter from Zunana to Zimri-Lim reports an oracle Dagan gave to Zunana concerning the recovery of her servant girl, Kittum-šimḫiya, who had been detained by government officials. Dagan informed Zunana that she could only secure her servant's release by the direct intervention of the king.

24. A.3424 = *ARM* X 117 = *AEM* 1/1, 240. [p. 208]

    This letter from Timlu to Adad-duri reports a dream Timlu had in which Belet-ekallim spoke to her. The text is broken before the content of the dream is narrated.

25. A.4996 = *ARM* XIII 23 = *AEM* 1/1, 209. [p. 208]

    This letter from Mukannišum to Zimri-Lim reports an oracle of the respondent of Dagan of Tuttul. In it Dagan addresses Babylon, questions its hostile actions, and threatens to destroy it and hand its treasures over to Zimri-Lim. The letter also contains a fragment of an oracle of the respondent of Belet-ekallim against Ḫammurabi of Babylon.

26. M.13841 = *ARM* XIII 112 = *AEM* 1/1, 234. [p. 210]

    This letter from Kibri-Dagan to Zimri-Lim reports a dream in which the god warns the governor not to rebuild a ruined house.

27. M.13842 = *ARM* XIII 113 = *AEM* 1/1, 235. [p. 212]

    This letter from Kibri-Dagan to Zimri-Lim reports a dream which a man saw and which Aḫum the priest relayed to the governor. In the dream an enemy army looted and occupied the major cities of Zimri-Lim's kingdom.

28. M.13843 = *ARM* XIII 114 = *AEM* 1/1, 210. [p. 212]

    This letter from Kibri-Dagan to Zimri-Lim reports on an oracle brought by a woman who claimed that Dagan sent her with a message of reassurance to Zimri-Lim. He need not worry, because the god would take care of Ḫammurabi of Babylon.

29. A.765 = *AEM* 1/1, 191 = *Syria* 19 (1938) 126. [p. 214]

    This letter from Zimri-Lim to the deified river refers to a sign that the river god had given to Zimri-Lim in the past and asks the deity to fulfill that past promise.

30. M.9714 = *AEM* 1/1, 192. [p. 214]

    This tablet contains a letter from the god Adad to Zimri-Lim promising the king support in his war against the Elamites, a letter from the goddess Ištar of Ninet dealing apparently with the same impending battle, and a letter from the god Šamaš which is badly broken.

31. A.2666 = *AEM* 1/1, 193. [p. 216]

    This tablet begins with a letter from the god Ištaran to the god of gods. This is followed by a letter from Ur-bel-šukurrim to Ur-lugal-banda. It may be a school text or practice tablet.

32. A.3719 = *AEM* 1/1, 196. [p. 218]

    This letter from Šamaš-naṣir to Zimri-Lim contains a fascinating account of a divine trial in which Dagan announces judgment on Tišpak, the patron deity of Ešnunna, proclaiming that Tišpak would soon receive his day of judgment just as Ekallatum had. This judgment is announced in an assembly of the gods, and the goddess Ḫanat urges Dagan not to be negligent in carrying out this judgment. This trial scene follows immediately after a break, but it was probably part of an oracular dream or vision. The trial may be compared to Psalm 82.

33. A.3912 = *AEM* 1/1, 198. [p. 220]

In this badly broken text Šelebum complains of his neglect and mistreatment.

34. A.925 + A.2050 = *AEM* 1/1, 199. [p. 220]

This letter from Sammetar to Zimri-Lim reports on a series of oracles brought by Lupaḫum, the respondent of Dagan, from Dagan of Terqa, Dagan of Tuttul, and Diritum of Dir, and follows this with the report of an oracle brought by a *qammatum* of Dagan of Terqa. Lupaḫum has an interesting discussion with the goddess Diritum, who warns the king not to make a treaty with Ešnunna without consulting the deity. The message of the *qammatum*, which cites the proverb about water running under straw, also warns the king not to make a treaty without consulting the deity. For this need to consult the deity before entering into a treaty, cf. Isa 30:2; 31:1. One should note that the expression for making a treaty varies from "touching his throat," used for the treaty with Ešnunna, and "killing the donkey of the Benjaminites," used for the treaty with the Benjaminites. Note that the *qammatum* requests payment for her oracle.

35. M.6188 = *AEM* 1/1, 200. [p. 224]

This letter from Aḫum, the high priest of Annunitum, reports an oracle of Ḫubatum, a female ecstatic. The highly metaphorical oracle is positive toward Zimri-Lim and negative toward the Benjaminites, both of whom are addressed directly.

36. M.11046 = *AEM* 1/1, 202. [p. 226]

This letter from Kanisan to Zimri-Lim reports on oracular reports contained in a letter from his father Kibri-Dagan. The proverb about water running under straw is repeated.

37. A.963 = *AEM* 1/1, 203. [p. 226]

This tablet contains the broken oracle of a *qammatum* who apparently asked for payment for her service in clothing.

38. M.7306 = *AEM* 1/1, 205 = *ARMT* XXV, 816. [p. 228]

This broken tablet contains an oracle of Dagan in which Dagan promises to open the battle for Zimri-Lim.

39. A.3893 = *AEM* 1/1, 206. [p. 228]

This letter from Yaqqim-Adad to Zimri-Lim reports on the oracle of an ecstatic of Dagan. It is remarkable for the symbolic action it contains. The ecstatic demands a lamb belonging to Zimri-Lim from Yaqqim-Adad, the governor of Sagaratim, eats it in front of the elders of the city while the lamb is still alive, and then proclaims an impending "divine eating" of the populace, or plague, if the people of the region do not demonstrate their repentance by concrete actions. The ecstatic demands and receives a garment for his service.

40. A.3178 = *AEM* 1/1, 211. [p. 230]

This letter from Šibtu to Zimri-Lim reports an oracle of Belet-ekallim in which she promises Zimri-Lim success.

41. A.2209 = *AEM* 1/1, 216. [p. 232]

This letter from Tebi-gerišu to Zimri-Lim reports that Tebi-gerišu assembled the prophets (*na-bi-i*[meš]) of the Haneans in order to pose an oracular question to them about the wellbeing of the king. This is the first occurrence of the term *nabî* in Akkadian to designate prophetic figures, though its cognate *nābîʾ* is the ordinary term in Hebrew for prophet. Note that they are assembled as a group to respond to the king's question. Cf. 2 Kgs 22:6. The response of the prophets is that the king should be very careful when outside the city walls.

42. M.8071 = *AEM* 1/1, 217. [p. 232]

This letter reports the oracle of a woman in which a god promises the king support but demands that the king send the deity's request to the deity in Naḫur.

43. M.14836 = *AEM* 1/1, 218. [p. 234]

This broken letter reports the demand of a god for a chariot and a monument that Zimri-Lim had promised the deity.

44. M.13496 + M.15299 = *AEM* 1/1, 219. [p. 236]

This broken text reports the oracle of a respondent of Nin-ḫursagga, in which the deity complains about Zimri-Lim's failure to provide what the deity had repeatedly requested.

45. A.3724 = *AEM* 1/1, 222 = *ARM* X, 106. [p. 236]

This letter from Ušareš-ḫetil to Dariš-libur reports an oracle of Irra-gamil demanding that the king be informed before he reaches Mari that his little girl has died. Cf. 1 Kgs 14:12.

46. M.9601 = *AEM* 1/1, 223. Too broken for translation. [p. 238]

47. A.2559 = *AEM* 1/1, 224. [p. 238]

This letter to Zimri-Lim reports a dream favorable to the king.

48. M.5704 = *AEM* 1/1, 225. [p. 240]

This letter to Zimri-Lim reports a disturbing dream which led the letter writer to have additional omens taken.

49. A.1516 and M.9034 = *AEM* 1/1, 226. [p. 240]

This letter reports a dream concerning the harvest.

50. M.9576 = *AEM* 1/1, 227. [p. 242]

This letter from Adad-duri to Zimri-Lim reports the odd dream of a woman in which two dead ecstatics are alive and appear before the god Abba where they call upon the women of Mari to have the ghosts of their stillborn babies bless Zimri-Lim.

51. M.13637 = *AEM* 1/1, 228. [p. 242]

This letter from Iddiyatum to Zimri-Lim reports the dream of Nanna-lutil in which Zimri-Lim defeats the Elamites.

52. A.1902 = *AEM* 1/1, 230. [p. 244]

This broken text reports the dream of a woman in which she sees an old man have a discussion with the god Itur-Mer.

53. A.2448 = *AEM* 1/1, 231. [p. 244]

This letter from Sammetar to Zimri-Lim deals with the offering of a hot dish to the gods Adad and Nergal based on an earlier dream concerning this offering.

54. A.4400 = *AEM* 1/1, 243. [p. 246]

This letter reports the repeated oracle of an ecstatic of Dagan to the effect that the god has cursed the brickwork of the house of Sammetar and that the brickwork should be removed and the foundation holes filled with dirt.

55. A.428 = *AEM* 1/2, 371. [p. 246]

This letter from Yarim-Adad to Zimri-Lim reports on the oracles of the respondent of Marduk against Išme-Dagan of Ekallatum which the respondent gave

---

Transliteration

1. A.1968

1 *a-na be-lí-ya qí-bí-ma*
2 *um-ma Nu-úr-*^{d}*Suen* ÌR-*ka-a-ma*
3 ^{m}*A-bi-ya a-pí-lum ša* ^{d}IM *be-el Ḫa-la-a*[*b*]
4 *il-li-kam-ma ki-a-am iq-bé-e-em*
5 *um-ma-a-mi* ^{d}IM-*ma ma-a-tam*$_{4}$ *ka-la-sa*
6 *a-na Ya-aḫ-du-Li-im ad-di-in*
7 *ù i-na* ^{giš}TUKUL^{meš}-*ya ma-ḫi-ra-am ú-ul ir-si*
8 *i-ya-tam i-zi-ib-ma ma-a-tam ša ad-di-nu-sum*
9 *a-na Sa-am-si-*^{d}IM *ad-*[*di-i*]*n*
10 [. . .] *Sa-am-si-*^{d}IM
(The bottom half of the tablet is broken off, and then it continues on the reverse.)

publicly at the gate of the house where the ill Išme-Dagan was staying in Babylon. He proclaims that Išme-Dagan will not escape the hand of Marduk.

56. FLP 1674 = Maria deJong Ellis, "The Goddess Kititum speaks to King Ibalpiel: Oracle Texts from Ishchali," *Mari: Annales de Recherches Interdisciplinaires* 5 (Paris: Éditions Recherche sur les Civilisations, 1987) 235–66. [p. 250]

This oracle from the goddess Kititum of Ešnunna to king Ibalpiel is a promise of well-being to the king, but its major importance is that along with the oracles of the respondent of Šamaš from Sippar and those of the respondent of Marduk from Babylon in the Mari collection, it demonstrates that the prophetic phenomena was not limited to the western periphery of the Amorite settlements of Mesopotamia.

57. M.13091 = *AEM* 1/1, 1. [p. 250]

The diviners' loyalty oath to the king requires the diviner to fully reveal to the king the results of any omens that the diviner takes or of which he is aware, and it prohibits the diviner from taking omens for an enemy of the king. The cultural presuppositions of this text suggests by analogy, among other things, some legal basis for Saul's judgment against Ahimelek, the priest of Nob, who inquired of God for David, Saul's enemy (1 Sam 22:9–16).

Translation

1. A.1968

1To my lord, speak:
2Thus says Nur-Suen, your servant:
3Abiya, the respondent of Adad lord of Aleppo,
4came to me and spoke to me as follows:
5Thus says Adad, "The whole land
6I gave to Yaḫdun-Lim,
7and thanks to my weapons he had no rival.
8But he deserted me, and the land which I had given to him
9I gave to Šamši-Adad.
10. . . Šamši-Adad
. . . . (long break). . .

1′*lu-t[e-e]r-ka a-na* ^{giš}G[U.ZA É *a-bi-ka*]
2′*lu-te-er-ka* ^{giš}TUKUL[^{meš}]
3′*ša it-ti te-em-tim am-ta-aḫ-ṣú*
4′*ad-di-na-ak-kum* Ì *ša nam-ri-ru-ti-ya*
5′*ap-šu-úš-*[*k*]*a ma-am-ma-an a-na pa-ni-ka*
6′*ú-ul iz-*[*zi-iz a*]*-wa-ti iš*$_7$*-te-et ši-me*
7′*i-nu-ma ma-am-ma-an ša di-nim*
8′*i-ša-as-sí-ik um-ma-*[*a*]*-mi*
9′*ḫ*[*a-ab-t*]*a-ku i-zi-iz-ma di-in-šu di-in*
10′[*i-ša-r*]*i-iš a-p*[*u-ul-šu*]
11′[*an*]*-ni-tam ša it-ti-ka e*[*-er-ri-šu*]
12′*i-nu-ma gi-ir-ra-am tu-u*[*ṣ-ṣú-ú*]
13′[*b*]*a-lum te-er-tim la tu-uṣ-*[*ṣí*]
14′[*i*]*-nu-ma a-na-ku i-na te-*[*e*]*r-ti-y*[*a*]
15′[*az-za-az-zu*] *gi-ir-ra-am ta-ṣí*
16′*šum-ma* [*la k*]*i-a-am-ma ba-ba-am*
17′[*la*] *tu-*[*u*]*ṣ-ṣí an-ni-tam a-pí-lum iq-bé-em*
18′*a-nu-um-*[*ma ša-ra-at a-pí-lim*]
19′*ù sí-*[*sí-ik-ta-šu a-na be-lí-ya*]
20′[*uš-ta-bi-lam*]

2. A.15 = *AEM* 1/1, 233

1*a-na be-lí-ya*
2*qí-bí-ma*
3*um-ma I-túr-Ás-du*
4ÌR-*ka-a-ma*
5*u*$_4$*-um ṭup-pí an-né-e-em a-na* [*ṣ*]*e-er*
6*be-lí-ya ú-ša-bi-lam*
7^{m}*Ma-li-ik-*^{d}*Da-gan* LÚ *Ša-ak-ka*^{ki}
8*il-*⟨*li*⟩*-kam-ma ki-a-am iq-b*[*é*]*-e-em*
9[*u*]*m-ma-a-mi i-na šu-ut-ti-ya a-na-ku ù* 1 LÚ *it-ti-ya*
10[*iš-t*]*u ḫa-la-aṣ Sa-ga-ra-tim*^{ki}
11*i-na ḫa-al-ṣí-im e-li-im a-na Ma-ri*^{ki} *a-na a-la-ki-im*
12*pa-nu-ya ša-ak-nu*
13*i-na pa-ni-ya a-na Ter-qa*^{ki} *e-ru-um-ma ki-ma e-re-bi-ya-ma*
14*a-na* É ^{d}*Da-gan e-ru-um-ma a-na* ^{d}*Da-gan*
15*úš-ke-en i-na šu-ke-ni-ya*
16^{d}*Da-gan pí-šu ip-te-e-ma ki-a-am iq-bé-e-em*
17*um-ma-a-mi* LUGAL^{meš}*-nu ša* DUMU^{meš} *Ya-mi-*{*na*}*-na*
18*ù ṣa-bu-šu-nu*
19*it-ti ṣa-bi-im* [*š*]*a Zi-im-ri-Li-im*

[1′]I returned you. To the thron[e of your father′s house]
[2′]I returned you. The weapon[s]
[3′]with which I fought with the sea
[4′]I gave to you. With the oil of my brilliance
[5′]I anointed you, and no one could sta[nd]
[6′]before you. My one word hear!
[7′]When someone who has a lawsuit
[8′]calls to you saying,
[9′]'I have been wronged!' stand up and judge his lawsuit.
[10′][Ju]stly ans[wer him].
[11′]This is what I d[esire] from you.
[12′]When you go out on a campaign,
[13′]do not go out without an oracle.
[14′]When I [step forth] in my oracle,
[15′]you will go out on a campaign.
[16′]If I do not,
[17′]you will [not] g[o] out the gate." This is what the respondent said to me.
[18′]Now [the lock of hair of the respondent]
[19′]and the h[em (of) his (garment) I have sent]
[20′][to my lord].

2. A.15 = *AEM* 1/1, 233

[1]To my lord
[2]speak:
[3]Thus says Itur-Asdu,
[4]your servant:
[5]On the day that I sent this my tablet
[6]to my lord,
[7]Malik-Dagan, a man of Šakka,
[8]came to me and spoke to me as follows:
[9]In my dream I, accompanied by another man
[10]from the district of Sagaratim,
[11]decided to go from the upper district
[12]to Mari.
[13]Before (going), I entered Terqa, and as soon as I entered,
[14]I entered the temple of Dagan, and to Dagan
[15]I bowed down. When I bowed down,
[16]Dagan opened his mouth, and he spoke to me as follows:
[17]"Have the kings of the (Ben)jaminites
[18]and their armies
[19]made peace with the army of Zimri-Lim

20*ša i-le-e-em*
21*[ì]s-li-mu-ú*
22*[u]m-ma a-na-ku-⟨ma⟩ ú-ul ìs-li-mu*
23*i-na pa-ni wa-ṣí-ya ki-a-am iq-bé-e-em*
24*um-ma-a-mi* DUMU^{meš} *ši-ip-ri*
25*ša Zi-im-ri-Li-im*
26*ka-ya-ni-iš ma-aḫ-ri-ya a-na m[i]-nim [l]a wa-aš-bu-ma*
27*ù ṭe*$_4$*-em-šu ga-am-ra-am ma-aḫ-ri-ya am-mi-nim*
28*la-a i-ša-ak-ka-an*
29*ú-ul-la-ma-an is-tu u*$_4$*-mi ma-du-tim*
30LUGAL^{meš}*-ni ša* DUMU^{meš} *[Ya]-m[i]-na*
31*a-na qa-at Zi-im-ri-Li-im um-ta-al-li-šu-nu-ti*
32*i-na-an-na a-li-ik áš-ta-pa-ar-ka*
33*a-na Zi-im-ri-Li-im ki-a-am ta-qa-ab-bi um-ma at-ta-a-ma*
34DUMU^{meš} *ši-ip-ri-ka a-na ṣe-ri-ya*
35*šu-u[p-r]a-[am-m]a ù ṭe*$_4$*-em-ka ga-am-ra-am*
36*ma-a[ḫ-ri-y]a [š]u-ku-un-ma*
37*ù* LUGAL^{meš}-*[ni ša* DUMU^{m}]^{es} *Ya-mi-na i-na* ^{giš}*sú-us-sú-ul*
38^{lú}ŠU.P[EŠ.A *lu-ša-a]p-ši-il-šu-nu-ti-ma*
39*ma-aḫ-ri-ka [lu-uš-ku]-un-šu-nu-ti*
40*an-ni-tam* LÚ *šu-ú [i-n]a šu-ut-ti-šu iṭ-ṭú-ul-ma*
41*ù a-[ya]-ši-im id-bu-ba-am*
42*i-na-an-na a-nu-um-ma a-na ṣe-er be-lí-ya áš-tap-ra-am*
43*wa-ar-ka-at šu-ut-ti-⟨im⟩ an-ni-tim be-lí*
44*li-ip-ru-us*
45*ša-ni-tam šum-ma li-ib-bi be-lí-ya*
46*be-lí ṭe*$_4$*-em-šu ga-am-ra-am*
47IGI ^{d}*Da-gan li-iš-ku-un*
48*ù* DUMU^{meš} *ši-ip-ri ša be-lí-ya*
49*a-na ṣe-er* ^{d}*Da-gan lu ka-ya-nu*
50LÚ *ša šu-ut-ta-am an-ni-tam*
51*[iq-b]é-e-em pa-ag-ra-am a-na* ^{d}*Da-gan*
52*i-na-ad-di-in-ma ú-ul aṭ-ru-da-aš-šu*
53*ù aš-šum* LÚ *su-ú ták-lu ša-ra-sú ù sí-sí-⟨ik⟩-ta-šu*
54*ú-ul él-qí*

3. A.222 = *AEM* 1/1, 229

1^{mí}*A-ya-la*
2*i-na su-ut-ti-ša*
3*ki-a-am iṭ-ṭú-ul*
4*um-ma-mi* 1 MUNUS *Ši-iḫ-ri-tum*^{ki}

[20]which came up
[21]here?"
[22]I said, "They did not make peace."
[23]Before I went out, he spoke to me as follows:
[24]"Why do the messengers of
[25]Zimri-Lim
[26]not sit before me continually?
[27]And why does he not place his complete report
[28]before me?
[29]If he had, I would have delivered
[30]the kings of the (Ben)jaminites
[31]into the hand of Zimri-Lim many days ago.
[32]Now go, I have sent you.
[33]To Zimri-Lim you will speak as follows:
[34]'Send your messengers to me
[35]and place your complete report
[36]before me,
[37]and the kings of the (Ben)jaminites I will cause to flop
[38]in a fisherman's basket,
[39]and [I will s]et them before you.' "
[40]This is what that man saw in his dream
[41]and told to me.
[42]Now then I have written to my lord.
[43]Let my lord decide the background of this
[44]dream.
[45]Moreover, if it pleases my lord,
[46]let my lord place his complete report
[47]before Dagan
[48]and let the messengers of my lord
[49]be constantly before Dagan.
[50]The man who told me this dream
[51]is offering a *pagrum*-sacrifice to Dagan,
[52]so I did not send him,
[53]and because that man is trustworthy,
[54]I did not take his lock of hair or his hem.

3. A.222 = *AEM* 1/1, 229

[1](The woman) Ayala
[2]saw in her dream
[3]as follows:
[4]A woman of Šiḫritum

5 1 MUNUS *Ma-ri-tum*^{ki}
6 [*i*]*-na ba-ab An-nu-ni-tim*
7 *te?-x?* (NULL?)
8 [*s*]*a ka-wi-tum*
9 *iṣ-ṣí-il-la*
10 *um-ma* MUNUS [*Š*]*i-iḫ-ri-tum*^{ki}
11 *a-na* MUNUS *M*[*a-r*]*i-tum*^{ki}
12 *e-nu-ti te-er-ri-im*
13 *ú-lu at-ti ši-bi*
14 *ú-lu-ma a-na-ku lu-ši-ib*
15 *i-na* MUŠEN$^{ḫi.a}$ *ḫu-ri-im*
16 *wa-ar-ka-sà ap-ru-ús-ma*
17 *na-aṭ-la-at*
18 *a-nu-um-ma ša-ra-sà*
19 *ú sí-*[*i*]*s-sí-ik-ta*[**-š*]*a**
20 *ú-ša-bi-lam*
21 *be-lí wa-ar-ka-sà*
22 *li-ip-ru-ús*

4. A.1121 + A.2731

1 *a-na be-lí-ya qí-bí-ma*
2 *um-ma Nu-úr-*^{d}EN.ZU ÌR*-ka-a-ma*
3 1*-šu* 2*-šu ù* 5*-šu aš-šum zu-uk-ri-im a-na* ^{d}IM *na-da-*[*nim*]
4 *ù ni-iḫ-la-tim ša* ^{d}IM *be-el Ka-al-la-sú*^{ki}
5 [*it-ti-n*]*i ir-ri-šu a-na be-lí-ya aš-pu-ra-am*
6 [*aš-šu*]*m zu-uk-ri-im a-n*[*a* ^{d}IM] *na-da-nim Al-pa-an*
7 IGI ^{m}*Zu-ḫa-at-nim A-bi-*K[UR*-i ù x-*]*x-ḫa-an*
8 *iq-bé-e-em um-ma-a-mi zu-uk-r*[*a-am ša ki ir-ri-šu*]
9 Ù ÁB$^{ḫi.a}$ *i-di-in be-lí* IGI LÚ[^{me}]^{š} XX[X][18]
10 *zu-uk-ra-am na-da-nam iq-bé-e-em um-ma-a-*[*mi*]
11 *a-na ur-ra-am še-ra-am la ib-ba-la-ka-ta-an-*[*n*]*i*
12 LÚ^{meš} *ši-bi aš-ku-un-šum be-lí lu-ú i-di*
13 *i-na te-re-tim* ^{d}IM *be-el Ka-al-la-as-sú*^{ki}
14 [*iz-z*]*a-az*[19] *um-ma-a-mi ú-ul a-na-ku-ú*
15 [^{d}I]M *be-el Ka-al-la-as-sú*^{ki} *ša i-na bi-ri-it*
16 *pa-ḫa-al-li-ya ú-ra-ab-bu-šu-ma a-na* ^{giš}GU.ZA É *a-bi-šu*
17 *ú-te-er-ru-šu iš-tu a-na* ^{giš} GU.ZA É *a-bi-šu*
18 *ú-te-er-ru-šu a-tu-ur-ma a-ša-ar šu-ub-ti*

18. Reading of Heintz in *Biblica* 52 (1971) 546.
19. Heintz reads *iq-bi-im*.

[5](and) a woman of Mari
[6]kept arguing with one another
[7]in the gate of Annunitum
[8]which is outside
[9]the wall.
[10]The woman of Šiḫritum said
[11]to the woman of Mari,
[12]"Return to me my furniture/high priesthood.
[13]Either you sit down
[14]or let me sit down."
[15]With (divination) by patridges
[16]I examined her case,
[17]and she has seen (this vision).
[18]Now her lock of hair
[19]and [he]r hem
[20]I have sent.
[21]Let my lord
[22]examine her case.

4. A.1121 + A.2731

[1]Speak to my lord:
[2]Thus says Nur-Suen, your servant:
[3]Once, twice, even five times I wrote to my lord with regard to giving to Adad
[4]the *zukrum* and the inheritance which Adad, lord of Kallasu,
[5]requested [from u]s.
[6][With rega]rd to giving the *zukrum* t[o Adad], Alpan
[7]said to me in the presence of Zuḫatnim, Abiš[adi, and . . .]ḫan,
[8]"Give the *zukr[um* just as he requested]
[9]and the cows. My lord told me in the presence of the men. . .
[10]to give the *zukrum*, saying:
[11]'In the future you will not doublecross me.' "
[12]I have placed witnesses for him. Let my lord know.
[13]By oracles Adad, the lord of Kallassu,
[14]confirms (stands), saying: "Am I not
[15]Adad lord of Kallassu who raised him on my lap
[16]and returned him to the throne of his father's house?
[17]After I returned him to the throne of his father's house,
[18]I turned and gave to him a dwelling place.

19 *ad-di-in-šum i-na-an-na ki-ma a-na* ^{giš}GU.ZA É *a-bi-šu*
20 *ú-te-er-ru-šu ni-iḫ-la-tam*[20] *i-na* É *a-bi-šu*
21 *šum-ma ú-ul i-na-ad-di-in be-el* ^{giš}GU.ZA
22 *e-pé-ri ù a-lim*^{ki} *a-na-ku-ma ša ad-di-nu*
23 *a-ta-ab-ba-al šum-ma la ki-a-am-ma*
24 *e-re-èš-ti i-na-ad-di-in* ^{giš}GU.ZA *e-li* ^{giš}GU.ZA
25 É-*tam e-li* É-*tim e-pé-ri e-li e-pé-ri*
26 *a-lam*^{ki} *e-li a-lim*^{ki} *a-na-ad-di-in-šum*
27 *ù ma-a-tam iš-tu ṣí-ti-ša*
28 *a-na er-bi-ša a-na-ad-di-in-šu*
29 *an-ni-tam* LÚ^{meš} *a-pí-lu iq-bu-ú ù i-na te-re-tim*
30 *it-ta-na-az-za-az i-na-an-na ap-pu-na-ma*
31 LÚ *a-*[*pí*]*-lum ša* ^{d}IM *be-el Ka-al-la-sú*^{ki}
32 *ma-aš-ka-nam ša A-la-aḫ-tim*^{ki} *a-na ni-iḫ-la-tim*⟨⟨ki⟩⟩
33 *i-na-aṣ-ṣa-ar be-lí lu-ú i-di*
34 *pa-na-nu-um i-nu-ma i-na Ma-ri*^{ki} *wa-aš-ba-ku*
35 LÚ *a-pí-lum ù* ^{mí}*a-pí-il-tum mi-im-ma a-wa-tam*
36 *ša i-qa-*[*ab-bu*]*-nim a-na be-lí-ya ú-ta-ar*
37 *i-na-an-*[*na i-na*] *ma-a-tim ša-ni-tim wa-aš-ba-ku*
38 *ša e-še-em-mu-ú ù i-qa-ab-bu-nim*
39 *a-na be-lí-ya ú-ul a-ša-ap-pa-a-ar*
40 *šum-ma ur-ra-am še-ra-am mi-im-ma ḫi-ṭ*[*ì-tu*]*m it-ta-ab-ši*
41 *be-lí ki-a-am ú-ul i-qa-ab-bi-i um-ma-a-mi*
42 *a-wa-tam ša* ^{lú}*a-pí-lum iq-bi-kum ù ma-aš-ka-an-ka*
43 *i-na-aṣ-ṣa-ar am-mi-nim a-na ṣe-ri-ya*
44 *la ta-aš-pu-ra-am a-nu-um-ma a-na ṣe-er be-lí-ya*
45 [*á*]*š-*[*p*]*u-ra-am be-lí lu-ú i-*[*di*]
46 [*ša-ni*]*-tam* ^{lú}*a-pí-lum ša* ^{d}IM *be-el Ḫa-la-ab*^{ki}
47 [*a-na A-bu*]*-ḫa-lim il-li-kam-ma ki-a-am iq-bé-e-em*
48 [*um-ma-a-mi*] *a-na be-lí-ka* [*šu-pu*]*-ur*
49 *um-ma-a-mi* ^{d}IM *be-el Ḫa-la-ab*^{ki} *ú-ul a-na-ku-ú*
50 *ša i-na sú-ḫa-ti-*[*y*]*a ú-ra-ab-bu-ka-ma*
51 *a-na* ^{giš}GU.ZA É *a-bi-ka ú-te-er-ru-ka*
52 *mi-im-ma it-ti-ka ú-ul e-er-ri-*[*i*]*š*
53 [*i*]*-nu-ma* ^{lú}*ḫa-ab-lum ù* ^{mí}*ḫa-bi-i*[*l-tum*]
54 *i-ša-as-sí-ik-kum i-zi-iz-ma di-*[*i*]*n-šu-nu di-in*
55 [*a*]*n-ni-tam ša it-ti-ka e-ri-šu*
56 *a-ni-tam ša aš-pu-ra-kum te-ep-pé-eš-ma*
57 *a-na a-wa-ti-ya ta-qa-al-ma*

20. The determinative is not written after *ni-iḫ-la-tim* here, nor in A.2731. It is probably an error in line 27. So Heintz, loc. cit.

[19]Now as I returned him to the throne of his father's house,
[20]I will take the inheritance away from his house
[21]if he does not give. I am lord of throne,
[22]land, and city. What I gave
[23]I will take away. If, on the other hand,
[24]he gives my request, I will give to him throne upon throne,
[25]house upon house, land upon land,
[26](and) city upon city.
[27]And the land from the east
[28]to the west I will give to him."
[29]This is what the respondents said, and by oracles
[30]it is continually confirmed. Now in addition
[31]the respondent of Adad, lord of Kallassu,
[32]is watching the tent shrine of Alaḫtum for the inheritance.
[33]Let my lord know.
[34]Formerly when I lived in Mari,
[35]I reported to my lord whatever word
[36]the male respondent or female respondent said to me.
[37]No[w] that I am living [in] another country
[38]shall I not write to my lord what I hear
[39]and what they say to me?
[40]If in the future any lo[s]s occurred,
[41]would not my lord say,
[42]"Why did you not write to me the word which the respondent said to you
[43]and that he was watching your
[44]tent sanctuary?" Now [I h]ave written to my lord.
[45]Let my lord kn[ow].
[46][Ano]ther matter. The respondent of Adad, lord of Aleppo,
[47]came here [to Abu]ḫalim and spoke here
[48][as follows]: "[Wr]ite to your lord.
[49]Thus (says the god), 'Am I not Adad, lord of Aleppo,
[50]who raised you on my breast
[51]and returned you to the throne of your father's house?
[52]I do not ask anything from you.
[53]When an oppressed man or an oppressed woman
[54]cries to you, step forth and render their judgment.
[55]This is what I request of you.
[56]If this that I have written to you, you will do,
[57]and you will pay attention to my words,

58 *[m]a-a-tam iš-tu ṣ[í-ti-ša] a-na er-bi-ša*
59 *ù ma-a-at x[x x-m]a a-na-ad-di-na-kum*
60 *an-ni-tam* ^{lú}*a-[pí-lum ša]* ^{d}IM *be-el Ḫa-la-ab*^{ki}
61 IGI *A-bu-ḫa-lim iq-bé-e-em*
62 *an-ni-tam be-lí lu-ú i-di*

5. A.4260 = *AEM* 1/1, 194

1 *[a-n]a Z[i-i]m-ri-L[i-im q]í-[bí-ma]*
2 *[u]m-ma a-pí-lum [š]a* ^{d}[UT]U-*ma*
3 *um-ma-a* ^{d}UTU-*ma be-el ma-a-t[im a-na-ku]*
4 ^{giš}GU.ZA GAL *a-na [š]u-ba-at la-l[i-ya]*
5 *ù* DU[MU].MUNUS-*ka ša e-ri-šu-ka*
6 *ar-ḫi-iš a-na* ZIMBIR.RA^{ki}
7 [UR]U *ba-la-ṭim li-ša-aḫ-mi-ṭú*
8 *[an]-nu-um-ma* LUGAL^{meš} *ša a-na [pa-ni-ka]*
9 *[iz-z]i-zu-ni-kum ù iš*$_{7}$*-[ta-aḫ-ḫi-ṭ]ú-n[i-ka]*
10 *a-[n]a q[a-t]i-ka i[t-ta-ad-d]u?*
11 *a[n-n]a-n[u]-um-ma* ^{giš}*gur-na-[tum*[21] *i-n]a ma-a-tim*
12 *n[a]-ad-na-at-[kum]*
13 *ù a[š-š]um a-sa-ak* ^{d}I[M]
14 *[K]a-ni-sa-nam la-ma da-am*$_{7}$*-de-e[m]*
15 *[aš-p]u-ra-kum a-sa-kam ka-la-šu*
16 *[p]u-ḫi-ir-ma*
17 *[a-na Ḫ]a-la-ab*^{ki} *a-na* É ^{d}I[M]
18 *[li]-ib-lu*
19 *[qí-i]š-ti* ^{d}*Da-gan*
20 *[ša a-pí]-lum iq-bé-k[um]*
21 *[an-ni]-tam i-di-i[n]*
22 *[x x x-k]a ù na-pí-i[š-ta-ka]*
23 *[li-š]a-re-e-[kum]*
24 *[š]a-ni-tam* ^{d}NÈ.IRI$_{11}$.GAL
25 [LU]GAL *Ḫu-ub-ša-lim*^{ki}
26 *i-na da-am*$_{7}$*-de-e-em a-na [i-d]i-ka*
27 *ù i-di um-ma-na-ti-ka iz-[z]i-iz*
28 *ma-al ta-ak-ru-bu*
29 *ù nam-ṣa-ra-am* ZABAR GAL
30 *šu-pí-iš-ma a-na* ^{d}NÈ.IRI$_{11}$.GAL

---

21. New word apparently connected to the root *garānu*, "to pile up," and the noun *gurunnu*, "heap, mound." The indication of wood in front of it suggests piles of wood for cremating the bodies of the slain enemy (Durand, *AEM* I/1, 419), cf. *gurun šalmāt ummānātīšu*, "funeral pile, pyre."

[58]the [l]and from the e[ast] to the west
[59]and the land.[. .] I will give to you.' "
[60]This is what the respondent of Adad, the lord of Aleppo,
[61]said here before Abuḫalim.
[62]Let my lord know this.

5. A.4260 = *AEM* 1/1, 194

[1][T]o Z[i]mri-L[im s]p[eak:]
[2][T]hus says the respondent [o]f [Ša]maš:
[3]Thus says Šamaš, "[I am the] lord of the lan[d].
[4]The great throne for my delightful [d]welling
[5]and your d[au]ghter which I requested of you
[6]let them bring swiftly to Sippar,
[7]the [ci]ty of life.
[8][N]ow the kings who [sta]nd against [you]
[9]and k[eep at]tacking [you]
[10]w[ill be throw]n in[t]o your h[an]d.
[11]N[o]w the burial hea[ps i]n the land
[12]will be g[i]ven [to you].
[13]And con[cer]ning the part dedicated to Ad[ad],
[14][I s]ent Kanisanum to you before (your)
[15]defeat (of them). All that dedicated part
[16][g]ather
[17][that] they may bring (it) [to A]leppo
[18]to the temple of Ad[ad].
[19]The [pre]sent for Dagan
[20][of which the resp]ondent spoke [to you],
[21][this] giv[e]
[22][that] he may bring [to you y]our [. . .]
[23]and [your] lif[e].
[24][M]oreover Nergal,
[25]the [k]ing of Ḫubšalum
[26]st[o]od by your [si]de
[27]and by the side of your army in the slaughter.
[28]Whatever you vowed,
[29]and a large bronze sword
[30]have made, and let them take (them) to Nergal,

31 *[L]*UGAL *Ḫu-ub-ša-lim*^{ki} *li-ib-lu*
32 *ù ša-ni-tam um-ma-a* ^{d}UTU-*ma*
33 ^{m}*Ḫa-mu-ra-bi* LUGAL *Kur-da*^{ki}
34 *[s]à-ar-ra-tim it-ti-ka i[d-bu-ub]*
35 *ù qa-as-sú a-šar ša-né-[em]*
36 *[š]a-ak-na-at qa-at-ka i-[ka-ša-sú]*
37 *ù i-na li-bi ma-ti-[šu]*
38 *[a]n-du-ra-ra-am tu-wa-[aš-ša-ar]*
39 *ù a-n[u-u]m-ma ma-a-tum k[a-lu-ša]*
40 *i-na qa-ti-ka na-ad-na-[at]*
41 *[k]i-ma a-la-am ta-ṣa-ab-[ba-tu-ma]*
42 *[a]n-du-ra-ra-am tu-wa-aš-ša-r[u]*
43 *[ak-ke]-em šar-ru-ut-ka [d]a-ri-[at]*
44 *[ù š]a-ni-tam Zi-im-ri-Li-im ša-ki-in* ^{d}*D[a-gan]*
45 *ù* ^{d}IM *ṭu[p-pa-a]m an-n[i]-a-am li-iš-me-ma [be-el]*
46 *di-ni a-na ṣe-er še-pí-ya li-iš-pu-r[a-am]*

6. A.455 = *AEM* 1/1, 215

1 *a-na be-lí-ya*
2 *qí-bí-ma*
3 *um-ma La-na-su-ú-um*
4 ÌR-*ka-a-ma*
5 *be-lí ki-a-am iš-pu-ra-am*
6 *um-ma be-lí-ma a-nu-um-ma* SISKUR$_2$.RE
7 *a-na* ^{d}*Da-gan ú-še-r[e]-e-em*
8 1 GU$_4$ *ù* 6 UDU.NITA$_2$ *[bi-i]l*
9 *i-na-an-na* SISKUR$_2$.RE *ša be-lí-ya*
10 *i-na ša-la-mi-im a-na a-lim ik-šu-da-am*
11 *ù* IGI ^{d}*Da-gan in-na-qí*
12 *ù ma-a-tum ip-tu-un*
13 *ù a-lum ka-lu-šu a-na* SISKUR$_2$.RE *ša be-lí-ya*
14 *[m]a-di-iš ḫa-di[-x]*
15 *ù mu-uḫ-ḫu-um* IGI ^{d}*Da-gan*
16 *[i]t-bi-ma ki-a-am iq-bi*
17 *u[m]-ma-a-mi šu-ú-*{A DI}*-ma*
18 *ad-ma-ti me-e za-ku-tim*
19 *ú-ul a-ša-at-ti*
20 *a-na be-lí-ka šu-pu-ur-ma*
21 *ù me-e za-ku-tim li-iš-qé-en*$_6$*-ni*
22 *i-na-an-na a-nu-um-*{MA}*-ma*
23 *et-qa-am ša qa-qa-di-šu*

[31][k]ing of Ḫubšalum."
[32]And, moreover, thus says Šamaš,
[33]"Ḫammurabi, the king of Kurda,
[34]sp[oke t]reachery with you,
[35]but his hand was [p]laced somewhere [else].
[36]Your hand will [capture him],
[37]and in the midst of [his] land
[38]you will dec[lare] a [r]elease.
[39]And n[o]w a[ll] the land
[40]is give[n] into your hand.
[41][A]s soon as you captur[e] the city,
[42]you shall declar[e a re]lease
[43][in or]der that your kingship be [f]orev[er].
[44][And, m]oreover, let Zimri-Lim, the governor of D[agan]
[45]and Adad, hear th[i]s tab[let], and let him sen[d] the [one]
[46]who has a lawsuit to my feet."

6. A.455 = *AEM* 1/1, 215

[1]To my lord
[2]speak:
[3]Thus says Lanasum,
[4]your servant,
[5]"My lord wrote to me as follows,
[6]thus my lord, 'Now a sacrifice
[7]to Dagan I have had s[e]nt.
[8]One ox and 6 male sheep [tak]e.'
[9]Now the sacrifice of my lord
[10]in peace at the city has arrived
[11]and before Dagan it was offered.
[12]And the land feasted
[13]and the whole city rejoi[ced] [ex]ceedingly
[14]at the sacrifice of my lord.
[15]And the ecstatic [r]ose before Dagan,
[16]and spoke as follows,
[17]saying:
[18]'How long shall I not drink
[19]pure water?
[20]Write to your lord
[21]that he may give me pure water to drink.'
[22]Now then
[23]the lock of his head

24 *ù sí-sí-ik-ta-šu a-na ṣe-er be-lí-ya*
25 *ú-ša-bi-la-am be-lí l*[*i*]*-za-ak-ki*
26 *ša-ni-tam aš-šum si-ri-im ša be-lí-ya*
27 *i-na* ÌR^{meš} *ša be-lí-ya* 1 LÚ *ták-lu-um*
28 *li-il-li-ka-am-ma ù si-ra-am*
29 *sa be-lí-ya it-ti* DUMU^{meš} *a-lim*
30 [*l*]*i-il-qí*
31 *ù* DUMU^{meš} *a-lim ba-lu-ya*$_8$ {LU YA}-*x*
32 2? ^{giš}IG$^{\text{ḫi.a}}$ *a-na* ^{d}*Da-gan*
33 *is-sú-ḫu*

7. A.4865 = *ARM* II, 90 = *AEM* 1/1, 220

1 *a-na be-lí-y*[*a*]
2 *qí-bí-ma*
3 *um-ma Ki-ib-ri-*^{d}*Da-gan*
4 ÌR-*ka-a-ma*
5 ^{d}*Da-gan ù* ^{d}*Ik-ru-ub-Il ša-al-mu*
6 *a-lum Ter-qa*^{ki} *ù ḫa-al-ṣú-um* [*š*]*a-lim*
7 *ša-ni-tam* ⟨*i-na*⟩ *a-ḫa-ra-tim* UDU$^{\text{ḫi.a}}$ *na-wu-um*
8 [*ša* DUMU^{me}]^{s} [*Y*]*a-mi-na a-na* GÚ ^{íd}BURANUN^{ki}
9 [*it-ru-ú*]*-ma it-ti* UDU$^{\text{ḫi.a}}$ *na-we-e-em*
10 [*ša* ^{lú}ḪA.NA^{meš}] *ri-tam i-ka-la*
11 [*mi-im-ma ḫi-ṭì*]*-tum ú-ul i-ba-aš-ši*
12 [*li-ib-bi be-lí-ya l*]*a i-na-aḫ-ḫi-id*
13 [*u*$_4$*-um ṭup-pí an*]*-né-e-em*
14 [*a-na ṣe-er*] *be-lí-ya*
15 [*ú-ša-bi-lam*]
16 [^{lú}*mu-uḫ-ḫu-ú-u*]*m*
17 *ša* ^{d}*Da-gan a-w*[*a-tam ki-a-am iq-bi*]
18 *um-ma-a-mi aš-šum* ZUR.ZUR.R[I *pa-ag-ra-i*]
19 *e-pé-ši-im* ^{d}*Da-gan iš-pu-r*[*a-an-ni*]
20 *a-na be-lí-ka šu-pu-ur-*[*m*]*a*
21 ITU *e-re-ba-am i-na* UD 14 KAM
22 ZUR.ZUR.RI *pa-ag-ra-i li-in-né-pí-*[*i*]*š*
23 *mi-im-ma* ZUR.ZUR.RI *še-tu la ú-še-te-qú*
24 *an-ni-tam* LÚ *šu-ú iq-bé-e-em*
25 *i-na-an-na a-nu-um-ma a-na be-lí-ya*
26 *áš-ta-ap-ra-am be-lí a-na ki-ma*
27 *mu-uš-ta-lu-ti-šu*
28 [*š*]*a e-li-šu ṭà-ba-at li-pu-úš*

[24]and his hem I have sent to my lord.
[25]Let my lord clear (the matter).
[26]Moreover, concerning the plaster(?) of my lord,
[27]let one trustworthy man from the servants of my lord
[28]come that he may take the plaster
[29]of my lord with the citizens of
[30]the city.
[31]And the citizens of the city without my permission
[32]have removed
[33]the two door-leafs for Dagan.

7. A.4865 = *ARM* II, 90 = *AEM* 1/1, 220

[1]To m[y] lord
[2]speak:
[3]Thus says Kibri-Dagan,
[4]your servant:
[5]Dagan and Ikrub-Il are well.
[6]The city Terqa and the district are [w]ell.
[7]Another matter: On the far bank [they have brought] the encampment sheep
[8][of the (Ben)j]aminites to the bank of the Euphrates,
[9]and they are grazing with the encampment sheep
[10][of the Haneans].
[11]There has been [no los]s.
[12][The heart of my lord should n]ot worry.
[13][The day I sent t]his [tablet of mine]
[14][to] my
[15]lord,
[16][the ecstati]c
[17]of Dagan [spoke a] wo[rd as follows],
[18]saying, "Dagan sent [me] concerning
[19]the performance of a sacrifice for the [dead].
[20]Write to your lord
[21]that a sacrifice for the dead be performed
[22]next month on the fourteenth day.
[23]By no means shall they miss the term for that sacrifice."
[24]This is what that man said to me.
[25]Now then I have written to my lord
[26]that my lord
[27]may do what pleases him
[28]according to his deliberations.

8. A.2030 = *ARM* III 40 = *AEM* 1/1, 221

1 *[a-n]a be-lí-ya*
2 *[q]í-bí-ma*
3 *um-ma Ki-ib-ri-*^{d}*Da-gan*
4 ÌR-*ka-a-ma*
5 ^{d}*Da-gan ù* ^{d}*Ik-ru-ub-Il [ša]-al-mu*
6 *a-lum Ter-[q]a*^{ki} *ù ḫa-al-ṣú-⟨um⟩ ša-lim*
7 *ša-ni-tam u*$_{4}$*-um ṭup-pí an-né-e-em*
8 *a-na [ṣ]e-er be-lí-ya ú-[š]a-[b]i-lam*
9 ^{lú}*[m]u-uḫ-ḫu-um ša* ^{d}*[D]a-gan*
10 *il-li-[ka]m-ma*
11 *a-wa-tam ki-a-am [i]q-bé-e-[em]*
12 *[u]m-ma-a-mi*
13 DINGIR-*lum iš-pu-ra-an-[ni]*
14 *ḫu-mu-uṭ a-na* LUGAL
15 *šu-pu-ur-ma*
16 *ki-ìs-pí a-na i-ṭe*$_{4}$*-em-m[i-im]*
17 *ša Ya-aḫ-du-un-L[i-im]*
18 *li-ik-si!-pu*[22]
19 *an-ni-tam* ^{lú}*mu-uḫ-ḫu-um šu-u*
20 *iq-bé-e-em-ma a-na be-lí-ya*
21 *aš-ta-ap-ra-am*
22 *be-lí ša e-li-šu ṭà-ba-at*
23 *li-pu-úš*

9. A.4934. = *ARM* III 78 = *AEM* 1/1, 221.

1 *[a-na be-l]í-ya*
2 *[qí]-bí-ma*
3 *[um-ma] Ki-ib-ri-*^{d}*Da-gan*
4 [ÌR]-*ka-a-ma*
5 *[*^{d}*D]a-gan ù* ^{d}*Ik-ru-ub-Il ša-al-mu*
6 *[a-l]um Ter-qa*^{ki} *ù ḫa-al-ṣú-um ša-lim*
7 *[a-n]a [š]e-i-im ša ḫa-al-ṣí-ya e-ṣé-di-im*
8 *[ù] a-na* KI.UD$^{ḫi.a}$ *na-sa-ki-im*
9 *[a-ḫa-a]m ú-ul na-de-e-ku*
10 *[ša-ni-ta]m aš-šum a-bu-ul-lim* GIBIL
11 *[e-pé-ši]-im i-na pa-ni-tum*
12 [X X X] ^{lú}*mu-uḫ-ḫu-ú-um*

22. Or *li-ik-ri-bu*, so Durand (unless otherwise noted, all references to Durand are to his discussion in *AEM* I/1).

8. A.2030 = *ARM* III 40 = *AEM* 1/1, 221

[1]To my lord
[2]speak:
[3]Thus says Kibri-Dagan,
[4]your servant:
[5]Dagan and Ikrub-Il are well.
[6]The city Terqa and the district are well.
[7]Another matter. On the day that I sent
[8]this my tablet to my lord,
[9]the ecstatic of Dagan
[10]came to me, and
[11]spoke a word to me as follows,
[12]saying:
[13] "The god sent m[e].
[14]Hurry! Write to
[15]the king, that
[16]they offer
[17]funerary offerings for the ghost
[18]of Yaḫdun-Lim."
[19]This is what that ecstatic
[20]said to me, and I have written
[21]to my lord
[22]that my lord may do
[23]what seems good to him.

9. A.4934. = *ARM* III 78 = *AEM* 1/1, 221.

[1][To] my [lor]d
[2][sp]eak:
[3][Thus says] Kibri-Dagan,
[4]your [servant]:
[5][D]agan and Ikrub-Il are well.
[6]The [c]ity Terqa and the district is well.
[7]I am not negligent
[8][t]o harvest the [g]rain of my district
[9][and] to pour it out on the threshing floors.
[10][Another m]atter: Concerning [the mak]ing of the new gate
[11]earlier
[12][PN], the ecstatic,

13 *[il-li-ka]m-ma* /or *[iq-bé-e-e]m-ma*
14 *[i-ta-aš-ša]-aš*
15 *[um-ma šu]-ma*
r16 *[a-na ši-pí-ir a-bu]-ul-lim [š]a-a-ti*
17 *[qa-at-ka šu-k]u-un*
18 *[i-na-an-na* u_4*-u]m ṭup-pí an-né-e-em*
19 *[a-na ṣe-e]r be-lí-ya ú-ša-[b]i-lam*
20 *[*lú*mu-u]ḫ-ḫu-ú-um šu-ú i-tu-ra-am-ma*
21 *[ki-a-am] iq-bé-e-em*
22 *[ù da]n-na-tim iš-ku-na-am um-ma-a-mi*
23 *[šum-ma]*[23] *a-bu-ul-lam ša-a-ti*
24 *[ú]-ul*[24] *te-ep-pé-ša*
25 *[ku-r]u-ul-lum*[25] *iš-ša-ak-ka-an*
26 *[ú-u]l ka-aš-da-tu-nu*
27 *[an-n]i-tam* lú*mu-uḫ-ḫu-ú-[u]m šu-ú*
28 *[iq-b]é-e-em ù a-na e-b[u-ri-im]*
29 *[pu-u]l-lu-sa-ku sú-ḫu-u[r]*
30 *[ki-ša]-di-ya*[26] *ú-ul e-l[e-e]*
31 *[šum-ma] be-lí i-qa-ab-bi*
32 *[né-eḫ-ra-rum li-il-l]i-kam-ma*
[continues on left side, but broken]

10. A.368. = *ARM* VI 45 = *AEM* 1/1, 201.

1 *a-na be-lí-ya*
2 *qí-bí-ma*
3 *um-ma Ba-aḫ-di-Li-im*
4 ÌR-*ka-a-ma*
5 *a-lum Ma-ri*ki É.GAL-*lum*
6 *ù ḫa-al-ṣum ša-lim*
7 *ša-ni-tum A-ḫu-um* SANGA
8 *ša-ar-tam ù sí-sí-ik-tam x x*
9 *[š]a* mí*mu-uḫ-ḫu-tim u[b-l]am*
10 *ù i-na ṭup-pi-i[m]*
11 *ša A-ḫu-um a-na ṣe-er be-[lí-ya]*
12 *ú-ša-bi-l[am]*
13 *ṭe*$_4$*-em-ša ga-am-ru-um ša-ṭe*$_4$*-er*
14 *[a-n]u-um-ma ṭup-pí A-ḫi-im*

23. Von Soden reads [*i-na-an-na*] (*UF* 1 [1969] 198–99).
24. Von Soden reads [*mi-im-ma ú-*]*ul* (loc. cit.).
25. Von Soden reads [*ma?-ti? d*]*u-ul-lum* (loc. cit.).
26. Or [*wa-a*]*r-di-ya*.

[13][cam]e to me /or [spok]e to me, and
[14][being troub]led,
[15][he] spoke [as follows]:
[16]["To the work on] that [ga]te
[17][pu]t [your hand."]
[18][Now on the da]y that I sent this my tablet
[19][to] my lord,
[20]that [ecs]tatic returned to me, and
[21]spoke [as follows] to me,
[22][and] he put it to me strongly, saying:
[23]["If] that gate
[24]you do [no]t make,
[25][a cal]amity will take place.
[26]You have accomplished no[thing at all."]
[27][Th]is is what that ecstatic
[28][to]ld me, but with the har[vest]
[29]I am [preo]ccupied. I am not able
[30]to turn my neck.[27]
[31][If] my lord commands,
[32][let some help co]me to me, and
. . . .

10. A.368. = *ARM* VI 45 = *AEM* 1/1, 201.

[1]To my lord
[2]speak:
[3]Thus says Baḫdi-Lim,
[4]your servant:
[5]The city Mari, the palace,
[6]and the district are well.
[7]Another matter: Aḫum the priest
[8]bro[ug]ht to me the hair and hem
[9][o]f the female ecstatic,
[10]and in the tablet
[11]which Aḫum sent h[ere]
[12]to [my] lor[d],
[13]the complete report about her is written down.
[14][N]ow then [I ha]ve sent

27. Or "to turn aside my servants."

15 *[š]a-ar-tam ù sí-sí-ik-tam ša mu-uḫ-ḫu-tim*
16 *[a-na ṣ]e-er be-lí-ya*
17 *[ú-ša-bi]-lam*

11. A.996 = *ARM* X 4 = *AEM* 1/1, 207.

1 *a-na be-lí-ya qí-bí-ma*
2 *um-ma* ^{mí}*Ši-ib-tu* GEME$_2$*-ka-a-ma*
3 *aš-šum ṭe*$_4$*-em ge-er-ri-im*
4 *ša be-lí i-la-ku it-ta-tim*
5 *zi-ka-ra-am ù sí-in-ni-iš-tam*
6 *aš!-qí!*[28] *áš-ta-al-ma i-ge-er-ru-ú-um*
7 *a-na be-lí-ya ma-di-iš da-mi-iq*
8 *a-na Iš-me-*^{d}*Da-gan qa-tam-ma*
9 *zi-ka-ra-am ù s[í]-in-ni-iš-tam*
10 *áš-ta-al-ma i-ge-er-ru-šu*
11 *ú-ul da-mi-iq*
12 *ù ṭe*$_4$*-em-šu ša-pa-al še-ep be-lí-ya*
13 *ša-ki-in um-ma šu-nu-ma be-lí ḫu-ma-ša-am i[š-ši]*
14 *a-na Iš-me-*^{d}*Da-gan ḫu-ma-ša-am iš-ši-ma*
15 *um-ma i-na {i-na} ḫu-ma-ši-im e-le-i-ka*
16 *ši-it-pu-ṣú-um ši-it-pa-aṣ-ma*
17 *i-na ši-it-pu-ṣú e-le-i-ka*
18 *um-ma a-na-ku-ma be-lí a-na ka-ak-ki*
19 *i-ṭe*$_4$*-eḫ-ḫe-e um-ma šu-nu-ma*
20 *ka-ak-ku*
21 *ú-ul in-né-pé-šu*
22 *ki-ma ka-ša-di-im-ma*
23 *ti-il-la-tu-[š]u*
24 *is-sà-ap-pa-[ḫ]a*
25 *ù qa-qa-[ad Iš-me]-*^{d}*Da-gan i-na-ki-sú-ma*
26 *ša-pa-al še-ep [b]e-lí-ya*
27 *i-ša-ak-ka-nu um-ma-a-mi*
28 *ṣa-bu-um ša I[š-m]e-*^{d}*Da-gan*
29 *ma-ad ù šum-ma [a]-[ka-aš-š]a-ad*[29]
30 *til-la-tu-šu is-sà-ap-[pa-ḫ]a-šu*

28. Following Durand. Berger (*UF* 1, 221), following a suggestion by von Soden, reads *ú!-qí*, "I awaited." Römer (*Frauenbriefe*, 50) tentatively accepts this reading and transposes it to the end of line 4: "I awaited oracles. A man and a woman I questioned."

29. Dossin (*ARMT* X) and Durand read *ṣ[a-bu-šu m]a-ad*, "even if his troops are numerous, they will be scattered from him," but this creates difficulties with the following context.

[15]the tablet of Aḫum (and)
[16]the [h]air and hem of the female ecstatic
[17][to] my lord.

11. A.996 = *ARM* X 4 = *AEM* 1/1, 207.

[1]To my lord speak:
[2]Thus says Šibtu, your maidservant:
[3]With regard to the report on the campaign
[4]on which my lord plans to go, (to obtain) oracles
[5]I caused a man and a woman
[6]to drink. I questioned (them), and the omen
[7]is very favorable for my lord.
[8]In the same way for Išme-Dagan
[9]I questioned the man and the woman,
[10]and the omen for him
[11]is not favorable.
[12]And the report for him is that he will be placed under the foot
[13]of my lord. They said: My lord l[ifted] the fist.
[14]Against Išme-Dagan he lifted the fist, and
[15]said, "With the fist I will overpower you.
[16]Wrestle all you want, but
[17]in wrestling I will overpower you."
[18]I asked, "Shall my lord draw near to battle?"
[19]They answered,
[20] "A battle
[21]will not be fought.
[22]As soon as he (Zimri-Lim) approaches,
[23]his (Išme-Dagan's) auxiliary troops
[24]will be scattered
[25]and they will cut off the hea[d of Išme]-Dagan,
[26]and under the foot of my lord
[27]they will place (it)." (Should my lord) say,
[28] "The army of I[šm]e-Dagan
[29]is large. Even if [I arri]ve
[30](and) his auxiliary troops are scattered from him,

31 *til-la-ti-i ya-at-tu-ú-um*[30] ^{d}*Da-gan*
32 ^{d}IM[31] ^{d}*I-túr-Me-er ù* ^{d}NIN-*é-kál-lim*
33 *ù* ^{d}IM-*ma be-el pu-ru-us-sé-e-em*
34 *ša i-na i-di be-lí-ya i-l[a-ku]*
35 *as-sú-ur-ri be-lí ke-em i-[qa-ab-bi]*
36 *um-ma-a-mi i-na nu-la-ni*[32] *ú[-ša-ad-bi-ib-š]u-ni-ti*
37 *mi-im-ma ú-ul ú-[š]a-ad-ba-[ab-šu-nu-ti]*
38 *šu-nu-ma i-da-ab-bu-bu šu-nu-[ma]*
39 *im-ta-ḫa-[ru]*
40 *um-ma šu-nu-ma til-la-at Iš-me-*^{d}*[Da-gan]*
41 ^{lú}*a-sí-ru i-na sà-ra-tim-[ma]*
42 *[ù] di-ṣa-tim it-ti-šu it-ta-na-⟨la⟩-ku*
43 *[a-wa]-sú ú-[u]l i-le-qú-ú*
44 *[a-n]a pa-ni be-lí-ya ṣa-bu-šu*
45 *[is]-sà-ap-pa-aḫ*

12. A.3217 = *ARM* X 6 = *AEM* 1/1, 212.

1 *a-na be-lí-ya*
2 *qí-[b]í-ma*
3 *um-ma* ^{mí}*Š[i-i]b-tu* GEME$_2$-*ka-a-m[a]*
4 *é-kál-l[um] ša-lim*
5 ^{m}*Ì-[lí-ḫa-a]z-na-a-ya* ^{lú}*a[s-s]í-[i]n-n[u]*
6 *ša An-[nu-ni-tim il]-li-ka[m]*
7 *i-na l[i-ib-bi* É *An-nu-ni-tim]*
8 [o o o o o o o]*-x-ma*
9 *[ṭe$_4$-mu-um aš-šum* KÁ.DINGIR.R]A^{ki}
10 *[a-na be-lí-ya iš-š]a-ap-ra-šu*
11 *[um-ma-mi Ḫa-am-mu-r]a-bi*

30. Following Berger (*UF* 1, 221) and Römer (*Frauenbriefe*, 51). Moran's reading is *til-la-ti-⟨im⟩ i-ya-at-tu eš-ra*, "they have hemmed in my auxiliary troops," which assumes an error *yattu(n)* for *yatti(n)* (*Biblica* 50, 47). Moreover, it has the added difficulty that it forces him to read the preceding clause as interrogative, though it does not have the lengthened vowel one expects. The lengthening of *ya-at-tu-ú-um* shows where the question really is. Dossin reads *til-la-ti i-ya-at-tu-ú-um* ^{d}*Da-gan*, "my auxiliary troops are Dagan, etc. (*ARMT* X)," but Dagan clearly begins the next clause, which has a different speaker, since Zimri-Lim is now referred to in the third person.

31. Durand reads ^{d}UTU, but the copy clearly has ^{d}IM, and one wonders if his reading is not motivated by the desire to avoid the repetition of the same divine name in the next line, but if one construes the next line as a parenthetical expression as I do, the repetition is not troubling.

32. Durand reads *be-la-ni*. Cf. *ARM* 8, 8:5. The sense of the term, whatever its correct vocalization, is "trickery, pretext, evil intentions." That is, Šibtu is making the oracle givers speak a positive message, because she wants to put Zimri-Lim in a difficult situation.

[31]what are my auxiliary troops?” [33] It is Dagan,
[32]Adad, Itur-Mer, and Belet-ekallim—and
[33]Adad is indeed the lord of decisions—
[34]who g[o] at the side of my lord.
[35]Heaven forbid that my lord should s[ay],
[36] “With evil intentions she is [making] them [speak].”
[37]I am not making [them] say anything.
[38]They are speaking on their own. They
[39]are agre[eing] on their own.
[40]They say, “The auxiliary troops of Išme-Dagan
[41]are prisoners. With lies
[42][and] treachery they are going around with him.
[43]They will not accept his [command].
[44][I]n the presence of my lord his (Išme-Dagan’s) army
[45]will be [sc]attered.”

12. A.3217 = *ARM* X 6 = *AEM* 1/1, 212.

[1]To my lord
[2]speak:
[3]Thus says Šibtu, your maidservant:
[4]The palace is well.
[5]I[li-Ḫa]znaya, the cult homosexual
[6]of An[nunitum ca]me to m[e].
[7]In the m[idst of the temple of Annunitum]
[8]. . . , and
[9][a message concerning Babylo]n
[10][was] sent by him [to my lord],
[11][saying, “Ḫammu-r]abi

33. That is, even if Išme-Dagan’s auxiliaries are scattered, his army is still large without them, and Zimri-Lim doesn’t have any auxiliaries to speak of. Against this lack of confidence Šibtu reminds him that the gods march at his side, including Adad, the god who renders the decisions about the outcome of battles.

12 [o o o o o o]-*ku*
(One third of tablet is missing.)
1′ *[aš-šu-um ṭe*$_{4}$*-e]m!* KÁ.DING[IR.RA^{ki}]
2′ *it!-ta!-tim! aš!-qí!*[34] *áš-ta-al-m[a]*
3′ LÚ *šu-ú ma-da-tim a-na ma-a-tim an-ni-tim*
4′ *ú-ša-am*[35] *ú-ul i-ka-aš-ša-ad*
5′ *be-lí i-im-ma-ar ša* DINGIR-*lum* LÚ *ša-a-ti*
6′ *i-ip-pé-šu ta-ka-aš-ša-as-sú*
7′ *ù e-li-šu ta-az-za-az*
8′ *u*$_{4}$*-mu-šu qé-er-bu ú-ul i-ba-al-lu-uṭ*
9′ *be-lí an-ni-tam lu-ú i-[d]e*
10′ *la-ma ṭe*$_{4}$*-em Ì-lí-Ḫa-az-na-a-[y]a*
11′ *ša An-nu-ni-tum iš-pu-ra-aš-[š]u*
12′ *u*$_{4}$-5-KAM *a-na-ku áš-ta-a-a[l-m]a*
13′ *[ṭe*$_{4}$*-]mu-um ša An-nu-ni-[tum]*
14′ *[iš-p]u-ra-ak-kum*
15′ *ù ša a-ša-lu*
16′ *iš-te*$_{9}$*-en*$_{6}$*-ma*

13. A.100 = *ARM* X 7 = *AEM* 1/1, 213.

1 *a-na be-lí-ya*
2 *qí-bí-ma*
3 *um-ma* ^{mí}*Ši-ib-tu*
4 GEME$_{2}$-*ka-a-ma é-kál-lum ša-lim*
5 *i-na* É *An-nu-ni-tim u*$_{4}$-3-K[A]M
6 ^{m}*Še-li-{bu}-bu-um*
7 *im-ma-ḫu-um-ma An-nu-ni-tum-ma*
8 ^{m}*Zi-im-ri-Li-im*
9 *i-na ba-ar-tim*
10 *i-la-at-ta-ku-ka*
11 *pa-ga-ar-ka ú-ṣú-ur*
12 ÌR^{meš} *eb-bi-ka*[36]
13 *ša ta-ra-am-mu*
14 *i-ta-ti-k[a]*
15 *šu-ku-un*
16 *šu-zi-is-sú-nu-ti-ma*
17 *li-iṣ-ṣú-ru-k[a]*

34. The reading follows Durand. Each of these signs is partially broken.
35. The verb is presumably the D stem of *šeʾûm*. Cf. von Soden, *UF* 1, 198.
36. Durand reads ⟨*li*⟩-*ib-bi-ka*, "servants of your heart," because he claims that the *ebbu* are never concerned with the personal protection of the king.

12 . . . .
(One third of tablet is missing.)
1′ [Concerning the messa]ge about Baby[lon]
2′ (To obtain) oracles I caused to drink. I questioned,
3′ and (the response was), “That man plots many things against this country,
4′ but he will not succeed.
5′ My lord will see what the god will do
6′ to that man. You will capture him
7′ and you will stand upon him.
8′ His day is near. He will not live.
9′ My lord should know this!”
10′ Five days before the message of Ili-Ḫaznaya
11′ which Annunitum sent,
12′ I made inquiry, and
13′ the [me]ssage which Annuni[tum]
14′ [s]ent to you
15′ and that which I obtained by inquiry
16′ are one (i.e., agree completely).

13. A.100 = *ARM* X 7 = *AEM* 1/1, 213.

1 To my lord
2 speak:
3 Thus says Šibtu,
4 your maidservant: The palace is well.
5 On the third day in the temple of Annunitum
6 Šelibum
7 fell into an ecstatic trance, and Annunitum said,
8 “Zimri-Lim,
9 in a rebellion
10 they will test you.
11 Guard yourself.
12 Your reliablc servants
13 whom you love
14 put
15 at your sides.
16 Station them that
17 they may protect you.

18 *a-na ra-ma-ni-k[a-ma]*
19 *la ta-at-ta-na-a[l-la-a]k*
20 *ù* LÚ^{meš} *ša i-la-a[t-ta-ku-k]a*
21 *a-na qa-ti!-ka a-[wi-li*^{meš} *š]u-nu-ti*
22 *ú-ma-al-[la-am]*
23 *i-na-an-na a-[nu-um-ma]*
24 *ša-a[r]-ta-[am ù sí-sí-ik-tam]*
25 *ša as-sí-[in-nim]*
26 *a-na ṣ[e-er be-lí-ya]*
27 *ú-ša-bi-[lam]*

14. A.671 = *ARM* X 8 = *AEM* 1/1, 214.

1 *a-na be-lí-ya*
2 *qí-bí-ma*
3 *um-ma* ^{mí}*Ši-ib-tu*
4 GEME$_2$-*ka-a-ma*
5 *i-na* É *An-nu-ni-tim ša li-ib-bi a-lim*
6 $^{\text{m mí}}$*A-ḫa-tum* MUNUS.TUR ^{d}*Da-gan-ma-lik*
7 *im-ma-ḫi-ma ki-a-am iq-bi*
8 *um-ma-mi Zi-im-ri-Li-im*
9 *ù šum-ma at-ta mi-ša-ta-an-ni*
10 *a-na-ku e-li-ka*
11 *a-ḫa-ab-bu-ub*[37]
12 *na-ak-ri-ka*
13 *a-na qa-ti-ka*
14 *ú-ma-al-la*
15 *ù* LÚ^{meš} *šar-ra-qí-ya*
16 *a-ṣa-ab-ba-at-ma*
17 *a-na ka-ra-aš* ^{d}NIN-*é-kál-lim*
18 *a-ka-am-mi-is-sú-nu-ti*
19 *i-na ša-ni-i-im u*$_4$*-mi-im*
20 ^{m}*A-ḫu-um* ^{lú}SANGA *ṭe*$_4$*-ma-am*
21 *an-né-e-em šar-ta-am*
22 *ù sí-is-sí-ik-tam*
23 *ub-la-am-ma a-na be-lí-ya*
24 *aš-pu-ra-am šar-ta-am*
25 *ù s[i-i]s-sí-ik-tam*
26 *ak-nu-ka-am-ma*
27 *a-na ṣe-er be-lí-ya*
28 *uš-ta-bi-lam*

---

37. Durand reads *a-ḫa-ab-bu-uṣ*$_4$, "I will massacre on your behalf."

[18]By yousel[f]
[19]do not wal[k aroun]d.
[20]And as for the men who will t[est y]ou
[21]those m[en] I will deliv[er]
[22]into your hand."
[23]Now t[hen]
[24]the ha[ir and the hem]
[25]of the cult homo[sexual]
[26]to [my lord]
[27]I have hereby s[ent].

14. A.671 = *ARM* X 8 = *AEM* 1/1, 214.

[1]To my lord,
[2]speak:
[3]Thus says Šibtu,
[4]your maidservant:
[5]In the temple of Annunitum which is inside the city
[6]Aḫatum, the servant girl of Dagan-Malik,
[7]fell into an ecstatic trance, and she spoke as follows,
[8]saying, "Zimri-Lim,
[9]even though you have neglected me,
[10]I will bend over you
[11]in love.
[12]Your enemies
[13]I will deliver
[14]into your hand.
[15]And the men who rob me
[16]I will seize, and
[17]to the destruction of Belet-ekallim
[18]I will gather them.
[19]On the following day
[20]Aḫum, the priest, brought me
[21]this report, the hair,
[22]and the hem,
[23]and to my lord
[24]I have written. The hair
[25]and the h[e]m
[26]I sealed, and
[27]to my lord
[28]I have sent.

15. A.2233 = *ARM* X 9 = *AEM* 1/1, 208.

1 *a-na be-lí-ya*
2 *qí-bí-ma*
3 *um-ma* ^{mí}*Ši-ib-tu*
4 GEME$_2$-*ka-a-ma é-kál-lum ša-lim*
5 ^{m}*Qí-iš-ti-*^{d}*Di-ri-tim*
6 *a-pí-lu-um ša* ^{d}*Di-ri-tim*
7 [U]$_4$-2-KAM *a-na ba-ab! é-kál-l[im il-li-kam]*
8 *[k]i-a-am iš-pu-ra-am [um-ma-mi]*
9 *a-na pa-ni* ^{giš}GU.ZA *Ma-[ri*^{ki}*]*
10 *ma-am-ma-am ú-ul i-i[l!-le-em]*
11 *a-na Zi-im-r[i-Li-im-ma]*
12 *a-la-i-tum na-ad-[na-at]*
13 ^{giš}SUKUR LÚ *E-l[a-am-tim*^{ki} *iš-še-bi-ir]*
14 *an-ni-tam [iq-bé-e-em]*
15 *ša-n[i-tam*
(. . .)
1′ *um-ma* ^{d}*[É-a-ma . . . .]*
2′ *ki-im-t[um . . . .]*
3′ *ni-i[š* DINGIR-*lim i ni-iḫ-sú-us]*
4′ *a-šar m[u-ú i-ba-aš-šu-ú]*[38]
5′ *ni-iš* DINGIR-*lim ni-i[ḫ-sú-us]*
6′ ^{d}*A-su-me-e-[e]m iš*$_7$*-[ta-si]*
7′ ^{d}*A-su-mu-um ar-[ḫi-iš il-li-ik-ma]*
8′ *a-wa-tam a-na* ^{d}*É-[a iq-bi]*
9′ *ša* ^{d}*A-sú-mu-um [a-na* ^{d}*É-a iq-bu-ú]*
10′ *ú-ul es-me it-[bé-ma* ^{d}*É-a]*
11′ *iq-bi um-ma-mi [ki-ma ni-iš* DINGIR-*lim]*
12′ *ni-za-ak-ka-ru ru-[ša-am]*
13′ *ù sí-ip-pa-am ša ba-ab [Ma-ri*^{ki}*]*
14′ *li-il-qú-nim-ma ni-iš* DINGIR-*lim [i ni-iḫ-s]ú-us*
15′ *ru-ša-am ù sí-ip-pa-am ša ba-[ab M]a-ri*^{ki}
16′ *il-qú-ni-im-ma i-na me-e im-ḫu-[ḫ]u-ma*
17′ DINGIR^{meš} *ù i-la-tum i[š]-te-e*
18′ *um-ma* ^{d}*É-a-ma a-na* DINGIR^{meš}
19′ *ti-ma-a*[39] *ša a-na li-bi-it-ti*
20′ *Ma-[r]i*^{ki} *ù ra-bi-iṣ*
21′ [〈*Ma-ri*^{ki}〉 *la-a tu]-ga-al-la-lu*[40]

38. Following the restoration of Moran (*Biblica* 50, 50).
39. Following Moran (ibid.). Durand reads *ṭì-ba-a*.
40. Following Moran (ibid.). Durand reads [*Ma-ri*^{ki} *ú*]*-ga-al-la-lu*.

15. A.2233 = *ARM* X 9 = *AEM* 1/1, 208.

[1]To my lord
[2]speak:
[3]Thus says Šibtu,
[4]your maidservant: The palace is well.
[5]Qišti-Diritum,
[6]the respondent of Diritum,
[7][came here] on the second [da]y to the gate of the pala[ce].
[8][T]hus he sent me [saying],
[9] "Against the throne of Ma[ri]
[10]no one will co[me up].
[11]To Zimr[i-Lim alone]
[12]the upper country is giv[en].
[13]The lance of the man of El[am will be broken."]
[14]This [is what he said to me.]
[15]Ano[ther matter. . . .]
(. . .)
[1′]Thus said [Ea. . . .]
[2′]fami[ly. . . .]
[3′][Let us take/remember] the oat[h.]
[4′]There where wa[ter is]
[5′]let us t[ake] the oath.
[6′]He c[alled] Asumum.
[7′]Asumum [came] q[uickly, and]
[8′][spoke] a word to E[a.]
[9′]What Asumum [said to Ea]
[10′]I did not hear. [Ea] ro[se up, and]
[11′]spoke as follows, ["Since an oath]
[12′]we are taking, let them take the di[rt]
[13′]and the doorjamb of the gate of [Mari,]
[14′]that [we might take] the oath."
[15′]They took the dirt and doorjamb of the ga[te of M]ari,
[16′]dissolved (it) in water, and
[17′]the gods and goddesses drank.
[18′]Thus said Ea to the gods,
[19′] "Swear that against the brickwork
[20′]of Mari and the protective deity of
[21′][Mari you will do no] wrong."

22′ [DINGIR^{me}]^{š} *ù i-la-t*[*um it-mu-ú*][41]
23′ [*um-m*]*a-mi a-na li-bi-it-ti*
24′ [*Ma*]-*ri*^{ki} *ù ra-bi-iṣ*
25′ *Ma-ri*^{ki}
26′ *ú-ul nu-ga-al-la-a*[*l*]

16. A.2437 = *ARM* X 10 = *AEM* 1/1, 236.

1 [*a-na be-lí-ya*]
2 [*qí-bí-*]*m*[*a*]
3 [*u*]*m-ma* ^{mí}*Š*[*i-i*]*b-tu* GEME$_2$-*ka-a-m*[*a*]
4 É DINGIR^{meš} DINGIR^{meš} *é-kál-lum*
5 *ù ne-pa-ra-tum ša-al-ma*
6 *ša-ni-tam* ^{mí}*Ka-ak-ka-li-di*
7 *i-na* É ^{d}*I-túr-Me-er i-mu-ur*
8 *um-ma-a-mi* 2 ^{giš}MÁ *ma-al-lu-ú*
9 *ra-ab-bu-tum na-ra-am pa-ar-ku-ma*
10 LUGAL *ù* LÚ^{meš} *re-du-um*
11 ŠÀ-*ba ra-ki-ib ša i-mi-it-tim*
12 [*a-n*]*a šu-mé-lim*
13 [*i*]-*ša-as-su-ú*
14 [*u*]*m-ma šu-nu-ma šar-ru-tum*
15 [*ḫa-a*]*ṭ-ṭú-um* ^{giš}GU.ZA
16 *pa!-lu!-um! ma!-tum e-*[*l*]*i-tum*
17 *ù ša-ap-li-tum*
18 *a-na Zi-im-ri-Li-im*
19 *na-a*[*d*]-*na-*[*a*]*t ù* LÚ^{meš} *re-du-ú-um*
20 *ka-lu-š*[*u i*]-*ip-pa-al*
21 *a-na Zi-im-ri-Li-im-ma*
22 *na-ad-na-at*
23 ^{giš}MÁ *m*[*a-a*]*l-lu-ú šu-nu*
24 *a-na b*[*a*]*-ab é-kál-lim*
25 [. . .]-*ma*
26 [. . .]-*šu*
. . . .

41. Following Moran (ibid.). Durand reads *i-la-t*[*um iq-bé-ni-im*].

22′ [The god]s and the godd[esses swore,]
23′ [say]ing, “Against the brickwork of
24′ [Ma]ri and the protective deity
25′ of Mari
26′ we will do no wrong.”[42]

16. A.2437 = *ARM* X 10 = *AEM* 1/1, 236.

1 [To my lord]
2 [spe]a[k:]
3 [T]hus says Š[i]btu, your maidservant:
4 The temples, the gods, the palace,
5 and workrooms are well.
6 Another matter: Kakkalidi
7 has seen (a vision) in the temple of Itur-Mer,
8 saying, “Two large barges
9 were blocking the river, and
10 the king and soldiers
11 were riding in it. Those on the right
12 were calling out
13 to (those on) the left,
14 saying, ‘The kingdom,
15 [the sc]epter, the throne,
16 the rule, the u[p]per land,
17 and the lower (land)
18 are given
19 to Zimri-Lim.’ And all the soldiers
20 were answering,
21 To Zimri-Lim alone
22 it is given.
23 Those barges
24 [arrived] at the g[a]te of the palace,
25 and
26 . . . .
. . . .

42. If one adopted Durand’s reading (all references to Durand are to his discussion of the individual passages in *AEM* 1/1), the translations would be, “ ‘Is it good that they do wrong to the brickwork and the protective deity of [Mari]?’ The [go]ds and goddes[ses spoke, sa]ying, ‘To the brickwork of Mari and the protective deity of Mari we will do no wrong.’ ”

17. A.994 = *ARM* X 50 = *AEM* 1/1, 237.

^{1}*a-na be-lí-ya qí-bí-ma*
^{2}*um-ma* $^{\text{mí.d}}$IM-*du-ri* GEME$_2$-*ka-a-ma*
^{3}*iš-tu šu-lu-um* É *a-bi-ka*
^{4}*ma-ti-ma šu-tam an-ni-tam*
^{5}*ú-ul a-mu-ur it-ta-tu-{tu}-ya*
^{6}*ša pa-na-nu-um*
^{7}*[an]-ni-it-ta-an*
^{8}*i-na šu-ut-ti-ya a-na* É ^{d}NIN-*é-kál-lim*
^{9}*e!-ru-ub-ma* ^{d}NIN-*é-kál-lim*
^{10}*ú-ul wa-aš-ba-at ù* ALAM$^{\text{ḫi.a}}$
^{11}*ša ma-aḫ-ri-ša ú-ul i-ba-šu-ú*
^{12}*ù a-mu-ur-ma ar-ṭú-up ba-ka-a-am*
^{13}*šu-ut-ti an-ni-tum ša ba-ra-ar-tim*
^{14}*a-tu-ur-ma Da-da* ^{lú}SANGA
^{15}*[š]a Eš$_4$-tár bi-iš$_7$-ra*
^{16}*[i]-na* KÁ ^{d}NIN-*é-kál-lim*
^{17}*iz-za-az-ma pí-ú na-ak-rum*
^{18}*[ki]-a-am iš-ta-na-ás-si*
^{19}*um-ma-mi t[u-r]a* ^{d}*D[a-g]an*
^{20}*tu-ra* ^{d}*D[a-g]an ki-a-am*
^{21}*iš-ta-na-ás-si ša-ni-tam*
^{22} ^{mí}*mu-uḫ-ḫu-tum i-na* É *An-nu-ni-tim*
^{23}*it-bé-e-ma um-ma-mi Zi-im-ri-Li-im*
^{24}*a-na* KASKAL.A *la ta-al-la-ak*
^{25}*i-na Ma-ri*^{ki} *ši-ib-ma*
^{26}*ù a-na-ku-ma a-ta-na-ap-pa-al*
^{27}*a-na pa-ag-ri-šu na-ṣa-ri-im*
^{28}*be-lí a-aḫ-šu la i-na-ad-di*[43]
^{29}*a-nu-um-ma ša-ar-ti*
^{30}*ù s[í-s]í-ik-ti*
^{31}*a!-[na-ku] ak-nu-ka-am-ma*
^{32}*a-na ṣe-er be-lí-ya*
^{33}*ú-ša-bi-lam*

18. A.122 = *ARM* X 51 = *AEM* 1/1, 238.

^{1}*a-na be-lí-ya*
^{2}*qí-bí-ma*
^{3}*um-ma* $^{\text{mí.d}}$IM-*du-ri*

43. Lines 27 and 28 are transposed in Dossin's copy according to Durand.

17. A.994 = *ARM* X 50 = *AEM* 1/1, 237.

[1]To my lord speak:
[2]Thus says Adad-duri, your maidservant:
[3]Since the end of your father's house,
[4]I have never seen this dream.
[5]My signs
[6]which (I saw) before
[7]are (like) [th]ese.
[8]In my dream I entered the temple of Belet-ekallim,
[9]but Belet-ekallim
[10]was no longer seated, and the statues
[11]which are before her were not there.
[12]When I saw, I kept on weeping.
[13]This dream of mine was in the first watch.
[14]I dreamed again (turned), and Dada, the priest
[15]of the Bishrian Ištar
[16]was standing in the gate of Belet-ekallim,
[17]and a strange voice
[18]kept crying out as follows,
[19]saying, "Re[tur]n O D[ag]an!
[20]Return O D[ag]an." Thus
[21]it kept crying out. Another matter:
[22]a female ecstatic rose in the temple of Annunitum,
[23]and said, "Zimri-Lim,
[24]you shall not go on campaign.
[25]Stay in Mari,
[26]and I will keep on responding (to you)."
[27]My lord should not be negligent
[28]in protecting himself.
[29]Now my hair
[30]and my h[e]m
[31]I [myself] have sealed, and
[32]I have sent (them)
[33]to my lord.

18. A.122 = *ARM* X 51 = *AEM* 1/1, 238.

[1]To my lord
[2]speak:
[3]Thus says Adad-duri:

4 ^{m}*I-din-Ì-lí* ^{lú}SANGA
5 *ša* ^{d}*I-túr-Me-er*
6 *šu-ut-ta-am iṭ-ṭú-ul*
7 *um-ma šu-ú-m*[*a*]
8 *i-na šu-ut-ti-ya*
9 ^{d}NIN-*bi-ri iz-zi-iz-za-am-ma*
10 *ki-a-am iq-bé-em*
11 *um-ma ši-i-ma*
12 *šar!-ru-tum na-al!-ba!-*[*n*]*a!-as!-s*[*ú*]
13 *ù pa-lu-um du-ur-šu*
14 *a-na* ^{giš}*di-im-tim*
15 *a-na mi-ni-im i-*te_9*-né-él-le*
16 *pa-ga-ar-šu l*[*i-i*]*ṣ-ṣ*[*ú*]*-ur*
17 *i-na-an-na be-lí a-na na-ṣa-ar*
18 *pa-ag-ri-šu*
19 *la i-ig-ge*

19. A. 3420 = *ARM* X 53 = *AEM* 1/1, 195.

1 [*a-na*] *be-lí-ya*
2 [*qí*]*-bí-ma*
3 [*um*]*-ma* $^{mí.d}$IM-*du-ri-ma*
4 [GEM]E_2-*ka-a-ma*
5 [*a-p*]*í-lum i-na* É ^{d}[*Ḫ*]*i-ša-me-tim*
6 [^{m}]*I-ṣí-a-ḫu šu-um-šu*
7 [*i*]*t-bi-*[*m*]*a um-ma-mi*
8 [*š*]*a*[44] *wa-ar-ki-ka-ma*
9 [*a-ka-a*]*l!-ka*[45] *i-ka-lu*
10 [*ù k*]*a-as-ka*
11 [*i-š*]*a-tu-ú*
12 [*it-t*]*i-ka la dam!-qa-a-tim*
13 [*le-e*]*m-né-e-tim*
14 [LÚ^{meš} *b*]*e-el a-wa-ti-ka*
15 [*uš-te-n*]*é-ṣú-ú*
16 [*a-n*]*a-ku-ma ka-ab-sà-ak-šu-nu-ti*
[. . . .]

44. Reading with Moran (*Biblica* 50, 34). Durand reads [*i-n*]*a wa-ar-ki-ka-ma*, "after your departure," and takes it to refer to servants misusing his provisions, but it is difficult to see how that fits the context. The eating and drinking idiom seems to imply a covenant meal, see *ARM* VIII 13:11–13.

45. Moran reads [*kar-k*]*a*, "your [ram]," based on *ARM* VIII 13 (ibid.).

4 Iddin-Ili, the priest
5 of Itur-Mer,
6 saw a dream.
7 Thus he said:
8 "In my dream
9 Belet-biri stood, and
10 spoke to me thus,
11 saying,
12 'Kingship is his brickwork,
13 and the rule is his wall.
14 Why does he keep climbing up
15 to the siege tower?
16 Let him protect himself.' "
17 Now my lord should not be negligent
18 in protecting
19 himself.

19. A. 3420 = *ARM* X 53 = *AEM* 1/1, 195.

1 [To] my lord
2 [sp]eak:
3 [Th]us says Adad-duri,
4 your [maidser]vant:
5 [A res]pondent named Iṣi-aḫu
6 rose in the temple of [Ḫ]išametum,
7 and said,
8 Only [tho]se who follow you
9 will eat your [brea]d
10 [and dr]ink
11 your [c]up.
12 Unfavorable
13 [(and) ev]il (words)
14 your [opp]onents
15 [keep ex]pressing [ag]ainst you.
16 But I alone have trampled them. . . .
[. . . .]

20. A.1047 = *ARM* X 80 = *AEM* 1/1, 197.

1 *a-na Ka-ak-ka-bi*
2 *qí-bí-ma*
3 *um-ma* ^{mí}*I-ni-ib-ši-na-ma*
4 *i-na p*[*a*]*-ni-tim Še-le-bu-um as-sí-in-nu*
5 *te-er-tam id-di-*[*na*]*m-ma aš-pu-ra-kum*
6 *i-na-an-na* 1 ^{mí}*qa-ma-*[*t*]*um*
7 *ša* ^{d}*D*[*a-gan*] *ša Ter-qa*^{ki}
8 [*i*]*l-li-ka-am-ma*
9 [*k*]*i-a-am iq-bé-e-em*
10 [*u*]*m-ma ši-i-*[*m*]*a*
11 *sa-li-ma-tum ša* LÚ ÈŠ.N[UN.NA]^{ki}
12 *da-aṣ-tum-ma*
13 *ša-pa-al* IN.NU.DA *mu-ú*
14 *i-il-la-ku ù a-na še-tim*
15 *ša ú-kà-aṣ-ṣa-ru a-ka-am-mi-is-sú*
16 *a-al-šu ú-ḫa-al-la-aq*
17 *ù ma-ak-ku-ur-šu*
18 *ša iš-tu aq-da-mi*
19 {*šu*} *šu-ul-pu-tam ú-ša-al-p*[*a-a*]*t*
20 *an-ni-tam iq-bé-e-em*
21 *i-na-an-*[*n*]*a pa-ga-ar-ka*
22 *ú-ṣú-ur ba-lum te-er-tim*
23 *a-na li-ib-bi a-lim*
24 *la te-er-ru-u*[*b*]
25 *ki-a-am eš-me um-ma-a-mi*
26 *a-na ra-ma-ni-šu iš-ta-na-ar-*[*ra*]*-a*[*r*]
27 *a-na ra-ma-ni-ka la ta-áš-t*[*a*]*-na-ar-ra-a*[*r*]

21. A.2264 = *ARM* X 81 = *AEM* 1/1, 204.

1 *a-na Ka-ak-ka-bi*
2 *qí-bí-ma*
3 *um-ma* [^{m}]^{í}*I-ni-ib-ši-na-ma*
4 $^{\text{m.mí}}$*In-ni-ba-na a-pí-il-tum*
5 *it-bi-ma ki-a-am id-bu-*[*u*]*b*
6 *um-ma-a-mi Zi-im-r*[*i*]*-Li-im*
7 *a-dì! ša-ar-ra-qí*{*a ya bi*}*-šu!* [46]

46. So Durand. The copy suggests that the *ya* is not an erasure, but Durand is probably correct in assuming that the writer anticipated the *a-ya-bi-šu* of the next line before realizing that he had not completed the current word *ša-ar-ra-qí-šu*.

20. A.1047 = *ARM* X 80 = *AEM* 1/1, 197.

[1]To my Star[47]
[2]speak:
[3]Thus says Inibšina:
[4]Earlier Šelebum, the cult homosexual,
[5]gave me an oracle, and I sent it to you.
[6]Now a *qammatum*
[7]of D[agan] of Terqa
[8][c]ame to me, and
[9]spoke as follows,
[10]saying:
[11] "The peaceful words of the man of Ešnunna
[12]are only treachery.
[13]Below the staw water
[14]runs. But into the net
[15]which he ties I will gather him.
[16]His city I will destroy,
[17]and his treasure
[18]which is from ancient times
[19]I will surely plunder."
[20]This is what she said to me.
[21]Now guard
[22]yourself. Without an oracle
[23]do not enter
[24]into the center of the city.
[25]Thus I have heard them say,
[26] "By himself he keeps moving around."[48]
[27]Do not keep moving around by yourself.

21. A.2264 = *ARM* X 81 = *AEM* 1/1, 204.

[1]To my Star
[2]speak:
[3]Thus says Inibsina:
[4]Inni-bana, the female respondent,
[5]arose, and spoke as follows,
[6]saying, "Zimri-Lim
[7]together with his robbers

47. "My Star" is a nickname for the king, Zimri-Lim.

48. The meaning of the verb *šarāru* is uncertain. It might mean "go ahead" or "move around" (cf. *CAD*), but Durand thinks the sense is "to distinguish oneself (in battle)."

8 [*ù*] *a-ya-bi-šu ù ša i-ta-ti-šu*
9 [*i*]-*sà-aḫ-ḫu-ru*
10 [o o o o o]-*šu*
11 [o o o o o o]
12 [o o o] x x x
13 [*la it*]-*ta-al-la-ak*
14 [o o *la*] *i-ša-am-ma*
15 *la i-š*[*a*]-*ak-ka-an*
16 *a-nu-um-ma ša-ar-ti*
17 *ù sí-sí-ik-ti ad-di-na-ki-im*
18 *li-za-ak-ku-ú*
19 *i-na-an-na a-nu-um-ma*
20 *ša-ar-tam ù sí-sí-ik-tam*
21 *a-na Ka-ak-ka-bi ú-ša-bi-lam*
22 ^{m}*K*[*a*]-*ak-ka-bi te-er-tam*
23 [*li-še*]-*pí-iš-ma a-na zi-im*
24 *te-re-ti-šu Ka-ak-ka-bi*
25 *l*[*i*]-*pu-úš* ^{m}*Ka-ak-ka-b*[*i*]
26 *pa-ga-ar-šu li-iṣ-ṣú-ur*

22. A.2858 = *ARM* X 94 = *AEM* 1/1, 239.

1 *a-na be-lí-ya* [*qí-bí-ma*]
2 *um-ma* ^{mí}*Ši-ma-t*[*um* GEME$_2$-*ka-a-ma*]
3 *iš-tu u*$_4$*-mi-im ša iš-*[*tu Ma-ri*^{ki} *ú-še-ṣú-ni*]
4 *ma-di-iš al-ta-*[*as-su-um*]
5 *ù a-la-ni ka-la-šu-nu a-*[*mu-ur*]
6 *ša k*[*i-m*]*a šu-ba-at be-lí-ya-*[*ma*]
7 *ù ša ki-ma be-lí-ya i-*[*mu-ru-ni*]
8 *i-na-an-na šum-ma be-lí a-n*[*a I-la-an-ṣú-ra*^{ki}]
9 *a-*[*n*]*a a-la-ki-im pa-nu-šu ša-*[*ak-nu*]
10 [o o o] *li* x x x [o o o]
Break
1′ [o o o] *a-na pa-an* [*b*]*e-l*[*í-y*]*a*
2′ [o] x *ú-ṣa-ab-ba-*[*at*]
3′ *ù pa-an be-lí-ya ú!-ṣa!-ba!-*[*at*][49]
4′ *ù aš-šum* DUMU.MUNUS [*š*]*a Te!-pa!-*[*ḫi-im*]
5′ *i-na šu-*[*u*]*t-ti-y*[*a-m*]*a* LÚ-*lum*
6′ *iz-zi-iz-ma u*[*m-m*]*a šu-m*[*a*]

49. Following Durand. The traces on the copy look more like *l*[*u-m*]*u-*[*u*]*r*, "let me see," which is what Moran reads (*Biblica* 50, 43).

8 [and] his enemies and those who
9 circle around his borders
10 . . .
11 . . .
12 . . .
13 [He shal]l not go away
14 [. . .] he will [not] buy, and
15 he will not place.
16 Now my hair
17 and my hem I have given to you
18 Let them clear (the matter)."
19 Now then
20 the hair and hem
21 I have sent to my Star.
22 [Let] my Star have an oracle
23 performed, and according to the appearance
24 of his oracles let my Star
25 act. Let my Star
26 protect himself.

22. A.2858 = *ARM* X 94 = *AEM* 1/1, 239.

1 To my lord [speak:]
2 Thus says Šimat[um, your maidservant]:
3 From the day that [they sent me out] from [Mari,]
4 I have ru[n about] very much,
5 and I have s[een] all the cities
6 which are like the dwelling of my lord.
7 And those like my lord s[aw me].
8 Now if my lord had de[cided]
9 to go to [(the city) Ilan-ṣura],
10 . . . .
Break
1′ [. . .] to the front of my lord
2′ [. . .] he/I will set out.
3′ And he/I will march at the front of my lord.
4′ And concerning the daughter of Tepa[ḫum],
5′ in my dream a man
6′ stood and said,

7′MUNUS.TUR DUMU.MUNUS ^{mí}[*T*]*e-pa-ḫi-i*[*m*]

8′$^{\text{m.mí}}$*Ta-gi-id-na-we-e li-i*[*š*$_{7}$*-ta-sú*]

9′*an-ni-tam iq-bé-e-em i-na-an-na*

10′*be-lí wa-ar-ka-tam* DUMU MÁŠ.ŠU.SU$_{13}$.SU$_{13}$

11′*li-ša-ap-ri-is-ma šum-*[*m*]*a* [*š*]*u-*[*u*]*t-tum š*[*i-i*]

12′*n*[*a-a*]*ṭ-la-at be-lí* MUNUS.TUR *T*[*a!-g*]*i!-i*[*d!-na-we-e li-ís-si*]

13′*ke-em-*[*m*]*a li-iš-ša-si*

14′*ù šu-lum be-lí-ya lu-ú* [*k*]*a-*[*y*]*a-a*[*n*]

23. A.907 = *ARM* X 100 = *AEM* 1/1, 232.

1*a-na be-l*[*í*]*-y*[*a*]

2*qí-bí-ma*

3[*u*]*m-ma* ^{mí}*Zu!-na-na* GEME$_{2}$*-ka-a-ma*

4*i-nu-ma i-na Ga-ni-ba-ti-im*^{ki} *úš-bu*

5^{mí}*Ki!-tum!-ši-im-ḫi-ya a-na Ru-ub-bé-en aš-pu-ur-ma*

6*i-na a-la-ki-ša it-ba-lu-ši*

7Ù [^{d}*D*]*a-gan be-el-ka ú-ṣa-al-l*[*i*]*-la-am-ma*

8*ma-am-ma-an ú-ul il-pu-t*[*a-a*]*n-ni*

9[^{d}*D*]*a-gan ki-a-am iq-bé-em um-*[*m*]*a š*[*u-m*]A

10*pa-nu-ki e-li-iš ša-a*[*p-l*]*i-iš*

11*um-ma a-na-ku-ma ša-ap-li-i*[*š*]*-ma*

12*al-li-ka-am-ma*

13MUNUS.TUR*-ti ú-ul a-mu-*[*u*]*r*

14*i-nu-ma a-na An-da-ri-ig*^{ki}

15*be-lí il-li-ku*

16*zi-im-zi-mu ša* MUNUS.TUR*-ti-ya*

17*it-ti Sa-am-me-e-tar*

18*i-le-em-ma*

19*al-li-ik-šu-um-ma a-an-na-am i-*[*p*]*u-l*[*a*]*-a*[*n-ni*]

20*i-tu-úr-ma ib-ba-al-ki-ta-an-ni-ma*

21MUNUS.TUR*-ti ú-u*[*l i*]*d-di-na-am*

22^{d}*Da-gan ki-a-*[*a*]*m iq-bé-em um-ma šu-ma*

23*a-di it-ti Zi-im-ri-Li-im* MUNUS.TUR*-ta-ki*

7′ “The little girl, the daughter of (lady) Tepaḫum,
8′ let them n[ame] Tagid-nawe.”
9′ This is what he said to me. Now
10′ let my lord have the diviner
11′ decide the matter. If [this] dream
12′ was seen, let my lord [name] the girl Tagid-nawe.
13′ Thus let her be named,
14′ and let the wellbeing of my lord be constant.

23. A.907 = *ARM* X 100 = *AEM* 1/1, 232.

1 To my lord
2 speak:
3 [T]hus says Zunana, your maidservant:
4 When I lived in Ganibatim,
5 I sent Kittum-šimḫiya to Rubben, and
6 as she was going they carried her off.
7 But [D]agan your lord protected me, and
8 no one touched me.[50]
9 [D]agan spoke to me as follows, say[ing]:
10 “Is your face up or down?”[51]
11 I answered, “Down.
12 I came here,
13 but I did not see my servant girl.
14 When my lord went
15 to Andarig,
16 the *zimzimu*[52] of my servant girl
17 came up here
18 with Sammetar.
19 I went to him, and he answered me yes,
20 but he turned and doublecrossed me, and
21 did not give me my servant girl.”
22 Dagan responded to me as follows, saying,
23 “Until one brings out your servant girl by the

50. Durand takes the verb *ṣullulu* as the D stem of *ṣalālu*, “to sleep,” and assigns it the meaning “to see during sleep.” He renders the passage, “Then I saw Dagan, your lord, during my sleep, though no one had performed the *liptum* ritual for me.”

51. There is a debate how to take this expression. Moran understands it as a question of direction, “Did you head up (or) down?” Durand takes it to refer to one’s mood, “Are you happy (or) sad?”

52. The meaning of this word is unclear. Durand takes it in the normal sense of “shalots.” According to him, Zunana received a box of shalots from her maidservant, and that is how she learned that her maidservant was being held by Sammetar.

24 *la ú-še-ṣé-*[*e*]*m ma-am-ma-an*
25 *ú-ul ú-*[*w*]*a-aš-ša-ra-*[*k*]*i-iš*
26 *i-na-an-na ki-ma qí-ib-it*[53] ^{d}*Da-gan*
27 MUNUS.TUR-*ti be-lí la i-ka-al-la*

24. A.3424 = *ARM* X 117 = *AEM* 1/1, 240.

1 *a-na* $^{mí.d}$IM-*du-ri be-*[*e*]*l-ti-ya*
2 *qí-bí-ma*
3 *um-ma* ^{mí}*Ti-im-lu-ú* GEME$_2$-*k*[*i-ma*]
4 *lu-ú it-tum-ma ša i-nu-ma {i na}*
5 *i-na li-ib-bi Ka-sa-pa-a*^{ki}
6 *Ya-ar-ip-*^{d}*Ab-ba ú-še-ṣi-i*[*n-ni*]
7 [*ù a*]*-na ṣe-ri-ki al-li-ka-a*[*m-ma*]
8 [*ki-a-am*] *aq-bé-ki-im um-ma-a*[*-mi*]
9 [*šu-ut-t*]*a-am a-mu-ra-ak-ki-i* [*m-ma*]
10 [*ù i-na š*]*u-ut-ti-ya* ^{d}*Be!-el!-ti-*[*é-kál-lim*]
11 [*ki-a-am iš-p*]*u-ra-an-ni*
12 [*um-ma-a-mi* . . .]
Break
1′ [. . . . . .]
2′ [. . . .*i*]*-ba-aš-ši*
3′ [. . . . .] X X X
4′ [. . . .] . . DUMU^{meš} BÀD.TIL.X^{ki}
5′ [*ša* X X *i-n*]*a-aš-šu-ú!* 6 L[Ú^{meš}]
6′ [*šu-nu-ti*] *qí-pí-ši-ma tu?-ur-*[. . .]
7′ [. . . .]*-úš-qí ša-ni-tam*
8′ [1 TÚG X]-X-*at-tam*
9′ [*ù* 1] TÚG BAR.S[I *š*]*a qa-qa-di-ki*
10′ *šu-bi-li-im*
11′ *e-ri-iš be-el-ti-ya*
12′ *lu-ṣe!-*[*e*]*n*$_4$*_ma* [X]
13′ *li-i* [*b-b*]*i mi-tu*
14′ *li-ib-*[*l*]*u-u*[*ṭ*]

25. A.4996 = *ARM* XIII 23 = *AEM* 1/1, 209.

1 [*a*]*-na be-lí-ya*
2 *qí-bí-ma*

53. Following Durand, though the writing *qí!-ib-it* for *qibit* is very odd. Moran reads *ki* ŠÀ.DI.IB *ša*, "in accordance with the wrath of Dagan" (*Biblica* 50, 54). This reading fits the traces on the copy very well.

[24]order of Zimri-Lim, no one
[25]will release her to you."
[26]Now according to the command of Dagan
[27]my lord should not detain my servant girl.

24. A.3424 = *ARM* X 117 = *AEM* 1/1, 240.

[1]To Adad-duri, my lady,
[2]speak:
[3]Thus says Timlu, your maidservant,
[4]It was clearly a sign that when
[5]Yar᾿ip-Abba made m[e] go out
[6]from Kasapa,
[7][and] I came to you,
[8]I spoke to you [as follows], saying,
[9] "I saw a [dre]am for y[ou,]
[10][and in] my [d]ream Belet-[ekallim]
[11][se]nt me [as follows],
[12][saying, . . .]
Break
[1′] . . . .
[2′] . . . . there is.
[3′] . . . .
[4′] . . . . . . citizens of Durum-labirum
[5′][which . . .] carry. [Those] six me[n]
[6′]assign to her . . .
[7′] . . . . Another matter:
[8′][One] . . . garment
[9′][and one] turban of your head
[10′]send me.
[11′]Let me smell
[12′]the perfume of my lady,
[13′]that my dead he[ar]t
[14′]might live.

25. A.4996 = *ARM* XIII 23 = *AEM* 1/1, 209.

[1][T]o my lord
[2]speak:

^{3}*um-ma Mu-ka-an-ni-šum*
^{4}ÌR-*ka-a-ma* SISKUR$_{2}$.RE *a-na* ^{d}*Da-ga*[*n*]
^{5}*a-na ba-la-aṭ be-lí-ya aq-qí-i-ma*
^{6} ^{lú}*a-ap-lu-ú-um ša* ^{d}*Da-gan ša Tu-ut-t*[*u-ul*^{ki}]
^{7}*it-bé-e-ma ki-a-am iq-bi*
^{8}*um-ma-a-mi* KÁ.DINGIR.RA^{ki} *mi-na-am*
^{9}*te-et-te-ne-e-pé-eš a-na pu-gi-im / ù ša!-ka-ri-im*
^{10}*ú-pa-aḫ-ḫa-ar-ka*
^{11}É$^{ḫi.a}$ 7 LÚ^{meš} *at-ḫi-i*
^{12}*ù ma-ak-ku-ur-šu-nu*
^{13}*a-*[*n*]*a* [*q*]*a-at Z*[*i-i*]*m-ri-L*[*i-im*]
^{14}*lu-m*[*a-a*]*l-l*[*e-e*]*m*
^{15}*ù* ^{lú}*a-ap-*[*lu*]*-ú-um ša* ^{d} NIN!.É!.GAL!
^{16}*i*[*t!-b*]*e!-e!-*[*ma*]
^{17}[*k*]*i-a-a*[*m*] *i*[*q-bi um-ma-mi*]
^{18}*Ḫa!-*[*a*]*m!-m*[*u!-ra*]*-b*[*ì!*]
The last four lines are missing.

26. M.13841 = *ARM* XIII 112 = *AEM* 1/1, 234.

^{1}*a-na be-lí-ya*
^{2}*qí-bí-ma*
^{3}*um-ma* [*K*]*i-ib-ri-*^{d}[*D*]*a-gan*
^{4}Ì[R]*-ka-a-ma*
^{5} ^{d}*D*[*a-gan*] *ù* ^{d}*Ik-ru-bé-el ša-al-mu*
^{6}*a-l*[*um Ter-qa*^{ki} *ù*] *ḫa-al-ṣú-um ša-lim*
^{7}*ši-*[*ip-rum ša*] *be-lí!* [*ú-wa-e-ra-a*]*n-ni*
Break of about 11 lines
$^{1'}$*ki-a-am* [*i*]*ṭ-ṭú-ul um-ma-*[*a-mi* DINGIR-*lum-ma*]
$^{2'}$É *an-né-e-em ḫa-ri-ba!-am la te-e*[*p-pé-ša*]
$^{3'}$É *šu-ú in-ne-ep-pí-iš-ma*
$^{4'}$*a-na na-ri-im ú-ša-am-qa-as-sú*
$^{5'}$*i-na u*$_{4}$*-mi-i*[*m š*]*a š*[*u*]*-u*[*t*]*-ta-am ša-a-ti*
$^{6'}$[*i*]*ṭ-ṭú-lu* [*a-na*] *ma-*[*a*]*m-ma-an ú-ul iq-*[*b*]*i*
$^{7'}$*ša-né-em u*$_{4}$*-ma-am i-tu-ur šu-ut-ta-am*
$^{8'}$*iṭ-ṭú-ul um-ma-a-mi* DINGIR-*lum-ma*
$^{9'}$*é an-né-e-em la te-ep-pé-ša*
$^{10'}$*te-ep-pé-ša-šu-ma a-na na-ri-im*
$^{11'}$*ú-ša-am-qa-as-sú i-na-an-na*
$^{12'}$*a-nu-um-ma sí-sí-ik-ti* ^{túg}*ṣú-ba-t*[*i*]*-šu*
$^{13'}$*ù et-qa-am ša qa-qa-di-šu*
$^{14'}$*a-na ṣe-er be-*[*l*]*í-ya*

^{3}Thus says Mukannišum,
^{4}your servant: A sacrifice to Daga[n]
^{5}I offered for the life of my lord,
^{6}and the respondent of Dagan of Tutt[ul]
^{7}rose, and spoke as follows,
^{8}saying, "O Babylon, why
^{9}do you keep doing (it)? I will gather you
^{10}to the net and to the lance.
^{11}The houses of seven confederates
^{12}and their treasure
^{13}into the hand of Zimri-Lim
^{14}I will surely deliver."
^{15}And the respondent of Belet-ekallim
^{16}r[os]e,
^{17}and spoke as follows, saying,
^{18} "O Ḫammu-rabi. . . .
The last four lines are missing.

26. M.13841 = *ARM* XIII 112 = *AEM* 1/1, 234.

^{1}To my lord
^{2}speak:
^{3}Thus says Kibri-Dagan,
^{4}your servant:
^{5}D[agan] and Ikrub-El are well.
^{6}The ci[ty Terqa and] the district is well.
^{7}The w[ork concerning which] my lord [gave] me [instructions]
. . . Break of about 11 lines
$^{1'}$he saw as follows, [the god] says:
$^{2'}$ "You will not rebu[ild] this ruined house.
$^{3'}$If this house is rebuilt,
$^{4'}$I will make it fall into the river."
$^{5'}$On the day [in w]hich he saw this dream
$^{6'}$he did not speak [to] anyone.
$^{7'}$The next day he saw the dream again,
$^{8'}$and the god said,
$^{9'}$ "You will not rebuild this house.
$^{10'}$If you rebuild it, I will make it fall
$^{11'}$ into the river." Now
$^{12'}$then the hem of his garment
$^{13'}$and the lock of hair of his head
$^{14'}$I have sent

15′ *uš-ta-bi-[l]am*
16′ *iš-tu u*$_4$*-m[i-im ša]-a-tu*
17′ ^{lú}*tur š[u-ú]*
18′ *ma-ru-[uṣ]*

27. M.13842 = *ARM* XIII 113 = *AEM* 1/1, 235.

1 *[a-na be-l]í-[ya]*
2 *[qí]-bí-ma*
3 *um-[m]a Ki-ib-ri-*^{d}*Da-gan*
4 ÌR-*ka-a-ma*
5 ^{d}*[Da]-gan ù [*^{d}*]Ik-[ru-b]é-È[l] ša-[a]l-mu*
6 *[a-lum] Ter-qa*^{ki} *[ù] ḫ[a-al-ṣú-um ša]-lim*
7 *[ša-n]i-tam 1 lú šu-ut-[tam i-mu-u]r-ma*
8 *[ù A]-ḫu-um ú-ša-an-[ni]*
9 *[um-ma-m]i ṣa-bu-um [na-ak-rum]*
10 *[i-n]a a-la-ni dan-n[a-tim]*
11 *[Ma]-ri*^{ki} *Ter-qa[*^{ki}*]*
12 *[ù Sa]-ga-ra-tim*^{k}*[*^{i}*]*
13 *[er-bu m]i-im-ma iš-t[a-ḫi-ṭú]*
14 *[ù i-na] dan-na-at be-[lí-ya]*
15 *[wa-aš]-bu*
16 *[A-ḫu-um] šu-ut-ta-šu an-ni-tam*
17 *[ú-ša-an-n]i-ma ar-nam e-li-ya*
18 *[ú-t]e-er-ma um-ma-a-mi šu-pu-ur a-na* LUG[AL]
19 *ù aš-šum ki-[a-am] a-na b[e-l]í-ya*
20 *aš-pu-[r]a-a[m]*

28. M.13843 = *ARM* XIII 114 = *AEM* 1/1, 210.

1 *[a-na be-lí-ya]*
2 *[q]í-bí-ma*
3 *um-ma Ki-ib-ri-*^{d}*D[a-gan]*
4 ÌR-*ka-a-ma*
5 *u*$_4$*-um ṭup-pí an-né-e-em a-na ṣe-er be-[l]í-y[a]*
6 *ú-ša-bi-lam*
7 *la-m[a] ti-ri-ik ša-di-im*
8 1 MUNUS.DAM LÚ *il-li-kam-ma*
9 *aš-šum ṭe*$_4$*-em* KÁ.DINGIR.RA^{ki}

15′ to my lord.
16′ Since [th]at da[y]
17′ t[his] servant
18′ has been sic[k].

27. M.13842 = *ARM* XIII 113 = *AEM* 1/1, 235.

1 [To my lo]rd
2 [sp]eak:
3 Thus says Kibri-Dagan,
4 your servant:
5 [Da]gan and Ik[rub]-E[l] are we[l]l.
6 [The city] Terqa [and] the dis[trict is w]ell.
7 [Anot]her matter: a man [sa]w a drea[m],
8 [and A]ḫum[54] repeated it (to me),
9 [say]ing, "The [enemy] army
10 [had entered in]to the str[ong] cities,
11 [Ma]ri, Terqa,
12 [and Sa]garatim.
13 They lo[oted s]ome,
14 [and in] the strongholds of [my] lor[d]
15 [they dw]elt.
16 [Ahum repeate]d this dream,
17 and the responsibility he [tu]rned upon me,
18 saying, "Write to the ki[ng]."
19 And that is why I have written
20 to my l[or]d.

28. M.13843 = *ARM* XIII 114 = *AEM* 1/1, 210.

1 [To my lord]
2 [s]peak:
3 Thus says Kibri-D[agan,]
4 your servant:
5 On the day I sent this tablet of mine
6 to my lord,
7 before the shade of the mountain,[55]
8 the wife of a man came to me
9 and concerning the news of Babylon

54. Aḫum was the high priest of Annunitum.

55. This expression is apparently a traditional expression for late afternoon that originated elsewhere than in the Terqa or Mari region (cf. Durand).

10 *ki-a-am iq-bé-em um-ma-a-mi*
11 ^{d}*Da-gan iš-pu-ra-an-ni*
12 *šu-pu-ur a-na be-lí-k*[*a*]
13 [*l*]*a i-ḫa-aš ù ma-a-*[*tum*]*-ma*
14 [*la*] *i-ḫa-a*[*š*]
15 [^{m}*Ḫa*]*-am-mu-ra-bi*
16 [LUGAL *š*]*a* KÁ.DINGIR.RA^{ki}
Reverse is not readable. One edge gone.
Remaining lateral edge:
1′ [. . . . .] *a-na ḫa-la-qí-šu*
2′ [*i/a-ḫa-am-mu*]*-uṭ*

29. A.765 = *AEM* 1/1, 191 = Syria 19 (1938) 126.

1 *a-na* ^{d}I$_7$ *be-lí-ya*
2 *qí-bí-ma*
3 *um-ma Zi-im-ri-i-im*
4 ÌR*-ka-a-*[*m*]*a*
5 *a-nu-um-ma* GAL KÙ.GI *a-na be-lí-ya*
6 *uš-ta-bi-lam i-na pa-ni-tim*
7 *ṭe*$_4$*-mi a-na be-lí-ya aš-pu-ra-*[*am*]
8 *be-lí it-tam! ú-ka-al-l*[*i-ma-an-ni*]
9 *be-lí it-tam ša ú-ka-al-li-ma!-a*[*n!-ni*]
10 *li-ša-ak-li-lam*
11 *ù a-na na-ṣa-ar na-pí-*[*iš-ti-ya*]
12 *be-lí a i-g*[*i*]
13 *a-šar ša-ni be-lí pa-n*[*é-šu*]
14 *a ú-sa-aḫ-ḫi-ir*
15 *ul-la-nu-ya*
16 *be-lí ša-né-e-e*[*m*]
17 *a iḫ-še-eḫ*

30. M.9714 = *AEM* 1/1, 192.

1 [*a-na Zi-im-ri-li-im*]
2 [*qí-bí-ma um-ma* ^{d}IM*-ma*]
3 [*a-na* . . . .*-ka*]
4 *ú-ta-ar-ka* [O O O]*-ka*
5 *i-*[*n*]*a bi-it-qa-ti-im i-ša-kum*
6 [^{giš}]*ka-ak-*[*k*]*i-ya da-an-nu-tim*
7 [*a-n*]*a pa-ni-ka aṭ-ru-ud*
8 *ù* 7 *ša-pa-ar-re a-n*[*a*] *lú*^{meš} *elam.ma*
9 [*s*]*à-ḫa-pí-im aṭ-ru-u*[*d*]

10 she spoke to me as follows, saying,
11 "Dagan sent me.
12 Write to yo[ur] lord
13 that he should not worry and the land
14 should [not] worry.
15 [Ḫa]mmu-rabi,
16 [the king o]f Babylon
. . . .
. . . .
1′ [. . . .] to destroy him
2′ [I/he will has]ten.

29. A.765 = *AEM* 1/1, 191 = *Syria* 19 (1938) 126.

1 To the divine River, my lord,
2 speak:
3 Thus says Zimri-Lim,
4 your servant:
5 Now a golden goblet I have sent
6 to my lord. Formerly
7 I sent my report to my lord,
8 and my lord showe[d me] a sign.
9 May my lord bring to pass for me
10 the sign which he showed m[e].
11 And to protect [my] life
12 may my lord not be neg[ligent.]
13 May my lord
14 not turn [his] face elsewhere.
15 Apart from me
16 may my lord not desire
17 another.

30. M.9714 = *AEM* 1/1, 192.

1 [To Zimri-Lim]
2 [speak: Thus says Adad:]
3 [To your. . . . .]
4 I will return you. . . . Your. . .
5 I have for you in the losses.
6 My strong weapons
7 I sent before you.
8 And 7 nets I sent
9 to overwhelm the Elamites.

10 *[iš-t]u* u_4*-15-kam a-di* u_4*-[x-ka]m*
11 *[ti]-iṣ-bu-tam tu-ṣa-m[a-a]d-ma*
12 [. . . . .]
13 [. . . . .]
14 [. . . . .]
(one blank line)
15 *[a-na Zi-im-ri-L]i-im*
16 *[qí]-bí-ma um-ma Eš*$_4$*-tár Ni-ne-[et*^{ki}]
17 *[i-n]a* ^{giš}*ka-ak-ki-ya da-an-nu-t[im]*
18 *az-za-az-za-kum* É*-tam ma-ṣa-la-a[m]*
19 *i-na Ma-ri*^{ki} *bi-né-em*
20 *ki-a-am ú-wa-e-er-ka um-ma a-na-ku-ma*
21 *i-nu-ma a-na* LÚ^{meš} *na-ak-ri-ka*
22 1 *bé-ra-am* A.ŠÀ *šu-ri-ḫa-am*
23 *i-ša-tam ú-pu-uḫ-ma ù Ḫa-ab-du-Ma-lik*
24 [^{l}]^{ú}SUKKAL *li-ba-li-{ši}-ši*
(one line blank)
25 *[a-n]a Zi-im-ri-Li-im*
26 *[qí-b]í-ma um-ma* ^{d}UTU*-ma*
27 *[a-na Ma]-ri*^{ki} *i-na e-re-bi-ka*
28 [. . . . .]
29 [. . . . .]
30 [. . . . .]
31 [. . . . .]*-tam ša ú-ša-[* . . . . .]
32 [. . . . .] *i-na ki-na-ti[m* . . . .]
33 [. . . . .] *qa-r[a-a]n ṣu-ba-ti-k[a* . .]
34 [. . . . .] X *sí-[sí-ik-ti-ka* . . . .]

31. A.2666 = *AEM* 1/1, 193.

1 *a-na* DINGIR DINGIR.DINGIR
2 *qí-bí-ma*
3 *um-ma* ^{d}IŠTARAN *ki-a-am-ma*
4 *um-ma* ^{d}IŠTARAN *ki-a-am-[ma]*
5 *a-na pa-an* ^{d}IŠTARAN LÚ
6 *li-ip-ḫu-ur*
7 *a-na* UR-^{d}LUGAL.B[ÀN.D]A
8 *qí-bí-[ma]*
9 *um-ma* UR-^{d}LUGAL-^{giš}*[š]u-k[u]-ri-im-ma*
10 ^{m}*I-din-*^{d}MAR.TU *ṣa-ab-ta-ku-ma*
11 ^{m}ÌR-^{d}EN.ZU *ú-ka-bi-su-šu-ma*
12 ^{d}SIPA SIPA.SIPA

10 [Fr]om the fifthteenth until the . . .
11 you will join the [b]attle, and
12 [. . . . .]
13 [. . . . .]
14 [. . . . .]
(one blank line)
15 [To Zimri-L]im
16 [sp]eak: Thus says Ištar of Ninet:
17 ["W]ith my strong weapons
18 I will stand by you. Build me a house, a shepherd's hut,
19 in Mari.
20 I have commanded you as follows, saying,
21 'When the distance to your enemies
22 is 1 *beru* (over 10 kilometers), hurry,
23 light a fire, and let Ḫabdu-Malik,
24 the vizier, quench it.
(one line blank)
25 [T]o Zimri-Lim
26 [sp]eak: Thus says Samas,
27 "When you enter [into Ma]ri,
28 [. . . . .]
29 [. . . . .]
30 [. . . . .]
31 [. . . . .] x which I [. . . . . . .]
32 [. . . . .] in trut[h. . . . .]
33 [. . . . .] the "horn" of your garment
34 [. . . . . your] h[em. . . . .]

31. A.2666 = *AEM* 1/1, 193.

1 To the god of gods
2 speak:
3 Thus says Ištaran, "It is so."
4 Thus says Ištaran, "It is so.
5 Before Ištaran let the people
6 gather."
7 To Ur-lugal-banda
8 speak:
9 Thus says Ur-bel-sukurrim:
10 "I have seized Iddin-Amurrum,
11 and as for Warad-Suen, they dropped the charges against him.
12 So the shepherd of the shepherds

13 *ṭu-ur-dam-ma*
14 *li-ba-al-li-sú-nu-ti*
Left edge: KA

32. A.3719 = *AEM* 1/1, 196.

1 *a-na be-lí-ya*
2 *qí-bí-ma*
3 *um-ma* ^{d}UTU-*na-ṣir*
4 ÌR-*ka-a-ma*
5 *i-nu-ma be-lí a-na ge-ri-im*
6 *pa-né-*[*šu*] *iš-ku-nu ki-a-am ú-wa-e-ra-an-ni*
7 *um-m*[*a-mi*] *i-na a-al* DINGIR-*lim wa-aš-ba-at*
8 *i-g*[*e-e*]*r-ru-ú-um ša i-na* É DINGIR-*lim*
9 *i-*[*ba-a*]*š-š*[*u*]*-ú ú te-še-mu-ú*
10 *a-*[*n*]*a ṣe-r*[*i-y*]*a šu-up-ra-am*
11 [*iš*]*-tu* u_4-[*mi-i*]*m ša-tu mi-im-ma*
12 [*i-na* É DINGIR-*lim ú-ul eš-te-em*]*-mé*
Break
1′ [*um-ma-mi a-na pa-ni-ya*]
2′ [^{d}TIŠPAK *li-ì*]*s-su-ú*
3′ *ši-ip-ṭ*[*á-a*]*m lu-ud-di-in*
4′ ^{d}TIŠPAK [*ì*]*s-su-nim-ma*
5′ *a-na* ^{d}TIŠPAK ^{d}*Da-gan ki-a-am*
6′ *iq-bi um-ma-a-mi iš-tu* ŠI-*na* X-*dí?*
7′ *ma-a-tam te-bi-il i-na-an-n*[*a*]
8′ *ú-ut-ka it-ta-al-kam*
9′ *ú-ut-ka ki-ma É-kál-la-tim*^{ki}
10′ *ta-ma-ḫa-ar an-ni-tam*
11′ IGI ^{d}*Da-gan ù* ^{d}*Ya-ak-ru-bé-Èl*
12′ [*i*]*q-*[*b*]*i um-ma* ^{d}*Ḫa-na-at-ma*
13′ *a-na ši-ip-ṭi*$_4$*-im ša ta-ad-di-nu*
14′ *a-aḫ-ka la ta-na-ad-di-in*
15′ [*š*]*a-ni-tam še-em ša* ^{giš}APIN$^{\text{ḫi.a}}$
16′ *ša é-kál-lim*
17′ [*š*]*a ḫa-la-aṣ Ter-qa*^{ki}
18′ *a-na Ter-qa*^{ki} *šu-ru-ub*

[13]send to me, that
[14]he may settle their accounts."
. . . .

32. A.3719 = *AEM* 1/1, 196.

[1]To my lord
[2]speak:
[3]Thus says Šamaš-naṣir,
[4]your servant:
[5]When my lord decided to go
[6]on campaign, he instructed me as follows,
[7]saying, "You are dwelling in the city of the god.
[8]Any chance oracle that h[app]ens in the
[9]temple of the god and that you hear,
[10]write to me."
[11]Since that day [I have hear]d nothing
[12][in the temple of the god].
Break
[1′][saying, "Before me]
[2′][let] them [sum]mon [Tišpak]
[3′]that I may render judg[me]nt."
[4′]They [s]ummoned Tišpak, and
[5′]Dagan spoke to Tišpak as follows,
[6′]saying, "Since. . .
[7′]you have ruled the land. Now
[8′]your day has come.
[9′]Just as Ekallatum you will receive
[10′]your day." This
[11′]before Dagan and Yakrub-El
[12′]he said, " Thus says Ḫanat,
[13′] 'To the judgment which you have rendered
[14′]do not be negligent.'"
[15′]Another matter: the grain of the plows
[16′]of the palace
[17′]of the district of Terqa
[18′]has been brought into Terqa.

33. A.3912 = *AEM* 1/1, 198.

. . . .

1′ *ù Zi-im-ri-L[i-im a-na Ma-ri*^{ki}]
2′ *i-sà-aḫ-ḫu-ru* 2 U[DU$^{ḫi.a}$ *li-iq-qú-ú*]
3′ *ša-ni-tam Še-le-bu-[um il-li-kam-ma]*
4′ *ki-a-am iq-bi um-ma [šu-ú-ma]*
5′ KAŠ *i-da-tam it-ti An-nu-[ni-tim i-ki-mu]*
6′ *i-nu-ma a-na i-ša-tim* Z[Ì.DA *aḫ-ši-ḫu*]
7′ *ù i-na mu-ši-iḫ-tim ba-b[a-sà-am]*
8′ *ki-ma* ZÌ.DA *i-di-n[u-nim]*
9′ *i-na pa-ni-ya a-aṭ-ṭú-[ul-ma]*
10′ *ši-ni-šu iš-tu a-di na-ak-[ri-im]*
11′ *ak-šu-du i-na-an-na ša-al-[ši-šu]*
12′ É-*tam úš-ba ù a-na-ku m[a]-di-i[š]*
13′ *ze-e ù ši-na-ti wa-aš-ba-ku*
14′ [*ù*] G[I] *t[i]-mi-nim a-ka-a[l]*
(All of the reverse has disappeared)
1″ *[a-n]a pí Še-le-bu-um i[q-bé-em aš-ṭú-ur]*
2″ *[i]-na-an-na a-nu-um-ma ša-ar-tam*
3″ *ù sí-sí-ik-tam ša Še-le-[bi-im . . . .]*
Break

34. A.925 + A.2050 = *AEM* 1/1,199.

1 *a-na be-lí-ya*
2 *qí-bí-ma*
3 *um-ma Sa-am-me-e-tar*
4 ÌR-*ka-a-ma*
5 ^{m}*Lu-pa-ḫu-um* ^{lú}*a-pí-lum ša* ^{d}*Da-gan*
6 *iš-tu Tu-ut-tu-ul*^{ki} *ik-šu-dam*
7 *ṭe*$_4$*-ma-am ša be-lí i-na Sa-ga-ra-tim*^{ki}
8 *ú-wa-e-ru-šu um-ma-mi a-na* ^{d}*Da-gan ša Ter-[q]a*^{ki}
9 *pí-iq-da-an-ni ṭe*$_4$*-ma-am ša-a-ti*
10 *ú-bi-il-ma ki-a-am i-pu-lu-šu um-ma-mi*
11 *e-ma ta-al-la-ku ṭú-ú-ub li-ib-bi*
12 *im-ta-na-a[ḫ-ḫ]a-ar-[k]a* ^{giš}*ya-ši-bu-um*
13 *ù* ^{giš}*[d]i-im-tum [n]a-ad-nu-ni-kum*
14 *i-na i-di-ka i-il-[l]a-ku tap-pu-ut-ka i-il-la-ku*
15 *ṭe*$_4$*-ma-am an-né-e-em i-na Tu-ut-tu-ul*^{ki}
16 *i-pu-lu-šu ù iš-tu Tu-ut-tu-ul*^{ki}
17 *ki-ma ka-ša-di-šu-ma a-na Di-ir*^{ki} *ú-še-er-di-ma*
18 ^{giš}*sí-ik-ku-ri a-na* ^{d}*Di-ri-tim ú-bi-il*

33. A.3912 = *AEM* 1/1, 198.

. . . .
1′and Zimri-L[im] returns [to Mari,]
2′[let them sacrifice] two sh[eep].
3′Another matter: Šelebu[m came to me],
4′and spoke as [follows]:
5′[“They took away] the *idatum* beer from Annu[nitum].
6′When [I requested] f[lour] for the fire,
7′then barl[ey soup] they gav[e to me]
8′in the container as flour.
9′I had to lo[ok] to myself.
10′Twice, since I went to the ene[my],
11′(and) now a thir[d time],
12′they are inhabiting the house, while I
13′am inhabiting nothing but shit and piss,
14′[and] I eat the reeds of the enclosure.
(All the reverse has disappeared)
1″[I have written what he said to me] at the dictation of Šelebum.
2″Now then the hair
3″and hem of Šele[bum. . . .]
Break

34. A.925 + A.2050 = *AEM* 1/1,199.

1To my lord
2speak:
3Thus says Sammetar,
4your servant:
5Lupaḫum, the respondent of Dagan,
6arrived here from Tuttul.
7The message which my lord
8commanded him in Sagaratum, saying, “With Dagan of Ter[qa]
9recheck the oracle concerning me.” This message
10he brought, and they answered him as follows:
11 “Wherever you go, happiness
12will constantly meet you. The battering ram
13and the siege tower are given to you.
14They will go at your side. They will be your companions.”
15They had answered him with this same message
16in Tuttul. As soon as he had arrived from Tuttul,
17I had him go down to Dir.
18He carried my deadbolt to the goddess Diritum.

19 *pa-na-nu-um še-er-nam ú-bi-il um-ma-mi*
20 *še-er-nu-um* {ZA} *ú-ul sà-ni-iq-ma mu-ú* {*ú*}
21 *i-ṣú-up-pu še-er-nam du-un-ni-ni*$_5$
22 *i-na-an-na sí-ik-ku-ri ú-bi-il*
23 *ù ki-a-am ša-pí-*{*ir*}*-ir*
24 *um-ma-mi as-sú-ur-ri a-na sa-li-mi-im*
25 *ša* LÚ ÈŠ.NUN.NA^{ki} *ta-ta-ka-li-ma*
26 *a-aḫ-ki ta-na-ad-di-i*
27 *ma-aṣ-ṣa-ra-tu-ki e-li ša pa-na-nu-um*
28 *lu-ú du-un-nu-na*
29 *ù a-ya-ši-im ki-a-am iq-bé-e-em um-ma-mi*
30 *as-*[*sú*]*-ur-ri* LUGAL *ba-lum* DINGIR-*lim ša-li-im*
31 *a-na* LÚ [ÈŠ].NUN.NA^{ki} *na-pí-iš*$_7$*-ta-šu*
32 *i-la-ap-pa-at ki-ma ša i-na pa-ni-tim*
33 *i-nu-ma* DU[MU^{m}]^{eš} [*Y*]*a-*[*m*]*i-na*^{ki} *ur-du-nim-ma i-na Sa-ga-ra-tim*^{ki}
34 *úš-bu ù a-na* LUGAL *aq-bu-ú um-ma a-na-ku-ma*
35 ^{anše}*ḫa-a-ri ša* DUMU^{meš} *Ya-mi-na la ta-qa-ṭá-al*
36 *i-na* {*b*[*u*]} *ḫu-bu-ur-re-e qí-na-ti-šu-nu*
37 *a-ṭà-ra-as-sú-nu-ti ù* I$_7$-DA *ú-ga-am-ma-ra-kum*
38 [*i-n*]*a-an-na ba-lum* DINGIR-[*la*]*m i-š*[*a-a*]*l-lu*
39 *n*[*a-pí-iš*$_7$]*-ta-šu la i-la-ap-pa-at*
40 *ṭe*$_4$*-ma-am a*[*n-n*]*é-e-em* ^{m}*Lu-pa-ḫu-um id-bu-ba-am*
41 *wa-ar-ki-šu-ma i-na ša-ni-i-im* [*u*$_4$*-m*]*i-im*
42 1 ^{mí}*qa-ma-tum ša* ^{d}*Da-gan ša T*[*er-qa*]^{ki}
43 *il-li-kam-ma ki-a-am iq-bé-e-*[*em um-ma*]*-mi*
44 *ša-pa-al* IN.NU.DA *mu-ú i-il-*[*la-ku*]
45 *a-na sa-li-mi-im iš*$_7$*-ta-na-ap-p*[*a-ru-ni-kum*]
46 DINGIR^{meš}-*šu-nu i-ṭà-ar-ra-du-*[*ni-kum*]
47 *ù ša-ra-am ša-né-e-em-ma*
48 *i-na li-ib-bi-šu-nu i-ka-ap-pu-du*
49 LUGAL *ba-lum* DINGIR-*lam i-ša-al-lu*

19 Formerly he had carried a *šernum*, saying,
20 "The *šernum* is not tight, the water
21 pours out. Strengthen the *šernum*."[56]
22 Now my deadbolt he carried,
24 and he was sent with a message as follows,
24 saying, "I am afraid you (Diritum) may trust in
25 the peace talk of the man of Ešnunna,
26 and become negligent.
27 Let your guards be strengthened
28 more than before."
29 And to me she spoke as follows, saying,
30 "I am afraid the king, without consulting the god,
31 may make a treaty[57] with the man of Ešnunna.
32 Just as formerly
33 when the Benjaminites descended and dwelt in Sagaratum.
34 and I spoke to the king saying,
35 'Do not make a treaty[58] with the Benjaminites.
36 With the dispersement of their nests
37 I will drive them away and the divine River will finish them off for you.'
38 Now without consulting the god,
39 he shall not make a treaty."
40 This is the message Lupaḫum told me.
41 Aftcr that, on the next day,
42 a *qammatum* of Dagan of Terqa
43 came to me, and thus she spoke to me, saying:
44 "Under the straw water is run[ning].
45 They keep sending [to you] messages for peace.
46 Their gods they will send [to you],
47 but another treachery
48 they plot in their heart.
49 The king without consulting the god

56. The *šernum* is an object made of wood, perhaps a container of some kind or a plug. Both the bolt and the *šernum* are apparently being used in a symbolic fashion. The goddess is being asked to secure the bolt against the enemy and secure the *šernum* so that the enemy not flood the land.

57. Literally, "He will not touch his throat for the man of Ešnunna." "To touch his throat is an idiomatic expression for making a treaty based on a ritual gesture of self-cursing sometimes used in treaty making. The same expression is found in line 39, but a different expression for treaty making is used in line 35.

58. Literally, "You will not kill the donkey of the Benjaminites." This is another idiomatic expression for making a treaty based on the ritual killing of a donkey in the treaty making ceremony.

50 *na-pí-iš*$_7$*-ta-šu la i-la-ap-pa-at*
51 1 ^{túg}SI.SÁ *la-ḫa-r[e-e]-em ù ṣé-er-re-tam*
52 *[i]-ri-iš-ma ad-[di-in-š]i-im ù wu-ú-ur-ta-ša*
53 *i-na* É ^{d}NIN-É.GAL *a-[n]a* D[AM.DINGIR.RA ^{mí}*I-ni*]*-ib-ši-na*
54 *id-di-in ṭe*$_4$*-e[m a-wa-tim ša]*
55 *id-bu-bu-nim-ma a-na ṣe-er be-lí-ya*
56 *aš-pu-ra-am be-lí li-iš*$_7$*-ta-al-ma*
57 *ša šar-ru-ti-šu* GAL *li-pu-uš*
58 *ù aš-šum Ya-an-ṣí-ib-*^{d}*Da-gan be-eḫ-ri-im*
59 LÚ *Da-aš-ra-an*^{ki} *ša a-na qa-qa-di-šu na-ka-si-im be-lí iš-pu-ra-am qa-tam*

60 *a-na qa-tim A-bi-E-pu-uḫ aš-pu-ur* LÚ *ša-a-ti ú-ul i-mu-ru-ma* É*-sú ù ni-[š]e*$_{20}$*-š[u]*
61 *a-[na* Ì]R*-du-t[im i]d-di-in i-na ša-ni-i-im u*$_4$*-mi-im ṭup-pí Ya-si-im-*^{d}*Da-gan ik-š[u-da]m*
62 *[u]m-ma-mi* LÚ *šu-ú ik-ta-áš-dam i-na-an-na an-ni-tam la an-ni-tam be-lí li-iš-pu-ra-[am] ni-še*$_{20}$*-šu lu-wa-aš-še-er*

35. M.6188 = *AEM* 1/1, 200.

1 *[a-na] be-lí-y[a]*
2 *[qí]-bí-ma*
3 *[um]-ma A-ḫu-um* ^{lú}SANGA *ša [An-nu-ni-tim]*
4 [Ì]R*-ka-a-ma*
5 ^{mí}*Ḫu-ba-tum mu-uḫ-ḫu-tum*
6 *[t]e-er-tam ki-a-am id-di-in*
7 *um-ma-a-mi* {2} *ša-ru a-na ma-t[im]*
8 *i-te-eb-bé-em ù ka-a[p]-pí-š[u]*
9 *ù* 2 *ta-ak-ka-[ti-šu]*
10 *a-ša-al-šu-nu-t[i]*
11 ^{m}*Zi-im-ri-Li-i[m]*
12 *ù* DUMU *si-im-a-[al]*
13 *e-bu-ra-[am li-pu-šu]*
14 *[i]š-tu qa-[ti-ka]*
15 ^{m}*Zi-im-r[i-Li-im]*
16 *ma-a-tam [k]a-la-š[a la tu-še-ṣí]*
17 *ù i-tu-ur-ma ki-a-a[m iq-bi]*
18 *um-ma-a-mi* DUMU^{meš} *Ya-mi-[na]*
19 *am-mi-nim tu-pa-al-la-a[s]*
20 *a-ša-al-ka*
21 *an-ni-tam mu-uḫ-ḫu-tum ši-i i[q-bi]*
22 *ù a-nu-um-ma ša-ar-tam*
23 *ù sí-sí-ik-tam ša* MUNUS *ša-a-t[i]*
24 *[a-na ṣ]e-er be-lí-ya uš-ta-bi-lam*

50 shall not make a treaty."
51 One *laḫarûm* garment and a nose ring
52 she requested, and I gave (them) to her. Her command
53 she gave in the temple of Nin-ekallim to the high priestess, Inib-šina
54 The mess[age of the words which]
55 they said to me, I have sent to my lord.
56 Let my lord consult, and
57 let him act according to his great kingship.
58 And concerning Yanṣib-Dagan, the soldier,
59 the man of Dašran, whom my lord commanded me to cut off his head immediately,
60 I sent Abi-Epuḫ. They did not find that man, but his household and his people
61 he gave into slavery. On the next day the tablet of Yasim-Dagan reached me,

62 saying, "This man has come." Now let my lord write me whether I should release his people or not.

35. M.6188 = *AEM* 1/1, 200.

1 [To] m[y] lord
2 [sp]eak:
3 [Th]us says Aḫum, the high priest of [Annunitum],
4 your [servant]:
5 Ḫubatum, the female ecstatic,
6 gave an oracle as follows,
7 saying, "A wind will rise up against the land.
8 And its wings
9 and [its] two necks
10 I will call to account,
11 so that Zimri-Lim
12 and the Bensimalite
13 [may make] the harvest.
14 [F]rom [your] han[d],
15 O Zimr[i-Lim],
16 [you shall not let] the whole land escape."
17 Then she [spoke] again as follows,
18 saying, "O Benjamin,
19 why do you cause trouble?
20 I will hold you to account."
21 This is what that female ecstatic s[aid].
22 And now the hair
23 and hem of that woman
24 I have sent [to] my lord.

36. M.11046 = *AEM* 1/1, 202.

1 *a-na be-lí-ya*
2 *qí-bí-ma*
3 *um-ma Ka-ni-sa-an*
4 ÌR-*ka-a-ma*
5 *a-bi Ki-ib-[r]i-*^{d}*D[a-gan]*
6 *a-na Ma-ri*^{ki} *[iš-pu-ra-am um-ma]*
7 *šu-ma a-wa-tim [ša i-na* É ^{d}*Da-gan]*
8 *in-[n]e-ep-ša [eš-me]*
9 *[k]i-a-am i[d-bu-bu-nim]*
10 *[u]m-ma-a-mi ša-[pa-al* IN.NU.DA]
11 *mu-ú i-il-l[a-ku]*
12 *il-li-ik-ma* DINGIR-*lum ša be-[l]í-y[a]*
13 LÚ^{meš} *a-ya-bi-šu a-na qa-ti-šu*
14 *ú-ma-al-li i-na-an-n[a]*
15 ^{lú}*mu-uḫ-ḫu-[um k]i-ma pa-na-nu-u[m-m]a*
16 *ir-ṭú-ub ši-[t]a-sa-am*
17 *an-ni-tam Ki-ib-[ri-*^{d}*Da-g]an is-pu-r[a-am]*
18 *be-lí a-na šu-u[l-mi-šu te-r]e-tim*
19 *šu-pu-ši-im ù [*
20 [o o *la-a] e-g[i* . . . .]
21 [. . . .]
22 [. . . .]
23 [. . . .]
24 *be-lí la ú-la-ap-pa-tam*
25 SISKUR$_{2}$.RE *li-iq-qé-em-ma*
26 *li-it-ta-al-kam*

37. A.963 = *AEM* 1/1, 203.

The obverse is totally lost.
1′ ^{m}*Z[i-im-ri-Li-im]*
2′ [. . . .]
3′ [. . . .]
4′ [. . . .]
5′ [. . . .]
6′ [. . . . .] *u*$_{4}$*-mu-um [ku-ṣú-um]*
7′ *i[t-tu-ú]r ù sa-ra-bu-u[m]*
8′ *pa-né-ya i-da-ak*
9′ *i-na-an-na u*$_{4}$*-um* SISKUR$_{2}$*-ya*
10′ *a-na* É*-ti-ya lu-ru-ub*
11′ *[a-nu-u]m-ma ša-ar-tam ù sí-sí-ik-[tam]*

36. M.11046 = *AEM* 1/1, 202.

[1]To my lord
[2]speak:
[3]Thus says Kanisan,
[4]your servant,
[5]My father, Kibri-D[agan],
[6][wrote to me] in Mari
[7]as follows, “ [I heard] the words [which]
[8]were produced [in the temple of Dagan].
[9][They] s[poke] as follows,
[10]saying, ‘Be[low the straw]
[11]water ru[ns].
[12]He came, and the god of my lord
[13]delivered his enemies into his hand.’
[14]Now
[15]the ecstatic, just as before,
[16]keeps on crying out.”
[17]This is what Kib[ri-Dag]an wrot[e me].
[18]My lord should [not] be negligent
[19]in having [ora]cles performed
[20]for [his] well being and . . . .
[21][. . . .]
[22][. . . .]
[23][. . . .]
[24]My lord should not tarry.
[25]Let him offer the sacrifice that
[26]he may depart.

37. A.963 = *AEM* 1/1, 203.

[1′]Z[imri-Lim]
[2′][. . . . .]
[3′][. . . . .]
[4′][. . . . .]
[5′][. . . . .]
[6′][“. . . . .] a [cold] day
[7′]re[turn]ed, and the cold
[8′]will smite my face.
[9′]Now on the day of my sacrifice
[10′]let me enter my temple.”
[11′][No]w the hair and hem

12′ [*ša* ^{mí}*qa*]-*am-ma*-[*tim*]
13′ [*a-na ṣe-e*]*r be-lí*-[*ya ú-ša-bi-lam*]
14′ [*ša-ni-tam* 1] ^{túg}*uṭ*-[*ba* GAL]
15′ [X ^{túg}S]I.SÁ [*a-na* MUNUS *ad-di-in*]
16′ [*i-n*]*a-an*-[*na* . . . .]

38. M.7306 = *AEM* 1/1, 205 = *ARM*T XXV, 816.

About half the tablet is lost.
1′ [*ù i-n*]*a i-di b*[*e-l*]*í*-[*ka lizzizu / lilliku*]
2′ *i-na ša-al-ši-im ka-ra*-[*ši-im*]
3′ *ka-sa-am li-iḫ-pu-ú*
4′ *a-na ma-ti-im ša-pí-il*-[*ti-im*]
5′ *du-ʾu*$_5$*-um-ma-tum iš*-[*ša-ka-an*]
6′ *iš-at a-na* TILLAT *tu-še-š*[*e-er-ši*]
7′ ^{d}*Da-gan ú-ša-ḫi-za*-[*an-ni*]
8′ *um*-[*m*]*a-a-mi* ^{giš}TUKUL$^{ḫi.a}$ *lu-up-ti*-[*i*]
9′ [*wa-a*]*r-di Zi-im-ri-Li-im*
10′ [*pu*]-*sú*-[*n*]*u al-pu-ut-ma*
11′ [*wa-a*]*r-ki*-[*k*]*a aṭ-ru-dam*
12′ [*ú-u*]*l ik-ta*-[*aš-du-ma*]
13′ [*i-na* U$_4$]-4-KAM *iš*-[*ša-la-mu*]
14′ [*wa-ar-ki*]-*šu ša-ni-iš i*-[O O O]
15′ [*um-ma a-n*]*a-ku-m*[*a i-na pa-ni*]
16′ [U$_4$]-4-KAM-*mi lu-m*[*u-ur-ma ṣa-bu-um*]
17′ [*li-ik-šu*]-*ud* [. . . .]
18′ ^{giš}*sí-ik-ka-ti* x [. . . . .]
19′ *ša-ni-tam a-na um-ma*-[*na-tim* . . . .]
20′ [*u*]*š-ta-bi-i*[*l*
21′ 1 NINDA X-[. . . .

39. A.3893 = *AEM* 1/1, 206.

1 *a-na* [*be-lí-ya*]
2 *qí*-[*bí-ma*]
3 *um-ma* [*Ya-qí-im*-^{d}IM]
4 ÌR-[*ka-a-ma*]
5 1 ^{lú}*mu-uḫ-ḫu-u*[*m ša* ^{d}*Da-gan*]
6 *il-li-kam-ma ki*-[*a-am iq-bi*]
7 *um-ma šu-ú-ma w*[*u-di mi-nam*]
8 *ša Zi*-[*im-ri-Li-im*]
9 *a-ka-al* 1 SI[LA$_4$ *i-di-in-m*]*a*
10 *lu-ku-ul* 1 SILA$_4$ [*ad-di-in*]-*šum-ma*

12′ [of the *qa*]*mma*[*tum*]
13′ [I have sent to my] lord.
14′ [Another matter: 1 large] *uṭbu* garment
15′ [and x gar]ment [I gave to the woman].
16′ [N]o[w. . . .]

38. M.7306 = *AEM* 1/1, 205 = *ARMT* XXV, 816.

1′ [Let them stand/go [at] the side of [your] lord.
2′ In the third cam[p]
3′ let them break the goblet.
4′ For the lower land
5′ darkness will be e[stablished].
6′ There will be confusion; you will sen[d it] as an auxiliary troop.
7′ Dagan instructe[d me]
8′ saying, "I will open the battle.
9′ [The serva]nts of Zimri-Lim—
10′ I have touched th[ei]r [for]ehead,
11′ and [af]ter your departure I sent (them).
12′ If [they have no]t arrived,
13′ [on the] fourth they will be sa[fely there].
14′ [After] this, a second. . . .
15′ [I sai]d, [Before]
16′ [the] fourth, let me s[ee, and let the army]
17′ [arr]ive. . .
18′ The stakes. . . .
19′ Another matter: to the arm[y. . .
20′ I have sen[t. . .
21′ one bread[. . . .

39. A.3893 = *AEM* 1/1, 206.

1 To [my lord]
2 sp[eak]:
3 Thus says [Yaqim-Adad],
4 [your] servant:
5 An ecstatic [of Dagan]
6 came and [spoke] as fo[llows],
7 saying, "S[urely what]
8 belonging to Zi[mri-Lim]
9 shall I eat? [Give] 1 lam[b] that
10 I may eat." [I gave] to him 1 lamb,

11 *ba-al-ṭú-us-sú-ma [i-n]a [p]a-an a-bu-lim*
12 *[i]-ku-ul-šu*
13 *ù* LÚ^{meš} SU.GI
14 *i-na pa-an a-bu-ul-li-im*
15 *ša Sa-ga-ra-tim*^{ki}
16 *ú-pa-ḫi-ir-ma*
17 *ki-a-am iq-bi um-ma šu-ú-ma*
18 *ú-ku-ul-tum iš-ša-ka-an*
19 *a-na* ⟨*a*⟩*-la-né-e ru-gu-um-ma*
20 *a-sà-ak-ka-am li-te-er-ru*
21 LÚ *ša ri-i-sa-am i-pu-šu*
22 *i-na a-lim*^{ki} *li-še-ṣú-ú*
23 *ù a-na ša-la-am be-lí-ka Zi-i[m-ri-Li-im]*
24 1 TÚG *tu-la-ab-ba-ša-an-ni*
25 *an-ni-tam iq-bé-e-em-m[a]*
26 *a-na ša-la-am be-lí-[ya]*
27 1 TÚG *ú-la-ab-b[i-is-sú]*
28 *a-nu-um-ma te-[er-tam ša]*
29 *id-bu-ba-a[m aš-ṭú-ur-ma]*
30 *a-na ṣe-er [be-lí-ya]*
31 *áš-tap-ra-[am]*
32 *ù te-er-ta-šu i-na sí-mì-iš-tim*
33 *ú-ul iq-bé-e-em i-na pu-ḫu-ur* LÚ SU.GI
34 *te-er-ta-šu id-di-in*

40. A.3178 = *AEM* 1/1, 211.

1 *a-na be-lí-ya*
2 *qí-bí-ma*
3 *um-ma* ^{mí}*Ši-ib-tu*
4 GEME$_2$-*[ka]-a-m[a]*
5 1 [$^{mí.d}$*Iš-ḫa*]*-ra-*[o o o]*nu-um*
6 [.....................................]
7 [*ša* ^{d}NIN-É].GAL
8 *iz-zi-i[z-ma]*
9 *ki-a-am iq-bé-e-em*
10 *um-ma ši-ma Zi-im-ri-Li-im*
11 *a-šar il-li-ku*
12 *ú-ul i-ba-aš*
13 *ḫa-da-an-šu i-ka-aš-ša-ad*
14 *ki-in-ni-ke-em a-ra-ʾu$_5$-ub*
15 *ù i-na li-tim az-za-az*

11 and while it was still alive, in front of the city gate
12 he ate it.
13 And the elders
14 in front of the city gate
15 of Sagaratim
16 he had gathered,
17 and he spoke as follows, saying:
18 “A devouring (plague) will take place.
19 Issue a claim against the cities
20 that they return the sacred things.
21 The man who has committed violence
22 let them expel from the city.
23 And for the wellbeing of your lord, Zi[mri-Lim]
24 clothe me in a garment.”
25 This is what he said to me.
26 For the well-being of [my] lord
27 I cloth[ed him] in a garment.
28 Now the or[acle which]
29 he spoke t[o me, I wrote down, and]
30 to my [lord]
31 I have sent (it).
32 And his oracle he did not tell me in secret.
33 In the assembly of the elders
34 he gavc his oracle.

40. A.3178 = *AEM* 1/1, 211.

1 To my lord
2 speak:
3 Thus says Šibtu,
4 your maidservant
5 [The woman Išḫa]ra. . . .
6 [. . . . .]
7 [of Belet-e]kallim
8 stoo[d, and]
9 thus she spoke to me,
10 saying, “Zimri-Lim,
11 where he has gone,
12 will not experience shame.
13 His goal he will reach.
14 There I will rage
15 and stand in triumph.”

41. A.2209 = *AEM* 1/1, 216.

1 *a-na be-lí-ya*
2 *qí-bí-ma*
3 *um-ma Te-bi-ge-ri-šu*
4 ÌR-*ka-a-ma*
5 *u*$_4$*-um a-na ṣe-er Aš-ma-a[d]*
6 *ak-šu-du i-na ša-ni-i-im u*$_4$*-m[i-im]*
7 ^{lú}*na-bi-i*^{meš} *ša* ḪA.NA^{meš} *ú-pa-ḫ[i-ir]*
8 *te-er-tam a-na ša-la-am be-lí-y[a]*
9 *ú-še-pí-iš um-ma a-na-ku-ma*
10 *šum-ma be-lí i-nu-ma ra-ma-[ak-šu]*
11 *i-pé-šu u*$_4$-7-KAM *i-na ka-[wa-tim]*
12 *[ú]š-[š]a-ab-ma i-na šu-ul-mi-[im]*
13 *[a-na a-l]im*^{ki} *[i-tu-ur-ra-am]*
Break of about 8 lines
1′ *[um-ma-mi u*$_4$*]-um [a-na An-nu-ni-tim]*
2′ *ša ka-wa-tim [be-lí il-la-ku]*
3′ *be-lí pa-ga-a[r-šu]*
4′ *li-iṣ-ṣú-ur [ṣa-bu-um]*
5′ *i-na re-eš be-lí-[ya li-zi-iz]*
6′ *ù ma-ṣa-ra-at [a-lim*^{ki}*]*
7′ *lu-ú dan-[na]*
8′ *a-na na-ṣa-ar pa-ga-ri-[šu]*
9′ *be-lí a-aḫ-šu la i-na-ad-di*

42. M.8071 = *AEM* 1/1, 217.

The first 10 lines of the obverse are illegible.
11 *[i]-na li-ib-[b]i* É-*ya* X X *ú-w[a-* O O]
12 *id-di-nam-ma* ^{giš}IG *š[a?* O O] X-*mi a-n[a ṣe-ri-ya]*
13 *šu-pu-ur* X [O O O O] *a* [?]
14 *iš-tu ṣú-uḫ-ri-ka ú-[k]a-na-ak-ka-ma*
15 *ú e-em ša-al-ma-tim at-ta-na-ba-al-ka*
16 *ú i-ri-iš-ti i-ri-iš-ka-ma*
17 *ú-ul ta-na-ad-di-nam*
18 *[i-n]a-an-na a-na Na-ḫu-ur*^{ki}
19 *[šu-le]-em-ma i-ri-iš-ti*
20 *[ša aq-b]i-kum-ma id-na-aš-ši*
21 *[ša iš-t]u pa-na-num a-na qa-a[t]*
22 *[ab-bé-ka] aš-ru-ku*
23 *[i-na-an-na a-n]a ka-šu-um a-ša-[ra-ak]*
24 *[na-ak-rum ša] i-ba-aš-šu-ú*

41. A.2209 = *AEM* 1/1, 216.

[1]To my lord
[2]speak:
[3]Thus says Tebi-gerišu,
[4]your servant:
[5]On the next day after I arrived
[6]before Ašmad,
[7]I assemb[led] the prophets of the Haneans.
[8]I had them take an oracle for the wellbeing of
[9]my lord. I said,
[10] "If my lord, when he makes [his] ablutions,
[11]stays outsi[de the walls] for seven days,
[12][will he return to the c]ity in safet[y]?"

Break of about 8 lines
[1][saying, "On the d]ay [my lord goes]
[2][to Annunitum] outside the walls,
[3]let my lord guard himself.
[4]Let [the army]
[5][stand] at the disposal of [my] lord,
[6]and let the guard over [the city]
[7]be reinfor[ced].
[8]In guarding himself
[9]my lord should not be negligent.

42. M.8071 = *AEM* 1/1, 217.

The first 10 lines of the obverse are illegible.
[11]In the heart of my temple. . . he. . .
[12]he gave to me, and a door. . . t[o me]
[13]send!. . .
[14]Since your infancy I have always treated you kindly,
[15]and where good things were I always led you.
[16]But my request that I ask of you,
[17]you do not give me.
[18][N]ow [sen]d up to Naḫur
[19]and my request,
[20][about which I spok]e to you, give to me.
[21][What fr]om ancient times I gave
[22]into the hand [of your fathers]
[23][now] I will gi[ve t]o you.
[24][The enemy who] comes to be,

^{25}[*ša-pa-a*]*l še-pí-ka ú-ka-am-ma-*[*ar*]
^{26}[*ma-a-at*]*-ka a-na nu-uḫ-ši-im ù ḫe-ga-a*[*l-l*]*im*
^{27}[*ú-ta*]*-ar* MUNUS *ši-i an-né-tim id-bu-ba-am-ma*
^{28}[*a-w*]*a-at pí-ša a-na be-lí-ya aš-pu-ra-am*
^{29}*a-nu-um-ma ša-ra-as-sà ù sí-sí-ik-ta-ša*
^{30}*a-na be-lí-ya ú-ša-bi-lam be-lí te-re-tim*
^{31}*li-še-pí-iš-ma a-na ki* DINGIR *be-lí i-ip-pa-lu li-*[*pu*]*-úš*
^{32}*ša-ni-tam aš-šum še-im a-na be-lí-ya áš-ta-na-pa-ra-am-ma*
^{33}*še-em ú-ul ub-lu-nim a-nu-um-ma i-na-an-na*
^{34}*Ya-ap-ṭú-ur iš-tu Sa-ri-im a-di Bu-úš-a-an*[^{ki}]
^{35}*ib-b*[*a-a*]*l-ki-it ni-kur-ta-šu-nu ú-we-du-ú*
^{36}*ù* [^{lú}*n*]*a-aṣ-rum ú-ṣé-em-ma*
^{37}[*ki-a-am id-b*]*u-ba-am um-ma-mi* {X} [*šu-ma*]
^{38}[*it-ti* 4 *l*]*i-mi* 5 *li-mi ṣa-bi-im* [
^{39}[*a-na Na-ḫu-u*]*r*^{ki} *ni-sa-an-ni-i*[*q*
^{40}[. . . .*-š*]*u-nu a-na Na-ḫu-*[*ur*^{ki}
Break of about 5 lines
$^{1'}$[. . . . . . . *ú*]*-še-ṣí*

43. M.14836 = *AEM* 1/1, 218.

^{1}[*a-na be-lí-ya*]
^{2}[*qí-bí-ma*]
^{3}[*um-ma* . . . .]
^{4}[ÌR-*ka-a-ma*]
^{5}[*i-na pa-ni-tim* ^{d} . . . . *iq-bi*]
^{6}[*um-ma-a-mi* ^{m}*Zi-im-ri-Li-im*]
^{7}*ḫu-mu-sà-am i-n*[*a* . . . . . ^{ki} *li-iḫ-mi-is*]
^{8}*ù šum-šu a-na da-ri-ti*[*m*] *úš-*[*za-az*]
^{9}*ù* $SISKUR_2$.RE *ša ḫu-mu-sí-*[*im*]
^{10}*še-tu ú-ul na-qí ù be-lí ki-*[*a-am*]
^{11}*iq-bé-e-em um-ma-a-mi i-na Ma-ri*^{ki}
^{12}*sà-pa-ra-am lu-ša-bi-la-kum*
^{13}*i-na ḫu-mu-sí-im še-tu šu-ku-*[*un*]
^{14}[*i-na-a*]*n-na be-lí Ma-ri*^{ki} *ik-*[*šu-ud*]
^{15}[*sà-pa*]*-ra-am ú-ul ú-ša-b*[*i-lam*]
^{16}[O O] *ni iš* X [. . . . .]
About 8 lines and all of the reverse missing.
$^{1'}$[. . . . . *b*]*e-lí ša* LUGAL-*ti-šu* [*li-pu-úš*]
$^{2'}$[. . . . .] X *ni* [. . . . .]

25 I will hea[p] up [beneat]h your feet.
26 [I will re]turn your [land] to abundance and prosperity."
27 That woman said these things to me,
28 and [the w]ords of her mouth I wrote to my lord.
29 Now her hair and her hem
30 I have sent to my lord. Let my lord
31 have oracles taken, and as the god answers my lord, let him do.
32 Another matter: Concerning grain I keep writing to my lord,
33 but they have not brought the grain. Now then
34 Yapṭur has crossed over the border from the Wadi Sarum as far as Bušan.
35 They have made known their hostility,
36 and a secret agent has come out to me,
37 [and sp]oken to me [as follows],
38 ["With 4 th]ousand or 5 thousand troops. . .
39 we will approach [to Naḫu]r. . .
40 their . . . to Naḫ[ur. . .
Break of about 5 lines
[. . .]brought out.

43. M.14836 = *AEM* 1/1, 218.

1 [To my lord]
2 [speak]:
3 [Thus says . . .],
4 [your servant]:
5 [Formerly the god. . . spoke],
6 [saying, "Let Zimri-Lim]
7 [set up] a *ḫumusum* monument in the [city . . . .],
8 and his name I will est[ablish] for ever."
9 But the sacrifice for that *ḫumusum* monument
10 has not been offered, and my lord
11 spoke to me as follows, saying, "(When I am) in Mari
12 I will send to you a chariot.
13 Pu[t] (it) in that *ḫumusum* monument."
14 [No]w my lord re[ached] Mari,
15 but he did not se[nd me] the [char]iot.
16 . . . .
About 8 lines and all of the reverse missing.
1′ [. . . . let] my [l]ord [act] according to his kingship.
2′ . . . .

44. M.13496 + M.15299 = *AEM* 1/1, 219.

1′*ak-ki-ma 7 me-tim ṣa-b[a-am . . . . . .]*
2′*ù a-lum ka-l[u-ša a-n]a [b]e-lí-ya i[k-ru-ub]*
3′*ù da-mi-iq-t[i be-lí]-ya iq-[bi]*
4′*ša-ni-tam* U$_4$ SISK[UR$_2$].R[E *i-n*]*a* É ^{d}[N]IN.ḪUR.[SAG.GÁ]
5′1 *a-pí-lum š[a* ^{d}NIN].ḪUR.SAG.GÁ *it-[bi-ma]*
6′*ki-a-am id-bu-u[b um]-ma-a-mi šu-[ma]*
7′1-*šu* 2-*šu ù* 3-[*šu*] IGI ^{m}*Zi-im-[ri-Li-im]*
8′*e-ri-iš-ti e-[ri-i]š-ma ù [m]i-[im-ma]*
9′*ú-ul id-di-n[am . . . .]*
10′*[u]m-ma a-na-ku-[ma . . . .]*
11′X X X X [. . . .]
12′*aš-šum ḫ[a . . . .]*
13′*[šu]m-ma ṣa/ḫ[a . . . .]*
14′[. . . .]
15′[. . . .]
16′[^{m}]*Zi-i[m-ri-Li-im . . . .]*
17′*ù ša-ni-tam [it-bi-ma* 1 *. . . . .]*
18′1 MUNUS.TEGUNU.BAR *ša mu la-[a . . .]*
19′*ta-ma-ra-am ša-n[i?-tam* 1 *. . . . .]*
20′*dam-qa-am ša šum-ka [ša-aṭ-ra-am]*
21′*šu-bi-lam an-né-tim* 1 *a-[pí-lum]*
22′*id-bu-ub ù a-nu-um-ma š[a-ar-tam ù sí-sí-ik-tam]*
23′*ša a-pí-lim a-na be-lí-ya ú-[ša-bi-lam]*
24′*be-lí ša e-pé-ši-šu li-pu-ú[š . . . .]*
25′*[ù ša-ni-ta]m Ṣú-ra-ḫa-am-mu* X-[
26′[O O *iš-t]a-na-ap-pa-a[r*

45. A.3724 = *AEM* 1/1, 222 = *ARM* X, 106.

1*a-na Da-ri-iš-li-bur*
2*qí-bí-ma*
3*um-ma* U$_4$-ŠÁR-RE-EŠ$_{15}$-ḪE-TIL
4[DUMU]-*ka-a-ma*
5[*aš-šum* MUNUS.TUR *š*]*a* ^{mí}*Be-el-tim*
6*[im-ma-ḫe]-e-em*
7[DUMU.MUNUS *b*]*e-lí-ya*
8*[ú-ul ib-lu-uṭ]*
9*[i-na-an-na i]m-tu-[ut]*
10[U$_4$]-X-KAM *wa-al-da-at*
11[X] X X X
12*[u$_4$-mi-šu-m]a* ^{d}*Ìr-ra-ga-mil*

44. M.13496 + M.15299 = *AEM* 1/1, 219.

1′In order that 700 sold[iers. . .
2′and the wh[ole] city b[lessed] my lord,
3′and sa[id] favorable things about my [lord].
4′Another matter: the day of the sacrifice in the temple of Nin-ḫursagga
5′a respondent of [Nin]-ḫursagga a[rose],
6′and spoke as follows, saying,
7′ "Once, twice, three times before Zimri-Lim
8′I made my request, but
9′he did not give [me anything. . . .]"
10′I said, ...
11′. . . . .
12′concerning. . . . .
13′if. . . . .
14′. . . . .
15′. . . . .
16′Zi[mri-Lim. . . .
17′and another matter: [a. . . arose. . .]
18′one female . . . . which . . . not. . .
19′you will procure for me. An[other matter: One
20′good. . . on which your name [is written]
21′send to me." These things the res[pondent]
22′said. And now the h[air and the hem]
23′of the respondent I [have sent] to my lord.
24′Let my lord do what must be done. . . .
25′[And another matt]er: Ṣura-ḫammu. . . .
26′[. . . ke]eps writing. . . .

45. A.3724 = *AEM* 1/1, 222 = *ARM* X, 106.

1To Dariš-libur
2speak:
3Thus says Ušareš-ḫetil,
4your [son]:
5[Concerning the little girl o]f the queen
6[he fell into a tr]ance.
7[The daughter of] my [l]ord
8[did not live].
9[Now s]he has die[d].
10[The . . . th day she was born.
11. . . .
12[On that day] Irra-gamil

13[*im-ma*]-*ḫe-e-em*
14[*um-ma š*]*u-ma*
15[*ú-ul i-ba-l*]*u-uṭ*
16[*la-ma* LU]GAL *a-na Ma-ri*^ki
17[*i*]-*ka-aš-ša-dam*
18*ki-ma* MUNUS.TUR *ši-i mi-ta-at*
19*qí-bí-šum-ma lu-ú i-de*
20[*a*]*s-sú-ur-ri a-na Ma-ri*^ki
21*i-na e-re-bi-šu*
22*mu-ut* MUNUS.TUR *ša-a-ti* LUGAL
23*i-še-em-me-e-ma*
24*i-ṣa-ab-ba-*[*at*]
25*i-ta-aš-šu-úš-ša-a*[*m*]

46. M.9601 = *AEM* 1/1, 223. Too broken for translation.

47. A.2559 = *AEM* 1/1, 224.

1[*a-na be-lí-ya*]
2*qí-b*[*í-ma*]
3*um-ma Su-m*[*u* . . . .]
4 ÌR-*ka-a-*[*ma*]
5*šu-ut-tum a-na be-l*[*í-ya ma-di-iš da*]*m-qa-at*
6*be-lí i-na e-t*[*e-qí-šu*]
7*i-na Sa-ma-nim*^ki *a-na An-nu-ni-tim*
8*li-iq-qí ù-lu-ma*
91 UDU.NITA$_2$ *be-lí li-il*$_5$*-pu-ut-ma*
10*li-ib-lu-ma li-iq-qú-ú*
11*ki-ma ta-ši-im-ti-šu be-lí li-pu-úš*
12[*ù aš-š*]*um a-la-ak b*[*e-lí-ya*]
13*u*$_4$*-ma-am ša be-lí i-ka-aš-ša-dam*
14*u*$_4$-1-KAM *ṭup-pí be-lí-ya*
15*li-bu-a-am* {MA}
16*aš-šum* KAS.SIG$_5$.GA *ra-sa-nim*
17[O O] X GA {X} *ša a-na* NÌ.GUB *be-lí-ya*
18[*i-na qa-ti-ya iz*]-*za-az*
19[O O O O O] X X *mi-im-ma*
20[O O O O O O O O O O]-X
. . . .
1′[*a-na* N]Ì.GUB GU$_4$ *šu-ú*
2′[*iṣ-ṣ*]*a-bi-it*

13 [fell into a tr]ance
14 [and s]aid:
15 "[She will not l]ive.
16 [Before the ki]ng reaches
17 Mari,
18 say to him that
19 this little girl is dead that he may know.
20 Lest, when he enters
21 into Mari,
22 the king should hear
23 about the death of that little girl, and
24 he choke up
25 and be profoundly troubled."

46. M.9601 = *AEM* 1/1, 223. Too broken for translation.

47. A.2559 = *AEM* 1/1, 224.

1 [To my lord]
2 spe[ak]:
3 Thus says Sumu. . . . ,
4 your servant:
5 The dream is [very] favorable for [my] lord.
6 Let my lord, when [he] crosses over
7 into Samanum, offer to Annunitum
8 a sacrifice, or
9 let my lord touch one male sheep,
10 that they may bring and sacrifice it.
11 According to his counsel let my lord act.
12 [And con]cerning the trip of [my] l[ord],
13 the day that my lord arrives,
14 on the same day let the tablet of my lord
15 come to me.
16 Concerning the soaking of the good beer
17 . . . . which is for the repast of my lord,
18 [s]tands [in my hands].
19 . . . . anything
20 . . . .
. . . .
1′ [For the r]epast this ox
2′ [has be]en taken.

48. M.5704 = *AEM* 1/1, 225.

1 [*a-na be-lí-ya*]
2 [*qí-bí-ma*]
3 [*um-ma* . . . . .]
4 [ÌR-*ka-a-ma*]
5 [*ṭup-pa-am ša be-l*]*í ú-*[*ša-bi-lam eš-me*]
6 [*be-lí ki-a-a*]*m iš-pu-ra-am um-m*[*a-a-mi*]
7 *šu-ut-tum ša a-mu-ru pa-ar-da-at*
8 *as-sú-ur-ri* ^{mí}DAM-KÙ.GI *ù ka-a-ta*
9 LÚ^{meš} *Su-tu-ú i-ṣa-ab-ba-at-ni*
10 *um-ma-a-mi a-di ta-šu-ba-at-ni*
11 *la tu-ta-ar-ru*
12 *ú-ul nu-wa-aš-ša-ar-šu-nu-ti*
13 [*an*]*-ni-tam be-lí iš-pu-ra-am*
14 [*k*]*i-ma ṭup-pí be-lí-ya*
15 *eš-me-mu-ú* DUMU^{meš} MÁŠ.ŠU.SU_{13}.SU_{13}
16 *ás-si-ma a-wa-tam ki-a-am*
17 *a-ša-al-šu-nu-ti um-ma a-na-ku-ma*
18 [*be-l*]*í ú-da-an-ni-na-am-ma*
19 [*iš-pu*]*-ra-am ki-i ta-am-li-ka*
20 [*ki-a-am aš-t*]*a-al-šu-nu-ti-ma*
21 [*na-pa-al-tam i*]*d-di-nu-nim um-ma-mi*
22 [. . . .]X *m*[*a-a*]*m-ma-an*
[. . .]
1′ [. . . . .] GE[M]E_2 *be-lí-ya*
2′ [. . . . . *li/ú-ša*]*-al-li-mu*
3′ [. . . . .] *ka-lu-ša*
4′ [. . . . . *li-il-l*]*i-ik*

49. A.1516 and M.9034 = *AEM* 1/1, 226.

1 [*a-na be-lí-ya*]
2 [*qí-bí-ma*]
3 [*um-ma* . . . . . .]
4 [ÌR-*ka-a-ma*]
5 [O O O O O]*-mu*
6 [O O O O O]*-di-ši*
7 [O O O O O]*-ya-*X
8 [*šum-ma i-na* O O O]*-tim*^{ki}
9 [^{lú}ENGAR *a-di pa-an m*]*u-ši-im*
10 [*ma-aš-q*]*í-tam la i-ṣí-id*
11 [*i-na m*]*a-aḫ-re-e-em-ma*

48. M.5704 = *AEM* 1/1, 225.

1 [To my lord]
2 [speak:]
3 [Thus says . . .],
4 [your servant],
5 [The tablet which] my [lord] s[ent me I heard].
6 [My lord] wrote me [as follow]s say[ing],
7 "The dream which I saw was disturbing.
8 I fear lest the Suteans should capture
9 Dam-ḫuraṣu and you,
10 saying, 'Until you return
11 our dwellings,
12 we will not release them.' "
13 [Th]is is what my lord wrote me.
14 As soon as I heard the tablet of my lord,
15 I summoned the diviners, and
16 the question as follows
17 I asked them, saying,
18 ["M]y lord made an urgent question
19 and [wro]te to me. What do you counsel?"
20 [Thus I have q]uestioned them,
21 and they gave me [an answer], saying:
22 . . . . no one
. . . .
1′ . . . . wife of my lord
2′ . . .] they [will ac]complish.
3′ . . . . all of it
4′ . . . . let h]im go.

49. A.1516 and M.9034 = *AEM* 1/1, 226.

1 [To my lord]
2 [speak]:
3 [Thus says . . . .],
4 [your servant]:
5 . . .
6 . . .
7 . . .
8 [If in the city . . .]tum
9 [the farmer before nigh]tfall
10 has not harvested the [irrig]ated land,
11 [pr]omptly

12 [^{giš}MAR.G]ÍD.DA$^{\text{ḫi.a}}$ *a-na* KI.UD
13 [*lu-ú u*]*ṣ*$_4$*-ṣú-ba*
14 [*a-nu-u*]*m-ma ša* LÚ *a-mi-ir šu-ut-tim*
15 [*ša-ra-s*]*ú ù sí-sí-ik-t*[*a*]*-šu*
16 [*a-na ṣe*]*-er be-lí-ya uš-ta-bi-lam*
17 [*w*]*a-ar-ka-at šu-ut-tim*
18 [*š*]*a-ti li-ip-ru-ús*

50. M.9576 = *AEM* 1/1, 227.

1 [*a-na be-lí-ya*]
2 [*qí-bí-ma*]
3 [*um-ma* ^{mí}]^{d}IM*-du-ri-ma*
4 [^{mí}X*-b*]*i-la-ú šu-ut-tam*
5 [*iṭ-ṭú*]*-ul um-ma ši-ma*
6 [*i-na šu-u*]*t-ti-ya*
7 [^{m}*Ḫa-a*]*d-nu-*DINGIR
8 [*ù*] *I-din-Ku-bi*
9 [^{lú}*m*]*u-uḫ-ḫu-ú*
10 *i* [*b*]*-l*[*u-ṭ*]*ú-nim-ma*
11 *a-na* [*l*]*e-et* ^{d}*Ab-ba*
12 *i-ru-bu-ma*
13 *ki-a-am iq-bu-ú*
14 *um-ma šu-nu-ma*
15 *a-na ku-bi-ki-na*
16 *qí-bé-e-ma*
17 *e-bu-ur šu-ul-mi-im*
18 ^{m}*Zi-im-ri-Li-im*
19 *li-pu-uš*
20 [^{m}*Z*]*i-*[*i*]*m-*[*ri-L*]*i-im*
21 [. . . .]
About 6 lines missing

51. M.13637 = *AEM* 1/1, 228.

1 [*a-na be-lí-ya*]
2 [*qí-bí-ma*]
3 [*u*]*m-ma I-*[*d*]*i-ya-*[*tum*]
4 ÌR*-ka-a-m*[*a*]
5 $^{\text{m.d}}$NANNA-LÚ.TIL ÌR*-ka*
6 *šu-ut-ta-am*
7 *i-mu-ur um-ma-a-mi*
8 *i-na šu-*[*u*]*t-t*[*i-y*]*a*

12 [let the cha]riots [be ad]ded
13 for (carrying grain) to the threshing floor.
14 [No]w concerning the man who saw the dream,
15 his [hair] and his hem
16 I have sent [to] my lord
17 that he may make a decision
18 about this dream.

50. M.9576 = *AEM* 1/1, 227.

1 [To my lord]
2 [speak]:
3 [Thus says] Adad-duri:
4 [The woman. . . . b]ilau [sa]w a dream,
5 saying,
6 ["In] my [dre]am
7 [Ḫa]dnu-El
8 [and] Iddin-Kubi,
9 [the ec]statics,
10 were alive, and
11 before the god Abba
12 they entered, and
13 they spoke as follows,
14 saying,
15 "To the ghosts of your stillborn babies
16 speak, that
17 Zimri-Lim
18 may make
19 a harvest of wellbeing.
20 Zimri-Lim
21 . . . ."
About 6 lines missing

51. M.13637 = *AEM* 1/1, 228.

1 [To my lord]
2 [speak]:
3 [T]hus says I[dd]iya[tum],
4 your servant:
5 Nanna-lú.til, your servant,
6 saw a dream,
7 saying,
8 "In my dream

9 TILLAT[^{meš} LUGA]L
10 X[. . . .]
11 [. . . .]
12 [^{m}]*Z*[*i-im-ri-Li-im*]
13 [*da-am*]$_{7}$*-da-am ša E-la-am-tim*
14 [*i-du-uk*] *ù i-na li-i-tim*
15 [*iz-zi-iz i*]*-tu-ur*
16 [. . . .]-X

52. A.1902 = *AEM* 1/1, 230.

1 [*um-ma* O O O O]*-ma i-na šu-ut-ti-ša* 1 LÚ.SU.GI
2 [*i-na sí-ka*]*-na-tim ša* ^{d}*Da-gan wa-ši-ib* {MA}
3 [IGI ^{d}*I-túr-Me*]*-er a-na šu-ke-nim um-ma šu-ma* (su.gi)
4 [*a-na ma-nim ták*]*-la-tu-nu* BA.UG$_{7}$
5 [*ad-bu-b*]*a-ak-kum-ma a-wa-ti-ya ú-ul te-še-em-mi*
6 [*iš-me-e*]*-ma* ^{d}*I-túr-Mé-er ki-a-am i-pu-ul-šu*
7 [*um-ma šu-m*]*a* ^{d}*Da-gan ù* ^{d}NIN-ḪUR.SAG.GÁ *ši-me-e*
8 [*i-na-an-n*]*a* 1 LÚ.SU.GI *a-na* 2 ^{lú}*eṭ-lu-tim*
9 [*mi-it-ḫa-ri-i*]S *iz-za-az-zu al-ka*
10 [*a-lam*^{ki}] *e-le-em er-ba-ma ša-pa-at*
11 [DINGIR^{meš} *ši*]*-me-e-nim*
12 [*a-wa-tim š*]*a a-wi-lu-tim ni-iš-me-e-em-*{MA}
13 [*ù* LÚ.SU.GI] *a-an-na-a*[*m*] *i-pu-ul-šu*

53. A.2448 = *AEM* 1/1, 231.

1 *a-na be-lí-*[*ya*]
2 *qí-bí-m*[*a*]
3 *um-ma Sa-am-me-e-t*[*ar*]
4 ÌR*-ka-a-m*[*a*]
5 *aš-šum bu-uḫ-ra-tim a-na* ^{d}IM *n*[*a-qé-em*]
6 *be-lí iš-pu-ra-*[*am*]
7 [*i*]*-na pa-ni-tim-ma aš-šum bu-uḫ-ra-t*[*im*]
8 *šu-ut-tum in-na-me-er-ma*
9 *iš-tu Bu-zu-ur-ra-an*^{ki}
10 *a-na ṣe-er be-lí-ya aš-pu-r*[*a-am*]
11 *um-ma a-na-ku-ma u*$_{4}$*-um* U$_{4}$-20-KAM
12 *bu-uḫ-ra-tam a-na* ^{d}IM *ù* [*k*]*e-em-*[*ma*]
13 *a-na* ^{d}NÈ.IRI$_{11}$.GAL *li-iq-q*[*ú*]
14 *ù qa-tam-ma a-na re-eš* ITU
15 *u*$_{4}$*-um* U$_{4}$-1-KAM *ù ša-al-ši-i*[*š*]
16 *u*$_{4}$*-um* U$_{4}$-[X-KAM *li-in-n*]*a-aq-q*[*í*]

[9]the auxiliary troops [of the king]
[10]. . . .
[11]. . . .
[12]Z[imri-Lim]
[13][accomplished the de]feat of the Elamites
[14]and [stood] in triumph.
[15][He] turned
[16]. . . .

52. A.1902 = *AEM* 1/1, 230.

[1][Thus says. . . .], and in her dream an old man
[2]was sitting [among the stel]as of Dagan
[3]to do obeisance [before Itur-M]er. He said,
[4][“In whom do] you [tr]ust? The dead.
[5][I spok]e to you, but you will not hear my words.”
[6]Itur-Mer [heard], and answered him as follows,
[7][sayin]g, “Dagan and Nin-ḫursagga listen!
[8][No]w one old man to two young men
[9]will stand [equally]. Go!
[10]Enter the upper [city], and hear
[11]the speech of [the gods]!
[12]We have heard [the words o]f humankind.”
[13][Then the old man] answered him, “Yes!”

53. A.2448 = *AEM* 1/1, 231.

[1]To [my] lord
[2]speak:
[3]Thus says Sammetar,
[4]your servant:
[5]Concerning the o[ffering] of the hot dish to Adad
[6]my lord has written [to me].
[7]Formerly concerning the hot dish
[8]a dream was seen, and
[9]I wrote to my lord
[10]from Buzurran,
[11]saying, “On the twentieth (of the month)
[12]let them offer the hot dish to Adad and
[13]the same for Nergal.
[14]And in the same way for the beginning of the month,
[15]on the first, and a third time
[16]on the . . . th [let it be] offered.”

^{17}[*an*]-*ni-tam* [*a-na be-lí-ya*]
^{18}[*aš-pu-ra-am*]
^{19}[*ki-ma* . . . .]
^{20}[*an-ni-tam i-n*]*a pa-ni-tim-m*[*a*]
^{21}[*a*]-*na be-lí-ya aš-pu-ru*
^{22}*a-di e-bu-ri-im* 3-*šu*-[*ma*]
^{23}*bu-uḫ-ra-tum ù ke-em ú-u*[*l*]
^{24}*in-na-aḫ-ḫ*[*i-ra*]
^{25}*a-na an-né-tim ma-aḫ-re-m*[*a be-lí li-qú-ul*]

54. A.4400 = *AEM* 1/1, 243.

^{1}[*a-na be-lí-ya*]
^{2}[*qí-bí-ma*]
^{3}*um-m*[*a* . . . . . .]
^{4}ÌR-*ka-a*-[*ma*]
^{5}*aš-šum* É *Sa-am-me-e*-[*tar*]
^{6}*ša i-na pa-ni-tim-ma qí-du*-[*tam il-li-k*]*u*
^{7} ^{lú}*mu-uḫ-ḫu-ú* {X} *ša* ^{d}*D*[*a-gan*]
^{8}*ka-a-ya-an-tam i-d*[*a*]-*a*[*b*]-*b*[*u-b*]*u-ni*[*m*]
^{9}*um-ma-a-mi* SIG$_4$ḪI.A *ša* É *ša-a-tu*
^{10}DINGIR-*lum i-ru-ur*
^{11}*li-ib-bi m*[*a*]-*y*[*a*]-*lim ù úš-še*$_{20}$ *li-ib-n*[*a-tim*]
^{12}*e-pí-re li-iš-pu-k*[*u*]
^{13}*an-ni-tam* ^{lú}*m*[*u-uḫ-ḫ*]*u-ú ša* ^{d}*D*[*a-gan*]
^{14}*i-da-ab-bu-bu-nim*
^{15}[*i*]-*na-an-na a-nu-um-ma*
^{16}*a-na be-lí-ya aš-ta-ap*-[*pa-ar*]
^{17}*be-lí li-iš-ta-al-ma*
^{18}*ak-ki-ma* [*mu-u*]*š-ta-l*[*u-tim*]
^{19}*ša be-lí iš-ta-al*-[*lu*]
^{20}*me-ḫe-er ṭup-pí-ya li-il-li*-[*kam*]
^{21}*šum-ma be-lí i-qa-ab*-[*bi*]
^{22}SIG$_4$ḪI.A *ša* É *ša-a-tu lu-ša*-[*aš-ši*]
^{23}*a-na mu-uḫ-ḫi* BÀD^{ki} *lu*-[*ša-bi-lam*]
^{24}*ù e-pí-re* [. . . .]
^{25}[o o –*t*]*e-si* [. . . . .]
break of 3 lines

55. A.428 = *AEM* 1/2, 371.

^{1}[*a-na be-lí-ya qí-bí-ma*]
^{2}[*um-ma*] *Ya-ri-im*-^{d}[IM ÌR-*ka-a-ma*]

[17][Th]is [I wrote]
[18][to my lord].
[19][In agreement with. . .]
[20][this tha]t I wrote
[21]to my lord formerly,
[22]until the harvest the hot dish offering
[23]will be made three times, and thus
[24]they will not be delayed.
[25]To these things [let my lord give] prompt [attention].

54. A.4400 = *AEM* 1/1, 243.

[1][To my lord]
[2][speak]:
[3]Thu[s says. . . .],
[4]your servant:
[5]Concerning the house of Samme[tar]
[6]which formerly [fell into] disrepair,
[7]the ecstatic of Dagan
[8]is constantly speaking to me,
[9]saying, "The god has cursed
[10]the brickwork of that house.
[11]Into the living area and the foundation of bricks
[12]let them pour dirt."
[13]This is what the ecstatic of D[agan]
[14]keeps saying to me.
[15]Now then
[16]I have writ[ten] to my lord
[17]that my lord may take counsel,
[18]and according to the [cou]nse[l]
[19]which my lord takes,
[20]may a response to my tablet come to me.
[21]If my lord commands (it),
[22]I will have them re[move] the brickwork of that house
[23]and ca[rry] it to the city wall.
[24]And dirt. . . .
[25]. . . .
break of 3 lines

55. A.428 = *AEM* 1/2, 371.

[1][To my lord speak]:
[2][Thus says] Yarim-[Adad, your servant],

3 *aš-šum ṭe*$_{4}$*-em e-le-e Iš-[me-*^{d}*Da-gan]*
4 *a-na É-kál-la-tim*[^{ki}]
5 *[š]a be-lí iš-te-né-mu-ú mi-im-[ma]*
6 *a-na É-kál-la-tim*^{ki} *ú-ul i-[le-e]*
7 *a-wa-tu-šu it-ta-ab-še-e-m[a]*
8 *i-ta-ti-šu ir-ṭú-pu sa-ḫa-ra-am*
9 ^{lú}*a-pí-lum ša* ^{d}AMAR.UTU *i-na ba-ab é-kál-lim*
10 *iz-zi-iz-ma ki-a-[a]m iš*$_{7}$*-ta-na-as*$_{6}$*-si*
11 *um-ma šu-ma Iš-me-*^{d}*D[a-g]an i-na qa-at* ^{d}AMAR.UTU
12 *ú-ul uṣ-ṣí ša-ḫa-ar-ra-am*
13 *i-ka-aṣ-ṣa-ar*
14 *ù iḫ-ḫa-ab-ba-as-sí-im*
15 *an-né-e-tim i-na ba-ab é-kál-lim*
16 *iš*$_{7}$*-ta-ás-si-ma*
17 *[ma-am-ma-a]n mi-im-ma ú-ul iq-bi-šum*
18 *ki-ma pa-ni-šu-un-ma i-na ba-ab Iš-me-*^{d}*Da-gan*
19 *iz-zi-iz-ma i-na pu-ḫu-ur ma-a-tim ka-li-ša*
20 *ki-a-am iš*$_{7}$*-ta-na-ás-si um-ma-a-mi*
21 *a-na sa-li-mi-im ù dam-qa-tim ša-ka-nim*
22 *a-na ṣe-er* SUKKAL ELAM.MA*-tim ta-al-li-ik-ma*
23 *ki-ma dam-qa-tim ša-ka-nim*
24 *ni-ṣi-ir-ti* ^{d}AMAR.UTU *ù a-lim* KÁ.DINGIR.RA^{ki}
25 *[a]-na* SUKKAL ELAM.MA*-tim tu-še-ṣí*
26 *[ka]-re-e ù na-ak-ka-ma-ti-ya ta-ag-mu-ur-ma*
27 *[g]i-mi-il-li ú-ul tu-te-e-er*
28 *[ù] a-na É-kál-la-tim*^{ki} *ta-at-ta-al-la-ak*
29 *[ša] ki-ma ni-ṣi-ir-ti ú-še-ṣú-ú*
30 *[ta-a]r-di-is-sà la i-ša-al-la-an-[ni]*
31 *[an-né-]e-tim i-na pu-ḫu-ur m[a-a-tim]*
32 *[ka-li-ša iš*$_{7}$*-t]a-na-ás-su-ú*
33 *[ma-am-ma-an ú]-ul iq-bi-š[um]*
34 [. . . . .]
35 [. . . . .]
36 [. . . . . *m]u-ur-ma*
37 [. . . . .*u]ḫ-šu-nu-ma*
38 [. . . . . *É-k]ál-la-tim*^{ki}
39 *iṭ-ṭà-ra-ad ù* LÚ *šu-ú*
40 *mu-ur-ṣa-am ra-bé-e-em*
41 *ma-ru-uṣ ba-la-as-sú*
42 *ú-ul ki-in*

[3]Concerning the report about Iš[me-Dagan] going up
[4]to Ekallatum,
[5]which my lord keeps hearing, he
[6]did not [go up] to Ekallatum at all.
[7]Words about him have started,
[8]and they constantly circulate around him.
[9]The respondent of Marduk stood in the gate of the palace,
[10]and keeps crying out as follows,
[11]saying, "Išme-D[ag]an will not escape from
[12]the hand of Marduk. As a sheath (of grain)
[13]it (the hand of Marduk) will tie (him),
[14]and he will be chopped up by it."
[15]These things he kept crying out in
[16]the gate of the palace,
[17][and no on]e said anything to him.
[18]In the same way he stood before them in the gate
[19]of Išme-Dagan and in the assembly of the whole land
[20]he keeps crying out as follows, saying,
[21] "To make peace and friendship
[22]you went to the ruler of Elam,
[23]and in order to make friendship
[24]you took out the treasure of Marduk and the city of Babylon
[25]to the ruler of Elam.
[26]The [si]los and my stores you used up, and
[27]you did not return my favor.
[28][And] will you go away to Ekallatum?
[29][The one who] removed my treasure
[30]shall not ask me for its [int]erest."
[31][Thes]e things [he kep]t crying out
[32]in the assembly [of the whole] la[nd].
[33][No one] spoke [to him].
[34]. . . .
[35]. . .
[36]. . .
[37]. . .
[38][. . . . to E]kallatum
[39]he sent, and that man
[40]is sick with a serious illness.
[41]His life
[42]is not firm.

56. FLP 1674

1 LUGAL *I-ba-al-pi-El*
2 *um-ma* ^{d}*Ki-ti-t*[*um-m*]*a*
3 *ni*$_{5}$*-iṣ-re-tum ša* DIN[GIR]^{meš}
4 *maḫ-ri-ya ša-ak-na*
5 *aš-šum zi-ik-r*[*u-u*]*m*
6 *ša šu-mi-ya i-na pí-ka*
7 *ka-ya-nu ni*$_{5}$*-iṣ-re-et* DINGIR^{meš}
8 *ap-ta-na-at-ti-a-ak-kum*
9 *i-na mi-il-ki*
10 *ša* DINGIR^{meš} *i-na ši-ip-ṭì*
11 *ša An-nim ma-tum*
12 *a-na be-li-im*
13 *na-ad-na-at-ku-um*
14 *ši-in ma-tim e-li-tim*
15 *ù ša-ap-li-tim ta-pa-ṭà-ar*
16 *ma-ak-ku-ur ma-tim e-li-tim*
17 *ù ša-ap-li-tim te-pé-ed-di*
18 *ma-ḫi-ir-ka ú-ul i-ma-aṭ-ṭì*
19 *e-em ma-tim ša qa-at-ka*
20 *ik-šu-du a-ka-*[*al*]
21 *ta-ne-eḫ-tim i-*[*ka-al*]
22 *iš-di* ^{giš}GU.ZA*-ka*
23 *a-na-ku* ^{d}*Ki-ti-tum*
24 *ú-da-na-an la-ma-s*[*a*]*-a*[*m*]
25 [*n*]*a-ṣé-er-tam aš-ta-ak-na-ak-*[*kum*]
26 [*ú*]*-zu-un-ka li-ib-ba-ši-a-am*

57. M.13091 = *AEM* 1/1, 1.

1 [*i-na te-re-e-et Zi-im-ri-Li-im be-lí-ya*]
2 [*i-na ne-pé-eš*$_{15}$*-tim ma-li i*]*š-ša-k*[*a-nu-ma a-am-ma-ru*]
3 [*ú-lu-ma i-na te-re-et mu-ú*]*š-ke-nim*
4 [*i-na ne-pé-eš*$_{15}$*-tim ma-li i*]*š-ša-ka-nu-ma a-am-ma-r*[*u*]
5 [UZU *le-em-na-am ù la da*]*m-qa-am ma-li a-am-ma-ru*
6 [*a-na* ^{m}*Zi-im-ri-Li-im be-lí-ya*] *lu-ú a-qa-ab-bi la a-ka-at-ta-mu*
7 UZ[U *l*]*e-*[*em-na-am ù la dam-qa-a*]*m ša i-na te-re-e-et*
8 ^{m}*Zi-im-ri-L*[*i-im be-lí-ya i-n*]*a* ^{uzu}*iz-bi-im ù i-na* ^{uzu}IZ.MI*-im*
9 *iš-ša-ak-ka-nu-ma a-am-ma-ru*
10 *a-na* DUMU *a-wi-lu-tim šum-šu la a-qa-ab-bu-ú*
11 *ù a-wa-tam na-ṣ*[*í-i*]*r-tam ša a-na te-re-e-tim e-pé-ši-im*
12 ^{m}*Zi-im-ri-Li-im b*[*e*]*-lí i-qa-ab-bé-e-em*

56. FLP 1674

[1]King Ibal-pi-El,
[2]thus says Kititum:
[3]The secrets of the gods
[4]are set before me.
[5]Because the mention
[6]of my name is constantly in your mouth,
[7]the secrets of the gods
[8]I keep on opening for you.
[9]By the advice
[10]of the gods (and) by the judgment
[11]of Anu, the land
[12]is given to you
[13]to rule.
[14]The tooth?/shoe? of the upper
[15]and lower land you will loosen.
[16]The treasure of the upper
[17]and lower land you will amass?/redeem?.
[18]Your economy will not diminish.
[19]Wherever in the land your hand
[20]has reached, it will enjoy
[21]the food of peace.
[22]The foundations of your throne
[23]I, Kititum,
[24]will strengthen. A protective
[25]spirit I have established for you.
[26]Let your ear be attentive to me.

57. M.13091 = *AEM* 1/1, 1.

[1][In the taking of oracles for Zimri-Lim my lord],
[2][in the extispicy, all that i]s pro[duced and that I see],
[3][or in the taking of oracles for an ord]inary person,
[4][in the extispicy, all that i]s produced and that I see,
[5][the bad and unf]avorable omen, all that I see,
[6]I will surely tell [to Zimri-Lim, my lord]; I will not conceal it.
[7]The b[ad and unfavorab]le omen which is produced and I see
[8]in taking oracles
[9]for Zimri-L[im, my lord, i]n an abnormal birth or in an *izmum*
[10]I will not tell to anyone whomever.
[11]The secret word which which Zimri-Lim, my lord,
[12]will say to me for the purpose of making oracular inquiry,

13 *ù a-na* DUMU MÁŠ.ŠU.SU$_{13}$.SU$_{13}$ *tap-pé-e-ya i-qa-ab-bí-ma e-še-em-mu-ú*
14 *ú-lu-ma i-na te-re-e-tim e-pé-ši-im i-na qa-at* M[ÁŠ.ŠU.SU$_{13}$.SU$_{13}$ *tap-p*]*é-ya*
15 *ši-ra-am ša-a-tu a-am-ma-ru*
16 *a-wa-tam ša-a-ti lu-ú a-na-aṣ-ṣa-a*[*r*]
17 [*a-wa-a*]*t* DUMU *a-wi-lu-tim šum-šu ša pé-em na-ak-*[*ra-am i-da-bu-bu-ma*]
18 [*l*]*a ú-še-eṣ-ṣú-ú-ši be-lí ša-*[*lu-um-ma i-ša-lu-ma*]
19 *a-na ba-ar-tim le-mu-un-tim ù* [*a-na la ba-la-ṭì-im*]
20 *ša Zi-im-ri-Li-im be-lí-ya te-re-*[*tim ú-še-pé-šu*]
21 *a-na* DUMU *a-wi-lu-tim šum-šu la e*[*-ep-pé-šu*]
(Three lines erased)
22 *ù e-pí-iš ba-ar-tim* [*l*]*e-mu-un-tim* [*a-na na-pí-iš-tim*]
23 *ša Zim-ri-Li-im be-lí-*[*ya*]
24 *ša a-na te-re-e-tim e-pé-*[*š*]*i-im i-qa-ab-bé-e-em*
25 *ù* [*a-na*] DUMU M[ÁŠ.ŠU].SU$_{13}$.SU$_{13}$ *tap-pé-e-ya i-qa-ab-bé*
26 [*e-še-em*]*-m*[*u-ú*] *ú-lu-ma i-na te-re-e-tim*
27 [*i-na qa*]*-at* DUMU MÁŠ.ŠU.SU$_{13}$.[SU$_{13}$] *tap-pé-e-ya* [*a*]*-a*[*m-m*]*a-ru*
28 [*la a-ka*]*-at-ta-mu-šu i-na u$_4$-mi-šu-ma*
29 [*a-na Zi-im*]*-ri-Li-im be-lí-ya lu-ú a-qa-ab-*[*b*]*i*
30 [*lu a-ša-a*]*p-p*[*a-a*]*r la a-ka-ta-mu-š*[*u p*]*a-né-šu la ub-ba-lu*
31 [É]*-ti-ya ù ra-pa-aš* É*-ti-ya*
32 [*a-na*] *na-pí-iš-ti Zi-im-ri-Li-im be-lí-ya*
33 [ ] *li-ib-bi-ya ga-am-ri-im*
34 [ ] *ra-tim-ma* [

. . . .

1′ [ ] *ki-ma ša ša-la-mi-ya ù ku-si-ri-ya*
2′ [*la*] *e-ep-pé-su ša na-ṣa-ar na-pí-iš-ti*
3′ [ ]*-ya Zi-im-ri-Li-im be-lí-ya ep-pé-*[O]
4′ [*a-di*] *ba-al-ṭà-ku lu-*⟨*ú*⟩ *e-ep-pé-eš*

13 or which he will say to a diviner, my colleague, and which I hear,

14 or in the making of an oracular inquiry by the hand of a diviner, my colleague,

15 that ominous sign I see,

16 that word I will certainly guard.

17 The word of anyone whomever who [speaks] with hostile intent,

18 and does not want it brought out, who wishes [to attack] my lord,

19 and [who wants] ora[cles taken] in preparation for an evil rebellion

20 or [for an assassination] of Zimri-Lim, my lord,

21 for any such person, whomever it is, I will not d[o it].

(Three lines erased)

22 And the one who makes an evil rebellion [against the life]

23 of Zimri-Lim, [my] lord,

24 who speaks to me about taking oracles,

25 or who speaks to a diviner, my colleague,

26 [and I he]a[r] or I see in the oracles

27 [performed by the h]and of a diviner, my colleague,

28 [I swear I will not] conceal it. In that very day

29 I will surely tell [Zim]ri-Lim, my lord,

30 [or I will wri]te him. I swear I will not conceal it. I will not show him favor.

31 . . . of my house and the enlargement of my house

32 . . . for] the life of Zimri-Lim, my lord,

32 . . . of my complete heart

33 . . . .

break

1′ . . . . as my wellbeing and my success

2′ . . . I swear I will not] do. With regard to protecting the life

3′ . . . of Zimri-Lim, my lord, I will act.

4′ . . . as long] as I live, I will surely act.

Part 3

Solving Difficult Problems: New Readings of Old Texts

Chapter 15

A New Root for an Old Crux, Psalm 22:17c

Ps 22:17c is an old crux which has never been satisfactorily explained. The MT's *kāʾărî yāday wĕraglāy*, "like a lion my hands and my feet," makes no sense,[1] and most modern scholars agree the text is corrupt. They also agree in locating the problem in the word *kāʾărî*, "like a lion." All the ancient versions with the exception of the Targum read a verb here,[2] and following their lead, most modern scholars emend the consonantal text from *kʾry* to *kʾrw* or *krw* in order to obtain a verb in the 3mpl suffix conjugation.[3] The correction is very slight. Intrusive *alephs* are well-known,[4] the confusion between *y* and *w* is common,[5] and there is some manuscript support for the emendation.[6] Thus

---

1. Attempts to extract some sense from these enigmatic words without resorting to textual emendations generally take one of two forms. Either one assumes an ellipsis of a verb in the line, or one redivides the line. Neither approach has produced a credible meaning, however. The Targum, following the first route, supplies a verb not found in the *MT*: *nktyn byk kʾryʾ ʾydy wrgly*, "they *gnaw* my hands and my feet like a lion," but such an ellipsis is incredibly hard and totally unexpected in the context. A. B. Ehrlich provides an example of the second approach. He takes *kʾry* with the preceding line and makes *ydy wrgly* objects of the following verb *ʾspr*, which results in the rather unique translation:

> der Bösewichter Rotte umgibt mich wie einen Löwen.
> Mit Händen und Füssen
> wehr' ich mich,
> mit all meinen Gliedern-
> (*Die Psalmen neu übersetzt und erklärt* [Berlin, 1905] 46).

Ehrlich's explanation is worthless for several reasons. While *kʾry* could fit grammatically with 17b, this redivision of the lines makes 17b too long for its parallel in 17a and destroys the rather clear imagery in 18a. Moreover, Ehrlich's assumption that *ydy wrgly* and *kl ʿṣmwty* are both objects of *ʾspr* is hard, his contrived meaning for *spr* is completely ad hoc, and his imprecise translation of *ʾṣmwty* is unacceptable. One simply cannot make sense of the line without correcting the text.

2. For the Targum's reading see above, n. 1.

3. See the commentaries. Dahood is an exception, but his analysis of the form as an infinitive absolute from *kry*, "to dig" (*Psalms I* [The Anchor Bible: Garden City, New York, 1966] 140–41), whatever its merit in preserving the *MT*, results in the same general translation and interpretation as those based on the reading *krw*.

4. See the numerous examples collected by Friedrich Delitzsch, *Die Lese- und Schreibfehler im Alten Testament* (Berlin, 1920) par. 31a.

5. Ibid., par. 103.

6. Accordding to Kennicott, the reading *krw* is found in one manuscript and in the margins of three, while seven manuscripts contain the reading *kʾrw* (Benjaminus Kennicott [ed.], *Vetus Testamentum Hebraicum; cum Variis Lectionibus* II [Oxford, 1780] 323).

one could readily accept an interpretation of the line based on this correction if it yielded a meaning consistent with the requirements of the context.

On this semantic level, however, the text remains recalcitrant. There are two commonly proposed derivations for the reconstructed verb form: (1) Following the *LXX* and the Syriac, some commentators derive the form from the well-attested Hebrew root *kārā(h)* I, "to dig."[7] (2) Others, following the other Greek versions and the Vulgate, posit an otherwise unattested root *kārā(h)* IV, "to tie together."[8] Yet neither of these proposed derivations yields a really satisfactory meaning. The lexical difficulties, if not insurmountable, are quite apparent. While the root *kārā(h)* I is well-attested, it is never used anywhere else in a metaphorical sense for "piercing" or "disfiguring" human extremities. The root *kārā(h)* IV, on the other hand, is not otherwise attested and may be no more than a contextual guess.[9]

The major difficulty with both these derivations lies at a deeper level than a simple lack of lexigraphical attestation, however. Neither provide a meaning compatible with the context. Both derivations are forced to take vv. 17c with 17ab, since by the meaning these derivations give, the only possible subject for 17c is the evildoers of 17ab. At best that yields a tricola, but the third stich does not offer a very good parallel to the other two, so the result really appears to be a bicola followed by an independent stich:

> For dogs have surrounded me,
> A congregation of evildoers have encircled me.
> They have pierced/tied my hands and my feet.

The evildoers are the subject again in 18b–19ab:

> They gave, they stare at me.
> They divide my garments among themselves,
> And for my clothes they cast lots.

That leaves 18a, where the subject is in the first person, isolated: "I can count all my bones."[10] Moreover, as D. Winton Thomas pointed out some years ago,[11] the phrase *ʾspr kl ʿṣmwty* is a description of the physical condition of the

7. This is the opinion of Deissler, Kittel, Kirkpatrick, and Nötscher.

8. This is the view of Kraus, Maillot and Lelievre, and Podechard.

9. G. R. Driver's attempt to provide evidence for this root from the cognate languages (*ET* 57 [1945–46] 193) is not very impressive. His Akkadian *karāru*, "to tie, to be twisted," is really *q/garāru*, "to wind, coil" (von Soden, *AHw*, 902–3) or "to turn, roll over" (*CAD* G, 47–48); *karāru* means "to put in place" (*CAD* K, 207). His Arabic and Syriac evidence is not too much better; at best he must press to get a root meaning "to tie."

10. The difficulty created by this isolated first-person verb has produced a secondary change to the easier 3pl reading in some Greek manuscripts and the Syriac—and at least one modern commentator, Deissler, has accepted it.

11. "Two Psalm Notes," *JTS* 37 (1936) 386.

one praying—he can count all his bones because his flesh is dried up and shrunken upon them. Verse 18b, however, drops the description of the poor man's physical condition and resumes the account of the evildoers' actions. Thus 18a has no genuine parallel and stands as an erratic phrase in an alien context on either of these interpretations.

One can remove this difficulty only by finding a parallel stich for 18a, and, in the context, 17c offers the sole possible candidate. Thomas, following this line of reasoning, rejected the usual corrections of *kʾry* to a verb form and analyzed it instead as the inseparable preposition *k* + a noun *ʾry*, for which he suggested the meaning "hearth."[12] Thus the line would read, "My hands and my feet are as a hearth," i.e., burnt up with fever. That would fit the context better than either of the two ordinary treatments of the line, but it is not convincing either. Fevered hands and feet present a somewhat strange image, and the lack of any verb in the line makes the comparison forced; Ps 102:4, which Thomas quotes as a parallel,[13] contains a verb that makes the comparison clear. Moreover, it is hard to disregard the almost unanimous tradition of the early translations which found a verb in 17c. Whatever the shortcomings of the two common interpretations, their agreement in looking for a verb behind *kʾry* can hardly be wrong.

It was an advance, therefore, when Kissane, who saw the same problem as Thomas, tried to resolve it with a new verbal interpretation.[14] His statement of the problem's solution is unusually lucid and deserves to be quoted:[15]

> In seeking a solution, we may assume that 17c is to be joined to 18a to form a couplet. The meaning of the second clause is quite clear. It describes a man whose body is so emaciated that his bones can be seen. Now in a precisely similar context in Job we find the following passage:
>
> His flesh is *consumed* from sight
> And his bones that were not seen are laid bare.
> (Job 33:21).
>
> The second clause is clearly the equivalent of 18a. Is the first clause in the psalm intended to have somewhat the same meaning as the first clause in the passage of Job? To get this meaning we have but to substitute the verb 'consume' used in Job for the obscure word in the psalm. They differ by a single letter, and it is well known that the two letters *lamed* and *resh* have often been confused; the sense obtained is the exact equivalent of the first clause of the passage of Job. The original *kālû* became *kārû*, then by the insertion of the vowel-letter *kāʾărû*. This seems to be the most probable solution of this difficult problem.

12. Ibid.
13. Ibid.
14. E. J. Kissane, *The Book of Psalms Translated from a Critically Revised Hebrew Text with a Commentary* (2 vols.; Westminster, Maryland, 1953) 97–101.
15. Ibid., 100–101.

Kissane's parallel from Job is impressive; it makes his interpretation almost convincing. There are difficulties, however. The orthographic replacement of *lamed* by *resh* due to the indistinctness of part of the original *lamed* is a relatively late phenomenon;[16] in the earlier form of the script the two letters are quite distinct. Can one assume, therefore, that this error could have taken place early enough to have been leveled through all the translations? Moreover, the verb *kālā(h)* does not occur with "hands" or "feet" as the subject in any other passage. Neither of these objections necessarily destroys the possibility of Kissane's emendation, but it remains no more than a mere possibility, and one is compelled to continue searching for a better explanation.

The ideal solution would be to keep a verbal root *kārā(h)*, while assigning it a meaning compatible with the context. It may be possible to do just that on the basis of Syriac and especially Akkadian cognates. Both languages contain a root *karû*, "to be short," which is used in certain contexts to indicate physical or mental infirmities.[17] Particularly significant for this discussion is the occurrence of the Gt stem of this root in Akkadian diagnostic texts to describe illness-induced deformities of human hands and feet:

> *šumma ina murṣīšu pâšu ṣabitma qātāšu u šēpāšu iktarâ ul mišitti murussu ētetiq*
>
> "If in his sickness his mouth is paralyzed and his hands and his feet are shrunken, it is not a stroke, his sickness will pass."[18]

There is no particular merit in "discovering" vast numbers of "hitherto unrecognized" Hebrew roots, particularly when the passages being explicated make sense with the old established roots. Nevertheless, classical Hebrew undoubtedly possessed a much richer vocabulary than has been preserved in our limited corpus of texts, and where none of the old roots make sense in the context, as is certainly the case in Ps 22:17c, it is legitimate to suggest a new root. The only requirements are that the root be well-attested in a cognate language or languages, the difference in root consonants, if any, be explainable by the principles of Semitic phonology, and the meaning suggested for the new root be consistent with its attested meaning in the cognate languages and with the context in the other language where it is posited. A root *kārā(h)* V, "to be short, shrunken, shriveled," which I would posit for Ps 22:17c, meets all these crite-

16. I assume this is what he is referring to when he appeals to the well-known confusion of *lamed* and *resh*, cf. Delitzsch, *Die Lese- und Schreibfehler*, par. 119b.

17. J. Payne Smith (Mrs. Margoliouth) (ed.), *A Compendious Syriac Dictionary* (Oxford, 1967³) 224; *CAD* K, 229–30.

18. René Labat, *Traité akkadien e diagnostics et pronostics médicaux* (2 vols.; Leiden, 1951) 160: 30; see also 142: 6′–8′.

ria. Hence one may accept the commonly adopted reading *kāru*, interpret it as a verb form, and translate Ps 22:17c–18a as follows:

> My hands and my feet are shriveled up,
>   I can count all my bones.[19]

---

19. The presence of this couplet between lines dealing with the psalmist's enemies might suggest transposing 17c–18a above, between 16ab and 16c, where one also has a description of the psalmist's bodily condition. Even a number of scholars who hold to one of the commonly accepted interpretations have suggested a rearrangement of the lines (Podechard, Maillot and Lelievre, and G. R. Driver, though only one part of Driver's interpretation, his derivation of *krw*, is widely accepted). This transposition is not necessary for my argument though, and one should note that vv. 17–18a reflect the same progression of thought found in vv. 13–16—the psalmist moves from the enemies who surround him to his own physical condition. Thus the repetition may be art, or attempted art, not error.

Chapter 16
The Young Lions of Psalm 34:11

The MT of Ps 34:11 contains a reference to young lions that, at least on the first reading, seems rather odd:

> *kpyrym ršw wrʿbw*
> *wdršy yhwh lʾ yḥsrw kl ṭwb*
>
> Young lions become poor and starve.
> But those who seek Yahweh will not lack any good.

The verb *rwš*, "to be poor," is normally used of human beings, not animals; the contrast between "young lions" and "those who seek Yahweh" is not immediately apparent; and, in the absence of any animal imagery in the preceding verses, the introduction of "young lions" here appears rather abrupt. Moreover, the LXX and the Syriac do not read "young lions," but "the rich" (πλούσιος, '*tyr*'), a reading which seems to fit the context better. Therefore it is not surprising that many commentators correct the MT by these versions.[1]

The evidence for correcting *kpyrym* is not as strong as it appears at first sight, however. If one considers the principle of *lectio difficilior*, one must at least question whether the LXX's rendering is really based on a different Hebrew *Vorlage*. Schmidt dismisses the LXX reading as a "deutende Übersetzung,"[2] and since no one has produced a convincing parallel for any of the corrections proposed for the hypothetical Hebrew *Vorlage*,[3] this writer is inclined to agree.

Furthermore, a similar use of lion imagery occurs in Eliphaz's first speech to Job, a passage often cited by commentators who retain the MT:

> Consider, what innocent ever perished,
> Or where have the righteous been destroyed?

1. So, for example, Castellino, Deissler, Duhm, Gunkel, Herkenne, Kraus, Leslie, Nötscher, Oesterley, and Podechard. Dahood and Kissane are more inclined to preserve the MT reading, but they still avoid the young lions by assigning *kpyrym* different meanings than it normally possesses.

2. H. Schmidt, *Die Psalmen* (HAT 15; Tübingen 1934) 63.

3. The three most common corrections are *kĕbēdîm*, *kabbîrîm*, and *kōpĕrîm*.

I have observed that they who plow evil
And sow trouble reap the same.
At a breath of God they perish,
A blast of His anger, and they vanish.
The lion may roar, the old lion growl,
But the young lion's teeth are broken.
The lion perishes, robbed of prey,
The lioness' whelps are scattered. (Job 4:7–11)[4]

In comparing this passage to Ps 34:11 several similarities become evident. To begin with, both passages are expounding the doctrine of individual retribution with its clear-cut contrast between the respective fates of the pious and the impious. Both passages also use the lion as an example of the impious, and both texts introduce this image rather abruptly; in neither case is the figure prepared for by previous animal imagery. Finally one should observe that in both texts the lion perishes from hunger.

These similarities, particularly the abruptness with which the image is introduced, suggest one is dealing with a well-known traditional motif, and this suggestion is strengthened by the occurrence of what appears to be the same motif in an earlier Akkadian text which bears noteworthy resemblances to both Psalm 34 and Job. The Babylonian *Theodicy*, written about 1000 B.C., is an acrostic poem just as is Psalm 34, and it deals with the problem of divine justice under the literary form of a dialogue between a sufferer and his friend, much as Job.[5] In the course of this dialogue, as the sufferer is pointing to examples of the impious who prosper, he mentions the lion:

ag-gu la-bu šá i-tak-ka-lu du-muq ši-r[*i*]
[*ak-k*]*i-mil-ti ìl-ti-i šup-ṭu-ri ú-bil mas-ḫat-s*[*u*]

The savage lion who devoured the choicest flesh,
Did it bring its flour offering to appease the goddess's anger?[6]

In other words, the lion, a creature who never bothers to offer sacrifice to the gods, has steak more often than the pious man who does honor the gods. Note that the lion's crime resides not so much in the moral quality of his action as it does in the self-assertive autonomy with which he acts. He commits the religious sin of ignoring the gods, of trusting in himself rather than in the gods.

4. The translation is M. Pope's (*Job* [AB 15; Garden City, 1965] 34).

5. The presence of this motif in a wisdom text prior to Job destroys the credibility of Fohrer's confident assertion about the image of the lion in Job 4:10–11: "Dieses Bild ist sicherlich aus den Psalmen übernommen, denen der Vergleich des Frevlers mit dem Löwen geläufig ist . . ." (*Das Buch Hiob* [KAT 16; Gütersloh 1963] 139). Psalm 34 also has close ties to the wisdom tradition (H.-J. Kraus, *Psalmen* [BK 15/1; Neukirchen 1961] 267), so one should rather look for the origin of the motif in the wisdom movement.

6. W. G. Lambert, *Babylonian Wisdom Literature* (Oxford 1960) 74: 50–51.

This is even clearer in the *Kutha Legend* about Naram-Sin where the motif occurs again. There, after Naram-Sin has offered his sacrifices but has failed to receive a positive response from the gods, the disgruntled king muses on the value of the traditional religious preparations for war:

a-a-ú nēšu (UR.MAḪ) *bi-ri ib-ri*
a-a-ú barbaru (UR.BAR.RA) *i*[*š*]*-al šá-il-tú*
lul-lik ki-ma mār (DUMU) *ḫab-ba-t*[*i ina*] *me-gir libbīya* (ŠÀ-*ya*)

What lion ever observed omens?
What wolf ever inquired of a dream interpreter?
I will go like a bandit in the good pleasure of my own heart.[7]

Of course this skeptical denial of the practical value of piety, while it might be stated, could not go unanswered. The *Theodicy* refutes such skepticism through the response of the sufferer's friend:

gi-ir bu-li la-ba šá taḫ-su-su ga-na bit-ru
gi-il-lat nēšu (UR.MAḪ) *i-pu-lu pi-ta-as-su ḫaš-tum*

Come, consider the lion that you mentioned, the enemy of cattle.
For the crime which the lion committed the pit awaits him.[8]

In the *Kutha Legend* the following narrative is quite sufficient to show up the folly of such impious self-confidence; the three huge armies Naram-Sin sends out without the approval of the gods "in the good pleasure of his own heart" are almost totally annihilated in rapid succession.[9] Man must trust in his gods, not in himself, *ina ramānīšu*.

With these passages in mind, the contrast between "young lions" and "those who seek Yahweh" no longer seems strained. The Hebrew expression *drš yhwh*, "to seek Yahweh,"[10] can sometimes be used as an almost exact cultural equivalent of the Akkadian *barû bīrī*, "to observe omens," an activity in which, as the impious Naram-Sin remarks, lions show no interest. The further contextual characterization of the *dršy yhwh* as the pious[11] who trust in Yahweh marks their opposite numbers as impious creatures who trust in them-

7. O. R. Gurney—J. J. Finkelstein, *The Sultantepe Tablets*, I (Occasional Publications of the British Institute of Archaeology at Ankara 3; London 1957) Nr 30:80–82; O. R. Gurney, "The Sultantepe Tablets (Continued): IV. The Cuthaean Legend of Naram-Sin," *Anatolian Studies* 5 (1955) 102–3: 80–82.

8. Lambert, *BWL*, 74: 61–62.

9. Gurney, *Anatolian Studies* 5, 102–3: 84–87.

10. Gen 25:22; Exod 18:15; 1 Sam 9:9; 1 Kgs 22:8; 2 Kgs 3:11; passim.

11. The expression *yr'yw*, "those who fear him," has the same range of meaning as the Akkadian *pāliḫ ili*. It designates those people who humbly observe the rules and regulations laid down by the deity.

selves,[12] the precise way in which the figure of the lion is used in the other passages we cited. Moreover, the poor starving lion of Ps 34:11 is only the pious man's pictorial response to the skeptic's image of the surfeited, steak-gorging lion. In short, the image of the young lions in Ps 34:11, far from being the result of textual corruption, stems from an old pre-Israelite proverbial motif which, if not created by, was at least at home in the wisdom literature, and through this channel Israel inherited it.

12. Weiser has seen this and expressed it very well: ". . . der Vergleich mit der Not der sich selbst überlassenen Kreatur offenbart ein tiefes Verständnis dessen, was dem Menschen ihr gegenüber in der Gemeinschaft mit Gott geschenkt ist" (*Die Psalmen* [ATD 14/15; Göttingen 1966] 201).

Chapter 17

The Religio-political Setting of Psalm 47

Recent scholarly treatment of Psalm 47 has limited itself to basically three interpretations: cultic, eschatological, and historical.[1] The historical interpretation is undoubtedly the least fashionable at the moment, and those who opt for it seem to prefer a relatively late moment in Israelite history as the setting for Psalm 47—the rebuilding of the temple after the exile.[2] Such a view is clearly inadequate to explain the language of the text, so its unpopularity is not surprising. Others, notably Weiser and Kraus, have modified the cultic interpretation by incorporating historical traditions as part of the content of what is cultically celebrated, but the cultic aspect remains dominant nevertheless. The historical events remembered in the traditions and celebrated in the psalm do not constitute the immediate background for the composition of the text. To my knowledge, no recent scholar has attributed a primary role to early historical-political realities as providing the *Sitz im Leben* for Psalm 47. That is the purpose of this paper, which may thus be seen as a sequel to my earlier study, "The Davidic Origin of the Zion Tradition."[3]

The Text

(2) All ye peoples, clap your hands,
Shout to God with jubilant voice.
(3) For Yahweh is awesome Elyon,
The great king over all the earth.
(4) He subjugated peoples beneath us,
Nations underneath our feet.

---

1. For the literature on the Psalms of Yahweh's kingship see Lipiński (1965) and more recently, on Psalm 47, Perdue (1974). The commentaries consulted in the preparation of this paper include Briggs (1906), Castellino (1965), Dahood (1966–70), Gunkel (1968), Kraus (1958–60), Nötscher (1960), Oesterley (1962), and Weiser (1966).

2. Ewald as cited by Gunkel (1968) 203, Briggs (1906) 398 dates it even later, in the Persian period subsequent to Nehemiah.

3. Roberts (1973). That paper would probably never have been published without the strong and enthusiastic support of Dr. Wright, so this sequel seemed a particularly appropriate tribute to his memory.

(5) He chose us for his possession.
The pride of Jacob whom he loved.
(6) God has gone up with a shout,
Yahweh at the sound of a trumpet.
(7) Sing, o gods, sing!
Sing to our king, sing!
(8) For he is king of all the earth,
O gods, sing a skillful song.
(9) God has become king over the nations.
Yahweh has sat down on his holy throne.
(10) The princes of the peoples have assembled to the God of Abraham,
For truly God is suzerain of the earth,
He is highly exalted.

Notes on the Text

V. 2. Dahood' treatment of *lʾlhym* as a vocative plural, "acclaim, you gods," is syntactically possible, but the normal construction of *hryʿ* + *l* + indirect object (Ps 66:1; 81:2; 95:1–2; 98:4; 100:1) strongly supports the traditional rendering. Moreover, the traditional interpretation is supported by the artistic fashion in which the author has returned to the imagery of 2b–3a in v. 6. The *ʿlh* of v. 6 seems to play on *ʿlywn* of 3a, *ʾlhym btrwʿh* picks up *hryʿw lʾlhym*, and *yhwh bqwl šwpr* lifts the *yhwh* of 3a and puts it with the *bqwl rnh* of 2b. The resultant chiastic artistry may be diagrammed as follows:

2b–3a *hryʿw lʾlhym* *bqwl rnh . . . yhwh* *ʿlywn*

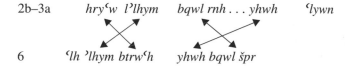

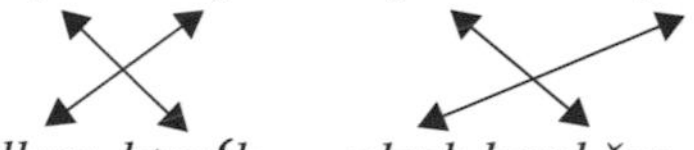

6 *ʿlh ʾlhym btrwʿh* *yhwh bqwl špr*

Since there is no question of the identity of *ʾlhym* in v. 6, the parallels and contacts between vv. 2 and 6 make it difficult to read *lʾlhym* of v. 2 as anything but the indirect object "to God."[4]

This support cannot be countered by considerations based on Dahood's conjectured **ʿam* II, "strong," since the evidence for that vocable is extremely tenuous,[5] and the traditional, well-attested meaning for *ʿam*, "people," fits the present context perfectly. In v. 10 *ʿm* is to be read *ʿim* and hence has no bearing on the question.

4. I must credit Father John Kselman for bringing this and a number of other stylistic observations to my attention.
5. See Dahood (1966–70) on Ps 18:28.

V. 3. The traditional rendering of *ky yhwh ʿlywn nwrʾ*, "For Yahweh, the Most High, is awesome," takes *ʿlywn* as an appositional epithet and *nwrʾ* as the predicate, but in so doing it misses the point of the line. The foreign peoples are called upon to worship God, not simply because he is awesome, but because he is Elyon, the Most High, the *legitimate* ruler of the divine world, and hence of the human as well.

Whatever the status of the god Elyon in the Canaanite pantheon,[6] in Israelite thought he was clearly the overlord of the gods. He assigned the nations their respective territories and entrusted them to their national gods (Deut 32:8), and these national gods were thought of as the sons of Elyon (Ps 82:6).

Thus when Yahweh is identified with Elyon, latent imperialistic claims are being made that sometimes come to explicit expression. Psalm 97, a hymn to Yahweh as king, stresses Yahweh's dominion over the divine world: *kʾth yhwh ʿlywn ʿl kl hʾrṣ mʾd nʿlyt ʿl kl ʾlhym*, "For you, Yahweh, are Elyon over all the earth, You are highly exalted over all the gods" (v. 9), but that heavenly dominion also finds expression in the human sphere (vv. 5–7). Psalm 83, a prayer for help against rebellious vassals, emphasizes precisely these earthly implications of Yahweh's dominion: *wydʿw ky ʾth šmk yhwh lbdk ʿlywn ʿl kl hʾrṣ*, "And let them know that your name is Yahweh[7] / That you alone are Elyon over all the earth."

Because these implications of overlordship implicit in the name touched both the divine and human spheres, *ʿlywn* could also be used figuratively of the Davidic ruler: *ʾp ʾny bkwr ʾtnhw ʿlywn lmlky ʾrṣ*, "Yea, I will make him the first born, Elyon to the kings of the earth" (Ps 89:28). That is, the Davidic ruler would occupy a position of suzerainty vis-á-vis other human monarchs corresponding to Elyon's position vis-á-vis the gods.

Such imperialistic use of *ʿlywn* makes it clear that *ʿlywn* and *mlk gdwl* are parallel terms in Ps 47:3—the expression *ʿl kl hʾrṣ* attached to *mlk gdwl* here, is attached to *ʿlywn* in Ps 83:19 and 97:9—but that parallelism finds adequate expression only when *ʿlywn* is taken as the predicate. This would have been obvious to everyone were it not for the adjective *nwrʾ*, but the addition of this element merely functions to give perfect poetic balance to the two parallel terms. Both *ʿlywn nwrʾ* and *mlk gdwl* are composed of noun + adjective, and there is no more justification for inserting a copulative between the first set than there is for the second.[8] That this analysis is correct is also supported by the inclusio it forms with the final parallelism of *mgn* // *nʿlh* (v. 10).

V. 5. The MT reading *ybḥr lnw ʾt nḥltnw*, "He chose for us our possession," does not provide a good parallel to the following line, and the ideological con-

6. See my reflections in Roberts (1973) 342.

7. Accepting Dahood's analysis based on the Ugaritic *šmk at*.

8. A similar pattern is found in Ps 95:3, *ky ʾl gdwl yhwh wmlk gdwl ʿlkl ʾlhym*, which Dahood translates very nicely, "Yahweh is the great El, the Great King over all the gods."

tacts with Deut 32:8–9 and Psalm 82 suggest correcting *nḥltnw* to *nḥltw* with the LXX and the Syriac. The corruption must go deeper than that, however, for *ybḥr lnw ʾt nḥltw*, to judge from our extant sources, is not a good Hebrew construction.[9] I suggest that an original *ybḥr ʾtnw lnḥltw* has become garbled, though the precise stages in what was probably a progressive corruption are not recoverable. For the translation of *nḥlh* see Harold O. Forshey, *The Hebrew Root NḤL and Its Semitic Cognates* (Harvard dissertation, 1973), and his paper in *BASOR* 220.

V. 7. The traditional rendering of *ʾlhym* in this verse as the accusative object of *zmrw* may be supported by a few parallels (Isa 12:5; Ps 147:1; 68:33), but normally *zmr* is followed by *l* + the indirect object (Judg 5:3; 2 Sam 22:50; Ps 9:12; 18:50; 27:6; 30:5; 33:2; 59:18; 66:4; 71:22, 23; 75:10; 92:2; 98:5; 101:1; 104:33; 105:2; 135:3; 144:6; 146:2; 147:7; 149:3; 1 Chr 16:9). There is some textual evidence for such a construction here, but it is probably due to assimilation to the parallel line.

Assuming the text is correct as it stands, the difference in construction between *zmrw ʾlhym* and *zmrw lmlknw* suggests a difference in meaning. Given the context in which Yahweh's rule over the nations is being affirmed, it is probable that *ʾlhym* should be taken as the subject of the verb. The pagan gods are commanded to praise God. A similar motif is found in the closely related Ps 97:7, in Ps 29:1–2, in Deut 32:43 (LXX and 4QDt),[10] and in Ps 148:2.

This interpretation is also supported by the word order in v. 8b where *ʾlhym* almost has to be the subject. One can avoid that only by attaching *ʾlhym* to the preceding line as the LXX does, but this destroys the metrical balance. Moreover, one should note the envelope construction that a similar understanding of *ʾlhym* in both verses produces:

(7)	*ʾlhym*	Pagan gods
	mlknw	Yahweh
(8)	*mlk*	Yahweh
	ʾlyhm	Pagan gods

V. 9. One does not expect the simple repetition of the same noun in parallel phrases, so *ʾlhym* in 9b has been corrected to *yhwh* in accordance with the parallelism of v. 6, and the order of occurrence of the two terms in 2b–3a.[11] One

9. Dahood's attempt to save the text by reading *lannū*, "for himself," founders on two difficulties. The direct object normally precedes the indirect in this construction with *bḥr*, and the meaning he must assign to *nḥltnw* is completely *ad hoc*.

10. See Skehan (1954), Cross (1958) 182–83, and Wright (1962) 33, n. 23.

11. That *ʾlhym* appears as the A word and *yhwh* as the B word should occasion no surprise in the Elohistic Psalter. From my treatment of the text it should be obvious that I reject the methodological procedure of retroverting Elohistic Psalms back into their *assumed* Yahwistic originals.

could also consider simply deleting *ʾlhym*. Either choice would improve the present metrical balance, but neither has a significant metrical advantage over the other.

V. 10b. *ʿm* should be read as *ʿim* with LXX and Syriac, but it has here the meaning "to," well attested in Ugaritic,[12] and found elsewhere in biblical Hebrew in parallelism with *l*, as, for example, in Deut 32:43 (4QDt):[13]

hrnynw šmym ʿmw	Shout to him with joy, O heavens,
whšthww lw kl ʾlhym	And bow down to him, all ye gods.

The widely adopted emendation of Ps 47:10 to *ʿim ʿam* is a mistake which reflects the LXX's similar double rendering of *ʿmw* in Deut 32:14.[14]

V. 10c. The rendering of *ky lʾlhym mgn (y) ʾrṣ* is dependent on the analysis of the similar expression in Ps 89:19: *ky lyhwh mgnnw wlqdwš yśrʾl mlknw*. Dahood has argued convincingly for interpreting the *l*'s in the Psalm 89 passage as emphatic: "Truly Yahweh is our Suzerain, the Holy One of Israel our King!" Given the striking similarity between the two passages, Ps 47:10 can hardly be saying anything different. Correct *mgny* to *mgn* accordingly.

Note how the parallelism between *mgn* "suzerain" and the root *ʿlh* in this verse forms a chiastic inclusio with the parallelism of *ʿlywn* and *mlk gdwl* in v. 3. It is striking that both lines are introduced by *ky*. One should also note the artistic use of the same verbal root *ʿlh* in the middle of the poem (v. 6) to mark Yahweh's triumphal accession to the throne.

12. It has this sense in the cliche, *idk . lttn pnm . ʿm X*, "They set their faces toward X" (X equals the name of a person or place; Gordon [1965] 49:I:4; IV:31–32; 51:VIII:1–2, etc.). In addition to this cliché, *ʿm* in the sense "to" occurs (in clear passages) with the verbs *hlk*, "to go," (*Krt* 124), *lsm*, "to run" (Gordon [1965] *ʿnt* III:16; cf. *ʿnt* IV:55, 56) and in the expression *ʿmy twtḥ išdk* (*ʿnt* III:16–17; *ʿnt* IV:56; *ʿnt*, pl. ix:III:11). The preposition is used not only of motion toward a thing, but of speaking to a person (*wṣḥhm . ʿm nǵr . mdrʿ*, "They call to the Guardian of the Sown"; Gordon [1965] 52:61) and of sending word to someone (*w . lak ʿmy*, "and send word to me"; Gordon [1965] 54:10–11; cf. line 19, *b . spr . ʿmy*; Gordon [1965] 77:16; 138:8). It is used like biblical Hebrew *ʿad* in the expression *ʿm ʿlm*, "forever, to eternity" (Gordon [1965] 51:IV:41–42; *ʿnt* pl. vi:V:39). Finally, in business documents *ʿm* occurs as a substitute for *l*: *kd . l . ašr* [*y*]*m kdm . ʿm .*[ ]*n* (Virolleaud [1957] 89:4, cf. 143:1, 3). For this analysis of the Ugaritic material I am indebted to Prof. D. R. Hillers, who graciously allowed me to use his notes on the subject. He also suggested a number of biblical parallels to this use of *ʿm*, including Deut 32:34.

13. See Cross (1958) 183. This is the best example of this usage of *ʿim*, but others may be cited, the most certain being the following: *ʾt ʿm ʿny tšʿ wʿnm rmt tšpl*, "You look with favor on the lowly, but haughty eyes you humble" (Ps 18:28 = 2 Sam 22:28; reading *tšʿ* from *šʿh*, cf. Gen 4:4–5). The traditional *ʿam*, "people," is objectional here because all talk has been in the singular), *wʾwlm my ytn ʾlwh dbr wypth śptyw ʿmk*, "But would that God would speak and open his lips to you" (Job 11:5).

14. See Strugnell's observation noted with approval by Cross (1958) 183.

The Sitz im Leben

Even from my translation it is evident that the cultic interpretation of Psalm 47 has much to commend it. The repeated command to praise God, the allusions to a cultic procession (v. 6) and enthronement (v. 9), and the mention of a cultic assembly (v. 10) underline the sacral nature of the ceremony reflected in this psalm. But what is the character of the event celebrated in this religious ceremony? Yahweh's kingship, certainly, but how is one to understand his rise to monarchical, nay more than that, to absolute imperial power?

One can hardly accept the view that attributes the exalted language of this psalm to simple borrowing from the Canaanites. The psalm makes no mention of the mythic victories Yahweh inherited from Baal or Anat. Neither can one follow those scholars who dismiss such praise as Israelite aping of the ideology of the great Mesopotamian empires, since these scholars neglect to cite contemporary analogies for such aping, and they fail to note that the Mesopotamian ideology was rooted in *historical* realities.[15] Verse 4 has been taken as a reference to the conquest, but it is also difficult to see the celebration behind Psalm 47 as a simple reflection of the Ritual Conquest, a re-enactment of the long past days of the Settlement. That view is inadequate to explain the presence of "foreign gods" in the worship. The presence of both points beyond the boundaries of Israel proper, Yahweh's own possession, where rival gods and non-Israelite princes could hardly be tolerated, to the subject states of the Davidic empire where the local rulers and their national gods were granted at least a modicum of toleration.

This observation suggests a setting for the psalm in a cultic celebration of Yahweh's imperial accession, based on the relatively recent victories of David's age, which raised Israel from provincial obscurity to an empire of the first rank. That would make it analogous to the similar phenomena from Mesopotamia. Just as Ishtar rose with Akkad's imperium, Marduk with Babylon's, and Aššur with Assyria's, so Yahweh rose with Israel's. Such a background would also explain the ideological contacts with Deuteronomy 32 and Psalm 82, and it would have the advantage of taking v. 10 with exegetical seriousness. The foreign princes present at the ceremony would be the princes of the subject nations who had come to Jerusalem to pay homage to the Israelite king and his divine suzerain. In the days of the Davidic-Solomonic empire that would not be idle talk or a vague hope for the future, but a periodic reality. Tribute had to be paid, presumably yearly (2 Sam 8:2, 6, 10–12), new accessions in the subject countries probably had to be approved in Jerusalem, a new accession in Jerusalem probably required a trip by the subject rulers to pledge

15. See Roberts (1973) 341–42 and now the very important article of Thorkild Jacobsen (1975).

their allegiance to the new Davidide,[16] and the dedication of certain royal buildings also called for the presence of foreign vassals (1 Kgs 8:65). Such a religio-political *Sitz im Leben* must assume an early date for Psalm 47, but there is nothing in the psalm which argues against its antiquity, and the content as well as the archaic use of emphatic *l* and *ʿim* meaning "to," argue for it.

16. This is the most probable background for the exhortation to the foreign kings in Ps 2:10–12a.

References

Briggs, C. A. 1906. *A Critical and Exegetical Commentary on the Book of Psalms*. The International Critical Commentary. Edinburgh: T. & T. Clark.

Castellino, D. G. 1965. *La Sacra Bibbia*. Rome: Marietti.

Cross, F. M. 1958. *The Ancient Library of Qumran*. Garden City, NY: Doubleday (Anchor).

Dahood, M. 1966–70. *Psalms*. 3 vols. The Anchor Bible 16, 17, 17A. Garden City, NY: Doubleday.

Forshey, H. O. 1973. The Hebrew Root *NḤL* and its Semitic Cognates. Unpublished Ph.D. dissertation, Harvard.

_____. 1975. The Construct Chain *naḥᵃlat YHWH/ʾᵉlōhîm*. *Bulletin of the American Schools of Oriental Research* 220: 51–53.

Gordon, C. H. 1965. *Ugaritic Textbook*. Analecta Orientalia 38. Rome: Pontificium Institutum Biblicum.

Gunkel, H. 1968. *Die Psalmen*. Reprint of the 5th edition. Handkommentar zum Alten Testament II. 2. Göttingen: Vandenhoeck and Ruprecht.

Jacobsen, Thorkild. 1975. Religious Drama in Ancient Mesopotamia. In *Unity and Diversity: Essays in the History, Literature, and Religion of the Ancient Near East*, ed. H. Goedicke and J. J. M. Roberts, pp. 65–97. Baltimore: Johns Hopkins University.

Kraus, H.-J. 1958–60. *Psalmen*. 2 vols. Biblischer Kommentar. Altes Testament. Neukirchen: Neukirchener.

Lipiński, E. 1965. *La royauté de Yahwé dans la poésie et le culte de l'ancien Israël*. Brussels: Paleis der Academiën.

Nötscher, F. 1960. Das Buch der Psalmen. In *Die Heilige Schrift in Deutscher Übersetzung*, ed. F. Nötscher, Vol. 4, pp. 1–312. Würzburg: Echter.

Oesterley, W. O. E. 1962. *The Psalms*. London: S.P.C.K.

Perdue, Leo G. 1974. "Yahweh is King over All the Earth." An Exegesis of Psalm 47. *Restoration Quarterly* 17: 85–98.

Roberts, J. J. M. 1973. The Davidic Origin of the Zion Tradition. *Journal of Biblical Literature* 92: 329–44.

Skehan, P. W. 1954. A Fragment of the "Song of Moses" (Deut 32) from Qumran. *Bulletin of the American Schools of Oriental Research* 136: 12–15.

Virolleaud, Charles. 1957. *Le Palais royal d'Ugarit*, II. *Textes alphabetiques des Archivs Est Ouest et Centrales*. Mission de Ras Shamra 7. Paris: Imprimere nationale.

Weiser, A. 1966. *Die Psalmen*. Das Alte Testament Deutsche 14/15. Göttingen: Vandenhoeck & Ruprecht.

Wright, G. E. 1962. The Lawsuit of God. In *Israel's Prophetic Heritage: Essays in Honor of James Muilenburg*, ed. Bernhard W. Anderson and Walter Harrelson, pp. 26–67. New York: Harper.

Chapter 18

Of Signs, Prophets, and Time Limits: A Note on Psalm 74:9

Our signs we have not seen;	אותתינו לא ראינו
There is no longer a prophet;	אין־עוד נביא
And there is not anyone with us who knows "How long?" (Ps 74:9)	ולא־אתנו ידע עד־מה:

This apparently straightforward verse has engendered an incredible divergence of opinion. The meaning of each member of its tricolon has been debated. If I understand him, H.-J. Kraus correctly interprets **אותתינו** here as " 'the revelatory signs' through which Yahweh announces his intervention,"[1] but Kraus has not been widely followed. W. A. Young, in fact, argues, "With the verb **ראה** these signs are apparently tangible. This rules out omens or promises of divine action."[2] He suggests with others that it could refer to the Sabbath or circumcision as signs of the covenant, or to other divine symbols, but "the most likely meaning is some sort of deed showing God's power."[3] This interpretation of **אותתינו** as "miracles" is widely adopted.[4] Evode Beaucamp and Jean-Pascal de Relles even assert that signs in v. 9a can only mean "the manifestations of the power and of the *ḥesed* of the God of the covenant."[5]

The second expression, "There is no longer a prophet," has also caused problems. It was one of the arguments for a Maccabean dating of this psalm,

1. H.-J. Kraus, *Psalmen* I (BKAT 15/1; 2d ed.; Neukirchen-Vluyn: Neukirchener Verlag, 1961) 517.

2. William Arthur Young, *Psalm 74: A Methodological and Exegetical Study* (Doctoral Dissertation, U. of Iowa, 1974) 86.

3. Ibid.

4. Thus, for example, H. Schmidt says, "Ein Wunder hätte geschehen sollen, als die Äxte der Fremden gegen den Tempel donnerten, als das alte Zedernholz plötzlich lichterloh in Flammen stand" (*Die Psalmen* [HAT 15; Tübingen: Mohr, 1934] 142); and M. Dahood comments, "The psalmist thinks of his time as characterized by the absence alike of miracles ('signs') and prophecy" (*Psalms* II [AB 17; Garden City: Doubleday, 1968] 202).

5. E. Beaucamp and J.-P. de Relles, "Si s'écroulait le temple, donjon de justice," *BVC* 66 (1955) 30.

since 1 Macc 4:46 clearly reflects the view that there was no prophet in those days.[6] Kraus[7] and others[8] have pointed to similar references to the absence or scarcity of the prophetic word in earlier periods (1 Sam 3:1; Ezek 7:26; Lam 2:9), but this observation has fared only a little better than the correct interpretation of אותתינו. Young, following a long scholarly tradition, argues that "to compare 74:9 to passages which lament that prophets are not discharging their office is misleading. Unlike 74:9, neither of these passages [Lam 2:9; Ezek 7:26] denies the existence of נביאים."[9] Apparently it was to meet this same objection that H. Schmidt, who dates the psalm sometime after 587 B.C., retorted, following an equally old scholarly tradition, "At that time there was no prophet on the spot. Jeremiah was in chains, and Ezekiel was in a distant land."[10]

It is the third member of the tricolon, however, which has been most mutilated in recent treatments. M. Dahood revocalizes to לֹא אָתָנוּ יֹדֵעַ עֵדִם, and translates, "No one who understands the evidence has come to us."[11] Young deletes עד־מה as a dittography of the first two words of v. 10 and comes up with the translation, "there is no sage among us."[12] Neither of these changes is at all compelling.

All three lines are textually unobjectionable,[13] all three lines reflect a concern over the absence of a reliable oracle—a frightening situation often threatened by the prophets (Hos 5:6; Amos 8:11–12; Mic 3:6–7; Ezek 7:26)—and each can be correctly interpreted only in relation to the other two and against the background of the oracular practices of Israel and the ancient Near East.

אות has several different meanings in Hebrew, but in the context of oracular practice its meaning is far more limited. It can refer to visual or auditory phenomena which serve as omens in their own right. Thus Jonathan tells his armor bearer, "But if they (the Philistines) say, 'Come up to us,' we shall go up, for Yahweh has given them into our hand. And this will be our omen" (וזה־לנו האות 1 Sam 14:10). Note that this usage may emphasize either the phenomenon which provides the omen or the oracle derived from that phenomenon. The term is used this way by Jeremiah when referring to pagan practices:

---

6. See H. Donner's evaluation of this argument in his "Argumente zur Datierung des 74. Psalms," *Wort, Lied und Gottesspruch: Festschrift für Joseph Zeigler* (ed. Josef Schreiner; Würzburg: Echter Verlag, 1972) 2.45.

7. *Psalmen* I, 517.

8. See, for example, H. Hupfeld, *Die Psalmen* (Gotha: Perthes, 1860) 3.310–11; and F. Nötscher, *Die Psalmen* (Echter Bibel; Würzburg: Echter Verlag, 1962) 162.

9. W. A. Young, *Psalm 74*, 86–87.

10. H. Schmidt, *Die Psalmen*, 142.

11. M. Dahood, *Psalms* II, 198.

12. W. A. Young, *Psalm* 74, 87.

13. The textual variations in the versions suggest simple misunderstandings of the MT, not a different Hebrew *Vorlage*.

Thus says Yahweh:
Learn not the way of the nations,
Nor be dismayed at the signs (ומאתות) of the heavens,
Though the nations are dismayed at them. (Jer 10:2)

One can find many parallels to this usage in the Babylonian texts with *ittu.*[14] It may be what is intended by the passage in *Ludlul*: "[In] waking hours he sent the message and showed his favourable sign (*ittuš damqatu*) to my peoples."[15] A passage in one of the literary texts from Ras Shamra is more obscure, but it probably means something similar: *ul itarraṣ bārû purussâya* / *itta ul inamdananni*, "The haruspex does not put forth a decision concerning me / He does not give me a sign."[16] One could also point to the use of *dīnu* in a Babylonian historical epic: *išteniʾū dīn Mar*[*duk*]. "They kept seeking a judgment of Marduk."[17] The context makes it clear that what the Babylonians sought was an omen that the period of Marduk's wrath was over. A similar meaning is to be attached to Isa 44:25, and, in Israelite usage, to Ps 86:17.

Show me a sign of your favor (אות לטובה),
that those who hate me may see and be put to shame.

Note the similarity between this passage and the similar passage in *Ludlul* where the oracular interpretation is secured by the context.

In Israel the symbolic actions of the prophets functioned in a similarly ominous fashion. Thus in Isa 20:3–4:

Yahweh said, "As my servant Isaiah has walked naked barefoot for three years as a sign (אות) and a portent against Egypt and Ethiopia, so shall the king of Assyria lead away the Egyptian captives and the Ethiopian exiles, both the young and the old, naked and barefoot, with buttocks uncovered, to the shame of Egypt."

---

14. *CAD* I, 306–7.

15. W. G. Lambert, *Babylonian Wisdom Literature* (Oxford: Clarendon, 1960) 50–51: 46–47.

16. *Ugaritica* V (Mission de Ras Shamra 16; Paris: Imprimerie Nationale, 1968) 267:3′–4′ (= No. 162, RS 25.460). This reading accepts Nougayrol's suggestion that the text *i-nam-na-an da-a-a-nu* contains a double error. An original *i-nam-da-na-an-ni* suffered an internal transposition to *i-nam-na-an-da-ni*, and them, by an unhappy attempt at interpretation, was separated into two words *inamnan dayyānu* (ibid., 270). The verb *tarāṣu* with *purussû* also seems strange. One expects *parāsu*, "to decide, render a decision," and I suspect an error somewhere in the course of the transmission of this text, perhaps involving a misreading of the ideogram *KUD.*

17. G. Smith, *The Cuneiform Inscriptions of Western Asia* III (London: Bowler, 1870) 38 no. 2, rev. 5. See H. Tadmor, "Historical Implications of the Correct Rendering of Akkadian *dâku*," *JNES* 17 (1958) 137–39, but note J. A. Brinkman's correction (*A Political History of Post-Kassite Babylonia* [AnOr 43; Rome: Pontifical Biblical Institute, 1968] 106, n. 575).

Or again in Ezek 4:1–3, after commanding Ezekiel to portray a siege with a model city, siegeworks, battering rams, and the like, Yahweh says, "This is a sign (אות) to the house of Israel." Compare also Isa 8:18.

On the other hand, אות is often used, not for the phenomenon from which the oracle is derived nor for the oracle itself, but as a sign given to confirm the oracle. Thus when Yahweh informed Hezekiah that he would recover from his illness, Hezekiah asked for a confirmatory sign, and the sign of the receding shadow was given (2 Kgs 20:8–9; Isa 38:7, 22). Such signs could be miraculous as in this case or as in the offer made to Ahaz (Isa 7:11; see also Deut 13:2–3; Judg 6:17ff.; Exod 3:12; 4:8ff.), but they need not be. The sign could consist simply in a natural event or sequence of events which the prophet describes to his hearers before the fact. Thus the signs given to Saul are simply a prophetic description of several encounters he would experience after leaving the seer (1 Sam 10:7, 9). The sign given to Eli was the predicted death of his two sons on the same day (1 Sam 2:34), and Jeremiah's sign of judgment upon his rebellious countrymen was the projected death of Pharaoh Hophra at the hand of his enemies (Jer 44:29–30).

Occasionally the sign appears even less striking and may in fact seem almost redundant, i.e., the sign that God will fulfill his word will be when he fulfills it. On closer examination, however, this type of sign normally has a time limit involved. Note, for example, 2 Kgs 19:29 (= Isa 37:30):

> And this shall be the sign (האות) for you: This year you shall eat what grows of itself, and in the second year what springs of the same; then in the third year sow, and reap, and plant vineyards, and eat their fruit. . . .

In other words, Isaiah's prophecy against the Assyrian king will be fulfilled within three years. The famous Immanuel sign is quite similar. The sign apparently resided not in any unusual feature of the child's conception or birth, but merely in the usual time it would take this child to reach an age of discretion:

> For before the child knows how to refuse the evil and choose the good, the land before whose two kings you are in dread will be deserted. (Isa 7:16)

Such time limits for the fulfillment of a prophecy are often given even when they are not specifically designated as signs. Isaiah prophesied the fall of Kedar within a year (Isa 21:16) and the desolation of Moab within three years (Isa 16:14). Jeremiah predicted the death of Hananiah within the very year of their famous encounter (Jer 28:16). Moreover, several prophets assigned temporal limits to the periods of divine punishment. The infamous Hananiah predicted the release from Babylonian bondage within two years (Jer 28:3), Isaiah predicted a seventy-year desolation of Tyre (Isa 23:15, 17), Jeremiah predicted a seventy-year Babylonian captivity for Judah (Jer 25:11–12; 29:10), and Ezekiel prophesied a forty-year desolation of Egypt (Ezek 29:11–13).

This idea that there were predetermined limits to the periods of divine wrath which the gods might reveal through omens or oracles was widespread in the ancient Near East. In addition to Marduk's famous decision to leave Babylon for seventy years,[18] one could point to the omen text dealing with the Elamite captivity of Bel:

> . . . the Umman-manda will arise and rule the land. The gods will depart from their daises, and Bel will go to Elam. It is said that after thirty years vengeance will be exercised, and the gods will return to their place.[19]

One should also note the statement in the Marduk prophecy, "I fulfilled my years."[20] which may be compared to Nabonidus' comment:

> For twenty-one years he (Marduk) established his seat in Ashur, but when the days were fulfilled and the set time (*adannu*) arrived, his anger abated, and the heart of the king of the gods, the lord of lords, remembered Esagil and Babylon, the seat of his lordship.[21]

This view is directly connected with the question found over and over again in both Israelite and Near Eastern laments, "How long?" It was a crucial question during times of tribulation, whether those tribulations affected a group or only a single individual. The failure to get a divine response to the question added to the sense of God-forsakenness and intensified the despair of the lamenting party. Note the plaint of the sufferer in *Ludlul: u adanna siliʾtīya bārû ul iddin*, "Nor has the diviner put a time limit on my illness."[22] Compare the similar line from the Ras Shamra text: *ummānū šaršubašâya uštamû ul iqbû ada(n) murṣīya*. "The experts have carefully pondered my tablets, but they have not set a limit to my illness."[23] However, it was even more disillusioning when a time limit was given,[24] and it passed without the hoped-for change. To quote

18. R. Borger, *Die Inschriften Asarhaddons Königs von Assyrien* (*AfO* Beiheft 9; Graz: E. Weidner, 1956) 14–15, episodes 6–10.

19. G. Smith, *Cuneiform Inscriptions* III, 61 no. 2:21′–22′.

20. R. Borger, *BO* 28 (1971) 8:12.

21. H. Winckler, "Einige Bemerkungen zur Nabunid-Stele," *MVAG* 1/1 (1896) 73–83 (copy), i 23–34.

22. Lambert, *Babylonian Wisdom Literature*, 44–45:111.

23. *Ugaritica V*, 267:7–8.

24. We have many examples of such time limits being given in the so-called diagnostic texts (R. Labat, *Traité akkadien de diagnostics et pronostics médicaux* I–II [Academie Internationale d'Histoire des Sciences; Leiden: Brill, 1951]). After discussing the symptoms of the sick person in the protasis, these texts often contain a statement in the apodosis to the effect that the sick person will recover (or die) within a set period of time. The time mentioned in the positive prognoses varies from the vague "quickly" (*Traité* I, 6:3; 10:33, 45, passim), to the very concrete "on the same day" (I, 10:44; 12:49), "within two or three days" (I, 156:3, 9), "within three days" (I, 116:8), "within five to seven days" (I, 158:13), "after seven days" (I, 156:7; 164:76), "after fourteen to twenty days" (I, 230:115), "after twenty-one days"

Ludlul again: *akšudma ana balat adanna īteq asaḫḫurma lemun lemunma*, "I survived to the next year; the appointed time passed. As I turn around, it is terrible, it is terrible."[25] Something of the same concern may be reflected in Zechariah's account of the angel's allusion to Jeremiah's prophecy of a seventy-year captivity:

> Then the angel of Yahweh said, "O Yahweh of hosts, how long will you have no mercy on Jerusalem and the cities of Judah, against which you have had indignation these seventy years." (Zech 1:12)

Moreover, if the people of Zechariah's day were concerned that Jeremiah's seventy-year limit might have passed without the promised intervention of Yahweh occurring, think what effect the non-fulfillment of Hananiah's more optimistic prophecy would have had on an earlier generation. Hananiah prophesied in the fifth month of the fourth year of Zedekiah (Jer 28:1, correcting the MT by the LXX) that within two years Yahweh would break the yoke of the king of Babylon, return all the vessels of Yahweh's house to the temple in Jerusalem, and restore Jehoiakin and all the exiles to Judah (Jer 28:2–4, 11). To judge from Jer 27:16–18, many other prophets of the time supported Hananiah, and from Jeremiah's bitter polemic one may surmise that most of the people believed these prophets rather than Jeremiah. When Hananiah's two years passed without any change, the faith of many was apparently devastated. Ezekiel bears witness to an attitude widespread among those left in Jerusalem in a prophecy dated to the sixth month of the sixth year (Ezek 8:1), or less than a month after Hananiah's absolute deadline had passed: "Yahweh does not see us. Yahweh has forsaken the land" (Ezek 8:12, 9:2). The same attitude is expressed even more clearly in a popular proverb reported by Ezekiel:

> Son of man, what is this proverb that you have about the land of Israel, saying, "The days grow long, and every vision comes to naught"? (Ezek 12:22)

The proverb irritates Yahweh, who promises to put an end to it by doing away with false visions and flattering divinations, and by bringing to fulfillment his threatened judgments (Ezek 12:23–25). One should note the curious dichotomy in this prophecy. The fulfillment of the prophetic words spoken by an Ezekiel or a Jeremiah was hardly what the people desired. Their despair, in fact, seems to have little to do with the prophecies of either Jeremiah or Ezekiel. They despair because the favorable prophecies of the false prophets do not materialize, and this leads them to debunk prophecy almost as though they had never heard of Jeremiah or Ezekiel.

(I, 230:116), "within thirty-one days" (I, 112:25), and "after a year" (I, 8:18). I wish to thank my student, Father Michael Barré, both for reminding me of this formulation in these texts and for supplying references.

25. Lambert, *Babylonian Wisdom Literature*, 38–39:1–2.

This observation is important in evaluating the meaning of our psalmist's expression, "There is no prophet." Almost all the commentators treat the psalm passage as though its author shared our view of Jeremiah and Ezekiel, which is based on their canonical status. Thus, the psalmist, living in the time of these two great prophets could not have said, "There is no prophet," or, at best, he could have said it only if they were somehow out of the way, in prison or in exile or the like. What does not appear to have occurred to any commentator is that the psalmist, particularly if he were a contemporary of these two figures, may have held a radically different view of them than we. Jeremiah was considered by many of his contemporaries as a traitor, and Ezekiel must have been regarded as crazy, or at best, entertaining by many of those who knew him. Moreover, there were probably circles so impressed by the other prophets of the period that Jeremiah and Ezekiel made hardly any impact on them. For such circles, the general loss of credibility which prophecy had suffered due to the failure of the optimistic prophecies of weal would have also affected their attitude toward Jeremiah and Ezekiel. It is this historically conditioned failure of confidence in the prophetic word, fought by Ezekiel and reflected in Lam 2:9, that finds expression in our verse.[26]

"Our signs we have not seen" means that the signs which the prophets promised as a confirmation of their oracles of salvation have not come to pass. The Babylonian empire had not collapsed, and the furniture of the temple had not been returned to Jerusalem. "There is no longer a prophet" need mean no more than that the speaker, like the author of Lamentations, had lost all confidence in those prophets still around. In his opinion the contemporary prophets did not deserve the name. Moreover, it may well be that the disrepute into which prophecy fell in the early exilic period caused a sharp reduction in the number actually involved in that profession.[27] "There is not anyone with us

26. To insist that אין־עוד נביא is a superficial denial of the very existence of anyone claiming to be a prophet will not do. One should compare Ezek 33:33 where God promises Ezekiel that when his words come to pass, the people "will know that a prophet has been among them." Yet from the preceding verses it is clear that outwardly no one was denying that Ezekiel was a prophet—he certainly acted the part, and the people came to him to hear the word from Yahweh—but on a deeper level no one took his word seriously. That was tantamount to taking Ezekiel's prophetic office lightly, of failing to recognize the prophet in their midst. The issue was not whether Ezekiel was a prophet, but whether he was a *real* prophet, i.e., one whose words would come to pass. In the same way the negative predication in Ps 74:9 may be interpreted on a similarly profound level. It was not that there was no prophet; there was simple no *real* prophet, i.e., no prophet whose words could be counted on to come to pass.

27. In my judgment, Second Isaiah's constant polemic and repeated appeals for a confident trust in God's unfolding deliverance suggests that even this prophet of salvation had to contend with a rather skeptical attitude toward prophecy in that period. Zech 13:1–6 shows how disreputable prophecy had become in a somewhat later period.

who knows 'How long?' " means that the prophetic attempts to set a limit to the period of divine wrath had failed. We may assume that many projections of Yahweh's time schedule for restoring his people's fortune had, like Hananiah's, passed without any noticeable improvement in Israel's lot. The result would have been a reluctance on the part of any contemporary prophet to make such a projection, and a reluctance on the part of the people to believe any that was made or any that remained outstanding. It is perhaps noteworthy that the first reference to Jeremiah's seventy-year prophecy in the later literature is found, not in Second Isaiah, but in Zechariah, about eight years *after* the return from exile. To summarize, every member of the tricolon in Ps 74:9 can best be understood in relation to ancient Israelite oracular practice; and thus the verse, far from suggesting a later date, actually supports a date for the psalm in the early exilic period.

Chapter 19

Blindfolding the Prophet

Political Resistance to First Isaiah's Oracles in the Light of Ancient Near Eastern Attitudes toward Oracles

In Isaiah 29:9–12 the prophet announces the following threat:

(9.) Astound yourself[1] and be astounded,
Blind yourself and be blinded!
You who are drunken,[2] but not from wine,
Who stagger,[3] but not from beer.[4]
(10.) For Yahweh has poured upon you
A spirit of stupor.
He has shut your eyes, the prophets;[5]
And your heads, the seers, he has covered.

---

1. The translation assumes the correction of MT's הִתְמַהְמְהוּ, the *hithpalpel* imperative of מהה, "to tarry," to הִתַּמְּהוּ, the *hithpa'el* imperative of תמה, "to be astounded." The correction is suggested by the same idiom in Hab 1:5 and by the versions. The LXX, Vulgate, Syriac, and Targum, each in its own way, treat the paired imperatives as synonymous and then make the two pairs synonymous with one another. Without the correction, the MT would appear to say something like: "Tarry and be astounded; Dally and blind yourself ."

2. The two 3mpl Qal perfects, שָׁכְרוּ and נָעוּ are often corrected to Qal imperatives because the shift from second person to third person is felt to be abrupt. It is preferable to retain the MT and read these clauses as asyndetic relative clauses functioning as vocatives (see William Henry Irwin, *Isaiah 28–33: Translation with Philological Notes* [Rome, Biblical Institute Press, 1977] p. 56).

3. See preceding note.

4. The reference to beer and wine seems to be a clear allusion to Isaiah's oracle against the Judean priests and prophets (כהן ונביא), whom Isaiah accused of being drunk when having their vision or giving their arbitration (28:7). This flight to alcohol and corresponding dereliction of duty may be a byproduct of government pressure to insure only oracles and decisions supportive of government policy (see below). In any case, it resulted in a people staggering drunkenly, not from alcohol, but from a lack of divine guidance (cf. 5:11–13).

5. The choice of the term הנביאים, "the prophets," is probably to make the allusion to the oracle preserved in 28:7 clear. Isaiah was critical of the נביא who failed to appropriately fulfill his function in society (3:2; 9:14; 28:7), just as he was critical of the priest (כהן, 28:7), royal official (שׂר, 1:23), or any other important member of his society who failed to perform his task appropriately. There is no evidence, however, that Isaiah regarded the נביא as an illegitimate functionary or that he attempted to distance himself from being identified as a נביא. That is the title assigned to Isaiah by the tradents of the Isaiah tradition (37:2; 38:1; 39:3), and Isaiah himself had no reservation about referring to his wife with the feminine form of this noun (נביאה, 8:3).

(11.) And the vision of everything has become to you like the words of the sealed book which they give to one who knows how to read saying, "Read this, please!" and he says, "I cannot read it because it is sealed."
(12.) Then the book is given to one who does not know how to read saying, "Read this, please!" and he says, "I do not know how to read."

If one interprets this text as it stands,[6] it sounds like a divine threat to blindfold the prophets. Read that way, it would be a simple variation on a recurring and well known motif in Old Testament prophetic literature—the threat of the cessation of prophetic oracles. Amos threatens a famine, not of food and water, but of hearing the word of Yahweh, and he pictures a frantic wandering about through the land in a fruitless attempt to consult Yahweh (8:11–12). Micah threatens the prophets themselves with a night without a vision, with darkness without revelation, with disgrace because there will be no answer to them from God (3:5–7). Hosea describes the people as going with their flocks and their cattle to inquire of Yahweh, but not finding him because he had withdrawn from them (5:6). And according to Ezekiel, God will not allow himself to be inquired of by people who do not take the prophetic word seriously, but who go to inquire of the prophet while retaining their idols and sins in their heart (14:1–11; 20:3, 31). Such threats are a response to the people's refusal to heed an unwelcome prophetic word (Micah 2:6, 11), to official attempts to silence the prophets (Amos 2:12; 7:12–17), or to the prophets' own attempts to gain a hearing by making the prophetic word more palatable to their audience (Micah 3:5). A similar background to Isaiah's threat is suggested by his notice in 30:9–10 that Judah has rejected the genuine word of Yahweh and has attempted to silence the prophets or to pressure them into offering a more acceptable message.

This Isaianic use of a common prophetic motif suggests a new angle for examining the nature of Isaiah's struggle with the political leadership of his day, but before focusing on Isaiah, it is important to put this threat of the cessation of prophetic oracles in a broader context. While the threat presupposes opposition to the prophetic message, its value as a threat is utterly dependent on the assumption that the culture takes seriously the importance of prophetic communication from the divine world. Something of a paradox here can be seen in

6. Most modern commentaries delete the words "prophets" and "seers" from v. 10 as secondary glosses and dismiss vv. 11–12 as a prosaic expansion from a much later period. The evidence for such a judgment is highly subjective, however. There is not the slightest textual evidence for deleting "prophets" and "seers," and the metrical argument is not convincing. Vv. 11–12 do read like prose, but the assumption that prose passages must be late expansions on the prophet's original, purely poetic oracles, remains simply that, an unproven assumption. It is worth considering, therefore, what sense the received text might make both in the larger context of the Old Testament and in the more particular context of First Isaiah's struggle with the leaders of his day.

the narratives detailing Jeremiah's interactions with Zedekiah, and then with the pitiful remnant following the murder of Gedaliah. Powerful government officials under king Zedekiah were adamantly opposed to Jeremiah and wanted him killed because his message was undermining morale in Jerusalem (Jer 38:4). Though the king could not prevent these officials from putting Jeremiah under arrest (37:15–16; 38:7), and though Zedekiah himself did not heed Jeremiah's prophetic oracles, king Zedekiah continued to call for Jeremiah to hear what word Yahweh had given to the prophet (37:17; 38:14–28). Likewise, after Gedaliah was murdered, the people and their leaders approached Jeremiah with the request that he pray for them and obtain directions from Yahweh as to what they should do. But, when he returned with the prophetic word that they should remain in the land and trust Yahweh to protect them from Babylonian retaliation (Jer 42:1–22), they rejected Jeremiah's message as a lie (Jer 43:1–4). This resistance to Jeremiah's message cannot be explained as rooted in a rival prophetic message—at this stage in Jeremiah's career the rival prophets appear to have been discredited (see Jer 37:19). Nor can it be explained as a principled rejection of a woe oracle. In his oracle to Zedekiah Jeremiah did urge surrender to Babylon, but this was accomplished by the promise that such a course of action would save the city from destruction and Zedekiah and his family from death. Jeremiah's oracle to the remnant after Gedaliah's murder was likewise a conditional oracle of divine protection. Indeed much of the older discussion of prophetic conflict which often assumed clear and obvious distinctions, sometimes terminologically marked, between true and false prophecy corresponding to such contrasts as cultic versus non-cultic, professional versus non-professional, group versus individual, salvation versus judgment, was never convincing, and deserves to be consigned to oblivion.

Perhaps the expanding corpus of other Ancient Near Eastern texts dealing with oracular communications from the divine world, particularly those from Mari, may provide a broader context in which to discuss these questions more realistically. It is clear from the Mari archives that in a culture where oracles were taken very seriously, political leaders could occasionally act contrary to the oracles, even when those oracles were given with some insistence. Nur-Su'en, Zimri-Lim's agent in Aleppo, claims that he had written to Zimri-Lim as many as five times with regard to the *zukrum*-festival and the *niḫlatum*-property that Adad of Kallasu had demanded from Zimri-Lim, and while Zimri-Lim eventually gave orders to provide the *zukrum*-festival, he continued to delay turning over the *niḫlatum*-property even in the face of serious threats from the god Adad.[7] Kibri-Dagan, the governor of Terqa, reports the renewed demand by the ecstatic that the governor begin work on a new gate, but through the god threatens Kibri-Dagan with a plague if he does not carry

7. *RA*, 78 (1984), pp. 7–18.

out the divine command, the governor informs Zimri-Lim that he is totally involved in bringing in the barley harvest and cannot attend to the gate at the moment without assistance from the king.[8] When Zimri-Lim began peace treaty negotiations with Eshnunna in his fourth year, there was considerable religious opposition to such a treaty, and both the goddess Dîritum and Dagan of Terqa give oracles warning Zimri-Lim not to conclude the treaty.[9] They warn that beneath his peaceful words the king of Eshnunna is plotting treachery, they promise victory over Eshnunna, and they urge Zimri-Lim not to conclude the treaty without first consulting the god.[10] The final point is worth stressing. Twice in text No. 199 one finds the divine admonition: *šarrum balum ilam išallu napištašu la ilappat*, "the king without consulting the god shall not touch his throat, i.e., conclude the treaty."[11] Nevertheless, despite the prophetic opposition, it is clear that Zimri-Lim went ahead with the ratification of the treaty,[12] and there is no evidence that he waited for a positive oracle from either Dîritum or Dagan of Terqa before this action.

Moreover, such political resistance to particular divine oracles is not limited to those issued by prophetic type figures. Oracles obtained through liver omens could also be resisted. One normally did not set out on a military campaign without favorable oracles.[13] If the situation were not critical, one simply continued making inquiry until one received a favorable oracle.[14] When the situation was critical, however, one could urge action despite the lack of favorable oracles. The writer of the letter published by Durand as No. 190[15] claims he kept formulating inquiries for the departure of the army and the execution of battle, but the oracle did not answer him. Nonetheless, he goes on to say that, in accordance with his deliberations, he will send out the army with the prayer, "And may the god of my lord let our campaign prosper!" In another text Meptûm urges the king to come see and encourage his troops whether the oracles for such a trip are favorable or not.[16] Perhaps the most striking example of this resistance to oracular instruction is the response of a certain Ḫammânum who was reluctant to hand over barley to another official. When that official suggested that Zikri-Ḫanat should take oracles to decide

8. *AEM* 1/1, No. 221.

9. *AEM* 1/1, 400. Dominique Charpin, "Un traité entre Zimri-Lim de Mari et Ibâl-pî-El II d'Ešnunna," in D. Charpin and F. Joannès (eds.), *Marchands, diplomates et empereurs: Etudes sur la civilisation mésopotamienne offertes à Paul Garelli* (Paris, Éditions Recherches sur les Civilisations, 1991) pp. 164–65.

10. Ibid.

11. *AEM* 1/1, No. 199: 38–39, 49–50.

12. Charpin, "Un traité," p. 165.

13. *AEM* 1/1, p. 28, n. 104.

14. *AEM* 1/1, No. 182: 4–12.

15. *AEM* 1/1, No. 190.

16. *AEM* 1/1, p. 28, n. 104.

whether the barley should be handed over, Ḫammânum is purported to have replied, "When he will have taken the oracles, even if they are favorable in every regard, I will not give a single seah of barley!"[17]

One of the difficulties that reliance on oracles presented to political leaders was the problem of preserving state secrets. It was not possible to make meaningful oracular inquiries of the deity without revealing to the divination priests or prophetic respondents a great deal of the state's secret plans and concerns. The so-called protocol of the diviners, a kind of loyalty oath taken by diviners in which, among other things, one swore not to reveal the content of oracular consultations to unauthorized persons, was an attempt to deal with such potential security leaks,[18] but it did not solve the problem. The problem was particularly acute when such oracular inquiry took place in the presence of foreign political allies who were potential enemies. During the period of joint Mari-Babylonian activity, Ibâl-pî-El complained to Zimri-Lim that certain servants of Išme-Dagan had won the confidence of Ḫammurabi and were constantly present during the oracular consultation of the Mari diviners Ḫâlî-Ḫadûn and Inib-Šamaš, though those consultations should have been kept secret.[19] This may explain the background behind the complaint of the diviners Ḫâlî-Ḫadûn and Ilu-šu-naṣir that Ibâl-pî-El had excluded them from his secret council and refused to supply them with lambs to perform oracular inquiry.[20] In halting the inquiries Ibâl-pî-El may merely have been trying to plug a serious security leak.

Government officials also preferred secret oracles for another, though related reason. One not only feared divulging state secrets to the enemy; one was also concerned about the morale and support of one's own subjects. Oracles given publicly and thus liable to affect public opinion and morale had to be handled more carefully than those delivered to government officials in private. Thus Yaqqîm-Addu makes a point of informing Zimri-Lim that the ecstatic of Dagan who threatened Saggarâtum with a plague did so in public: "And it was not in secret that he spoke to me his oracle; in the assembly of the elders he gave his oracle."[21] A public oracle against government policy could have a devastating effect on public order, both demoralizing those loyal to the government policy and encouraging dissidents who might be looking for an opportune time to revolt. In the Old Testament, Amos was accused of conspiring (קשׁר) against Jeroboam because of his oracles, which Amaziah claims were too much for the land to bear (Amos 7:10), and during the last days of the Judean kingdom the royal officials in Jerusalem demanded that Jeremiah be

17. *AEM* 1/1, No. 154: 20–29.
18. *AEM* 1/1, pp. 11–22.
19. *AEM* 1/1, No. 104.
20. *AEM* 1/1, No. 101.
21. *AEM* 1/1, No. 206: 32–34.

put to death because his oracles were demoralizing the soldiers and citizens left in Jerusalem (Jer 38:4).

In the light of this general background one may return to Isaiah's threat. As mentioned above, his threat seems to be a reaction to Judean political repression against the prophetic opposition to government policy. Note especially the oracle in Isa 30:8–11:

(8.) Now come, write it down on a tablet,
Go,[22] on a plaque inscribe it,
That it might be for a later day,
For a witness[23] unto the future.
(9.) Because this is a rebellious people,
Deceitful children,
Children who are unwilling
To hear the teaching of Yahweh;
(10.) Who say to the seers,
"Do not see!"
And to the visionaries,[24]
"Do not envision[25] for us what is right!
Speak to us smooth things!
Prophesy deceptions!
(11.) Turn aside from the way.
Lead astray from the path!
Remove from before us
The Holy One of Israel!"

If one takes the wording of this passage seriously, it not only implies that Isaiah personally encountered opposition to his prophetic utterances; it also implies that other prophets and seers contemporary with him were under public pressure either to keep silence or to support the public policy. The public policy at issue was the formation of a military alliance with Egypt in order to break away from Assyria. This is clear both from the concluding judgment

22. Reading MT's אִתָּם וְעַל as אֶֽתְמוֹ עַל and analyzing the form אתמו as the Qal msg imperative of אתה plus enclitic *mem*. This analysis provides a good parallel to the imperative בוא in the first line and does not require radical emendation of the consonantal text. See W. H. Irwin, *Isaiah 28–33*, p. 79.

23. Reading לְעֵד with the Syriac, Vulgate, and Targum.

24. The translation is an attempt to preserve the parallelism between ראים and חזים, two designations for "seers" from synonymous roots meaning "to see." Isaiah's choice of חזים here rather than נביאים, "prophet," is probably because of his desire to exploit the notion of seeing. It should not be taken as an implicit critique of the נביאים, *contra* Wildberger, *Jesaja*, III, 1171).

25. The translation is an attempt to preserve the word play on the root חזה, "to see," though the verb probably implies the act of speaking and could certainly be translated simply as "prophesy." Note that the same verb is used in parallel with דבר, "to speak," at the end of verse 10, where I have translated חזו, "prophesy."

attached to this oracle and from the larger context of the chapter. The concluding judgment (vv. 12–14) speaks of rejecting the prophetic word and trusting instead in "oppression" and "cunning" (30:12), though this sin, far from gaining Judah a strong protective wall, would result in the disastrous collapse of such protection (30:13–14). Then the following verses (30:14–17) elaborate on the contrast between the rejected prophetic message and the political path chosen by the government. Isaiah had urged trust in Yahweh, but the political leaders had chosen to rely instead on horses:

> For thus says my lord Yahweh, the Holy One of Israel:
> In returning and rest you will be saved,
> In quietness and trust will be your strength.
> But you were not willing, and you said:
> "No! But on a horse we will flee."
> Therefore you will flee.
> "And upon a swift steed we will ride."
> Therefore your pursuers will be even swifter.
> A thousand at the rebuke of one,
> At the rebuke of five you will flee,
> Until you are left
> Like a flagpole on the top of the mountain,
> Like a standard on the hill.

This reference to horses is obviously an allusion to the horses Judah expected to get from Egypt as Isa 31:1 makes clear.[26] Judah's rejection of trust in Yahweh for dependence on Egypt is even more evident from the larger context of Isaiah 30. Vv. 1–5 contains a *hôy*-oracle against these same rebellious children (בנים סוררים) who reject God's counsel in order to go down to Egypt to seek the protection of the Pharaoh, and vv. 6–7 contain a מַשָּׂא-oracle which makes clear reference to the sending of treasures to Egypt, presumably tribute to secure Judah's defensive alliance with Egypt against Assyria.

This larger context also suggests that the political authorities tried to cut the prophets out of the government deliberations that led up to these policy decisions. Just as certain of the Mari prophets were upset by Zimri-Lim's negotiations with Eshnunna and urged Zimri-Lim not to make the treaty with Eshnunna without first consulting the deity, so Isaiah appears to have been upset by Hezekiah's negotiations with Egypt that precluded prophetic consultation. Yahweh's complaint that the Judean government follows advice that is not from him, pours out a drink offering to conclude a covenant that is not of God's spirit, and goes down to Egypt without inquiring of Yahweh's mouth (ופי לא שׁאלו, Isa 30:1–2), implies the adoption of a political policy without first consulting the deity through the prophets. The same must be said for the

26. Compare also Deut 17:16.

complaint that these officials in following their plan to take refuge in a treaty with Egypt "did not look to the Holy One of Israel and did not consult (דרשו) Yahweh" (Isa 31:1).[27] Indeed, Isa 29:15 may well suggest that the authorities tried to keep these negotiations secret from Isaiah and thus by extension, according to Isaiah's point of view, from Yahweh himself:

> Hey, you who try to hide counsel deep from Yahweh,
> Whose deeds are in the dark,
> Who say, "Who sees us, and who knows us?"

It does not take much imagination to understand these counselors' reasons for secrecy. Such negotiations with Egypt involved a breach of Judah's vassal obligations to Assyria. They were tantamount to revolt from Assyria. If word of these negotiations reached Assyria before they were successfully completed, Assyria might retaliate before Judah had made the necessary defensive preparations for a successful revolt. It was important, therefore, to keep these negotiations hidden from Assyrian agents, and Isaiah was clearly a serious security risk. His opposition to reliance on defensive alliances with foreign powers had long been known. Moreover, neither Isaiah's public confrontations with Ahaz during the Syro-Ephraimitic War of 735–732 B.C. (Isaiah 7–8) nor his outlandish public behavior in opposition to Ashdod's reliance on Egypt in the abortive revolt of 714–711 (Isaiah 20) were calculated to go unnoticed. Both his actions and his words were politically indiscrete; they clearly indicated that the prophet was not to be trusted with sensitive state secrets. It is worth noting that the narrative about the embassy from Merodach-Baladan to Hezekiah suggests that Isaiah was initially uninformed about the purposes of this state visit. It was only after the conclusion of Hezekiah's discussion with the Babylonian embassy that Isaiah demanded and received an explanation from the king who these foreigners were and what they wanted (Isa 39:1–4).

The government attempt to keep Isaiah out of the policy-making loop was not simply a concern to preserve state secrets from foreign powers, however. His opposition to government plans could have a destabilizing influence on public support for royal policy. Ahaz's reluctance in the earlier period to ask for confirmation of Isaiah's oracle of salvation (Isa 7:10–14) should probably

27. Wildberger's attempt to deny the concrete meaning of these expressions is unconvincing. It depends on his assumption of a radical discontinuity between Isaiah, the true prophet, and the cultic prophets, the false prophets (*Jesaja*, III, 1152–53). When he argues that these expressions no longer mean "to seek an oracle" but now mean "They have not concerned themselves with the word of Yahweh proclaimed by Isaiah" (ibid., 1153), Wildberger is setting up a false contrast. Isaiah is clearly miffed that the government officials have not sought an oracle from him and have ignored the oracles he has offered unbidden, but the expressions probably mean more than that. The government officials appear to have tried to avoid the public exposure and potential security problems any prophetic consultation would have created for their delicate negotiations with Egypt.

be understood in this light. To publicly ask for and receive a sign confirming the reliability of a divine oracle would create public expectation that the king and his court act in accordance with the oracle. If one were already planning on a different course of action, it were better not to have such an oracle confirmed. Moreover, the somewhat obscure command, "Do not say, 'Conspiracy!' (קשר) to everything that this people says, 'Conspiracy!'" may imply that some people regarded Isaiah's public opposition to royal policy just as treasonous as Amaziah considered Amos's or the later Judean officials considered Jeremiah's.

Isaiah's message was certainly capable of stirring up civil unrest. His biting critique of the corruption of Judean society, which implicated the wealthy, the powerful, and every level of the royal bureaucracy, must have struck a responsive chord in the hearts of many who felt themselves oppressed by the rich and powerful, and defrauded by a governmental system that denied them access even to judicial redress. Moreover, Isaiah's opposition to Hezekiah's policy of a defensive alliance with Egypt played on these social concerns. Hezekiah's policy involved a secret breach of Judah's sworn agreement with Assyria. It also required a significant transfer of capital to Egypt for tribute and to acquire horses for the army (30:6–7), a transfer of funds that would have to be made up by taxation. Hezekiah's military preparations for the inevitable defense of Jerusalem also involved government confiscation and destruction of houses in order to fortify the walls of the city (22:10), a move that must have exacerbated the social dislocation that was already a problem in Judean society (5:8–10). No wonder Isaiah characterized the reliance on this policy as reliance "on oppression and deceit" (30:12). Over against this policy, Isaiah urged trust in Yahweh: "In returning and rest you will be saved, in quietness and trust will be your strength" (30:15). Such trust would enable the Judean government to provide genuine security and relief to its oppressed citizens: "This is rest; give rest to the weary. And this is relief; give relief to the needy" (28:12).[28]

Initially the royal counselors were probably more concerned with security leaks than with public opinion. The revolt against Assyria seems to have had popular nationalistic support, and on the level of Realpolitik, treaties with other enemies of Assyria seemed both reasonable and prudent. It is doubtful whether the ordinary citizen was as confident of Yahweh's protection as Isaiah was. There were probably few who feared only Yahweh as Isaiah had urged in an earlier crisis (8:12–13). Early on Hezekiah's royal advisors, though irritated by Isaiah's meddling in secret affairs of state, seem to have humorously scoffed at Isaiah's reservations about their policy advice (Isa 28:9–10; cf. 5:19). As the economic and social cost of Hezekiah's policy became more and more obvious, however, it would have been more and more difficult to find a receptive

28. J. J. M. Roberts, "A Note on Isaiah 28:12," *HTR* 73 (1980), pp. 48–51.

audience for such scoffing. Isaiah's opposition to royal policy, his bitter denunciation of the royal counselors' so-called wisdom (Isa 5:21; 29:14), and his claim that Yahweh was the truly wise one who would surely bring to pass his prophetic word (Isa 31:2) would have had an increasingly negative impact on public opinion. No wonder the authorities wanted to hush Isaiah and kindred prophetic spirits (Isa 30:10–11). Better that his eyes be shut and his head covered than that he further undermine royal policy (Isa 29:10).

Chapter 20

Yahweh's Foundation in Zion (Isaiah 28:16)

Isa 28:16 is one of the most notable cruxes in the Hebrew Bible. For a single verse it has more than its share of textual, lexigraphical, stichometric, and syntactical difficulties: What is the correct parsing and pointing for *yissad*? Is the preposition before Zion a *beth essentiae*, or is it used in its ordinary locative sense? Is the doubling of *ʾeben* and *mûsād* the result of textual corruption, that is, dittography, or is it an intentional device of the poet? What does *bōḥan* mean? How is the syntax of *pinnat yiqrat mûsād* to be explained? With what is the second *mûssād* to be construed? What does the hiphil of *ʾmn* mean in this context? What does the root *ḥûš* mean, and how does it fit in this context?

Moreover, in addition to harboring this host of difficulties within its narrow compass, Isa 28:16 is also the central verse in the larger pericope of which it is a part, so that the satisfactory resolution of its internal difficulties is essential to an adequate interpretation of this larger context. What is more, this larger context seems to involve some of the most central issues in Isaiah's theology, so in the case of Isa 28:16 the struggle to resolve the technical difficulties is at the same time a struggle to understand one of Isaiah's central theological affirmations.

I. The Problems of Translation

With this apology for devoting so much attention to the problems of a single verse, let us turn to the technical problems of translation.

yissad

If one follows the pointing of the MT, one must analyze the piel perfect third masculine singular *yissad* as introducing an unmarked relative clause modifying the first person suffix on *hinnî*. The sense would be approximately, "Look, I am the one who founded. . . ." This analysis is defended by William Irwin and a number of the older commentators.[1] Irwin cites the three other

1. W. H. Irwin, *Isaiah 28–33: Translation with Philological Notes* (BibOr 30; Rome: Biblical Institute Press, 1977) 30–31. To cite only a few of the older commentators, see Franz Delitzsch, *Das Buch Jesaia* (Biblischer Commentar über das Alte Testament 3/1; 4th ed.;

examples listed in GKC §55f (*hinnî yôsīp* in Isa 29:14 and 38:5, and *hinnî nāṭîtî* in Ezek 25:7) and a similar Ugaritic construction from *UT* 51 VII:49–50: *aḥdy dymlk ʿl ilm* ("I alone am he who will rule over the gods").[2] One should note, however, that Irwin's Ugaritic example has a relative pronoun to introduce the relative clause and that the introductory word is not the Ugaritic equivalent of Hebrew *hinnēh*.

Irwin's Hebrew examples are not any more convincing. The two that evidence the same shift from the first person of *hinnî* to the third person of the following finite verb both contain the same verb *yāsap*, pointed as a defective hiphil imperfect. They provide no evidence for the use of the perfect after *hinnēh*, and since *yôsīp* differs in vocalization from the third masculine singular qal participle only in having *ī* for *ē* in the second syllable, one has the overpowering suspicion that the form in both passages is just a mispointed qal participle.[3] The use of the first person perfect is attested after *hinnî*, though it is extremely rare (Jer 44:26; Ezek 25:7; with more complicated constructions, Ezek 34:11, 20; 36:6), but Isa 28:16 would be the only example of the third person perfect introduced by *hinnî*. After *hinnēh* with other pronominal suffixes the perfect is not attested at all. In contrast, the participle is the normal continuation of the construction introduced by all the suffixed forms of *hinnēh*.

Irwin tries to turn this liability into an advantage by claiming that *yissad*, as the *lectio difficilior*, should be the preferred reading, since "it is indeed hard to explain how the more common construction with the participle could have corrupted [sic] into the very rare construction of MT."[4] The construction of the MT is not just very rare, however; it is totally unparalleled. Moreover, the form *yissad*, with Yahweh as the subject, occurs in Isa 14:32, a passage that reflects a theology very similar to that of Isa 28:16, and the preterite orientation of this earlier passage is probably responsible for the anomalous pointing of the form in 28:16. In short, this is one case where the *lectio difficilior* is not to be preferred.

What one really expects after *hinnî* is a participle, which is what both the Isaiah scrolls from Qumran have. IQIsa[a] has the piel participle *mysd*, and 1QIsa[b] has the qal participle *ywsd*. The Peshitto, the Targum, and Saadya translate with a participle, and the renderings of both the LXX and the Vg

Leipzig: Dörffling & Franke, 1889) 316–17; August Dillmann, *Der Prophet Jesaia* (Kurzgefasstes exegetisches Handbuch zum Alten Testament 5; 5th ed.; Leipzig: S. Hirzel, 1890) 255; Bernhard Duhm, *Das Buch Jesaia* (HKAT 3/1; 3d ed.; Göttingen: Vandenhoeck & Ruprecht, 1914) 175; and J. Skinner, *The Book of the Prophet of Isaiah, Chapters I–XXXIX* (Cambridge Bible for Schools and Colleges; Cambridge: University Press, 1925) 225.

2. Irwin, *Isaiah*, 31.
3. So already GKC, §155f.
4. Irwin, *Isaiah*, 31.

presuppose the Hebrew participle.[5] The simplest correction is to revocalize as the qal participle *yôsēd*. If one adopts this reading, the construction with *hinnēh* should probably be construed as a *futurum instans*, "I am about to lay as a foundation. . . ."

bṣiyyon

Irwin, following GKC (§119i), takes the *b* of *bṣywn* as *beth essentiae* and translates as, "I have founded Zion as a stone."[6] Syntactically this is very problematic, since the object of the verb is *ʾāben*. In most of GKC's examples, the *beth essentiae* introduces the term that is translated by "as a. . . ." In other words, Irwin is translating the phrase as though the text had *ṣywn bʾbn*, not *bṣywn ʾbn*. One might render, "I am about to lay a foundation stone, which is Zion," but the issue is debatable, and it seems safer to stick with the ordinary locative sense of the preposition: "I am about to lay in Zion a foundation stone."

ʾeben bōḥan

One must return to the textual and stichometric questions raised by the repetition of *ʾbn* later; the present paragraph is concerned only with the meaning of the rare word *bōḥan*. The traditional derivation of the word from the verb *bāḥan* ("to test, examine") gives a noun meaning "testing," and the expression in Isa 28:16, "a stone of testing," is then explained as meaning "touchstone," "a stone for testing other stones," or "a tested stone." Given the building imagery in the context and the total absence of any reference to gold, the word can hardly mean touchstone in its primary sense as a stone for testing the purity of gold. The second meaning is also problematic, since there is little evidence that the ancients used one stone as the model for cutting other stones. The third interpretation has the support of the exegetical tradition represented by all three later Greek translations (*lithon dokimon*, "approved stone"),[7] the Vg (*lapidem probatum*, "tested stone"), and the Peshitto (*kʾpʾ bḥyrtʾ*, "a chosen stone"). The second element in LXX's double translation (*lithon polytelē eklekton*, "an expensive, choice stone") also belongs in that exegetical tradi-

5. Unless otherwise noted, my citations of the versions are drawn from the following editions: Peshitto: Antonio Maria Ceriani, *Translatio syra Pescitto Veteris Testamenti ex codice ambrosiano sec. fere VI photolithographice edita*, I (1876); Targum: Alexander Sperber, *The Latter Prophets according to Targum Jonathan* (The Bible in Aramaic 3; Leiden: Brill, 1962); LXX: Joseph Ziegler, *Isaias* (Septuaginta Vetus Testasmentum Graecum auctoritate Academiae Litterarum Gottingensis editum 14; Göttingen: Vandenhoeck & Ruprecht, 1967); Vg: Robertus Weber, *Biblia sacra iuxta vulgatam versionem*, II (2d ed.; Stuttgart: Württembergische Bibelanstalt, 1975). Saadya is cited according to Joseph Derenbourg and Hartwig Derenbourg, *Version arabe d'Isaïe de R. Saadia ben Iosef al-Fayyoûmî* (Oeuvres complètes de R. Saadia ben Iosef al-Fayyoûmî 3; Paris: Ernest Leroux, 1896).

6. Irwin, *Isaiah*, 31.

7. Ziegler, *Isaias*, 218.

tion, and the MT pointing probably reflects this tradition.[8] Nevertheless, this interpretation would be more convincing if the verb *bāḥan* were ever used in connection with building stones. The translation "tested stone" is anomalous, not to say ad hoc, and it does not fit particularly well in the context. What is being tested is the building upon the foundation stone, not the stone itself. Given the subsequent testing of the superstructure with line and plummet, it is quite possible that Isaiah was playing with double entendre here—he is a master at it—but it seems very unlikely that "testing" is the primary meaning of *bōḥan* in this passage.

Moreover, the first element in LXX's translation (*polytelē*, "expensive") points toward a different interpretation. It suggests, as Laberge correctly surmised, that *bḥn* designates a particular type of valuable stone.[9] Thus, it is not surprising that scholars have searched the languages which were either cognate with Hebrew or which heavily influenced the Hebrew vocabulary for stone names that could explain Hebrew *bōḥan*. The best candidate that has emerged from that search is the Egyptian word *bḫn*, a word that designates schist gneiss, a black or green siliceous schist that was used in Egypt for making statues,[10] and a number of scholars have explained the Hebrew *bōḥan* as a loanword from this Egyptian term.[11] H. Wildberger and M. Tsevat reject this identification, because this stone is not found in Palestine, and there is no evidence that the Israelites imported it into Israel for building purposes.[12] This is not a fatal objection, however, because as a loanword *bḥn* could easily have come to designate fine building stones quite distinct from the original Egyptian stone designated by the term. Nonetheless, there is no convincing positive evidence for this equation.

---

8. Joseph Ziegler, *Untersuchungen zur Septuaginta des Buches Isaias* (Alttestamentliche Abhandlungen 12/3; Münster i. W.: Aschendorf, 1934) 67. Leo Laberge suggests an alternative to Ziegler's double translation (*La Septante d'Isaïe 28–33: Étude de tradition textuelle* [Ottawa: privately published, 1978] 10). According to Laberge, *polytelē*, could be a gloss introduced to explain that *bḥn* here designates a stone of quality and should not be taken in the sense of "tested." His distinction between the meaning of *polytelē* and *eklekton* is probably correct, but I see no reason to take *polytelē* as a secondary gloss. If either word were a secondary gloss, *ekleton*, which moves in the direction of the later Greek interpretation *dokimon*, would be the far more likely candidate.

The MT pointing seems to be a conscious attempt to distinguish between *baḥan* ("fortress, tower") and *bōḥan* ("testing"). See below.

9. Laberge, *La Septante*, 10.

10. Adolf Erman and Hermann Grapow, *Wörterbuch der aegyptischen Sprache* (Leipzig: Hinrichs, 1926) 1.471; Thomas O. Lambdin, "Egyptian Loan Words in the Old Testament," *JAOS* 73 (1953) 148–49; and Ludwig Koehler, "Zwei Fachwörter der Bausprache in Jesaja 28, 16," *TZ* 3 (1947) 392.

11. Koehler, "Zwei Fachwörter"; W. Baumgartner et al., *HALAT*, 115.

12. Hans Wildberger, *Jesaja* (BKAT 10/3; Neukirchen-Vluyn: Neukirchener Verlag, 1982) 1066; M. Tsevat, "בחן *bḥn*; בָּחוֹן *bāchôn*," *TDOT*, 2.72.

There is a strong possibility, however, that *bōḥan* should be connected with *baḥan*, another loanword from Egyptian, which means "fortress, tower, watch tower."[13] This word occurs twice in the OT and, interestingly enough, both times in Isaiah, the only book with an undisputed occurrence of *bōḥan*.[14] Its clearest attestation is in Isa 32:14: *ky ʾrmwn ntš hmwn ʿyr ʿzb ʿpl wbḥn hyh bʿd mʿrwt*, "For the citadel is forsaken, the noisy city is deserted, the fortified hill[15] has become a nest of dens for ever." The other occurrence is found in Isa 23:13, though there the word is written either as *bḥyn* or *bḥwn*:

> *hn ʾrṣ kśdym zh hʿm lʾ hyh ʾšwr ysdh lṣyym hqymw bḥynyw ʿrrw ʾrmnwtyh śmh lmplh*. Look at the land of the Chaldeans! This people no longer exists. Assyria assigned it to the creatures of the desert. They had raised its towers, they had erected its citadels, but he turned it into a ruin.[16]

The Hebrew of this passage is very difficult and the translation only provisional, but the word *bḥyn* does seem to stand in parallel to *ʾrmnh* ("citadel").

The connection with *baḥan* is suggested also by the three occurrences of *bḥn*, so written, in the Qumran literature in passages dependent on Isa 28:16: (1) 1QS 8:7b–8a; (2) 1QH 6:25d–27a; and (3) 1QH 7:8–9. As P. Wernberg-Møller has noted, the Qumran community vocalized *bḥn* in Isa 28:16 as *baḥan*, not *bōḥan*.[17] Both 1QS and 1QH consistently write "o"-class segholates with a *mater*,[18] so if they had read *bōḥan* with the MT, they would have written *bwḥn*. This is more than just a difference in vocalization, however, as

13. Erman, *Wörterbuch*, 1.471.

14. Ezek 21:18 is textually obscure, and if the reading *bḥn* is correct, it must probably be analyzed as a verb form, most likely a qal passive perfect.

15. I assume that *ʿpl wbḥn* ("hill and fortress") is a hendiadys.

16. This translation is heavily dependent on that found in the *Ancien Testament* (Traduction oecuménique de la Bible; Paris: Cerf, 1975) 798.

17. P. Wernberg-Møller, "Studies in the Defective Spellings in the Isaiah-Scroll of St. Mark's Monastery," *JSS* 3 (1958) 248.

18. So *qwdš* (1QS 2:25; 4:5, 21; 5:6, 13, 18, 20; 8:5–6, 8, 11, 16, 17, 20, 21, 23; 9:2, 3, 6, 8; 10:3, 4, 5, 9, 12, 22; 11:8, 19; 1QH 3:34; 6:20; 7:7, 10; 8:10, 12, 13; 9:32; 12:2, 12, 28; 13:1; 14:6, 13; 15:23; 16:2, 3, 7, 12; 17:26 and fragments; see Karl Georg Kuhn, *Konkordanz zu den Qumrantexten* [Göttingen: Vandenhoeck & Ruprecht, 1960] 190–91); *bwšt* (1QS 4:23; 1QH 4:23; 5:35; 9:20, 22); *ʿwrp* (1QS 4:11; 5:5, 26; 6:26; 1QH frag. 12:4); *mwšh* (1QS 1:3; 5:8; 8:15, 22; 1QH 17:12); *qwṣr* (1QS 6:26); *ḥwdš* (1QS 7:3, 4, 5, 6, 8, 9, 12, 18; 10:3); *ḥwšk* (1QS 1:10; 2:7; 3:3, 19, 21 [3 times], 25; 4:11, 13; 10:2; 11:10; 1QH 9:26; 12:6; 18:29; frags. 2:11; 5:13); *ʾwrk* (1QS 4:3, 7; 1QH 13:18); *ʾwzn* (1QS 4:11; 1QH 1:21; 6:4; 7:3; 18:4, 20, 27; frags. 4:7, 12; 5:10; 18:2; the single exception is the form *ʾznym* in 1QH 2:37, and from the photograph it is very difficult to make out the actual reading here, since it is on a discolored part of the scroll close to where it is eaten away; see E. L. Sukenik, *The Dead Sea Scrolls of the Hebrew University* [Jerusalem: Magnes Press, 1955] plate 36); *ḥwmṣ* (1QH 4:11); and *šwrš* (1QH 3:3; 4:14; 8:7, 10; there are two exceptions, the only two occurrences of the construct plural with the third masculine singular suffix: *šršyw*, 1QH 6:16; 8:23).

Benedikt Otzen correctly observed.[19] They apparently interpreted *bḥn* in Isa 28:16 in the light of *bḥn* in Isa 32:14 and *bḥyn* in Isa 23:13 as "fortress" or "tower."[20]

A closer look at these Qumran passages will make that obvious. 1QS 8:1–7a stresses that as long as the council of the community includes twelve laymen and three priests who truly fulfill their role, the council of the community shall be established in truth as an everlasting plantation, a sanctuary (*byt qwdš*) for Israel, and a most holy assembly (*swd qwdš qwdšym*) for Aaron. They shall be witnesses at the judgment and participate in rendering to the wicked their due. Then in 7b–8a the text continues with a play on Isa 28:16:

> *hyʾh ḥwmt hbḥn pnt yqr bl yzdʿzʿw yswdwtyhw wbl yḥyšw mmqwmm*
> This is the wall of the fortress, the cornerstone of preciousness; its foundations will not be shaken, and they will not move from their place.

Grammatically one should note that the masculine suffix on *yswdwtyhw* ("foundations") must refer back to *baḥan*, since it is the only masculine antecedent, and if the *baḥan* has foundations, the meaning "fortress" or "tower" is more appropriate than any attempt to identify it with a particular type of stone.

The psalmist in 1QH 6, after recounting the danger he had been in, describes in lines 24d–29a how he had found refuge with God, presumably in the Qumran community:

> *wʾhyh kbʾ bʿyr mṣwr wnʿwz bḥwmh nśgbh ʿd plṭ wʾś[mḥh b]ʾmtkh ʾly ky ʾth tśym swd ʿl slʿ wkpys ʿl qw mšpṭ wmšqlt ʾ[mt] l[ns]wt ʾbny bḥn lb[n]w[t ḥwmt] ʿwz llwʾ ttzʿzʿ wkwl bʾyh bl ymwṭw ky lʾ ybwʾ zr [bšʿr]yh dlty mgn lʾyn mbwʾ wbryḥy ʿwz llwʾ yšwbrw bl ybwʾ gdwd bkly mlḥmtw ʿm twm kwl ḥ[rbwt* (?)] *mlḥmwt ršh*
> And I have become like one who enters a fortified city and takes refuge behind a high wall until deliverance comes. I re[joice (?) in] your truth, my God, for you set the foundation on a rock, and [lay] the rafters according to a line of justice and a plummet of t[ruth] in order to test the stones of the fortress, to b[u]il[d] a strong [wall], so that it cannot be shaken and those who enter it cannot be moved. For no stranger shall enter. [In (?)] its [gates] are doors of protection which permit no entry and strong bars which cannot be broken. No raiding party with its weapons of war will enter until all the s[words (?)] of the wars of wickedness have come to an end.

In this passage the imagery of the fortified city and the high wall within which the psalmist takes refuge suggests strongly that the *ʾbny bḥn* are "stones of the fortress" with which the wall is built. The plural *ʾbny* would appear to rule out both the meaning "touchstone" and the meaning "testing stone." Why should there be a plurality of either? It would be possible to take the expression as

19. Benedikt Otzen, "Some Text-problems in 1QS," *ST* 11 (1957) 94–95.
20. Ibid., 95 n. 1.

designating the kind of stones normally used in the construction of fortresses, however. If this is what is meant by "fortress stones," they would presumably be huge ashlars like those used in the lower courses of Solomon's temple (1 Kgs 5:31; 7:9–12).

In 1QH 7:8b–9 the psalmist praises God for making him secure in the face of adversity:

> *wtśymny kmgdl ʿwz kḥwmh nśgbh wtkn ʿl slʿ mbnyty wʾwšy ʿwlm lswdy wkwl qyrwty lḥwmt bḥn llwʾ tzdʿzʿ*
> And you made me like a strong tower, like a high wall, and you fixed my building on a rock, with eternal foundations for my foundation, and all my walls for a fortress wall, so that it shall not be shaken.

Given the imagery of the strong tower, high wall, and firmly founded building, *baḥan* in this passage is best understood as fortress. The psalmist's walls are like the wall of a fortress in that they are thick, solid, and heavy so that they cannot be shaken.

Indeed all three of the Qumran passages interpret Isa 28:16 as referring to a place of refuge and therefore emphasize the solidity of the structure envisioned. Since the expression *ʾbn bḥn* in Isa 28:16 is in apposition to *ʾbn* and, as such, a second object of the participle *yôsēd*, and since the expression is also in parallel to *pnt yqrt mwsd*, *ʾbn bḥn* must designate a particular kind of stone that served as a part of the foundation and as such had great value. The Qumran texts suggest that the value of this stone lay precisely in its size, weight, and strength, and Tsevat is probably correct when, following the lead of the Qumran interpretation, he defines *ʾbn bḥn* as "a stone used in building a fortress," "an ashlar."[21]

Wildberger objects to introducing the Qumran material into the discussion as evidence, since "in these passages it is just a matter of free citations of Isa 28:16 which do not lead any further."[22] On that basis he urges that one stick with the "traditional" rendering of *bḥn* as "testing."[23] What this overlooks, however, is that the exegetical option reflected in the Qumran texts has quite as impressive a tradition supporting it as the "traditional" interpretation. Whatever one thinks of the double translation in the LXX, it seems clear that the Targum's messianic interpretation, with its emphasis on the strength of the future king, understands *bḥn* in Isa 28:16 as the same word found in 32:14 and 23:13:

> *hʾnʾ mmny bṣywn mlk mlk tqyp gybr wʾymtn ʾtqpynyh wʾḥsnynyh ʾmr nbyʾ wṣdyqyʾ dhymynw bʾlyn bmyty ʿqʾlʾ yzdʿz ʿzwn*

21. Tsevat, "בחן *bḥn*," *TDOT*, 2.72. On the other hand, I am unable to accept his theory of an inscription on the ashlar as an explanation for the last clause in Isa 28:16.

22. Wildberger, *Jesaja*, 1066.

23. Ibid., 1067.

> Look, I am about to appoint in Zion a king, a strong king, powerful and terrible. I will make him strong and I will make him powerful, says the prophet; and the righteous who have believed in these things will not be shaken when distress comes.

The medieval Jewish commentators Rashi and David Kimchi both explained *bḥn* in 28:16 as *mbṣr* ("fortress") by reference to Isa 32:14,[24] and Ibn Ezra, although he does not use the term *mbṣr*, does define the term from the expression *ʿpl w bḥn* ("citadel and tower") in Isa 32:14.[25] Saadya translates *bḥn* in all three passages by the same Arabic word, *ṣnʾm* ("fortress").[26] This tradition is continued in David Luzzatto's nineteenth-century commentary, defended by Tsevat, and incorporated in an odd form in the new JPS translation: "Behold, I will found in Zion, Stone by stone, A tower of precious cornerstones, Exceedingly firm. . . ."[27] JPS's stichometric analysis can hardly be correct, but the recognition that *bḥn* means "tower" or "fortress" is correct.

pinnat yiqrat mûsād

The presence of *yqrt* in the middle of a construct chain has troubled some scholars, and, in order to avoid this difficulty, it has been suggested that *yqrh* is a noun rather than an adjective. This is unnecessary, however; the construction is not unparalleled. The phrase *ʾšt ypt tʾr*, "a woman beautiful of form" (Deut 21:11), also has a construct noun followed by an adjective in construct followed by a noun. I would translate the phrase in Isa 28:16 as "a cornerstone valuable for a foundation."

mûssād

How does the second *mwsd* fit into the syntax of the verse? The Masoretic distinction between the noun and the following participle seems to me to be highly artificial. On the other hand, there seems to be no good textual evidence for deleting either *mwsd* as simple dittography.[28] Moreover, the doubling of *ʾbn* in the preceding line gives support to the doubling of *mwsd* here. Irwin refers to this repetition of the last word of a line at the beginning of the next line

24. For Rashi I have used the edition of I. Maarsen, *Parshandath: The Commentary of Rashi on the Prophets and Hagiographs, Part II. Isajah* (Jerusalem: Central, 1933). Kimchi is cited according to the popular edition of *Miqraʾot Gedolot* (New York: Tanach, 1959).

25. M. Friedlaender, *The Commentary of Ibn Ezra on Isaiah*, vols. 1 and 3 (London: Trübner, 1873, 1977).

26. Derenbourg, *Vesion arabe*.

27. Samuel Davide Luzzatto, *Il profeta Isaia volgarizzato e commentato ad uso deglʾ Israeliti* (Padua: Antonio Bianchi, 1867) 325; Tsevat, "בחן *bḥn*," *TDOT*, 2.72. *The Prophets, Neviʾim: A new translation of the Holy Scriptures according to the Masoretic text*, section 2 (Philadelphia: Jewish Publication Society of America, 1978).

28. Laberge, *La Septante*, 10–11.

as anastrophe,[29] and I think his observation is important for the correct sticho-metric division of 28:16. I would divide the verse into three lines following the introductory formula:

hnny ywsd bṣywn ʾbn (10)
ʾbn bḥn pnt yqrt mwsd (10)
mwsd hmʾmyn lʾ yḥyš (9)

Each of the three lines is approximately the same length. The first two lines have ten syllables, and the last line has nine, if one counts syllables by the Masoretic vocalization. However one measures, the poetic line length is not so skewed as to rule out this stichometric analysis.

Against Irwin, however, I would vocalize the second *mwsd* as a construct form of the same noun with the same meaning as the first *mwsd.*[30] Just as the second *ʾbn* further defined what kind of stone Yahweh was laying down in Zion, so the second *mwsd* further defines what kind of foundation that stone would constitute. Before one can translate the line, however, one must discuss the meaning of *hmʾmyn* and *yḥyš.*

hmʾmyn

The only passage where the hiphil of *ʾmn* may preserve the root meaning "to be firm" is Job 39:24, where some commentators assign the verb the meaning "to show firmness, remain still," but the sense of the passage is obscure and this meaning hardly certain.[31] The ordinary meaning of the hiphil of *ʾmn* is "to believe"[32] or "to believe in," the latter meaning being the equivalent of "to trust."[33] Ps 78:22, in fact, puts *hʾmn bʾlhym* ("to believe in God") in parallel with *bṭḥ byšwʿtw* ("to trust in his salvation"). When used in the sense of "to trust," the meaning of the verb can often be more precisely defined as "to believe what someone says or promises, and to act in accordance with that belief." That seems to be the sense of the verb in Isa 7:9, the only other time that *hʾmn* occurs in First Isaiah:[34] *ʾm lʾ tʾmynw ky lʾ tʾmnw*; "If you do not believe, you will not be established." In v. 7 Isaiah had just given God's promise that

29. Irwin, *Isaiah*, 30.

30. Ibid., 31.

31. See the discussions in Robert Gordis, *The Book of Job: Commentary, New Translation, and Special Studies* (New York: Jewish Theological Seminary, 1978) 462–63; and in Marvin H. Pope, *Job* (AB 15, 3d ed.; Gardin City, NY: Doubleday, 1973) 313.

32. Gen 15:6; 45:26; Exod 4:1, 5, 8, 9, 21; 19:9; 1 Kgs 10:7 = 2 Chr 9:6; Job 9:16; 29:24; Ps 27:13; Prov 14:15; 26:25; Isa 53:1; Jer 12:6; 40:14; Lam 4:12; Hab 1:5; Jonah 3:5.

33. Exod 14:31; Num 14:11; 20:12; Deut 1:32; 9:23; 1 Sam 27:12; 2 Kgs 17:14; 2 Chr 32:15; Job 4:18; 15:15, 22; 39:12; Ps 78:22, 32; 106:12, 24; Isa 43:10; Mic 7:5.

34. Isa 30:21 should not be listed under *ʾmn*, since as the parallel with *hśm ʾl* ("to turn to the left") shows, there the verb form *tʾmynw* must be seen as a denominative hiphil from *ymyn* with the meaning "to turn to the right."

the wicked plot of Damascus and Samaria against the Davidic house would not succeed. This promise seems to be rooted in the ancient tradition of God's covenant with David (vv. 8–9), the head of Jerusalem, the capital of Judah,[35] though it is given explicit contemporary application to Ahaz and his royal advisers. But, Isaiah adds, unless Ahaz and his royal advisers believe the promise and act accordingly—that is, trust God for deliverance from the Syro-Ephraimite coalition and forgo an appeal for Assyrian assistance—they shall not be established. Despite Wildberger's demurral, 2 Chr 20:29 remains the best commentary on the meaning of *hʾmn* in Isa 7:9.[36] Following the prophet Jahaziel's oracle of salvation in 2 Chr 20:15–17, King Jehoshaphat encourages the people in v. 20: *hʾmynw byhwh ʾlhykm wtʾmnw hʾmynw bnbyʾyw whṣlyḥw*, "Believe Yahweh your God and be established; believe his prophets and succeed." In effect, believe Jahaziel's oracle and act accordingly in the upcoming battle, and you will be successful.[37] In the light of this interpretation of Isa 7:9, *hmʾmyn* in 28:16 should designate the person who believes in God's promise to provide a secure foundation and acts accordingly, that is, the one who trusts God as the ground of one's security.

yḥyš

Neither the meaning "hasten" nor the meaning "be worried" appears to be the appropriate meaning for *ḥûš* in the context of Isa 28:16. The Qumran text 1QS 8:8—*wbl yḥyšw mmqwmm*, "they [the foundations] will not *ḥûš* from their place"—suggests a meaning "waver, shake, quake" or the like, and this meaning is also suggested by the parallelism with *zwʿ* ("to tremble, quake"). Moreover, CAD lists a rare root *ḫâšu/ḫiāšu*, found in lexical texts, with precisely this connotation.[38] I would assign the presumably cognate Hebrew verb this meaning in Isa 28:16 and would see the verb clause as modifying the foundation, not the believer. After all, the verse has been stressing the solidity of the foundation God is laying. Given that emphasis, it should be the foundation, not the believer, that is unshakable. The verb clause follows *hmʾmyn* ("believer") rather than *mwsd* ("foundation"), the word it actually modifies, because *mwsd* is in construct with *hmʾmyn*, which prohibits the clause from intervening between the two words. The line may be translated, then, as, "a foundation which will not shake for the one who trusts."

35. Wildberger, *Jesaja*, 282–83.

36. Ibid., 285.

37. Wildberger trivializes the Chronicles passage when he dismisses the use of *hʾmn* in it as meaning simply "to regard the prophetic word as true," and his treatment of Isa 7:9 leaves "trust" a curiously empty concept (ibid.). Trust, in this context, can mean only "to believe God's promise and act in reliance on him to keep it."

38. *CAD*, Ḫ/vol. 6 (Chicago: Oriental Institute, 1956) 147, under *ḫâšu* C.

II. Translation

In the light of the preceding discussing, Isa 28:16 may be translated as follows:

> Therefore, thus says the Lord Yahweh:
> Look, I am about to lay in Zion a stone,
> A massive stone, a cornerstone valuable for a foundation,
> A foundation which will not shake for the one who trusts.

III. The Larger Issues

Context

The precise limits of the pericope in which Isa 28:16 stands is a disputed point.[39] My own view is that 28:1–4 was a *hôy* oracle, originally addressed to the northern kingdom at the time of the Syro-Ephraimite War, that Isaiah reused in the Assyrian period to introduce his oracle against the Judean leaders, who were just as irresponsible as the northerners had been (28:7–13).[40] If one may judge by the opening of v. 7, which can hardly be regarded as a typical opening for a prophetic oracle, it is doubtful that vv. 7–13 ever existed independently of the older *hôy* oracle in vv. 1–4. At the heart of the oracle in vv. 7–13 is the question where one can find true security or rest (v. 12), and Yahweh's answer seems set in contrast to the Judean leaders' attempt to find such security elsewhere. That elsewhere is only evident when one looks back to vv. 1–4. The proud crown of the drunkards of Ephraim probably refers to the city walls of Samaria ("at the top of the rich valley"), though, given Isaiah's penchant for double entendre, it could also refer to garlands worn by the Israelite revelers. Thus, Yahweh's assertion that security lay in relieving the oppressed is set in contrast to the Judeans' drunken reliance on military fortifications like that of the drunken Israelites a few years earlier. The link between v. 13 and v. 14 may be a secondary literary link, as Wildberger and others have argued, but the theme of Isa 28:14–22 is similar to that of Isa

---

39. Some scholars treat the unit as vv. 1–22, often with the omission of vv. 5–6 (so G. R. Driver, "Another Little Drink"—Isaiah 28:1–22," in *Words and Meanings: Essays Presented to David Winton Thomas* [ed. Peter R. Ackroyd and Barnabas Lindars; Cambridge: University Press, 1968] 47–67; and J. Lindblom, "Der Eckstein in Jes. 28, 16," in *Interpretationes ad Vetus Testamentum pertinentes Sigmundo Mowinckel septuagenario missae* [Oslo: Fabritius & Sons, 1955] 123–32, esp. 128). Others would limit the pericope to Isa 28:14–22 (so Friedrich Huber, *Jahwe, Juda und die anderen Völker beim Propheten Jesaja* [Berlin and New York: de Gruyter, 1976] 89–101; and Wildberger, *Jesaja*, 1063–82).

40. The original insight I owe to William L. Holladay, *Isaiah: Scroll of a Prophetic Heritage* (Grand Rapids: Eerdmans, 1978) 59. Whether vv. 5–6 are a later insertion as most scholars assume remains uncertain to me.

28:1–13.[41] Again the theme or central issue is the question where true security is to be found. Against the rulers' reliance on a deceitful refuge that will fail the test of the first big storm (28:15, 17b–18), Isaiah points to the refuge that Yahweh himself will establish (28:16–17a). Since both passages share the same theme and may stem from the same historical setting,[42] it is possible that Isaiah himself is responsible for the secondary editorial connection between Isa 28:1–13 and Isa 28:14–22—if, in fact, the connection is secondary. At any rate, this wider literary context of 28:1–22, as well as other passages that share the same themes and reflect the same historical setting, may be drawn in to elucidate Isaiah's meaning in Isa 28:16.

To begin with the immediate context, however, there can be little doubt that 28:16 is the central verse in the section 28:14–22. Verse 14 begins with a new call to the audience to pay attention, and v. 15 quotes the audience's former statements as the grounds for Yahweh's impending action. That action is announced in v. 16 with a new introductory formula, and then the consequences of Yahweh's action for the audience's previously mentioned boasts are spelled out in vv. 17–18. The following verses simply elaborate the thought with additional imagery. Since v. 16 is bracketed by the references to the deceitful refuge in the invective (v. 15) and the threatened judgment (v. 17b), the centrality of v. 16 seems assured. Brevard S. Childs avoids that conclusion by treating 28:16–17a as an independent oracle secondarily inserted into 28:14–22,[43] but I find his form-critical analysis insufficient justification for this radical surgery. By itself, Isa 28:16–17a is a mere fragment, beginning abruptly and ending even more abruptly, as even Childs must admit;[44] it could never have existed alone as an independent oracle. Moreover, without vv. 16–17a, the transition from invective to threat is lacking the normal transition markers. It is not at all clear that the order in 17b–18 has been disturbed,[45] and Childs's assumption that Isaiah could not deviate from the normal form of the "invective-threat," in which an embedded promise would be unusual,[46] seems to impose an inappropriate "form-critical" straitjacket on a prophet of Isaiah's creativity. Threat and promise are often mixed in Isaiah's oracles (1:19–20; 1:21–26; 7:7–9; 29:1–8; 31:4–9), and the foundation promised in v. 16 actually functions analogously to the offer of rest in 28:12 or the strength and security proffered in 30:15; it

41. Wildberger, *Jesaja*, 1068.

42. Wildberger admits that it is possible (*Jesaja*, 1069), but I think it is probable that both passages come from the same historical setting sometime during the Assyrian crisis in Isaiah's later years.

43. Brevard S. Childs, *Isaiah and the Assyrian Crisis* (SBT 2:3; London: SCM, 1967) 30–31.

44. Ibid., 65.

45. Contra Childs, *Isaiah*, 31.

46. Ibid., 30.

serves as a foil to highlight the disobedience of Yahweh's people. Thus, the structure of the oracle is not as unique as Childs thought, and with the majority of interpreters one may continue to interpret Isa 28:16 as an integral and central element in its present context.[47]

In other words, Isaiah's use of building imagery in Isa 28:16–17 has both a negative and a positive aspect. On the one hand, Yahweh is building a very solid structure with an unshakable foundation. On the other hand, the rival refuge constructed by the human rulers of Jerusalem will be swept away by the first rainstorm. The contrast between these rival structures suggests two different backgrounds for Isaiah's choice of imagery.

1. The Temple in the Zion Tradition

Part of what lies behind Isaiah's choice of imagery is the Zion tradition with its old theological concept of Yahweh as the founder of Jerusalem and its temple.[48] According to Ps 78:68–69, Yahweh chose Jerusalem and built his sanctuary like the heavens and founded it like the earth, and there are other passages where Yahweh is described as the builder of Zion (see Ps 51:20; 102:17; 147:2).

This tradition of the temple's stability had certain roots in earthly reality; the physical temple was solidly built. According to 1 Kgs 5:31, the king commanded and they quarried great stones (*ʾbnym gdlwt*), quality stones (*ʾbnym yqrwt*), in order to found the temple, ashlars (*ʾbny gzyt*). 1 Kgs 7:9–12 further specifies the size, presumably length, of these stone blocks as being some of 10 and some of 8 cubits, or 15 and 12 feet apiece. Yet the physical impressiveness of the temple complex was not as important to this tradition as the theological belief that Yahweh lived in the temple on Zion. Because Yahweh made Jerusalem firm and resided within it, Jerusalem could not be shaken (Pss 48:9; 87:1, 5). Isaiah held to this theology as is clear from Isa 8:18: *mʿm yhwh ṣbʾwt hškn bhr ṣywn*, "from Yahweh of Hosts who lives in Mount Zion." Isa 14:32 gives even more striking evidence of Isaiah's rootage in this theology:

> *wmh yʿnh mlʾky gwy ky yhwh ysd ṣywn wbh yḥsw ʿnny ʿmw*
> And what will he answer the messengers of the nations? That Yahweh founded Zion, and in it the poor of his people will find refuge.

47. Childs himself notes that the great majority of commentators regard 28:16–17a as integral to the larger passage (*Isaiah*, 30).

48. For a discussion of this tradition see my study "Zion in the Theology of the Davidic-Solomonic Empire," in *Studies in the Period of David and Solomon and Other Essays* (ed. Tomoo Ishida; Tokyo: Yamakawa-Shuppansha, 1982) 93–108 [[here: pp. 331–347]], and compare the even more recent work of Moshe Weinfeld, "Zion and Jerusalem as Religious and Political Capital: Ideology and Utopia," in *The Poet and the Historian: Essays in Literary and Historical Biblical Criticism* (ed. Richard Elliott Freidman; HSS 26; Chico, CA: Scholars Press, 1983) 75–115.

The "poor of his people" in Isa 14:32 corresponds to the "one who trusts" in 28:16, and this touches the point at which Isaiah corrected the Zion tradition in which he was steeped. He made the promise contingent upon trust and behavior appropriate to trust.

This becomes clearer if one continues with the imagery in Isa 28:17 and then compares it with a related passage later in Isaiah. The role of the line and plummet in v. 17 is to test whether the superstructure is built upon, and in precise alignment with, the solid foundation God is laying. Line and plummet were used both in demolition work preceding repairs and in building (Lam 2:8; Isa 34:11; 2 Kgs 21:13; Job 38:5–6). The concern for building on the foundation was architecturally based, but, when it came to temples, it also had a religious dimension, and that may be helpful for understanding Isaiah's imagery.

In ancient Near Eastern thought one could build a temple only where the god directed and according to the plan given by the god. The classic text in this regard is Gudea's famous dream,[49] but the idea permeated all of Mesopotamian culture and is also found in Israel. Thus, Moses built the tabernacle according to the plan shown to him on the mountain (Exod 25:40), and David was given a divine blueprint for the construction of the temple (1 Chr 28:19). Moreover, the logic of this conception meant that one could not deviate from the original design of a temple when renovating it unless the god residing in the temple had given specific approval for the proposed changes. Thus, Tukulti-Ninurta I emphasized that he changed the site of an earlier temple at the request of Ishtar,[50] and Sennacherib mentions the divine approval for his change of a temple's doors.[51] When doing repair work on temples, therefore, it was important to find the original foundations, so that the renovated temple could be rebuilt exactly as the god had ordered.[52] The Neo-Babylonian kings, in particular, consistently claim to have sought and found the original foundation trenches of temples they were repairing.[53] Nabonidus boasts that his repairs

---

49. A. Falkenstein and W. von Soden, *Sumerische und akkadische Hymnen und Gebete* (Die Bibliothek der alten Welt; Zurich and Stuttgart: Artemis, 1953) 137–82, Nr. 32.

50. Albert Kirk Grayson, *Assyrian Royal Inscriptions* 1 (Records of the Ancient Near East; Wiesbaden: Harrassowitz, 1972) 111 §731.

51. Daniel David Luckenbill, *The Annals of Sennacherib* (OIP 2; Chicago: University of Chicago Press, 1924) 144–45:8–15.

52. Richard S. Ellis, who has written the basic work on Mesopotamian foundation deposits, *Foundation Deposits in Ancient Mesopotamia* (New Haven and London: Yale University Press, 1968), plays down the importance of the divine sanction in temple building, asserting that only Esarhaddon among Assyrian kings put much stress on it (p. 7), but his position is belied by the passages already noted.

53. Stephen Langdon, *Die neubabylonischen Königsinschriften* (Vorderasiatische Bibliothek 4; Leipzig: Hinrichs, 1912) 62, Nr. 1, 2:44–46 (Nabopolassar); 76, Nr. 1, 2:12–35; 78, Nr. 2, 3:22–27; 92, Nr. 9, 2:56–59; 96, Nr. 10, 2:2–6; 98, Nr. 11, 2:7; 110, Nr. 13, 3:37–43; 142, Nr. 16, 2:17–20; 194, Nr. 27a, 2:17–21; Nr. 27b:13–15 (all Nebuchadnezzar); 216,

did not vary from the old foundation by a single finger's breadth.[54] The most interesting statement, however, is the following:

> Ebarra, his house, which is in the midst of Sippar, the lofty dwelling which befits his divinity, the pure cella, the seat of appeasement, the dwelling of his lordship, whose temenos had been destroyed for many days, whose building plan had been obscured—a former king sought the old foundation, but he did not find it. From himself he made a new house for Shamash which did not befit his lordship, which was not appropriate to the splendor of his divinity. The top of that house sank down before it should have, its top parts had collapsed. I looked carefully, and I was afraid, trembling seized me. To firmly lay the foundation, to restore the building plan of his house, to make the cella and dwellings as befits his divinity, I prayed to him every day, I offered sacrifices to him for this, and I took omens. Shamash, the exalted lord, had paid attention to me since long ago. An agreeable yes, a firm decision agreeing to my work and establishing the sanctuary, Shamash and Adad fixed by my oracles. I greatly trusted in their firm decision which cannot be annulled. I took the hand of Shamash my lord, and I made him dwell in another house on the first day of the year. Right and left, front and back of the cella and in the midst of the dwellings I dug trenches, and I gathered the elders of the city, the citizens of Babylon, the mathematicians, the wise, the inhabitants of the temple academy, the keeper of the secrets of the great gods, who establishes the face of kingship, for council. I sent to them, and thus I said to them, "Find the old foundation. The cella of Shamash the judge see, and a lasting house for Shamash and Aya, my lords, build." With prayer to Shamash my lord, with his prayer to the great gods, the assembly of the scholars looked for the old foundation, cella and dwellings they sought, and quickly they returned and said to me, "I found the old foundation of Naram-Sin, an ancient king, the legitimate cella of Shamash, the dwelling of his divinity. My heart rejoiced, my face shone, I viewed the cella of his lordship and the dwellings, and in joy and rejoicing I laid its foundation over the old foundation. . . .[55]

In other words, if one does not build precisely according to the divine plan, if one does not raise the walls in perfect alignment upon the god's appointed foundation, the building will not stand.

2. *The Royal Building Program to Fortify Jerusalem*

If the emphasis in Isa 28:16 on Yahweh's laying a firm foundation points to the background of the Zion tradition and its inherited temple ideology, Isaiah's graphic portrayal of the government's worthless shelter collapsing under a violent rainstorm (28:17–18) probably points to another background. This

---

Nr. 2, 2:21–22 (Neriglissar); 224–26, Nr. 1, 2:49–65 (Nabonidus); passim. For the translation of *temennu* as "foundation," see Ellis, *Foundation Deposits*, 148–49.

54. Ibid., 226, Nr. 1, 2:64–65.

55. Ibid., 254–56; Nr. 6, 1:16–40.

imagery, which may seem peculiar at first, strikingly reflects topographical and architectural realities of ancient Jerusalem.[56] Since Jerusalem was built on a rather steep hill and much if its fortifications rested on artificial stone platforms, the rapid runoff from a violent rainstorm would tend to erode the base of these platforms or terraces, producing a massive stone slide and the collapse of the undermined superstructure. The confused jumble of rocks found by archaeologists along the eastern slope of ancient Zion bears eloquent testimony to the stark realism of Isaiah's imagery.

Strikingly similar imagery of a collapsing wall reappears in Isa 30:12–14:

> Therefore thus says the Holy One of Israel:
> Because you have rejected this word,
> And have trusted in oppression and deceit,
> And relied upon it;
> Therefore this sin shall be to you
> Like a spreading breach bulging out in a high wall.
> Whose collapse comes suddenly, in an instant.
> And its collapse will be like the shattering of a potter's vessel,
> Smashed beyond repair,
> So that among its fragments no sherd may be found
> To scoop fire from a hearth
> Or to skim water from a cistern.

This passage has a number of features that tie it rather closely to 28:2–22 and suggest that both passages originated in the same historical setting and deal with the same theological problem. The high wall, bulging out of alignment, recalls the line and plummet of 28:17, and its collapse into useless rubble parallels the fall of the useless shelter swept away by the rain torrents in the same verse. Moreover, both passages are linked, at least secondarily, with strikingly similar thematic verses—Isa 28:12 and 30:15—to which we must return.

If both passages originate in the same historical context, and if they both choose imagery of collapsing buildings to develop their polemic against Judah's rulers, one should ask whether the choice of that metaphor may not be dictated by actual, government-sponsored building activity in Jerusalem. In the larger contexts of both passages, Isaiah is attacking the attempt of the Judean rulers to achieve national security through political agreements, presumably with Egypt.[57] Such agreements apparently involved acquiring chariot or cavalry horses from Egypt (Isa 30:16; 31:1), and obviously demanded mil-

56. I owe this insight to the helpful observations of my former colleague at the University of Toronto, the archaeologist John S. Holladay, Jr.

57. Isa 28:15 remains a crux, but behind the strangely allusive language most critics would still see political intrigue with a foreign ally, and unless the passage is dated as early as the Syro-Ephraimite War, Egypt remains the most likely candidate. In the larger context of Isaiah 30, Egypt is clearly the culprit.

itary preparation against the inevitably Assyrian response.[58] Part of that military preparation would involve the strengthening of Jerusalem's fortifications to withstand a siege. Isa 22:8b–11, which shares the same general theme with our passages and may stem from the same historical setting, illustrates the kind of building activity such refortification of Jerusalem would involve and may well report the very government actions that caused Isaiah to employ the building metaphors in his polemic against Jerusalem's rulers:

> On that day you looked to the arms in the House of the Forest, and you saw that the breaches in the City of David were many. You collected the waters of the lower pool. The houses of Jerusalem you counted, and you pulled down the houses to fortify the wall. You constructed a basin between the walls for the water of the old pool. But you did not look to him who did it, and the one who planned it long ago you did not consider.

Such a building program must have been socially painful. It does not require much imagination to guess who lost their houses to these defense projects or to surmise who was drafted to do the labor on the projects; it was hardly the nobility. Micah, Isaiah's contemporary, spoke of those who "build Zion by blood and Jerusalem by injustice" (Mic 3:10), and he may have had in mind just such expropriation of houses and use of forced labor as one may legitimately infer from Isa 22:8b–11.[59]

Isaiah's Theological Message

Faced with such a public policy with its inevitable social dislocations and hardships, which Judah's leadership probably justified as necessary evils to achieve security, peace, and well-being for Jerusalem, Isaiah responded with a prophetic critique of both poetic and theological depth. Metaphorically drawing on the ancient temple ideology of the Zion tradition, Isaiah contrasted the solid foundation Yahweh was laying to the government's flimsy fortifications,

---

58. The link between Isa 30:12–14 and 30:15–17 *may* be a secondary literary connection, but just as in the case of the relation between 28:7–13 and 28:14–22, there is no reason to look for a different historical setting.

59. There is archaeological evidence now for Hezekiah's refortification of Jerusalem. He is apparently responsible for building the recently discovered city wall which incorporated a large part of the western hill within the city's fortifications and in doing so cut through a number of older buildings in that area. See especially M. Broshi, "The Expansion of Jerusalem in the Reigns of Hezekiah and Manasseh," *IEJ* 24 (1974) 21–26; idem, "Excavations on Mount Zion, 1971–72, Preliminary Report," *IEJ* 26 (1976) 81–88. Note also N. Avigad, "Excavations in the Jewish Quarter of the Old City of Jerusalem, 1970 (Second Preliminary Report)," *IEJ* 20 (1970) 129–40; idem, "Excavations in the Jewish Quarter of the Old City of Jerusalem, 1971 (Third Preliminary Report)," *IEJ* 22 (1971) 193–200; idem, "Excavations in the Jewish Quarter of the Old City, 1969–1971," in *Jerusalem Revealed: Archaeology in the Holy City 1968–1974* (ed. Y. Yadin; Jerusalem: Israel Exploration Society, 1975).

hastily built on inadequate foundations. Those fortifications would be measured for alignment with Yahweh's foundation, and, found wanting, they would be swept away, clearing the ground for Yahweh's new structure.

The nature of those measurements, however, is the real key to Isaiah's meaning. His identification of the divine builder's line and plummet as justice and righteousness shows that Isaiah was not referring to the foundation of an actual physical temple, whether contemporary or future. The temple symbolized Yahweh's presence in Jerusalem, and, according to the Zion tradition, it was Yahweh's presence that provided the city's security, that constituted its real walls and towers (Pss 48:2, 6, 8, 12; 48:4). But just as Near Eastern gods refused to live in temples that were not built according to their specifications, upon the foundations laid out in their ground plans, so Yahweh would not live in a Jerusalem built in violation of his blueprint. His blueprint, the foundation he would relay, called for a city built by justice and righteousness. The present government's policy of trying to found Jerusalem's security on the human strength of political alliances and military preparation, a policy vividly embodied in the actual refortification of Jerusalem going on at the time, failed to meet the divine standard. Not only did it shift the ground of security from divine strength to human might, but that human might was bought at the cost of injustice and oppression. That is brought out quite strongly in Isa 30:12, which defines the sin that will result in the collapsing wall as Judah's trust in "oppression and deceit." Yahweh's rival program for government policy is well spelled out in the two thematic passages referred to earlier. As Isa 28:12 makes clear, God's concern seems to be for the unfortunate victims of the government's oppressive program to rebuild Jerusalem's defenses:

zʾt hmnwḥh hnyḥw lʿyp
wzʾt hmrgʿh ⟨hrgyʿw lʾbywn⟩[60]
wlʾ ʾbw šmwʿ
This is rest: give rest to the weary;
This is repose: give repose to the needy;
But they refused to listen.

The prophetic word suggests that Israel's true security would come by giving relief to the citizens who were paying for the royal fortifications with their houses, labor, taxes, and time. This thought is closely paralleled in the other thematic passage, Isa 30:15:

bšwbh wnḥt twšʿwn
bhšqṭ wbṭḥh thyh gbwrtkm
wlʾ ʾbytm

60. See my reconstruction of this passage in "A Note on Isaiah 28:12," *HTR* 73 (1980) 49–51.

> In returning and rest you will be saved;
> In quietness and trust will be your strength;
> But you were not willing.

Isaiah goes on to say that Judah's refusal of this policy in favor of building up their cavalry or chariot corps would simply result in their being able to flee in panic that much faster (vv. 16–17).

Isaiah's message, put simply, is this. Jerusalem's security is dependent on Yahweh's presence in the city. However, that presence depends on the righteous and just behavior of the human inhabitants of Jerusalem, particularly that of the king and his officials, who are largely responsible for the quality of life in a monarchical society. Because the present rulers of the city had not fostered righteousness and justice, Yahweh was about to institute an urban renewal project for Jerusalem. His demolition work, however, was simply a necessary step in his restoring righteousness and justice as the foundation for Jerusalem's life. But this required faith. The one who trusted God to provide Jerusalem's security could afford to promote righteousness and justice. If one did not trust God, if one looked to human means for security, justice and righteousness would eventually be sacrificed to that higher goal of security, but, paradoxically, the hoped-for security would remain elusive. It could only come in God's way; it could not be achieved by human shortcuts.

PART 4

Kingship and Messiah

Chapter 21

The Davidic Origin of the Zion Tradition

I

There is fairly general agreement among scholars as to the content of the Zion tradition. Edzard Rohland, in what remains the basic work on the subject, analyzes the tradition into the four following motifs: (1) Zion is the peak of Zaphon, i.e., the highest mountain; (2) the river of paradise flows out of it; (3) God has defeated the assault of the waters of chaos there; and (4) God has defeated the kings and their peoples there.[1] Others have criticized many of Rohland's conclusions, but even the severest critics seem to accept his four motifs as the basic elements contained in the Zion tradition. Günther Wanke, for example, differs from Rohland only in terminology, and even this difference is very slight.[2] The one notable exception to this general consensus is Hans Wildberger who embellishes the above analysis by adding a fifth motif, that of the pilgrimage of the nations to Jerusalem.[3] This is simply an addition, however, not a radical change, and the acceptance or rejection of this minor elaboration has little bearing on the following discussion.[4]

When one moves from the question of content to the more difficult question of the original *Sitz im Leben* of the Zion tradition, it is no longer possible to speak of a general consensus. One can speak, however, of a dominant position. Most of the OT scholars who have published detailed treatments of the Zion tradition trace its formation back to the pre-Israelite inhabitants of Jerusalem.[5]

1. *Die Bedeutung der Erwählungstraditionen Israels für die Eschatologie der alttestamentlichen Propheten* (Heidelberg: dissertation, 1956) 142.

2. *Die Zionstheologie der Korachiten in ihrem traditionsgeschichtlichen Zusammenhang* (BZAW 97; Berlin: Töpelmann, 1966) 64, 70.

3. "Die Völkwallfahrt zum Zion, Jes. II 1–5," *VT* 7 (1957) 62–81.

4. Wildberger's view is attractive. Such a motif certainly plays a part in certain prophetic texts which use the Zion tradition (Isa 2:1–5; Mic 4:1–7; Zech 14:16–19). There is a possible trace of it in one Zion song (Ps 76:11–13), and it occurs in a related royal psalm (Ps 2:10–11). Its inclusion would also strengthen the argument of this paper. Nevertheless, to remain on common ground, I shall simply follow the more commonly accepted analysis of Rohland and Wanke.

5. So, e.g., Herbert Schmid, "Jahwe und die Kulttraditionen von Jerusalem," *ZAW* 26 (1955) 168–98; A. R. Johnson, *Sacral Kingship in Ancient Israel* (Cardiff: U. of Wales, 1955); E. Rohland, *Erwählungstraditionen*, 142; Hans-Joachim Kraus, *Psalmen* (BKAT

The obviously pagan origin of some of the individual motifs in the tradition give this view a certain presumptive appeal, and while its proponents have often made unproven and unprovable assumptions about the Jebusite role in Davidic Jerusalem,[6] they can at least show a plausible channel by which such a pagan tradition, if it existed, could have been transmitted to Israel.[7]

The Jebusite theory has its critics, but they have failed to topple it from its dominant position. Günther Wanke's recent monograph is a case in point.[8] He makes some good individual observations in his detailed criticism of the Jebusite theory, but, judged as a whole, his arguments are inconclusive, his treatment of the evidence often arbitrary, and his own reconstruction far more improbable than the theory he attacks.[9] A more promising critique of the hy-

---

15/1; 2d ed.; Neukirchen: Nuekirchener Verlag, 1961) 197–201; G. von Rad, *Old Testament Theology* (2 vols.: New York: Harper, 1962–65) 1.46–47; 2.156–58; John H. Hayes, "The Tradition of Zion's Inviolability," *JBL* 82 (1963) 419–26; Josef Schreiner, *Sion-Jerusalem Jahwes Königssitz, Theologie der heiligen Stadt im Alten Testament* (StANT: Munich: Kösel, 1963); Werner Schmidt, "Jerusalemer El-Traditionen bei Jesaja, ein religionsgeschichtlicher Vergleich zum Vorstellungskreis der göttlichen Königtums," *ZRGG* 16 (1964) 302–13; Hans-Martin Lutz, *Jahwe, Jerusalem und die Völker, zur Vorgeschichte von Sach 12, 1–8 und 14, 1–5* (WMANT; Neukirchen: Neukirchener Verlag, 1968); Fritz Stolz, *Strukturen und Figuren im Kult von Jerusalem, Studien zur altorientalischen vor- und frühisraelitischen Religion* (BZAW 118; Berlin: de Gruyter, 1970).

6. Stolz's discussion may serve as a typical example of the tendency to multiply unprovable assumptions. He assumes that (1) David captured Jerusalem without any significant bloodshed (ibid., 7); (2) the previous Jebusite nobility, including Uriah the Hittite, formed David's court (ibid., 7–8); (3) Zadok was originally a Jebusite priest of the city god of Jebusite Jerusalem (ibid., 8); and, even more problematically, that (4) Nathan may have been a Jebusite cult prophet (ibid., 8). The evidence at our disposal is inadequate to make any of these suppositions probable.

7. The account of David's purchase of the threshing floor of Araunah the Jebusite (2 Sam 24:18–24) suggests David spared at least part of the former population of Jerusalem. This is the only concrete evidence, however, for the preservation of the earlier inhabitants, and it is valid only if one regards Araunah as a historical figure contemporary with David. If one removes David's Jebusite subject from this account, either by turning him into the god Varuna (Stolz, ibid., 10) or by making him a much earlier figure than David (Werner Fuss, "II Samuel 24," *ZAW* 74 [1962] 164), one can no longer cite this passage as evidence for David's treatment of the earlier inhabitants of Jerusalem. Fuss sees this quite clearly, but neither he nor Stolz seems to recognize that this is the one piece of solid ground on which the rest of the Jebusite theory rests. Without it one loses the only fixed point in the whole reconstruction.

8. *Zionstheologie*, 70–113. One could also mention R. de Vaux, "Jérusalem et les prophètes," *RB* 73 (1966) 495–97; Th. C. Vriezen, *Jahwe en zijn Stad* (Amsterdam: N. V. Noord-Holland, 1962) 3–4, 11–16.

9. See the excellent critique of Wanke's book by H.-M. Lutz (*Jerusalem und die Völker*, 213–16). The earlier review of R. Tournay (*RB* 74 [1967] 124–25) is more favorable, but it adds nothing to strengthen Wanke's arguments, the weaknesses of which Lutz has since made painfully obvious.

pothesis was hinted at in the earlier work of R. Lack[10] and E. Lipiński,[11] but neither carried through with their insight, and the actual form in which they stated their objection has little weight.[12] Thus the Jebusite theory remains the most popular view, and it must be destroyed before a new hypothesis can be constructed in its place.

II

Unfortunately we have very little information about Jebusite beliefs, but the little there is suggests that the Jebusites shared the same theological views as the Canaanites. If one may judge from Gen 14:18–22,[13] the pre-Israelite city god of Jerusalem was El Elyon, a deity with clear Canaanite affinities. At least the elements El and Elyon, taken separately, are Canaanite. El is attested as the head of the Canaanite pantheon in the Ugaritic texts,[14] and El and Elyon are both attested as independent Canaanite deities in Sanchuniathon's later work on Phoenician religion.[15] In the latter El is again portrayed as the head of the pantheon, while Elyon, who comes two generations before El, has a much less important role as one of the cosmogonic deities.

The combination of the two names in Genesis 14, therefore, is a little strange. Since Elyon means "most high," and El can be used as a determinative, the syntax permits one to interpret El Elyon three ways: (1) the god Elyon, (2) El the most high, or (3) as a compound divine name, El-Elyon. One could argue for the third alternative on the basis of the "El and Elyon" which

10. "Les origines de *Elyon*, le Très-haut, dans la tradition cultuelle d'Israël," *CBQ* 24 (1962) 59.

11. *La royauté de Yahwé dans la poésie et le culte de l'Ancien Israël* (Verhandelingen van de koninklijke vlaamse academie voor wetenschappen, letteren en schone kunsten van België, Klasse der letteren XXVII, 55; Brussels: Paleis der Academiën, 1965) 119.

12. Lipiński (ibid.) merely repeats in slightly different words the earlier objection of Lack (*CBQ* 24 [1962] 59): "Sans doute, les Jébuséens n'ont jamais pensé que leur colline de 760 m. était la montagne de Dieu au coeur de l'Aquilon. Pour eux, comme pour tous les Cananéens, cette montagne existait, localisée au Mont Casius. Nous savons que, cultuellement parlant, l'aire cananéenne était extrêmement uniformisée." This criticism is good as far as it goes, but it does not go far enough. See below, p. [[317]], and n. 32.

13. One has questioned whether this pericope contains either a premonarchical (R. de Vaux, *Histoire ancienne d'Israël des origines à l'installation en Canaan* [Études Bibliques; Paris: Gabalda, 1971] 262) or a Jerusalem tradition (J. G. Gammie, "Loci of the Melchizedek Tradition of Genesis 14:18–20," *JBL* 90 [1971] 385–96); but since my argument is with the defenders of the Jebusite theory, who do not share this skepticism, it is not necessary to deal with these problems (i.e., even granting the existence of a premonarchial, Jerusalem Melchizedek tradition, does the Jebusite theory hold up?).

14. F. M. Cross, "אל," *TWAT* (Stuttgart: Kohlhammer, 1971) 1.260.

15. Eusebius, *Praep. evang.* 1.10, 14–16; Carl Clemen, *Die phönikische Religion nach Philo von Byblos* (MVAG 42/3; Leipzig: Hinrichs, 1939) 24–25; M. Pope, *El in the Ugaritic Texts* (VTSup 2; Leiden: Brill, 1955) 55–56.

occurs in an intermediate position between the major deities and the cosmogonic pairs in a list of divine witnesses to an eighth century B.C. Aramaic treaty from Sefire.[16] Yet the construction is not exactly the same, and El Elyon in Genesis 14 is not a largely otiose cosmogonic deity, but the major figure in the cult of Jerusalem who is very active in human affairs. The same observation militates against reading the name as the god Elyon, since Elyon does not occur outside Israelite texts as a major, active deity. Thus Cross is probably correct in preferring the second translation, El the most high, which takes Elyon as an epithet for El that stresses El's exalted position as head of the pantheon.[17] The relationship between this epithet and the divine name Elyon, however, remains to be explained, and the question whether it was applied to El by the pre-Israelite inhabitants of Jerusalem must at least be raised. One should note that El Elyon's epithet in Gen 14:19, 22, *qnh śmym wʾrṣ*, "creator of heaven and earth," is very similar to *qn ʾrṣ*, "creator of earth," an epithet used simply of El in inscriptions from Karatepe.[18] Leptis Magna,[19] and Palmyra,[20] and possibly under the form Elkunirsha in a Hittite translation of a Canaanite myth from Bogazkoi.[21] There is some weight, therefore, to the view of Levi della Vida,[22] quoted with approval by Pope,[23] that the original form of the title in Gen 14:19, 22 was simply *ʾl qn hʾrṣ*, "El creator of the earth."[24] At any rate, the El of Gen 14:18–22 appears to be the Canaanite El.

Thus, if the Zion tradition goes back to the pre-Israelite inhabitants of Jerusalem, and particularly to their cult of El, that tradition should be compatible with the *extra-biblical* traditions about this Canaanite deity.[25] However, such is not the case.

16. H. Donner, *KAI* (3 vols.; Wiesbaden: Harrassowitz, 1962–64) Nr. 222A:11. Note that *ʾl wʿlyn* occurs in the list after the major gods—even after a summary statement, if Donner's interpretation of *wqdm ʾlhy rḥbh wʾdm[h]*, "and before all the gods of the desert and the fertile land," is correct—and immediately before the cosmogonic pairs, "heaven and earth," "depths of the sea and springs," and "day and night." Thus *ʾl wʿlyn* seems to mark the transition in the list from the cultically important deities to those deities who, apart from their role as witnesses, seldom occur outside cosmogonies. See F. M. Cross, *TWAT,* 1.268.

17. Ibid., 274.

18. *KAI*, No. 26 A III 18.

19. *KAI*, No. 129:1.

20. J. Cantineau, "Tadmorea," *Syria* 19 (1938) 78–79, No. 31; but correct the reading with G. Levi della Vida ("El ʿElyon in Genesis 14:18–20," *JBL* 53 [1944] 8).

21. Heinrich Otten, "Ein kanaanäischer Mythus aus Boğazköy," *Mitteilungen des Instituts für Orientforschung* (Berlin: Akademie, 1953) 1.135–40; Harry A. Hoffner, "The Elkunirsa Myth Reconsidered," *Revue hittite et asianique* 23 (1965) 5–6, n. 4.

22. *JBL* 63 (1944) 9.

23. *El in the Ugaritic Texts*, 52.

24. The translation is Pope's (ibid.); Levi della Vida maintained the less probable rendering "lord of the earth" (*JBL* 63 [1944] 1, n. 1).

25. Of course, one could explain any conflict between the two by assuming that the Jebusite theology reflected a slightly variant form of Canaanite beliefs, but that would reduce one to the circular process of reconstructing the Jebusite beliefs from the OT and then

Two of the four motifs in the Zion tradition deal with what one may term the mythological topography of Zion. This mythological portrayal of Zion as a high mountain from which a paradisiacal river flows agrees in general with the Canaanite tradition about El's abode. In the Ugaritic texts El appears to dwell on a mountain, Mt. *Ll*, where the assembly of the gods met,[26] and his abode is elsewhere referred to as the "spring of the two rivers, the source of the two seas."[27]

Nonetheless, the identification of Mt. Zion with El's mythological abode must be secondary. Sacred mountains in Canaanite mythology, like Mt. Olympus in Greek mythology, are not only mythological peaks; they are also real mountains, and their mythological description bears a close resemblance to the actual topography of the real mountain.[28] Baal's Mt. Zaphon, for instance, was known in Hurrian as Mt. Hazzi, passed from there into the classical sources as Mt. Casius, and from these sources may be identified with the modern Jebel el-Aqraᶜ, an imposing peak 1770 meters high, located on the Mediterranean coast about 30 kilometers north of Ras Shamra.[29] El's abode cannot be located with the same confidence, but Pope's identification with modern Khirbet Afqa, at the majestic mountain source of the Nahr Ibrahim, has much to commend it.[30] Nevertheless, whether one prefers this identification or a site somewhere in the Amanus range, as proposed by Cross,[31] it is in any case clear that El's mountain originally had nothing to do with the hill on which Jerusalem was built. In the first place, the Jebusite city was built on thc lowest hill in the vicinity, and, in the second place, there was no river in Jerusalem.

Of course, it is conceivable that the Jebusites transplanted the cult of El from its original sacred mountain to Jerusalem.[32] There are parallels for such

explaining thse same OT texts from the reconstructed Jebusite faith. Such circular reasoning is a fundamental weakness in Stolz's monograph.

26. Andrée Herdner, *Corpus des tablettes en cunéiformes alphabétiques découvertes à Ras Shamra-Ugarit de 1929 à 1939* (2 vols.; Mission de Ras Shamra, 10; Paris: Imprimerie Nationale, 1963) 2 I 14, 20. Pope tries to identify *ǵr ll* with Mt. Zaphon (*El in the Ugaritic Texts*, 102); but see n. 39 below.

27. Herdner, *Corpus*, 2 III 4; 3 E V 14–15; 4 IV 21–22; 6 I 33–34; 17 VI 47–48.

28. This must be stressed against those who would find throughout the ancient Near East a common mythological pattern in which every sacred mountain is somehow a mere embodiment of the original cosmic mountain. One may legitimately question whether such an incorporeal, universal ideal mountain ever existed in Near Eastern thought.

29. O. Eissfeldt, *Baal Zaphon, Zeus Kasios und der Durchzug der Israeliten durchs Meer* (Halle: Niemeyer, 1932) 5–9; "Die Wohnsitze der Götter von Ras Schamra," *Forschungen und Fortschritte* 20 (1944) 25 (= *Kleine Schriften* [Tübingen: Mohr, 1963] 2.503); Hatice Gonnet, "Les montagnes d'Asie Mineure d'après les textes hittites," *Revue hittite et asianique* 26 (1968) 146–47.

30. *El in the Ugaritic Texts*, 72–81.

31. *TWAT*, 1.266.

32. This possibility, which Lack and Lipiński did not consider (see n. 12 above), destroys the force of their criticism, at least in the form in which they stated it.

a transfer. As Otto Eissfeldt has demonstrated in a number of studies,[33] when the cult of a Canaanite mountain deity was transplanted from its original setting to another area, the daughter cult often attached the name and traditions of the mother cult to the new site, even when the topography of the new site made such a transfer awkward. As an example, Eissfeldt points to the name Casius for the low rise, slightly over 13 meters high, near Pelusium in Egypt.[34] In spite of its unimpressive height, it was not only called a mountain, but one even thought of it as a high mountain.[35]

There are, however, difficulties with this expansion. In the examples cited by Eissfeldt, the new cult sites bore the same name as the original sacred mountain. This is not true of Jerusalem. The Jebusites, if we may judge from the OT, called the hill on which Jerusalem was built Mt. Zion. Even in passages where there is an identification with a mythological mountain, Zion is clearly the real name of Jerusalem's hill. Moreover, Ps 48:2–3 identifies Mt. Zion, not with Mt. *Ll*, El's mountain, but with Mt. Zaphon, Baal's mountain:

> Great is Yahweh, and greatly to be praised.
> In the city of our God is his holy mountain,
> The most beautiful peak, the joy of all the earth.
> Mt. Zion is the heights of Zaphon, the city of the great king.

This identification is obscured by the standard English translations which render the crucial phrase *yrkty ṣpwn*, "in the far north." While it is true that *ṣpwn* is normally used in Hebrew as an ordinary noun meaning "north," this usage is secondary, derived from Mt. Zaphon's location far to the north of Palestine. There are at least two other passages in the OT where the term is used in its primary sense as the name of a sacred mountain. It occurs in Ps 89:13 along with the name of four other sacred mountains:[36]

> Zaphon and Amana[37] you created,
> Tabor and Hermon shout for joy at your name.

---

33. *Baal Zaphon*; "Der Gott des Tabor und seine Verbreitung," *Archiv für Religionswissenschaft* 31 (1934) 14–41 (= *Kleine Schriften* 2, 29–54); "Die Wanderung palästinisch-syrischer Götter nach Ost und West im zweiten vrochristlichen Jahrtausend," *JPOS* 14 (1934) 294–300 (= *Kleine Schriften* 2, 55–60).

34. *Archiv für Religionswissenschaft* 31 (1934) 33–34 (= *Kleine Schriften* 2, 46–47).

35. Ibid.

36. O. Eissfeldt, *Baal Zaphon*, 12; M. Pope and W. Röllig, "Syrien, die Mythologie der Ugariter und Phönizier," *Wörterbuch der Mythologie: I. Götter und Mythen im vorderen Orient* (ed. H. W. Haussig; Stuttgart: Ernest Klett, 1962) 258; Oswaldus Mowan, "Quatuor Montes Sacri in Ps. 89, 13?" *VD* 41 (1963) 11–20.

37. Mowan (ibid., 15) emends *ymyn* to the *ʾmnh* of Cant 4:8 and identifies this mountain with Mt. Amanus. This identification, however, is problematic, because the name for Amanus is normally written in Akkadian sources with an initial *ḫ*, which would not correspond to a West Semitic *aleph* (Simo Parpola, *Neo-Assyrian Toponymns* [Alter Orient und Altes

Isa 14:13–14 also mentions Zaphon in what appears to be an old mythical motif about the revolt and subsequent fall of one of the divine beings:

> You said in your heart, "I will scale the heavens.
> I will exalt my throne above the stars of El.
> I will sit enthroned on the mount of assembly, on the heights of Zaphon.
> I will mount up on the backs of the clouds.
> I will make myself equal to Elyon."
> But to Sheol you will be cast down, to the depths of the pit.

This last OT passage seems to make Zaphon the mount of assembly and implies some connection between El and Mt. Zaphon. Some scholars have tried to explain that connection by assuming Zaphon originally belonged to El and that he was driven from it by the younger and more vigorous Baal.[38] The theory is, however, extremely dubious. In the first place, a biblical text cannot be cited uncritically as good Canaanite evidence.[39] In the Canaanite texts themselves there is no direct evidence to tie El to Mt. Zaphon.[40] The expression *il ṣpn*, which Herbert Schmidt[41] and Oldenburg[42] cite as evidence for such a connection, is no exception. As Pope has pointed out,[43] *il ṣpn* can be translated as "the god of Zaphon," referring to Baal, or even as "the god Zaphon," referring to the sacred mountain itself, since, contrary to Oldenburg,[44] the sacred mountains were deified.[45] In the second place, the textual evidence for an

Testament 6; Neukirchen: Nuekirchener Verlag, 1970] 145). It is easier to identify *ʾmnh* with Mt. Ammana (na), apparently a different mountain (ibid., 16). It occurs in one text along with Mt. Amanus and Mt. Lebanon: ^{KUR}*Ḫa-*[*m*]*a-na* ^{KUR}*Lab-na-na* u_3 ^{KUR}*Am-ma-na-na* (Paul Rost, *Die Keilschrifttexte Tiglat-Pilesers III., nach den Papier-abklatschen und Originalen des Britischen Museums* [2 vols.; Leipzig: Eduard Pfeiffer, 1893] 74.26), which is probably to be identified with a part of the Anti-Lebanon range (J. Simons, *The Geographical and Topographical Texts of the Old Testament* [Leiden: E. J. Brill, 1959] 2; cf. Hatice Gonnet, *Revue hittite et asianique* 26 [1968] 116–17, and literature cited there).

38. Pope, *El in the Ugaritic Texts*, 102; Ulf Oldenburg, *The Conflict between El and Baʿal in Canaanite Religion* (Supplementa ad Numen, altera series, dissertationes ad historiam religionum pertinentes, 3; Leiden: Brill, 1969) 104–6, 123–25.

39. This is a major weakness in Pope's attempt to identify *ǵr ll* with Mt. Zaphon (see n. 26 above). Since Mt. Zaphon is never called the mount of assembly in the Ugaritic texts, it is methodologically unsound to identify the two Ugaritic toponyms connected to two different gods on the basis of a late Israelite text which associates the god and function belonging to one toponym with the other place. One could as easily argue that the place of assembly changed with the growing prominence of Baal.

40. Pope, *El in the Ugaritic Texts*, 102.

41. *ZAW* 26 (1955) 188.

42. *The Conflict between El and Baʿal*, 104–6.

43. *El in the Ugaritic Texts*, 102.

44. *The Conflict between El and Baʿal*, 78, 105, n. 1.

45. They occur in sacrificial lists (Herdner, *Corpus* 35:34, 42; 36:4, 7; Ch. Virolleaud, "Chapitre III. Les nouveaux textes mythologiques et liturgiques de Ras Shamra [XXIVe

assault of Baal on El's mountain is virtually non-existent. Oldenburg reconstructs this episode from the extremely broken and fragmentary fifth column of Herdner, *Corpus*, 1, though this reconstruction forces him to follow Cassuto's[46] drastic rearrangement of the tablet.[47] Neither the reconstruction nor the renumbering of the columns is convincing.[48]

Frank M. Cross also sees a connection between El and the *yrkty ṣpwn* in Canaanite tradition,[49] but this contradicts his own attempt to locate El's mountain in the Amanus range,[50] since the expression *yrkty ṣpwn* must refer to Mt. Zaphon;[51] it cannot possibly refer to the mountains on the other side of Zaphon, i.e., the Amanus, as Cross suggests.[52] Moreover, the description of El's abode

campagne, 1961]," *Ugaritica* 5 [Mission de Ras Shamra 16; Paris; Imprimerie Nationale, 1968] 9 R° 1, 6 V° 5, 7 [note that both *bʿl ṣpn* and *ṣpn* receive a sheep]; 12:10; 13:9–10, 34) and as witnesses in treaties (E. F. Weidner, *Politische Dokumente aus Kleinasien; Die Staatsverträge i akkadischer Sprache aus dem Archiv von Boghazköi* [Boghazköi-Studien 8–9; Leipzig: Hinrichs, 1923] 1, rev. 41 [read "Seris (and) Hurris, the mountains Nanni (and) Hazzi" with Goetze (*ANET*², 205)], 2, rev. 12; 3 IV 10, 36–37; 4, rev. 3–4). [Marvin Pope and Jeffrey H. Tigay, in a work which came to my attention after this article was finished ("The Description of Baal," *Ugarit-Forschungen* 3 [1971] 122–23), have now demonstrated that *il ṣpn* must be taken as the deified mountain.]

46. U. Cassuto, *The Goddess Anath, Canaanite Epics of the Patriarchal Age* (Jerusalem: Bialik Institute, 1951) 91–92.

47. Oldenburg, *The Conflict between El and Baʿal*, 123–25.

48. Note Herdner's comment: "Il est donc matériellement impossible de considérer avec Cassuto que les col. V et IV sont à numéroter respectivement I et II, tandis que nos. col. II et III seraient les col. VI et V" (*Corpus*, 1).

49. *TWAT*, 1.265–66.

50. Ibid.

51. Where *yrkty* is used in construct before a clear topographical term other than *ṣpwn*, it designates the most remote part of *that* site: *yrkty* (*h*) *byt*, "the back part of the house" (1 Kgs 6:16; Amos 6:10; Ps 128:3); *yrkty hmʿrh*, "the back of the cave" (1 Sam 24:4); *yrkty hspynh*, "the hold of the ship" (Jonah 1:5); *yrkty hr ʾprym*, "the heart of Mt. Ephraim" (Judg 19:1, 18); *yrkty bwr*, "the bottom of the pit" (Isa 14:15; Ezek 32:23); and *yrkty lbnwn*, "the heights of Lebanon" (2 Kgs 19:23; Isa 37:24). The expression never points to a region *beyond* that designated by the *nomen rectum* of the construct chain, i.e., *yrkty lbnwn* means "the heights of Lebanon," not "the Anti-Lebanon."

52. The suggestion is based on the use of this expression in Ezek 38:6, 15; 39:2 to designate the homeland of Beth-Togarmah and Gog, which does lie considerably north of Mt. Zaphon. Ezekiel, however, uses *yrkty ṣpwn* in precisely the same way as Jeremiah uses *yrkty ʾrṣ*, "the remotest parts of the earth" (Jer 6:22; 25:32; 31:8; 50:41). Since Jeremiah's expression has no specific geographical reference point, one must question whether *ṣpwn* in Ezekiel's expression stands for anything more than the vague noun of direction, "north." Ezekiel apparently tried to combine Jeremiah's enemy from the north and the peoples from the remotest parts or the earth in one expression. In doing so, he used an old topographical expression, but with a new and far less concrete meaning; "the heights of Zaphon" have become "the far north" in Ezekiel. Thus Ezekiel's usage should be regarded as secondary and cannot be cited to locate *yrkty ṣpwn* in the Amanus.

as the source of the two rivers does not fit a location on Mt. Zaphon, as Pope also recognized. He attributed that feature to the site that El supposedly took after losing Zaphon.[53] Thus, even if Zaphon was at one time El's mountain, the mythological topography of Mt. Zion is a composite picture of two completely distinct holy places. And, on the basis of the Canaanite evidence, these two sacred places belonged to two different gods, Mt. Zaphon to Baal, Mt. *Ll* to El.

There is no reason to believe the Jebusites would have fused the separate mythological traditions of El and Baal. Yet the third motif in the Zion tradition, a tradition supposedly inherited from the El cult, is also derived from the Baal tradition. In Ugaritic mythology it is Baal, the storm god, who battles the sea and defeats the forces of chaos. This motif is widespread in the ancient Near East, but the protagonist always has the features of a storm god whether his name be Enlil, Marduk, Tishpak, Addu, Teshub, or Baal. El, however, is not a storm god. As Cross succinctly puts it:

> One cannot describe El as a god of heaven (like Anu), as a storm god (like Enlil or Zeus), as a chthonic god (like Nergal) or as a grain god (like Dagan). The only picture of El which can comprehend all his myths is that of the patriarch. He is the primeval father of gods and men, sometimes strong, often compassionate, always wise in his judgments.[54]

On the basis of the Canaanite evidence it is impossible to assign the Baal functions to El as an original part of his character.[55]

The fourth motif in the Zion tradition presents the Jebusite theory with a different, but equally serious problem. While the first three motifs were obviously mythological, this last motif, the vain assault of the kings and the nations against Jerusalem, is not. Though it may use imagery drawn from the myth of the storm god's battle with chaos, the motif refers to a historical event involving human kings and human peoples as the antagonists. Such a motif is difficult to explain from Canaanite traditions. Stolz has attempted to demonstrate non-Israelite parallels for it.[56] But his parallels are too general to be convincing. Otherwise, as far as I can see, the proponents of the pre-Israelite origin of this motif have made only three serious arguments to support their view.

First, they point to the Jebusite belief in the invincibility of Jerusalem attested in 2 Sam 5:6.[57] The passage is somewhat obscure as the text now stands, but it does seem to reflect Jebusite overconfidence prior to David's assault on the city. One need not attribute, however, this sense of security to a sacred tradition. Mt. Zion, while not high, was very steep, and with its strong defenses

53. *El in the Ugaritic Texts*, 68–80, 102.
54. *TWAT*, 1.270.
55. Against Stolz who seems to do precisely this (*Strukturen*, 154–55).
56. Ibid., 72–85.
57. Schreiner, *Sion-Jeusalem*, 277.

it was a difficult city to capture. Such mundane factors are quite sufficient to explain the Jebusite attitude.

The second argument is based on Ps 110:4–5, which mentions Yahweh's defeat of the kings in the same context with Melchizedek. Since the tradition about Melchizedek is unquestionably pre-Israelite, the mention of Yahweh's defeat of the kings in the same context suggests this motif is also pre-Israelite.[58] This argument has two weaknesses. In the first place, the occurrence of Melchizedek can be questioned. The traditional rendering, "You are a priest for ever after the order of Melchizedek,"is suspect; elsewhere *ʿl dbrt(y)* means "because," not "after the order of." If one alters the traditional rendering, however, the reference to Melchizedek becomes less obvious, and one could consider taking the element not as a proper name, but as two common nouns.[59] In the second place, the connection between Melchizedek, if that reading is correct, and Yahweh's smiting of the enemies is rather loose in the passage. It is not necessary to assume that both had the same origin.

The third argument for the Jebusite origin of this motif is purely negative. We know of no event in the Israelite history of Jerusalem that could have given rise to the motif, so it must be pre-Israelite.[60] Whether the premise of this argument is true we will have to consider later. For the present one may simply note that it is an argument from silence. Such arguments are precarious, for we are not that well informed on Israelite history. If it were not for fortunate discoveries of Assyrian records, for instance, we would not know that Ahab played an important role in the Syrian coalition that fought against Shalmaneser III at the battle of Qarqar, or that Azariah of Judah headed the Syrian coalition against Tiglath-pileser III.[61] These two examples should make one hesitate, at least briefly, before accepting a historical argument based on the silence of the biblical record.

In short, the arguments for the Jebusite origin of this fourth motif are not convincing in and of themselves. Their force depends largely on the association of this motif with the three mythological motifs whose origin in the Jebusite cult is uncritically assumed.[62] But if, as I have attempted to show, the formulation of the mythological motifs cannot be attributed to the Jebusites, there is certainly no reason to attribute this motif to them.

---

58. Hays, *JBL* 82 (1963) 420; Rohland, *Erwählungstraditionen*, 141.

59. Cf. Gammie, *JBL* 90 (1971) 388, n. 23.

60. Rohland, *Erwählungstraditionen*, 140; Schreiner, *Sion-Jerusalem*, 230; von Rad, *Old Testament Theology*, 2.157.

61. Hayim Tadmor, "Azriyau of Yaudi," *Scripta hierosolymitana* 8 (Jerusalem: Magnes, 1961) 232–71.

62. Rohland, *Erwählungstraditionen*, 137.

III

On the other hand, Wanke's attempt to explain the origin of the fourth motif as an exilic development out of a legendary conception of a mysterious, terror-inspiring foe from the north—a conception Wanke traces back to the movement of the Sea People ca. 1200 B.C.[63]—is even less convincing than the Jebusite theory of his opponents. To maintain his late dating, he must deny any connection between this motif and the very similar motif which occurs in the royal Psalms.[64] Note, for example, Ps 2:1–11:

Why do the nations grow restive, the peoples make vain plans?
The kings of the earth plot together,[65] the rulers take counsel together
Against Yahweh and against his anointed:
"Let us snap their bonds, let us cast off their ropes."
He who sits enthroned in the heavens laughs, the Lord scoffs at them.
Then he speaks to them in his anger, in his wrath he terrifies them:
"I myself installed my king on Zion, my holy mountain."
Let me recount the decree of Yahweh.
He said to me, "You are my son, today I have begotten you.
Ask of me and I will give you nations as your inheritance, the ends of the earth as your possession.
Break them with a rod of iron, like a potter's vessel smash them."
Now, O kings, be wise, accept reproof, O rulers of the earth.
Serve Yahweh with fear, rejoice (before him) with trembling.

The similarity between the thought in this royal psalm and the motif in the Zion tradition can be seen by comparing this passage with the Zion song Ps 48:3–7:

Mt. Zion is the heights of Zaphon, the city of the great king.
God is in its citadels, he is known as a refuge.
For, lo, the kings gathered together, they crossed over together.
They saw, then they were astounded, they were terrified, they fled in fright.
Trembling seized them there, pangs like a woman in labor.

There are two differences that one should observe. The part played by the earthly king in the royal psalm is lacking in the Zion song, and in the Zion song the enemy kings are defeated before the very walls of Jerusalem (cf. Ps 46:6–7; 76:4), while the royal psalm does not indicate the site of the battle, though it does stress that Zion is Yahweh's holy mountain and thus, by implication, that Yahweh would protect it. Apart from these two differences the passages are

63. *Die Zionstheologie*, 92.
64. Ibid., 74, n. 18.
65. Reading *ytyʿṣw* because of the parallelism with *nwsdw* and the following direct quotation, which suggests a verb denoting verbal activity; cf. Ps 83:4.

very similar. In both passages the kings and their nations plot together against Yahweh; in both cases the enemy plot is portrayed as a revolt of vassals—this is less clear in Psalm 48 than in Psalm 2, but it is suggested by the expression in 48:3 that designates Yahweh the great king, *mlk rb*, since this is a good Semitic expression for a suzerain[66]—and in both cases Yahweh's intervention creates a panic among the enemy. In view of these similarities, Wanke's attempt to disassociate the motif in the Zion tradition completely from the material in the royal psalms must be judged a failure, and since the royal psalms make sense only in the period when Israel still had a king, an exilic date for the origin of this motif is out of the question.[67]

IV

So far this paper has attempted to show that one cannot derive the Zion tradition from the pre-Israelite cult of Jerusalem. At the same time I have agreed with the representatives of this dominant view in rejecting Wanke's exilic dating. Now one is free to suggest a better hypothesis. I suggest that all the features in the Zion tradition can be explained most adequately by positing an original *Sitz im Leben* in the era of the Davidic-Solomonic empire.

The Zion tradition's identification of Yahweh with El and Elyon (Ps 46:5; cf. Ps 47:3; 83:19; 97:9) is probably earlier than David's empire; it is attested in the oracles of Balaam (Num 24:16), which Albright dates to the 13th century B.C.,[68] and the old poem in Deuteronomy 32, which Albright and Eissfeldt date to the time of Samuel in the last half of the 11th century B.C.[69] Nevertheless, David's imperial conquests must have given added impetus to this identification. David's empire, which stretched from the Mediterranean in the west to the edge of the Arabian desert in the east, and from the river of Egypt in the south northward to Lebo Hamath in the Lebanon, with at least marginal control as far as the Euphrates, was the largest empire of its day.[70] Such an empire

66. Cf. the similar expressions *mlk yrb* (Hos 5:13; the words should probably be divided as *mlky rb*; see the commentaries), *hmlk hgdwl* (2 Kgs 18:18, 28), and the common Akkadian expression *šarru rabû*, all of which mean "great king, suzerain."

67. Lutz also noted the similarities between some of the royal psalms and the Zion songs and raised the question, "Sollte zwischen diesen Texten, die anscheinend von einer weitverbreiteten 'Königsideologie' gespeist werden . . . und der Vorstellung vom Ansturm der 'Könige' and 'Völker' gegen die Gottesstadt ein Zusammenhang bestehen . . . ?" (*Jerusalem und die Völker*, 175–76, n. 3).

68. *Yahweh and the Gods of Canaan* (Garden City: Doubleday, 1968) 15.

69. Albright, ibid., 17; Eissfeldt, *Das Lied Moses Deuteronomium* 3^{21-43} *und das Lehrgedicht Asaphs Psalm 78 samt einer Analyse der Umgebung des Mose-Liedes* (Berichte über die Verhandlungen der sächsischen Akademie der Wissenschaften zu Leipzig, Philologisch-historische Klasse 104/5; Berlin: Akademie, 1958) 42.

70. 2 Samuel 8; John Bright, *A History of Israel* (2d ed.; Philadelphia: Westminster, 1972) 200.

needed theological legitimation. What better way was there than to stress the imperial god's older identification with the supreme head of the pantheon, thus undergirding Yahweh's divine right to grant world dominion to his earthly regent in Jerusalem?

If one can accept Albright and Eissfeldt's early dating of Deuteronomy 32,[71] one can even detect a development in the conception of Yahweh's universal rule between the time of Samuel and the Davidic empire. According to Deut 32:8–9, Elyon, who is apparently identified with both El and Yahweh, assigned the various nations to their territories and appointed the various pagan national gods to rule over their respective peoples, but he kept Israel under his own direct rule.[72] In contrast, Psalm 82, which Eissfeldt dates to the Davidic period,[73] portrays a judgment scene in which Yahweh condemns all these pagan gods for misrule, the implication being that now Yahweh will exercise direct rule over the pagan nations as well.[74] Such a change in ideology certainly reflects the desire to justify imperial expansion, but it was made possible by the empirical fact that the pagan kings, who formerly served their own

---

71. G. E. Wright dates the present form of the poem between 900–600 B.C., but he assumes that much older material has been used in the poem ("The Lawsuit of God: A Form-Critical Study of Deuteronomy 32," *Israel's Prophetic Heritage: Essays in Honor of James Muilenburg* [eds. B. W. Anderson and A. W. Harrelson; New York: Harper, 1962] 66–67). My argument will stand, therefore, even if one accepts his dating, as long as one assigns the theologoumenon expressed in Deut 32:8–9 to the older, premonarchic material which was taken up in the later poem. R. Meyer's attempt ("Die Bedeutung von Deuteronomium 32, 8f. 43 (4Q) für die Auslegung des Moseliedes," *Verbannung und Heimkehr: Beiträge zur Geschichte und Theologie Israels im 6. und 5. Jahrhundert v. Chr., Wilhelm Rudolph zum 70. Geburtstage* [ed. A. Kuschke; Tübingen: Mohr, 1961] 197–209) to date Deuteronomy 32 to ca. 400 B.C. precisely on the basis of this theologoumenon is totally unconvincing. Not only does Meyer fail to explain the many archaic features in the poem, his assumption that an Israelite writer, after Deutero-Isaiah, would create *de novo* a legitimate realm in which the pagan national gods could exercise their authority is simply incredible. While the motif does occur in late texts, its origin must be sought in the earlier period when the existence of the pagan national gods was freely admitted (Judg 11:24) and there was a need to bring this fact into harmony with Israel's claim for Yahweh's supremacy.

72. Eissfeldt's view that Elyon refers to a deity other than and superior to Yahweh ("El and Yahweh," *JSS* 1 [1956] 29–30 [= *Kleine Schriften* 3, 390]) cannot be accepted if one is interpreting the Israelite text. The *bny ʾl* are clearly subservient to Yahweh (vs. 43 LXX), which suggests quite strongly his identification with the head of the pantheon. The same is true in Psalm 82. In fact, one must question whether Elyon or El ever occur in Israelite poetry other than as terms for Yahweh. This of course does not deny the ultimately Canaanite origin of the terms or of certain expressions in which they occur. See Wright's judicious statement (*Israel's Prophetic Heritage*, 28, n. 7).

73. *JSS* 1 (1956) 36–37 (= *Kleine Schriften* 3, 396).

74. Psalm 82 obviously represents a conscious transformation of the theologoumenon found in Deut 32:8–9, which it therefore presupposes. This consideration alone makes James S. Ackerman's attempt to date Psalm 82 to the premonarchic period (*An Exegetical Study of Psalm 82* [Cambridge: Harvard Divinity School dissertation, 1966] 442–55) highly improbable.

gods, now had to pay tribute to Yahweh, and may have been required to participate in important cultic celebrations honoring him, such as the dedication of Solomon's temple (1 Kgs 8:65).

This kind of development, where religious ideology reflects and justifies political realities, has many analogies in the ancient Near East. One could cite the elevation of Ishtar under the Sargonic empire of Akkad[75] or that of Marduk which began under the first Babylonian dynasty.[76] An even better example for our purposes is the Assyrian god Asshur. He was apparently the head of the Assyrian pantheon from very early times, but the Assyrians were heavily influenced during most of their history by the culturally superior Babylonians, much as Israel was influenced by her culturally superior neighbors, the Canaanites. As a result, the Assyrians adopted the standard Mesopotamian pantheon, including Marduk. Nevertheless Asshur, sometimes called the Assyrian Enlil,[77] remained the real head of the Assyrian pantheon. Nowhere is this more evident than in the periods of Assyrian imperial expansion, especially when those expansionist policies led to conflict with Babylon. One text from the time of Sennacherib, for instance, appears to describe a judicial proceeding in which Asshur, as the head of a divine court, condemns Marduk to prison for some wrongdoing.[78] Assuming that von Soden's interpretation of this very difficult text is correct, it presents a clear example, strikingly parallel to Psalm 82, of propagandistic religious literature used to justify political developments, in this case Sennacherib's sack of Babylon. The same tendency is also reflected in some copies of the *Enuma Elish* from Asshur, where Asshur, though he is not really a storm god, has replaced Marduk as the hero of the epic.[79] More-

75. J. J. M. Roberts, *The Earliest Semitic Pantheon: A Study of the Semitic Deities Attested in Mesopotamia before Ur III* (Baltimore/London: The Johns Hopkins University, 1972) 153–54; W. W. Hallo and J. J. A. van Dijk, *The Exaltation of Inanna* (New Haven/London: Yale University, 1968) 9–11.

76. Marduk eventually supplants Enlil as the main executive force in the universe, but exactly when this takes place is disputed. W. G. Lambert dates this change to the time of Nebuchadnezzar I, ca. 1100 B.C. ("The Reign of Nebuchadnezzar I: A Turning Point in the History of Ancient Mesopotamian Religion," *The Seed of Wisdom: Essays in Honour of T. J. Meek* [ed. W. S. McCullough; Toronto: University of Toronto, 1964] 3–13); but J. van Dijk has pointed to other evidence which suggests an earlier date in the late Old Babylonian period ("L'hymne à Marduk avec intercession pour le roi Abīʾešuḫ," *Mitteilungen des Instituts für Orient-Forschung* 12 [1966] 57–74). Cf. also W. W. Hallo and J. J. A. van Dijk, *The Exaltation of Inanna*, 66–67.

77. Knut Tallqvist, *Akkadische Götterepitheta* (Studia orientalia edidit societas orientalis fennica, 7; Helsinki: Societas orientalis fennica, 1938) 266.

78. W. von Soden, "Gibt es ein Zeugnis, das die Babylonier an Marduks Wiederauferstehung glaubten?" *ZA* ns 16–17 (1952–55) 130–66; "Ein neues Bruchstück des assyrischen Kommentars zum Marduk-Ordal," *ZA* ns 18–19 (1957–59) 224–34.

79. Erich Ebeling, *Keilschrifttexte aus Assur religiösen Inhalts* (Ausgrabungen der deutschen Orient-Gesellschaft in Assur, E: Inschriften; ed. F. Delitzsch; Leipzig: Hinrichs, 1919) 117, rev. 3–4 = Tablet I 80–81; 173, obv. 10 and rev. 19 = Tablet II 10, 138.

over, the Assyrian poet has identified Asshur with the similar sounding Anshar, one of the primeval gods, the father of Anu, apparently to suggest Asshur's priority and, hence, superiority over his rivals in the Mesopotamian pantheon, though this identification creates a contradiction in the development of the narrative.[80] Politico-religious propaganda has never been overly concerned with keeping its mythology straight.

This last analogy suggest the source of the mixed mythology one finds in the Zion tradition. The Israelites, who may have had a somewhat garbled understanding of Canaanite mythology to begin with, wanted to make Yahweh the undisputed head of the pantheon. To do that it was not enough to identify him with El, since, in Canaanite thought, Baal had come to play a far more important role in the actual exercise of divine authority than the putative head of the pantheon.[81] Thus to give Yahweh full supremacy, the Israelites had Yahweh absorb some of the mythological traits and functions of Baal, as well as those of El.

The same concern to underscore Yahweh's absolute supremacy might also explain the rather curious identification of Elyon, a cosmogonic deity, with El and Yahweh. With some hesitancy I suggest this identification was an Israelite innovation, analogous to the Assyrian identification of Asshur and Anshar, motivated by an attempt to elevate Yahweh still higher than the simple identification with the enfeebled Canaanite El could. Unlike the Asshur-Anshar equation, however, it was not the similarity in sound that suggested the identification, but the actual meaning of the divine name Elyon.

Since this identification is attested in early pre-monarchical sources, it may have first been broached in response to Yahweh's triumphs over the Canaanite gods and their peoples during the early period of the conquest. Nevertheless, just as Marduk's definitive elevation to the head of the pantheon took place sometime later than the first attempt to exalt him, and under the impact of a more recent historical development than that which had first gained him prominence, so Yahweh's exaltation really reached its climax only with the rise of the Davidic-Solomonic empire. It is precisely in the monarchical period, after the creation of David's empire gave new relevance and added credence to the imperial claims always implicit in the use of the epithet Elyon, that the epithet enjoyed its greatest popularity.[82]

80. This is clear from a comparison of Ebeling, ibid., 173, obv. 10, 13, with the standard Babylonian edition of the epic. In this Assyrian edition Asshur has a double role, unless one assumes the scribe distinguished between Asshur and Anshar while writing their names in identical fashion.

81. According to Sanchuniathon, Baal ruled as king through the consent of El (Eusebius, *Praep. evang.* 1.10, 31; Clemen, *MVAG* 42/3, 29 §31), and the Ugaritic texts give the same picture.

82. The pre-monarchic references in Gen 14:18–22; Num 24:16; and Deut 32:8 were edited in the monarchic period; Isa 14:14; Pss 18:14 (= 2 Sam 22:14); 21:8; 46:5; 47:3; 86:6;

The Davidic-Solomonic era also provides the most logical setting for the glorification of Jerusalem as Yahweh's abode, a central theme in the Zion tradition. After David captured Jerusalem and made it his capital, he transferred to it the central cultic object of the old Israelite league, the ancient ark of the covenant. This was obviously part of David's plan to make Jerusalem both the religious and political center of the nation—David had seen in Saul's reign what conflict could result when the political and religious authorities were too far apart—but this transfer of the ark to Jerusalem needed justification. Jerusalem, after all, had no league traditions to justify its new religious importance under David.[83] The answer to this problem apparently came in the form of a prophetic oracle (Ps 132:13–14). It laid the foundation for the belief that Yahweh had chosen Mt. Zion for his dwelling place just as he had chosen David for his king. Such a tradition was clearly an innovation; in the older Yahwistic poetry the mountain of Yahweh was not Mt. Zion, or any particular peak, but the land of Palestine as a whole.[84] Nevertheless, the divine authority of the prophet, presumably Nathan, backed by the impressive royal power of an undoubtedly pleased king, quickly overcame any resistance to this radical localizing of Yahweh's mountain abode. One may dispute precisely when this tradition of the choice of Zion was first formulated, but it can hardly be later than Solomon's construction of the temple in Jerusalem, which presupposes it, and the tradition had already become firmly fixed prior to Solomon's death, for when Jeroboam revolted, he could not set up a counter cult without provoking a negative reaction among some of his political supporters (1 Kgs 14:1–18). Apparently the tradition of Yahweh's choice of Zion was more widely accepted in northern circles than the parallel tradition of Yahweh's choice of David and his dynasty.

Finally, the action of the enemy kings in plotting against Jerusalem, and Yahweh's response to their wicked plans can best be understood if one traces the origin of this motif back to the Davidic-Solomonic era. At that time all, or at least most, of the surrounding states were vassals of Israel, and as vassals they were expected to pay tribute to the Israelite king and the Israelite national god, in whose name they undoubtedly had to swear an oath of allegiance.[85] In this context, any attempted rebellion on the part of a vassal, even

83:19; 89:28 (in a derivative sense); 91:1, 9 are monarchical texts; Lam 3:35, 38 is clearly exilic and probably reflects monarchic usage; and a number of the other psalm passages (7:18; 9:3; 57:3; 77:11), though difficult to date, could be pre-exilic.

83. M. Noth, "Jerusalem und die israelitische Traditionen," *OTS* 8 (1950) 28–46 (= *Gesammelte Studien zum Alten Testament* [Munich: Kaiser, 1957] 172–87).

84. Lack, *CBQ* 24 (1962) 59. Exod 15:17 and Ps 78:54 seem very clear on this point.

85. If one includes the pilgrimage of the nations to Jerusalem as a fifth motif in the Zion tradition (see above, nn. 3–4), these political realities of the David-Solomonic empire would also form the obvious *Sitz im Leben* for the origin of that motif.

the simple failure to pay the yearly tribute, would be regarded from the Israelite point of view as a grave sin and a direct challenge to the imperial claims of Yahweh.

We are not informed of any such external revolts in the time of David, though the internal revolts and crises that racked Israel in the last years of his reign certainly provided ample opportunity for revolt. The biblical historian records at least three revolts in the time of Solomon, however, two of them involving vassal states and at least partially successful. According to 1 Kgs 11:14–25, Hadad attempted to restore Edomite independence, and Rezon set up an independent Aramean state in Damascus. It is not at all unlikely that there were other attempts which were successfully crushed and receive no mention in the biblical text. These are enough, however, to create the motif of the nations plotting against Yahweh and his anointed.

There is no record of these rebellious vassals in the Davidic-Solomonic era actually attacking Jerusalem as the Zion tradition suggests, but this is not an insurmountable objection. One can explain the difficulty in one of two ways.

David, apparently soon after he had captured Jerusalem, had to fight two crucial defensive battles with the Philistines who had encamped in the Valley of Rephaim just outside Jerusalem (2 Sam 5:17–25). The Philistines were not his vassals at the time; in fact, he was their former vassal whom they were attempting to retain, but it is conceivable that these victories at the beginning of his reign in Jerusalem provided the crystallization point around which the tradition of the unsuccessful attack of rebellious vassals later developed. In favor of this view one should note that Psalm 76, a Zion song which describes Yahweh's defeat of the enemy at Jerusalem, does not picture them as rebellious vassals, though the incident seems to be cited as a warning to Israel's present vassals not to take Yahweh lightly. One should also observe that David's victory over the Philistines is portrayed as Yahweh's victory over the pagan gods (2 Sam 5:21).

The other possibility is to assume that the location of the battle at Jerusalem is a secondary development. As I noted earlier, the similar motif in the royal Psalms stresses Yahweh's attachment to Zion and implies he will protect his holy mountain, but it does not locate the scene of the battle at Jerusalem. This suggests that the Zion tradition may have originally told only of Yahweh's defeat of the rebel kings threatening Zion's rule, without specifying the location of that defeat. In this case, a later incident, possibly the remarkable deliverance of Jerusalem in Hezekiah's day, would have led to the motif of Yahweh's defeat of the vassal kings being further specified as a defeat of the enemy before the very gates of Jerusalem. The fact that Sennacherib was not Hezekiah's vassal is irrelevant, since according to the Israelite ideology he was Yahweh's vassal whether he knew it or not. Religious ideology often outlives the political realities it was in part created to justify.

I think the first development more probable, but either way one can posit an original setting for the fourth motif in the Davidic-Solomonic period. Thus there is no reason to attribute the formation of the Zion tradition to a largely unknown pre-Israelite cult or to relegate it to the weird apocalyptic fantasies of exilic or post-exilic prophecy. It is best understood as a product of Zion's most glorious days, the golden age of David and Solomon.

Chapter 22

Zion in the Theology of the Davidic-Solomonic Empire

I wish to thank Prince Mikasa, The Society for Old Testament Studies in Japan, and the Medical Tribune Japan for their gracious hospitality and for the kind invitation to participate in this symposium. I am particularly pleased with the chance to read a paper at this meeting because of the opportunity it affords me to make up what I have long felt to be a deficiency in my earlier study on the Zion tradition. My *JBL* article of 1973 was largely a negative critique of other scholars' attempts to find a suitable *Sitz im Leben* for the Zion tradition.[1] I basically accepted Rohland's analysis of that tradition, and, while I did give positive arguments for dating its formation to the period of the Davidic-Solomonic empire, I did not offer my own positive analysis of the tradition. It is to that task this paper is dedicated.

Ideally, the study of any aspect of the theology of the Davidic-Solomonic era should be limited to texts written in that period. Unfortunately, the nature of our sources for the glorification of Zion precludes such a direct approach. The prose sources from this era have been reedited at a later period, and it is often difficult in the key passages to separate the early material from the later editing. Moreover, the prose sources have relatively little to say on the topic. The far richer poetic sources, on the other hand, often lack the historical specificity that makes it possible to date the prose sources, and, as a consequence, there is even less agreement about the dating of the relevant poetic texts. Therefore, it is necessary to approach the problem obliquely. I will begin with a composite picture of the Zion tradition drawn from texts of varied date. Then, following an analysis of its main features, I will attempt to show which of these features can be dated to the Davidic-Solomonic period.

The Zion Tradition

The main features of the Zion tradition may be schematically represented in the following outline:

1. J. J. M. Roberts, "The Davidic Origin of the Zion Tradition," *JBL* 92 (1973) 329–44 [[here: pp. 313–330]].

I. Yahweh is the great king.
II. He chose Jerusalem for his dwelling place.
   A. Yahweh's choice has implications for Zion's topography.
      1. It is on a high mountain.
      2. It is watered by the river of paradise.
   B. Yahweh's choice has implications for Zion's security.
      1. Yahweh protects it from his enemies:
         a. The unruly powers of chaos, and
         b. The enemy kings.
      2. At Yahweh's rebuke:
         a. The enemy is undone,
         b. War is brought to an end,
         c. And plunder is taken.
      3. The nations acknowledge Yahweh's suzerainty.
   C. Yahweh's choice has implications for Zion's inhabitants.
      1. They share in the blessings of God's presence.
      2. But they must be fit to live in his presence.

Analysis

Yahweh Is the Great King

One of the two fundamental conceptions of the Zion tradition is that Yahweh is the great king. Ps 48:3 actually refers to God as מלך רב,[2] while Ps 46:5 designates him עליון, a title synonymous to מלך גדול in Ps 47:3. Both terms imply that Yahweh is king not just over Israel but over the other gods and their nations as well.[3] The development of this conception requires some discussion.

That Yahweh was praised as king in Israel prior to the monarchic period seems certain. Exod 15:18 explicitly says, "Yahweh will reign for ever and

2. Malamat, in his essay in this volume [[not reproduced here]], has suggested that this title refers to Solomon, the builder of Jerusalem, but, while I recognize the Ugaritic and Aramaic antecedents for מלך רב, I am not convinced that as a Hebrew title it is more archaic than מלך גדול or that it refers to the human king. Both Ugarit and the Aramean area were under strong cultural influence from Mesopotamia, so their usage could be due to the influence of the Akkadian title *šarru rabû*, attested as early as the Old Babylonian period for the king of Aleppo and widely used in the last half of the second millennium B.C. (M.-J. Seux, *Épithètes royales akkadiennes et sumériennes* [Paris, 1967] 298–300. מלך גדול is the Hebrew counterpart of מלך רב, but it can be very early. Psalm 48 is probably no earlier than the late eighth century, while Psalm 47 appears to be Solomonic. Moreover, the parallels in the Psalms point to מלך רב as a divine title.

3. This is explicit in Psalm 47, but it is also clear from Ps 97:9, where עליון is construed exactly as מלך גדול in Ps 47:3. See my article, "The Religio-Political Setting of Psalm 47," *BASOR* 221 (1976) 129–32 [[here: pp. 266–273]].

ever," and the work of Albright, Cross, Freedman, and David Robertson should have established beyond reasonable doubt the antiquity of the old poem that this verse concludes.[4] If one rejects their early dating, one must at least answer their arguments, which, as far as I am aware, no one has bothered to do.[5] Stig Norin's recent book, *Er spaltete das Meer*, is one of the very few European works I have seen which seriously grapples with the issue, and he concludes that the original Song of the Sea was contemporary with or at most a century younger than the event it portrays.[6] For Norin that original song included vv. 3, 6–7a, 9, 7b, 10–13, 15ab, 16a, and 17–18.[7] His reasons for the numerous deletions are in general no more convincing than his attempt to derive *leviathan* and *tanin* from the Egyptian *apophis* monster,[8] but Norin's acceptance of an early date for the kernel of the song, including v. 18, points up the force of the typological argument, at least with regard to this poem. I am also convinced of the premonarchic date of Num 23:21 and Deut 33:5, two other texts which refer to Yahweh as king, but here the evidence is less overwhelming. Robertson's purely linguistic criteria do not speak to the date of these texts.

The major argument against such an early designation of Yahweh as king has been the conception that kingship was foreign to Israelite experience and that a people would only choose its religious metaphors from the range of their own culture's fundamental structures of reality. Behind this argument lies the conceptual model of Israel as uncultured Bedouins from the desert for whom Canaanite culture and institutions were a brand new experience, but that model is outdated to say the least.[9] Whatever one's view of the conquest/settlement, nearly everyone today agrees that much, if not most, of later Israel was already

4. W. F. Albright, *Yahweh and the Gods of Canaan* (Garden City, 1968); F. M. Cross, Jr. and D. N. Freedman, *Studies in Ancient Yahwistic Poetry* (Baltimore, 1950); Cross, "The Song of Miriam," *JNES* 14 (1955) 237–50; idem, "Song of the Sea and Canaanite Myth," *JTC* 5 (1968) 1–25; idem, *Canaanite Myth and Hebrew Epic* (Cambridge, MA/London, 1973); Freedman, *Prolegomenon to G. B. Gray's The Forms of Hebrew Poetry* (New York, 1971); idem, "Divine Names and Titles in Early Hebrew Poetry," *Magnalia Dei: The Mighty Acts of God. Essays on the Bible and Archaeology in Memory of G. E. Wright* (eds. F. M. Cross et al.; Garden City, 1976) 55–102; D. A. Robertson, *Linguistic Evidence in Dating Early Hebrew Poetry* (SBLDS 3, 1972).

5. D. W. Goodwin's book, *Text Restoration Methods in Contemporary U.S.A. Biblical Scholarship* (Naples, 1969), is only an apparent exception. It was dated before it appeared and was thoroughly demolished in a devastating response by Cross and Freedman ("Some Observations on Early Hebrew," *Bib* 53 [1972] 413–20).

6. Norin, *Er spaltete das Meer* (CBOTS 9, 1977) 92–93.

7. Ibid., 103.

8. Ibid., 42–75.

9. See most recently N. K. Gottwald, *The Tribes of Yahweh* (Maryknoll, 1979). One does not have to accept all of Gottwald's views to see that he has established this point, a point which everyone should have already known, but which many ignored in their treatment of Israelite religion.

in Canaan when Moses' group arrived. Moreover, it is difficult to assign such a cultural blank even to the group that left Egypt with Moses. Canaanite culture and religion had already made great inroads in Egypt, particularly in the delta region where the Israelites were settled,[10] and one can hardly see how they could be unaffected by it. In Canaanite religion, as throughout the Near East, the gods were arranged in political hierarchies with a divine king. Thus Israel would have been familiar with such religious use of royal language from the cultural environment they shared with their neighbors, and it would be very strange if that environment left no imprint on Israel's own religious language.

Furthermore, the late development of the monarchy in Israel appears to reflect a conscious rejection of political structures that had been experienced as oppressive, and in the context of such a political decision the metaphor of Yahweh as king could function polemically against human kingship. If Deut 33:4–5 is premonarchical, it suggests that this conception of Israel's political structure as a confederation of tribes under Yahweh as king originated in the Mosaic covenant:

> Moses commanded for us torah
> A possession of the assembly of Jacob.
> Then (Yahweh) became king in Yeshurun
> When the leaders of the people gathered together,
> The assembly of the tribes of Israel.[11]

In other words, this community of newly liberated slaves took the metaphor of God as king, known from their environment, and introduced it into their political structure as part of their conscious rejection of human kingship.

The recognition of Yahweh as king, however, meant that two important theological problems would have to be faced. The first concerned Yahweh's relationship to the other members of the Canaanite pantheon. In Canaanite mythology Baal was the king of the gods, while El was the titular head of the pantheon. Where was Yahweh to fit into this preexisting pattern of divine rule? It appears that Israel identified Yahweh and El without any serious difficulty, but Baal presented more of a problem. The course eventually chosen was simply to replace Baal with Yahweh. One can already see the process at work in Exodus 15, where the poet uses the pattern of the Baal myth in structuring his poem.[12] It is more blatant in Psalm 29, where an original hymn to Baal has

10. R. de Vaux, *The Early History of Israel* (Philadelphia, 1978) 117–19; W. Helck, *Die Beziehungen Ägyptens zu Vorderasien im 3. und 2. Jahrtausend v. Chr.* (2d ed.; Wiesbaden, 1971) 446–73.

11. Following P. D. Miller's translation (*The Divine Warrior in Early Israel* [Cambridge, 1973] 82).

12. Cross, *Canaanite Myth and Hebrew Epic*, 112–44.

been adapted by the simple expedient of replacing the name Baal with the name Yahweh.[13] The process eventually results in Yahweh despoiling Baal of all his mythology that was compatible with Israel's God.

The same problem was presented in a slightly different form by those members of the pantheon who were also national gods of the rival neighboring states. To some extent Yahweh's struggle with Baal was an in-house quarrel. In the process of replacing Baal, Yahweh was identified with him often enough to create religious confusion. Their conflict was basically a religious conflict, not just the ideological reflection of political conflict, though that was also involved. Yahweh's position vis-à-vis the national gods of her neighbors, however, was a different matter. Here there was no question of identification or replacement. Here the conflict was to a large extent the reflex of political conflict. How then was Yahweh's relationship to these deities to be understood?

Deut 32:8 presents an early attempt to resolve this question:

> When Elyon allotted the nations as an inheritance,
> When he parceled out the sons of men,
> He established the boundaries of the peoples
> According to the number of the sons of El.
> Yahweh's portion is his people,
> Jacob his allotted inheritance.[14]

According to his text the national gods have a legitimate function within their own assigned territory, similar to Yahweh's function within Israel. Jephthah enunciated this point of view when he asked the king of Moab,[15] "Do you not take possession of that which Chemosh your god gives you as a possession? All that Yahweh our God has given us as a possession we will take in possession" (Judg 11:24). This legitimate sphere of hegemony was assigned to the national gods by a higher deity, however, Elyon, the Most High. One must ask whether the poet intended to distinguish between him and Yahweh. Eissfeldt thought that he did.[16] It is just possible that at one point in Israel's theological reflection Yahweh, though king, was assigned a subservient position vis-à-vis Elyon, much as Baal, though king, was ranked under El. I am not convinced, however. The identification of El, Elyon, and Yahweh took place very early,

13. Ibid., 152, and earlier bibliography cited there. More recently, A. Fitzgerald, "A Note on Psalm 29," *BASOR* 215 (1974) 61–63.

14. For the discussion of the text and date of this passage, see my earlier study, *JBL* 92 (1973) 339–40 [[here: pp. 324–325]], nn. 69–72.

15. The text has "king of the Ammonites," but it is questionable whether Jephthah would have characterized the Moabite god as the god of the Ammonite king, *contra* Boling (*Judges* [AB 6A, 1975] 201–4). The compositional history of this piece is rather complicated, however, and the last word has certainly not been written.

16. "El and Yahweh," *JSS* 1 (1956) 29–30 = *Kleine Schriften* 3 (Tübingen, 1966) 390.

and I think the poet is stressing rather Israel's special privilege.[17] The other nations were parceled out to various gods, but the suzerain himself chose to keep Israel and rule her directly.

The same motif is picked up in Psalm 82 and given a new twist.[18] In this text from the Elohistic Psalter, God stands in the council of El giving judgment against the gods. He accuses them of judging unjustly, of showing partiality to the wicked, of failing to acknowledge his order to vindicate the poor and orphan, the needy and oppressed. As a result the foundations of the earth were endangered. Therefore, despite the fact that the gods were divine, the sons of Elyon, nonetheless they are condemned to die like mere mortals. The text then ends with a prayer to God to rise and execute this judgment. The closest extrabiblical parallel to this text is the Assyrian text that tells of Marduk's trial before Ashur, a text that von Soden has convincingly interpreted as a propaganda piece to justify Sennacherib's sack of Babylon.[19] Psalm 82 may be interpreted along similar lines. Though the national gods had once been assigned the task of ruling their respective nations, they had botched the job, and now Yahweh was to remove them and rule their nations directly. Such a text can best be understood as an oracle justifying and encouraging David's imperial wars.

Yahweh's status as king undoubtedly took on new significance as a result of David's conquests. They demonstrated Yahweh's kingship in the same way that Ishtar's position in the pantheon was established by Sargon's conquests, in the same way that the ascendancy of Marduk was correlated with the political ascendancy of Babylon, and in the same way that Ashur's supremacy was demonstrated by the success of Assyrian arms.[20] Moreover, they established Yahweh as the great king. He was no longer just the king of Israel; he was now suzerain over the whole earth with vassal states who actually acknowledged his suzerainty. This situation is reflected in Psalm 47,[21] and it is the necessary background for Ps 2:1–3:

> Why do the nations rage
> And the peoples vainly scheme?
> Kings of the earth plot together

17. El and Elyon (Num 24:16) and Yahweh and El (Num 23:8) are equated in the Balaam oracles, and Yahweh and Elyon are identified in Ps 47:3 (cf. *BASOR* 221 [1976] 129–32 [[here: pp. 266–273]]; *JBL* 92 [1973] 340 [[p. 325]], n. 72).

18. See *JBL* 92 (1973) 340–42 [[here: pp. 325–327]]. I agree with most of the conclusions of H.-W. Jüngling, *Der Tod der Götter* (Stuttgarter Bibelstudien 38, 1968), but we part company on the date and *Sitz im Leben* of Psalm 82.

19. W. von Soden, "Gibt es ein Zeugnis, dass die Babylonier an Marduks Wiederauferstehung glaubten?" *ZA* NS 16–17 (1952–55) 130–66; "Ein neues Bruchstück des assyrischen Kommentars zum Marduk-Ordal," *ZA* NS 18–19 (1957–59) 224–34.

20. *JBL* 92 (1973) 341 [[here: p. 326]].

21. *BASOR* 221 (1976) 129–32 [[here: pp. 266–273]].

And rulers take council together
Against Yahweh and against his anointed (saying):
"Let us break his bonds.
Let us cast off his yoke ropes."
. . .

This is the speech of rebellious vassals, and the necessary conceptual background for such speech is an ideology of Yahweh's suzerainty. In the ancient Near East such ideologies were normally rooted in political realities, if not of the present, then of some more favored time in the past. They were seldom spun out of whole cloth or simply borrowed from another culture without reference to the political realities in the target culture.

The second theological problem inherent in the conception of Yahweh as king arose with the institution of human kingship. How is the human king related to the divine suzerain? Once Israel overcame her earlier reluctance to accept a human monarch, she settled the problem along the same lines followed in Assyria and Babylon. The real king was the deity; the human king was just his representative or regent, elected by the deity to carry out his earthly tasks.[22] One even reads of the gods making an oath to the king.[23] The tradition of Yahweh's choice of David and his house, therefore, is not completely unparalleled, although one can hardly cite a parallel where such a tradition has had the same impact on later developments as the covenant with David did in later Israelite history.

Yahweh Chose Jerusalem for His Dwelling Place

The second fundamental conception of the Zion tradition is that Yahweh chose Jerusalem for his dwelling place. This is explicitly stated in Ps 78:68 and 132:13, but it is implicit in the Zion songs' affirmations that Zion is God's city (Pss 46:5; 48:2–3, 8–9; 87:2), that he resides within her (Pss 46:6; 48:4), and that his covert or lair is within her (Ps 76:3). This last reference could refer to the tent sanctuary or temple in Jerusalem, though that is not certain. Israelite religious poetry moves easily back and forth between a specific reference to

22. In the Assyrian enthronement ritual the kingship of Ashur is significantly proclaimed prior to the crowning of the human king (K. F. Müller, *Das assyrische Ritual* 1 [MVAG 41/3, 1937] 8–9, line 29). The Babylonian view is well reflected in the prologue to the Code of Hammurabi, i 1–52, vv. 14–24.

23. Thus Marduk claims to have made a covenant with the future king of Babylon who will destroy Elam (*anākuma . . . ittišu salmāku*) in the Marduk prophecy text (R. Borger, "Gott Marduk und Gott-König Šulgi als Propheten," *BO* 28 [1971] 11, 17, iii 21′–22′). Note also K2401 ii 10′–32′, which records an oracle of Ashur promising salvation to Esarhaddon, and which refers to the tablet containing the oracle as "the sworn tablet of Ashur" (*ṭup-pi a-de-e an-ni-u šá* ^{d}*Aš-šur*, S. A. Strong, "On Some Oracles to Esarhaddon and Ashurbanipal," *Beiträge zur Assyriologie* 2 [1894] 639, obv. ii 27; the complete text is translated in H. B. Huffmon's forthcoming volume on prophecy.).

the temple and a more general reference to the city as a whole. Thus Yahweh founds his sanctuary like the earth and builds it like the heavens (Ps 78:69), but he also founds Zion (Pss 48:9; 87:1, 5) and builds Jerusalem (Ps 102:17; cf. Pss 51:20; 147:2).

Topography

From these two fundamental conceptions of the Zion tradition several subsidiary motifs follow. Since Zion was the abode of Yahweh, the divine king, any of the language used to describe the abode of the comparable Canaanite deities whom Yahweh had despoiled could now be transferred to Zion.

The High Mountain

West Semitic deities were generally conceived of as having their abode upon high mountains, and Yahweh appears to have been no exception. His original mountain abode seems to have been Mt. Sinai/Horeb, the mountain of God (Exod 3:1; 18:5; 24:13; Num 10:33) which he left (Deut 33:2; Judg 5:4; Hab 3:3) to take up his abode in Canaan (Exod 15:17; Ps 78:54). At first it would appear that the central hill country as a whole was thought of as his holy mountain (Ps 78:54),[24] but with David's transfer of the ark to Jerusalem, Mt. Zion became Yahweh's chosen mountain (Ps 78:68–69). Since Yahweh had replaced Baal as king of the gods, it was possible to identify Mt. Zion with Baal's famous Mt. Zaphon (Ps 48:3).[25] Even when this precise identification is not made, however, Mt. Zion is constantly thought of as a high mountain appropriate for the dwelling of the divine king.[26]

At this point it is worth noting that there is no necessary contrast, at least in the early material, between the deity residing in heaven and the deity residing on his mountain.[27] By definition the top of the sacred mountain reached into heaven, as is clear from Isa 14:13–14, where "to sit enthroned on the mount of assembly, on the heights of Zaphon" is equivalent with scaling heaven, putting one's throne above the stars of El, and rising above the clouds. One should also observe that the traditions about Yahweh's giving the law at Mt. Sinai sometimes describe him as speaking from heaven, sometimes as speaking from the mountain without any apparent distinction in meaning (Exod 19:18–

24. D. N. Freedman, however, would take this as a reference to the wilderness mountain sanctuary ("Early Israelite History in the Light of Early Israelite Poetry," *Unity and Diversity* [eds. H. Goedicke and J. J. M. Roberts; Baltimore/London, 1975] 8–9).

25. For the rendering of צפון as a proper name for a mountain, see the discussion in *JBL* 92 (1973) 334–35 [[here: pp. 318–321]] and Roberts, "*Ṣāpôn* in Job 26, 7," *Bib* 56 (1975) 554–57.

26. Pss 2:6; 68:17; 87:1; 99:9; Isa 2:2; 27:13; 66:20; Ezek 40:2; Zech 14:10; etc.

27. See the fine discussion by Mettinger in his article in this volume [[not reproduced here]].

19; 20:22). The deuteronomistic theologians introduced a distinction with their name theology, but that distinction seems relatively late. One should not read the deuteronomistic contrast into every poetic passage where Yahweh is said to have done something from heaven, particularly if the same piece speaks of God as living in Zion or acting from Zion.

The River

The standard epithet for El's abode in the Ugaritic texts is *mbk nhrm qrb apq thmtm*, "at the sources of the two rivers midst the streams of the two seas."[28] Since Yahweh was identified with El, it is not surprising that the watery nature of his abode also makes its imprint on the Zion tradition. Ps 46:3 speaks of a river whose streams make glad the city of God. This motif plays a major role in late prophetic descriptions of the new Jerusalem (Ezek 47:1–12; Joel 4:18; Zech 14:8), and it also occurs in a rather peculiar form in Isaiah 33, a text that may be Isaianic.[29] In the context of his description of a redeemed Jerusalem the prophet says in vv. 21–23a:

> But there Yahweh will be majestic,
> For us a reservoir[30] of rivers,
> Of streams broad and wide.
> No galley with oars will travel it.
> No mighty ship will cross it.
> For Yahweh is our judge,
> Yahweh is our lawgiver,
> Yahweh is our king,
> He will save us.
> Its rigging will hang loose;
> They cannot hold the mast in place,
> They cannot spread the sail.

The references in both Psalm 46 and Isaiah 33 are tantalizing because it is not quite clear syntactically what Yahweh's relation to this river or reservoir of rivers is. Is Yahweh himself the stream? It is evident from Jer 2:13 and 17:12–13 that Yahweh could be described metaphorically as a spring of living waters. Whether the original motif had already been so transformed in Psalm 46, it is

---

28. *CTA* 2 iii 4; 3 E v 14–15; 4 iv 21–22; 5 vi 2*–1*; 6 i 33–34; 17 vi 47–48; cf. the only slightly variant form found in *Ugaritica* 5 (1968) no. 7 (RS 24.244) 3: *mbk nhrm. bʿdt. thmtm*, "at the sources of the two rivers, at the gathering of the two seas."

29. Most recent studies date the piece to the postexilic period, but I hope to show in a forthcoming article that the Isaianic attribution given by many of the older scholars (e.g., S. R. Driver, *An Introduction to the Literature of the Old Testament* [New York, 1912] 225) is more credible.

30. Reading *miqwē-m* with W. H. Irwin, *Isaiah 28–33: Translation with Philological Notes* (BibOr 30, 1977) 158–59.

at least clear in the later texts that the source of the stream is found in the very presence of God. One may be dealing with a very early transformation of a geographical feature into a religious metaphor about the source of life.

One other feature about El's abode seems to be reflected in Ezekiel's description of Tyre's abode in the garden of God. Tyre is described as "on the holy mountain of God, in the midst of the stones of fire" (Ezek 28:14–16). The precise meaning of the term "stones of fire" is still debated, but some have seen its background in the incident in the Baal epic where a fire burns in Baal's new palace to melt down the silver and gold needed for the building. Nothing appears to be made of this motif in the Zion songs, but one wonders whether Isaiah's references to Yahweh, "who has a fire in Zion and a furnace in Jerusalem" (31:9), who is "a devouring fire, a perpetual burning" (33:14), and who threatens to purify Jerusalem by smelting (1:25), may not have their background in such a mythological setting.[31]

Security

Another consequence of Yahweh's living in Jerusalem is the absolute security his presence provides. With Yahweh in it, the city cannot be shaken (Ps 46:7). He is its stronghold (Pss 46:8; 48:4), and he is more than a match for any hostile power.

The Enemy

These hostile powers are sometimes described under the mythological imagery of the unruly sea (Ps 46:2–4), sometimes more historically as hostile kings or nations (Pss 46:7; 48:5–7; 76:6–8), and sometimes the two merge into one (Isa 17:12–14). The mythological imagery of the unruly sea was undoubtedly borrowed from the Canaanite myth of Baal's struggle with Prince Yamm, but there has been no consensus on the source of the imagery for the hostile nations.[32] In my earlier study I rejected any possibility of finding its antecedents in the Baal myth and argued for its derivation from some historical incident early in the history of the united monarchy.[33] Though I still think historical events helped shape the motif, I am now convinced that there are also mythological antecedents. *CTA* 4 vii 30–37 seems to refer to an attempt to storm Baal's mountain after he has established his palace there, an attempt, one should note, that Baal turns back by the thunder of his voice:

> Baal gives forth his holy voice
> Baal discharges the utterance of his lips

31. Other passages, however, associate Yahweh's fire with storm imagery (29:6; 30:27–30).

32. *JBL* 92 (1973) 337–39 [[here: pp. 321–324]].

33. Ibid., 337–39 [[here: pp. 321–324]], 343–44 [[here: pp. 328–330]].

His holy voice convulses the earth, . . . the mountains quake,
  A-tremble are . . .
East and west, earth's high places reel,
Baal's enemies take to the woods,
Hadd's foes to the sides of the mountain.[34]

The gory picture of Anat's slaughter of the people of the seashore and of the sunrise may refer to the same enemies (*CTA* 3 B ii 3–39). *CTA* 3 D iii 43–iv 47 may even contain a reference to a successful assault against Baal's mountain that temporarily drove Baal from Zaphon.

Perhaps one should also discuss Ps 48:8 under this rubric. After describing the panic of the enemy kings the psalmist adds, "With an east wind you smashed the ships of Tarshish." In the context of an attack on Jerusalem this is a rather strange statement. Nevertheless, the "ships of Tarshish" reappear as a metaphor for human arrogance in Isaiah's magnificent portrayal of Yahweh's solitary exaltation (2:16), a portrayal with strong mythological overtones. One should also note the image of the stately ship in Isa 33:21, where it clearly stands for powers hostile to Yahweh's well-watered Jerusalem. Moreover, the ship there is also disabled, if not smashed, by the wreckage of its tackle. The continuity of the metaphor and the difficulty of explaining it from Israelite historical experience suggests that it too may be derived from Canaanite tradition, perhaps a seaborne assault on Baal's abode. Where, after all, did the "men of the seashore" in the Baal epic come from?

Yahweh's Rebuke

As in the Baal epic, Yahweh turns back these hostile forces by his thunderous rebuke (Pss 46:7; 76:7, 9).[35] But, from where does Yahweh thunder? The verse transmitted in both Amos 1:2 and Joel 4:16 has Yahweh roar from Zion, but Ps 76:9 says he makes his judgment heard from heaven. Nonetheless, there is probably no difference intended in Psalm 76, since that Psalm has already described Yahweh as having his lair in Zion. The temple mount and heaven are probably also equivalent in Psalm 18, where Yahweh utters his voice from "his temple" (v. 7), "in heaven" (v. 14), and sends help from "the heights" (v. 17)—the same term that Ps 78:69 uses to describe how Yahweh built his sanctuary and that Isa 33:5 parallels with Zion. Ps 48:6 suggests that the enemy is turned back by visual phenomena,[36] and this is followed by the verse that tells of the

34. Following Ginsberg's translation, *ANET* (2d ed. Princeton, 1955) 135.

35. Cf. Ps 2:4–5; Isa 17:13; 29:6; 31:4–5; 33:3.

36. Ps 48:6 does not specify what "they saw," but its structural correspondence to Yahweh's "rebuke" in the parallel passages suggests the visual counterpart to Yahweh's "roar." His "roar" appears to be drawn from thunderstorm imagery, so the visual phenomena implied

east wind wrecking the ships of Tarshish. All these clues taken together suggest that the original phenomenon behind the mythological pattern in its original setting was the experience of a sudden thunderstorm sweeping down over the Mediterranean from the heights of the Jebel Aqra. This was given a mythological transformation in the Baal epic, and it received a further historical transformation when it was taken up in Israel and applied to Jerusalem.

The defeat of Yahweh's enemies has several results. In the first place the weapons of war are shattered and peace is established in the earth (Pss 46:10; 76:4, 9). There may be Canaanite antecedents for this theme in Baal's command to Anat to banish war from the earth, if the relevant Ugaritic lines have been correctly understood (*CTA* 3 C iii 10–15; D iv 51–54, 71–75). Another result of Yahweh's victory is the collection of a vast amount of booty. This may be referred to in the very difficult lines of Ps 76:5–6,[37] and it is very clear in some of the later texts (Isa 33:4, 23; Ezek 39:9–10; Zech 14:14). Finally, the nations must acknowledge Yahweh's sovereignty and honor him with praise and tribute. Ps 76:11–13 gives much fuller expression to this motif than Psalms 46 and 48, which are satisfied with vague statements about Yahweh's exaltation among the nations.[38] The motif finds its most elaborate expression in Zech 14:16–19.

Implications for Zion's Inhabitants

The fact that Yahweh lives in Zion has at least three implications for the human inhabitants of Jerusalem. These implications are not spelled out in the Songs of Zion, but they do appear in other texts that are heavily dependent on the Zion tradition. In the first place, only those who meet God's righteous standards can live in his presence (Isa 33:13–16; Ps 24:3–4). One of the duties of God's regent, the human king, was "to cut off the doers of iniquity from the city of Yahweh" (Ps 101:8). In the second place, the inhabitants, and especially the king, have the duty of building God's city. The texts normally speak of God doing the building or they express it in the passive, but it is clear from Hag 1:2–11 that God expected help from his human agents. Ps 78:69 says that

---

should also be understood from that same background: lightning, etc. This is strongly suggested by Ps 50:2, "From Zion, the perfection of beauty, Yahweh shines forth. Our God comes and will not be silent; a fire devours before him, and around him a tempest rages." Isa 29:6 also portrays Yahweh's sudden intervention in the imagery of the thunderstorm with both the loud thunder, קול גדול, and the devouring fire, להב אש אוכלה.

37. The verb אשתוללו points in that direction.

38. I read v. 11 as follows:

כי חמת אדם תודך
שארית חמת תחגך

Surely the fortress (?) of Edom will praise you.
The remnant of Hamath will celebrate your festival.

God built his sanctuary like the heavens, but Solomon was the human agent in that construction, and he claims as much in 1 Kgs 8:13, "I have indeed built a princely house for you, a place for you to dwell forever."[39] Finally, those inhabitants who are fit to live with God will rejoice in the security and abundant life that Yahweh's presence brings.[40]

Date

It should be clear from the preceding analysis of the Zion tradition that all that was required for its crystallization was the belief that Yahweh, the suzerain, had chosen to make his dwelling in Zion. Once that step had been taken, the glorification of Zion with motifs drawn from Canaanite mythology about the abode of the great gods would follow as a matter of course. Historical events might shape the use of these motifs, but the historical events themselves could also be shaped by the pattern of the myth. Given this situation, what can one say about the historical development of the tradition?

First, its crystallization point must still be sought in the Davidic-Solomonic era. Most of my earlier arguments against the wholesale adoption of a prepackaged Jebusite tradition remain valid, but the beginning of the tradition must have followed shortly on David's movement of the ark to Jerusalem. That act presupposes oracular approval. One did not set up sanctuaries in antiquity without the prior approval of the deity to be housed in the sanctuary, and Jerusalem had no ancient Yahwistic tradition to commend it. Whether that move was originally conceived of as a permanent move, it is clear that David's desire to build a temple implied the establishment of Yahweh's permanent residence in Jerusalem, and that step, which marked a major departure from Israel's past religious practice, certainly required divine validation. In the Israelite tradition that validation came in the form of an oracle that coordinated Yahweh's choice of David with his choice of Jerusalem (2 Sam 7; Pss 78:68; 132:10–18). Whatever the precise date at which these texts were written, there is no reason to doubt the original linkage of the choice of David and the choice of Jerusalem. This pattern is also found outside Israel, in the prologue to the Code of Hammurabi, for instance, where the divine election of Hammurabi and his capital city Babylon are coordinated. But, if the two were originally linked, the tradition of Yahweh's election of Jerusalem cannot postdate David's reign, because the tradition of Yahweh's election of David certainly

39. Thus Micah is actually criticizing the Zion tradition from within that tradition when he attacks all of Jerusalem's leaders for exercising their legitimate functions in the wrong way and includes the line "who build Zion with blood and Jerusalem with wrongdoing" (3:10).

40. Ps 48:12–14; 132:13–18; 133:3; 147:13; Isa 33:17–24.

comes from David's own time. It was a necessary part of his struggle for legitimation in view of his suspiciously irregular succession to the throne, and it is paralleled by numerous examples from Mesopotamia, where a king often refers to his divine election. Solomon no doubt cultivated David's religious propaganda for his own purposes, but there is no compelling reason to make him the creator of these traditions. I doubt that there are many examples, if any, where one can show that a Near Eastern king created a tradition of divine election for his predecessor on the throne.

But, if it is clear that the necessary crystallization point for the development of the Zion tradition existed from the time of David's later years, it is also clear that many of the motifs in its later elaboration are also attested as early as Solomon's reign. Psalm 68 would appear to be from that period. Its mention of the temple in v. 30 dates it after Solomon's construction of that edifice, but other indications in the text make it difficult to see a *terminus ad quem* later than Solomon. The poem contains a number of archaic linguistic features such as the use of זו or זה as a relative (vv. 9, 29; cf. Exod 15:17). Many of its formulas have their closest parallels in the old poetry: v. 2 is parallel to the old formula in Num 10:35, vv. 8–10 have their closest parallel in Judg 5:4–5, and vv. 34–35, which speak of God as riding in the heavens, are closely paralleled in Deut 33:26. Psalm 68 also has many more contacts with the Baal myth than one might expect in a later work. Verses 21b–24 are very difficult to interpret, but they seem to speak of Yahweh's power over Mot, his smiting of his enemies, his conquest of Yamm, and his wading in the gore of his slain foes:

> From Yahweh the lord is the escape from death.
> Surely God smote the head of his enemies,
> He split[41] the crown of him who walked in sin.
> The Lord said, "I will repulse the Serpent,[42]
> I will muzzle the depths of the Sea."
> So that your foot plunged in blood,
> The tongue of your dogs had their share of the enemy.[43]

One should note, also, that this passage is followed by a victory processional of the divine king. The description of that cultic procession in vv. 25–28, with its mention of the princes of Zebulon and Naptali as well as Benjamin and Judah, would also suggest a period before the northern tribes split off from the south. The religious and political rivalry between Jerusalem and the Aramean territory, expressed in the motif of Mt. Bashan's jealousy toward Mt. Zion,

41. Reading the verb שער, "to split," following Dahood, *The Psalms* 2 (AB 17, 1968) 144.

42. Attaching the *mem* to the end of אדני as an enclitic with Dahood, *The Psalms* 2, 145, but reading אשיב as the hiphil of שוב.

43. Following Dahood, *The Psalms* 2, 145–46.

would also be easier to explain against the background of David's Aramean conquests than at any later period. The parallel usage of ישב and שכן to describe the nature of Yahweh's abiding on his mountain is the same as the usage found in the old poetic fragment from the book of Yashar embedded in Solomon's prayer of dedication of the temple (1 Kgs 8:12–13). It is clearly a pre-deuteronomistic usage and also antedates the later technical distinction between ישב and שכן exploited by the P tradition.[44]

Of course, all these bits and pieces help in dating the Psalm only if the Psalm is, in fact, a literary unit. If Albright's thesis that Psalm 68 is simply a series of incipits were correct,[45] one could not argue from material in one verse of the Psalm for the date of any other verse. Albright's view is unconvincing, however. Although I do not understand much of the Psalm and certainly cannot at this point reconstruct an orderly whole with a nice progression of thought throughout the Psalm, there are large blocks where there are more logical connections than one would expect in a random collection of incipits. Verses 16–17, even taken by themselves, are long for an incipit, but it is possible that v. 15 is connected (Ṣalmon could be the name for the Jebel Druze) and vv. 18–19, with the triumphant entrance into the sanctuary, perhaps even the transfer of the sanctuary from Sinai to Jerusalem, could also be a continuation of the same thought. Verse 19c, "In the presence of God no rebel can dwell," picks up the same theme as v. 7. Verses 22–24 also appear to be connected and may lead into the description of the processional in vv. 25–28. Verses 29–33 appear to be connected by the theme of the tribute of the foreign nations. One should also note that it is not easy to follow the logical progression in Judges 5 or in long Mesopotamian hymns.

If one accepts this dating for Psalm 68, one already has the motif of Yahweh choosing Mount Zion as the high mountain on which he desires to dwell and where his temple in Jerusalem is to stand (vv. 16–17, 30). The poem also tells of his victory over the mythological powers as well as over the enemy kings, and it mentions Yahweh's thunder against his foes, as well as the plunder which results from the flight of the enemy. Finally, it mentions the tribute of the nations and Yahweh's exaltation in the world.

The oldest of the Zion songs, Psalm 76, may also date this early. It coordinates Judah and Israel in a way compatible with a date in the united monarchy, in contrast with the Judean orientation of Psalm 48, and it breathes the same air of imperialism that one finds in Psalms 47, 68, and 82. There is a certain resemblance to Psalm 2, but one should note that Psalm 76 does not characterize

44. See the discussion of these terms in Cross, *Canaanite Myth and Hebrew Epic*, 97, n. 24.

45. W. F. Albright, "A Catalogue of Early Hebrew Lyric Poems (Psalm LXVIII)," *HUCA* 23 (1950–51) 1–39.

the enemy kings as Yahweh's vassals until after the battle. In effect, it is his victory which establishes his rule as in Psalm 68. In both Psalms 68 and 76 there seem to be reflexes of David's imperial wars, suggesting that the tradition is shaped by both the mythological pattern and the actual course of history. I take Ps 76:4 to reflect David's defeat of the Philistines in the vicinity of Jerusalem, and vv. 10–13 I see as rooted in his imperial wars against Aram and Edom.

The Zion tradition is certainly older than Isaiah, whose message is permeated by it. In his inaugural vision he saw Yahweh as the king sitting enthroned upon a high and lofty throne in the temple (Isa 6:1). For him Yahweh dwelt on Mount Zion (8:18; 12:6), and his conception of Yahweh's plan to save Jerusalem through purging (1:25), when it is spelled out in detail, involves an adaptation of the assault of the nations motif (10:16–17; 14:24–25; 17:12–14; 29:1–8; 31:8–9; 33:1–24). Isaiah appears to innovate in making Yahweh fight against Jerusalem before saving it (29:1–4)—an innovation that is further developed in Zechariah 12 and 14—but otherwise he appears to stay very much within the contours of the tradition. There are good reasons for connecting both Isaiah 33 and Psalm 48, which have striking contacts with each other, with the Assyrian crisis of Hezekiah's time, and specifically with Sennacherib's failure to take Jerusalem. This must have given added weight to the Zion tradition, but since both Psalm 48 and Isaiah 33 treat the freshly experienced deliverance (Psalm 48) or the soon-to-be-expected deliverance (Isaiah 33) as a new realization or confirmation of an old tradition—"As we had heard, so now we have seen" (Ps 48:9; cf. Isa 33:3–5)—it is clear that that event did not create the tradition. The Zion tradition, in fact, probably shaped Israel's perception of that event and no doubt heightened its miraculous quality.

Conclusion

The fundamental point necessary for the formation of the Zion tradition was the belief that Yahweh had chosen Jerusalem as his permanent abode. That dogma could not date much later than David's decision to move the ark to Jerusalem, and certainly not later than the decision to build the temple there. Once this dogma was accepted, it brought in its wake the glorification of Jerusalem, with mythological traditions associated with the abode of those gods with whom Yahweh was identified or whom he had displaced. Some of these traditions had points of contact with Israel's historical experience in the period of David's imperial wars, and the precise form the Zion tradition took was probably due to the mutual influence of myth and history. Certainly the political ascendancy of Jerusalem in the imperial period had a great deal to do with both the imperial conception of Yahweh's suzerainty and the glorification of his capital. The Zion tradition was basically fixed by the end of this period. It was reinforced by Jerusalem's deliverance from Sennacherib, though the interpretation of that event was largely colored by the preexisting Zion tradition; however, about this time the first major innovations in the tradition were introduced by Isaiah and Micah. Working from within the tradition, they introduced the notion of Yahweh's fighting against Zion, in order through judgment to realize the ideals embodied in the tradition.

Chapter 23

The Divine King and the Human Community in Isaiah's Vision of the Future

Isaiah's inaugural vision of the divine king seated on his exalted throne dominates the prophet's conception of the future as indeed it dominates all his theology.[1] In the words of the refrain to his powerful vision of Yahweh's coming day of judgment, "Yahweh alone will be exalted in that day."[2] Judgment, deliverance, and future bliss are all focused in the divine initiative. Yahweh may use human agents as his tools for working out the future, but Isaiah leaves no doubt that the plan and its execution are Yahweh's plan and Yahweh's work. Within this impressively theocentric theology, therefore, it may be profitable to look at the role of the human community. What, if anything, remains as human responsibilities?

Judgment

Yahweh's judgment of his people is provoked by their rebellion. The people as a whole,[3] their political and religious leaders,[4] including even the royal house[5]—though Isaiah seems curiously reticent to attack the Davidic kings—and the women of means,[6] are all forced to bear the blame for God's

Author's note: It is a pleasure to contribute this study in honor of a scholar [[George Mendenhall]] whose creative treatment of the Old Testament has remained a stimulating influence on me since I first read his *Law and Covenant* almost twenty years ago.

1. Isa 6:1. The attempts by Jacob Milgrom (*VT* 14 [1964] 164–82) and others to treat this chapter as a later commissioning during Isaiah's prophetic career is unconvincing. It does show close similarities to the Micaiah ben Imla episode in 1 Kings 22, but it also has certain features in common with the call narratives that are absent from 1 Kings 22. The fiery cleansing of Isaiah's sins, centered on his lips, is surely to be understood as enabling him to take up the prophetic task, and as such it is analogous, though not identical, to the divine actions in Jer 1:9 and Ezek 2:8–3:3. The literary placement of Isaiah 6 is no argument against this interpretation, as the placement of Amos's call narrative demonstrates (Amos 7:10–16). Moreover, the evidence of Isa 1:5–9 shows that Isaiah's oracles are *not* arranged in chronological order.
2. Isa 2:11, 17.
3. Isa 1:3–4.
4. Isa 1:10, 23; 2:12–15.
5. Isa 7:13.
6. Isa 3:16–4:1; 32:9–14.

impending judgment. As an agent of judgment Yahweh had used Aram,[7] the Philistines,[8] Ephraim and Manasseh against themselves and both against Judah,[9] and he threatened to use Assyria as his staff to punish both Israel and Judah.[10] But Assyria's role was to be a limited one, and any transgression of those limits, any attempt to elevate themselves and rival Yahweh, would be crushed by God.[11] Yahweh alone will be exalted.

Deliverance

While God's plan to judge his people had its human agents, it is far more difficult to find any human agents for Yahweh's deliverance for the remnant, symbolized in his deliverance of the city of Jerusalem. In Isaiah's early oracles from the period of the Syro-Ephraimitic war it is true that Assyria is mentioned at least once and perhaps several times as the agent that would remove this northern threat,[12] but other passages which may date to this period simply speak of Yahweh frustrating the plan of Judah's enemies without naming any historical agent for Yahweh's deliverance.[13] The ultimate source of this deliverance is far more important to Isaiah than its proximate source, and the demand he places on his hearers is for faith in God's promises, not for confidence in his analysis of the external political situation.[14]

In his later prophecies from the period of the Assyrian crisis there is no attempt to point to the human agent of Judah's deliverance.[15] In fact, the prophet quite explicitly denies that God will use any human agent: "Assyria shall fall by a sword, not of man; and a sword, not of man, shall devour him."[16] The

---

7. Isa 9:11.

8. Isa 9:11.

9. Isa 9:20.

10. Isa 10:5ff.; cf. 5:26–29.

11. Isa 10:12, 15ff. I remain unconvinced by Hermann Barth's (*Die Jesaja-Worte in der Josiazeit* [WMANT 48; Neukirchen-Vluyn: Neukichener Verlag, 1977]) and R. E. Clements's (*Isaiah and the Deliverance of Jerusalem* [JSOTSup 13; Sheffield: JSOT, 1980] and *Isaiah 1–39* [New Century Bible Commentary; Grand Rapids: Eerdmans, 1980] 5–6) attempts to redate most of the oracles against Assyria to the Josianic period.

12. Isa 8:4. See also 7:18, 20.

13. Isa 7:7–9, 16; 8:9–10; 17:12–14.

14. Isa 7:9.

15. Some recent scholars have again defended an eighth century date for the references to the Elamites and the Medes in chapters 13, 21, and 22 (Seth Erlandsson, *The Burden of Babylon* [Coniectanea Biblica, OT Series 4; Lund: CWK Gleerup, 1970]; and the more limited and nuanced work of A. A. Macintosh, *Isaiah xxi: A Palimpsest* [Cambridge: Cambridge University, 1980]), but whatever one's response to their argument, it does not affect my point. The Medes and Elamites do not deliver Judah from Assyria in these passages if they are read in an eighth century context.

16. Isa 31:8.

deliverance is portrayed as pure miracle, as due to the direct intervention of Yahweh himself.[17]

In view of this emphasis, it is important to note the relatively secondary role the Davidic ruler plays in the *inauguration* of this era of salvation. Neither in Isaiah 9 nor 11 does the messianic king overthrow the foreign enemy. Rather, in both cases, he inherits and enhances the results of Yahweh's prior intervention. This is especially clear in 11:1 where the growth of the messianic shoot is immediately preceded by Yahweh's lopping off of the arrogant, overbearing forest of Jerusalem's enemies.[18] It is less clear in chapter 9, but one should note that Yahweh's smashing of the enemy power (9:3) precedes the prophet's comments on the rule of the Davidic monarch, and the whole section is concluded with the statement: "The zeal of Yahweh of hosts shall accomplish this."[19]

Nonetheless, this messianic figure is not totally passive. He judges, he reproves, he smites the earth, he slays the wicked—in short he exercises royal rule in justice and righteousness.[20] While he apparently does this in response to the prior deliverance of Yahweh, the king still plays an active role, and that forces one to ask about the role or task of the human community in the coming age of salvation.

Age of Salvation

While Jerusalem's deliverance may be attributed to the intervention of Yahweh alone and human participation in that deliverance be reduced to mere obedient faith in God's promise,[21] a more active role is assigned to the human community in the coming age of salvation. Isa 32:1–8 provides a good framework for the discussion of Isaiah's point of view:

See, a king will reign in righteousness,
And ministers will govern with justice,

---

17. Isa 10:16–17, 25–27, 33; 14:24–27; 29:6–8; 30:31–33; 31:4–9; 33:10–12.

18. Isa 10:32–34. The common critical insistence that Isa 11:1 begins a new oracle, and should therefore be read in antiseptic isolation from its present literary context, is a bit puzzling. Not only does the image of the hacked-down forest provide a meaningful setting for the image of new growth, but this decimated forest imagery appears elsewhere referring both to Assyria's downfall (10:17–19) and to Judah's restoration through and after judgment (29:17; 32:15–19).

19. Isa 9:6.

20. Isa 9:6; 11:3–4.

21. Isa 7:9; 30:15. I use the term "obedient faith" because Isaiah is speaking of a confidence in God that expresses itself by turning away from frantic attempts to achieve security by oppressive political and military planning, and concentrates instead on easing the oppression of the poor (Isa 28:12; see my note on this passage in *HTR* 73 [1980] 49–51).

Everyone of them will be like a refuge from the wind,
A shelter from the rainstorm,
Like streams of water in a desert,
Like the shade of a massive rock in a weary land.
Then the eyes of those who see will not be closed.
And the ears of those who hear will listen attentively,
The minds of the thoughtless will attain understanding,
And the tongues of the stammerers will speak fluently,
No longer will the villain be called noble,
Nor will "gentleman" be said of a knave.
For the villain speaks villainy,
And his mind plots treachery:
To act impiously,
And to advocate disloyalty against Yahweh.
To leave the craving of the hungry unsatisfied
And deprive the thirsty of drink.
As for the knave, his weapons are evil.
He devises wicked schemes
To destroy the poor with lies
Even when the plea of the needy is just.
But the noble plans noble actions,
And he is constant in noble deeds.[22]

Since many modern critics regard this passage as secondary, it is necessary to treat that question before one can use this text as a source for Isaiah's vision of the future. The arguments against Isaianic authorship are actually not very impressive. Wildberger, while admitting the weakness of the arguments, nonetheless rejects the passage on the basis that "for Isaiah the שׂרים would hardly have had a place next to the Davidide in such a vision of the future."[23] But this judgment flies in the face of the clearly Isaianic 1:26, where Yahweh, following his refining judgment on Zion, promises to restore her judges and counselors as at the beginning. Isaiah's vision of the future included a place for royal officials, and it is not surprising to find them mentioned here.[24] R. E. Clements argues that 32:1 does not foretell the advent of the king who rules justly, but simply describes him as a present figure,[25] but against him one must insist that

22. The translation is the author's, though heavily influenced by the RSV and the new JPS rendering.

23. Hans Wildberger, *Jesaja* (BKAT X; Neukirchen-Vluyn: Neukirchener Verlag, 1978) 1253.

24. Cf. Hans-Jürgen Hermisson, "Zukunftserwartung und Gegenwartskritik in der Verkündigung Jesajas," *EvT* 33 (1973) 67; J. Skinner, *Isaiah* (The Cambridge Bible for Schools and Colleges; Cambridge: University, 1925) 255; Bernh. Duhm, *Das Buch Jesaia* (HzAT; Göttingen: Vandenhoeck & Ruprecht, 1892) 210–11.

25. R. E. Clements, *Isaiah 1–39*, 259.

vv. 1–5 are all clearly construed in the future. Moreover, the oracle is placed in a context where it follows Yahweh's deliverance of Zion, just as 11:1 follows Yahweh's destruction of Zion's enemies.[26] The oracle may originally have been independent of its present context, but it had a context, and I see no reason to fault the ancient editor, who apparently understood the oracle to refer to the era of salvation after Yahweh will have destroyed Assyria.

Hermisson, who accepts 32:1–2 as genuine, rejects vv. 3–5, since these verses deal with the altered nature of humans or particular human types in the age of salvation. He cannot see any connection between a change in human nature and the coming kingdom.[27] Wildberger similarly claims that Isaiah envisioned a particular political-social action of Yahweh, not the creation of a new humanity.[28] Both of them miss the point. In his critique of his contemporaries Isaiah had blamed the leaders for misleading the people.[29] The political and religious leadership was largely responsible for Judah's blindness, deafness, and folly.[30] The promise is that when the leaders rule justly, these defects will fall aside. It is precisely the political-social establishment of just government which will lead to a transformation of society. This is not an individualistic vision of a transformed humanity, but a vision of transformed society!

If my argument for the authenticity of at least 32:1–5 is sound,[31] what kind of framework does this passage provide for exploring Isaiah's vision of the future king, his officers, and the populace as a whole?

King

The role the king plays in this passage's portrayal of the future is similar to the function of the messianic king in Isaiah 9 and 11. All these passages give expression to the very ancient ideals of Davidic royal theology. Isa 32:1, though it uses a different verb, resembles in thought and expression the de-

26. Moreover, 31:9 contains the fire imagery so dear to Isaiah for describing Yahweh's deliverance through judgment that leads to a renewed community (cf. 1:25–26; 10:17; 30:33; 33:10–14).

27. Hermisson, "Verkündigung Jesajas," 57, n. 12.

28. Wildberger, *Jesaja*, 1252.

29. Isa 3:12.

30. Their refusal to look to the Holy One of Israel (5:12; 22:11), their desire not even to hear of him (30:9–11), ultimately led to the loss of their wisdom (29:9–14). Precisely what the "tongue of the stammerer" refers to is not clear. The word "stammerer" (*ʿlg*, 32:4) occurs nowhere else in the OT. The closest parallel is in the expressions *blʿgy śph*, "by those of strange lips" (28:11), and *nlʿg lšwn ʾyn bynh*, "who stammer in a tongue you cannot understand" (33:19). In 32:4, however, the stammerer is not a foreigner, but an Israelite.

31. The authenticity of 32:6–8 is more seriously questioned, but I am not convinced that even these verses are secondary. They have a wisdom flavor to them, but Isaiah's contacts with wisdom are well established, and he could well have adapted wisdom material to make his point. These verses are not central to my argument, however.

mands that Yahweh imposed on the human king in his covenant with David as recorded in the "Last Words of David": "Rule over men in righteousness, rule in the fear of God."[32] Isa 11:1–5 is full of phraseology that can be paralleled in the royal Psalms. It is particularly close to Psalm 72. In Isaiah the king is equipped for his task by the "spirit of Yahweh" which rests upon him, so in Psalm 72 it is God's gift of his own divine justice and righteousness that enables the king to fulfill his task. In both passages that task is defined as primarily judicial in nature. The king judges the poor in righteousness and reproves the humble of the earth in equity (*wšpṭ bṣdq dlym whwkyḥ bmyšwr lʿnwy ʾrṣ*; Isa 11:4a). He judges God's people in righteousness and his humble ones in justice (*ydyn ʿmk bṣdq wʿnyyk bmšpṭ*; Ps 72:2). In both passages his vindication of the poor involves the slaying of the wicked (*whkh ʾrṣ bšbṭ pyw wbrwḥ śptyw ymyt ršʿ*; Isa 11:4b; "and he crushes the oppressor," *wydkʾ ʿwšq*, Ps 72:4). On this point compare also Ps 2:9: "You will shatter them with an iron staff, you will smash them like a potter's vessel" (*trʿm bšbṭ brzl kkly ywṣr tnpṣm*), and Ps 101:8: "Each morning I will destroy all the wicked of the land, cutting off all the evildoers from the city of Yahweh" (*lbqrym ʾṣmyt kl ršʿy ʾrṣ lhkryt mʿyr yhwh kl pʿly ʾwn*). The staff with which the king smashes the evil is a staff of equity (*šbṭ myšr*, Ps 45:7), and he establishes his throne by justice and righteousness (Isa 9:6; cf. Prov 20:28; 25:5).

It is important to recognize that in all these activities not only is God at work (Isa 9:6), but the king is participating in what is really the work of the divine king. Yahweh judges the peoples (Isa 2:4), including the poor (Ps 10:18), in righteousness (Ps 9:8–9; 67:5; 96:13; 98:9). He slays the wicked (Ps 9:6; 129:4; 145:20), and the foundations of his throne are righteousness and justice, while mercy and truth stand before him (Ps 89:15; cf. 9:8; 97:2). In other words, the human king is simply the regent of the divine sovereign, participating in what is ultimately the divine rule. His authority comes from God and rests in the conformity of his human rule to the divine will, a view of kingship adumbrated in the ancient Davidic covenant.

Isaiah's vision of the future is controlled by the ancient concept even though it was never fully realized in the past and the monarchs of his own day fell woefully short of the ideal. Despite that experience, Isaiah could not, or at least did not, conceive of a future without a power structure centered in a human king, and he assigned that king the same day to day tasks of judicial administration that the monarchs of his own day were botching.

32. 2 Sam 23:3. Reading *mšl* with 4QSam[a] and vocalizing as an imperative following G[L]. See F. M. Cross, *Canaanite Myth and Hebrew Epic* (Cambridge: Harvard University, 1973) 235–36, n. 70; and E. C. Ulrich, Jr., *The Qumran Text of Samuel and Josephus* (HMS 19; Missoula: Scholars Press, 1978) 114.

Ministers

It is worth noting, however, that the portrayal of the age of salvation in Isa 32:1 includes a role for ministers or officers alongside the role of the king. This corresponds to the Isaianic promise in 1:26 that God would restore Jerusalem's judges as at the first and her counselors as in the beginning. The reference here is clearly to the idealized Davidic period, and it indicates that just as Isaiah could not envision a future for his people without a monarch, so he could not envision monarchical rule without the royal officials to carry out royal policy. In that sense his vision for the future is very much tied to history and to this world.[33]

Even more interesting, however, is the imagery used to characterize the role of king and ministers in Isa 32:2. The metaphors found there are elsewhere in the Old Testament associated primarily with Yahweh's role. The word *mḥbʾ*, "refuge," does not occur again in a similar context, but *str*, "shelter," is used most often of God as the place of refuge for his people (Ps 27:5; 32:7; 61:5; 91:1; 119:114), and *mḥsh*, a synonym of *mḥbʾ*, is similarly used of Yahweh (Ps 61:4; Isa 25:4). Though the expression *plgy mym*, "streams of water," is not elsewhere used as a metaphor for Yahweh (see, however, Ps 1:3),[34] it calls to mind the numerous passages that do compare Yahweh to water or the source of water (Jer 2:13; 17:13; 18:14–15; Isa 33:21; Pss 42:2; 63:2). The use of *ṣl*, "shade," as an image for Yahweh's protection is widespread (Pss 17:8; 36:8; 57:2; 63:2), as is also the metaphor of Yahweh as the rock (Pss 18:3; 31:4; 42:10; 71:3). The closest parallel to Isa 32:2 is found in the Isaiah apocalypse, where a number of the same elements are picked up and applied to Yahweh:

> For you will be a refuge to the weak,
> A refuge to the needy in his affliction,
> A shelter (*mḥsh*) from the rainstorm (*zrm*),
> a shade (*ṣl*) from the heat. . . . (Isa 25:4)

The continuation of this text, with its interpretative identification of the "winter rainstorm" (*zrm qr*[35]) and "heat in the desert" (*ḥrb bṣywn*) as the "spirit of the ruthless" (*rwḥ ʿryṣym*), suggests that it is dependent on Isa 32:2. If so, it

33. If Isa 8:23–9:6 originated as an enthronement oracle for Hezekiah as a number of scholars think, that would underscore just how closely Isaiah's glorious hopes could be tied to mundane realities. His concrete threats to Shebna and promises to Eliakim (22:15–24) might also provide a paradigm of how Isaiah himself understood this business of restoring just officials.

34. The expression is used of a human king in Prov 21:1, but the meaning of the metaphor is quite different there.

35. The correction from *qyr*, "wall," to *qr*, "cold," is suggested by the contrast with *ḥrb*, "heat." *Qyr* is probably the result of a mistaken vocalization of a form written in a defective orthography.

simply underscores the degree to which metaphors appropriate to the deity have been applied to the human king and his human ministers in Isa 32:2.

In short, in the age of salvation, king and ministers alike will participate in Yahweh's salvific activity. Yahweh's vindication of the needy among his people will be the concern of his human agents, and when that takes place, when Israel's leaders truly pursue justice, the moral blindness and hypocrisy which marred the society of Isaiah's contemporaries will cease to exist.

People

That brings one to the role of the people in the age of salvation. If just monarchical rule is truly to strip away pretense and sham, if reality is again to be called by its true name, if Zion is once again to be known as the faithful city of righteousness (Isa 1:26), this drastic change in Judean society must demand something of God's people as well as its leaders. Just as a radical purging of corrupt officials and their replacement by righteous judges appears as a prerequisite for the unfolding of the age of salvation, so the rest of society must also experience the purging effect of God's judgment. It is through judgment that Jerusalem is to be saved, and that judgment involves both the death of sinners and the transformation of those who survive (Isa 1:27–28).[36]

Isaiah sees this transformation arising out of the glorious yet terrifying experience of Yahweh's deliverance of Jerusalem. This theme is touched on in a number of passages, but nowhere is it more clearly stated than in Isa 33:10–16.[37] After describing how he would rise up to punish his enemies and deliver

36. Those scholars who regard the "remnant" as a purely negative motif in Isaiah must not only delete these verses as secondary, they must also dismiss them as a misinterpretation of Isaiah's message. But the interpretation of 1:21–26 offered by such modern critics is not as convincing as the ancient one found in 1:27–28. How can one speak of purifying and restoring a city, if there is to be no continuity between the present and future inhabitants? Hermisson argues for a continuity focused totally on the city as an institution, ignoring its population, and he claims that the contrary view rests on rationalistic considerations (*EvT* 33 [1973] 68, n. 38). This rigid distinction between city and people appears unbiblical and a bit artificial, not to say irrational, however. Had Moses used similar logic, there would have been no Israel (Exod 32:9–14), and one might hope that interpreters could be as sensitive to the implications of a divine action as Moses was. Moreover, one cannot cut away every passage which sees a positive future for a segment of the people without appearing to trim the evidence to fit the theory (cf. the judicious remarks of Joseph Jensen in "Woe and Weal in Isaiah: Consistency and Continuity," *CBQ* 43 [1981] 167–87). A righteous remnant is clearly presupposed by 14:32; "For Yahweh has founded Zion, and in it the humble of his people will find refuge."

37. Cf. 4:3–4; 10:20–23; 29:17–21; 30:18–26; 30:27–33; 31:4–9. Unfortunately most of these passages, including 33:10–16, are generally dismissed by modern scholars as non-Isaianic and therefore ignored in treatments of Isaiah's view of the future. The question is too complex to treat in an article of this scope—see my study of Isaiah 33 in the forthcoming Festschrift for Noel Freedman and the more limited treatment of 30:18–21 in "The Teaching

Jerusalem, Yahweh calls upon people far and near to observe what he has done. Then he describes the impact of that experience on the inhabitants of Zion. The sinners and impious in Zion are thrown into a panic. God's devastating judgment on his enemies forces them to raise the question, "Who among us can sojourn with such a devouring fire?" The response comes in the form of an entrance torah similar to those in Psalms 15 and 24.[38] The kind of person who will live in the purified Jerusalem with Yahweh, this never-dying fire, is

> The one who walks in righteousness,
> Who speaks uprightly,
> Who refuses the profit from oppression,
> Who shakes out his hands from taking a bribe,
> Who closes his ears from participating in plots to shed blood,
> Who shuts his eyes from looking at evil. (33:15)

The moral transformation of Zion's surviving remnant is expressed here in very traditional Israelite categories. In this, as in his description of the messianic king and his enlightened ministers, Isaiah remains very much a man of his time, rooted in ancient tradition. But the catalyst behind this transformation is a new experiential awareness of God's character, a new openness to his activity in history. As Isaiah's inaugural vision of the awesome, holy, divine king transformed the prophet, so the people's vision of Yahweh's terrifying judgment and awesome deliverance would transform their lives. When that experience forced them to hallow the Holy One of Jacob and stand in awe of the God of Israel, a change in behavior would follow (29:23–24).

Summary

In Isaiah's vision of the future the initiative belongs to Yahweh. Whether in judgment, deliverance, or the following age of salvation, Yahweh remains the dominant actor. In Isaiah's description of the age of salvation, however, something is expected of all segments of the transformed human society. It is a

---

Voice in Isaiah 30:20–21," *Christian Teaching: Studies in Honor of LeMoine G. Lewis*, ed. Everett Ferguson (Abilene: Abilene Christian University, 1981) 130–37—but I do not share the prevailing judgment. Some of the passages appear to have been glossed or to have otherwise suffered in the course of textual transmission, but the underlying theology is thoroughly compatible with that of Isaiah. One might attribute some of this material to close disciples, but to assign it to the postexilic or even Josianic period and then set up sharp contrasts between it and Isaiah's own, very narrowly construed, thought, is utterly unconvincing.

38. Since Psalm 24 most likely dates to the very early monarchic period (Cross, *Canaanite*, 91–94), this form was certainly at home in Jerusalem prior to Isaiah's time. That he should adapt it for his own use is no more surprising than his use of the Zion tradition or his references to festival processions (30:29) in the course of which such liturgies apparently had their place.

transformed society, not because the form of the society is changed—Isaiah foresees a monarchical community basically similar to the one he knew—but because its experience of divine judgment and deliverance has been so profound that king, official, and commoner alike are motivated to realize the ancient ideals for their station.

Chapter 24

In Defense of the Monarchy: The Contribution of Israelite Kingship to Biblical Theology

It is very difficult to write a dispassionate evaluation of the contribution that the Israelite monarchy made to biblical theology. The monarchy arose and developed in controversy, and that ancient debate continues to provoke sharp controversy in modern attempts to evaluate the theological significance of the Israelite kingdom. In the ancient debate some voices claimed that the mere request for a human king was tantamount to a rejection of God, to a rebellion against divine rule (Judg 8:22–23; 1 Sam 8:7; 12:12, 17–20). Others, arguing less theologically but equally opposed to the monarchy, saw kingship as a totally unnecessary and unproductive drain on the resources of a healthy society (Judg 9:7–15; 1 Sam 10:27). Still others, the ancient promonarchists, viewed kingship as God's gift that finally brought order to an irresponsibly chaotic society in which formerly "every man did what was right in his own eyes" (Judg 17:6; 21:25; cf. 18:1; 19:1). Which of these ancient opinions is the voice of authentic Yahwism? Or, more to the point, which of these ancient opinions, if any, represent the authentic word of God?

Given these several discordant opinions, all of which are preserved and positively presented in Scripture, one might have expected contemporary scholars to be cautious about adopting any of them uncritically. Nonetheless it is fairly common today for biblical scholars to characterize the monarchy as an essentially alien development in Israelite history.[1] Its development, and especially the creation of an imperialistic ideology to undergird it, is typically seen as the progressive paganization of Israel,[2] and some scholars who hold this

1. One may cite S. Herrmann (*A History of Israel in Old Testament Times* [2d ed.; Philadelphia: Fortress Press, 1981] 132) as fairly representative of this view: "All this confirms the common view that the monarchy was a late phenomenon in Israel, forced on it by historical circumstances and essentially alien to its original nature." Herrmann goes on to argue that Israel was by nature a tribal alliance and ideally remained so throughout its history, and this in turn is the major reason why the monarchy was not renewed in the postexilic period once it had collapsed (ibid.).

2. This view is expressed in its strongest form in a number of studies by G. E. Mendenhall. In his article "The Monarchy" (*Interpretation* 29/2 [April 1975] 155–70), he argues that "a systematic reversion to Bronze Age paganism took place in less than two generations"

view are quite extreme in rejecting any theological construct that is dependent on the monarchy for its creation or development.[3]

---

with the development of the monarchy (p. 157). Since Israel's formative period was the time of Moses and the covenant legal tradition, this "reversion to the old Bronze Age paganism of the United Monarchy" was "a process of rapid erosion of the basic principles of the new religious ethic" that Moses introduced (p. 158). The process began under Saul's rule, and the erosion took place so fast that by David's time little was left of the basic convictions of the Old Yahwist federation outside isolated segments of the society (p. 161). David and Solomon finished the job. Mendenhall assumes that David simply took over the Jebusite bureaucracy of Jerusalem, and he identifies Zadok, Nathan, and Bathsheba as Jebusites (pp. 162–64). He admits that he cannot prove that Zadok and Nathan were Jebusites, but he asserts, "What we can prove is the fact that the cultic/political system of Jerusalem during the Monarchy had nothing to do with the Yahwist revolution and was actually completely incompatible with that religious movement" (p. 166). Similar blasts against the monarchy may be found in his book *The Tenth Generation: The Origins of the Biblical Tradition* (Baltimore: Johns Hopkins University Press, 1973), where he blames the state with breaking down both the old tribal structure of early Israelite society and the religiously centered value system, thus making possible the corruption of the law courts so bitterly denounced by the prophets (p. 209), and in his contribution to the Wright Festschrift, "Social Organization in Early Israel," *Magnalia Dei, The Mighty Acts of God* (ed. F. M. Cross, W. E. Lemke, and P. D. Miller; Garden City, N.Y.: Doubleday & Co., 1976) 132–51—note esp. 140.

Other scholars who in some way share Mendenhall's negative view of the monarchical development are far more restrained and careful. Cross is not especially critical of the "limited monarchy" of Saul and David, but while he spares Saul and David, he has hardly anything good to say about Solomon, who, according to Cross, began a pattern of innovations that "Canaanized" the royal ideology and cult (*CMHE*, 233–34, 239–41). J. Bright's reconstruction of the historical development of the monarchy has much in common with that of both Mendenhall and Cross, but in sharp contrast to Mendenhall and far more explicitly than Cross, Bright points to the ambiguity in the institution: "From our modern point of view at least, the new order brought to Israel so much that was good and so much that was bad that no simple evaluation is possible. It is, therefore, scarcely surprising that Israel was herself never of one mind on the subject. The monarchy was a problematical institution that some believed divinely given and that others found intolerable. In speaking of Israel's notion of kingship and state we are warned never to generalize" (*A History of Israel* [3d ed.; Philadelphia: Westminster Press, 1981] 224; see also 225–28).

In recent years a third group of scholars has attacked the basic underlying notion according to which the monarchy was an alien development in Israel. As long ago as 1967, G. Buccellati vigorously and brilliantly debunked this idea (*Cities and Nations of Ancient Syria* [Rome: Istituto di Studi del Vicino Oriente, 1967] 240–41), and his conclusion is well worth quoting: "And, to my mind, the conclusion is that the monarchy, far from being an 'alien institution,' was the natural development of forces present among the Israelites and stimulated by circumstances such as the conquest of Palestine and the fight against the Philistines. In other words, the monarchy was the institution which best met the political exigencies of the Israelites at a given time: since institutions could originate and develop freely, there is no reason to deny the monarchy validity and authenticity as a real Israelite institution" (p. 241). J. A. Soggin also raises questions about the standard treatment of the monarchical development in his new history, though he approaches the question quite differently from Buccellati. Basically he rejects the reconstruction of the premonarchical period as the formative period

The implications of such a stance are profound, because many of what have been taken to be central biblical themes owe their existence or their peculiar biblical shape to the imperial theology first developed in the David-Solomonic court and then transmitted and elaborated in the royal cult of the subsequent Judean court. I have discussed the formation and the shape of that imperial theology extensively elsewhere,[4] so here I will simply list some of the central biblical themes that are dependent on this royal theology.

While the conception of Yahweh as king is premonarchical in origin[5] and at one stage in Israelite history even functioned polemically to retard the development of human kingship,[6] the imperial conquests of David played an

---

of Israelite identity when Yahwism was pure and orthodox. The monarchy could not represent the progressive paganization of an originally pure Yahwism, because that golden age of noble and pure origins never existed (J. A. Soggin, *A History of Ancient Israel* [Philadelphia: Westminster Press, 1985] 167–68).

3. J. L. McKenzie, who basically follows Mendenhall's historical reconstruction, is even more radical, or at least more explicit, than Mendenhall in drawing such radical theological conclusions from this historical reconstruction. Since he believes "the monarchy makes sense only as the imposition of a foreign aristocracy upon Israel," in his *A Theology of the Old Testament* (Garden City, N.Y.: Doubleday & Co., 1974) 267–317, he "refused to include the theme of messianism as proper to the theology of the Old Testament" ("The Sack of Israel," *The Quest for the Kingdom of God: Essays in Honor of George E. Mendenhall* [ed. H. B. Huffmon, F. A. Spina, and A. R. W. Green, Winona Lake, Ind.: Eisenbrauns, 1983] 34). Moreover, the section on messianism in his article "Aspects of Old Testament Thought," *The Jerome Biblical Commentary* (ed. R. E. Brown, J. A. Fitzmyer, and R. E. Murphy; Englewood Cliffs, N.J.: Prentice-Hall, 1968) art. 77, secs. 152–63, was, according to McKenzie, added by the editors without his knowledge or consent, and he publicly disavowed it ("The Sack of Israel," 34).

4. See especially my article, "Zion in the Theology of the Davidic-Solomonic Empire," *Studies in the Period of David and Solomon and Other Essays* (ed. T. Ishida; Winona Lake, Ind.: Eisenbrauns, 1982) 93–108 [[here: pp. 331–347]]. Cf. also my earlier studies: "The Davidic Origin of the Zion Tradition," *JBL* 92 (1973) 329–44 [[here: pp. 313–330]]; "The Religio-Political Setting of Psalm 47," *BASOR* 221 (1976) 129–32 [[here: pp. 266–273]]; and "Zion Tradition," IDBSup, 985–87.

5. For further discussion of this point, see T. N. D. Mettinger, "YHWH Sabaoth—The Heavenly King on the Cherubim Throne," *Studies in the Period of David*, 130 n. 87.

6. Despite F. Crüsemann's recent attempt to date this religious rejection of kingship to the post-Solomonic period (*Der Widerstand gegen das Königtum. Die antiköniglichen Texte des Alten Testamentes und der Kampf um den frühen israelitischen Staat* [WMANT 49; Neukirchen-Vluyn: Neukirchener Verlag, 1978] 74–81, 124), K. H. Bernhardt's earlier discussion that situated this outlook to the transitional period between tribal league and monarchy is far more convincing (*Das Problem der altorientalischen Königsideologie im Alten Testament* [VTSup 8; Leiden: E. J. Brill, 1961] 154–55). As Bernhardt says, the total rejection of kingship presupposes a situation in which the decision whether to remain with the patriarchal rule of the tribal leaders or to adopt monarchical rule was still in doubt, and this transitional period prior to the monarchy is the only period in which the alternative, patriarchate or kingdom actually existed for Israel: "Wenn es gilt, einen Ursprungsort für die gründsätzliche Ablehnung des Königtums zu finden, dann dürfte keine Epoche israelitischer

essential role in the development of the theological claim that Yahweh's rule was universal, that he was the great king over all the earth.[7] The royal theology's claim that God had chosen David and his dynasty as God's permanent agent for the exercise of the divine rule on earth was the fundamental starting point for the later development of the messianic hope, and the particular contours that this hope took reflect to a large extent the portraits of the ideal king projected in the royal cult.[8] Those portraits include mythological elements, some borrowed from other cultures, but Christians have claimed that even these mythological elements find a surprisingly literal fulfillment in Jesus Christ.[9] Finally, the imperial theology's claim that Yahweh chose Jerusalem for his dwelling place, a claim that resulted in the creation of a mythological mystique for this royal city, is the ultimate source for the later prophetic vision of universal peace and for the hope of eternal life in the new Jerusalem.[10]

Geschichte so geeignet sein wie diese Übergangszeit von der patriarchalischen Herrschaft der Stammeshäupter zur Monarchie. Es ist die einzige Situation, in der die Alternative Patriarchat oder Königtum überhaupt für Israel bestanden hat. Die grundsätzliche Verneinung des Königtums setz eine Situation voraus, in der das gewohnte Nomadendasein mit der neuen Notwendigkeit des Königtums noch im Streite lag; nicht anders, als die spätere polemische Kritik an einzelnen Regenten ein durch lange Erfahrung mit der Monarchie zur festen Norm gewordenes Königsideal zur unbedingten Voraussetzung hat. Kein Anzeichen aber deutet darauf hin, dass die antimonarchischen Äusserungen im Alten Testament allmählich aus dieser Kritik an unbeliebten Fürsten zur grundsätzlichen Ablehnung der Königsherrschaft herangewachsen sind" (pp. 154–55). For further discussion of the historical and theological background of this ancient Israelite debate, see below.

7. Roberts, "Zion in the Theology of the Davidic-Solomonic Empire," 98–99 [here: pp. 336–337]]; idem, "The Religio-Political Setting of Psalm 47," 129–32 [[here: pp. 266–73]].

8. Cross, *CMHE*, 263–65. For my own views on this development, see J. J. M. Roberts, "The Divine King and the Human Community," *The Quest For the Kingdom of God*, 127–39 [[here: pp. 348–357]], esp. 132–33 [[pp. 352–353]]; idem, "Isaiah in Old Testament Theology," *Interpretation* 36/2 (1982) 130–43, esp. 138–39.

9. The Christian claims that Jesus is the Son of God and that he shares the divine nature with the Father have their scriptural roots in the royal theology's mythologumenon of the divine birth of the Davidic king which raises him to the position of Yahweh's firstborn (Pss 2:7, 89:27–28; perhaps 110:3; and possibly Isa 9:5) and secondarily in the hyperbolic deification of the king which took place in the extravagant language of the royal cult so that the king on occasion was addressed with divine titles, e.g., "Mighty God" (Isa 9:5), "Elyon" (Ps 89:28), and "God" (Ps 45:7–8).

10. Roberts, "Isaiah in Old Testament Theology," 136–37; idem, "Isaiah 33: An Isaianic Elaboration of the Zion Tradition," *The Word of the Lord Shall Go Forth: Essays in Honor of David Noel Freedman in Celebration of His Sixtieth Birthday* (ed. C. L. Meyers and M. O'Connor; Winona Lake, Ind.: Eisenbrauns, 1983) 15–25; idem, "Isaiah 2 and the Prophet's Message to the North," *JQR* 75 (1985) 209–308; idem, "Yahweh's Foundation in Zion (Isa 28:16)," forthcoming in *JBL* [[here: pp. 292–310]]; and the excellent study by B. C. Ollenburger, *Zion, the City of the Great King: A Theological Investigation of Zion Symbolism in the Tradition of the Jerusalem Cult* (1982 Princeton Theological Seminary diss. soon to appear in the *JSOT* Supplement Series, no. 41).

If one dismisses the imperialistic theology of the Davidic-Solomonic court as sheer apostasy, as nothing but the progressive paganization of the Yahwistic faith, what does that do to the content of biblical theology? Must all of those biblical themes dependent on this theology for their development or elaboration also be condemned as pagan aberrations? If so, biblical theology as it has been traditionally understood will be gutted. The knife will have to remove far more than just the messianism that J. L. McKenzie is willing to sacrifice to his antimonarchical principle.

Before undergoing radical surgery, a patient is always wise to get a second opinion, and before sacrificing so much of the traditional content of biblical theology, one should question whether the Israelite monarchy has been correctly diagnosed as an alien, malignant growth in the body of genuine Yahwism. This negative diagnosis is based on several arguments: (1) The establishment of the monarchy involves significant borrowing from the surrounding, non-Israelite cultures; (2) the setting up of a human king stands in fundamental opposition to the recognition of God as king; and (3) the motivations behind the royal theology are transparently human and reflect all too clearly the inevitable coercive abuse of any human monopoly on power. Each of these arguments must be reappraised to see whether it justifies such a negative appraisal of the royal theology.

Foreign Elements

The monarchy is generally regarded as alien to genuine Yahwism, because the development of the monarchy in Israel involved the adaptation of elements taken over from the surrounding cultures. This is indicated by the Deuteronomic and Deuteronomistic motif that Israel asked for a king "like all the nations" (Deut 17:14; 1 Sam 8:5) or "to be like all the nations" (1 Sam 8:20). Moreover, a comparison of the Israelite monarchy with the monarchies in the surrounding states shows that Israel obviously adapted many features from these older models. Egypt, in particular, appears to have exercised a strong influence over the development of the Israelite monarchy. This is not surprising, given the fact that Egypt had been the nominal overlord of Palestine down to the time of the formation of the Israelite monarchy and that Egypt experienced a resurgence of its imperial power while the Israelite monarchy was still quite young, during the reign of Solomon and especially of Rehoboam, his successor. David and Solomon both appear to have followed Egyptian models in setting up their imperial administrations,[11] the Israelite coronation service seems

11. See especially T. N. D. Mettinger, *Solomonic State Officials: A Study of the Civil Government Officials of the Israelite Monarchy* (Lund: Gleerup, 1971), and the earlier literature cited there.

to have adapted the Egyptian practice of giving five royal names,[12] and the conception of the new king as the offspring of the deity has certain connections to the Egyptian material.[13] The practice of anointing the new king may also go

---

12. S. Morenz, "Ägyptische und davidische Königstitular," *Zeitschrift für ägyptische Sprache* 79 (1954) 73–74 = *Religion und Geschichte des alten Ägypten* (Cologne and Vienna: Bölan Verlag, 1975) 401–3. For the Egyptian enthronement ritual, see H. Bonnet, "Krönung," *Reallexikon der ägyptischen Religionsgeschichte* (Berlin: Walter de Gruyter, 1952) 395–400; H. Brunner, *Die Geburt des Gottkönigs. Studien zur Überlieferung eines altägyptischen Mythos* (Ägyptologische Abhandlungen 10; Wiesbaden: Otto Harrassowitz, 1964); and note especially the accounts of the coronation of Horemhab (G. Roeder, *Der Ausklang der ägyptischen Religion mit Reformation, Zauberei und Jenseitsglauben* [Die ägyptische Religion in Text und Bild 4; Zurich and Stuttgart: Artemis Verlag, 1961] 72–89) and Thutmosis III (G. Roeder, *Kulte, Orakel und Naturverehrung im alten Ägypten* [Die Ägyptische Religion in Text und Bild 3; Zurich and Stuttgart: Artemis Verlag, 1960] 195–215). For the Israelite evidence, see A. Alt's seminal study, "Jesaja 8, 23–9, 6. Befreiungsnacht und Krönungstag," *Kleine Schriften zur Geschichte des Volkes Israel* (Munich: C. H. Beck'sche Verlagsbuchhandlung, 1964) 2.206–25, and the careful treatment by H. Wildberger, *Jesaja* (BKAT X/1; Neukirchen-Vluyn: Neukirchener Verlag, 1972) 362–89.

13. Cross thinks any Egyptian influence on Israelite royal ideology must have been indirect, mediated through the Canaanites, both because "the Egyptian royal theology with its conception of the king as a physical son of the god and the Israelite conception of the adoptive sonship of the king were not identical" and because of "the rapidly increasing evidence of the specifically Canaanite origin of Israelite ideas of the king as son of god" (*CMHE*, 247). Unfortunately, Cross does not give any specifics as to what makes up this "rapidly increasing evidence." The Keret Epic does suggest that the Canaanites, at least those circles from which this text came, considered their kings as in some sense the offspring of the deity. Keret is referred to as the "lad of El" (*ǵlm il*, *CCA* 14.40–41, 61–62, 306; 15.2.16, 20), El is called his father (14.40, 49, 169), and as the son and progeny of El, immortality was expected of Keret—he should not die like a mere mortal (16.3–23, 98–111). Since Keret is king and the text is about kingship, one may conclude that this text reflects a conception of the divine sonship of the king, but nothing suggests that it is adoptive rather than physical. If anything, the emphasis on the expected immortality of the king points in the other direction. Moreover, I see nothing in the Ugaritic or El Amarna texts that suggests that Canaanite conceptions, in contrast to Egyptian conceptions, were more influential in the Israelite development. There are quite striking parallels between the Egyptian and the Israelite coronation ritual. Besides the giving of the royal names, note the similar divine acknowledgement of the human king as his offspring using the language of birth. Amon's words to Horemhab, "You are my son and my heir who has come out of my members" (G. Roeder, *Zauberei und Jenseitsglauben*, 88 [my translation of the German], and Yahweh's words to the Davidic king, "You are my son, today I have given birth to you" (Ps 2:7), are similar, if not identical, and both were apparently spoken on the day of the king's enthronement.

It may be that the Israelite conception is adoptionistic, Yahweh's word being a performative utterance, as Mettinger has very skillfully argued (*King and Messiah: The Civil and Sacral Legitimation of the Israelite Kings* [Coniectanea Biblica, OTS 8; Lund: Gleerup, 1976] 265–66), but, contrary to Cross, that does not rule out direct Egyptian influence on the Israelite conception. Mettinger believes that there is a genetic connection between the two conceptions, and he suggests that this may reflect a deliberate Israelite "adaptation and reinterpretation of the Egyptian mythological conception" (ibid.). While I think Mettinger has

back to Egyptian antecedents, but this is debated.[14] Other elements associated with the monarchy seem to have connections with Mesopotamia,[15] though these may have been mediated through the smaller kingdoms that lay between Israel and the major empires of Assyria and Babylon.

Nevertheless, despite these borrowings, it is not at all clear whether one is justified in characterizing the monarchy as alien to the essence of Yahwism.

---

demonstrated that there is a subtle difference between the Israelite and the Egyptian conception of the king's sonship, I am dubious whether the Israelite conception was as free of mythological color as Mettinger would have us believe. In that regard I share the skepticism that H. Donner ("Adoption oder Legitimation? Erwägungen zur Adoption im Alten Testament auf dem Hintergrund der altorientalischen Rechte," *OrAnt* 8 [1969] 87–119, esp. 114), G. W. Ahlström (*Psalm 89, Eine Liturgie aus dem Ritual des leidenden Königs* [Lund: Gleerup, 1959] 112), M. Görg ("Die 'Wiedergeburt' des Königs [Ps 2, 7b]," *Theologie und Glaube* 60 [1970] 413–26, and P. A. H. de Boer ("The Son of God in the Old Testament," *OTS* 18 [1973] 204) have expressed toward the adoptionist interpretation of the Israelite conception. In short, I think Egypt, with all its differences, still provides the best background for understanding this aspect of Israelite royal theology, and it is probably the dominant influence on Canaanite royal theology as well.

14. R. de Vaux argued for an Egyptian influence behind the Israelite practice ("Le roi d'Israël, vassal de Yahvé," *Mélanges Eugène Tisserant* 1 [Studia e Testi 231; Città del Vaticano: Biblioteca Apostolica Vaticana, 1964] 119–33), E. Kutsch suggested a Hittite background mediated through Canaan (*Salbung als Rechtsakt im Alten Testament und im alten Orient* [BZAW 87; Berlin: Walter der Gruyter, 1963] 56), and Mettinger argues for an autochthonous development in Israel (*King and Messiah*, 185–232). Mettinger's argument against de Vaux's view is dependent on Mettinger's historical reconstruction of the development of the rite in Israel (ibid., pp. 210, 232), however, and I cannot accept his reconstruction, according to which the rite was originally secular and only became sacralized in the time of Solomon (ibid., pp. 207, 229–30). His dating of the texts seems arbitrary, if not circular—e.g., he makes the tradition of Saul's anointing dependent on the "late" tradition of Samuel's anointing of David, thus enabling him to reject the anointing of Saul as unhistorical! (ibid., pp. 194–97)—and he assigns far more significance to the use of the plural form of the verb *māšaḥ* ("anoint") than seems justified (ibid., p. 208).

15. The characterization of the king's rule as "from sea to sea" (Ps 72:8) picks up Mesopotamian geographical terminology ("from the upper sea [Mediterranean] to the lower sea [Persian Gulf]"), though the borrowing of such imperialistic language actually grows out of the imperialistic expansion of David's rule (see H.-J. Kraus, *Psalmen* [BKAT 15/1; 2d ed.; Neukirchen-Vluyn: Neukirchener Verlag, 1961] 14, 498). Note that the similar motif in Ps 89:26 is colored by the Canaanite cosmogonic myth. Other motifs that Israel's royal ideology shared with Mesopotamia include the divine election of the king and his royal city (Pss 78:72; 132; see the prologue to the Code of Hammurabi [E. Bergmann, *Codex Hammurabi, Textus Primigenius* (Rome: Pontificium Institutum Biblicum, 1953), i 1–50]) as well as the conception that the real king was the imperial deity (Code of Hammurabi, ibid., and the Assyrian enthronement ritual—K. Fr. Müller, *Das assyrische Ritual, Part 1: Texte zum assyrischen Königsritual* [*MVAG* 41/3; Leipzig: J. C. Hinrichs Verlag, 1937], esp. i 29; and compare the similar text edited by E. F. Weidner in *AfO* 13, 210ff., esp. line 15). The king's responsibility for maintaining justice is common to Egypt, Mesopotamia, and Canaan, so one cannot attribute that element of Israelite royal theology to any one specific background.

As far as one is able to judge, given the nature of the sources, Yahwism has always been characterized by the adaptation of elements from its surroundings. If one can characterize the Mosaic period as the period when Yahwism was born, following the biblical tradition about the revelation of the name Yahweh, one finds a religious faith quite open to external religious influences. The revelation of the divine name takes place at a mountain site that had apparently long been sacred to tribes in the area (Exod 3:1), and in organizing the new religious community, particularly with regard to its cultus, Moses seems to have been heavily influenced by his Mideonite family connection (Exod 18:1–27).[16] Moreover, Israel's earliest religious poetry seems to have been heavily dependent on the poetic canons and the religious motifs of contemporary Canaanite culture.[17] It is difficult to speak of the essence of Yahwism without speaking of its ability to take up elements of its environment, even hostile elements, and transform them into supporting structures for the Yahwistic faith. In view of this well-attested power of absorption, the mere presence of foreign elements in the development of the Israelite monarchy is hardly sufficient grounds for rejecting it as pagan aberration.

The Conflict between Human and Divine Kingship

But is not the conception that Yahweh is king fundamentally at odds with any attempt to set up a human king? Is not the desire for a human king tantamount to the rejection of Yahweh as king? Such a view was current in ancient Israel. Both Gideon (Judg 8:22–23) and Samuel (1 Sam 8:7; 10:19; 12:12, 17–20) give expression to it, but the modern theologian would do well to consider the issue carefully before simply adopting this view as the authentic word of God on the matter.

In the first place, this is only one of the points of view preserved and positively presented in the biblical text. Even the Deuteronomistic historian (Dtr), who is normally considered rather critical of kingship, preserves both the promonarchical and the antimonarchical sources in his account of the transition from tribal confederacy to monarchy, and he, along with many other biblical writers, invests the monarchy with the sanction of Yahweh's promissory covenant to the Davidic dynasty.[18] If one takes canon seriously as an important

16. Cross, *CMHE*, 200–201; D. N. Freedman, "Early Israelite History in the Light of Early Israelite Poetry," *Unity and Diversity: Essays in the History, Literature, and Religion of the Ancient Near East* (ed. H. Goedicke and J. J. M. Roberts [Baltimore and London: Johns Hopkins University Press, 1975]) 6–7, 25 n. 16; Herrmann, *A History of Israel in Old Testament Times*, 75–77.

17. Cross, *CMHE*, 121–34, 141–44.

18. According to Cross, God's promise to David and his dynasty is one of the two major themes in the first edition of the Deuteronomistic History (*CMHE*, 278–85).

factor in theological debate, then it must be significant that the voices of the promonarchists were not erased from the biblical record in the editing process. If the critique of kingship preserved in the biblical record relativizes kingship and destroys any claim which that form of human government may make to being *the* divinely authorized form of government,[19] the positive appreciation for kingship relativizes the claims of any competing form of human government. In fact, one can hardly find any clear portrayal of a rival form of government. The tribal alliance remains a nebulous scholarly reconstruction even for the period when it functioned politically, and after the establishment of the monarchy there seem to have been no efforts to return to this earlier form of organization. Both the prophetic visions of the future government and the actual forms the government took when Israel gained a measure of independence, as in the Maccabean era, were in some sense monarchical.[20] Contrary to S. Herrmann,[21] there was even an attempt to restore the monarchy in the early postexilic period.[22] Its failure was due to Israel's status as an insignificant but potentially

19. J. D. Levenson, *Sinai and Zion: An Entry Into the Jewish Bible* (Minneapolis: Winston Press) 74–75.

20. One may argue about the authenticity of the passages concerned, but at least in the form in which the oracles of Amos (9:11), Hosea (3:5), Micah (5:1–5), Isaiah (8:23–9:6; 11:1–9, 10; 32:1–8), Jeremiah (23:5–6; 33:14–22), and Ezekiel (34:23–31; 37:24–28) have come down to us, they envision a future Davidic monarchy. Isaiah of Jerusalem's vision of the future government hardly differed in structure from the government of his own day (Roberts, "The Divine King and the Human Community," 132–33), and while the Davidic king plays no significant role in Second or Third Isaiah or in the Isaianic Apocalypse, none of these collections really address the issue of the structure of the future government of Yahweh's community; they are content to concentrate on the divine king (Roberts, "Isaiah in Old Testament Theology," 140–42). The question has been raised, however, whether the monarchs in Ezekiel 40–48 and in First Zechariah are actually envisioned as functioning politically in a manner that would justify the term "monarchy" for their government. Levenson characterizes the Davidic prince of Ezekiel 40–48 as no more than a liturgical figurehead (J. D. Levenson, *Theology of the Program of Restoration of Ezekiel 40–48* [HSM 10; Missoula, Mont.: Scholars Press, 1976] 143), and D. L. Petersen sees the governmental ideal portrayed in the oracles of Zechariah as a diarchy rather than a monarchy (*Haggai and Zechariah 1–8* [OTL; Philadelphia: Westminster Press, 1984] 118). Given the higher status assigned to the royal figure in Zech 6:9–15 (ibid., p. 277), however, I am dubious whether diarchy is really a more appropriate designation than monarchy.

21. Herrmann, *A History of Israel in Old Testament Times*, 132.

22. The oracles concerning Zerubbabel in Haggai and Zechariah (Hag 2:20–23; Zech 3:8; 4:6–10, 11–14; 6:9–15) clearly express the expectation that God will elevate Zerubbabel to royal honor, even if Petersen is right in suggesting that Haggai, at least, was very careful in his formulation of this expectation so as not to stir up political problems with the Persians (*Haggai and Zechariah 1–8*, 104–6). The textual problems in Zech 6:9–15 still suggest to me, contrary to Petersen (ibid., pp. 273–81), that Zechariah was not so cautious, that the expectations attached to Zerubbabel were rudely dashed, probably by the Persian authorities, and that the text was secondarily corrected away from the emphasis on the crowning of Zerubbabel.

troublesome part of the Persian empire. Israel simply did not have the freedom to choose its own form of government.

The apparent assumption of later Israel that a free Israel would be constituted as a kingdom and Dtr's clear incorporation and preservation of both promonarchical and antimonarchical sentiments in his history suggest that one be very careful in evaluating Dtr's attitude toward the monarchy. It is doubtful whether one can simply identify the antimonarchical sentiments of either Gideon or Samuel with the opinion of Dtr. The law of the king (Deut 17:14–20) found in the Deuteronomic law code, the theological base for Dtr's treatment of history, contains no trace of the notion that the appointment of a human king implies the rejection of Yahweh as Israel's king.[23] While Dtr incorporates traditions in his history that attribute that notion to Gideon and Samuel, two of his heroes, his treatment of both contains certain undercurrents which, taken seriously, tend to distance the narrator from his leading character. As has long been noted, while Gideon rejected the popular attempt to make him and his son after him "ruler" over Israel since only Yahweh should be Israel's "ruler," this rejection appears to have been more the rejection of a title than of the substance behind that title.[24] Immediately after rejecting this title, Gideon asks for tribute from his followers (Judg 8:24), establishes a cult center in his city of Ophrah (Judg 8:27), and creates a large harem for himself (Judg 8:30). Abimelech, his son through the concubine, clearly understood that despite Gideon's disclaimer, his father did in fact "rule," and he assumed that that rule would pass to Gideon's sons (Judg 9:2). Some ancient sources have probably been conflated in Judges 8–9,[25] but Dtr has allowed these texts to stand together, thereby relativizing Gideon's rejection of the "rule" and at the same time distancing himself from this rigid position.

Dtr similarly distances himself from the opinion of Samuel voiced in 1 Samuel 8 and 12. In addition to preserving the more promonarchical narratives in 1 Samuel 9–11, including the notice in 10:27 that identifies those who opposed Saul's rule as "worthless fellows," Dtr gives some justification to the people's demand for a king even in 1 Sam 8:1–5, when he preserves the tradition that the sons of Samuel perverted justice and ruled unjustly.[26] Moreover, in 1 Sam 8:7 Yahweh has to remind Samuel that the people are rejecting Yahweh, not Samuel, as their ruler, and it is curious how easily Yahweh, in contrast

23. Bernhardt, *Das Problem der altorientalischen Königsideologie*, 136–39.

24. J. Gray, *Joshua, Judges and Ruth* (NCB; London: Oliphants, 1977) 175–76.

25. G. F. Moore indicates the tensions in the narrative quite clearly (*Judges* [ICC; Edinburgh: T. & T. Clark, 1895] 229), even if one is not convinced by his analysis of the sources.

26. A. Weiser: *Samuel, Seine geschichtliche Aufgabe und religiöse Bedeutung* (FRLANT 81; Göttingen: Vandenhoeck & Ruprecht, 1962) 30; H. J. Stoebe, *Das erste Buch Samuelis* (KAT 8/1; Gütersloh: Gerd Mohn, 1973) 183; J. Mauchline, *1 and 2 Samuel* (NCB; London: Oliphants, 1971) 88–89.

to the irate Samuel, gives in to the people and grants their request. R. Klein comments that the rationale for this paradoxical behavior of Yahweh is not satisfactorily explained.[27] I would suggest that Yahweh's paradoxical behavior is a better reflection of Dtr's views than the antimonarchical formulations that God, no less than Samuel, utters. Dtr found this antimonarchical polemic in his sources, preserved it, but by interspersing it within and thereby juxtaposing it to other traditions he softened it, thereby bringing it more into line with his own qualified acceptance of kingship.

In the light of Yahweh's reminder to Samuel that it was not Samuel that the people were rejecting, it may be profitable to examine Samuel's attitude toward kingship more closely, paying attention both to the narrative and the possible historical realities behind the narrative. Yahweh's comment suggests that Samuel's unhappiness over the people's request (1 Sam 8:1–6) had a large personal element in it. In fact, whatever else the people may have been doing, they *were* rejecting the rule of Samuel and his sons. The transition to royal rule would certainly weaken the authority of Samuel, and it would seriously undercut any attempt to hand down any of his authority to his children.

It is difficult to evaluate Samuel's opposition to Saul in the following stories in 1 Samuel 13–15. On the narrative level, Saul is portrayed as too weak, fearful, rash or self-willed to wait for and follow God's direction, but it is easy for the reader, at least the modern reader, to regard the king sympathetically as a tragic character. In contrast, Samuel appears brutally harsh, particularly in 1 Sam 13:5–14, since the prophet was late (v. 8) and the situation was desperate.[28] P. K. McCarter apparently does not respond to the text in the same way, or he assumes that the ancient Israelite readers would not have responded in that way. He attributes this material to a pre-Deuteronomistic prophetic author who took over an older, pro-Saulide complex of traditions, and revised it in order to "introduce paradigmatically the relationship between king and prophet" and "to establish the ongoing role of the prophets."[29] I have difficulty with this analysis. McCarter sees no sign of prophetic reworking of the Davidic material in 1 Samuel 16–31, except for the introduction in 16:1–13, a late addition in 19:18–24, the brief notice in 25:1, and the séance at En-dor (28:3–25).[30] But it is clear that the older Davidic material consciously portrays David as having precisely those virtues which Saul was lacking. Saul was too impatient to wait for the divine oracle (1 Sam 13:8–14; 14:18–19, 36), but David scrupulously consulted it (1 Sam 23:2–4, 6–12; 30:7–9; 2 Sam 2:1–2; 5:19, 22–25). Saul

27. R. Klein, *1 Samuel* (Word Biblical Commentary 10; Waco, Tex.: Word Books, 1983) 75.

28. Ibid., 126–27.

29. P. K. McCarter, *1 Samuel* (AB 8; Garden City, N.Y.: Doubleday & Co., 1980) 20.

30. Ibid., 20–21.

was antagonistic toward the priestly bearers of the old religious traditions and eventually slaughtered most of them (1 Sam 22:12–19),[31] but David respected the traditions (1 Sam 21:6; 22:14–15) and saved the survivor of that slaughter (1 Sam 22:20–23). Saul apparently showed no concern for the ancient religious symbol of Yahweh's presence, the Ark,[32] but David returned it to a place of honor in Israel's religious life (2 Samuel 6). Finally, while Saul disobeyed the divine oracle in his campaign against the Amalekites (1 Samuel 15), David followed the oracle in his campaign against the same people (1 Sam 30:7–8).[33]

These contrasts were apparently a part of the History of David's Rise, David's apologetic justifying his irregular succession to the throne.[34] If that is so, the religious critique of Saul antedates any use of it that a later prophetic writer may have made, and it suggests that the tensions reflected in the narrative between the older religious authorities, including Samuel, and the new king Saul are actually rooted in early historical realities.

On the historical level, the text seems to reflect a conflict between representatives of the old order trying to maintain their former prerogatives and a representative of the new order, forced to move forward cautiously because of the jealous reluctance of the older religious authorities to give up their former control over political life in Israel. The religious opposition to Saul all seems to have come from professional religious types whose status was threatened by any growth in Saul's royal power. Samuel attacks Saul for usurping his old prerogative of presiding over the sacrifices at state functions (1 Sam 13:8–14; cf. 1 Sam 7:5–10; 9:12–13), even though Saul acts out of concern for the well-being of his army. Samuel also attacks him for failing to adhere rigidly to Samuel's prophetic call for the ban (1 Samuel 15). Finally, the narrative faults him for not directing his campaigns according to the oracular responses of the priests (1 Sam 14:18–19, 36–38). One wonders whether Saul's hostile attitude toward the priests of Nob (1 Sam 22:12–19), the successors of the influential Shiloh priesthood, may not have had deeper roots than the incident that provoked Saul's massacre of this priestly clan. The restrictions on Saul's freedom already noted suggest that the representatives of the old order did their best to limit Saul's kingship. The *mishpaṭ* of the kingdom that Samuel wrote in a document at Mizpah (1 Sam 10:25) was probably a treaty specifying the rights and

31. Note how Ahimelek's initial fear on seeing David coming alone (1 Sam 21:2) parallels Samuel's fear when told to go anoint David (1 Sam 16:2).

32. The reference to the Ark in the MT of 1 Sam 14:18 is generally considered a textual corruption for "ephod" which most critics adopt as the correct reading (McCarter, *1 Samuel*, 237).

33. One should note, however, that the same harsh sacral demands were never imposed on David; no one complained when he returned from his campaign loaded with booty.

34. For the identification of the date, genre, and purpose of this History, see McCarter, *1 Samuel*, 27–30.

limitations of the king.[35] and the comment in 1 Sam 14:47 that Saul "seized the kingship over Israel" may suggest that Saul had extended his authority beyond the limits that the older authorities had envisioned for an Israelite king.[36]

If many ancient biblical writers, including Dtr, did not share the view of Gideon and Samuel that the choice of a human king implies the rejection of Yahweh, that notion can hardly be regarded as self-evident. In fact, seen in the broader perspective of general Near Eastern thought, the notion is anything but self-evident. In Mesopotamia the human king was easily accepted as the agent or regent of the real king, the deity. Thus in the Assyrian enthronement ritual one stresses that the real king is Asshur, but the human king is allowed his place in the scheme of things nevertheless.[37] Likewise in Babylon, the real king is Marduk, but his human agent is still permitted the title king of Babylon.[38] The accommodation of human kingship to divine kingship appears to have taken place without any serious theological friction. Moreover, once Israel developed the monarchy, it related the human king and the divine monarch to each other in precisely the same way as had been done in Mesopotamia.[39] The texts that come out of the royal cult betray no indication that the presence of a human king compromises the position of the divine king.

35. Ibid., 194.

36. The use of the term *lākad* for assuming kingship is unusual; it is nowhere else attested either for assuming kingship or any other office, and this leads McCarter to adopt the reading *mlʾkh* ("territory") for MT's *hmlwkh* ("the kingdom") (*1 Samuel*, 253). But McCarter can show no real parallel for translating *mlʾkh* as "territory" (p. 255), and to translate it and the following prepositional phrase as "territory outside of Israel" is simply an unjustified tour de force. H. J. Stoebe points out that the use of the verb *lākad* here picks up on its use in 1 Sam 10:20–21, where Saul was "taken" by lot to be Israel's king (*Das erst Buch Samuelis*, 276). The use of the active voice here suggests that Saul was now grasping after royal authority rather than simply allowing himself to be grasped by God's call, and the placement of this fragment of tradition (14:47–52) between Saul's clash with sacral tradition in the account of his botched success in chap. 14 and his final rejection in chap. 15 heightens the impression that it functions editorially to prepare for Saul's approaching downfall.

37. K. Fr. Müller, *Das assyrische Ritual*, esp. i 29, where the priests proclaim, "Asshur is king! Asshur is king!," ii 30–31, where Asshur and Ninlil are referred to as the lords of the royal crown that has just been placed on the head of the new king, and iii 5–7, where the first present brought to the newly enthroned king is taken away to the temple of Asshur and presented to the god. Note also the ritual for King Asshur-ban-apal edited by E. F. Weidner (*AfO* 13, 210ff.; = E. Ebeling, *Literarische Keilschrifttexte aus Assur* [Berlin, 1953] no. 31). Lines 15–16 say: "Asshur is king! Asshur alone is king! Asshur-ban-apal is [the beloved] of Asshur, the creation of his hand. May the great gods establish his reign, may they protect [the life of Asshur-ba]n-apal, the king of Assyria."

38. See, e.g., the prologue to the Code of Hammurabi (Bergmann, *Codex Hammurabi*, cols. i–v).

39. Levenson, *Sinai and Zion*, 70–71.

Human Motivations behind Kingship and the Royal Ideology

No one will deny that quite human and sometimes sinful motivations played a role in the formation of the kingship and of the imperialistic royal ideology that was developed to undergird it, but theologically one must ask, So what? The God portrayed in the Bible has never seemed averse to working through human agents who were less than perfect. Moreover, anyone with a basic theological understanding of human nature knows that there was never a time in Israel's history when quite human motivations were out of play, and that includes the creative Mosaic period.

In his canonization of this period as the ideal period that should serve as a touchstone for judging what is authentically Yahwistic, G. E. Mendenhall seems to imply that Israel's leaders at this time were completely open to God's leading, that the selfish human desires and motivations that later perverted this ideal situation were dormant or ineffective in this period.[40] Such a claim is heavily dependent on sheer hypothetical reconstruction. There is almost no direct historical evidence for this period and relatively little for the subsequent period of the Judges, so any reconstruction of the Israelite political and religious order during these formative periods is quite hypothetical at best. To canonize one such fragile reconstruction as the touchstone for deciding what is "authentically Yahwistic," as Mendenhall and other do, hardly seems compelling.

Even if one agrees in many respects with Mendenhall's reconstruction of early Israel's organization, it does not follow that the human motivations that led to that structure were as pure and devoid of the desire for power as Mendenhall suggests. In my opinion, Mendenhall is correct in seeing the Mosaic covenant as very early and as intimately tied to the idea of Yahweh's kingship over Israel.[41] Moreover, Israel's covenantal recognition of Yahweh as king and

---

40. Mendenhall's grudging admission that the old pagan tendency toward local aggrandizement at the expense of groups beyond the tribal border continued even under the *pax Yahweh* hardly affects his unrealistic idealization of this formative period (*Magnalia Dei*, 145).

41. Despite the recent tendency of some scholars to return to a Wellhausian late dating of the covenant concept following L. Perlitt (*Bundestheologie im Alten Testament* [WMANT 36; Neukirchen-Vluyn: Neukirchener Verlag, 1969]), and despite D. J. McCarthy's more restrained judgment that the earliest covenant form in Israel was a ritual covenant, that the treaty form was first called upon to express some profound ideas about the people's relation to God after the fall of Samaria by the circles that produced Ur-Deuteronomy (*Treaty and Covenant* [AnBib 21A; Rome: Biblical Institute Press, 1978] 290), Mendenhall has maintained the position he spelled out in his classic *Law and Covenant in Israel and the Ancient Near East* (Pittsburgh: Biblical Colloquium, 1955), and many Old Testament scholars, particularly in North America, would still agree with his claim that the religious foundations of

its acceptance of the covenantal law in the tribal assembly probably reflected a rejection of Pharaonic rule and of Canaanite kingship, both of which had been experienced by different elements in the assembly as oppressive.[42] Assuming that this is correct, however, the creation of this rival theological ideology for self-government was not without its selfish human motivation. By uniting under a divine overlord, the tribes gained a supratribal strength that aided them in their struggle to wrest living space from the established city-states in Canaan. Moreover, by vesting that unifying power in a divine king rather than in a human king they preserved the maximum freedom for the pursuit of their own tribal interests as well as scoring a propaganda victory against their opponents in the struggle for Canaan. The burden of taxation that was needed to support Israel's divine king was far less than that required to support the human kings of the Canaanite city-states. Thus, for large elements of the population of Canaan capitulation to the Israelites offered the advantage of lower taxes as well as relief from the economic disruption that hostile Israelites tribes could cause to the cities that opposed this confederacy. As N. K. Gottwald has correctly noted, the Israelite confederacy in no way represented the renouncement of the human exercise of coercive power; it simply redistributed the power in a

---

the premonarchic tribal federation "stemmed from Moses and the Sinai covenant" (Mendenhall, "The Monarchy," 158).

P. D. Miller has shown, following Wright, that Deut 33:4–5 links Israel's recognition of Yahweh as king, Israel's acceptance of covenantal law, and the constitution of the people of Israel in a tribal assembly (*The Divine Warrior in Early Israel* [HSM 5; Cambridge: Harvard University Press, 1973] 82). As translated by Miller, the text reads as follows:

> Moses commanded for us torah,
> A possession of the assembly of Jacob.
> Then (Yahweh) became king in Yeshurun
> When the leaders of the people gathered together.
> The assembly of the tribes of Israel.

It is difficult to assign a specific date to this text, but even if one agrees with Miller in regarding it as a secondary insertion in the very ancient introductory frame to the Blessing of Moses, the text is quite old (ibid.) and may reflect on authentic tradition about the formation of the Yahwistic federation. Given our limited knowledge of the premonarchic period, it is hard to take seriously Crüsemann's confident rejection of this possibility: "Es ist nach all unserer Kenntnis historisch-unmöglich, dass eine Versammlung des vorstaatlichen Israel Jahweh zum König über sich proklamiert hätte" (*Der Widerstand gegen das Königtum*, 81).

42. J. D. Levenson has shown quite convincingly that Israel's religious rejection of kingship stems from Israel's covenant conception in which God is seen as suzerain of the people: "If all Israelites are vassals of the great king, then it follows that one Israelite may not be set up over his fellows as king. There is no such thing as a 'vice-suzerain' to whom vassals in covenant may do homage without harming their relationship with the great king. In short, the directness of the two-party relationship of YHWH and Israel, including even the individual Israelite, precludes human kingship. YHWH is her suzerain, YHWH alone (*Sinai and Zion*, 72–73).

less centralized fashion than the contemporary monarchies.[43] While Yahweh was the acknowledged suzerain, the actual governmental power lay in the hands of the tribal leaders and the religious authorities. Moreover, while that power was diffuse and apparently ill-defined, it was clearly enough recognized that any shift in its distribution could provoke intertribal warfare.[44] Tribal leaders during the period of the league could be just as defensive of the status quo as any court theologian of the later monarchy, and I have already indicated the political stake that religious leaders like Samuel had in maintaining the old system.

Finally, while more diffuse, the exercise of coercive power during the league could be just as brutal as anything seen during the later monarchy, and because the power was so diffuse, its coercive exercise tended to be far more ad hoc and arbitrary. If one gives any credence to the texts, both the early wars of conquest and the intertribal conflicts were brutal, bloody affairs with no lack of what people today would consider atrocities. Thus when Mendenhall blasts Saul for the illicit conduct of war, David for his glorification of the professional soldier's "superior ability to commit murder," and the monarchy in general for the horrendous atrocities that marked the royal wars of the united monarchy and the divided monarchy of ancient Israel and Judah,[45] that critique appears anachronistic, self-contradictory, and hardly worthy of rebuttal. Unless one is prepared to accept G. von Rad's claim that the early wars of Israel were purely defensive wars.[46] a claim that contradicts the biblical tradition and represents perhaps the weakest point in his classic study,[47] one cannot sanitize the early wars of the "divine warrior." The *ḥerem*, that religious obligation which called for, among other things, the sacral execution of prisoners of war, is quite clearly a heritage from these early wars of conquest, and the great promoters of the *ḥerem* or ban were not the kings of Israel and Judah but the religious leaders of the league and their later successors among the prophets. Samuel condemned Saul for not carrying out the ban. If one wants to speak of atrocities, it was Samuel, not Saul, who hacked the living Agag into pieces before Yahweh (1 Sam 15:32–33), and it was the prophets who wanted to preserve this ancient practice against the tendency of the later kings to treat their captives with politically motivated clemency (1 Kgs 20:30–43). It was the Deuteronomistic heirs of the Mosaic tradition, not the court theologians of the

43. N. K. Gottwald, *The Tribes of Yahweh: A Sociology of the Religion of Liberated Israel 1250–1050 B.C.E.* (Maryknoll, N.Y.: Orbis Books, 1979) 226, 599–602.

44. Note especially the recurring motif of Ephraim's claim to hegemony in Israel (Judg 8:1–3; 12:1–6).

45. Mendenhall, "The Monarchy," 159.

46. G. von Rad, *Der heilige Krieg im alten Israel* (3d ed.: Göttingen: Vandenhoeck & Ruprecht, 1958) 26.

47. Miller, *The Divine Warrior*, 2.

Zion tradition, who preserved and codified in Deuteronomy 20 the rules of war so offensive to modern sensibilities.

The transition to royal rule took place in Israel because the old system was no longer working. Under the combined pressure of Philistine and Ammonite expansion, the loosely organized Israelite confederacy could not muster and maintain sufficient military forces to deal with the continuing threat. The advantages the league offered during the earlier period of the struggle with the Canaanite city-states no longer worked against the new enemies. An Israelite king might require taxes, but the alternative was to pay an even more onerous tribute to the Philistines, the Ammonites, or some other invading enemy. Some Israelites opposed the development, but apart from important officials in the old regime, it is difficult to identify these opponents. The opposition probably came from those who had the most to lose and the least to gain from such a change, that is, from tribal leaders whose own territories were least threatened by the growing Philistine and Ammonite power.[48]

With the establishment of the monarchy, a new religious ideology was developed to legitimate the human monarch as the chosen agent of the divine king, and under David this royal ideology was elaborated to provide justification for his imperial conquests. On the one hand, one can see how this ideology served to stabilize the power structure, but while it certainly served royal interests, that ideology can hardly be dismissed as all bad. The ideology of kingship emphasized the king's duty to promote justice, and the royal administration of justice probably offered the powerless the first effective check against the oppression of powerful local leaders that they had experienced in a long time: Judicial corruption did not begin with the monarchy; on the contrary, the monarchy was understood as offering a corrective to such corruption. While Israelite kings did not live up to the ideal promulgated in the royal ideology, the ideology promoted the understanding of justice that the prophets were later to exploit in their critique of particular kings and their royal officials.

Curiously enough, the same point may be made in regard to the imperialistic aspects of the royal ideology. The Zion tradition's conception that Yahweh would subject all the surrounding nations to the Davidic hegemony in Jerusalem, thus bringing about peace and well-being in the Davidic empire, is nationalistic, imperialistic, and even chauvinistic, but it also lies at the base of the great prophetic visions of universal peace. Again, the ideal reflected in the ideology could provide a weapon for criticizing any contemporary ruler. Though originally formulated to justify the Davidic imperial expansion, it

48. Thus, in contrast to McKenzie's claim that the elders pushed for a king in order to enrich an oligarchy (in *The Quest for the Kingdom of God*, 29), I would argue that much of the opposition to kingship came from an oligarchy that feared that its privileges and freedom would be curtailed by this new authority.

could be employed by an Isaiah to attack the militaristic activities of an Ahaz or a Hezekiah.[49] It will not do to dismiss this theology as a purely pagan development. Theologically the doctrine of the election of the Davidic dynasty is no more problematic than the doctrine of the election of the Israelite people. Both doctrines can and have been perverted by sinful human beings who want to claim privilege without responsibility, but even without that perversion the doctrines may seem offensive in their particularity. There is an undeniable human and self-serving element in the formulation of both these doctrines, yet despite this human element, both these doctrines are authentically Yahwistic and characteristically biblical. To reject either is simply to rebel against the particularity of biblical faith, to reject the God who chose to work his work through a particular nation and through particular individuals despite their sins and shortcomings.

---

49. See especially my forthcoming study, "Yahweh's Foundation in Zion (Isa 28:16)," *JBL* [[here: pp. 292–310]].

Chapter 25

The Old Testament's Contribution to Messianic Expectations

A discussion of the Old Testament's contribution to the development of the later messianic expectations can hardly be focused on the Hebrew word for messiah, מָשִׁיחַ. In the original context not one of the thirty-nine occurrences of מָשִׁיחַ in the Hebrew canon refers to an expected figure of the future whose coming will coincide with the inauguration of an era of salvation.

The word מָשִׁיחַ is an adjectival formation with passive significance from the verbal root מָשַׁח, "to anoint." It is used adjectivally in the expression הַכֹּהֵן הַמָּשִׁיחַ, "the anointed priest" (Lev 4:3, 5, 16; 6:15), to refer either to the Aaronid priests in general, all of whom were anointed (Exod 28:41; 30:30; 40:15; Num 3:3), or possibly to the high priest alone as the specific successor to Aaron, since the unction of high priest seems to be treated as something special (Num 35:25). The most common use of the term, however, is as a singular nominalized adjective in construct with a following divine name or with a pronominal suffix referring to the deity: מְשִׁיחַ יהוה "the anointed of Yahweh" (1 Sam 24:7, 11; 26:9, 11, 16, 23; 2 Sam 1:14, 16; 19:22; Lam 4:20); מְשִׁיחַ אֱלֹהֵי יַעֲקֹב, "the anointed of the God of Jacob" (2 Sam 23:1); and מְשִׁיחוֹ, מְשִׁיחִי, מְשִׁיחֶךָ "his, my, your anointed one" (1 Sam 2:10, 35; 12:3, 5; 16:6; 2 Sam 22:51; Isa 45:1; Hab 3:13; Pss 2:2; 18:51; 20:7; 28:8; 84:10; 89:39, 52; 132:10, 17; 2 Chr 6:42 [corrected from מְשִׁיחֶיךָ]). With one exception all these occurrences refer to the contemporary Israelite king, and the use of the term seems intended to underscore the very close relationship between Yahweh and the king whom he has chosen and installed.

The exception is Isa 45:1, where the Persian Cyrus is called Yahweh's anointed one: לְכוֹרֶשׁ כֹּה־אָמַר יהוה לִמְשִׁיחוֹ, "Thus says Yahweh to his anointed one, to Cyrus. . . ." This usage, like Yahweh's earlier reference to Cyrus as רֹעִי, "my shepherd" (Isa 44:28), is analogous to passages in Jeremiah where Yahweh refers to Nebuchadnezzar as עַבְדִּי, "my servant" (Jer 25:9; 27:6; 43:10), an expression that is otherwise reserved in Jeremiah for David (Jer 33:21, 22, 26) or the collective Jacob (30:10; 46:27, 28). This unusual designation of a non-Israelite king with terms normally used to express the very special relationship that the Israelite king had to Yahweh is clearly intended by both Jeremiah and Second Isaiah to shock their Israelite audiences into looking at historical events in a new way. Yet the role assigned to Cyrus by Second Isaiah is quite different from that assigned to Nebuchadnezzar by Jeremiah.[1] Nebuchadnezzar was an agent of judgment against God's people, a role never assigned to a native Israelite king. Cyrus, however, is assigned a role as an agent of salvation for God's people. This is quite compatible with Israelite expectations for their own native kings, and Isaiah's oracle concerning Cyrus could be seen as modeled on Israelite coronation oracles. Nonetheless, one should not regard Second Isaiah's treatment of Cyrus as messianic in the later sense of the term. Despite the positive expectations associated with Cyrus, he, like Jeremiah's Nebuchadnezzar, was a contemporary ruler, not an expected figure of the future. At most one could say that Second Isaiah endowed him with the same royal expectations that were formerly bestowed on any new incumbent of the Davidic throne at his coronation.

The plural nominalized adjective occurs twice (excluding 2 Chr 6:42, which should be corrected to a singular), both times with a first person singular suffix referring to Yahweh: אַל־תִּגְּעוּ בִמְשִׁיחָי וְלִנְבִיאַי אַל־תָּרֵעוּ, "Do not touch my anointed ones, and do not harm my prophets" (Ps 105:15; 1 Chr 16:22). The context makes it clear that the anointed ones here are the Israelite patriarchs seen as prophets (cf. Gen 20:7). Whether Israelite prophets, like Israelite priests and kings, were normally anointed at their installation, as 1 Kgs 19:16 might suggest, is disputed, but an early cultic practice of such anointing would help to explain the later metaphorical language that characterizes the prophet as anointed with the spirit of God (Isa 61:1; Joel 3:1).

One of the other three occurrences of מָשִׁיחַ is irrelevant for our discussion since it concerns the oiling of a shield (2 Sam 1:21) and should probably be corrected to מָשׁוּחַ, but the final two are significant since they involve the nominal use of מָשִׁיחַ in the absolute state (Dan 9:25–26), and they occur in a late text only a century earlier than datable texts that use מָשִׁיחַ or its Greek translation χριστός to refer to expected eschatological figures of the future. The usage in Daniel is not messianic in this later sense, however. The expression צַד־מָשִׁיחַ נָגִיד, "until an anointed one, a prince [comes]" (Dan 9:25), apparently has a historical figure of the distant past in mind, perhaps the high priest Joshua or the governor Zerubabbel mentioned in Haggai and Zechariah (Hag 1:1–14; 2:21–23; Zech 4:6; 6:9–14; cf. 4:14, where the expression שְׁנֵי בְנֵי־הַיִּצְהָר, "the two sons of oil," presumably refers to these two anointed officials). On the other hand, the expression יִכָּרֵת מָשִׁיחַ וְאֵין לוֹ, "an anointed one will be cut off and will have nothing" (Dan 9:26), is normally interpreted to refer to Onias III, the legitimate high priest who was deposed and eventually murdered during the reign of Antiochus IV. At the time of the writer of Daniel, both

1. I must thank Martin Hengel for reminding me of this during the discussion at the colloquium.

incidents were past events, so neither figure could be regarded as a messianic figure expected by him or his readers.

Passages Which Acquired a Later Messianic Interpretation

Even if some of these passages where מָשִׁיחַ occurs were later understood as prophetic predictions of the Messiah, as happened for example with Ps 2:2, such passages provide an inadequate base from which to discuss the Old Testament contribution to the development of messianic expectations. By far the majority of biblical passages given a messianic interpretation by later Jewish and Christian sources do not contain the word מָשִׁיחַ. The passages selected as these messianic proof texts remain remarkably consistent for both Jewish and Christian interpreters, however, and this suggests that one might approach our task by analyzing the different types of material included in this fairly consistent body of messianic texts.[2]

Ex Eventu *Prophecies*

Some of these texts in their original settings appear to have been prophecies *ex eventu*. Balaam's oracle about the star that would step forth from Jacob and the staff that would arise from Israel (Num 24:17) probably dates from the early monarchy and celebrates the victories of a Saul or a David in the guise of prophecy. This seems to be literary prophecy in a triumphalist mode, not so much propaganda to further a political agenda as nationalistic literature celebrating an already achieved hegemony. Jacob's comment that the scepter or staff would never depart from Judah (Gen 49:10) would also appear to date to the early monarchy and to refer to the Davidic dynasty. Whether it is pure celebration, however, or whether it was intended to undergird the inviolability of the Davidic dynasty by rooting it in a prophetic word remains debatable. One might challenge the characterization of these texts as prophecies *ex eventu* if one accepted a pre-monarchical date for them on linguistic grounds, but, in any case, they found their fulfillment in the early monarchical period, and it is only by ignoring that original setting that they can continue to function as prophecies for the future.

2. The basic consistency in the choice of texts can be seen by a simple comparison of the work of the Jewish scholar J. Klausner, *The Messianic Idea in Israel* (New York, 1955), to any of the countless works by Christian scholars on the same subject. Nor is this consistency a modern phenomenon. Early Christians, rabbinic sources, and the sectarians at Qumran cite the same biblical texts in their portrayals of the royal messiah, as A. S. Van der Woude has pointed out (*Die messianischen Vorstellungen der Gemeinde von Qumrân* [Studia Semitica Neerlandica 3; Assen, 1957], pp. 243–44).

Enthronement Texts

Other texts appear to have their original settings in the enthronement ceremonies of particular Israelite or Judean kings. Psalms 2 and 110 and Isa 8:23b–9:6 have been plausibly interpreted in this fashion. The divine promises contained in these texts were made to particular kings or their subjects at particular points in the history of the monarchy. They were not prophecies holding out hope for a distant future but oracles that gave expression to political, social, and religious expectations for the reign of a contemporary king just being installed into office. As such, they served a political as well as a religious function; the propaganda value of such texts and of the larger ceremonial occasion in which they were originally embedded should by no means be overlooked.

Such enthronement texts, though composed for particular occasions, reflect the Israelite royal theology as it was developed and transmitted in the kingdom of Judah, and it will be helpful to highlight aspects of that royal theology before turning to the next category of "messianic" texts. The particular historical developments during the reigns of David and Solomon led to the widely accepted theological claims that Yahweh had chosen David to be his king and Jerusalem to be his royal city. The choice of David extended to David's descendants so that the Davidic dynasty was to retain David's throne in perpetuity and the choice of Jerusalem meant that Yahweh would make his abode there, first in David's tent where David had the ark transferred with great fanfare and then in the Temple that Solomon eventually built. This double choice, of dynasty and royal city, which has numerous parallels in the ancient Near East, was firmly linked in the royal Zion theology (Pss 2:6; 132:10–18), but the implications of each choice could be spelled out independently of the other.

The choice of Zion was elaborated by the glorification of the city, sometimes in strongly mythological terms, but I have treated that subject extensively elsewhere,[3] and while it would be central to any discussion of Israel's general eschatological expectations, it is not central to a discussion of "messianic texts" narrowly conceived. One should note, however, that the tradition of Zion as Yahweh's city presupposes the Temple, the cultus, and the priesthood in one fashion or another.

The choice of David was elaborated by the tradition of the eternal covenant God made with him and his dynasty. This tradition is already attested in the "last words of David" (2 Sam 23:1–7), an old poem with close linguistic ties to the oracles of Balaam, and it is continued in such texts as Psalms 89 and 132, and 2 Samuel 7, to mention only the most prominent. Israelite royal theology resembled that of its Near Eastern neighbors in stressing the king's

3. See my article, "Zion in the Theology of the Davidic-Solomonic Empire," *Studies in the Period of David and Solomon and Other Essays*, ed. T. Ishida (Tokyo / Winona Lake, Ind.: 1982), pp. 93–108 [[here: pp. 331–347]], and the literature cited there.

responsibility to uphold justice, rule wisely, and ensure the general well-being and piety of his land, but David's imperial expansion gave the Israelite royal theology an added dimension. This royal ideology viewed David and his successors as regents of the divine suzerain; hence the surrounding nations should be their vassals, making pilgrimage to the imperial city to pay tribute to the Davidic overlord and his God and to submit their conflicts to the overlord's arbitration.

One other aspect of the enthronement texts should be noted—their strong mythological component. However the language was understood in the enthronement ceremony, Ps 2:7 speaks of God giving birth to the king; Ps 110:3, though textually difficult, also appears to refer to the divine birth of the king;[4] and Isa 9:5–6, after referring to the king's birth, assigns divine qualities to the king in the series of names that are given to him. These names in Isa 9:5–6 are best explained as royal names given to the new king in the coronation ceremony on the analogy of the five royal names given the new Pharaoh in the Egyptian enthronement ceremony,[5] and this suggests a strong Egyptian influence on the Judean coronation ritual. This influence may go back to the formative period of the Israelite state when Egyptian influence was quite strong. As is well known, Solomon married a daughter of the Pharaoh (1 Kgs 3:1; 7:8; 9:16), and even earlier David appears to have adopted Egyptian models for many of the high offices in his empire.[6] In any case, the Egyptian influence on the Israelite royal ceremony brought with it the strongly mythological language of the Egyptian royal protocol. This language was probably not taken literally in the Israelite court—the language of divine sonship, for instance, was presumably understood in Israel as adoptive sonship—but once this mythological language had been deposited and preserved in texts whose original roots in particular court ceremonies were forgotten, the possibility for new, literalistic readings of this mythological language arose. Much of the mythological dimension in the later messianic expectations can be traced back to the remythologization of this borrowed mythological language of the royal protocol.

---

4. Note H.-J. Kraus's emendation of the text to בְּהַרְרֵי־קֹדֶשׁ מֵרֶחֶם שַׁחַר כְּטַל יְלִדְתִּיךָ, "On the holy mountains, out of the womb of Dawn, like dew have I given birth to you" (*Psalmen* 2 [Biblischer Kommentar 15.2; Neukirchen, 1961[2]], pp. 752–53, 758–60).

5. S. Morenz, "Ägyptische und davidische Königstitular," *Zeitschrift für ägyptische Sprache* 79 (1954) 73–74; H. Bonnet, "Krönung," *Reallexikon der ägyptischen Religionsgeschichte* (Berlin, 1952), pp. 395–400; A. Alt, "Jesaja 8,23–9,6. Befreiungsnacht und Krönungstag," *Kleine Schriften zur Geschichte des Volkes Israel* (Munich, 1953), vol. 2, pp. 206–25.

6. See the discussion and further bibliography in T. N. D. Mettinger, *Solomonic State Officials: A Study of the Civil Government Officials of the Israelite Monarchy* (Coniectanea Biblica, Old Testament Series 5; Lund, 1971).

Restoration and Dynastic Texts

The third category of messianic texts differs from the first two in that these texts do in fact envision a future ruler not yet on the scene. Because Israelite royal theology, at least as transmitted in Judah, regarded the Davidic dynasty as eternally guaranteed by God, in times of severe crisis the tradition of Yahweh's eternal covenant with David could serve as basis for the hope that God would soon restore the monarchy to its former glory by raising up a new scion of the Davidic line. Sometimes this figure is not described as a descendant from the Davidic line, but simply as David himself. Nonetheless, it is extremely doubtful that this usage should be pressed to imply that the long-dead king would return to life to assume the throne again. It is more likely that the usage simply implies a new embodiment of the Davidic ideal, a new David. As the founder of the dynasty, creator of the Israelite empire, and dominant influence in the creation of the national cultus in Jerusalem, David was the model of the ideal king, and a new embodiment of that ideal could be called David for short.

A number of these passages cluster in prophetic collections that come from the late eighth century, but the originality of that literary context is disputed for every one of the passages in question. Isa 11:10, 32:1–8; Hos 3:5; Amos 9:11–12; and Mic 5:1–5 are generally taken as later expansions of the genuine eighth-century material in these books. The judgment on Isa 11:1–9 is more divided, but a significant number of scholars would also date this material much later than the eighth century. I am not convinced that this general skepticism is warranted. There are other indications that the political disasters of the late eighth century, including the destruction of the northern kingdom and the deportation of a significant portion of the population of the southern kingdom, produced widespread longing for the unity, strength, and justice of the idealized united monarchy of the past. Isaiah reflects that longing in a number of oracles dating from the period of the Syro-Ephraimite war,[7] it is clearly expressed in Isa 1:21–26, and Hezekiah's attempt to extend his control into the north presupposes it. One should also note that the oracle in Zech 9:1–10, as difficult as it is to interpret, contains a number of elements that strongly suggest an original eighth-century context. The linking of Hadrach (Hatarikka in the Akkadian texts), Damascus, Israel, Hamath, and the Phoenician cities inevitably reminds the historically informed interpreter of Tiglath-pileser's victory over Kullani (biblical Calneh) in 738 B.C.E., when the south Syrian coalition apparently led by Judah under Azariah/Uzziah collapsed. All these

7. J. J. M. Roberts, "Isaiah 2 and the Prophet's Message to the North," *JQR* 75.3 (1985) 290–308; and "Isaiah and His Children," *Biblical and Related Studies Presented to Samuel Iwry*, ed. A. Kort and S. Morschauser (Winona Lake, Ind., 1985), pp. 193–203.

states figure in that event according to the Assyrian sources, and it is impossible to find a later event of which the same could be said.[8]

If such a longing for the golden days of the Davidic empire were prevalent in the late eighth century, one should reevaluate these texts. As von Rad argued years ago,[9] Amos can be interpreted as rooted in the Zion theology, and an eighth-century Judean prophet rooted in that theology could well author such an oracle as Amos 9:11–12, which envisions the restoration of the Davidic empire. One should note that both Amos (6:2) and Isaiah (10:9) specifically mention the fall of Kullani as an event with profound consequences for Israelite and Judean security.

Hillers has suggested a similar background for Mic 5:1–5.[10] The reference to the seven shepherds and eight princes is most easily explained against the background of the south Syrian league active in the late eighth century and in which Judah apparently played a leading role prior to the battle of Kullani. Isa 11:1–9 would also fit this period as a statement of Isaiah's hope in the context of the Syro-Ephraimitic war.

Micah's promise of a new ruler from Bethlehem and Isaiah's promise of a shoot from the root of Jesse both suggest a new David is needed and thus imply a serious criticism of the current occupant of the Davidic throne as less than an adequate heir to David. Such criticism fits the time of Isaiah and Micah quite well. With Azariah/Uzziah's demise there was ample room for dissatisfaction with the Davidic house. Jotham is hardly noted, but Isaiah's disappointment with Ahaz is well documented. It would seem that both prophets expected a new embodiment of the Davidic ideal, but both expected a refining judgment on the nation beforehand. That is certainly the case with Isaiah, who envisioned a humbling of the royal house and of the royal city before both would experience a new embodiment of the ancient ideal (Isa 1:21–26, 11:1–9, 32:1–8).[11] Nonetheless, it also seems certain that Isaiah expected this new

---

8. The best and most comprehensive treatment of this event remains that of H. Tadmor ("Azriyau of Yaudi," *Studies in the Bible*, ed. C. Rabin [Scripta Hierosolymitana 8; Jerusalem, 1961], pp. 232–71), but it should be supplemented or corrected by at least the following articles: M. Weippert, "Menahem von Israel und seine Zeitgenossen in einer Steleninschrift des assyrischen Königs Tiglathpileser III. aus dem Iran," *Zeitschrift des Deutschen Palästinavereins* 89 (1973) 26–53; N. Naʾaman, "Sennacherib's 'Letter of God' on His Campaign to Judah," *BASOR* 214 (1974) 25–39; and K. Kessler, "Die Anzahl der assyrischen Provinzen des Jahres 738 v. Chr. in Nordsyrien," *Die Welt des Orients* 8 (1975–76) 49–63.

9. G. von Rad, *Old Testament Theology*, trans. D. M. G. Stalker (New York, 1960), vol. 2, pp. 130–38.

10. D. R. Hillers, *Micah* (Hermeneia; Philadelphia, 1984), pp. 65–69.

11. J. J. M. Roberts, "The Divine King and the Human Community in Isaiah's Vision of the Future," *The Quest for the Kingdom of God: Studies in Honor of George E. Mendenhall*, ed. H. B. Huffmon, F. A. Spina, and A. R. W. Green (Winona Lake, Ind., 1983), pp. 127–36 [[here: pp. 348–357]].

David in the near future. His use of very similar language in his coronation oracle for Hezekiah probably suggests that, for a time at least, he expected Hezekiah to fulfill these expectations.

Jeremiah, Ezekiel, and Related Texts

The next cluster of messianic texts envisioning a future king falls at the end of the Judean kingdom in the late seventh and early sixth century. These include Jer 23:5–8, 30:9, 33:14–27; Ezek 17:22–24, 34:23–24, 37:15–28. The originality of some of these passages in their present context or their attribution to the prophet in whose book they stand has been questioned, but there is little reason for redating any of the passages to a significantly later period. Jer 23:5–8 is normally attributed to Jeremiah, and the apparent play on Zedekiah's name in v. 6 suggests that the oracle comes from the period of that king's rule. The oracle seems influenced by several Isaianic passages. The צֶמַח ("sprout") for David recalls Isa 11:1, 10; the expression וּמָלַךְ מֶלֶךְ וְהִשְׂכִּיל וְעָשָׂה מִשְׁפָּט וּצְדָקָה בָּאָרֶץ "the king will rule and act wisely, and he will do justice and righteousness in the land," resembles Isa 32:1a, הֵן לְצֶדֶק יִמְלָךְ־מֶלֶךְ, "Then the king will rule in righteousness"; and the themes of the reunification of Judah and Israel and of the new exodus remind one of Isa 11:10–16, all of which suggest that these passages antedated Jeremiah and influenced his outlook. Jeremiah envisions a new Davidic ruler who will embody the ancient ideals of just rule. In this ruler's days the unity of north and south will again be realized, and the exiles from both states will return to Israel to live in their own land. Jer 30:8–9 may be originally from an early period in the prophet's ministry, perhaps from the time of Josiah, when Jeremiah was appealing to the north. It shows close connections to Hos 3:5 and to some Isaianic passages (Isa 10:27, 14:25). If this early dating for the original setting of Jer 30:8–9 is accepted, it may suggest that Jeremiah at one point in his ministry saw Josiah as the new David. Exactly how Jer 30:18–21 fits into this picture is not clear, though it also seems to be an early oracle addressed to the north. What is meant by the ruler who would arise from the midst of Jacob? Could the prophet refer to a Davidic king in so obscure a fashion? Could Josiah, for instance, have claimed kinship with the northerners in an effort to persuade them to accept his rule in preference to that of the foreign nobility who had controlled Samaria since the fall of the north? Or does this passage envision a genuine northerner to rule over the north? The issue remains obscure. Jer 33:14–26 is also problematic. Since the passage requires extensive discussion and its attribution to Jeremiah is questionable, we will return to it later.

The messianic oracles in Ezekiel are roughly contemporaneous with those of Jeremiah and basically only elaborate the themes already found in Jeremiah. The long-standing division between north and south will be healed under the new David, and the exiles will return to their own land to serve God, where a Davidic prince will always rule over them. This emphasis on the eternal rule of the promised Davidic prince appears to be a response to a problem of faith created by the Babylonian termination of the Davidic dynasty in Jerusalem. Given the tradition of God's eternal covenant with David, how could the dynasty possibly come to an end? When it was seriously threatened, one could approach God with the accusation of a breach of covenant, as Psalm 89 very well illustrates, but when the dynasty no longer existed, what was left to say? Were the promises of God not reliable? Ezekiel suggests the reinstallment of the dynasty in such a way as to respond at least implicitly to this existential concern.

That such an existential concern was a serious problem in this general period is clear from Jer 33:14–26, which addresses it explicitly. This pericope is full of problems that make its attribution difficult. It is missing in the LXX of Jeremiah, which has been taken as an indication that the pericope is a very late secondary addition to the book. The pericope begins after an introductory statement in v. 14 with a citation in vv. 15–16 of a slightly variant form of the genuine Jeremianic oracle of Jer 23:5–8. That in itself may also suggest secondary expansion of the Jeremianic corpus. The pericope, however, continues with a promise that God is not yet finished with the Davidic dynasty nor with the Levitical priesthood, and this promise is clearly formulated in response to a widespread opinion that was being expressed among the people. According to v. 24 the people were saying that God had rejected the two families that he had chosen. He had annulled his covenant with David so that a member of the Davidic dynasty no longer ruled before him, he had annulled his covenant with Levi so that the Levites no longer served as priests before him, and he had spurned his people so that they were no longer a nation before him. Whatever one may think of the authorship of this pericope, such murmurings among the people can hardly be temporally situated anywhere but in the exile. They presuppose the end of the Davidic dynasty, the cessation of the regular Temple cultus, and the loss of Judah's independent existence as a nation. With the restoration of the Temple cultus after the return, it is unlikely that such a claim about the Levitical priests could have gained currency, and the nature of the prophet's response to the opinion of the people gives no grounds for thinking that the Temple cultus had yet been restored.

One should note that the three things which the people claim God has rejected are three central dogmas of the deuteronomic theology: Yahweh's choice of and covenant with David and his successors to be his king; Yahweh's choice of and covenant with Levi and his successors to be his priests; and Yahweh's choice of and covenant with Israel to be his special people. It should be clear then that the prophetic defender of these threatened dogmas is to be sought in those theological circles that were trying to preserve the deuteronomic legacy from its apparent failure in history. In the face of external reality, the prophet simply asserts that God has not abrogated his covenants with these parties any more than he has abrogated his covenant that upholds the order of creation. The implication is that he will once again install Davidic kings and Levitical priests in office for his people Israel. Moreover, it is very clear from the passage that the prophet envisions a series of Davidic rulers and Levitical priests. Given the decimation of these families caused by the disaster of the Babylonian conquest, the prophet is constrained to apply the old Abrahamic promise of national fertility to these specific families: "Just as the host of heaven cannot be counted and the sand of the seashore cannot be measured, so I will multiply the seed of David my servant and the Levites who minister to me" (Jer 33:22). This is probably an important exegetical comment on earlier prophecies of a new David since it provides a good indication that there had not yet developed any expectation for a last David who in his own person would rule forever.

The mention of the Levitical priests deserves further comment. At first blush their inclusion in such a prophecy concerning a restoration of the Davidic dynasty seems surprising, but further reflection shows that such a move was only to be expected. From the beginning the Zion Tradition had linked the choice of David to the choice of Jerusalem, and Jerusalem as the city of God was first and foremost Jerusalem the site of God's sanctuary, the national Temple built for Yahweh by Solomon. If the Davidic ruler was Yahweh's regent for maintaining just political rule, the priests were Yahweh's chosen servants for maintaining the cultus that allowed Yahweh to remain in the midst of his city among his people. One should recall that Psalm 132, which celebrates Yahweh's linked choice of David and of Zion, twice mentions the priests of Yahweh (vv. 9, 16).

Moreover, the tradition of Yahweh's election of a particular priestly family probably predates any tradition of his choice of a royal line, though the variety of such traditions and their possible contamination by later struggles over the priesthood make any attempt at clarifying the history of the priesthood highly speculative. Nevertheless, one should regard the tradition of Yahweh's selection of Levi for the priesthood, attested among other places in the early blessing of Moses (Deut 33:8–11), as pre-monarchic, and the same is probably true for the tradition of Yahweh's election of Eli's predecessors to the priesthood (1 Sam 2:28–29), even though Eli's family was eventually rejected and replaced by Zadok (1 Kgs 2:27). Num 25:13 also speaks of an eternal covenant of priesthood which Yahweh gave to Phineas and his descendants as a result of his actions on God's behalf at Baal Peor. One should note that each of these traditions is traced back to pre-settlement days and that two of them make the bestowal of the priesthood a reward for the priest's violent actions of killing on behalf of Yahweh. Their similarity in this regard raises the possibility that all these traditions may be variants of a single original.

In any case, some form of such a priestly tradition was undoubtedly cultivated by the priestly family or families that dominated the Jerusalem priesthood. As long as the normal functioning of the cultus was uninterrupted, the average Israelite was probably not much concerned which priestly family had the upper hand in the Temple. The threats to the Davidic house in the late eighth century find their reflex in texts from that period, but despite occasional prophetic attacks on the priests, there is no indication that there was any threat to the continuity of the Jerusalem cultus sufficient to call forth widespread and serious reflection on claims of priestly election. Josiah's radical cultic reform in the late seventh century probably altered this situation, since the closing of so many local shrines and the consequence unemployment of the local priests in favor of Jerusalem and its priesthood must have exacerbated rival priestly claims for the right to serve as priests in the Temple. If one may judge from the book of Deuteronomy, the deuteronomic reform certainly brought the claims of the Levites to public awareness. Then when the Babylonians brought an end to the Davidic dynasty, destroyed Jerusalem, burned the Temple, and killed or deported the priests, it was not just Yahweh's election of David that seemed abrogated; it was also Yahweh's choice of Jerusalem, and for a deuteronomist, of Yahweh's servants, the Levitical priests. It is no more surprising that an exilic deuteronomist should mention the Levitical priests alongside the Davidic king in his vision for the future than that an exilic Zadokite should mention the Zadokite priests alongside the Davidic prince in his vision of the restored community (Ezekiel 40–48).

Postexilic Texts

The attention devoted to Jer 33:14–26 may seem disproportionate to the intrinsic value of the text, but it is crucial to a correct evaluation of the next cluster of messianic prophecies, those of the early postexilic period. After the first return from exile following the edict of Cyrus in 539 B.C.E., the faith issues raised by the people in Jer 33:24 were still not resolved. There was no Davidic king, the Temple was still in ruins, and, given the state of the temple, the priesthood was in no little disgrace. In 520 B.C.E. the prophets Haggai and First Zechariah began to address that situation, apparently initiating a campaign to rebuild the Temple. Haggai urged the Persian-appointed Davidic governor of Judah, Zerubabbel the son of Shealtiel, and the high priest, Joshua the son of Jehozadak, to finish the work, promising that God would soon intervene to make this disappointingly modest-looking building more glorious than the former Temple (Hag 2:1–9). Moreover, in a second oracle Haggai promised that on that day of divine intervention God would take Zerubabbel his servant and make him the signet ring on the divine finger, for God had chosen Zerubabbel (Hag 2:20–23). Given the context of God's promise to overturn other kingdoms, such an oracle clearly implied the elevation of Zerubabbel to the Davidic throne of his ancestors, a point that is even more explicit in the oracles of Haggai's contemporary Zechariah.

Zechariah addressed all of the issues raised by the complaint of the people in Jer 33:24. He proclaimed Yahweh's return to Zion and his reelection of Jerusalem as his place of abode among his people (Zech 2:5–17), and he promised that Zerubabbel who had begun the rebuilding of the Temple in Jerusalem would complete it (Zech 4:6–10). He proclaimed the rededication of the priesthood in a vision concerning Joshua, and he announced that God had renewed his covenant of priesthood with Joshua and his colleagues (Zech 3:1–10). Finally, picking up the older Jeremianic prophecies concerning the "sprout" (צֶמַח) of David, he announced that God was bringing his servant the צֶמַח (Zech 3:8), and in Zech 6:12 he identified the צֶמַח as the man who would build the Temple, that is, as Zerubabbel the Davidic governor. There can be little doubt that Zechariah identified Zerubabbel as the one who would restore the Davidic dynasty. Despite the secondary dislocations that the text of Zech 6:9–15 has suffered, the crown referred to there was originally intended for the head of Zerubabbel who would build the Temple and rule as king, while Joshua would be the priest who served by his throne and with whom the king would have amicable relations.

This linking of royal and priestly figures in Zechariah's prophetic expectations is not an innovation, since it simply continues that found in Jer 33:14–26, which may have influenced Zechariah, but Zechariah seems to be the first writer to call attention to the fact that both priest and king were anointed as God's chosen agents. That would seem to be the implication of his somewhat obscure reference, presumably to Zerubabbel and Joshua, as "the two sons of oil who stand before the lord of all the earth" (Zech 4:14). It is probably also the biblical source for the later dual expectations for "messiahs of Aaron and Israel." The secondary corrections to Zech 6:9–15 that resulted in the crown being placed on the head of the priest instead of the king may also have contributed to the superior position accorded the messiah of Aaron in priestly dominated circles like those of the Qumran community.

Sometime after Haggai and Zechariah, Malachi introduced a prophetic figure into Israel's expectations for God's future intervention with his announcement that God was sending Elijah the prophet before God's great day of judgment (Mal 3:23). This passage is dependent on his earlier oracle announcing God's sending of his messenger to prepare the way before him (Mal 3:1), though it is not clear in this earlier oracle that the מַלְאָךְ ("messenger") is even human, much less specifically a prophet. It is hard to determine the source for this new expectation of a particular prophetic figure. It does not seem dependent on the Mosaic prophet of Deut 18:15, though the introduction of Elijah as an eschatological figure may have influenced a new eschatological reading of this deuteronomic text. The more general announcements of the return of prophecy found elsewhere are less difficult to explain. Since the exile had raised doubts about the continuation of prophecy (Ps 74:9) just as it had about kingship and the priesthood, such prophecies as Joel 3:1–2 could be seen as a response to the longing for a reestablishment of the institutions of the idealized golden age. No particular family, however, had ever been promised an eternal prophetic line, so the hope for a prophetic future did not have the compelling tie to the progeny of a particular figure the way the expectations for a king or priest did, and as a result the later speculations about the prophet to come remain quite fluid.

Summary

This paper has only touched on the high points of the Old Testament's prophecies of a new David, a new priest, and a new prophet. There are major dimensions of the Bible's eschatological hopes that I have not discussed or have discussed far too inadequately. The new Jerusalem is far more prominent in prophetic visions of the future than the Davidic king, but such eschatological hopes are not specifically messianic, so I have only mentioned this outgrowth of the Zion Tradition in passing. Many prophets left no oracles expressing the hope for a new David, and some may have been opposed to such views. Second Isaiah applied God's commitments to David to the nation as a whole (Isa 55:3), thereby implicitly renouncing the expectations for a new David, and at least one voice in the Third Isaiah collection appears to have also rejected the priestly claims. He seems to oppose the rebuilding of the earthly Temple (Isa 66:1), and he extends the priestly role to all Israelites (Isa 61:6).

Moreover, I have characterized a number of passages as not really envisioning a future king in their original contexts, and I have ignored other more peripheral passages for the same reason. That cannot be the last word on these passages. Once the expectation of a new Davidic king became an important hope in large circles of the Israelite people, these passages would be subject to eschatological reinterpretation, to new readings that were genuinely prophetic.

Nonetheless, within the self-imposed limits of this study, several conclusions stand out: (1) Nowhere in the Old Testament has the term מָשִׁיחַ acquired its later technical sense as an eschatological title. (2) Old Testament expectations of a new David are probably to be understood in terms of a continuing Davidic line. There is little indication that any of these prophets envisioned a final Davidic ruler who would actually rule for all time to come, thus obviating the need for the continuation of the dynasty line. The language of some of the prophecies is open to that interpretation, and such a reading was eventually given to them, but such passages as Jer 33:14–26 and Ezekiel 40–48 indicate that the dynastic understanding was the dominant interpretation of such promises as late as the exilic period, and the repeated references to the בֵּית דָּוִיד, "the house of David," in Third Zechariah (Zech 12:7–12; 13:1) suggest that this interpretation remained dominant well into the postexilic period. (3)The mythological language of the royal protocol, influenced as it was by Egyptian conceptions of the royal office, provided a textual base for the development of later, far more mythological conceptions of the awaited Messiah. (4) The later expectations of a priestly Messiah can be traced back to the promises of the restoration of the priesthood found in Jeremiah 33 and in Zechariah's oracles concerning the high priest Joshua. (5) Finally, Malachi provided the catalyst for further speculation about prophetic figures who would precede the great day of Yahweh's coming judgment.

Part 5

Interpreting Prophecy

Chapter 26

Historical-Critical Method, Theology, and Contemporary Exegesis

Introduction

In recent years, one has seen a veritable explosion in the writing and publishing of biblical commentaries. All sorts of new commentary series have begun appearing, and some classical old series have resumed publication after a hiatus of many years. At the same time there is a great deal of discussion and no little uncertainty about what a biblical commentary should be, about the proper task of exegesis.[1] The discussion is due, in part, to the dissatisfaction preachers and church teachers have felt with the older commentaries. The complaint is often heard that the older commentaries are interested only in the dry and boring, if not deadly, details of textual minutiae and hypothetical historical reconstruction; and that they offer no theological direction for the preacher's reflection on the text. The reason for this, many critics say, is that professional biblical scholarship has been dominated too long by the historical-critical methodology introduced at the time of the Enlightenment.

Historical-critical methodology was always the bogeyman of fundamentalist biblical scholarship, but now it has become the bogeyman for much wider circles of theological scholarship in this so-called postcritical age. It is not uncommon today, even in scholarly circles, to blame historical-critical scholarship for making the Bible inaccessible to the average person. As the Yale theologian George Lindbeck formulates it, "It is now the scholarly rather than the hierarchical clerical elite which holds the Bible captive and makes it inaccessible to ordinary folk."[2] Though Lindbeck does not make the historical-critical method solely responsible, he does imply that it has contributed to the

---

1. One may gain an interesting insight into this debate by comparing Brevard Childs's "Interpretation in Faith: The Theological Responsibility of an Old Testament Commentary," *Int* 18 (1964) 432–49, with James Barr's "Exegesis as a Theological Discipline Reconsidered and the Shadow of the Jesus of History," *The Hermeneutical Quest: Essays in Honor of James Luther Mays on His Sixty-fifth Birthday*, ed. Donald G. Miller (Allison Park, Pa.: Pickwick, 1986) 11–45.

2. "Scripture, Consensus, and Community," *The World: A Journal of Religion and Public Life* 23/4 (1988) 16.

contemporary Christian community's loss of biblical literacy, to the loss "of a generally intelligible and distinctively Christian language within which disagreements can be expressed and issues debated."[3] Biblical scholars have also joined the chorus of critics. Brevard Childs has been a persistent and long-time critic of the theological inadequacies in the historical-critical approach to the Bible,[4] but even if one disagrees with his critique of traditional historical-critical scholarship,[5] his comments have been restrained and measured compared to the charges leveled against the method by other biblical scholars. Note the comments of James A. Sanders:

> Hans Frei has put it very well: the biblical story has become eclipsed by the work of the very professionals in seminaries and departments of religion who seem to know most about the Bible. In the rhetoric of today, the experts have lost perspective on the very object of their expertise. A colleague calls biblical criticism bankrupt. For some, it has reduced the Bible to grist for the historian's mill, the province of the professor's study. Something like the very opposite of what Albright and George Ernest Wright intended has taken place: often the Bible has been reduced to the status of a tell which only the trained expert with hard-earned tools can dig.[6]

---

3. Ibid. 5–6.

4. A critique of this method has been a persistent theme in his work throughout his career. See his comments, for example in "Interpretation in Faith: The Theological Responsibility of an Old Testament Commentary," *Int* 18 (1964) 432–49; *Biblical Theology in Crisis* (Philadelphia: Westminster, 1970) 141–42; *The Book of Exodus: A Critical, Theological Commentary* (OTL; Philadelphia: Westminster, 1974) xiii–xvi; *Introduction to the Old Testament as Scripture* (Philadelphia: Fortress, 1979) 39–41; *The New Testament as Canon: An Introduction* (Philadelphia: Fortress, 1984); and *Old Testament Theology in a Canonical Context* (Philadelphia: Fortress, 1985) 17. Moreover, these major works represent only a partial sampling of what Childs has written on this topic, as one can easily see from his bibliography published in *Canon, Theology, and Old Testament Interpretation: Essays in Honor of Brevard S. Childs* (ed. Gene M. Tucker, David L. Petersen, and Robert R. Wilson; Philadelphia: Fortress, 1988) 329–36.

5. Though addressing broader issues, James Barr has offered a trenchant critique of both Childs's negative theological assessment of the traditional historical-critical approach and of the theological value of Childs's own canonical approach. See Barr's "Exegesis as a Theological Discipline Reconsidered and the Shadow of the Jesus of History," 11–45; and his "The Theological Case Against Biblical Theology," *Canon, Theology and Old Testament Interpretation* (ed. Gene M. Tucker, David L. Petersen, and Robert R. Wilson; Philadelphia: Fortress, 1988) 3–19.

6. *From Sacred Story to Sacred Text: Canon as Paradigm* (Philadelphia: Fortress, 1987) 78–79. Barr's scathing review of this volume in *Critical Review of Books in Religion 1988: A Cooperative Venture of the Journal of the American Academy of Religion and the Journal of Biblical Literature*, ed. Beverly Roberts Gaventa, 137–41, is worth noting, particularly his comments on 139: "Able as Sanders may be in telling us what he thinks, nothing that he says about other people's thoughts or about trends in scholarship can be relied on. And this is no incidental remark, but bears upon the whole validity of the canonical criticism movement: its most powerful arguments, as I have said elsewhere, consisted in attacks on the

Or compare the following comments of Walter Wink, the colleague to whom Sanders referred, from a book whose first chapter bears the sensational title, "The Bankruptcy of the Biblical Critical Paradigm":

> Historical biblical criticism is bankrupt. . . . The historical critical method has reduced the Bible to a dead letter. Our obeisance to technique has left the Bible sterile and ourselves empty. . . . It was based on an inadequate method, married to a false objectivism, subjected to uncontrolled technologism, separated from a vital community, and has outlived its usefulness as presently practiced.[7]

Finally nontheological and theological critics alike attack the method for being overly concerned with historical questions, with the search for external referential meaning, for not being satisfied with the internal, narrative meaning of the text.[8] Given this widespread climate of opinion, and the fact that I have just finished one major commentary and am working on two more, my interest in these new trends is deeply existential. At the same time, I am concerned about the integrity and continuity of the scholarly enterprise. Though I feel no compulsion to offer a blanket defense of the historical-critical method as theoretically conceived, much less as it has been practiced by the many different scholars in the field, I am deeply suspicious of the current tendency to denigrate previous OT scholarship. The disparagement of the historical-critical method as a dead end that, if not responsible for all the current problems in the field of biblical exegesis, must be transcended if one hopes to achieve theologically relevant and compelling exegetical results for the contemporary community of faith, seems to me to lead to a far narrower dead end of its own.

The important article of George Lindbeck previously cited may serve as a useful framework for a discussion of these issues.[9] In it he argues that it was a particular way of reading the Bible that created and sustained the communal faith and identity of the early Church. Lindbeck defines this classic hermeneutic as reading the Bible "as a canonically and narrationally unified and internally glossed (that is, self-referential and self-interpreting) whole centered on Jesus Christ, and telling the story of the dealings of the Triune God with his people and his world in ways which are typologically . . . applicable to the

faults of previous scholarship; and, if previous scholarship is as badly misrepresented as it is in this volume, then the entire case for canonical criticism becomes all the weaker."

7. Walter Wink, *Transformation: Toward a New Paradigm for Biblical Study* (Philadelphia: Fortress, 1973) 1, 4, 15.

8. This has been a recurring theme among adherents of a literary approach to the Bible, and, at least in the form presented by Hans Frei, *The Eclipse of Biblical Narrative: A Study in Eighteenth and Nineteenth-Century Hermeneutics* (New Haven: Yale University Press, 1974), has exercised a major influence on "Narrative Theology."

9. "Scripture, Consensus, and Community," *This World: A Journal of Religion and Public Life* 23/4 (1988) 5–24. Fuller documentation of his views expressed here may be found in his book, *The Nature of Doctrine* (Philadelphia: Westminster, 1984).

present."[10] This hermeneutic began to break down at the time of the Enlightenment, according to Lindbeck, and its loss is largely responsible for the present biblical illiteracy and the lack of a central core of commonly acknowledged beliefs in Christendom today. In his view, the creation and sustaining of such communally held beliefs is dependent on a central core of privileged and familiar texts which project imaginatively and practically habitable worlds. That means that these privileged and familiar texts must supply followable directions for coherent patterns of life in new situations. According to Lindbeck, to again make the Bible followable in our day, one must regain this classic hermeneutic of the past.

How is a biblical scholar to respond to these claims of Lindbeck? In a very general way, I think one can agree with him. At least in broad terms, I would claim that to read the Bible as a unified whole means telling the story of the Triune God's dealing with his people and his world in ways that are typologically applicable to the present. I would certainly claim that scripture provides the interpretive framework for all reality for me, and for the Christian community to which I belong. On the other hand, Lindbeck's formulation harbors numerous problems when one tries to apply it in detail to the reading of the biblical text. What do canonical unity, narrational unity, and self-referentiality actually imply for the exegesis of particular prophetic texts?

Canonical Unity

First of all, what precisely is meant by "canonically unified whole"? Does this mean that one reads any particular book in the light of all the other canonical books? If that is so, the question as to which canon is meant rises immediately. Lindbeck speaks of the Hebrew scriptures and the Hebrew Bible in a way that suggests that he follows Childs in basically identifying the OT canon with the canon of the Masoretic Text.[11] That, however, was definitely not the OT canon of most Christian churches until the time of the Reformation. Their OT canons, whether they used the LXX, the Vulgate, or other translations, typically contained additional books and followed a different physical arrangement of the material. Any "canonical" reading of the biblical text that wants to

10. Ibid. 6.

11. Lindbeck, "Scripture, Consensus, and Community," 7. According to Childs, "The term 'canonical text' denotes that official Hebrew text of the Jewish community which had reached a point of stabilization in the first century A.D., thus all but ending its long history of fluidity" (*Introduction to the Old Testament as Scripture*, 100). Thus "the Masoretic text is not identical with the canonical text, but is only a vehicle for its recovery" (ibid.). In fact, "there is no extant canonical text" (ibid.). All that Childs means by these reservations, however, is that one must make some very minor textual corrections to the Masoretic text in order to recover the canonical text.

claim the support of early Christian interpretation must be broad enough, therefore, to accommodate this diversity in both content and arrangement of the canon.[12]

Second, how can one protect a canonical reading of the text, say of Isaiah, from the charge that one is simply reading all sorts of later Christian meanings into the text? How can one make sure that one is reading Isaiah and not simply using it as a pretext for hearing only Paul or some other NT writer? If one reads Isaiah as part of the ongoing story of God's dealing with his people, one can be open to the larger canonical context while respecting the historical fact that this represents an earlier chapter in the story. Openness to the canonical context of the fuller story need not result in collapsing the distinctive message of Isaiah into a carbon copy of later New Testament texts, but it does require a willingness to take historical development seriously in order to avoid this danger.

The necessity to take historical development seriously should make one cautious about playing off a canonical meaning of a text against a historical one, as though the canonical meaning were certain and the historical one were only putative and reconstructed. Lindbeck is guilty of this when he asserts that in the classic hermeneutic "the use and therefore meaning of the text . . . was the one it had in the canon-forming situation, not in some putative historically reconstructed originally one."[13] In addition to the lack of clarity as to what is meant by this expression, his formulation overlooks the fact that any "canon-forming situation" is itself the construct of a historical reconstruction.[14] The formation of the canon was a long process; it was not completed at one time, and the reasons for the particular canonical shape of individual books, and often even of individual pericopes within a book, are usually obscure and hardly to be attributed to a particular moment in the course of that process. "Canon-forming situation," then, is not a very helpful concept to clarify the appropriate approach to exegesis.

Third, to read a biblical book as scripture in the light of the larger canon need not imply any contrast to a reading motivated by philological or historical purposes. It is simply not true to say, as Lindbeck does, that "to read Homer's *Odyssey* for philological or historical purposes . . . is to turn it into something other than an epic poem."[15] Any decent historian who expected to

12. Childs's attempt to deal with this difficulty (*Introduction to the Old Testament as Scripture*, 659–71), can hardly be considered adequate. Cf. James Barr's critique in "Childs' Introduction to the Old Testament as Scripture," *JSOT* 16 (1980) 12–23.

13. "Scripture, Consensus, and Community," 7.

14. Barr points out how little is actually known about the community of the time of the canonizers and how in Childs's work that community may amount to no more than "an imaginative construct formed out of his (Childs's) own ideas about the centrality of canon" (*JSOT* 16 [1980] 21).

15. "Scripture, Consensus, and Community," 7.

extract useful historical information from Homer's *Odyssey* would have to be constantly aware of the text's genre. He or she would have to read the text as an epic poem before one could expect it to yield any useful historical information. Moreover, even canonical readings cannot dispense with philological and historical concerns. If one is going to read the Bible with any understanding at all, one must learn the scripts, the morphology, the syntax, the vocabulary, and the literary conventions of the languages and periods in which it was written. And for an ancient text like the Bible, that inevitably involves historical as well as philological research. The historical-critical method is not responsible for the difficulty of interpreting the biblical text. Any ancient text from a different culture composed in a foreign language would present similar difficulties, and neither Lindbeck's classical hermeneutics, nor any other kind, can sweep these difficulties away and magically clarify the meaning of the Bible to the general public.

Narrational Unity

Lindbeck's characterization of the Bible as a "narrationally unified whole" also needs further specification. If he means by that phrase that all parts of the Bible contribute generally to the one story of God's dealing with his people, it is a useful concept. However, one must be careful to avoid overstressing narrative as the fundamental theological category for revelation. If the older scholarship overstressed history as the mode for revelation, recent scholarship seems tempted to simply substitute narrative or story for history, forgetful of the fact that narrative is subject to many of the same objections that were raised against history.

In the first place, much of the Bible does not qualify as narrative in a meaningful sense. The legal collections, the wisdom books, most of the p phetic books, many of the Psalms, and the epistolary material of the NT simply not narrative literature. To try to interpret these materials in detail interpretive categories derived from narrative literature is sure to res gross misrepresentation.[16]

One can illustrate this issue with specific regard to a prophetic book ical prophetic book consists of a mixed collection of oracles give prophet at different times and occasions during his prophetic ministr collection is usually expanded by the commentary and additio

16. Claus Westermann, following Gerhard von Rad, tried to construe O historical categories, but he had to admit that Wisdom simply had no place (*Theologie des Alten Testaments in Grundzügen* [Göttingen: Vandenhoec 1978] 7). The "historical" construal of much of the other nonnarrative O outline also seems forced, and a simple switch from "history" to "narrativ ling category will not ease this fit in the slightest.

prophet's disciples, editors, and later scribes. Some of the oracles in a prophetic book may have a brief notice informing the reader what the historical occasion behind that particular oracle was, and such a notice may take the form of a more extended narrative. Yet even in the case of Jeremiah, which has relatively extensive narrative material, the majority of the oracles are without a narrative framework. Moreover, despite the enormous effort that has gone into the attempt to uncover the principles behind the present literary arrangement of the oracles in the various prophetic books, there is very little agreement on this matter with respect to most books. If one were to look for a contemporary analogy to the literary form of the prophetic book, the closest parallels would be a book of sermons or a collection of meditations with extensive marginal notations. Given this literary form and the fact that the principles of literary arrangement are uncertain and at least open to the possibility of being haphazard, meaningful reading of such a work will concentrate on individual oracles rather than on putative literary links between contiguous oracles. If one wants to put a particular oracle in a larger context within the book, one will read it over against other oracles on the same subject, or, when this can be known, against other oracles given by the prophet in the same historical context. Literary placement in the collection may count for less than similarity of message or of historical background. Thus a critical, if not *the* critical issue in the interpretation of a prophetic book will be the correct delimitation of the extent of a particular oracle. This way of reading the material is dictated by the genre, and no concept of canonical or narrational unity can override this elementary observation of the character of the material to be read.

One could, however, take Lindbeck's claim for canonical and narrational unity as a claim that the reading of a particular passage in a prophetic book should be controlled by the literary arrangement of oracles in the book. Brevard Childs clearly makes such a claim when he argues that the placement of Isaiah 40–66 in the same scroll with the oracles of Isaiah of Jerusalem has dehistoricized the oracles of Second Isaiah so that they should be read canonically as though they were from the eighth century B.C.E.[17] In my opinion, this is sheer nonsense, and it certainly cannot claim the support of the history of interpretation. It is true that Isaiah 40–66 was attributed to Isaiah of Jerusalem because these chapters were included in the same book as the oracles of the eighth-century prophet, but in terms of the actual interpretation of individual passages the ancient Christian interpreters paid very little attention to the literary shape of the book. Classical interpretation of a prophetic book actually interpreted discrete passages, not the prophetic book as a whole. Prophetic books were read, not as coherent, unified wholes, but as collections of discrete prophecies, each of which could stand on its own as a word of God. In general, there

17. *Introduction to the Old Testament as Scripture*, 325.

was very little interpretation of any biblical book, even the genuinely narrative ones, in terms of the structure of that book as a whole.[18] Interpretation concentrated not on books, but on relatively short pericopes. It tended to be quite atomistic, unified only by the belief that all of scripture was the word of God. Therefore any passage in the Bible could be invoked to help explain whatever difficult passage one was reading at the moment.

There are exceptions to my general portrayal of the literary character of prophetic books. In the case of Habakkuk, for example, I would argue that one was dealing with a work that reflected a self-conscious compositional unity. It may be composed of discrete oracles given on different occasions, but these oracles have been put together in such a way as to create a narrativelike structure in which the theological point depends on the text's sequential development of the argument. Even in the case of Habakkuk, however, one cannot elevate the final form of the text to the final arbiter of theological meaning, because after the creation of this compositional unity, late marginal glosses were added to the text which confuse the message.[19] In Hab 2:5–20 the nations who have been oppressed by the Babylonians sing a taunt song over the Babylonian king in which they describe his terrible oppression of other peoples. In 2:12 they address the Babylonian king as one who builds his city with bloodshed and establishes his town with iniquity. Following this address, in 2:13*b* one finds the statement:

> So that the peoples exhaust themselves only for the fire,
> And the nations grow weary for nothing. (author's translation)

In the context of this saying and in the context of the larger pericope's function within the book as a compositional unity, the meaning of Hab 2:13*b* can only be that Babylon's oppression of the other nations has prevented these nations from enjoying the fruits of their own labors. It is an indictment of the selfish cruelty of the Babylonians. This verse, however, is partially quoted in

---

18. Cf. Barr's comment: "Canon, meaning recognition as regulative scripture, may have conflicted with canonical form, in the sense of the guidance given by the total literary form of a work; for fixation as scripture could mean, and probably often did mean, that the sense for the total literary form was lost and meaning was seen in individual word-groups and locutions. The sense for the total literary form of a text was there in central OT times, and we have it also in modern times; it is not so certain that it was there in the late canonizing and supposedly canonically guided community" (*JSOT* 16 [1980] 18).

Even for the central OT times the possibility must remain open that the total literary form of some works suggested to the competent reader that he or she was dealing with a mere collection of discrete units more or less haphazardly arranged.

19. For a fuller discussion of these glosses see my commentary, *Nahum, Habakkuk, and Zephaniah: A Commentary* (OTL; Louisville, Ky.: Westminster/John Knox, 1991) 115–17. Such glosses correspond to what Barr calls "anti-hermeneutic" changes in the text (*JSOT* 16 [1980] 18).

the later oracle in Jer 51:58, and there it is applied to the doom of the Babylonians. A still later reader of Habakkuk, influenced by this Jeremiah passage, wanted to impose this interpretation on Hab 2:13*b*, and to do so he bracketed it with two glosses. He introduced it with the comment in 2:13*a*: "Are not these things from Yahweh of Hosts? and he ended it in 2:14 with a partial quotation of Isa 11:9: "For the earth will be filled so that it knows the glory of Yahweh as the waters cover the sea" (author's translation). Both comments miss the sense of the passage and are clearly recognizable as secondary glosses. One can interpret what the glosses mean, but one cannot interpret the whole context in the light of these glosses, because the glossator did not interpret, much less understand, the whole text. Why, then, should we accept any canonical or narrative theory that would allow the latest pre-Jamnia glosses to control our reading of whole pericopes?

Self-Referential and Self-Interpreting

Lindbeck's principle of scripture's self-referential and self-interpreting character is also problematic. It was formulated as a corrective to the tendency in historical-critical scholarship to be so concerned about the historical background of the text that the actual narrative meaning of the text was lost. A good example of the problem is presented by Speiser's treatment of the three stories in Genesis where the patriarch denies that the matriarch is his wife and claims instead that she is his sister. Speiser argued that the motif arose from a later misunderstanding of an early social custom, known from sixteenth-century B.C.E. Nuzi, where a man could give higher status to his wife if he also adopted her as his sister.[20] However one judges the accuracy of Speiser's historical argument, which has been seriously challenged by other scholars,[21] it does not have any clear bearing on the present form of any of the stories in Genesis. Whatever the background of those stories, the exegete must ask what they mean in their present shape, and Speiser largely ignores that question. Thus Lindbeck's principle is the reaffirmation of the importance of a narrative *qua* narrative. What does a story mean as a story? The introduction of historical information actually extraneous to the story is no contribution to the interpretation of the story as such, and far too much of that has been done. When interpreting literature composed of a people's myths, legends, sagas, or dramatic treatment of quasi-historical heroes of the past, one must allow the literary work to create its own world of reality. Particularly in books like Genesis

20. E. A. Speiser, *Genesis* (AB 1; Garden City, N.Y.: Doubleday, 1964) 91–94.

21. Barry L. Eichler, "Another Look at Nuzi Sisterhood Contracts," *Essays on the Ancient Near East in Memory of Jacob Joel Finkelstein*, ed. Maria de Jong Ellis, Memoirs of the Connecticut Academy of Arts and Sciences, 19 (Hamden, Conn.: Archon Books, 1977) 45–59; A. Skaist, "The Authority of the Brother at Arrapha and Nuzi," *JAOS* 89 (1969) 10–17.

or Job, the question of historicity should not be allowed to crowd out the more important question of meaning.

On the other hand, when a work like Samuel or Kings refers to known historical events, sometimes just in passing, it hardly makes sense to restrict interpretation to the internal referential world of the book itself. If a book refers to external events, a more profound knowledge of those events than what is actually narrated in the book itself may be necessary for a proper understanding of the work.

In modern fictionalized narratives set in the contemporary world, an author often depends on his or her audience's knowledge not only of contemporary culture, but of recent history as well, in order for the work to make sense. If one were to interpret such a work to a foreign audience five hundred years later, when such knowledge could not be presupposed, one would have to supply much of that missing "historical background" for that later audience to understand the work. The same is true for the interpretation of many biblical narratives.

Moreover, biblical books like Kings and Chronicles claim to be more than historical romances: they make theological claims based on their construal of Israel's history. When a modern work offers a theological critique of contemporary society based on historical events, say the internment of Japanese-Americans in World War II or the killing of civil rights activists in the South, an interpretation of the meaning of that work, if it is to go beyond saying what the work claims, to an evaluation of how one should react to those claims, must ask how accurately the work has portrayed those historical details. One need not get every historical detail right in order to sustain a particular interpretation, but a gross misrepresentation of historical facts would certainly render any interpretation dependent on that misrepresentation suspect. That is one reason why biblical scholars in general have a higher respect for the theology of Kings than that of Chronicles. It is rooted in a less tendentious treatment of historical detail. The point, however, is that the interpretation of biblical books that refer to external events requires the interpreter to raise historical questions. An interpretation of the Bible that limits itself to a referential system totally restricted to the biblical narrative itself does not take seriously the actual character of the biblical literature.[22]

If the referential system of even narrative literature cannot be restricted to the "imaginative" world created by the narrative itself, how much less is that the case with nonnarrative literature? Prophetic oracles in particular make all sorts of passing allusions to historical events without providing any narrative framework for an adequate understanding of those historical events. Even

22. On this point Childs is also quite critical of Lindbeck's program, *The New Testament as Canon: An Introduction*, 545.

when one reads the prophets in the context of the whole Bible, one still finds no clue to the significance of many of these allusions. References to Calno, Hamath, Carchemish, and Arpad (Isa 10:9) would remain unclear were it not for the Assyrian inscriptions and the historical reconstruction they make possible. Were it not for the Greek historians, the full significance of Second Isaiah's references to Cyrus would not be known, and this is not a modern discovery. The exegetes of the ancient Church, those model practitioners of the classic hermeneutic, also quoted Herodotus and other secular Greek sources in their interpretation of the biblical material.

Moreover, the understanding of a detail in the text may sometimes require the reconstruction of the historical event that lay behind that text from scattered hints in the biblical text itself. This controversial point may be illustrated from an equally controversial detail in Isa 7:3:

> And the Lord said to Isaiah, "Go forth to meet Ahaz, you and Shear-jashub your son, at the end of the conduit of the upper pool on the highway to the Fuller's Field. (author's translation)

An attentive reader will ask why God told Isaiah to take his son Shear-jashub with him when he went to meet Ahaz. The text in Isaiah 7 raises the question, but it provides no answer to it. We know from Hos 1:3–9, however, that prophets sometimes gave symbolic names to their children as a kind of living embodiment of their prophetic message. Isaiah (8:18) refers to the children God had given him as "signs and portents in Israel," and that suggests that he too gave symbolic names to his children. There were certainly two and probably three—Shear jashub, Immanuel (often identified as the king's son for insufficient reasons), and Maher-shalal-hash-baz. Now all of the symbolic names that Hosea gave to his children are explained in the passage that refers to their naming. The same is true of the name of Isaiah's third child, Maher-shalal-hash-baz. The name means "Hasten booty, hurry plunder!" and Isa 8:3–4 explains the prophetic judgment implicit in the symbolic name:

> The Lord said to me, "Call his name Maher-shalal-hash-baz; for before the child knows how to cry 'My father' or 'My mother,' the wealth of Damascus and the spoil of Samaria will be carried away before the king of Assyria." (author's translation)

If this was the normal pattern in the giving of symbolic names, why does Isaiah 7 not explain the significance of the name Shear-jashub? The name means "A remnant will return," but a remnant of whom shall return from where? Does it convey a positive meaning or a negative meaning? For whom is it positive or negative? If one limits oneself to the present text of Isaiah 7, these questions cannot be answered.

There is another passage in Isa 10:20–23, however, where the phrase Shear-jashub occurs twice. The present shape and context of this passage requires that one read it as an oracle from the period of the Assyrian crisis. There is impressive evidence, however, that verses 16–23 dated originally to the period of the Syro-Ephraimitic war and were intended at the time as a threat against Israel, the northern kingdom.[23] In other words, these verses were originally composed around the same time as the events described in Isaiah 7 took place, and they explain the meaning of the name Shear-jashub: "A remnant will return, the remnant of Jacob, to the mighty God. For though your people Israel were like the sand of the sea, only a remnant of them will return. Destruction is decreed, overflowing with righteousness" (Isa 10:21–23).

In the context of the Syro-Ephraimitic war, this can only mean that the Israelite army threatening Jerusalem will be destroyed, and only a remnant of the hostile northern kingdom will survive. Thus the name Shear-jashub originally conveyed a message similar to that of the name Maher-shalal-hashbaz. It pronounced judgment on the north, but hope for Judah. In my opinion, it is only by such a historical reconstruction of the original meaning of Shear-jashub's name that one can answer the long disputed question of whether Isaiah had a positive concept of the remnant. In the original historical context this ambiguous concept was positive for Judah but negative for Israel, and that suggests that Isaiah may have preserved a similar ambiguity in his later reuse of this concept when applied to Judean society alone. Judah's judgment was certain, but Isa 1:26 nonetheless implies the survival of a positively evaluated remnant. If this discussion has any merit, theological significance cannot be limited to the final form of the text as Lindbeck and Childs seem to demand: one's perception of earlier forms of the text affect the way one reads the final form.

Conclusion

Thus, three of the main principles of Lindbeck's definition of the classical hermeneutic are ambiguous, problematic, or subject to significant abuse. His critique of the way in which the historical-critical method has been applied has its valid points. Whether it is legitimate to criticize exegetes of the church for not carrying their task far enough, for stopping before addressing the theological concerns that the text raises, is not as self-evident as Lindbeck and other critics imply. There may, in fact, be some good reasons for the hesitancy of scholars to press on in this area. As Barr has persuasively argued, this hesitancy may arise out of the nature of the theological enterprise itself, from the fact that theological exegesis is an interaction that takes place between the

23. For a detailed discussion of this point, see my article, "Isaiah and His Children," *Biblical and Related Studies Presented to Samuel Iwry* (ed. Ann Kort and Scott Morschauser; Winona Lake, Ind.: Eisenbrauns, 1985) 193–203, especially 200–201.

factuality of the text and the prior theological expectations that people have due to the particularities of their own religious or nonreligious backgrounds.[24] Unless the commentator is addressing a very particular religious community whose theological presuppositions he or she knows well, the contemporary theological reflections of the commentator are apt to appear scattered and unfocused, and a commentary addressed to such a particular community is apt to strike other readers as tendentious or peculiar.

On the other hand, particularly if Barr's analysis is correct, Lindbeck and other critics of the historical-critical method do not have enough respect for the continuing contribution of this approach to the task of interpretation. One cannot dismiss this approach *in toto* as now outdated without losing the ability to achieve a critical understanding of ancient documents, and the preservation of this ability is a goal that has profound theological, not just historical, ramifications.

24. Barr, "Exegesis as a Theological Discipline Reconsidered and the Shadow of the Jesus of History," *The Hermeneutical Quest: Essays in Honor of James Luther Mays on His Sixty-fifth Birthday* (ed. Donald G. Miller; Allison Park, Pa.: Pickwick Publications, 1986) 22–23. Note also his elaboration of this point on 23–24: "In other words, the apparent reluctance of the commentary to address directly the theological and ethical questions of the present day is not necessarily a fault; nor is it a consequence of a "historical" orientation that refuses to face modern problems. It is, on the contrary, a decision perfectly seriously grounded in theological principle, in the fact that theological consequence does not follow directly from the text itself but only from its interaction with other texts and with preexisting theological tradition. Since the nature of that tradition is highly variable, it is a perfectly responsible theological decision that the commentary cannot handle all the possibilities of theological consequence but must concentrate on providing and discussing the evidence of the text itself, within its own environment, the impact of which evidence upon the theological assumptions forms the core of theological exegesis."

Chapter 27

A Christian Perspective on Prophetic Prediction

Prophecy in the Old Testament involves a great deal more than simple prediction. The prophets, as Yahweh's messengers and spokesmen, have much to say about social justice, individual righteousness, and the limited value of ritual practices when isolated from God's other demands. Nonetheless, prediction is an important element in biblical prophecy, and even those apparently "timeless ethical elements" are normally framed within or given urgency by threatening predictions or encouraging promises based on what God is about to do. Scholarship has come to recognize this once again in our day, and such pronouncements of the older scholarship as, "Prophets are forthtellers, not foretellers," have gone out of fashion. This shift in scholarly fashion, however, seems to have little connection with the popular understanding of the prophets in the churches. It is doubtful whether the older scholarship's denial of prophecy's predictive element ever filtered down to the average layman, and while there is certainly a renewed popular interest in prophetic prediction—note the popularity of Hal Lindsey's *The Late Great Planet Earth*—it stems more from neo-Pentecostalism and Christian Zionism than from serious scholarship. The popular approach to prophecy remains poorly informed, is largely inattentive to context, and tends to interpret predictions in an overly simplistic and highly dubious fashion. Serious scholarship, on the other hand, has been reluctant to address the larger theological issues raised by prophetic predictions.

I wish to contribute in some small way to correcting this situation by the present paper. First of all I would suggest classifying the various prophetic predictions into four main categories. There are probably some that will not fit into any of these categories, but the majority will, and it seems preferable to begin with as simple a schema as possible.

1. The first group of predictions are those contained in the Old Testament which have already come to pass. There are many of these of differing types and differing complexity, and I will cite only a few of the simplest—those about which there can be no argument. In Amos 7:9, Amos prophesied that Yahweh would rise up against the house of Jeroboam with a sword. Within a few years Zechariah, the son and successor of Jeroboam, was assassinated after only six months as king; and with his death Jeroboam's royal line was cut

off (2 Kgs 15:8–12). Hosea prophesied that Israel would "dwell many days without king, without prince, without sacrifice, without sacred stele, and without ephod and teraphim" (Hos 3:4), and shortly thereafter the Assyrians completely dismantled the Northern Kingdom. In 609 B.C. Jeremiah prophesied that God would do to the temple in Jerusalem as he had done to the earlier sanctuary in Shiloh (Jer 7:14; 26:1), and twenty-two years later in 587 B.C. the Babylonians burned the temple (2 Kgs 25:9). After the first captivity in 597 B.C., Jeremiah wrote to the exiles in Babylon urging them to settle down for a long stay in their new home, promising Yahweh would bring them back to Palestine only after seventy years had been fulfilled (Jer 29:10). Cyrus' edict permitting the Jews to return was issued in 539, or approximately sixty years later, which was close enough to Jeremiah's prediction to give him the edge over his contemporary opponents who were promising a quick return. These are only a few of the many prophecies contained in the Old Testament which were fulfilled in the lifetime or soon after the lifetime of the prophets who uttered them. It is precisely these fulfilled prophecies upon which the prestige of the classical prophets has been based. However adequate the rules given in Deut 18:18–22 for distinguishing between true and false prophets may or may not be, they underline the significance attached to accurate prediction by the contemporaries of the prophets. If a prophet's word did not come to pass, one could and should doubt whether he had really been sent by God (Jer 28, esp. v. 9). Were it not for the early fulfillment of many prophetic predictions, therefore, it is doubtful there would have been any incentive to preserve the prophetic works.[1]

2. The second category of predictions contains fewer examples, but, nonetheless, it is a category that deserves our careful consideration if we are to understand the nature of prophetic prediction. It may be characterized as that group of predictions which did not come to pass and will never come to pass. Let me illustrate this category with what I consider to be its clearest example. In Ezekiel 26, Ezekiel predicts the utter ruin of the city of Tyre. Verses 7–14 read as follows:

> For thus says the Lord God: I am now bringing up against Tyre from the north Nebuchadnezzar the king of Babylon, the king of kings, with horses and chariots, with cavalry and a great and mighty army.

1. I have not included *vaticinia ex eventu*, "prophecies after the event," in my grouping since they are not genuine prophecies and are in any case quite rare in the biblical material—the best examples occur in Daniel and 1 Kgs 13:2, though the last passage may simply reflect a Deuteronomic retouching of an older, genuine prophecy. Moreover, the inclusion of such texts would only confirm my argument. The concern with detailed correspondence between prophecy and fulfillment characteristic of these prophetic imitations further underscores the importance of accurate prediction for legitimation of the prophetic word.

> Your daughters on the mainland he shall slay with the sword;
> He shall place a siege tower against you.
> Cast up a ramp about you.
> And raise his shields against you.
> He shall pound your walls with battering-rams
> And break down your towers with his weapons.
> The surge of his horses shall cover you with dust,
> Amid the noise of steeds, of wheels and of chariots.
> Your walls shall shake as he enters your gates.
> Even as one enters a city that is breached.
> With the hoofs of his horses he shall trample all your streets;
> Your people he shall slay by the sword;
> Your mighty pillars he shall pull to the ground.
> Your wealth shall be plundered, your merchandise pillaged;
> Your walls shall be torn down, your precious houses demolished;
> Your stones, your timber, and your clay shall be cast into the sea.
> I will put an end to the noise of your songs.
> And the sound of your lyres shall be heard no more.
> I will make you a bare rock;
> A drying place for nets shall you be.
> Never shall you be rebuilt, for I have spoken, says the Lord God.

This oracle is followed by related oracles against Tyre in the remainder of chapter 26, all of chapter 27, and down through verse 19 of chapter 28. Later, in an oracle against Egypt, Ezekiel has occasion to comment on his earlier predictions about Tyre (note Ezek 29:17–20):

> On the first day of the first month in the twenty-seventh year [April 26, 571 B.C.], the word of the Lord came to me: "Son of man, Nebuchadnezzar, the king of Babylon, has led his army in an exhausting campaign against Tyre. Their heads became bald and their shoulders were galled; but neither he nor his army received any wages from Tyre for the campaign he led against it. Therefore, thus says the Lord God: I am now giving the land of Egypt to Nebuchadnezzar, king of Babylon. He shall carry off its riches, plundering and pillaging it for the wages of his soldiers, who did it for me; as payment for his toil I have given him the land of Egypt, says the Lord God."

Thus Ezekiel himself admits that his earlier predictions against Tyre did not come to pass. Nebuchadnezzar and his army worked hard to capture Tyre, but ultimately the siege failed. From Josephus we learn that the siege lasted some thirteen years and ended without success. As a result, to be fair, Yahweh promised Egypt to Nebuchadnezzar as a consolation prize. Whether Nebuchadnezzar actually collected even the consolation prize is uncertain—we have only a fragmentary text concerning a campaign of the Babylonian king against Egypt in 568 B.C., three years after Ezekiel's prediction, and the outcome of that campaign is unknown—but it is absolutely clear that the prediction against

Tyre failed to materialize. Since the prediction specifically named Nebuchadnezzar as the king who would despoil Tyre, and since Nebuchadnezzar has now long since departed from this world, I think one may go on to assert that not only has the prediction against Tyre not been fulfilled; in the nature of the case there is no reason to expect its fulfillment in the future. The context for the fulfillment of that specific prediction has passed.

Such unfulfilled and unfulfillable prophecies may or may not raise certain problems for faith, but they undoubtedly underscore the conditional nature of biblical prophecy. The biblical god, unlike the static, eternally unchanging god of Greek philosophy, can change his mind. He repents of proposed plans of action, he reacts to the changing attitudes of his human subjects, and this may result in a divinely inspired prediction failing to materialize.

A beautiful illustration of this is provided by the story of Jonah. When God finally convinces Jonah to carry out the divine commission, Jonah begins proclaiming to Nineveh: "Forty days more and Nineveh shall be destroyed" (Jonah 3:9). Note that the prophetic prediction is not couched in a conditional form. There is no indication that Jonah suggested any way of avoiding the fate prophesied. Indeed, when the people repent, it is not with any great confidence in the efficacy of repentance, but simply on the longshot, the mere possibility, that God might relent. "Who knows," they say, "God may relent and forgive, and withhold his blazing wrath, so that we shall not perish" (3:9). Nonetheless, "when God saw by their actions how they turned from their evil way, he repented of the evil that he had threatened to do to them; he did not carry it out" (3:10). That infuriated Jonah. Why Jonah became so upset is not made explicit in the text. He clearly wanted God to go ahead and destroy the city; he even took up residence outside Nineveh to see what would happen to the city. Some have thought Jonah's desire for the destruction of Nineveh was due to nationalistic hatred, but it seems to me that another factor is just as important. If the city is not overthrown, Jonah's reputation will be hurt. By the criteria given in Deut 18:22, Jonah would be considered a presumptuous prophet. This was a constant source of anguish to the true prophets. They did not want to see the punishment of their people which they were called upon to predict, but if the fulfillment of their predictions were delayed, the very people they were trying to save would make fun of them. Notice Jeremiah's bitter lament:

> Heal me, Lord, that I may be healed;
>   save me, that I may be saved,
>   for it is you whom I praise.
> See how they say to me,
>   "Where is the word of the Lord?
>   Let it come to pass!"
> Yet I did not press you to send calamity;
>   the day without remedy I have not desired.

> You know what passed my lips;
>   it is present before you.
> Do not be my ruin,
>   you, my refuge in the day of misfortune.
> Let my persecutors, not me, be confounded;
>   Let them, not me, be broken.
> Bring upon them the day of misfortune,
>   Crush them with repeated destruction. (17:14–18)

We do not know why Tyre escaped. Was Ezekiel just wrong, or did God change his mind? Did Tyre repent? Did Nebuchadnezzar become too haughty? Or were there perhaps other reasons? We are not told. Apparently even Ezekiel did not know. This example should make the point, however, that not every prophecy in the Old Testament can be expected to be fulfilled some time in the future just because it was not fulfilled in the past. There are predictions which were not fulfilled and will not be fulfilled because God changed his mind.

3. The third category of predictions I will simply mention without discussing in any detail. They are those prophecies which are yet to be fulfilled and for which we longingly look for fulfillment. If we may expand our horizons at this point to take in New Testament as well as Old Testament predictions, we may point especially to the promise of Jesus' second coming as an example of such predictions. Within the Old Testament one could point to numerous passages which speak of an earth purified of evil. Note, as an example, Isa 11:6–9:

> Then the wolf shall be a guest of the lamb,
>   and the leopard shall lie down with the kid;
> The calf and the young lion shall browse together,
>   with a little child to guide them.
> The cow and the bear shall be neighbors,
>   together their young shall rest;
>   the lion shall eat hay like the ox.
> The baby shall play by the cobra's den,
>   and the child lay his hand on the adder's lair.
> There shall be no harm or ruin on all my holy mountain;
>   for the earth shall be filled with the knowledge of the Lord,
>   As water covers the sea.

Oftentimes, however, such Old Testament passages, either through their context or through a surprisingly strong this-worldly orientation, raise difficulties that suggest the need for a fourth category of prophetic predictions.

4. This category is the one I want to spend the most time on, because the predictions contained in it are the most controversial and, I think, the most

open to misinterpretation. They are those predictions whose fulfillment, whether already past or yet to be expected, must be regarded as taking place in a way that is less—or more than—literal. Let me illustrate this by a rather lengthy passage from the Old Testament which most scholars would regard as a yet unfulfilled prediction, or series of predictions—Ezekiel's vision of the restored Israel in chapters 37–48. The problems this body of material presents for our question can be seen more clearly if we juxtapose the Ezekiel material with John's vision of the future in Rev 20:4–22:5. These two visions of a better future follow a common pattern.

In Ezekiel 37 the famous vision of the resurrection of a valley full of dry bones is recounted to give emphasis to Yahweh's promise to restore Israel to her land, where united under a Davidic ruler and blessed by God's beneficent presence they would live in peace. In Rev 20:4 those who had been beheaded for their witness to Jesus and the word of God came to life again to reign with Christ for a thousand years.

At this point in Ezekiel, Gog, Magog, and the hordes of the nations gather together to attack God's people in the promised land, but Yahweh intervenes and annihilates his enemies on the mountains of Israel (38–39). In Revelation, the millennium is followed by the loosing of Satan who musters the troops of Gog and Magog and brings them up against the beloved city of God's people; but fire falls down from heaven and destroys these forces of evil and Satan is thrown into hell (Rev 20:7–10).

Thus Yahweh will demonstrate his judgment to the nations and save Israel (Ezek 29:21–29), and the judgment follows at the same point in Revelation (20:11–15).

Then, in the Book of Ezekiel, God shows the prophet the new Jerusalem set on a high mountain, the way it is going to be reorganized in those days after the defeat of the nations (40). In Revelation, God shows John the new Jerusalem, coming down out of heaven, adorned as a bride for her husband (Rev 21:2), and this also transpires on the top of a very high mountain (Rev 21:10).

At this stage Ezekiel watches the angel with the measuring rod as he measures the temple that will exist in this new Jerusalem. Here there is a significant difference between Ezekiel and Revelation, though they remain structurally parallel. In Revelation the angel with the measuring rod measures the city, not the temple (21:15ff.). The reason is very simple. The new Jerusalem of Revelation has no temple (21:22). It has no temple because there is no need for one. God and the Lamb will themselves visibly live with their people, thus there is no point in representing God's presence symbolically through a temple.

The next thing that is mentioned in the Book of Ezekiel is the set of rules for animal sacrifice. All the various sacrificial rituals of the preexilic period are reconstituted and regulated in great detail in two long passages (40:38–47; 43:18–27). Revelation, however, makes no mention of animal sacrifice. The reason for this is obvious. Jesus is described as the Lamb slain before the foundation of the world (Rev 13:8), in whose blood the saints cleanse their garments (7:14), and through whose blood they overcome the devil (12:11). There is no need for animal sacrifice, for the true sacrifice, Christ Jesus, has now been revealed. The same argument, of course, is made in Heb 7:27.

Ezekiel also reaffirms the priestly prerogatives of the old Zadokite priesthood. Only the descendants of Aaron from the line of Zadok are to have full priestly rights in the new temple (Ezek 40:46). In Revelation, however, there is no mention of any special priest; for in line with the rest of the New Testament, Revelation considers all Christians priests. Those raised in the first resurrection, for instance, are said to "serve God and Christ as priests" (20:6). One should also compare Heb 7:12ff. where it is argued that the Levitical priesthood has been changed, that Jesus, stemming from Judah not from Levi, much less Aaron or Zadok, has become our one high priest.

The Book of Ezekiel is also very concerned about the proper division of the land of Palestine between the priests, the Levites, the king, and the various tribes. This was important to the prophet because he was visualizing an actual earthly life in the physical land of Israel. Thus he also speaks of the land as being ruled by a succession of Davidic princes (Ezek 45:7). The implication is that while life will be good in Ezekiel's new Jerusalem, the limitations of human existence will not be completely transcended. Generations will still come and pass on to be replaced by the new generations. Over against this picture, Revelation shows no concern for the proper division of its new Jerusalem. It is not a mundane realm where such mundane concerns are important. Moreover, it is ruled over by God and the Lamb, not by a series of human Davidides, because the limitations of death have been overcome.

Finally there is the picture in Ezekiel of the river that is going to flow down from the temple and turn the Dead Sea into a fresh water lake. It will be full of fish, and the river bank will be lined with all sorts of ever-bearing fruit trees whose leaves will be for the healing of the nations. Rev 22:1–3 presents the same picture, though the water of life in Revelation does not flow from under the temple but from the throne of God and the Lamb.

Looking back over these parallels, it should be clear that the prophetic prediction in Revelation is dependent on the prediction in Ezekiel. They follow the same pattern; the very same order of events is described. Restoration involving resurrection is followed by the assault of Gog and Magog, the defeat of evil, judgment, and the revelation of the new Jerusalem and its splendors. This close parallelism in thought and structure, however, makes certain contrasts between the two passages all the more striking; and it is precisely this combination of structural similarities and striking contrasts which should raise questions for the Christian reader. How can we from a Christian perspective visualize a future fulfillment of the prophecy in Ezekiel 37–48? Would a literal fulfillment have any theological significance for the Christian? What could a Christian make of animal sacrifice, Zadokite priests, contemporary—and very human—descendants of David, and parcels of land in Palestine? Can the Christian visualize a future fulfillment of Ezekiel's vision which ignores John's adaptation and revision of Ezekiel's material? It seems to me impossible. The vision of Revelation has taken up, but at the same time transcended, that of Ezekiel; and one can hold to the literal fulfillment of Ezekiel's prediction only at the expense of rejecting basic Christian doctrines.

This example from Ezekiel points to one serious problem, then, in this large category of prophetic predictions. That is, the less than total correspondence between original prediction and its final fulfillment. Very often the language of prophecy seems to imply one type of event when in reality the fulfillment, if it is to materialize, seems to have a somewhat different character. There is another problem, however, that often accompanies this first one. It may be illustrated by a much shorter passage from Hag 2:20–22:

> The message of the Lord came a second time to Haggai on the twenty-fourth day of the month: Tell this to Zerubbabel, the governor of Judah:
>
> I will shake the heavens and the earth;
> I will overthrow the thrones of kingdoms,
> destroy the power of the kingdoms of the nations.
> I will overthrow the chariots and their riders,
> and the rider with their horses
> shall go down by one another's sword.
> On that day, says the Lord of hosts,
> I will take you, Zerubbabel,
> son of Shealtiel, my servant, says the Lord,
> And I will set you as a signet ring;
> for I have chosen you, says the Lord of hosts.

This prophecy, dating sometime from 520 B.C. or shortly thereafter, predicts that Yahweh is about to shake the nations in judgment, and on that day he will set up Zerubbabel, the Judean governor, as his chosen one. Zech 6:11–14, a related prophecy dating to precisely the same period, makes it clear that both Zechariah and Haggai attached Messianic expectations to Zerubbabel. These expectations failed to materialize, and as a result there has even been some tampering with the text of Zechariah. At any rate Zerubbabel passed from the scene without witnessing anything so glorious as the overthrow of Persian rule. The temple was rebuilt, but the Persian empire remained, and any Messianic hopes attached to Zerubbabel were disappointed. One might be tempted, therefore, to classify this prophecy with that group of prophecies which were not and never will be fulfilled. At the very least, one must admit that Yahweh's shaking of the nations was more distant than the wording of the prophecy seemed to imply.

This feature is quite characteristic of prophetic predictions. They almost invariably fore-shorten the time element. The time one must wait before the fulfillment comes always seems to appear shorter in the wording of the prophecy than it turns out to be in reality. One can see the same problem in the New Testament. In Mark 13, for instance, in an admittedly difficult passage, presumably dealing with his second coming, Jesus speaks of the Son of Man coming with the clouds of heaven. Then in verse 30 he says, "I assure you, this generation will not pass away until all these things take place." That generation has passed, has long since passed, and many of these things, certainly the coming of the Son of Man with the clouds of heaven, has not taken place. Of course, in the same context Jesus says, "As to the exact day or hour, no one knows it, neither the angels in heaven nor even the Son, but only the Father" (v. 32). Nevertheless, whatever Jesus may have originally meant by his saying, and one can raise questions as to the precise meaning, the early church took it to mean that the second coming would be very soon. Thus there was a great expectation in the early church that Jesus would return within their own lifetime. Paul in the early part of his ministry was very confident that the coming would be while he was still alive, and he hoped for it in that way. It is only in the later Pauline books that he begins to realize that it is not going to be in his lifetime, and that he will probably die before Jesus returns. There is, then, this element of a fore-shortening of prophetic expectations as well as the problem that the character of the event prophesied somehow does not correspond exactly to the letter of the original prophecy. Can one account for these perennial problems or difficulties within this last category of prophetic predictions?

First of all let us look at the matter of the time element. There are at least three different points at which we could try to locate the source of the problem—at the level of the reader, at the level of the prophet, or, if we may be so bold to suggest it, at the level of God. Let me illustrate this by the passage in Mark 13:30. One could argue that the reason this prediction *seems* foreshortened is that we have misunderstood it. "Generation," on this view, means something different from the ordinary, normal meaning for the word. Or we could argue that Jesus himself, due to the historically conditioned limitations of his manhood, erroneously assumed that the second coming was to take place very, very soon. Remember the view of Albert Schweitzer and his disciples. Or, finally, one may try to find the basis for this perplexing problem in the purpose of God himself.

In dealing with any particular passage where the problem emerges, I think all three possibilities must be considered. First we have to ask ourselves as readers, "Have I really understood this passage?" If we cannot resolve the difficulty at this level, however, without arbitrary and *ad hoc* twisting of the language, we must raise the second possibility. Are there some limitations in the prophetic spokesman, whether in his character or in the conditioned historical context in which he stands, which would lead to some distortion of a prophetic message conveyed through such a messenger? Finally, one must ask whether such temporal distortion may not originate within the purposes of God himself.

It is on this final level that I would like to discuss the problem in this paper. What conceivable reason could God have for leading us to expect a prophetic fulfillment sooner than it will in fact occur? It strikes me that this tendency to fore-shorten expectations is a very human characteristic that even we as humans have to accommodate ourselves to when we encounter it in others. Those of you who have taken a long trip with little children know that as soon as you get in the car and drive around the block, the first thing they say is, "Daddy, are we almost there?" If you do not lay the law down, they repeat variations on the same question until you are almost ready to throw them out of the car. This same impatient expectancy is attributed even to the martyred saints in Revelation 6:10: "They cried out at the top of their voices: 'How long will it be, O Master, holy and true, before you judge our cause and avenge our blood among the inhabitants of the earth?' "

Now, if you will permit me to change the trip analogy slightly, I think we can see how the fore-shortened expectancy of others forces us to accommodate ourselves to the situation thus created. On a long automobile trip one can successfully cope with the problem only by getting the children's minds off the goal. Give them something to read or a game to play so that they will forget about the trip for as long as possible. Tell them, "It is a very long way to go; do not ask again!"

But if one is traveling by foot rather than by car, a totally different strategy is called for. If you tell the children in that context, "Oh, it is still another thousand miles," you have had it. They will say, "Carry me, I can't go any farther." In that context you have to keep encouraging the children to keep moving, to watch what they are doing, reassuring them they can make it. It seems to me that in some sense this is the problem God is confronted with. He has to get his people to move over what would seem to them a vast distance without giving up or becoming careless. Let me use another analogy. When I teach my children to swim, I try to get them to swim as far as possible. Normally I stand out in the water and say, "Come on, it is just a little way." When they get close I stark backing up, and they cry, "Don't back up!" They do not believe they can go one stroke farther, but, of course, I know they can swim across the pool. It is just a matter of them thinking they can. In a sense I think this is what is involved in some of the prophetic material. It is a matter of God saying, "Okay, keep coming, it is just a little bit farther." God is standing there in the pool of time, backing up and saying, "A little bit farther, a little bit farther." From his perspective, remember, one day is like a thousand years and a thousand years like one day. From his perspective it *is* just around the corner (cf. 2 Pet 3:8).

Thus, to some extent, one may explain the fore-shortening in prophetic prediction to God's desire to keep his people moving toward their goal.

What about the other problem, however? Why does the language of the prediction seem to imply an event somewhat different in character from the reality of the fulfillment? In reflecting on this problem it occurs to me that all human language involves a certain element of abstraction that to some extent falsifies the picture. Even when we are talking about past events, we only give expression to certain key elements abstracted from those occurrences. If I tell you about an afternoon I spent picking blackberries, for instance, I do not include a description of every blackberry bush I saw. If you assumed that my account included everything that happened and all that I saw on that trip, you would obviously have a very false picture of what was involved. In the same way, every human description of any kind of event, whether past, present, or future, involves an abstraction that to some extent falsifies the real event. The description is always less than reality because we never put into words every aspect of the reality we experience. In some respects it may be more than the physical reality, because we often use physical images to convey emotional reality. The fisherman describing the five pounder that got away may in fact be describing the emotional excitement that a one-and-a-half pounder made on him. To some extent I like to think of the prophecies in Isaiah 40–55 that speak of the return from exile as involving some element of this. If one reads Isaiah's account of how the desert will bloom for the Israelites returning to their homeland, and then compares his predictions to the historical accounts in Ezra and Nehemiah, one is struck by the contrast. The desert did not become a well-watered garden for the returning Israelites. If one sees such predictions as fulfilled in the return from Babylonian exile, one would have to see the fulfillment in the emotional impact, in the joy of a safe return, not as an actual physical transformation of the desert. At any rate I think one must take that into account.

In the light of this consideration, however, how can one judge the truth or falsity of a prophetic prediction? Let me use another analogy. When we go to a party at a home where we have never been, it is often necessary to have directions. Sometimes on such occasions hand-drawn maps are given out. Normally they include only the barest essentials and are wildly out of perspective. But if when we reach the crucial points on the way we can recognize them and thus attain our destination, the map has successfully conveyed the intended meaning. It seems to me that predictive prophecy is that way. If when one gets to the event one can say, "Aha! That is what he meant!" the prediction is truly fulfilled. Moreover, I think there is almost always this element of discovery.

Apart from the problem of abstraction inherent in any human language, however, one must be aware of a quite different problem. The imagery in a prophetic prediction has to be based on past experience. The prophet is in the peculiar situation of describing something that has not yet occurred, and the only language he has to describe it in is language drawn from his own past experience. Now it is extremely difficult to communicate something that is totally new to one's listeners. We had a guest this summer who told us of her difficulty in describing snow to the Nigerians. But the difficulty is compounded when the speaker himself has never experienced the reality he is describing. Suppose a Nigerian who had never been any place where there is snow had merely seen a vision about snow and tried to describe it to the Nigerians. The difficulty he would confront would be immense.

Going back now to Ezekiel, one should note that his predictions are drawn from his own past experiences. He was a priest from a priestly family, so his experiences of God's presence among his people is dependent on the priestly outlook that he inherited. That is, the way in which God was present among his people in the period in which he lived was in the temple that existed at Jerusalem. So in his view of the future, the temple plays a very important role. The sacrificial system is important to him because it was precisely this that maintained the relationship between God and his people. The Davidic monarchy is important because it was the princes of the Davidic line who ruled over his people according to the divine promises in the older passages of the Old Testament. At the same time that he uses these traditional images, however, he stretches them.[2] The idea of a river flowing down from the holy mountain has a long history in Palestine, though in Ezekiel's day and as far back before that as we know, there had never been a river in Jerusalem. Nonetheless, there was a spring on the east side of the temple mount, which is apparently seen as becoming a mighty river in the future. There was at least some element in his experience for him to attach this expectation to.

Now what happens when new experiences come along? We could use another analogy. When a child is very small and plays house, he may pretend he is married and has children which he and his wife must discipline. In short, a child has some conception of what marriage is like. When that same child becomes seventeen and starts dating seriously, he still has a conception of marriage, but it is a different and more developed conception than the one he had when he was six. Now it seems to me that prophetic prediction has to be regarded in somewhat the same way. God's people have a history, and within the light of later developments the expectations of the future change. In my opinion this is what takes place between the Book of Ezekiel and the Book of

2. Given the prophets' penchant for reworking traditional themes and motifs, one must raise the question to what extent they have deliberately used these in symbolical, non-literal fashion. It will require a separate paper to treat this question adequately, but one could read Ezekiel's description of the new land and new Jerusalem in this way, and the recurring prophetic themes of new exodus, new covenant, and new David might suggest such an intentional employment of "broken symbols." If this is the case, the later reworking of the same set of symbols would in no way invalidate a prophecy's fulfillment.

Revelation. In Ezekiel there is one expectation based upon the experiences of God's people up until the time of Ezekiel. By the time the Book of Revelation is written there have been new experiences. Jesus has come and brought his teachings. There is a new realization of how God can deal with his people and what sacrifice is really all about. This affects the character, the style of the expectation. In a sense, I would say that what we have in Ezekiel is a child's perception of the future of God's people with God. The Book of Revelation represents that of the teenager. It is a much clearer view of what is in store for God's people, and yet even here one has to say with Paul, we still see through a glass darkly. Or, in the words of 1 John 3:2, "It does not yet appear what we shall be, but we know that when he appears, we shall be like him." The implication is that even what we have in Revelation has to be taken provisionally. When the fulfillment comes, there will probably be an element of surprise that will cause us to cry out in delight, "That's what he meant!"

There is a sense in which prophecy always involves a mystery, and it is this element of the unexpected which puts a keener edge on our expectations.

Against this attempt to deal with the problems raised by predictive prophecy one could certainly raise the objection that it makes things complex. One can no longer read a prophetic prediction and say, "That is what it means, period." But life itself is quite complex. If things are so simple in Scripture that there are no problems that arise from the reading of the text, one must wonder whether the simplicity may not be in the reader rather than in the Scriptures. Anything that is too simple raises the suspicion that it has not been correctly understood—that it is not real. As Christians we have to be willing to recognize not only the simplicity of God's way—and there is a sense in which God's way is simple—but also the complexity that goes along with it. If one fails to notice the complexity, one falls into the danger of twisting the gospel in a way that raises all sorts of far more serious contradictions within the biblical message.

Index of Authors

Index of Scripture

Old Testament / Hebrew Bible

New Testament

Deuterocanonical Literature